Delinquency and Youth Crime

Second Edition

Gary F. Jensen
Vanderbilt University

Dean G. Rojek
University of Georgia

D1401604

WAVELAND
PRESS, INC.

Prospect Heights, Illinois

To Tony and Kris,
Dean

To Lois and Jense,
Gary

For information about this book, write or call:
Waveland Press, Inc.
P.O. Box 400
Prospect Heights, Illinois 60070
(708) 634-0081

Chapter Opener Photo Credits

Chapter 1, © Arthur Tress/Photo Researchers. Chapter 2, The Bettmann Archive. Chapter 3, AP/Wide World. Chapter 4, CLEO/Hillstrom Stock Photo, Inc. Chapter 5, Suzanne Arms-Wimberley. Chapter 6, © Armando F. Mola. Chapter 7, CLEO/Hillstrom Stock Photo, Inc. Chapter 8, © Armando F. Mola. Chapter 9, AP/Wide World. Chapter 10, The Bettmann Archive. Chapter 11, © Armando F. Mola. Chapter 12, Jim West/Hillstrom Stock Photo, Inc.

Table of Contents

Preface

It was only a few years ago that a delinquency text could be justified by pointing to skyrocketing crime rates for offenses involving the young, ever-growing arrest rates for juveniles, and the burgeoning number of youth being processed by the juvenile court. Juveniles are still responsible for a disproportionate share of arrests for property crimes and it is still the case that about one in four will acquire a juvenile court record. However, most of the last ten or fifteen years has been characterized by declining or stable rates of juvenile crime. Hence, the topic need not be approached with any sense of alarm but as *one* dimension of the crime problem — not necessarily the worst or most pressing and, yet, not a trivial dimension of the problem either.

Juvenile delinquency has been the subject of "scientific" research for more than half a century and this text attempts to capture and summarize the best of that research and to organize it in a manner that gives students a comprehensive understanding of delinquency and juvenile justice. We deal with delinquency as 1) a socio-legal category invented in conjunction with the juvenile court, 2) a label applied to youth at the end of a chain of decisions involving the public, police, and officials of the juvenile court, and 3) behavior which violates legal codes, regardless of its detection or processing. Whether conceived of as a legal category, a label, or a behavior delinquency cannot be understood without considering the social context shaping it.

The first four chapters of this text introduce delinquency in these several different senses. In Chapters 1 and 2 delinquency is discussed in the context of other dimensions of the crime problem, as part of the development of criminology in general, and as a social-cultural invention. Chapter 3 focuses on the production of official data on delinquency and youth crime and the "images" conveyed by such statistics as well as research on determinants of official processing. In Chapter 4 we examine other ways of measuring delinquency and the images they suggest, concentrating on consistencies as well as inconsistencies in the different types of information.

While Chapters 1 through 4 deal with the "construction" of delinquency as a social problem, Chapters 5 through 8 deal with issues involving the "causes" of delinquency. In Chapter 5 we try to provide an honest and, we hope, objective assessment of theory and research on biological, genetic, and psychological correlates of crime and delinquency. Though such research is often glibly dismissed by members of our particular discipline (sociology), too many of our students are majoring in other disciplines to dismiss entire traditions without discussing them. Chapter 6 summarizes sociological theories as "schools of thought" and focuses on crucial contrasts among them and on research relevant to their central claims.

Because scholars are typically interested in "theories," research that focuses on specific social institutions is often slighted both in textbooks and in class. Chapters 7 and 8 deal with specific social institutions and address enduring questions about the relevance of specific circumstances and forces for explaining delinquency. Chapter 7 discusses the influence of family, school, and peer groups. Chapter 8 deals with religious, media, and community influences. Religion and media are often ignored in textbooks written by sociologists, despite their centrality to common folklore about crime and their possible relevance to traditional sociological perspectives. Community influences were important in the earliest versions of many criminological theories and interest in this aspect has revived in the last several years.

Criminology has been defined as the scientific study of law-making, law-breaking, and reactions to law-breaking and the last four chapters deal with such "reactions." They are organized around major issues involving deterrence, labeling, imprisonment, correctional experiments, diversion, restitution, and prevention. We deal with general issues as well as the evaluation of specific programs and attempt to discern what appears promising as well as approaches that have failed.

The text is designed to be used with juniors and seniors and is written to enhance their familiarity with juvenile justice terminology, their ability to think critically, and their understanding of the delinquency problem. While we have attempted to keep jargon at a minimum, they will encounter complicated ideas, scientific and theoretical terms, and concepts that are crucial to debates and controversies in the field.

We would like to express our appreciation to those students who have taken our classes, asked us questions, and challenged us to think about our preconceptions and blind spots in the study of delinquency. We would also like to thank the staff who contributed to the many drafts of the text — Linda Kundell and Sandy Gary at the University of Georgia and Mary Clissold, Joyce Ogburn, and Linda Willingham at Vanderbilt University. We would also acknowledge the support provided by three great universities over the years it took to revise this text — the University of Arizona, the University of Georgia, and Vanderbilt University.

We are indebted to the many teachers and colleagues who had an impact on the text either directly through their comments or indirectly through their own work. Travis Hirschi, Ronald Akers, Herbert Costner, Jack Gibbs, and Malcolm Klein have had a particularly significant impact on our careers. We would like to give special tribute to Maynard Erickson, who died in 1986, and Donald Cressey, who died in 1987. We miss both of them and hope to carry on their commitment to careful thinking and critical research.

We had a great experience working with Waveland Press and its publisher, Neil Rowe, and appreciated the careful review by Jack Spencer of Purdue University. After dealing with large companies over the years it was refreshing to work with the same personnel from beginning to end. Laurie Prossnitz was outstanding as a copy editor and spotted problems that would have evaded us without her careful eye for detail.

Obviously our families deserve recognition. We would like to thank Sheila Carroll Jensen and Kathy Rojek for tolerating and helping us in the midst of their busy careers. We would also like to acknowledge our children who challenged us to revise our theories about human behavior on a daily basis—Jennifer Jensen, Jason Forni, Brian Forni, Wendy Jensen, Kevin Forni, Joel Rojek, and Eric Rojek.

chapter 1

Delinquency in Context

> *Let any man that hath occasion either to walk or ride through the Out-parts of this City (where mostly our poor people inhabit) tell but what he hath seen of the Rudeness of young Children, who for want of better Education and Employment, shall sometimes be found by whole Companies at play, where they shall wrangle and cheat one another, and upon the least Provocation, swear and fight for a Farthing, or else they shall be found whipping of Horses, by reasons of which, they sometimes cast their Riders, to the hazard or loss of their Lives or Limbs; or else they shall be throwing of Dirt or Stones into Coaches, or at the Glasses, insomuch that I have been a hundred times greatly troubled, to see the Rudeness and Misbehavior of the poorer sort of Children (especially of late year), they having been generally so much neglected, that they have neither been taught their Duties either towards God or Man.*
>
> —A 17th Century English Philanthropist

Introduction

John Jones, 17, stands before the juvenile court for disposition, having been adjudicated a delinquent minor child. In his intake interview John admitted that he and Roger Smith decided to break into the Ace Bike Shop to steal money. John said that he attempted to enter through an air conditioning vent but became scared and decided to back out. He was immediately apprehended outside the store together with Roger Smith. The burglar alarm system was torn off the wall, necessitating repairs costing approximately $200.

Since Roger Smith was an adult, he was taken to criminal court but the charges were dropped. John Jones was referred to the juvenile court where a petition for attempted burglary was filed. The petition was amended to trespass in the third degree. This is John's second referral to the juvenile court. His first was for taking a motorcycle. That referral was adjusted after the minor made restitution of $135 to the store owner for damages incurred.

The probation worker recommends supervised probation until his 18th birthday with the provisions that he 1) obey all laws; 2) attend school; 3) follow the reasonable demands of his parents and probation officer; 4) donate 50 hours of volunteer work to a nonprofit community organization; 5) discontinue all association with Roger Smith; and 6) make a formal apology to the owner of the bike shop. A review hearing on this matter should be held in approximately six months. The Court accepts this recommendation and sentences John Jones to probation as stipulated. (Pima County Juvenile Court Center, 1982)

Newspaper, magazine, and textbook introductions to the problem of delinquency often begin with dramatic examples of murder, rape, armed robbery, or other instances of young people preying on weak and defenseless victims or attacking people at random. No doubt such examples would grab your attention and hold it much better than the case of John Jones. Juveniles do commit such offenses and violent offenses are an important dimension of the problem of delinquency and youth crime.

The case of John Jones, however, is more typical of the problem of juvenile delinquency and more useful for beginning our study for several reasons. First, juvenile delinquency is a legal category which includes a wide range of criminal offenses committed by minors (nonadults) as well as activities that are only illegal for people under the age of 18. Most of the illegal activities dealt with as delinquency are neither dramatic nor extraordinary. John intended to steal money by illegally entering the bicycle shop—a form of property crime. It is such property crime which is most overrepresented among juveniles in arrest statistics when juveniles are compared to adults. Second, John was with his friend, Roger, which is consistent with the general finding that most delinquent offenses are committed while in the company of friends. Most delinquent activity is social activity. Third, because he was 17, John was processed not by the adult criminal justice system, but by a specialized justice system with its own unique terminology ("referral," "intake," "adjudicated," "petition"). Fourth, because he was 18, Roger was treated as an adult and actually suffered fewer consequences for his actions than John. This difference runs counter to the perception of the juvenile court as a "kiddies' court" meting out lesser consequences than would have been the case if the adult criminal justice system were involved. A comparative analysis of the adult and juvenile justice systems (see Chapter 2) shows John's experience to be more common than critics realize.

This text will address most of the questions (offender characteristics, police and court processing, and future criminal involvement) that come to mind when thinking about John's predicament. We will begin our study by focusing on delinquency as *one* dimension of the crime problem. We stress the word "one" because a comprehensive understanding of delinquency requires that we consider it in the context of adult crime. The picture at the beginning of this chapter of a small boy inside an old television set brandishing his toy gun was chosen as a reflection of a major theme to be elaborated in the following pages. Whether we are trying to understand John's predicament or why a boy wanders through a junkyard in search of adventure we have to consider them in the context of a larger world—one which is largely handed to them by adults.

An Enduring Concern

In a sense, juvenile delinquency is a relatively new dimension of the crime problem since juvenile courts and legislation dealing exclusively with the offenses of children are products of modern times. In the United States, Illinois was the first state to pass a juvenile court act (1899) and Wyoming the last to enact such legislation (1945). Toronto (1912) was among the first Canadian cities to establish a court for juveniles (Hagan and Leon, 1977). India passed its first juvenile statutes in 1920 (Priyadarsini and Hartjen, 1981). In England, where the court system has a long history, the youthful offender was not recognized until 1854 (Terrill, 1984). Thus, in view of the long legal tradition that accompanies much of the civil and criminal law throughout the world, juvenile statutes are relatively recent additions.

On the other hand, despite the infancy of "juvenile delinquency" as a legal concept there has been a persistent concern with youthful misbehavior and the offenses of youth throughout history, along with a tendency to view the situation as progressively worse than in preceding generations. Consider, for example, the following anguished statement: "Youth is disintegrating. The youngsters of the land have a disrespect for their elders, and a contempt for authority in every form. Vandalism is rife, and crime of all kinds is rampant among our young people. The nation is in peril" (Aries, 1962). Although this lament appears to be a contemporary critique of youth in modern industrial society, it actually dates back some four thousand years to a despondent Egyptian priest.

During the "Golden Age" of Greece (500-300 B.C.), Socrates was quite disgruntled with the youth of his day, as evidenced by his claim that "children today love luxury. They have bad manners, a contempt for authority, a disrespect for their elders, and they like to talk instead of work. They contradict their parents, chatter before company, gobble up the best at the table, and tyrannize over their teachers." As the cartoon on the following page suggests, "The world is always in the biggest mess it's ever been in" and young people have been suspected of contributing unduly to that mess for most of history.

The image of the young as recalcitrant or incorrigible persists in contemporary American society, where crime is typically depicted as a problem of youth. For example, in the late 1960s the President's Commission on Law Enforcement and Administration of Justice in the United States (1967:169-170) concluded that (1) "enormous numbers of young people appear to be involved in delinquent acts," (2) "youth is responsible for a substantial and disproportionate part of the national crime problem," and (3) "America's best hope for reducing crime is to reduce juvenile delinquency and youth crime." The crimes and delinquencies of the young are viewed as an enormous social problem and as a major, if

"Remember this, my child. The world is always in the biggest mess it's ever been in."

not *the* major dimension of crime in the United States. The popular press often depicts the problem even more dramatically, referring to the situation as the "youth crime plague" (*Time*, July 11, 1977:18). Alfred Regnery, a recent administrator of the Office of Juvenile Justice and Delinquency Prevention, viewed juvenile crimes as a "grave problem on a national scale" with a "staggering" range and intensity (1985: 65).

Juveniles in Conflict with the Law

It is a fact that a substantial proportion of young people have conflicts with the law before they reach adulthood. Based on several studies where youths' histories were compiled and analyzed, the National Center for Juvenile Justice estimates that about one-third of juveniles acquire a police record by the time they reach eighteen. For example, by the time a "cohort" of boys born in Philadelphia in 1945 reached their 18th birthdays, 35 percent of them had acquired a record with the police (Wolfgang et al,

1972). In a study conducted in rural Oregon, one-fourth of the males acquired records with the county juvenile department by that age (Polk, 1974). In Racine, Wisconsin more than one-half of male youths born in either 1942, 1949, or 1955 had some contact with the police before they were adults (Shannon, 1982). In an urban, white, working-class London neighborhood one-fourth of males born in 1953 had been convicted for "delinquency" by age 18 (West, 1982). In short, based on studies in a variety of communities in more than one nation it is safe to conclude that a considerable proportion of youth get into trouble with the law.

In some situations such trouble may be as much the rule as an exception. For example, in the Philadelphia cohort study about 50 percent of the nonwhite males, in contrast to nearly 30 percent of the white males, had acquired police records between ages 7 and 18. Such conflicts appear more likely for boys than for girls (Shannon, 1982), for urban youths than for rural youths (Snyder and Nimick, 1983) and for youths in urban, industrialized societies than for youths in agrarian nations (Clinard and Abbott, 1973; Priyadarsini and Hartjen, 1981). Thus, while conflict with the law is quite common, it is more common in some settings and categories of youth than in others.

Undetected Lawbreaking

While a sizable proportion of youth acquires an official record, an even greater proportion engages, without detection, in activities that are a potential source of conflict with the law. For example, in an interview study of delinquency in a representative national sample of youths age 13 to 16, Jay Williams and Martin Gold (1972) found that although 88 percent of the youths had done something that could have resulted in trouble with the law, only 22 percent had ever had any contact with police and only 2 percent had been under judicial consideration. In similar research among high school students in upstate New York, 75 percent of the male subjects and 45 percent of the female subjects reported committing one or more of the six criminal acts studied in the survey (Hindelang, 1973:474).

The most recent surveys of representative samples of American youth (see Elliott et al., 1985) continue to reaffirm this tendency. For example, data from a national survey of high school seniors show that during 1986, 19 percent of girls and 29 percent of boys admitted shoplifting within the twelve months preceding the survey. Twenty-seven percent of senior girls indicate having "Taken something not belonging to you worth under $50" as did 37 percent of senior boys. Nineteen percent of senior boys reported having hurt someone badly enough that they needed a doctor as compared to 3 percent of girls (Bachman et al., 1988). In statistical terms, involvement in some form of delinquency is normal adolescent behavior and surveys over several decades suggest that it has been statistically normal for a considerable period of time.

Similar results have been reported in studies of youth in parts of London (West and Farrington, 1973) and other communities in England (Belson, 1978) as well as Canada (Hagan et al., 1985). When youth are asked to report on their offense behavior they report much more delinquent activity than is ever reflected in police or court statistics. We will learn more about such surveys in Chapter 4.

Overrepresentation in Arrest Statistics

It is commonly assumed that juveniles represent a disproportionate amount of arrests compared to adults. In Figure 1-1 we have summarized the percentage of arrests accounted for by people age 10 through 17, as reported in the Federal Bureau of Investigation's *Uniform Crime Reports* for 1988. People age 10 through 17 made up about 12 percent of the population in 1988, which means that when they account for more than 12 percent of arrests they are *overrepresented* in the arrest statistics. Figure 1-1 shows that in 1988, youths were clearly overrepresented in arrests for motor vehicle theft, vandalism, arson, burglary, larceny, liquor law violations, receiving, buying or possessing stolen property, robbery, suspicion,

---

Figure 1-1

Percent of Arrests Accounted for by Youths Age 10-17

Motor Vehicle Theft	40 %	Aggravated Assaults	12 %
Vandalism	37	All Other Offenses	11
Arson	35	Murder	11
Burglary	32	Drug Abuse	9
Larceny	30	Forgery & Counterfeiting	8
Liquor Laws	25	Embezzlement	8
Stolen Property	25	Vagrancy	8
Robbery	22	Fraud	5
Suspicion	19	Family and Children	4
Weapons	16	Gambling	4
Other Sex Offenses	15	Drunkenness	3
Disorderly Conduct	15	Prostitution/Vice	1
Rape	14	Driving Under Influence	1
Simple Assaults	14	Total for All Offenses Listed Above	14

Source: *Uniform Crime Reports*, 1988.

and weapons violations. They were also somewhat overrepresented for rape and other sex offenses, simple assaults and disorderly conduct. When all offenses are added together juveniles account for only slightly more arrests than expected (14 percent). Theft of and attacks on property are the most distinctively juvenile offenses.

Juvenile Delinquency and Adult Crime

All the foregoing observations—the enduring historical concern with the misbehavior of the young, the proportion of juveniles involved in illegal activities, and the disproportionate number of juveniles arrested for property crimes—have been the traditional justifications for devoting an extraordinary amount of attention to delinquency as a major aspect of crime in America. To put juvenile delinquency in proper perspective, however, we need to make some observations about juvenile crime in relation to the adult world and adult crime.

Overrepresentation of Young Adults in Violent Crime

While government commissions, numerous politicians, and the popular press have dramatized the importance of addressing juvenile delinquency and youth crime as America's "best hope" for reducing crime in general, this point of view has certain shortcomings. For one thing, it should be reasserted that for some types of serious crime, juveniles are not over-represented relative to adults. It is *young adults* who contribute most disproportionately to crimes of interpersonal violence (other than robbery). As we will note again in Chapter 3, more types of offenses peak in the young adult years than at any other age.

Group Delinquency and Arrests

Second, arrest statistics may exaggerate the degree to which juveniles are responsible for crimes. In a report on delinquency in metropolitan and nonmetropolitan areas, Howard Snyder and Ellen Nimick (1983:49) argue that the *Uniform Crime Reports* "has led to a distorted perception of the actual contribution of juveniles to serious crimes." Juveniles are more likely than adults to commit their crimes in groups and, hence, although one offense may be committed it may result in several arrests. Snyder and Nimick estimate that while people under 18 accounted for four of every ten *persons arrested* for serious property crime in 1980, they actually accounted for about three in ten property *crimes cleared by an arrest*. Thus, the contribution of juveniles to crime statistics is more dramatic when number of persons arrested is considered than when crimes cleared by an arrest is the focus. The group nature of delinquency may exaggerate juvenile criminal activity and increase the visibility and hazard of arrest when juveniles commit an offense (Erickson, 1971:114-29).

In response to such criticism the *Uniform Crime Reports* began reporting crimes cleared by an arrest as well as the number of persons arrested (see Figure 1-2). The traditional way of analyzing arrests shows persons under 18 accounted for 29 percent of persons arrested for the FBI's eight index crimes while about 18 percent of offenses were cleared by the arrest of someone in that age group. The figure for violent crime is much lower when offenses cleared by an arrest is considered (9 percent) than when number of arrests is considered (15 percent). The group or "gang" nature of delinquency not only exaggerates arrest statistics but may also be relevant to understanding public fear of delinquency. Among the most readily dramatized crimes are those involving groups of youth attacking

---

Figure 1-2

Percentage of Crimes Cleared by Arrest and Percentage of People Arrested Who Are Under 18 Years of Age*

	Percentage of Crimes Cleared	Percentage of People Arrested
Arson	40%	45%
Larceny	22	32
Motor Vehicle Theft	21	40
Burglary	18	34
Robbery	10	22
Rape	9	14
Aggravated Assault	8	12
Murder	6	11
Property Crimes	21	34
Violent Crimes	9	15
All Index Crimes	18	29

*26% of the U.S. population was under 18 years of age in 1988.

Source: *Uniform Crime Reports*, 1988.

relatively helpless victims. Incidents of group attacks on randomly encountered victims such as the "Central Park jogger" in New York City arouse great public concern and establish an image of delinquency as senseless violence by groups of youths. Most delinquency does occur in groups and most juveniles engage in some form of group delinquency at some time but the outcome in terms of the proportion of crimes committed is not particularly dramatic compared to other age groups.

Changing Contribution to Arrest Statistics

Third, if we consider statistics from a few decades ago the contribution of juveniles to arrest statistics was much more dramatic then than it is now. In the decades following World War II, the "Baby Boom" led to large cohorts of young people and high national crime rates. At the same time, the crime rate within the juvenile age group increased as well, possibly as a product of economic deprivation and the overload on institutions of social control; i.e. the family and schools (Easterlin, 1987; O'Brien, 1989). During the 1960s and into the 1970s, both the size of the juvenile age group and rates of crime and delinquency within that group were continually on the rise. It appears that for all ages of youth subject to juvenile court jurisdiction, rates of arrests peaked around 1978, declined through 1985, and have been relatively stable since that time (see Figure 1-3)[Britt, 1985].

Underrepresentation of Serious Adult Crimes

A fourth point concerning juvenile delinquency in relation to adult crime is that our major body of statistics on crime in the United States presents a biased picture of the crime problem. The FBI's *Uniform Crime Reports* provides statistics on eight specific offenses—criminal homicide, forcible rape, robbery, aggravated assault, burglary, larceny, motor vehicle theft, and arson. Together these offenses constitute the *serious-crime index*. Four of the offenses included in the index (robbery, burglary, larceny, and motor vehicle theft) accounted for 92 percent of all index crimes in 1988. Larceny (theft) alone accounted for 55 percent of the index crimes in the United States in 1988. In sum, the index is heavily weighted with property offenses that are unusually common among juveniles.

Many crimes that are not included in the index of serious crime—for example, consumer fraud, fraud, child abuse, drunken driving, drunkenness, gambling, prostitution, and vice—are more characteristic of adults than juveniles. Further, there are innumerable offenses such as price fixing, income tax evasion, and shoddy business practices which are not treated as criminal offenses. These offenses are not included in the serious-crime index because they are more likely to go unreported than those that are

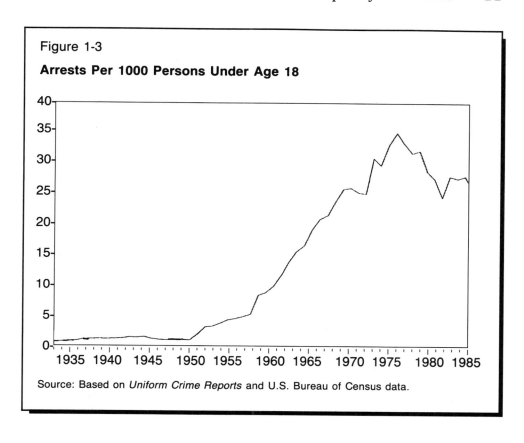

Figure 1-3

Arrests Per 1000 Persons Under Age 18

Source: Based on *Uniform Crime Reports* and U.S. Bureau of Census data.

included or because they are less reliably reported than other offenses. It seems clear, then, that there are grounds for challenging the view that adult crimes are "less serious" than those of juveniles.

In fact, in terms of economic cost to the American public, a President's Commission in 1967 estimated that the annual loss associated with consumer fraud alone was greater than that for all auto theft, burglary, larceny, and robbery in a given year. The Chamber of Commerce (1974) estimated that the cost of "white-collar" crimes in 1974 was at least $40 billion annually. The FBI's estimate for the four property crimes for that same year (burglary, larceny, motor vehicle theft, and robbery) was $3.2 billion. More recently, activities that are not even included as a category in crime data, such as price-fixing, insider trading, stock manipulations, and savings and loan scams, have been estimated to cost the public at least $50 billion a year. The Department of Health and Human Services has reported $2 billion lost annually to Medicare fraud. Juveniles are rarely, if ever, in a position to engage in such costly forms of criminal activity.

The failures of government-insured savings and loan institutions in the 1980s and 1990s will cost American taxpayers many times more than they will lose as a result of juvenile delinquency and youth crime. Considered "the biggest heist in U.S. history" (Pizzo et al., 1989), the failures were as much a product of intentional fraud and illegal practices as of economic conditions. Politicians, banking executives, and entrepreneurs played a major role in deregulating the thrift industry while maintaining government insurance on deposits. They then took advantage of the deregulation through reckless and questionable loans, illegal appraisals and collusion to artificially inflate their assets. When the outcome anticipated by opponents of deregulation occurred, the offenders escaped by taking advantage of bankruptcy laws and left the American public with the bill.

In 1978 a U.S. Senate investigation found that some 350 corporations had admitted to making bribes to officials of foreign governments (Roebuck and Weeber, 1978). Similarly, the Watergate Committee revealed that over 300 corporations made illegal contributions to President Nixon's 1972 election campaign (Clinard and Yeager, 1978).

The world of business is rife with documented cases of fraud. General Motors has put Chevrolet engines in Oldsmobiles. Life insurance companies have invented nonexistent insurance policies to inflate the price of their stock. Television evangelists have misappropriated funds for personal use. Stock scams have been estimated to cost the public hundreds of millions of dollars per year (Engardio and DeGerge, 1989).

Richard Hollinger and John Clark (1983) sampled workers in retail, manufacturing, and service sectors on workplace crime. They found over 35 percent of employees in the retail sector reported stealing from their employers, and a third of the hospital employees reported pilfering on the job. Further, only 5 percent of retail employees were apprehended and less than 1 percent of hospital employees were caught. Chemerinsky (1981) reports that the General Services Administration (GSA) estimates that $100 million is stolen annually by GSA employees, contractors, and suppliers. In another report, the GSA reported that collusion between employees and private contractors and false claims cost taxpayers $25 billion yearly. David Simon and D. Stanley Eitzen (1986) suggest that the diverse forms of what they refer to as "elite deviance" adds between $174 to $231 billion to prices for goods and services. The irony is that despite the enormous costs associated with white-collar crime, the penalties are typically quite lenient and they are routinely dismissed as merely civil infractions.

Organized crime is another costly enterprise run by and profitable for adults. Yet, organized crime activities are not likely to enter into crime statistics, and those caught engaging in such activities are not likely to be those who profit the most. Organized crime is involved in a host of illegal pursuits that range from fraud and corruption to murder—all of which are controlled by adults. Organized crime's involvement in gambling alone is estimated to result in greater economic loss than all eight of the "serious" crimes in the FBI's crime index. Moreover, organized crime uses the profits from the supply of illicit goods and services to gain control of other economic institutions and to corrupt the political system (Cressey, 1969). Syndicated criminal organizations are not the domain of juveniles. Juveniles are found within these criminal confederations only at the "street level," where profits and power are minimal.

It is easy to show that adult-controlled crimes result in far greater economic losses than juvenile crime. It is much more difficult, however, to assess the amount of misery, pain, and suffering that adult-controlled crime may generate. How many Americans have suffered as a result of fraudulent health devices and misrepresented drugs? How many have suffered because of price fixing and its impact on everyday budgets? How much do we suffer when government and big business violate or circumvent laws governing their activities? The public tends to react most severely to crimes involving direct attacks against people and property in which there are clearly defined victims and offenders. Yet, offenses that involve *indirect* and *collective* attacks against us all take a far greater toll.

To put juvenile delinquency in perspective, we also have to ask how fraud, corruption, and the violation of positions of trust affect attitudes toward law and authority. In the early 1940s Edwin Sutherland (1940:1-12) argued that white-collar crime or crimes committed by persons in violation of their positions of trust not only are a serious form of crime in terms of financial loss but, more importantly, also contribute to distrust on a wide scale. Unethical and illegal practices spread from person to person and from one business or occupational group to another, resulting in a general disrespect for the law by "noncriminals." Studies of occupational offenders indicate that while many feel *they* can violate the law with impunity ("business is business"), they also feel little shame in attributing the "crime problem" to others.

John Johnson and Jack Douglas have observed that in comparison to the thousands of studies of juvenile delinquency, social scientists have paid relatively little attention to business and professional deviance—despite the evidence that such adult-dominated crimes are "by far the most pervasive and massive forms of financial deviance in our society" (1978:1). They note that the traditional rationale of the social scientist who selects delinquency as a research topic has been that "street crimes" and those offenses disproportionately involving "the lower part of our social-economic spectrum" (and we would add "the young") involve more violence and thus generate more public concern than business or professional crime. However, Johnson and Douglas firmly believe that in terms of human suffering and the total threat to personal safety and human happiness, our attention has been misplaced.

Another type of crime that has only recently begun to generate national concern is child abuse. The image of the delinquent juvenile preying on a weaker victim is mirrored by parents who inflict considerable pain and suffering on their children. Yet, much child abuse does not make its way into police statistics. Richard Gelles and Murray Straus (1985) estimated that more than 1 million children were subject to severe physical abuse from their parents. The American Humane Association (1986) notes that over 2 million cases of child neglect and abuse were reported in 1986 and that this represents only a fraction of the actual number of cases. An interview study of a nationally representative sample of 1,146 families with children ages 3 through 17 living at home (Gelles and Hargreaves, 1981) measured those violent acts that had a high probability of causing injury and found that about 18 percent of mothers indicated at least one severe violent act towards one of their children. Gelles and Straus (1985) concluded that child abuse and neglect had reached epidemic proportions.

While child abuse appears to be a serious dimension of the crime problem, a review of all of the publications available on the topic through the National Center for Child Abuse and Neglect (Bolton et al., 1981) found that very little of the literature on the topic could qualify as scholarly or scientific research. Family violence and child abuse have only recently become a topic for systematic research by social scientists. If speculation that abused children may be likely to become abusive parents is correct, then child abuse becomes part of a vicious cycle where violence breeds violence. There is already evidence which suggests that abused children are more likely to acquire an adult criminal record than nonabused children, including a higher frequency of arrest for violent crimes as adults (Widom, 1989).

Public Opinion About Crime

Another justification for paying an inordinate amount of attention to juvenile crime might be public opinion. If there were a general consensus that the types of crimes disproportionately involving juveniles are the most serious crimes, then the severity of public condemnation would justify concentration on the topic. That, however, does not seem to be the case.

A 1984 study by the Bureau of Justice Statistics sought an answer to the question "How do people rank the severity of crime?" They surveyed 60,000 people 18 years of age or older assigning a score of 10 to the following crime: "A person steals a bicycle parked on the street." Respondents were asked to assign scores to a wide range of crimes in comparison to that crime. The Bureau concluded that:

> The overall pattern of severity scores indicates that people clearly regard
> violent crimes as more serious than property offenses. They also take

white-collar crime and drug dealing quite seriously, rating two offenses of this type higher than some forms of homicide. One of the highest scores (39.1) is awarded to the factory that causes the death of 20 people by knowingly polluting the city water supply. (Bureau of Justice Statistics, 1984:5)

A legislator who accepted a bribe received a higher severity score than many of the FBI's "serious" crimes. Doctors cheating on insurance claims received higher scores than most forms of larceny. A factory which pollutes city water and causes 20 people to become ill earned a score of about 20. The "serious" crime index includes data on crimes which, it would seem, are considered less serious than several kinds of crime which are not reflected in crime statistics. (See Box 1-1 for a sample of items from the survey).

One component of public opinion that might help explain the attention given to juvenile crime is the "nip-it-in-the-bud" philosophy which suggests that by dealing with juvenile delinquency we are dealing with the roots of the crime problem. However, we can find as much justification for the position that an attack on adult-controlled criminal organizations would combat crime just as effectively. Delinquency and the transgressions of the young must be viewed in context. It is misleading to concentrate on relatively powerless segments of American society when crime is intimately linked to institutions that adults control and to values and practices that are passed from one generation to the next. The youth crime "plague" is paralleled by numerous other patterns of crime that can be presented in equally dramatic terms. White-collar crime can be depicted as a pernicious plague as can political corruption, organized crime, and child abuse.

It is understandable that indignation and concern are readily expressed about crimes in which there are clear-cut victims and offenders. Moreover, such crimes may be of particular concern when the offenders are young. It is important to note, however, that there are other criteria for assessing the "seriousness" of crime and a variety of reasonable arguments suggesting that juvenile delinquency may not be *the* most significant dimension of the crime problem.

Why Study Delinquency?

If we accept the argument that delinquency is not the most serious dimension of the crime problem, then why devote an entire textbook to it? In the preceding discussion we have tried to put delinquency in the context of other forms of crime. We have pointed out that there are grounds for arguing that crime involving adults is far more costly than crime involving juveniles and that delinquency qualifies neither as the most

Box 1-1

How Do You Rank the Severity of Crime?

Suppose a person steals a bicycle parked on the street. If this offense were given a score of 10 to indicate its seriousness, what score would you assign to each of the following (e.g. a 20 would mean twice as serious, a 5 would be half as serious, etc.):

Score

1. A man forcibly rapes a woman. As a result of physical injuries she dies   _____

2. A man stabs his wife. As a result she dies.   _____

3. A woman stabs her husband. As a result he dies.   _____

4. A parent beats his young child with his fists. The child requires hospitalization.   _____

5. A factory knowingly gets rid of its waste in a manner that pollutes the water supply of a city. As a result twenty people become ill but none require medical treatment.   _____

6. A person robs a victim of $10 at gunpoint. The victim is wounded and requires hospitalization.   _____

7. A legislator takes a bribe of $10,000 from a company to vote for a law favoring the company.   _____

8. A person intentionally sets fire to a building causing $10,000 worth of damage.   _____

9. Ten high school boys beat a male classmate with their fists. He requires hospitalization.   _____

10. A person breaks into a school and steals equipment worth $1,000.   _____

11. A person snatches a handbag containing $10 from a victim on the street.   _____

12. A person breaks into a public recreation center, forces open a cash box, and steals $10.   _____

Offenses from National Survey of Crime Severity (Bureau of Justice Statistics Bulletin NCJ-92326). Average score: 1. 53, 2. 39, 3. 28, 4. 23, 5. 20, 6. 18, 7. 17, 8. 13, 9. 12, 10. 10, 11. 5, 12. 4.

serious nor as the primary dimension of our crime problem. On the other hand, it is only through years of study that we can begin to question popular images and conceptions of the crime problem and to put juvenile delinquency in proper perspective. Delinquency is *one* dimension of our overall crime problem — one that has generated considerable public and political concern.

Moreover, while offenses among youth may be facilitated by the messages conveyed and institutions controlled by the adult world, the probability of common forms of adult crime is greater among people who had trouble with the law when young. In fact, the single best predictor of adult criminality is childhood or juvenile criminality (see Gottfredson and Hirschi, 1990). If the probability of juvenile delinquency is reduced, it could have an effect on subsequent adult crime. We cannot say whether this holds true for white-collar crime. Some theorists argue that children who are raised in families where parents wield power and authority are encouraged to take risks and that this orientation is reflected in common forms of undetected delinquency (i.e. shoplifting) as well as entrepreneurial risk-taking as adults (Hagan et al., 1985). Such arguments imply a link between undetected delinquency among advantaged youth and white-collar crime. In sum, the correlation between delinquency and adult crime may be reciprocal with each reinforcing the other.

In addition, delinquency is an illustrative subject matter for studying the forces that affect our laws and human behavior. Since the study of delinquency looks at activities, conflicts, and experiences that are familiar to most of us, it is also a convenient mechanism for studying ourselves and the everyday experiences affecting our lives. Self-understanding and insight into the operation of our social world can be rewarding in their own right. To the degree that each of us influences young people as parents, teachers, or friends, understanding the impact of different styles of family life, school experiences, and other circumstances which contribute to or inhibit delinquency can be useful for our own choices and personal policies.

While few have challenged whether we need a criminal justice system, there is continual debate over whether we need a separate system for juveniles. The system has been criticized both for being too tough on juveniles and ignoring their rights and for being too soft and unconcerned with retribution or victims. Both positions have had their advocates throughout the history of the juvenile court. It is easy to lose sight of the social forces and arguments behind the development of a separate juvenile court system and to repeatedly discover the same inherent problems. While an understanding of the system's history will not resolve the debate, it is worthwhile to discern what issues are of continuing concern. If the juvenile justice system generates debate because it is expected to serve a variety of conflicting goals, then mere recognition of that fact might facilitate more constructive discussions and proposals. The study of juvenile justice provides us with lessons in the politics and sociology of law and legal institutions.

Whether the student of delinquency is radical, liberal, or conservative, he or she is likely to view delinquency as "a problem" about which "something" should be done. There are many different opinions about what form that "something" should take. For some people part of the delinquency problem can be attributed to the nature of the laws that define delinquency as a legal category. The laws are vague and encompass behaviors and situations calling for social rather than legal intervention. To others the answer rests with identifying the causes of delinquent behavior. If generating forces or circumstances can be identified, then delinquency might be reduced by altering such circumstances.

Still others believe that part of the problem is attributable to inadequacies in the juvenile justice system and our reactions to it. Some think the system is too punitive and others think it is too lenient. Proposed solutions range from revolutionary change in our social-economic-political system to programs aimed at early identification and intervention. Whenever we choose among alternative solutions or merely declare that "something" ought to be done, we are making a moral decision. Hence, the study of delinquency forces us to consider our own moral and political beliefs and commitments, their implications for responding to delinquency, and their accuracy in relation to years of research on the topic.

Finally, the study of delinquency is central to the development of a scholarly tradition or field of study called *criminology*. As we study delinquency we will learn about criminology and a variety of possible careers. The study of delinquency has been particularly central to the development of sociological criminology as an academic field in American universities. This text examines delinquency in the context of the larger discipline of criminology and is organized in terms of the topics which have come to define that discipline. Hence, we will briefly discuss criminology and its relevance for organizing our study of delinquency.

Criminology and the Study of Delinquency

Criminology is most simply defined as the "study of crime." Of course, the word "study" is a vague term which can encompass everything from a casual interest in crime to scientific research on determinants of criminal behavior. However, to most people the ". . . ologies" refer to fields of study involving specialists or people with special expertise on a topic.

The title "criminologist" is most likely to evoke an image of police investigators or forensic scientists analyzing evidence and solving crimes. Since crime is police business the study of crime is typically thought of by the public as a police activity. Yet, when people go to college and take courses on crime and delinquency or decide to pursue advanced degrees in criminology they soon discover that there are a variety of specialists and a wide range of different "criminologies." This diversity is reflected in the membership of the American Society of Criminology which includes sociologists, psychologists, anthropologists, biologists, economists, political scientists, lawyers, judges, police, and other professionals interested in crime.

One trait that most criminologists have in common is a commitment to the view that crime can be and should be studied following those standards or principles referred to as "the scientific method." No matter what the particular discipline, criminology tends to be treated as a "science" and such a designation has certain implications for the way in which criminology is approached. For one, as with a science, the aim is to discover and explain orderly patterns or regularities in the subject matter. A criminologist studying delinquency might be interested in whether certain types of delinquency are more common among central city youth than youth in rural settings. Others might be interested in whether children with a measurable value in terms of a certain characteristic (e.g., low grades, child abuse) have a greater probability of involvement in delinquency than children with a different value on that characteristic (e.g., high grades, nonabuse). Some criminologists spend their time trying to account for changes in the extent or nature of different types of crime over time. Whatever the specific topic, criminologists share an interest in uncovering some type of meaningful order to the crime problem and explaining what generates that order. Some take the additional step of drawing implications about the alleviation of the crime problem from such findings.

Modern criminologists are also committed to discerning such order and regularity through the systematic collection of data or evidence which can be verified by others. For much of the history of human discourse the standard for truth was the power or authority of the person making a declaration. While there is always some tendency to accept declarations of truth when they are advanced by people we respect or admire, the standard of truth in a science is verifiable evidence. For example, if a criminologist states that males commit more delinquent offenses than females, this statement should not be accepted merely because of the power or authority of the criminologist but on the basis of the data or information used to justify the claim. It should be "verifiable" in the sense that other people could gather and examine the same evidence and reach the same conclusion. The ability to do so may require some training but that is exactly the purpose of this book.

Since much of the evidence used by criminologists is statistical in nature it is common for people to claim that "You can say anything with statistics," implying that it is impossible to know when a researcher is lying or mistaken. If it is impossible, then there is no such thing as verifiable evidence and no way to decide what is truthful and what is not. However, if we really want to gain an understanding of crime, then our task is to learn about the types of scientific evidence that are used to study crimes. With such knowledge, we can hope to be able to determine whether evidence is convincing given what we know about the problems encountered when using such data or evidence in the past. Thus, to approach a matter scientifically requires that it be approached very critically. Evidence must be assessed and questioned.

One of the early and most influential texts on the subject defines criminology as the scientific study of "the processes of making laws, of breaking laws, and of reacting toward the breaking of laws" (Sutherland and Cressey, 1974:3). Each of these areas is a source of public concern and each may be studied with a view toward discovering, explaining, and tracing out the implications of regularities. Each of the three may be approached as a target for change.

Lawmaking

Historically, the search for the causes, or *etiology*, of lawbreaking and for ways of dealing with lawbreakers, *penology*, have dominated criminological inquiry. The central questions were: 1) "Why do some people become involved in crime or delinquency?" and 2) "What can we do about it either before or after the fact?" In the 1960s, however, a growing number of people became interested in a third question: "Why do we have the laws we have?" For these people the crime problem is, at least in part, a problem of *overcriminalization* (that is, treating too many types of behavior as crime) and the proliferation of laws "creating" crime. For example, after an extensive analysis of the drug problem in the United States, Erich Goode (1984) argued that our drug laws and their enforcement are primarily responsible for some of the most serious and harmful characteristics of the drug problem. He argued that by criminalizing drug use, the law actually sustains a subculture, supports an illicit market, drives users to crime, and creates a host of other secondary problems. The view that laws exist to prevent or solve problems and to protect society has been countered with arguments that laws originally designed to cope with social problems may create new problems or may transform minor social problems into more serious ones (Rose, 1968:33-43.)

Some critics of the juvenile justice system argue that too many kinds of youthful misbehavior can bring a child to the attention of the court and kids should be "left alone whenever possible" (Schur, 1973). A joint committee of the Institute for Judicial Administration and the American Bar Foundation (1977) has advocated removing noncriminal behavior and victimless crimes from juvenile court jurisdiction as well. The substance of laws governing children is a perennial target for proposals to help remedy the delinquency problem.

Thus, at present, there appears to be widespread consensus that a comprehensive study of crime and delinquency requires consideration of the forces and processes involved in the making, as well as the breaking, of laws. Our attempts to explain lawbreaking are often based on *implicit* theories and assumptions about the nature of criminal law and the relation of people in a society to those laws. Therefore, in considering the sources and causes of criminal behavior, we are often assuming a certain perspective on the nature of laws whether or not we realize that fact.

Lawbreaking

The explanation of who becomes "delinquent" and delinquent "behavior" has been a persistent concern in criminological inquiry, dominating much of the earliest work and much, if not most, of the research over the last two decades as well. In pursuit of an explanation, criminologists have examined physical, biological, psychological, social and cultural characteristics of people. Some criminologists have advanced explanations which stress "abnormality" while others have suggested that criminal and delinquent behavior are learned and that the processes involved are basically the same as those through which all behavior and lifestyles are acquired. Detailed case histories and ethnographies carried out in the 1920s and 1930s supported the view that crime or delinquency is learned and not inherited (Thrasher, 1927; Shaw, 1930, 1931, 1938; Sutherland, 1937). More recent research has shown that whether we learn to be law-abiding or law-violating individuals, this learning process is essentially the same.

The role of opportunities, values, and institutions such as the school, family, religion, and mass media in the causation of delinquency have been central foci in criminological research for several decades now. It is commonly presumed that if correlates or causes of lawbreaking can be identified, then one would be able to identify targets for preventative intervention or social change.

Reactions to Lawbreaking

We have already noted that an analysis of delinquency requires that we examine both lawmaking and lawbreaking. In addition, we should note that the study of law is one aspect of a larger concern—that is, the study of those forms of social control that involve "reactions to deviance." As Jack Gibbs (1972:4) has pointed out, a fundamental question in the study of social control is "What are the causes and consequences of variation in the character of reaction to deviance among social units over time?" The creation of laws or legal norms is one type of reaction to real or imagined problems and, hence, is a major aspect of the study of social control (Gibbs, 1989).

The dominant focus in the study of crime control has been *penology*— that branch of criminology concerned with the punishment and treatment of offenders and the administration of prisons (Fox, 1972). While the study of prisons and other correctional programs remains a vital concern in criminology, social scientists have been increasingly concerned with the administration of justice in general and have been extending the study of crime control processes to include the police and the courts. Moreover, researchers have begun exploring community reactions to crime and the sources of public attitudes, beliefs, and fears about crime and crime control (Conklin, 1986:325-45). Numerous observers and researchers have pointed out that the public plays a key role in the implementation (or lack thereof) of formal control processes and that decisions to call the police, to press for action, and to provide testimony are problematic themselves (Black, 1970; Black and Reiss, 1970; Hawkins, 1973; Black, 1989). Thus, the study of reactions to crime and delinquency has been extended to encompass not only the operation of the justice system but the causes of public reaction to crime as well.

Organizing Our Inquiry

Our study of delinquency will be organized around the three basic issues defining the subject matter of criminology as already outlined: lawmaking, lawbreaking, and reactions to lawbreaking. In Chapter 2 we will consider lawmaking. By exploring the nature, origin, and changes in juvenile law and juvenile justice we can gain an understanding of the forces that shape and sustain delinquency as a legal category and the juvenile court as a distinct legal institution.

In Chapters 3 and 4 we will deal with *delinquent* and *delinquency* as labels applied to some juveniles and some behaviors by police and the courts. Given the existence of such a legal category as delinquency, how is it actually applied? Who gets labeled and why? Do data on officially labeled acts and persons give an accurate picture of the nature and distribution of delinquent activity? Criminologists must deal with such questions in order to assess the adequacy of certain bodies of data for reaching conclusions about delinquency.

Not everyone engages equally in the types of activities that are defined as delinquency, and students of crime and delinquency have come up with a wide range of explanations for this variability. Sociologists focus on the social and cultural environment as sources of variation. Others look to biological or genetic characteristics of individuals and groups. Still others have searched for the cause of delinquency in the individual's personality. Biological, psychological and social psychological theory and research will be reviewed in Chapter 5 and sociological perspectives in Chapter 6.

While Chapter 6 concentrates on theories and the research which supports them, Chapters 7 and 8 summarize most of what is known about the role of the family, school, peers, religion, mass media, and neighborhoods in contributing to or inhibiting juvenile delinquency.

No study of delinquency is complete without a consideration of reactions to delinquency. At present, the basic issue of dominant concern to criminologists is the consequence of alternative reactions to delinquency. Does official processing, labeling, and punishment deter or encourage juvenile delinquency? Can community-based programs do a better job of inhibiting further delinquency than institutionalization of juvenile offenders? Can delinquency be reduced by diverting youth, making them compensate the victim or community, or scaring them straight? In Chapter 9, "Deterrence and Labeling," we will examine the first issue. The second will be the topic of Chapter 10, "Imprisonment and Alternatives," while Chapter 11, "Diversion, Restitution and Shock Therapy" will concentrate on the third issue.

The concluding chapter will consider a much broader issue involving social policy and juvenile delinquency: "Prevention: Dilemmas of Choice, Change, and Control." There we will grapple with complex and controversial issues: What meaning does all the research to date have for policy? If broad-scale change is called for, how far can we go and how far are we willing to go in dealing with the delinquency problem? What changes in our perspectives, values, and goals are we willing to consider? We cannot even take it for granted that "something" must be done. Such decisions involve moral evaluations of delinquency and of the social arrangements that help produce delinquency.

Summary

Although juvenile delinquency as a legal category is a relatively recent invention, there is a long history of concern for the misbehavior of the young, as well as an enduring tendency to view crimes of the young as the major dimension of the crime problem. The view that certain categories of juveniles are quite commonly involved in crime is supported by police and court statistics and by behavioral reports in surveys of juveniles. However, it should be emphasized that 1) juveniles are most distinct in their high arrest rates for related property offenses, 2) the group nature of their offenses may exaggerate their contribution to crime, 3) juvenile representation in arrest statistics peaked around 1978 and declined through the mid-1980s when it started up again, and 4) juveniles are underrepresented in numerous types of crime that have a higher economic cost than juvenile property crimes. Delinquency is one dimension of the crime problem, but there are reasonable grounds for challenging the view that it is the most serious or primary dimension.

Yet, the study of delinquency is the study of an important part of the crime problem, particularly since adult crime and juvenile delinquency can feed on each other. Such study also is a convenient vehicle for learning about ourselves and provides a foundation for making personal choices. Moreover, the study of delinquency has been central to the scientific discipline of criminology. Defining criminology as the scientific and critical study of lawmaking, lawbreaking, and reactions to lawbreaking, this text summarizes issues, theories, and research relevant to each of these topics in the study of juvenile delinquency.

References

American Humane Association. 1986. *Annual Report 1984. Highlights of Official Child Neglect and Abuse Reporting.* Denver: American Humane Association.

Aries, P. 1962. *Centuries of Childhood,* New York: Vintage Books.

Bachman, J. G., L. D. Johnston, and P. M. O'Malley. 1988. *Monitoring the Future, 1987.* Ann Arbor, MI: Institute for Social Research.

Belson, W. A. 1978. *Television Violence and the Adolescent Boy.* Farnborough: Saxon House.

Black, D. J. 1970. "Production of Crime Rates." *American Sociological Review* 35 (August): 733-48.

_____. 1989. *Sociological Justice.* New York: Oxford University Press.

Black, D. J., and A. J. Reiss, Jr. 1970. "Police Control of Juveniles." *American Sociological Review* 35 (February): 63-77.

Bolton, F. G., Jr., R. H. Laner, D. S. Gai, and S. P. Kane. 1981. "The 'Study' of Child Maltreatment: When is Research . . . Research?" *Journal of Family Issues.* Vol. 2 (December): 501-40.

Britt, C. 1989. "Constancy and Change in U.S. Age-Specific Arrest Rates, 1970-1984." Department of Sociology, University of Arizona.

Bureau of Justice Statistics. 1984. "The Severity of Crime." Bureau of Justice Statistics Bulletin, NCJ-92326.

Chamber of Commerce of the United States. 1974. *A Handbook on White-Collar Crime.* Washington, DC: Chamber of Commerce of the United States.

Chemerinsky, E. 1981. "Fraud and Corruption Against the Government: A Proposed Statute to Establish a Taxpayer Remedy." *Journal of Criminal Law and Criminology* 72: 1485-88.

Clinard, M. and P. Yeager. 1978. "Corporate Crime: Issues in Research." *Criminology* 2: 260-69.

Clinard, M., and W. Abbott. 1973. *Crime in Developing Countries: A Comparative Perspective.* New York: Wiley-Interscience.

Conklin, J. E. 1989. *Criminology.* New York: Macmillan.

Cressey, D. R. 1969. *Theft of the Nation.* New York: Harper & Row.

Easterlin, R. A. 1987. *Birth and Fortune: The Impact of Numbers on Personal Welfare.* Chicago, IL: The University of Chicago Press.

Elliott, D. S., D. Huizinga, and S. S. Ageton. 1985. *Explaining Delinquency and Drug Use.* Beverly Hills: Sage Publications.

Engardio, P., and G. DeGerge. 1989. "The Penny Stock Scandal." *Business Week* January 23: 74-82.

Erickson, M. L. 1971. "The Group Context of Delinquent Behavior." *Social Problems* 19 (No. 1): 114-28.

Federal Bureau of Investigation. 1988. *Crime in the United States.* Washington, DC: U. S. Government Printing Office.

Fox, V. 1972. *Introduction to Corrections.* Englewood Cliffs, NJ: Prentice-Hall.

Gelles, R. J., and E. F. Hargreaves. 1981. "Maternal Employment and Violence Towards Children." *Journal of Family Issues.* Vol. 2 (December): 509-30.

Gelles, R. J., and Murray Straus. 1985. *Is Violence Toward Children Increasing? A Comparison of 1975 and 1985 National Survey Rates.* Durham, NH: Family Violence Research Program.

Gibbs, J. P. 1972. "Social Control." New York: Warner Modular Publications, Module 1.

_____. 1989. *Control: Sociology's Central Notion.* Urbana, IL: University of Illinois Press.

Goode, E. 1984. *Drugs in American Society.* New York: Alfred A. Knopf.

Gottfredson, M. R., and T. Hirschi. 1990. *A General Theory of Crime.* Stanford, CA: Stanford University Press.

Hagan, J., and J. Leon. 1977. "Rediscovering Delinquency: Social History, Political Ideology and the Sociology of Law." *American Sociological Review* 42 (August): 587-98.

Hagan, J., A. R. Gillis, and J. Simpson. 1985. "Class Structure of Gender and Delinquency." *American Journal of Sociology* 90 (May): 1151-78.

Hawkins, R. 1973. "Who Called the Cops; Decisions to Report Criminal Victimization." *Law and Society Review* 7 (Spring): 427-43.

Hindelang, M. J. 1973. "Causes of Delinquency: A Partial Replication and Extension." *Social Problems* 20 (Spring): 471-87.

Hollinger, R. C., and J. P. Clark. 1983. *Theft by Employees.* Lexington, MA: D. C. Heath.

Institute for Judicial Administration and the American Bar Foundation. 1977. *Juvenile Justice Standards.* 24 Vols. Cambridge, MA: Ballinger Publishing Company.

Johnson, J. M., and J. D. Douglas. 1978. *Crime at the Top: Deviance in Business and the Professions.* Philadelphia: J. B. Lippincott.

O'Brien, Robert M. 1989. "Relative Cohort Size and Age-Specific Crime Rates: An Age-Period-Relative-Cohort-Size Model." *Criminology* 27 (Number 1): 57-78.

Pima County Juvenile Court Center. 1982. *Volunteer Handbook.* Volunteer Service, Pima County Juvenile Court, Tucson, Arizona.

Pizzo, S., M. Fricker, and P. Muolo. 1989. *Inside Job: The Looting of America's Savings and Loans.* New York: McGraw-Hill Publishing Company.

Polk, K. 1974. *Teenage Delinquency in Small Town America*, Research Report 5. Center for Studies of Crime and Delinquency. Rockville, MD: National Institute of Mental Health.

President's Commission on Law Enforcement and Administration of Justice. 1967. *The Challenge of Crime in a Free Society.* Washington, DC: U. S. Government Printing Office.

Priyadarsini, S., and C. A. Hartjen. 1981. "Delinquency and Corrections in India." Pp. 109-23 in *Sociology of Delinquency*, G. F. Jensen, (ed.). Beverly Hills, CA: Sage Publications.

Regnery, A. S. 1985. "Getting away with Murder: Why the Juvenile Justice System Needs an Overhaul."*Policy Review*, (Fall): 65-68.

Roebuck, J., and S. C. Weeber. 1978. *Political Crime in the United States: Analyzing Crime by and against Government.* New York: Praeger.

Rose, A. M. 1968. "Law and the Causation of Social Problems." *Social Problems* 16 (Summer): 33-43.

Schur, E. M. 1973. *Radical Non-Intervention: Rethinking the Delinquency Problem.* Englewood Cliffs, NJ: Prentice-Hall.

Shannon, L. 1982. *Assessing the Relationship of Adult Criminal Careers to Juvenile Careers.* Washington, DC: U. S. Department of Justice.

Shaw, C. R. 1930. *The Jack-Roller.* Chicago: University of Chicago Press.

_____. 1931. *Natural History of a Delinquent Career.* Chicago: University of Chicago Press.

_____. 1938. *Brothers in Crime.* Chicago: University of Chicago Press.

Simon, D. R., and D. S. Eitzen. 1986. *Elite Deviance.* Boston: Allyn and Bacon.

Snyder, H. N., and E. H. Nimick. 1983. "City Delinquents and Their Country Cousins: A Description of Juvenile Delinquency in Metropolitan and Nonmetropolitan Areas." *Today's Delinquent*, Vol. 2.

Sutherland, E. H. 1937. *The Professional Thief.* Chicago: University of Chicago Press.

_____. 1940. "White Collar Criminality." *American Sociological Review* 5 (February): 1-12.

Sutherland, E. H., and D. R. Cressey. 1974. *Criminology.* New York: J. B. Lippincott.

Terrill, R. J. 1984. *World Criminal Justice Systems: A Survey.* Cincinnati: Anderson Publishing.

Thrasher, F. M. 1927. *The Gang.* Chicago: University of Chicago Press.

Time. 1977. "The Youth Crime Plague." (July 11): 18-28.

West, D.J. 1982. *Delinquency: Its Roots, Causes and Prospects.* London: Heinemann.

West, D. J., and D. P. Farrington. 1973. *Who Becomes Delinquent?* London: Heinemann.

Widom, C. S. 1989. "Child Abuse, Neglect, and Violent Criminal Behavior." *Criminology* 27 (Number 2): 251-72.

Williams, J. R., and M. Gold. 1972. "From Delinquent Behavior to Official Delinquency." *Social Problems* 20 (Fall): 209-29.
Wolfgang, M. E., R. Figlio, and T. Sellin. 1972. *Delinquency in a Birth Cohort.* Chicago: University of Chicago Press.

chapter **2**

Juvenile Justice

AN INFANT DESPERADO.

> *The rights to a definite charge, counsel, a fair hearing, reasonably relevant and convincing evidence, and appeal are insured to a man on the most trivial issues of political administration, but not to the child. In a large proportion of specialized urban children's courts the child enters with what is in effect a presumption of his delinquency and, under the conditions of today's "chancery" procedure there, it is almost impossible for him to rebut that presumption, once a probation officer has found a personal problem in his history to work on. Who is to save the child from his saviors?*
>
> —Paul W. Tappan, *Juvenile Delinquency*, 1949

Introduction

"Who is to save the child from his saviors?" At a time when people are concerned that teenage "thugs" are treated too leniently and too much attention is paid to the rights of the accused, Tappan's question may seem absurd. Yet, in 1949 when he asked that question there had been no Supreme Court decisions extending rights of due process of law to juveniles in juvenile court proceedings. Delinquency rates were relatively low (see Chapter 3) and had not begun their long upward climb in the United States. American society had not yet experienced the decades of population growth associated with the post-war "baby boom." In fact, delinquency referral rates had been declining after a brief post-war surge and the juvenile arrest rate was low and stable.

In 1949 juveniles being processed by the juvenile court had few rights of due process. They were not entitled to an attorney, to question witnesses or testimony, or to notification of the charges against them. Despite a flourish of decisions beginning in the 1960s which extended rights to juveniles, there are still major differences between procedural protections required in the adult criminal justice system and those required in juvenile proceedings. Most of us are aware of rights in the adult system, and such terms as *bail, Miranda warnings, trial by jury, taking the fifth, right to an attorney,* and *notification of charges* sound familiar. Yet, if we asked what rights juveniles have or do not have, and what terms are used in juvenile court proceedings, they would likely be familiar only to a few.

In this chapter we will briefly describe contemporary juvenile justice and the social changes, precedents, and prerequisites to its invention. We will also review Supreme Court decisions defining the rights of juveniles as well as current court definitions of delinquency. Finally, we will ask "How tough are juvenile courts compared to adult courts?" The popular conception is expressed in the title of a recent critique of the system by Alfred Regnery (1986) in which he concludes that juveniles are literally "Getting Away with Murder." Are they getting away with murder to any greater degree than comparable cases processed through the adult system?

A Brief Overview of Juvenile Justice

Juvenile justice systems are the legal institutions that handle offenses and problems of nonadults in society. Such cases can be handled in juvenile courts that are separate organizations within a state's court system or in courts that are divisions of a larger court system. In some jurisdictions matters of juvenile justice are dealt with by *family courts*. While we will concentrate on the processing of offenses and offenders, it is important to note that family courts deal with a wide range of issues where the court seeks to protect the interests of children, including divorce, custody, neglect, abuse, child support, and adoption. In some jurisdictions the traffic offenses of juveniles are processed by the juvenile court while in others such offenses are handled by a separate traffic court. The full range of issues falling within their jurisdiction will vary from state to state and county to county. Juvenile courts do not handle as wide a range of legal issues as family courts, but they too deal with a wide range of juvenile matters, only one of which is juvenile delinquency.

The organization of juvenile justice systems varies among jurisdictions and similar procedures may be given different names. Figure 2-1 summarizes the major steps in a "generic" juvenile justice system and Figure 2-2 includes the definitions of important terms used in such systems. There is a wide range of options available at nearly every stage and several steps may occur at once (e.g. adjudication and disposition, detention and transfer).

The terms used can be contrasted with parallel terms in the adult system to illustrate distinctive features of juvenile court philosophy. Since the juvenile court is supposed to be helping, treating, or rehabilitating youth rather than punishing them, youth are not "arrested" but rather are "referred" to the court. Such referrals can come from agents of social control other than the police such as school officials, social workers, and parents. Juveniles can be referred for specific activities that would not be criminal for an adult (e.g. truancy, smoking, runaway) as well as for vague patterns of activities (e.g. ungovernable, incorrigible). Such offenses are called *status offenses* because it is the offender's juvenile status that warrants intervention by the juvenile justice system. Youth are also referred for offenses that are criminal for adults and make them liable to being

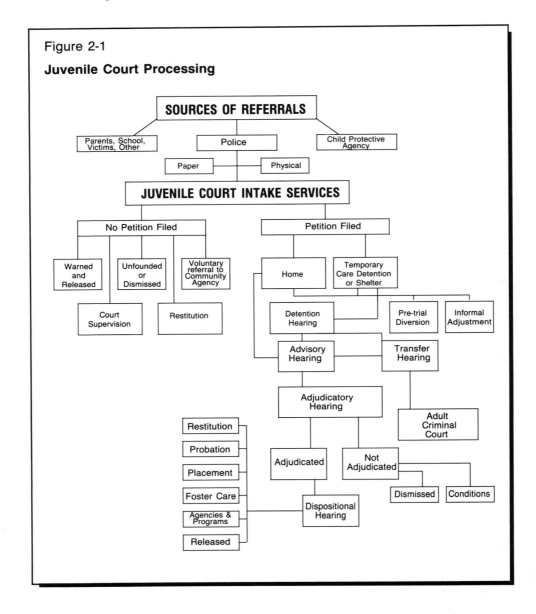

Figure 2-1

Juvenile Court Processing

processed as a "delinquent." As we elaborate later in this chapter, the differentiation among types of offenses and offenders and the various methods of treatment are a relatively recent development.

Police can make *paper referrals* or *physical referrals* to the juvenile court. A paper referral is much like a traffic citation in that an official document (paper) is issued to the youth's parent or guardian, requiring that the youth be brought to the juvenile court at a specific time to determine what additional action, if any, is needed. A physical referral is made when the youth is brought bodily to the juvenile court. Paper referrals are more likely for less serious offenses and in situations where a parent is readily available, willing, and able to accept custody of the child. In some instances a youth may not have to appear at the court. Rather, a case worker or probation officer may meet with the youth and his or her parents at the youth's residence to decide on further action.

A physical referral is made to an *intake unit* and an intake officer decides among a variety of options based on details of the case, characteristics and attitudes of the youth, and the youth's home and school situation. If a decision is made that the court needs to take further legal action, the juvenile is not charged but, rather, a *petition* is filed recommending one of several further proceedings. Juveniles have not been extended the right to have a lawyer present at this stage and the information compiled to make such intake decisions cannot be used in any subsequent *adjudication hearing*. While the next stage in an adult case after the accused is arraigned or indicted could be a trial to determine guilt, the comparable step in the juvenile justice system would be a *hearing* to *adjudicate* the case. The youth might also be recommended for *detention* at a secure facility while waiting for subsequent hearings and is entitled to a detention hearing. The petition filed could recommend transfer to the adult criminal justice system and that decision would be made in a hearing as well.

Rather than determining whether the accused is guilty as charged, the case is adjudicated and a decision is made by the judge (or the judge's representative, a "referee," with the judge subsequently reviewing the decision for approval). Juveniles are entitled to a lawyer (at the court's expense if necessary) at this stage, although a recent survey suggests that only 50 percent of juveniles are represented by attorneys (Feld, 1988). If the judge decides that there are insufficient grounds for adjudicating a youth as recommended, the youth is released. If the juvenile is adjudicated a delinquent or status offender, then the judge must decide on a *disposition*. Information gathered as part of the intake report can be used at this stage and a juvenile is not generally entitled to a lawyer unless state law requires it.

The most common disposition is *probation*. Typically, the youth will be on probation under the supervision of parents and must abide by a set of rules as well as report to or be supervised periodically by a probation officer. The juvenile might also be placed in an institution, treatment program, or foster home. The adjudicated offender may be required to make *restitution* (repay) the victim and/or to do service for the community.

In sum, consistent with the treatment-rehabilitation philosophy of the juvenile court, the terms used to describe the process do not carry the

Figure 2-2

Glossary of Juvenile Justice Terms

Adjudicated: Judicially determined to be a delinquent, status offender, or dependent/neglected.

Adjudication Hearing: Hearing to determine whether a child should be adjudicated.

Advisory Hearing: A preliminary hearing to determine what subsequent actions are necessary.

Delinquency: Acts or conduct in violation of criminal law.

Delinquent Act: An act committed by a juvenile for which an adult could be prosecuted in a criminal court, but when committed by a juvenile is within the jurisdiction of the juvenile court. Delinquent acts include crimes against persons, crimes against property, drug offenses, and crimes against public order when such acts are committed by juveniles.

Dependent/Neglected: Those cases covering neglect or inadequate care on the part of the parents or guardians. They include lack of adequate care or support resulting from death, absence, or physical or mental incapacity of the parents; abandonment or desertion; abuse or cruel treatment; and improper or inadequate conditions in the home.

Detention: Temporary incarceration of a child who requires secure custody for his/her protection or protection of the community.

Detention Hearing: Hearing to determine whether a child is in need of secure detention.

Disposition: Definite action taken or a treatment plan decided upon or initiated regarding a particular case. Case dispositions are coded into the following categories:

> Transfer to Criminal Court/Waive—Cases which were waived or transferred to a criminal court as the result of a waiver or transfer hearing.
>
> Release—Cases dismissed (including those warned, counselled, and released) with no further disposition anticipated.
>
> Probation—Cases in which youth were placed on informal/voluntary or formal/court-ordered probation or supervision.
>
> Placement—Cases in which youth were placed out of the home in a residential facility housing delinquent or status offenders.
>
> Other—A variety of miscellaneous dispositions not included above.

Disposition Hearing: A hearing held to determine what should be done after a child has been adjudicated.

Incorrigible: A juvenile law categorization in some jurisdictions encompassing youth who are repeatedly in conflict with authority.

Informal Adjustment: Subject to court approval, after investigation in a delinquent or unruly referral, the designated court officer concluded that a child is within the jurisdiction of the court and undertakes to remedy the situation by giving counsel and advice to the parties with a view toward informal adjustment of the case. If the informal adjustment is not successful, the court officer may terminate the informal adjustment and file a petition.

Intake Officer: Probation officer who first reviews a referral and makes a recommendation on proper court action in a case.

Intake Services: Unit at juvenile court center where referrals are initially processed.

Juvenile Court: Any court which has jurisdiction over matters involving juveniles.

Petition: A document filed in juvenile court alleging that a juvenile is a delinquent, status offender, dependent, abused, or for a special proceeding (i.e., child support, legitimation) and asking that the court assume jurisdiciton over the juvenile or asking that an alleged delinquent be transferred to criminal court for prosecution as an adult.

Referral: The filing of a complaint by a law enforcement officer; the child's parents, guardians, or custodians; the school system; a social service agency; or other individuals or agencies requesting the court to exercise its authority.

Restitution: Plan requiring offender to return property, make monetary compensation, or provide service to the victim and/or community to compensate for harm inflicted by the offender.

Source of Referral: The agency or individual filing a complaint with intake (which initiates court processing).

Status Offense: Behavior which is considered an offense only when committed by a juvenile (for example, running away from home).

Transfer Hearing: Hearing to determine whether a case should be remanded or waived to the criminal justice system.

Source: Compiled from J. Traugher, J. F. Lucas, and S. Parish, 1989, *Tennessee Juvenile Court Annual Statistical Report;* Pima County Collaboration for Children and Youth, 1980, *Juvenile Rights and Responsibilities;* Snyder et al., 1989, *Juvenile Court Statistics, 1985.*

adversarial and combative connotations of terms for comparable procedures and decisions in the adult system. The juvenile court is supposed to be acting in lieu of the parents to do something to help the youth or on "behalf of" the youth. Hence, procedural *due process of law* safeguards taken for granted in the adult system have not been as prominent in the juvenile system.

The organizational and procedural outgrowths of this treatment philosophy have come under attack by critics since the invention of the court. On the one hand, the treatment philosophy has been criticized for disguising a basically punitive system where the juvenile is neither helped nor protected by due process of law. On the other hand, the treatment philosophy and the leeway it accords intake officials, judges, and probation officers has been attacked for allowing lenient offender-centered decisions and dispositions.

The same debates involved in the invention of the juvenile justice system are carried out in public, scholarly, and political debates of the 1990s. Some exposure to the history of this special legal institution and the controversies that perennially surround it should prompt questions about the diverse and contradictory expectations that different groups or "publics" have for the juvenile justice system. It is expected to deter, treat, and respond to the offenses of juveniles in a just manner. It likely cannot do all three equally well at the same time and can always be attacked for ignoring one goal while pursuing another. A review of the history of the juvenile court should make us aware of conflicting expectations and help us understand the basis for perennial criticism.

Many features of the criminal justice system date to the eleventh century while most features of the juvenile court system emerged only in the twentieth century. Indeed, the juvenile justice system can be considered to be in its infancy and numerous issues of due process of law have yet to be resolved.

The perceived need for a special court to deal with juvenile offenders was preceded by the development of conceptions of age categories between infancy and adulthood that required special attention. Whether this attention is good or bad from the point of view of society or the people processed through it is still a controversy. The debates concerning the merits of creating a juvenile court in the nineteenth century have reemerged in the past few years, reflecting a never-ending tension between the view that special consideration should be given to children and that society should be protected from crime regardless of the age of the offender.

The Discovery of Childhood

It may seem ludicrous to propose that childhood was "discovered" just a few centuries ago, since the persistence of the human race obviously required that people had children. However, the number of stages that are acknowledged in human development varies among different societies and over time. For example, some historians argue that the concept of childhood as a socially distinct category developed sometime during the seventeenth century. Prior to that time, no one really considered these pre-adults to have any special problems or to have any unique position in the family. Life was short, and with so many children dying in infancy, what appeared to be callousness toward children was a natural response to a highly precarious stage of existence.

World population growth is a product of modern times with little change until the eighteenth century. There were fewer than 300 million people on earth in the year 1000 A.D. Infant mortality was extremely high with epidemics of plague and smallpox as well as such diseases as whooping cough, scarlet fever, diphtheria, typhus, dysentery, and measles serving as a natural check on population growth. Phillip Aries suggests in his book, *Centuries of Childhood*, "people could not allow themselves to become too attached to something that was regarded as a probable loss" (1962:38).

Researchers studying the fifteenth, sixteenth, and seventeenth centuries have noted that people tended to slow the rate at which they had children following disease epidemics (Wrigley, 1969). Some scholars suggest that plagues had devastating psychological as well as biological consequences and people rejected the idea of bringing new life into the world (Chambers, 1972). It was during such periods of stagnant population growth that the Catholic Church and numerous European governments mounted a campaign to encourage marriage and fertility and to discourage abortion, infanticide, and birth control.

Aries suggests that it was during this time period that the concept of childhood emerged. Based on an examination of family portraits, Aries argues that prior to the seventeenth century, all family members were represented as equals. Some members were tall and physically mature whereas others were short and somewhat scrawny, but there was no attempt to differentiate adults from children. Beginning in the seventeenth century, Aries noted a dramatic difference in family portraits, especially those depicted by Rubens and Van Dyck. Children ceased to be dressed like grown-ups and their placement in the portrait was typically of a dependent person held in the arms of his or her mother, or else sitting or leaning on an adult. Children wore clothing that set them apart from adults. Another historian suggested that "the decline in early mortality, therefore, can be seen as an independent variable that encouraged the deepening of emotional bonds between parents and children" (Zelizer, 1985:10).

Aries' interpretation of the discovery of childhood is a subject of debate and is not accepted by everyone. Linda Pollock (1983) argues that the assumption of indifference and neglect prior to the seventeenth century is exaggerated and based on inadequate documentary evidence. While abuse and neglect may have been exaggerated, there is agreement among historical demographers (people who study the nature, change, and distribution of populations) that people in Western European society were not having children at the rate that would be supported by available resources, nor rebounding from massive disease epidemics. Church and state felt it necessary to fight such tendencies and to enforce pro-natalist norms supporting the value of marriage, family, and children (Heinsohn and Steiger, 1982). Whether such policies had an impact on conceptions of age categories or the care and value of children cannot be determined. The certainty of survival beyond infancy did increase considerably beginning in the mid-1700s together with the decline in disease epidemics, famines, and increased public and personal hygiene.

The Discovery of Adolescence

The interim status between childhood and adulthood, which we call "adolescence," was a term that came into usage in the nineteenth century. Aries noted that in the French language there were three age references in the seventeenth century: childhood, youth, and old age, with youth signifying the prime of life. The word commonly used for referring to children from birth through their teens was "infant." Aries observed that the differentiation between infancy and childhood in the French language did not occur until the nineteenth century. What emerged in the sixteenth and seventeenth centuries was the perceived need by aristocrats to send their children to special schools for a classical education and, most importantly, for discipline, which was seen as an instrument of moral and spiritual improvement.

> A new moral concept was to distinguish the child, or at least the schoolboy, and set him apart: the concept of the well-bred child . . . (the concept) was the product of the forming opinions of an elite group of thinkers and moralists who occupied high positions in Church or State. The well-bred child would be preserved from the roughness and immorality which would become the special characteristics of the lower classes. In France this well-bred child would be the little bourgeois. In England he would be the gentleman, a social type unknown before the nineteenth century, and which a threatened aristocracy would create, thanks to the public schools, to defend itself against the progress of democracy. (Aries, 1962:327-28)

Aries tied the development or recognition of adolescence to the rise of an emphasis on militaristic discipline in the schools and the preparation of "boys of good family" for military careers. The adolescent was the young would-be soldier. Thus, the idea of adolescence as a distinct age group began in Europe and was related to the development of an educational system designed to produce disciplined, well-bred children whose further training in adolescence would prepare them for military careers.

According to Aries the differentiation of age grades between infant and adult, and the view of these stages as special and unique, may have reflected social and political development of the seventeenth and eighteenth centuries. In contrast, David Bakan (1971) has argued that "adolescence was added to childhood as a second childhood in order to fulfill the aims of the new urban-industrial society which developed so rapidly following the Civil War." Bakan's claim is that "adolescence" took shape as a distinct socio-legal age category in the last two decades of the nineteenth century in the United States as a result of three major social movements. These movements were aimed at 1) compulsory public education, 2) child labor legislation, and 3) the establishment of a juvenile court. During this so-called Progressive era, the state, according to Bremner (1970), became a kindly parent and the best interests of the child coincided with the best interests of the state.

According to Bakan, the term "adolescence" was an American "discovery" linked specifically to G. Stanley Hall, one of the most prominent psychologists of the nineteenth century and the person who is considered the father of the study of adolescence. In an 1882 publication entitled "The Moral and Religious Training of Children," Hall compared the stage of adolescence to the evolution of the human species from savagery into civilization. His so-called "storm and stress" hypothesis likens adolescence to a period marked by "a lack of emotional steadiness, violent impulses, unreasonable conduct, the previous selfhood is broken up and a new individual is in process of being born. All is solvent, plastic, particularly susceptible to external influence" (1882:29). While Hall's notion of adolescence as "a long pilgrimage of the soul" has been severely criticized, his dramatic highlighting of this stage of child development added fuel to the fire for greater care and concern for maturing children in the late nineteenth century.

Social Change in the Nineteenth Century

The social movements of the nineteenth century reflected the transformation of American society from a rural-agrarian economy to an urban-industrial one. This transformation took place as huge waves of immigrants poured into urban settings. Of particular importance were the reactions of the established Protestant middle and upper classes. It was from these ranks that social reformers and the leaders of the social movements would emerge. In New York in the early 1800s and Chicago in the late 1800s, upper- and middle-class reformers exhibited common concerns about establishing institutions and shaping policies to socialize the urban, lower-class immigrant into their conception of the American way of life.

The drive for compulsory public education of the young reflected the reformers' perceived need to integrate and control the masses and to prepare them for work. To acculturate the new Americans, children had to be taken out of the labor force and put in school. The importance of public education was also reinforced by an increasing industrial need for skilled labor and by the efforts of labor unions to gain control over working conditions. Cheap, readily available child labor was an impediment to successful unionization, and labor leaders were opposed to it on economic as well as social grounds. Also there emerged a need to control the labor supply in the United States as unrestricted immigration and an increasing number of children began to produce a labor surplus. Thus, a concern for creating special institutions that could socialize and control emerging problem populations preceded the development of a special legal status for certain age groups.

In summary, the prolongation of childhood and the delineation of adolescence as a distinct age category were ultimately the products of social, economic, and technological change. Such change led to the increasing emphasis of the uniqueness of children and the need of the state to take a more active role in the socialization of youth. Historian Christopher Lasch argues that Progressive reformers sought to shelter and preserve the family's influence on children, especially immigrant families, by creating new "agencies of socialized reproduction: educators, psychiatrists, social workers, and penologists" (1979:27). Lasch claims that these reformers sought to place the young under the benign influence of the state in order to insure the proper "American" socialization of children. Mary Carpenter, an influential penal reformer, stated in an 1875 address that it is the duty of the state to intercede and "stand *in loco parentis* and do its duty to the child and to society, by seeing that he is properly brought up" (Abbot, 1938). Having considered the social forces at work, particularly in nineteenth century America, we can now turn to an examination of the development of the juvenile court.

The Origins of Juvenile Justice

Several historical studies in recent years have dealt with the evolution of juvenile justice in the United States and Canada (Platt, 1969a; Bremner, 1970; Finestone, 1976; Schlossman, 1977; Hagan and Leon, 1977; Sutton, 1988). In some of these studies there is disagreement on the sources or meaning of certain important developments in the processing of juveniles. For instance, a popular work by Anthony Platt focuses on the "child-saving" movement in the late 1800s as the key to the establishment of the first juvenile court in Chicago. In their histories of juvenile justice, Steven Schlossman (1977) and Harold Finestone (1976) describe the social developments and legal justifications that ultimately led to a separate justice system for juveniles as occurring very early in the 1800s. Moreover, the social and religious forces of the late 1800s upon which Platt focuses are quite similar to the forces Schlossman and Finestone identify at earlier points in time. Schlossman and Finestone view the establishment of the juvenile court as a product of more benign forces than Platt, who suggests that such development was a reflection of pressure for increased social control by capitalists. As noted later in this chapter, an analysis of the history of Canadian juvenile court reform is critical of the vague references to the interests or needs of capitalists as the driving force behind the emergence of distinct juvenile laws and juvenile justice machinery. As we examine the development of the juvenile justice system it is important to recognize that there are conflicting interpretations of social history.

Compulsory Education and Houses of Refuge

An important development in the early evolution of juvenile justice in the United States was the establishment of the "house of refuge" in the 1820s. Such institutions were prison-like schools for juvenile offenders and impoverished children. Their development was intimately connected with the push for compulsory public education. Both compulsory education and the concept of the reformatory grew out of the efforts of middle- and upper-class reformers to deal with new problem populations through the extension of state control over children. In 1838, for example, a key court decision (*Ex parte Crouse*), which concerned the constitutionality of incarcerating a child in a house of refuge without due process of law, drew on the arguments that reformers used to advance compulsory education and helped establish the legal basis of the juvenile court.

The 1838 case involved Mary Ann Crouse, who was committed to the Philadelphia House of Refuge on the basis of a complaint lodged by her mother. Her father did not find out about the action until after Mary was committed, and he subsequently sought to have Mary released on the grounds that her rights had been violated. The court decided that the Bill of Rights did not apply to children and that the house of refuge was merely a type of school for problem children. The court ruled:

> The object of the charity is reformation, by training its inmates to industry; by imbuing their minds with principles of morality and religion; by furnishing them with means to earn a living; and above all, by separating them from the corrupting influence of improper associates. To this end, may not the natural parents, when unequal to the task of education, or unworthy of it, be superseded by the *parens patriae*, or common guardian of the community? It is to be remembered that the public has a paramount interest in the virtue and knowledge of its members, and that, of strict right, the business of education belongs to it (4 Wharton 9).

The concept of *parens patriae* (parent of the land), or the right of the state to care for minors and others who cannot legally take care of themselves, arose in fifteenth century law. The king as parent of the land was asked to become a guardian over those children whose natural parents were deceased. This legal right was used, ostensibly, to maintain the structure of feudalism and to assure the orderly transfer of feudal duties from one generation to the next. Similarly, the English Poor Laws of 1601 extended the original interpretation of *parens patriae* to the right of the state to remove children from destitute parents and apprentice them to others. These children were forced to serve their masters as agricultural laborers or domestic servants until age 21. Thus, the Poor Laws and the *Ex parte Crouse* case were predicated on the right of the state to intervene in the lives of children, even if the natural parents objected.

In the United States, the house of refuge movement and the notion of reform schools for delinquent children used the concept of *parens patriae* as its legal foundation. It is also important to note that compulsory school attendance was being advanced at the same time and this legal stipulation gave the state the right to mandate compulsory education for all children. Schlossman states that the advocates of public education and reform schools:

> urged the judges to place both types of facility, public school and reformatory, under the safeguard of the parens patriae doctrine, and to establish once and for all time that the state's provision of education for the poor was a legitimate exercise of its police powers.
>
> The court agreed entirely with (this) point of view. A reformatory, it insisted, was nothing but a residential school for underprivileged children, a horizontal expansion of the fledgling public school system. A reformatory was "not a prison but a school." Its objectives were in the broadest sense educational: to train children in industry, morality, the means to earn a living, and most importantly, to isolate them from the "corrupting influences of improper associates." The court went on: "As to the abridgment of indefensible rights by confinement of the person, it is no more than what is borne, to a greater or less extent, in every school; and we know of no natural right to exemption from restraints which conduce to an infant's welfare." In sum, the court concluded, the government's right to incarcerate children who had not committed criminal acts was neither capricious nor vindictive, for the house of refuge was nothing but a residential public school for unfortunate youth. (1977:10)

This conception of reformatories was disputed in 1870 in Illinois in the case of *People v. Turner*. The case involved a boy who had been committed to the Chicago Reform School on vague charges that did not involve a definable crime. The state appellate court ordered the boy's release and questioned the analogy that had been drawn between reformatories and public schools, as well as the right of the state to intervene in violation of children's rights and parents' rights. However, as Schlossman has pointed out, this decision had little impact on the spread of reformatories or on subsequent court challenges. The movement to deal with problem populations through compulsory education and the extension of governmental control was too widely supported by reformers, industrialists, and the dominant ideology of the times to be overturned by a court decision.

In the mid-1800s reformers, drawing on European views of juvenile corrections, challenged the idea of the "school-like" institution with its emphasis on discipline and work. The basic concept and practice of differential treatment of juveniles was accepted both in the United States and abroad, but the correctional model in Europe took the form of the "family reform school" (Schlossman, 1977:37).

Anti-institutionalists—such as Charles Loring Brace of New York and Samuel Gridley Howe of Massachusetts—opposed the use of prison-like institutions and advocated a greater reliance on the "family" as a tool for changing behavior. They particularly advocated using rural, frontier, or farm families to provide foster homes for the "vagabond," the "wretched," and the "homeless." In 1853 the New York Children's Aid Society was founded to stress prevention rather than simply correcting juvenile delinquents. Brace, as secretary of the Society, disparaged the "institutional child" and sent them west to "the best of all asylums...the farmer's home" (Bremner, 1970:672). This became known as the *placing out* doctrine.

However, this anti-institutionalist point of view was influenced by the religious and class conflicts of the time. Protestant ministers dominated the reform school movement and were accused of proselytizing Catholic youths and discriminating against children of free blacks. According to Bremner (1970) many reform schools and preventive societies sent older boys to fight for the North during the Civil War. Between 1855 and 1880, Brace, who attributed the crime problem "to the cheapness of spirit and the multitudes of low Irish Catholics," sent an estimated 50,000 Catholic orphans to Protestant families in the West (Hawes, 1971). In 1863 the New York Catholics Protectory was founded not only to protect poor children of Catholic parentage but also to protect them from institutions "having Protestant directors, Protestant superintendents, Protestant teachers, Protestant worship, and Protestant instruction and training" (Bremner, 1970:749).

The Juvenile Court

By the mid-1800s debates over the privately funded houses of refuge and the newly created, publicly funded reform schools in northeastern states had established the precedents for differential handling and processing of youthful "troublemakers" and problem children. As John Sutton (1988: 118) concludes in his historical analysis of the evolution of the juvenile court "the reform school served as the vehicle and prerequisite for the formal, legal creation of delinquency as a deviant role for children." As early as the 1880s some judges in New York were holding separate hearings for children, and a crude probation system had developed in Massachusetts (Schlossman, 1977:63-64).

A number of factors converged in Chicago at the end of the nineteenth century that led to the creation of a juvenile court. First, Chicago grew faster than any city in the world, reaching one million in 1890 and growing to two million by 1910 (Finestone, 1976). Second, more than 70 percent of the inhabitants of Chicago were immigrants. Third, the Chicago Bar Association was particularly concerned that the State of Illinois had no reform schools and no power regarding the conduct of juveniles. With pressure from a coalition of reformers and the Chicago Bar Association, the Illinois legislature passed a bill in 1899 establishing the first juvenile court. The legislation formally established a separate system of juvenile justice that was to be essentially noncriminal and oriented toward "treatment" rather than punishment of juvenile offenders.

The new juvenile court was not to be a mere extension of the jurisdiction of the criminal court, but rather an independent court system with complete jurisdiction over the affairs of juveniles. The founders of the juvenile court envisioned it as the cornerstone of a comprehensive child care system. "It was designed to treat the youthful offender as a child primarily and only incidentally as a law violator" (Finestone, 1976:45).

Some observers view the motivation for the creation of the juvenile court as a product of the same conservative reformist concerns that resulted in the establishment of houses of refuge and reformatories. Anthony Platt described the conservative nature of reform during the late 1800s as follows:

> Contemporary programs of delinquency control can be traced to the enterprising reforms of the child-savers who, at the end of the nineteenth century, helped to create special judicial and correctional institutions for the labeling, processing, and management of "troublesome" youth. Child-saving was a conservative and romantic movement, designed to impose sanctions on conduct unbecoming youth and to disqualify youth from enjoying adult privileges. The child-savers were prohibitionists, in a general sense, who believed in close supervision of adolescents' recreation and leisure. The movement brought attention to, and thus "invented," new categories of youthful misbehavior which had been previously unappreciated or had been dealt with on an informal basis. Child-saving was heavily influenced by middle-class women who extended their housewifely roles into public service and emphasized the dependence of the social order on the proper socialization of children. (1969b:21)

Elsewhere in his writings (1974:356-89), Platt extended his analysis to argue that the middle-class reformers were supported by an upper-class and industrial elite who would benefit from industrial discipline and who were concerned with establishing stability and order in a rapidly changing urban environment. Thus, Platt views the creation of the juvenile court as an outgrowth of middle- and upper-class interests, fears, and concerns that promoted an increase in the scope of state control.

In contrast to Platt, Schlossman and Finestone believe that what was most distinctive or "progressive" about the idea of the juvenile court was its emphasis on probation and on the home and family as the target for treatment. According to Finestone (1976:46), "Since the formation of the juvenile court represented the culmination and response to almost fifty years of criticism of the institutionalized handling of juvenile delinquents, it was primarily concerned with treatment in the community." Thus, the emphasis was on probation and the probation officer as an "agent of the court in the community." In an analysis of the development of juvenile court legislation in Canada, John Hagan and Jeffrey Leon (1977:597) presented a similar interpretation. They argued that an emphasis on probation and the family as the locus of treatment was central to such legislation. They also argued that the link between the interests of industrial and other elites, and the invention of the juvenile court emphasized by Platt is purely inferential and that most claims about the consequences of its invention are wrong.

Whether the creation of the juvenile court was progressive or conservative, or motivated by humanitarian concerns or class interests is a continuing source of controversy. However, there does appear to be agreement that the gap between the "promise" of the juvenile court and its actual implementation was considerable. Platt argued that treatment for lower-class youths took the form of "training schools" built as prisons and based on principles of reform through militaristic discipline and forced labor. The noncriminal nature of its proceedings gave the court greater control over the lives of juveniles in that it could deal with behavior that was not criminal but that was defined as "bad" by the reformers. In his analysis of the operation of the Milwaukee Juvenile Court in the early 1900s, Schlossman (1977:167) reported that 1) relations between the court and clientele "were generally hostile and always superficial," 2) the court showed little concern with fair proceedings, and 3) actual operations were infused with a view of youth (particularly lower-class immigrant youth) as threatening and perverse.

Overall, it appears that the establishment of the juvenile court represented a combination of humanitarianism and an anti-institutional ideology that emphasized probation. However, its popularity, support, and implementation also reflected anti-urban, anti-Catholic, anti-immigrant, and anti-lower-class biases. In short, a concern with gaining better legal control over threatening categories of people. Humanitarianism demanded that children be "saved" from the brutal realities of the adult criminal justice system, but at the same time many adults felt that they needed to be saved from the children of the "dangerous" classes. The criminal justice system was not controlling the young effectively. Judges were reluctant to deal with youth in the same fashion as adults, and were releasing them back to the streets. Something had to be done. That "something" was the creation of a separate justice system for juveniles that encompassed a far wider range of offensive behaviors than the adult criminal justice system.

Parens Patriae *and Due Process of Law*

The move toward separate legal institutions for juveniles was justified as an "obvious" extension of a doctrine in English common law known as *parens patriae* (parent of the land). This legal concept is reflected in virtually all juvenile codes and serves as the legal rationale for both the form and substance of juvenile justice in the United States. The major consequence of applying this concept to juvenile justice is that the court, acting on behalf of the state, can become the legal guardian of all juveniles in its jurisdiction and can thereby limit and possibly terminate the guardianship and custody rights of parents.

Under the common law in England and the United States, a child under seven years of age could not be charged with a criminal offense, and between the ages of seven and fourteen, the child was normally not considered responsible for violations of criminal law. Exceptions could occur if it were shown that the child understood the nature of the offense and could distinguish between right and wrong. Thus, it is conceivable that under common-law principles, juveniles between the ages of seven and fourteen could be found responsible and sentenced to prison or execution as if they were adult offenders. However, the evidence is extremely weak that such punishments were actually carried out in England (Sanders, 1945) or in the United States (Platt, 1969).

Nonetheless, the possibility of indiscriminate punishment and imprisonment of the juvenile and hardened adult offender alike in the criminal justice system was often cited in the first efforts to establish houses of refuge in New York, Boston, and Philadelphia. The argument was used again in the crusade for the creation of the juvenile court later in the nineteenth century. The amplification of the *parens patriae* doctrine in the United States allowed the relaxation of procedural safeguards and allowed the juvenile court to operate as a civil court not a criminal court, allowing far greater discretion in dealing with juveniles.

Under the spirit of *parens patriae*, the American juvenile court emerged and spread to every state in the Union within a few decades. The phenomenal spread of the juvenile court ideology serves as testimony to the reform movement of the anti-institutionalists and the organizing efforts of upper-class women who were in the forefront of the child-saving movement. Between 1899 and 1909, thirty-four states enacted some form of juvenile court law. Within twenty years all but two states (New York and Wyoming) had such legislation.

Of course, not all states immediately implemented features of the new system to the same degree. For example, an analysis of detention rates among states in 1910 by Rodney Stark and colleagues (Stark et al., 1983) shows that the extent of church membership in a state was correlated with the juvenile detention rate. States with high church membership were especially high in use of detention. Yet, there is no reason to believe that the delinquency problem was actually worse in those states. Rather, the researchers suggest that resources and support for implementation was particularly high in such states. By 1923, however, the situation had reversed. Once such a practice was established it tended to be states with high delinquency rates and low church membership that had high rates of detention. They interpret these data as suggesting that solitary communities with low offense rates were the first to utilize the new system but that "with the passage of time, as juvenile programs became universal they functioned in response to real conditions. That is, communities with the most severe rates of juvenile offenses became the ones with the highest rates of juvenile detention" (Stark et al., 1983:20).

In an extensive historical analysis of the "diffusion" of juvenile court reform, John Sutton (1988) found that the states that most rapidly innovated were those with large urban populations, well-developed educational systems, and relatively decentralized political systems. Proximity to Chicago was a major influence on the rapid innovation of the North Central states. These also were states in which the Progressive ideology was strong.

Although states varied in the implementation and use of the system, the basic features were well-established quite rapidly. A President's Commission on Law Enforcement and Administration of Justice (1967:3) summarizes the basic features of the system as follows:

> The juvenile court, then, was born in an aura of reform and it spread with amazing speed. The conception of the delinquent as a "wayward child" first specifically came to life in April, 1899, when the Illinois legislature passed the Juvenile Court Act, creating the first statewide court especially for children. It did not create a new court; it did include most of the features that have since come to distinguish the juvenile court. The original act and the amendments to it that shortly followed brought together under one jurisdiction cases of dependency, neglect, and delinquency—the last comprehending incorrigibles and children threatened by immoral associations as well as criminal lawbreakers. Hearings were to be informal and nonpublic, records confidential, children detained apart from adults, a probation staff appointed. In short, children were not to be treated as criminals nor dealt with by the processes used for criminals.

A new vocabulary symbolized the new order: Petition instead of complaint, summons instead of warrant, initial hearing instead of arraignment, finding of involvement instead of conviction, disposition instead of sentence. The physical surroundings were important too: They should seem less imposing than a courtroom, with the judge at a desk or table instead of behind a bench, fatherly and sympathetic while still authoritative and sobering. The goals were to investigate, diagnose, and prescribe treatment, not to adjudicate guilt or fix blame. The individual's background was more important than the facts of a given incident, specific conduct relevant more as symptomatic of a need for the court to bring its helping powers to bear than as prerequisite to exercise of jurisdiction. Lawyers were unnecessary — adversary tactics were out of place, for the mutual aim of all was not to contest or object but to determine the treatment plan best for the child. That plan was to be devised by the increasingly popular psychologists and psychiatrists; delinquency was thought of almost as a disease, to be diagnosed by specialists and the patient kindly but firmly dosed. (President's Commission on Law Enforcement and Administration of Justice, 1967:3)

Early Attacks

Early critics of the juvenile court questioned the concept of parens patriae as an adequate legal precedent. Because the notion had applied to protecting the property of children (Tappan, 1949:169-70), it was not a purely logical or automatic outgrowth of English Common Law tradition. Rather, the concept was extended by analogy as a legal basis for the court. The early critics challenged its constitutionality on the grounds that its application by the juvenile court violated notions of due process of law. Timothy Hurley (1905) who was influential in establishing the Chicago juvenile court, lamented in 1905 that the property rights of children have been clearly established but the legal rights of the child as a person are ignored. Similarly Thomas Eliot criticized the juvenile court as becoming a "department of maladjusted children" and for attempting to become "all things to all men" (1914:16). However, because the juvenile court defined its procedures as civil rather than criminal, constitutional guarantees of due process were not applicable.

Of course, the denial of due process was not entirely unique to the juvenile justice system. As Glen and Weber (1971:1) have pointed out, "State Court systems were relatively free to operate as they wished, bound only by their own constitutions and State Court interpretations." The autonomy of state courts allowed considerable variation in the extension of due-process guarantees to adults who were being processed for criminal offenses. Extension of guarantees of due process to minors began much later and is still in process. States have had considerable autonomy in the handling of juveniles, and in the 1940s and 1950s some began to extend due-process protections to juveniles (Glen and Weber, 1971). During those years, Wisconsin, Minnesota, Oregon, and California revised or rewrote their juveniles codes to extend greater due-process guarantees to juveniles. However, for the most part the juvenile court was considered to be concerned with rehabilitation rather than punishment and the trappings of criminal law and procedure were shunned.

Juvenile Justice and the Supreme Court

No sooner had the court been established than dissatisfaction arose with the juvenile justice system. For example, the Illinois legislature voted in 1912 to abolish the court, but the governor vetoed the measure (Decker, 1984). Robert Mennel (1973) cites several instances where the doctrine of *parens patriae* was challenged immediately after the juvenile court was created, but in each case there was a gradual strengthening of the powers of the court. It was not until 1966 that the United States Supreme Court handed down its first ruling that bore on the constitutionality and legal foundation of juvenile court proceedings. Since that time, the court has examined several matters that deal with the rights of juveniles and has questioned the *carte blanche* authority of the juvenile court. However, compared to the voluminous decisions that have been made in hammering out the legal rights of adults, we have only a handful of decisions that relate to juveniles. The following ten decisions represent the major cases that the Supreme Court has considered in the area of legal rights for juveniles.

1. *Kent v. United States*, 383 U.S. 541 (1966). The *Kent* case is a most significant decision because it was the first time that the United States Supreme Court agreed to hear a case regarding a juvenile. As late as 1955 the Court refused to rule on the issue of due process of law for juveniles stating that "Since juvenile courts are not criminal courts, the constitutional rights granted to persons accused of crime are not applicable to the children brought before them" (*In re Holmes*, 1089A, 2d 523). The Supreme Court argued that the juvenile court, operating under the doctrine of *parens patriae*, does not punish children but acts on their behalf. Due process of law does not apply to juveniles since the juvenile court is not a criminal court and the juvenile is not charged with committing a criminal act.

In 1966 the Court reversed its stand on the negation of due process in juvenile matters by ruling on the case of Morris A. Kent, Jr. The specifics of the case were as follows: 1) Kent, first arrested in 1959 at the age of 14 for housebreaking, was freed on probation; 2) in 1961 during the investigation of a theft, Kent's fingerprints were found at the scene of the crime;

3) the juvenile judge, after considering the charges against Kent, decided to waive jurisdiction and transferred the case from juvenile to adult court without stating a reason to the youth or his parents; 4) Kent stood trial as an adult and received a sentence of thirty to ninety years in prison. If Kent had appeared in juvenile court, the maximum sentence for the 16-year-old boy would have been five years (the court's jurisdiction does not extend beyond age 21).

The *Kent* case was appealed to the Supreme Court, and in 1966 the Court ruled that Kent's right of due process had been violated. In handing down its decision, the Supreme Court ruled that 1) a hearing must be held in juvenile court on the issue of remanding or transferring a juvenile case to an adult court; 2) the juvenile is entitled to counsel at the waiver proceeding; 3) counsel is entitled to have access to all the social records of the juvenile prepared by the staff of the court in presenting their decision to waive jurisdiction; 4) it is incumbent upon the juvenile court that a statement of reasons accompany the waiver order.

Although this 1966 decision is confined only to matters of waiver of jurisdiction, it marked the first significant step toward a review of the juvenile justice system. The Supreme Court appeared to open the door for further litigation by emphasizing the need for due process and fair treatment in the juvenile court. Mr. Justice Fortas added his personal observations to the *Kent* decision with the following statement:

> While there can be no doubt of the original laudable purpose of juvenile courts, studies and critiques in recent years raise serious questions as to whether actual performance measures well enough against theoretical purposes to make tolerable the immunity of the process from the reach of constitutional guarantees applicable to adults. There is much evidence that some juvenile courts, including that of the District of Columbia, lack the personnel, facilities, and techniques to perform adequately as representatives of the state in a *parens patriae* capacity, at least with respect to children charged with law violation. There is evidence, in fact, that there may be grounds for concern that the child receives the worst of both worlds; that he gets neither the protection accorded to adults nor the solicitous care and regenerative treatment postulated for children. (383 U.S. 541-555-56, 1966)

This poignant statement added to the Supreme Court's concern that the right to representation is "not a grudging gesture to a ritualistic requirement" but is the essence of justice. The *Kent* ruling set the stage for the landmark *Gault* case that was acted upon the following year.

2. *In re Gault*, 387 U.S. 1, 55 (1967). On June 8, 1964, the sheriff of Gila County, Arizona, arrested 15-year-old Gerald Gault. The sheriff was acting on a complaint from a neighbor, Mrs. Cook, that Gerald and another boy had made lewd and indecent remarks to her on the telephone. Gerald was

taken to the local detention facility, and his parents, who were both at work, were not informed of the arrest until later that evening. On June 9 an adjudication hearing was held, at which time Gerald and his parents were informed of the nature of the complaint. Mrs. Cook, however, did not appear. This hearing was conducted without any formal notice of charges, without legal counsel, without the presence of any witnesses, and without any record or transcript of the hearing. The dispositional hearing was held on June 15, and the juvenile court reported that "after a full hearing and due deliberation the court finds that said minor is a delinquent child, and that said minor is of the age of 15 years." The juvenile judge committed Gerald as a juvenile delinquent to an institution for boys "for the period of his minority"—that is, until Gerald was 21 years of age. As a juvenile, Gerald was sentenced to six years; had he been an adult, the maximum penalty would have been a fine of $50 or a jail sentence of not more than two months.

Arizona law permitted no appeal in juvenile cases. Instead, a petition for a writ of habeas corpus was filed with the Supreme Court of Arizona on August 3, 1964. Such a writ, in effect, demands that reasons be given concerning the detention of any individual. The writ was based on an alleged denial of the following rights: 1) notice of the charges; 2) right to counsel; 3) right to confrontation and cross-examination; 4) privilege against self-incrimination; 5) right to a transcript of the proceedings; and 6) right to appellate review.

The Supreme Court of Arizona dismissed the writ and each of the six allegations. This court argued against the first charge of denial of notice of charges by stating that the Gaults knew of the nature of the charges against Gerald by virtue of their appearance at the two hearings. Furthermore, the court stated that specific written charges are not necessary because "the policy of the juvenile law is to hide youthful errors from the full gaze of the public and bury them in the graveyard of the forgotten past." The court rejected the second charge of denial of counsel by arguing that "the parent and the probation officer may be relied upon to protect the infant's interests." In addition, the court maintained that the juvenile court has the discretion, but not the duty, to allow legal representation. The third and fourth charges (lack of cross-examination and protection from self-incrimination) were dismissed on the grounds that "the necessary flexibility for individualized treatment will be enhanced by a rule which does not require the judge to advise the infant of a privilege against self-incrimination." The final two charges concerning appellate review and a transcript of the proceedings were also denied. The court argued that Arizona law permitted no appeal of a juvenile court decision and that since juvenile proceedings are confidential, any transcript would have to be destroyed in due time.

The *Gault* case was then appealed to the United States Supreme Court, and on May 16, 1967, the Court reversed the decision of the Supreme Court of Arizona. The Supreme Court reexamined each of the six charges and found that the juvenile court's unbridled discretion "however benevolently motivated, is frequently a poor substitute for principle and procedure." Due process of law is provided for by the Constitution and "the condition of being a boy does not justify a kangaroo court."

The Supreme Court specifically stipulated: 1) Notice of charges must be given sufficiently in advance of juvenile court hearings to permit time to prepare for the court proceedings. 2) The probation officer cannot act as counsel for the child because he or she is in fact acting as the arresting officer. In any juvenile proceeding that may result in commitment to an institution, the juvenile and his or her parents must be notified of the child's right to be represented by counsel; if they are unable to afford counsel, the court must appoint an attorney to represent the juvenile. 3) Confrontation and sworn testimony by witnesses available for cross-examination are essential in delinquency hearings. Any order of commitment to a state institution cannot be sustained in the absence of these fundamental principles of the adversary process. 4) Although a juvenile hearing may in fact involve civil rather than criminal proceedings, the privilege of the right to remain silent as stipulated in the Fifth Amendment nonetheless applies in juvenile matters. The Constitution guarantees that no person shall be compelled to be a witness against her/himself when threatened with deprivation of liberty. The Supreme Court argued that juvenile proceedings that may lead to commitment to a state institution must be regarded as criminal hearings for the purposes of the privilege against self-incrimination.

The Supreme Court did not rule on the fifth charge, denial of the right to a transcript at juvenile hearings. Although such a practice is desirable, particularly in reconstructing the record in an appeals process, the Court did not enforce this procedure. Finally, regarding the sixth charge of denial of appellate review, the Supreme Court chose not to rule on the constitutionality of the Arizona statute that denied appeal in juvenile cases.

The importance of the *Gault* decision in the extension of juvenile rights cannot be minimized. Although it neither overturned the juvenile court system nor invalidated questionable procedures in dealing with the rights of juveniles, it did introduce the concept of due process of law into the juvenile court system. The Supreme Court heavily qualified the capacity of the doctrine of *parens patriae* to be the all-pervading philosophy of the juvenile court. The *Gault* decision also challenged the common assumption that juvenile court proceedings are noncriminal. In sum, this decision was not so much a culmination of the fight for juvenile rights as a call to arms in recognizing the dignity and respect that individuals under the age of majority must be accorded.

3. *In re Winship* 397 U.S. 358 (1970). The third case regarding juvenile rights came before the United States Supreme Court in 1970. A 12-year-old boy named Samuel Winship had been charged with stealing $112 from a woman's purse. This act, if committed by an adult, would constitute a crime of larceny, and the probable punishment would not be particularly severe. As a juvenile, however, Winship was ordered to be placed in a training school for a period of six years. The judge in the juvenile court relied on a provision of New York state law that states that proof of the matter in a juvenile case need not be established beyond a reasonable doubt but simply that an adjudicatory hearing be based on a "preponderance of the evidence."

The case was appealed to the United States Supreme Court on the grounds that the essentials of due process had been violated. In addition, the appellant contended that when a juvenile is charged with an act that would constitute a crime if committed by an adult, proof must be established beyond a reasonable doubt. The Court ruled that proof of a criminal charge beyond a reasonable doubt is constitutionally required for juveniles, as well as adults. Further, the Court argued, despite the rhetoric of the juvenile court, a delinquency adjudication is a conviction, and its proceedings are criminal. "Civil labels and good intentions do not themselves obviate the need for criminal due process safeguards in juvenile courts."

4. *McKeiver v. Pennsylvania* 403 U.S. 528 (1971). What appeared to be a steady progression of Supreme Court rulings extending the provisions of the Bill of Rights to juveniles received a temporary setback with the 1971 McKeiver ruling. The case involved a 16-year-old boy, Joseph McKeiver, who had been charged with three felonious acts in juvenile court. At the time of his adjudication hearing, a request made for a jury trial was denied, and McKeiver was adjudged delinquent and placed on probation. The case was appealed to the Supreme Court on the grounds that it violated the Sixth Amendment's guarantee of the right to an impartial jury and the Seventh Amendment's stipulation of the right to a trial by jury.

After a careful review of previous decisions relating to juvenile matters, the Court concluded that the right to a trial by jury in the juvenile court's adjudication stage is not a constitutional requirement. The precise reasons set forth entail the transformation of the juvenile proceeding into an adversary process that would jeopardize the "idealistic prospect of an intimate, informal protective proceeding." Mr. Justice Blackmun, who delivered the decision, stated: "If in its wisdom, any State feels the jury trial is desirable in all cases, or in certain kinds, there appears to be no impediment to its installing a system embracing that feature. That, however, is the State's privilege and not its obligation." The essence of this decision is the Supreme Court's refusal to equate juvenile proceedings with the proceedings of the adult criminal justice system. The Court believed that such an equation would negate "every aspect of fairness, of concern, of sympathy, and of paternal attention that the juvenile court system contemplates."

5. *Breed v. Jones* 421 U.S. 519 (1975). In 1971, a 17-year-old Los Angeles juvenile was arrested on the charge of robbery with a deadly weapon. The juvenile was ordered detained pending adjudication on the delinquency petition. The juvenile court sustained the delinquency petition, finding that the juvenile had committed the robbery, and ordered that the proceedings be continued for a dispositional hearing. At this subsequent hearing, the juvenile judge ruled that this juvenile was "not amenable to the care, treatment and training program of the juvenile court" and therefore remanded the juvenile to the adult criminal court for a new trial. Despite the defendant's objections that such an action would constitute double jeopardy, the juvenile was tried in the adult criminal court and found guilty of committing a felony.

A petition was filed in the federal district court on the grounds that the juvenile hearing and the adult trial on the same criminal act had placed the defendant in double jeopardy. The district court denied the petition, stating that the juvenile proceeding was civil and not criminal in nature, and that if the juvenile court had to follow the rigorous rules and formalities regarding double jeopardy, it would be deprived of its ability to function. The case was then taken to the court of appeals, which ruled that the double jeopardy clause of the Fifth Amendment is fully applicable to juvenile court proceedings. Furthermore,the court ruled that the application of the double jeopardy guarantee in the juvenile court would not interfere with that court's goal of rehabilitation. In 1975 the decision of the court of appeals was appealed to the United States Supreme Court. In a unanimous decision, the Court upheld the ruling of the appellate court.

In handing down its decision, the Supreme Court broadened the concept of double jeopardy beyond its traditional meaning of double punishment to include the "potential or risk of trial and conviction." The Court argued that the juvenile was put in double jeopardy even though the juvenile hearings did not run their full course and did not arrive at a final disposition. Although sentenced for punishment only at the adult criminal trial, the juvenile was subjected to the burden of two trials for the same offense and twice had to marshal resources against the state. The effect of this ruling was to require that decisions about the transfer of jurisdiction be made before the juvenile or criminal proceedings are initiated.

6. *Swisher v. Brady*, 438 U.S. 204 (1978). It is not unusual to find in many states substitute judges or referees who assist the actual judge in hearing cases. In the State of Maryland, such a referee is called a "master" who actually hears delinquency cases and rules on the matter. However,

in actuality the master submits his or her recommendation to the juvenile judge who officially rules on the matter. The *Swisher v. Brady* case involved a master who heard a case and found the juvenile not to be delinquent. The judge of the juvenile court reviewed the case and allegedly obtained new information that was not discussed in the juvenile's hearing before the master. The juvenile judge overruled the master and found the juvenile to be delinquent.

This case was appealed to the Supreme Court on the grounds that it constituted double jeopardy and was in violation of the Court's position taken in the *Breed v. Jones* case. However, the Supreme Court ruled that the juvenile was subjected to only one hearing under the Maryland system. The Court reasoned that the juvenile judge's review of the record constituted a combination of the original hearing before the master. Rather than being placed in jeopardy a second time, the master's findings are advisory only, subjected to final approval by the juvenile judge. In contrast both California and Illinois have ruled that reversal by a juvenile court judge of a referee's dismissal of charges constitutes double jeopardy if the charges are heard again (Guggenheim and Sussman, 1985:54-55).

7. *Fare v. Michael C* 442 U.S. 707 (1979). The applicability of Miranda (a Supreme Court decision extending certain rights to suspects in the process of arrest) to juvenile proceedings has never been ruled upon by the Supreme Court. Considerable disagreement exists whether a juvenile is competent to waive his or her Miranda rights or whether a parent or an attorney must be present (Davis, 1986:3-52). In California a 16-year-old boy with a prior record was arrested and read his Miranda rights. Since the boy was already on probation, he asked to see his probation officer. He informed the arresting officer that he was instructed to contact his probation officer if he ever got into any difficulties. The police officer said the juvenile could not see his probation officer but he could see an attorney. The boy chose not to see an attorney but repeatedly asked for his probation officer and finally confessed to the crime. The California Supreme Court ruled that the request for a probation officer was an invocation of his Fifth Amendment right. The U.S. Supreme Court ruled that a probation officer is not an attorney but an officer of the law and as such cannot give advice. Further, the boy was an "experienced, older juvenile who knew what he was doing" when he confessed to the crime. Justice Marshall vehemently disagreed with this decision. He stated that the "juvenile reached out for an adult to obtain advice . . . it is absurd to think that a juvenile would know an attorney." Justice Marshall also pointed out that the "record indicates he was immature and uneducated and vulnerable to pressures of interrogation." However, the Court held that the 16-year-old's waiver of counsel was valid and his confession was admissible.

8. *Smith v. Daily Mail Publishing Co.* 443 U.S. 97, 105 (1979).

Traditionally, a juvenile court hearing is a private matter where the press and the public are not invited. A West Virginia statute forbade the publishing of the name of any youth charged as a delinquent without the written approval of the juvenile court. In the case in question, two West Virginia newspapers reported the identity of a 14-year-old who was accused of murder. The newspaper published not only the name of the alleged offender but also his picture. The newspapers were indicted by the Grand Jury for failing to protect the anonymity of a juvenile offender. The Supreme Court held that the ban violated the First Amendment's freedom of the press guarantee. The newspapers had lawfully obtained the name of the alleged delinquent by monitoring a police band radio. Similar cases in Oklahoma and South Carolina seem to suggest that the Supreme Court will uphold restrictions on the gathering of certain information, but once the information is obtained, the Court will not forbid the publication of that information (Guggenheim and Sussman, 1985:49).

9. *New Jersey v. T.L.O.* 105 S Ct. 733 (1985). The Fourth Amendment right of juveniles regarding protection against unreasonable search and seizure has always been problematic. This is compounded by the fact that juveniles are also students and the doctrine of *in loco parentis* asserts that school officials take the place of parents and as such can claim parental immunity from Fourth Amendment limitations. In essence this means that school officials in many states could search lockers for drugs; trained dogs could be used to sniff out drugs in lockers; and in certain situations, school officials could search students without a search warrant. This issue becomes quite complex because the courts have made distinctions between searches of lockers which are jointly controlled by the student and the school, and the distinction of a teacher as a government representative and surrogate parent. Generally speaking, the limitations of the Fourth Amendment apply to law enforcement officials, not to private citizens.

The *New Jersey v. T.L.O.* case is a significant decision regarding school searches. The case arose out of an incident in which a teacher found two girls smoking in a lavatory. Because this violated school policy, the girls were taken to the assistant principal's office. The vice-principal then examined one of the girls' purse and found a pack of cigarettes but then also found marijuana, marijuana paraphernalia, a substantial quantity of money, index cards that appeared to be a list of students who owed the girl money, and two letters implicating the girl as a marijuana dealer. At the trial court level, the argument was made that the evidence was obtained illegally and therefore must be suppressed. The judge denied the motion to suppress stating that the school official acted in a reasonable manner. Upon appeal to the New Jersey Supreme Court, this court argued that the search violated the girl's constitutional rights and the evidence was not admissible. Finally, the case was appealed to the U.S. Supreme Court.

The Supreme Court stated that the *in loco parentis* doctrine is suspect and such reasoning is "in tension with contemporary reality and the teachings of this Court." Secondly, the Court argued that when teachers conduct searches of students, they cannot claim parental immunity from Fourth Amendment restrictions. Teachers are acting as representatives of the state and they are subject to Fourth Amendment limitations. However, the Court adopted a "reasonable ground" standard by asserting that school personnel may have to conduct searches in order to maintain safety, order, and discipline in the school. The test for reasonableness according to the Supreme Court is twofold: 1) was the action "justified at its inception," and 2) was the search "reasonably related in scope to the circumstances which justified the interference in the first place."

What is not known is just how far the "reasonable suspicion" standard extends. The Court left unresolved whether school personnel must have individualized suspicion before searching a student or whether the standards change if school personnel act as agents of the police. The Court did acknowledge that students are indeed entitled to some protection under the Fourth Amendment but "under the Court's expanded view of reasonableness, a search may be conducted if school personnel believe it will produce evidence of a violation of law or a school disciplinary rule" (Davis, 1986:3-23).

10. *Stanford v. Kentucky* 57 LW 4973 (1989). The final Supreme Court case to be discussed deals with the issuance of a death sentence for two individuals under the age of 18. The petitioners claimed that they had a right to treatment in the juvenile justice system since they were 16 and 17 years of age, and a death sentence constitutes cruel and unusual punishment. In one case a juvenile and an accomplice repeatedly raped and sodomized a gas station attendant during a robbery, drove the victim to a secluded area, and shot her point blank in the face. In the second case, a juvenile robbed a convenience store and repeatedly stabbed the victim, leaving her to die on the floor. As stated in their petition, the petitioners argued that the death penalty is contrary to the "evolving standards of decency that mark the progress of a maturing society."

What makes this case so fascinating is that in 1988 the Court in *Thompson v. Oklahoma* ruled that Oklahoma's imposition of a death sentence on an individual who was 15 years old at the time he committed the offense should be set aside. In this case it was argued that since Oklahoma did not have a minimum age for capital punishment they could not sentence a juvenile to death. Of the 37 states that permit capital punishment, 15 do not allow it in the case of 16-year-olds, and 12 for 17-year-olds. Oklahoma was one of the ten remaining states that permitted capital punishment but did not stipulate the minimum age.

In the *Stanford* case the Supreme Court made no direct reference to the

Thompson case of a year earlier and rejected outright any notion that 16- or 17-year-olds cannot be held responsible for their behavior and cannot be deterred. Further, the Court argued that no historical or current societal standard forbids the imposition of capital punishment for a person who murders at 16 or 17 years of age.

Box 2-1

Executing the Retarded

The Supreme Court's "Get Tough" Attitude: *Penry V. Lynaugh* (109 S. Ct. 2934, 1989)

In June of 1989 the Supreme Court handed down a decision that represents a "hard-line" approach in the area of captial punishment. John Penry, a 22-year-old who had the mental age of a six and a half-year-old was found guilty of murder and sentenced to death. The defense argued that Penry suffered from organic brain damage possibly caused by multiple injuries from his mother's beatings. His IQ was between 50 and 63, and his social maturity was that of a 9 or 10-year-old. Penry's mother indicated that he never finished the first grade, he was routinely locked in his room for long periods of time, and was in and out of state schools and hospitals. The jury found him competent to stand trial and rejected his insanity defense. On appeal to the U.S. Supreme Court, Penry's defense argued that it was cruel and unusual punishment to execute a mentally retarded person.

The Supreme Court agreed that "it may indeed be 'cruel and unusual' punishment to execute persons who are profoundly or severely retarded and wholly lacking the capacity to appreciate the wrongfulness of their actions. . . . Such a case is not before us today." The Court concluded that the concept of mental age is imprecise. It might be argued that a mildly retarded person could be denied the opportunity to marry or to enter into contracts based on the fact that this person had a mental age of a young child. However, the Court argued that the Eighth Amendment does not preclude the execution of any mentally retarded person simply on the basis of mental retardation alone. "While a national consensus against execution of the mentally retarded may someday emerge reflecting the 'evolving standards of decency that mark the progress of a maturing society,' there is insufficient evidence of such a consensus today."

Do you think that executing people with the mental age of children constitutes cruel and unusual punishment?

Overview: The Extension of Juvenile Rights

Starting with the 1966 *Kent* decision, the United States Supreme Court extended to juveniles basic constitutional rights that restrict in some fashion the open-ended authority derived from the doctrine of *parens patriae*. Although the Court did not radically alter the juvenile justice system, it introduced the concept of due process of law for children and adolescents.

In all its decisions regarding the rights of juveniles, including its McKeiver ruling, the Court expressed a growing disenchantment with numerous aspects of the juvenile justice system. Although the Court did not fully endorse the procedural rights of juveniles regarding a criminal hearing (for example, the right to be released on bail or the right to a jury trial), it seriously challenged the noncriminal nature of juvenile court proceedings. The Court has hesitated to negate what it feels is a unique function of the juvenile court system; it has not, however, specified the precise advantages of that system. In fact, recent Court decisions endorse aspects of the juvenile system (i.e. reversals of referee decisions) that would not be acceptable in criminal justice procedures.

It is hazardous to predict what future constitutional rights will be extended to juveniles. Significant gains have been made, but the basic doctrine of *parens patriae* will inevitably continue to produce legal difficulties in the future. Many questions pertaining to the rights of juveniles are still unanswered: the use of questionable search and seizure practices (Fourth Amendment rights), speedy and public hearings (Sixth Amendment rights), cruel and unusual punishments (Eighth Amendment rights), vague and ambiguous definitions of delinquency, and the precarious balance between the social work and legal posture of the juvenile court. Indeed it is not even clear whether juveniles can be technically arrested. In most states the phrase "taking into custody" is used rather than "arrest." Because of this, the Supreme Court has never ruled on the applicability of the Miranda decision in the juvenile system.

It should also be noted that the rights that the Supreme Court has extended to juveniles involve rules of evidence and due process at the adjudicatory hearing stage. Thus, when the juvenile stands accused he or she is now entitled to remain silent, to have an attorney (at state expense, if necessary), to be advised of his or her rights, notice of charges, and proceedings, and to subpoena witnesses. In addition, Court decisions suggest that rights to a transcript and appellate review are desirable. However, at the disposition level the judge is not bound by the rules of evidence nor is the juvenile entitled to have an attorney. Some commentators on the juvenile court (Glen and Weber, 1971) view the dual character of the juvenile justice system (that is, different standards for the adjudication hearing and the disposition hearing) as a means of protecting the rights of juveniles and at the same time serving the treatment aims of the court. Others (Edwards, 1973) feel that the rights of children should be protected at all stages of the proceedings and advocate ensuring due process at points beyond the adjudication hearing.

The Supreme Court has always sought to preserve the noncriminal nature of the juvenile court and has never stated that a juvenile hearing must conform to all the requirements of a criminal trial. In light of the current criticism of the adult criminal justice system, this brand of justice may not be the ideal model. The adult criminal justice system has been depicted (with considerable justification) as a system of "bargain-counter justice in which notions of due process and the adversary roles of defense and prosecution are secondary to efficiency and mass production (Blumberg, 1970). Platt and Friedman (1968) found that in the Chicago juvenile court, private attorneys for juveniles, even after the Gault decision, tended to be small-fee lawyers who neither represented their clients in an adversarial fashion nor negotiated or bargained for their clients. Similarly, public defenders appeared to spend very little time on behalf of their juvenile clients (Platt et al., 1968). On the other hand, Spencer Cox (1967) reported that in Philadelphia the percentage of juveniles represented by counsel increased from 5 percent to 40 percent following the Gault decision. Cox noted that this increase had a number of consequences for the processing of juveniles: 1) a reduction in detention before hearings, 2) a drop in commitment to institutions, and 3) a staggering backlog of cases awaiting disposition. It is important to note that Gault applies to alleged delinquents who are faced with potential commitment. It does not apply to instances of status offenders (noncriminal offenses like truancy, running away, or ungovernability), nor stages other than adjudication, such as intake, detention, or disposition (Wadlington et al., 1983).

Recent analyses of juvenile court processing reveal that many, if not most, juveniles are not represented by attorneys even at the adjudication stage. Barry Feld (1984) reports that in the decades following the Gault decision the promise of counsel has not been realized. In an analysis of court cases for Nebraska, Minnesota, and North Dakota at least 50 percent of delinquents and status offenders did not have lawyers (Feld, 1988). However, it did not appear to work to a youth's advantage to have a lawyer. Feld found that "representation by counsel redounds to the disadvantage of juveniles" (1988:419). Youths with representation did worse in terms of outcomes than youths without lawyers. Feld suggests a number of explanations for this perplexing finding, including the possibility that the lawyers are unskilled, inclined to go along with the judge, or prone to bad plea bargains. Youths without lawyers might also be less serious offenders.

The juvenile court, like the criminal court, is a system with characteristics and practices that are dictated by concerns for the efficient processing of thousands of cases rather than by legal notions of due process of law.

It is one thing to read the lofty ideals of the juvenile court set forth in the juvenile code and in Supreme Court decisions but it is another matter to view the system in operation. The modern juvenile justice system is fraught with judges who have an enormous backlog of cases, probation officers who carry an enormous case load, parents who do not want to get involved, and detention and juvenile institutions that are typically filled to capacity.

Current Definitions of Delinquency

While due process and the procedural rights of juveniles are in a state of flux and the subject of legal battles, legal definitions of what constitutes delinquent behavior have been criticized for their lack of precision and rigor as well. Even the meaning of the term "delinquent" is ambiguous and varies from jurisdiction to jurisdiction. For example, if we try to specify a legal definition of delinquent that would be generally applicable throughout the United States, all we can state is that a delinquent is a nonadult or a child who commits an offense against a law of the state. In some instances these offenses may be criminal acts and in other cases these behaviors may be noncriminal offenses such as running away from home.

The glossary of terms presented at the beginning of this chapter represents the current trend in defining delinquency. It is now common to maintain a distinction among categories and to limit the term "delinquent" to offenses and offenders that would be criminal if the youth were an adult. Moreover, patterns of conflict or misbehavior that could be the basis for deeming a youth "incorrigible" or "ungovernable" may now fall within the category of "status offenses" together with the specific activities typically included (e.g. runaway, smoking, drinking). Such differentiation between criminal offenses and status offenses grew out of recommendations by two national commissions and subsequent federal legislation (see Chapter 11) encouraging the *diversion* of status offenders from regular juvenile court processing. In the 1970s critics of the juvenile court (Lerman, 1971) were reporting that status offenders were dealt with as harshly as (or even more harshly than) youths who had committed criminal offenses. The lack of differentiation was particularly disadvantageous to girls since a larger proportion of their offenses were status offenses. A major theme characterizing juvenile justice reform in the late 1970s and 1980s was to differentiate among offenders and to reserve forms of confinement for serious offenders. In short, the limitation of the term "delinquent" to criminal activities is a recent development as are specific policies requiring differential responses to youth who have not been charged with criminal offenses.

The definition of nonadult varies from state to state, with age 18 the most common cutoff point between adult and nonadult. Figure 2-3 lists the *jurisdictional age* (that is, the age below which a person is subject to juvenile court jurisdiction) for each of the 50 states plus the District of Columbia. In some states the cutoff point is as low as age 16, while in others it may extend to age 19. The minimum age limit of children subject to the juvenile court's jurisdiction is rarely specified, although Massachusetts and New York require a child to be at least seven years of age and Colorado, Mississippi, Vermont, and Texas set the minimum age at 10. However, common-law traditions have in essence set an operational lower limit of at least seven years of age. A person younger than seven is presumed not to be responsible for his or her actions. In some states a child under eight years of age who enters the juvenile justice system may be dealt with as a "dependent," rather than a "delinquent," child.

The second column in Figure 2-3 lists the waiver or transfer age whereby juveniles may be tried as adults in criminal court. In the vast majority of cases, states specify the age at which a waiver hearing can take place. Some states list no age and three states do not provide for a waiver hearing. In those states where a waiver hearing is permitted, generally there is an added stipulation that the child must have committed a serious felony or that the child had been adjudicated for a previous juvenile offense. In a few instances the waiver criteria are exceedingly complex and the listing of such states in Figure 2-3 may be oversimplified. For example, in Connecticut a child may be transferred to the adult court if he or she is 14 and is charged with a serious juvenile offense. A waiver is mandatory for those 14 or older charged with murder or who have been previously adjudicated for a serious felony offense and are being charged for a second felony offense. The criteria for a waiver standard are generally vague, simply stating that the child is "not amenable to treatment or rehabilitation." Prior to the *Kent* and *Breed v. Jones* decisions, few states had checks against procedural arbitrariness in the waiver process. Typically, the juvenile courts use two factors in the decision to waive jurisdiction: the seriousness of the offense and the past history of the juvenile.

The third column in Figure 2-3 indicates the type of jurisdiction the juvenile court enjoys. In most instances the juvenile court has *exclusive jurisdiction*, which means that no other court can rule on the matter, regardless of the nature of the offense. The juvenile court generally has exclusive jurisdiction over delinquent behavior which is in violation of the criminal codes. The juvenile court will also have jurisdiction over noncriminal acts that constitute status offenses. Some states refer to such offenders as Persons in Need of Supervision (PINS) or Children in Need of Supervision (CHINS). Some states also extend juvenile court jurisdiction to children who are "in danger of leading an idle, dissolute, lewd or immoral life" or "those who are a danger to themselves or others." It bears repeating that status offenses are acts for which adults could not be arrested and yet these cases comprise "no less than one-third and perhaps close to one-half the workload of America's juvenile courts" (Fox, 1984:12). The rules for adjudication for status offenses differ from the rules applicable to delinquency cases. As discussed in the Winship case, the standard of proof for delinquency is "beyond a reasonable doubt." For status offenses, however, the standard of proof is generally "a preponderance of evidence" which is considerably less demanding.

Finally, the juvenile court has jurisdiction over a broad range of neglect and abuse situations. Such children are those who are without a parent or have been abandoned, abused, or who lack adequate parental care or supervision. Depending on the state, such a child may be referred to as *dependent, deprived,* or *neglected.* In those states where the jurisdictional age listed in Figure 2-3 is younger than 18, it invariably rises to 18 for abused, dependent or neglected children. In instances of abuse or neglect the juvenile court may place the child in a temporary shelter care or foster care home; in instances of serious mistreatment the court may terminate the parental rights of the child's parents.

The scope of juvenile court jurisdiction has often been criticized as vague. For example, it is not clear what a California statute means when it makes reference to a child under the age of 18 "who from any cause is in danger of leading an idle, dissolute, lewd, or immoral life." Similarly, a Texas statute described a child who "habitually so deports himself as to injure or endanger the morals or health of himself or others" as a delinquent. These statutes are exceedingly broad and very subjective. Challenges to such statutes have been made but no court has found them to be unconstitutional. In one instance a three-judge federal panel found the phrase "in danger of leading an idle, dissolute, lewd, or immoral life" to be vague but the U.S. Supreme Court vacated the judgement.

In some states, as shown in Figure 2-3, more than one court has jurisdiction over juveniles. *Concurrent jurisdiction* means that the juvenile court shares jurisdiction with the criminal court. In Arkansas the criminal and juvenile courts have joint jurisdiction over all children under age 18. In other states the jurisdiction is concurrent only for offenses that are punishable by death or life imprisonment (Florida and Georgia) or when the juvenile is 16 and has committed a serious felony offense (Utah). In these situations, the prosecuting attorney generally decides to which court the juvenile will be referred.

The last column in Figure 2-3 lists those states which exclude certain offenses from the jurisdiction of the juvenile court. Until recently, nearly every state gave the juvenile court full jurisdiction over all offenses. In the past few years, there has been a growing trend to exclude serious offenses from the jurisdiction of the juvenile court. Colorado has perhaps the most complicated exclusion provisions of any state. The juvenile court does not have jurisdiction over 14-year-olds who are charged with crimes of violence,

Figure 2-3

Jurisdiction of the Juvenile Court

State	Jurisdiction Age	Waiver Age	Type of Jurisdiction	Offenses Excluded
Alabama	18	14	Exclusive	None
Alaska	18	None stated	Exclusive	None
Arizona	18	None stated	Exclusive	None
Arkansas	18	No provision	Concurrent	None
California	18	16	Exclusive	None
Colorado	18	14	Exclusive	14 years-crimes of violence, 16 years-previous felony-arrested for felony
Connecticut	16	14	Exclusive	Capital offenses
Delaware	18	16	Exclusive	Capital offenses
District of Columbia	18	15-felony 16-under commitment	Concurrent	None
Florida	18	14	Concurrent for death or life imprisonment	None
Georgia	17	15	Concurrent for death or life imprisonment	Burglary if over 15
Hawaii	18	16	Exclusive	Serious felonies
Idaho	18	14	Exclusive	Capital offenses
Illinois	17	13	Exclusive	Serious felonies
Indiana	18	14-mandatory if serious felony	Exclusive	Serious felonies
Iowa	18	14	Exclusive	None
Kansas	18	16	Exclusive	16 years of age and 2 prior felonies
Kentucky	18	16	Exclusive	None
Louisiana	17	15	Exclusive	Serious felonies
Maine	18	None stated	Exclusive	None
Maryland	18	15	Exclusive	Serious felonies
Massachusetts	17	14	Exclusive	None
Michigan	17	15	Exclusive	None
Minnesota	18	14	Exclusive	None
Mississippi	18	13	Exclusive	Capital offenses
Missouri	17	14	Exclusive	None
Montana	18	16	Exclusive	None

Nebraska	18	No provision	Concurrent for felonies	None
Nevada	18	16	Exclusive	Murder
New Hampshire	18	None given	Concurrent for felonies	None
New Jersey	18	14	Exclusive	None
New Mexico	18	16	Exclusive	None
New York	16	No provision	Exclusive	Serious felonies
North Carolina	16	14	Exclusive	Capital offenses
North Dakota	18	14	Exclusive	None
Ohio	18	15	Exclusive	Serious felonies
Oklahoma	18	None stated	Exclusive	Serious felonies
Oregon	18	16	Exclusive	None
Pennsylvania	18	14	Exclusive	Murder
Rhode Island	18	16	Exclusive	None
South Carolina	17	16	Exclusive	None
South Dakota	18	None stated	Concurrent for felonies	None
Tennessee	18	16	Exclusive	None
Texas	17	15	Exclusive	None
Utah	18	14	Concurrent for felonies	None
Vermont	16	10 for serious felonies	Exclusive	Serious felonies
Virginia	18	15	Exclusive	None
Washington	18	None stated	Exclusive	None
West Virginia	18	16	Exclusive	None
Wisconsin	18	16	Exclusive	None
Wyoming	19	None stated	Concurrent	None

Source: Davis, S. M. 1986. *Rights of Juveniles: The Juvenile Justice System.* New York: Clark Boardman. Reprinted with permission Clark Boardman Callaghan, Copyright © 1988.

or 16-year-olds who have adjudicated delinquent for a felony in the past two years and have been charged with a felony, or children 14 or older who are charged with a felony and had been transferred to the criminal court for a previous felony.

How Tough Is the Juvenile Court?

In a critique of the juvenile court Alfred Regnery calls for the juvenile court to move towards a more punitive, deterrence-based philosophy so that delinquents can "feel the sting of the justice system" (1986:44). He cites examples of youth who have committed murder and the likelihood of more lenient consequences if the case were dealt with in juvenile court rather than criminal court. It is quite common to challenge the treatment orientation of the juvenile court by focusing on dramatic cases where the juvenile court can be made to appear "soft." However, it is misleading to focus on such cases for several reasons.

First, as we will detail further in Chapter 3, murder is rare among youths who fall under the jurisdiction of the juvenile court. Such cases tend to attract a lot of attention and to arouse alarm—but they are not typical of juvenile court cases. Second, the type of case where a lenient disposition would generate public outcry is the type of case most likely to be remanded or transferred to the adult court by one of the means discussed in the previous section. Third, such critiques *presume that the criminal justice system is tougher than the juvenile justice system.* Indeed, the most consequential of the Supreme Court decisions, *In re Gault* (1967), was a case in which the consequences were considerably more severe for the juvenile than they would have been for an adult. Chapter 1 began with an example of an actual court case in which a minor was dealt with more harshly than his adult accomplice. We noted then, and it bears repeating, that his experience was more common than conceptions of the juvenile court as a "kiddie's court" imply.

A comparison of criminal and juvenile court handling of serious offenders was carried out by Howard Snyder and John Hutzler of the National Center for Juvenile Justice in 1982. Their analysis suggests that in some ways the juvenile court is tougher than criminal court. While less than 40 percent of serious adult offenders (392 out of 1,000) are convicted and sentenced, 44 percent of juvenile cases result in some form of adjudication. Another 2 percent are convicted after transfer to adult court. It should also be noted that about 11 percent of serious youthful offenders are placed on "informal" probation at the intake stage. Such informal probation does involve consequences for a juvenile, ranging from curfews to community service. Thus, overall, juvenile courts were more likely to take some form of action for juvenile cases than criminal courts were for adult cases. Once a criminal case reached the conviction stage there was a greater probability of imprisonment while juveniles were more likely to receive probation.

A more recent report compared juvenile court dispositions for violent offenders to similar adult cases in the criminal courts. Considering all dispositions in which the court restricted or monitored the behavior of the offender as well as transfers of juveniles to criminal courts the report concluded that:

> Juvenile courts intervened in the lives of a greater proportion of violent
> offenders than did criminal courts. In all, 59 percent of 16- and 17-year-

olds charged with violent acts were transferred to criminal court or placed in residential facilities or on formal probation, while only 46 percent of adults charged with a violent crime were incarcerated or placed on probation. (Office of Juvenile Justice and Delinquency Prevention, 1989:4)

As summarized in Figure 2-4, adults were more likely to be released with no restrictions. In contrast, 35 percent of adults were incarcerated compared to 23 percent of juveniles. Moreover, since the juveniles transferred to the adult system have a high probability of imprisonment it is conceivable that the difference for imprisonment could be as small as 2 percent.

Other government data suggests a difference in time served. The average length of stay for juveniles committed to institutions in 1984 was about eight months (Bureau of Justice Statistics, 1989). In 1982 it was about seven months. The average time served by adult offenders in state prisons in 1983 was about 26 months. The criminal justice system, therefore, is more likely to imprison and typically imposes longer sentences.

In sum, systematic comparisons of the two justice systems does not support a simplistic conclusion that the juvenile justice system merely slaps youth on the hand or lets them "get away with murder." For common types of serious offenses, the juvenile system is more likely to impose some form of restriction than the adult system and is nearly as likely to imprison, although youth are not incarcerated nearly as long as adults. The idea that treating juveniles more like adults means "getting tough" assumes that the adult system is tougher than the juvenile system. But as we have learned that is not always the case.

Continuing Controversy

The juvenile court will continue to be a source of controversy and conflicting opinions because it deals with people who are not quite adults and not quite children. Adults are likely to resist extending to juveniles all of the rights of adults. At the same time, however, when youths commit "adult" offenses there will be pressure to treat them like adults.

Activities that are legally acceptable for adults will continue to be legally unacceptable for youth. In fact, to deal with alcohol consumption states have uniformly raised the legal drinking age. To keep youth in school, state lawmakers are contemplating legislation that would deny driving licenses to drop-outs. Such actions are based on the presumption that the state has more leeway to regulate and control the behavior of juveniles than the behavior of adults and that youths do not have the right to resist such efforts. Thus, the ambiguous status of youth creates a double bind in that there is pressure to treat them as adults when dealing with their transgressions but to deny them a full range of rights in other regards.

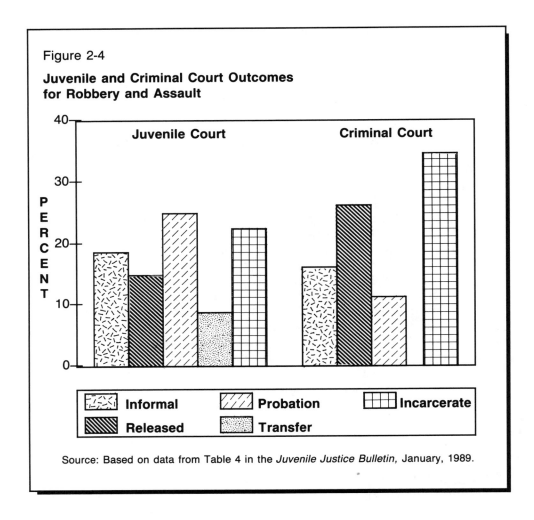

Figure 2-4

**Juvenile and Criminal Court Outcomes
for Robbery and Assault**

Source: Based on data from Table 4 in the *Juvenile Justice Bulletin,* January, 1989.

As the composition of the Supreme Court changes, so will interpretations of the nature of "rights" and "due process of law" for both adults and juveniles. In reality, rights are not stable, constant, and unambiguous but are instead subject to human interpretation. Abraham Blumberg summarized the situation as follows:

> The legal concept of due process serves much the same function in the legal system as does the joker in a card game: it has a shifting meaning and application. Just as the structure of legal and judicial systems are a reflection of group structure and the individuals who comprise it, so the content of due process of law (whether at the Supreme Court or state

level) may have a particular meaning, purpose, and character that mirror the unique angle or mission of a historical and social location. In a rational-legal society, the "rule of law" is invoked as a source of legitimacy. In dealing with a wrongdoer, the question is not guilt or innocence, but rather a demonstration of the "approved way" in which evidence can be used legitimately vis-a-vis a given individual. In American society the "approved way" means due process of law, which in essence refers to the normatively established, institutionalized recipes for invoking and using legal machinery. (1970:20)

Even if standards of due process are clearly defined and extended to minors who have committed criminal offenses, a significant proportion of adolescents—"incorrigible" youths and status offenders—will continue to be processed through the juvenile court system without having committed a criminal offense. Rather than reducing the involvement of the court in the lives of youth, as was intended by many advocates of diversion, more and more programs have developed dealing with a growing range of youthful misbehavior, leading one critic of the juvenile justice system to ask whether youth are "being abused at higher prices?" (Schwartz, 1989). While some court processes are reserved for the most serious offenders, the juvenile justice system has been dealing with a wider range of youth with the implementation of diversion programs. The proliferation of such programs has generated new controversies involving the same perennial conflicts—due process and justice for juveniles versus the government's right to control the behavior of youth.

Some radical critics have argued that the only effective approach to the problem is to attack the economic and social marginality of youth directly. In other words, rather than developing programs that rely on the courts to cope with the consequences of the marginal position of youth, we should attack the "marginalization" itself (Schwendinger and Schwendinger, 1979). This approach calls for major changes in the American economy: the elimination of unemployment and subemployment through government control of industry and extensive public works programs. Although such an approach upsets many people, it does direct our attention to the fact that the juvenile justice system was developed to deal with an age category that did not (and still does not) quite fit into the American economic system.

In Chapters 10, 11, and 12, we will review a wide range of experimental programs for dealing with delinquency within the juvenile justice system. Unfortunately, few of these programs have had a significant effect on either the prevention or inhibition of delinquent activity. Such pessimistic findings, together with the alleged failure of the juvenile justice system to cope with delinquency problems, have led critics to seriously question whether modifications within the system can make any difference.

The behavior and attitudes of the young should be understood in the context of a largely adult-controlled and adult-defined world. Children can easily become scapegoats for the grief and woes of modern industrial society. In America today, adolescents are seen as the cause of many of society's shortcomings. Crimes against persons and property, drug-related problems, lack of respect for authority, overweening ambition, and widespread apathy are considered as the unique problems of youth; in fact, they are as much, if not more so the problems of society as a whole.

Summary

The origin and development of the juvenile justice system was influenced by a variety of social forces including declining infant mortality rates, industrial development, urbanization, and such reform movements as compulsory public education, child labor legislation, and houses of refuge. Such forces helped establish childhood, adolescence, delinquents, and status offenders as bio-social-legal categories between birth and legal adulthood.

The legal groundwork and philosophical precedents of the juvenile court can be traced to the development of houses of refuge and reform schools for troublesome youth in the early and mid-1800s. The legal doctrine invoked in establishing such institutions was *parens patriae*, the concept that the state has the right to act as a parent. However, the establishment of houses of refuge and reform schools, the later "anti-institutionalist" movement, and the eventual creation of the juvenile court did not flow purely from humanitarian concerns; these movements also reflected the religious, ethnic, and class interests of the time.

The debate among scholars about the forces that shaped the juvenile justice system has not been resolved. Anthony Platt interprets the emergence of the juvenile court in the late 1800s as an extension of religious and class conflicts. In contrast, Schlossman, Finestone, Hagan and Leon argue that the emergence of the juvenile court reflected an anti-institutional ideology that stressed probation, the home, and family as targets of treatment. However, scholars do agree that there was and is a considerable gap between the professed aims and the actual operation of the juvenile justice system.

Although the first juvenile court was established in 1899, it was not until 1966 that the United States Supreme Court first ruled on a constitutional issue relating to juvenile court proceedings. In a modest number of cases since 1966, the Supreme Court extended several rights of due process to juveniles at the adjudicatory level. These rulings do not, however, apply to the pre- or post-adjudicatory stages of the juvenile justice system. Moreover, the Court has not addressed several of the constitutional protections extended to adults in terms of their applicability to juveniles.

Whether the Court's decisions have had a significant impact on juveniles processed through the system is still a subject of dispute. The mass-processing, "bargain-justice" aspects of the administration of justice, whether for adults or for juveniles, may make Supreme Court decisions irrelevant to the everyday operation of juvenile justice systems.

The creation of a separate juvenile court was more than a matter of instituting new procedures. It involved the extension of state control over a wider range of activities than criminal law had ever encompassed. An examination of current statistics shows several overlapping categories of activity or problems that can bring a juvenile to the attention of the juvenile court. The nature of the offense alone does not automatically enable us to decide whether a youth is a delinquent, a status offender, or a dependent. Such categorization may also depend on age, gender, past behavior, and community reaction. Moreover, while distinctions between categories are made in statutes, the relevance of these distinctions for the actual processing and ultimate disposition of cases remains a subject of debate (see Chapter 11).

Despite evidence of similarities in outcomes when comparing adult and juvenile justice systems, the juvenile court will continue to be a subject of controversy and will be attacked by some factions as harsh and repressive and by others for being lenient and sympathetic. Justice Blackmun's remarks in the McKeiver decision seem to echo the uncertain fate of the juvenile court:

> If the formalities of the criminal adjudicative process are to be superimposed upon the juvenile court system, there is little need for its separate existence. Perhaps that ultimate disillusionment will come one day, but for the moment we are disinclined to give impetus to it. (*McKeiver v. Pennsylvania*, 403 U.S. at 550-51)

References

Abbot. 1938. *The Child and the State*. Vol. 1 and 2. Chicago: University of Chicago Press.

Aries, P. 1962. *Centuries of Childhood*. New York: Vintage Books.

Bakan, D. 1971. "Adolescence in America: From Idea to Social Fact." *Daedalus* (Fall): 979-95.

Blumberg, A. S. 1970. *Criminal Justice*. Chicago: Quadrangle Books.

Bremner, R. H. 1970. *Children and Youth in America: A Documentary History*. Vols. I & II. Cambridge, MA: Harvard University Press.

Chambers, J. D. 1972. *Population, Economy and Society in Pre-Industrial England*. London: Oxford University Press.

Cox, S. 1967. "Lawyers in Juvenile Court." *Crime and Delinquency* 13 (October): 488-93.

Davis, S. M. 1986. *Rights of Juveniles: The Juvenile Justice System*. New York: Clark Boardman.

Decker, S. H. 1984. *Juvenile Justice Policy: Analyzing Trends and Outcomes*. Beverly Hills: Sage.

Edwards, L. 1973. "The Rights of Children." *Federal Probation* 37 (June): 34-41.

Eliot, T. D. 1914. *The Juvenile Court and the Community*. New York: The Macmillan Company.

Feld, Barry C. 1984. "Criminalizing Juvenile Justice: Rules of Procedure for Juvenile Court." *Minnesota Law Review* 69: 141-276.

_____. 1988. "*In re Gault* Revisited: A Cross State Comparison of the Right to Counsel in Juvenile Court." *Journal of Research in Crime and Delinquency* 34 (October): 393-424.

Finestone, H. 1976. *Victims of Change*. Westport, CT: Greenwood Press.

Fox, S. 1984. *Juvenile Courts in a Nutshell*. 3rd edition. St. Paul: West Publishing Co.

Glen, J. E., and J. R. Weber. 1971. The Juvenile Court: A Status Report. Washington, DC: Center for Studies of Crime and Delinquency.

Guggenheim, M., and A. Sussman. 1985. *The Rights of Young People*. New York: Bantam Books.

Hagan, J., and J. Leon. 1977. "Rediscovering Delinquency: Social History, Political Ideology and the Sociology of Law." *American Sociological Review* 42 (August): 587-98.

Hall, G. S. 1882. "The Moral and Religious Training of Children" *Princeton Review* (January): 26-48.

Hawes, J. 1971. *Children in Urban Society*. New York: Oxford University Press.

Heinsohn, G., and O. Steiger. 1982. "The Elimination of Birth Control and the Witch Trials of Modern Times." *International Journal of Women's Studies* 5 (No. 3): 193-210.

Hurley, T. D. 1905. "Necessity for the Lawyers in the Juvenile Court." Proceedings of the National Conference of Charities and Correction, 173-77.

Lasch, Christopher. 1979. *Haven in a Heartless World: The Family Besieged*. New York: Basic Books.

Lerman, P. 1971. "Child Convicts." *Trans-Action* 8 (July/August): 35-45.

Mennel, Robert M. 1973. "Origins of the Juvenile Court: Changing Perspectives on the Legal Rights of Juvenile Delinquents." *Crime and Delinquency*, 68: 18-36.

Office of Juvenile Justice and Delinquency Prevention. 1989. "The Juvenile Court's Response to Violent Crime." *Juvenile Justice Bulletin*. U. S. Department of Justice: U. S. Government Printing Office.

Pima County Collaboration for Children and Youth. 1980. *Juvenile Rights and Responsibilities*. Tucson, Arizona.

Platt, A. 1969a. *The Child Savers: The Invention of Delinquency*. Chicago: University of Chicago Press.

_____. 1969b. "The Rise of the Child-Saving Movement: A Study in Social Policy and Correctional Reform." *Annals of the American Academy of Political and Social Science* 381 (January): 21-38.

Platt, A. 1974. "The Triumph of Benevolence: The Origins of the Juvenile Justice System in the United States." In R. Quinney (ed.), *Criminal Justice in America.* Boston: Little, Brown.

Platt, A., and R. Friedman. 1968. "The Limits of Advocacy: Occupational Hazards in Juvenile Court." *Pennsylvania Law Review* 116: 1156-84.

Platt, A., H. Schechter, and P. Tiffany. 1968. "In Defense of Youth: A Case Study of the Public Defender in Juvenile Court." *Indiana Law Journal* 43: 619-40.

Pollock, L. A. 1983. *Forgotten Children: Parent-Child Relationships from 1500 to 1900.* New York: Cambridge University Press.

President's Commission on Law Enforcement and Administration of Justice. 1967. *Task Force Report: Juvenile Delinquency and Youth Crime.* Washington, DC: U.S. Government Printing Office.

Regnery, Alfred. 1986. "A Federal Perspective on Juvenile Justice Reform." *Crime and Delinquency* 326 (January): 39-51.

Sanders, W.B. 1945. "Some Early Beginnings of the Children's Court Movement in England." *National Probation Association Yearbook* 39: 58-70.

Schlossman, S.L. 1977. *Love and the American Delinquent.* Chicago: University of Chicago Press.

Schwartz, I. M. 1989. *(In)justice for Juveniles: Rethinking the Best Interests of Children.* Lexington, MA: D. C. Heath and Company.

Schwendinger, H., and J. R. Schwendinger. 1979. "Delinquency and Social Reform: A Radical Perspective." In L. Empey (ed.), *Juvenile Justice: The Progressive Legacy and Current Reforms.* Charlottesville: University Press of Virginia.

Snyder, H. N., and J. L. Hutzler. 1982. "The Serious Juvenile Offender." *Justice Assistance News* 3 (April): 12-13.

Snyder, H. N., T. Finnegan, E. H. Nimick, M. H. Sickmund, D. P. Sullivan, and N. J. Tierney. 1989. *Juvenile Court Statistics, 1985.* Pittsburgh, PA: National Center for Juvenile Justice Statistics.

Stark, Rodney, W. S. Bainbridge, R. D. Crutchfield, D. P. Doyle, and R. Finke. 1983. "Crime and Delinquency in the Roaring Twenties." *Journal of Research in Crime and Delinquency* 20 (January): 4-23.

Sutton, John R. 1988. *Stubborn Children: Controlling Delinquency in the United States, 1640-1981.* Berkeley, CA: University of California Press.

Tappan, P. W. 1949. *Juvenile Delinquency.* New York: McGraw-Hill.

Traugher, J., J. F. Lucas, and S. Parish. 1989. *Tennessee Juvenile Court Annual Statistical Report.* Nashville, TN: Tennessee Council of Juvenile and Family Court Judges.

U.S. Department of Justice, Bureau of Justice Statistics. 1989. *Children in Custody: 1975-85 Census of Public and Private Juvenile Detention, Correctional, and Shelter Facilities.* Washington, DC: U. S. Government Printing Office.

Wadlington, W., C. H. Whitehead, and S. M. Davis. 1983. *Cases and Materials on Children in the Legal System.* Mineola, NY: Foundation Press.

Wrigley, E. A. 1969. *Population and History.* New York: McGraw-Hill Book Company.

Zelizer, V. 1985. *Pricing the Priceless Child: The Changing Social Value of Children.* New York: Basic Books.

chapter 3

Images of Delinquency
Police and Court Statistics

> *No one can dismiss the juvenile contribution to violent crime as inconsequential, but if we were to lock up all 60 million persons under the age of 18 today, the number of murders committed tomorrow would drop by only 5 percent, the number of rapes by 9 percent, the number of robberies by 16 percent, and the number of aggravated assaults by 10 percent. Juvenile crime is, and should be, a major social concern, but it is imperative that each of us develop an accurate understanding of the problem. Misinformation about the dimensions of juvenile crime is currently a formidable barrier to the development of a coherent response.*
>
> —Howard Snyder and Ellen Nimick, 1983:51

The "Facts" About Delinquency

"Everyone does it! I just got caught!" Most of us have either heard someone make such a proclamation or have said it ourselves when caught doing something wrong. And, as was noted in Chapter 1, there is an element of truth to such statements. Most people do break laws but only a tiny fraction are ever caught. Most offenses which occur are never even reported to the police. Yet, for most of the history of criminology the "facts" about crime and delinquency have been based on the small percentage of crimes that *have* been reported and the offenders who *have* been caught.

If those few who are caught mirror the characteristics of all those involved (i.e. are a representative sample) and if the same proportion of delinquent episodes occur in different settings and times, then we can have some confidence that our facts, based on official statistics, accurately reflect the nature of the delinquency problem. It is exactly these "ifs" that disturb criminologists. Many criminologists suspect that some types of people are more likely to be suspected and labeled by officials than others. It is quite commonly argued that blacks and other minority youths are more likely to become official statistics than white youths engaged in similar delinquent activity. Girls are believed to be more likely than boys to be labeled delinquent based on their sexual behavior. In addition, because they are less likely to have a parent at home, children in single-parent families may run a greater risk of being taken to a juvenile court or detention center than children who can be taken home and turned over to their parents. If such biases are real, then the characteristics of those youth who are processed through the juvenile court system and therefore contribute to official statistics are *not* representative of youth committing delinquent acts.

Similarly, if criminal and delinquent episodes are more likely to be detected at one time or place than at another, then observations about location and variations over the years may be misleading. An increase in the number of facilities for processing delinquents may be responsible for an increase in the number of delinquent youths who are processed. A state or community that develops special programs and devotes new resources to juvenile justice may be rewarded by an "increase" in the number of cases and have a worse statistical record than a state or community that does not make such investments.

It is important to recognize that these questions about official statistics are the topic of criminological research and have not been answered conclusively. Such questions have prompted criminologists to explore ways of acquiring information about delinquency which do not depend on official data. One such technique has been to ask samples of youth to report on their own delinquent activities, whether or not they were ever caught. An even more recent technique has been to ask people about their experiences as victims and, if possible, the characteristics of the people who have victimized them.

In this chapter and the next, we focus on "images" of delinquency rather than "facts" about delinquency because facts may differ, depending on the source of information. The images suggested by different methods of measuring delinquency may also differ because each method measures more than just involvement in delinquency. Official statistics reflect the behavior of the public in recognizing and reporting delinquency, the behavior of the police in defining and responding to crime and delinquency, as well as the characteristics and activities of offenders. Similarly, surveys of youths may merely reflect their desire to present certain images of themselves. Even victims' reports are affected by memory and willingness to acknowledge such experiences. By considering different images and thinking about the disparities, we should end up with a less simplistic view of delinquency than that conveyed by the "facts." However, we will also find areas of agreement and images that recur.

The Official Creation of Delinquent Events and Persons

We are continually bombarded with statistical information about the state of society and our collective well-being. "The cost of living increased by 10 percent!" "The value of the dollar has declined 20 percent!" "Crime increased by 5 percent!" Moreover, during political campaigns we are likely to find various candidates using the same statistics to support very different positions. It is not surprising then that so many people conclude that "one can say anything with statistics." However, the more detailed our knowledge about the collection and use of statistics, the better able we are to assess their meaning and to differentiate between proper and improper interpretations.

As already noted, most events and people who *could* enter into official statistics do not, because they go undetected or they are never reported. A major reason why many criminal victimizations never become crimes recorded by the police or the courts is that the public does not take the initial step of reporting the crime (see Chapter 4). Since most police activity is in response to public complaints, the public's willingness to report crimes is a major factor affecting the number of youths who are caught and processed through the juvenile justice system. For example, the annual Bureau of Justice Statistics' National Crime Survey shows that the public reports only about one-third of the victimizations experienced by members of their households.

Whether people report their victimizations varies, depending on the seriousness of the crime and such characteristics as the victim's sex, age, household income, and home ownership. Violent crimes are more likely to be reported than theft and the rate at which theft victimizations are reported varies by seriousness. Close to three-fourths of motor vehicle thefts are reported as compared to about one-tenth of thefts under $50 where there is no personal contact. While the major determinant of public reporting appears to be the seriousness of the offense, crimes are more likely to be reported when the victim is 1) female, 2) elderly, 3) in a high income group, 4) a homeowner, or 5) suspects (if known) are strangers, than when the victim is 1) male, 2) young, 3) in a low income group, 4) a renter and/or 5) suspects are non-strangers.

Why do people choose not to report crimes against them? The most common reasons given by respondents to the National Crime Survey vary by offense. With rape victims, the most common reasons given are that 1) it is a personal or private matter (35%), 2) nothing can be done (18%), or 3) fear of reprisal (16%). For less serious crimes, another common reason is that the event was "not important enough." The views that nothing could be done or that the event was not important enough to report are particularly common reasons for not reporting thefts.

Research in England in the early 1970s suggested a similar gap between victimization and reporting. In a study of three areas of London, researchers found that only one-third of those victimized indicated having reported such incidents to the police. They concluded that "in general, completed crimes were more likely to be reported than attempts; assaults which caused some degree of physical injury were more likely to be reported, and for property crimes reporting increased, the greater the value of the property said to be involved" (Sparks, Genn, and Dodd, 1977:120).

Because the decision to report an offense has been found to play a key role in the creation of official statistics, criminologists have studied the way interaction between the public and the police affects the "production of crime rates." Donald Black (1970) has reported on a study of encounters between police and citizens in the cities of Boston, Chicago, and Washington, D.C. In cases in which there was no suspect, police decided to take action on 72 percent of the most serious offenses (felonies) and 53 percent of the less serious offenses (misdemeanors). However, if the complainant did not want the police to take further legal action, the police abided by this wish in every encounter observed. On the other hand, if the complainant pressed for further action, the police were apparently influenced by other considerations. Police abided by such preferences more often when 1) the offense was a felony rather than a misdemeanor, 2) the suspected offender was a stranger to the complainant rather than an acquaintance, and 3) the complainant was respectful to the police rather than disrespectful. There was also some indication that for serious offenses, police were more likely to honor the preferences of middle-class complainants than those of working-class complainants. However, there was no evidence that white complainants received more preferential treatment than black complainants.

A more recent study (Smith et al., 1984) using direct observations of 611 police-citizen encounters in St. Louis, Rochester, and Tampa-St. Petersburg did find evidence of preferential treatment of white victims as compared to black victims. Police were more likely to arrest a suspect when the complainant was white than when the complainant was black. Such results may reflect differences among cities studied or differences in police response in different time periods. It is conceivable that during the most active period of civil rights activity (the 1960s) police were less likely to respond differently by race than in the late 1970s. As we will note later in the chapter, some scholars argue that the outcome of different "waves" of research on discrimination has varied in different periods of time (Zatz, 1987).

Black and Reiss (1970) also examined the circumstances leading to encounters between police and juveniles and to police decisions to arrest. They found that most arrest situations (78 percent) developed through citizen complaints rather than police initiative—that is, most contacts represented *reactive* rather than *proactive* police action. Furthermore, the police were found to be quite lenient, arresting only 57 percent of felony suspects and 48 percent of misdemeanor suspects. The probability of being arrested, however, was enhanced when 1) the offense was serious, 2) the suspect was a stranger to the complainant, and 3) the suspect was unusually respectful or disrespectful. Black juveniles were more likely to be arrested than white juveniles, but the greater hazard for black juveniles was found to reflect a tendency for black complainants to press for arrest. Nearly identical results were obtained in one subsequent replication of the Black and Reiss (1970) study in other settings (Lundman et al., 1978).

There has been a huge number of studies of biases in juvenile processing and we will return to that topic later in this chapter. We have touched on such research here to stress that criminal or delinquent events and persons represent only a small proportion of events and persons that could be so labeled. Whether an event or a person *is* so labeled is a product of legal constraints, complainant preference, relationships between suspects and complainants, and the interaction between police, complainants, and suspects. The fact that a variety of distinct circumstances affect the probability that persons and events make their way into government statistics as criminal or delinquent should be kept in mind as we examine the images suggested by such information.

Police Reports and Court Statistics

Statistics compiled by police and other law enforcement agencies have been a major component of public and governmental perceptions of the crime problem. Such statistics were first collected in Germany, France, Belgium, and England in the early and mid-1800s, and are now collated on a national scale in numerous modern industrial nations. In the United States, the Federal Bureau of Investigation centralized and organized the national collection of crime statistics in the 1930s and that report has grown from a relatively small document to an annual report several hundred pages long.

The FBI amasses great quantities of crime information on an annual basis and publishes these crime statistics in a volume referred to as the *Uniform Crime Reports* (UCR). More than 16,000 law enforcement agencies, which cover 96 percent of the United States population, submit monthly and annual reports to the FBI on the number of offenses known to the police, arrest statistics, statistics on characteristics of persons arrested, and law enforcement employee data. Most Americans have encountered these statistics in one form or another in proclamations about "crime" in the United States.

For the eight offenses that constitute the serious-crime index, the annual report provides statistics on *crimes known to the police* (that is, offenses officially recognized by the police as crimes), as well as arrest statistics. For other offenses, arrest data alone are provided. Only at the point of arrest does the *Uniform Crime Reports* provide any information on the age of the suspect. Since only a small percentage of most offenses ever results in arrest, arrest statistics do not necessarily provide an accurate or representative picture of offenders. Rather, they tell us who is being caught and arrested out of a much larger universe of people liable to arrest. As shown in Figure 3-1 the *clearance rate* (crimes cleared by an arrest relative to crimes known to the police) varies from 72 percent for murder to 14 percent for burglary.

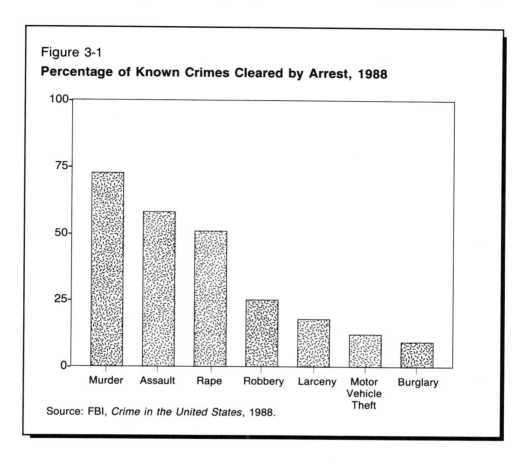

Figure 3-1

Percentage of Known Crimes Cleared by Arrest, 1988

Source: FBI, *Crime in the United States*, 1988.

It is also important to note that FBI arrest statistics generally refer to the *number of arrests* (incidence) rather than *the number of different people arrested* (prevalence). A very high arrest rate for a particular category of people may reflect a large incidence of offending by a few rather than common involvement of the majority. This point is well illustrated in a study by Lyle Shannon (1978). In an analysis of police-contact statistics for youths born in Racine, Wisconsin in 1949, Shannon found that around 5 percent of the white males accounted for over 38 percent of police contacts with white males and that 16 percent of the black males accounted for over 50 percent of police contacts with persons in that category. This disproportionate contribution of a few was found for females as well, with 8 percent of the black females accounting for 41 percent of all contacts with black females and 5 percent of white females accounting for 44 percent of contacts with that group.

Tracy et al., (1985) report that among youths born in Philadelphia in 1958, about 22 percent of male delinquents could be considered *chronic* delinquents (i.e. repeatedly in trouble with police). Chronic male delinquents accounted for 61 percent of all offenses involving males in that birth cohort and an even greater share of the most serious delinquent offenses. Among girls born in 1958, about 7 percent of those acquiring a police record by age 18 could be considered chronic, but that small group accounted for 27 percent of total offenses committed by girls. Thus, among males, the majority of incidents were attributable to a small category of chronic offenders. The chronic offender was less of a problem among girls but still contributed disproportionately to incidents recorded by the police.

Just as a single offender may account for numerous arrests, a single incident may result in several different people being arrested. We noted this possibility in Chapter 2 because it can exaggerate the image of the contribution of juveniles to crime. Suppose three juveniles were arrested for one incident of shoplifting and in another case that day, one adult was arrested. Juveniles would account for 3 of 4 arrests but only one of two incidents. Beginning in 1985, the *Uniform Crime Reports* added information on the number of offenses cleared by arrest where only young people under age 18 were involved. When measured in that fashion, juveniles do not account for as large of a share of crime as when number of arrests for that age group is considered.

In addition to the *Uniform Crime Reports*, a second source of official statistics on delinquency in the United States has been *Juvenile Court Statistics*, issued by various government agencies since 1929. For most of the history of such statistics, that report summarized information on total numbers of cases, gender, location of the court, and method of handling the case. There were no breakdowns by offense since the philosophy behind juvenile justice was that the state was intervening to decide whether the child needed help as a "delinquent" and not convicting her or him for a specific crime (see Chapter 2). In 1982 the National Center for Juvenile Justice issued a report, *Delinquency in the United States*, which provided much more detail than previously available. That Center now collates and stores information in a National Juvenile Court Data Archive. A recent report of court-level statistics and summary data on cases processed (published in 1989 covering 1985) comes from courts with jurisdiction over about 59 percent of the juvenile population in 1985. Detailed characteristics of each case are available as well, but limited to courts encompassing about 49 percent of the juvenile population in the United States. Thus, while the National Center now provides considerable detail on juvenile delinquency, reports are still limited in their coverage. Again, we should approach such national data with a view towards constructing images which can be compared and contrasted with other data sources.

While the National Center does not report prevalence rates, their 1982 data allow us to make an estimate of such a rate. For each age category, the Center reported on the number of cases referred to juvenile court where there was a prior record with the court and the number of new cases. Using these data, we estimate that out of over three million youths age 12 or younger in 1980, about one-half million will have been referred to the juvenile court by their 18th birthdays, which represents about 18 percent of them. About 25 percent of boys and 12 percent of girls will come to the attention of the juvenile justice system for some form of delinquency before they are eighteen.

These figures are lower than those reported for the 1958 cohort of youth in Philadelphia mentioned earlier. However, the Philadelphia cohort has a much larger proportion of black youth than the nation as a whole. If the data from Tracy et al., (1985) are adjusted to estimate the prevalence of delinquency for the nation, the estimate based on their study would be about 18 percent, reflecting a rate of about 26 percent for males and about 11 percent for females. In sum, it appears safe to conclude that about *one-fourth of males in the United States get into trouble with the law before they are 18 years of age and that girls are less than one-half as likely as boys to do so.*

Patterns Based on Police and Court Statistics

What do data on crime and delinquency show about variations or patterns over time, in different settings, and among different categories of people? We have touched on some differences already. Most people believe that crime and delinquency have been increasing, that they are primarily urban problems, and that males, minority groups, the disadvantaged, and the young account for an unusual amount of the crime problem. Such images have been supported by police and court statistics for the United States and a number of other societies.

There are, however, contrasting points of view. Since police and court statistics on crime and delinquency reflect the behavior of 1) the public, 2) the police, 3) the courts, and 4) offenders, there is obviously room for disagreement about how much each contributes to whatever patterns are observed. Changes in public willingness to report offenses or in police and court procedures can affect the volume and rate of recorded crime and delinquency. In addition, differences in public, police, and court response to crime and delinquency in different settings or among different categories of people can lead to differences in crime and delinquency statistics— differences that do not accurately reflect criminal and delinquent activity. Hence, the patterns outlined below can be given *several* interpretations and cannot be taken as conclusive statements of the "facts" about delinquent behavior.

Variations over Time and Space

Crime and delinquency can be thought about in several different ways. We dealt with delinquency as a legal category in the last chapter. In this chapter, we have been dealing with crime and delinquency as legal labels applied to experiences, events or activities at the end of a chain of decisions by control agents, including the public. One way to summarize such events has been to compile or *aggregate* data on such events and to use them together with other bodies of data to create "rates." For example, when criminologists and others refer to "crime rates" in the United States, they are likely to be referring to the *Uniform Crime Reports'* crimes known to the police. When the number of crimes known is divided by the population of the United States it gives us an estimate of the risk of crime "per capita." When multiplied times 100,000 the crime rate becomes the number of crimes per 100,000 population. The number of crimes can increase due merely to an increase in the population. The crime "rate" takes the population into account and has been used to estimate trends in crime and variations among regions, states, and communities.

Other data can be used to generate rates as well. National juvenile court statistics can be used to estimate trends and variations in rates of court-recorded delinquency and status offenses. *Uniform Crime Reports* data can be used to estimate trends in arrest rates among juveniles. When all sources of data "converge" and yield similar patterns, our confidence that the data are accurately describing a real pattern in officially recognized crime and delinquency is greatly enhanced.

Time. For most of the last several decades, crime and delinquency were viewed as *growing* social problems in the United States, getting worse year after year. Police statistics were typically cited in support of this observation. Moreover, similar reports were heard from Canada, England, and several European countries (Rutter and Giller, 1984:65-89). Studies of developing African nations and India indicated rising crime rates as well (Clinard and Abbott, 1973).

The major source of data on crime over time in the United States is the *Uniform Crime Reports*. The FBI's data on "crimes known to the police" are generally viewed as better than arrest statistics for assessing crime trends since they are not influenced by the contingencies affecting arrest. At the "crimes known" level, the statistics merely refer to those incidents recognized by the police as crimes whether or not they are ever solved or ever result in an arrest. Because the age of the offender is not known, these statistics do not provide information specifically on crimes by juveniles. However, since male juveniles account for especially high proportions of property "crimes known to the police," these statistics are relevant to assessing trends in crimes commonly associated with juveniles.

Figures 3-2 and 3-3 summarize six categories of crimes known to the police per 100,000 persons between 1933 and 1988. Rates for most crimes were declining or stable in the 1930s and early 1940s. Assault began climbing in the early to mid-1940s, as did burglary. Motor vehicle theft began its upward trend in the early to mid-1950s. Forcible rape increased gradually between 1933 and the early 1960s, after which it began to increase dramatically. Murder rates were stable or declining during most of the years between 1933 and 1965 but started climbing in the mid-1960s. Sometime between the late 1970s and early 1980s the rates for these crimes leveled out or began to decline.

We have summarized the trend in larceny for 1960 through 1988 in Figure 3-3 as well. Larceny rates are graphed separately for several reasons. Until 1973 a theft had to involve at least a $50 loss before it was counted in these national statistics. Thus, the measure of larceny was limited to what were considered to be serious thefts. However, since estimates of value were highly subjective it was easy for police departments to alter their crime rates by varying their estimates of the value of property. Furthermore, inflation could raise the crime rate as more and more items became worth $50 or more. A solution to such problems was the inclusion of all reported thefts in the larceny index. The data in Figure 3-3 are from a report which adjusted the data from 1960 to 1973 to compensate for that change in definition.

Larceny (the unlawful taking of property) occurs at such a high rate that it has to be graphed on a much larger scale than the other offenses. It peaked at a rate more than twice that of the next most frequent offense, burglary (the unlawful entry of a building to commit a theft). As noted earlier, it accounts for most of the FBI's serious crime index. However, the trend in larceny is quite similar to other property crimes and crimes of interpersonal violence. The major increases occurred during the 1960s and 1970s. Larceny declined from 1980 through 1984 but started another upward climb between 1985 and 1988. It has not returned to its earlier peak but is very close to it.

Juvenile court statistics follow a similar pattern over time. In 1957, with an estimated 22,173,000 people age 10 to 17, juvenile courts handled 440,000 cases, yielding a rate of about 20 cases per 1,000 juveniles. The rate hovered around 20 per 1,000 until 1962 when it started climbing. By the mid-1960s, the rate was 25 cases per 1,000. By 1969 it had reached 30 per 1,000, climbing to 45 per 1,000 by 1975 (Snyder et al., 1985). The rate remained at 45 for the remainder of the 1970s, rose to about 47 in 1980 and ranged between 47 and 49 through the most recent report.

Referral rates for youths age 10 through 17 years based on a variety of government reports from 1939 through 1984 are summarized in Figure 3-4. The trends are quite similar to arrest rates for persons under 18 using

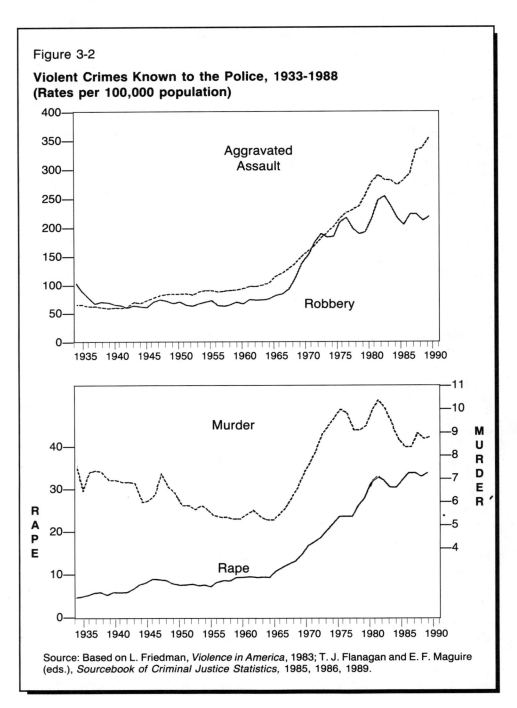

Figure 3-2

**Violent Crimes Known to the Police, 1933-1988
(Rates per 100,000 population)**

Source: Based on L. Friedman, *Violence in America*, 1983; T. J. Flanagan and E. F. Maguire (eds.), *Sourcebook of Criminal Justice Statistics*, 1985, 1986, 1989.

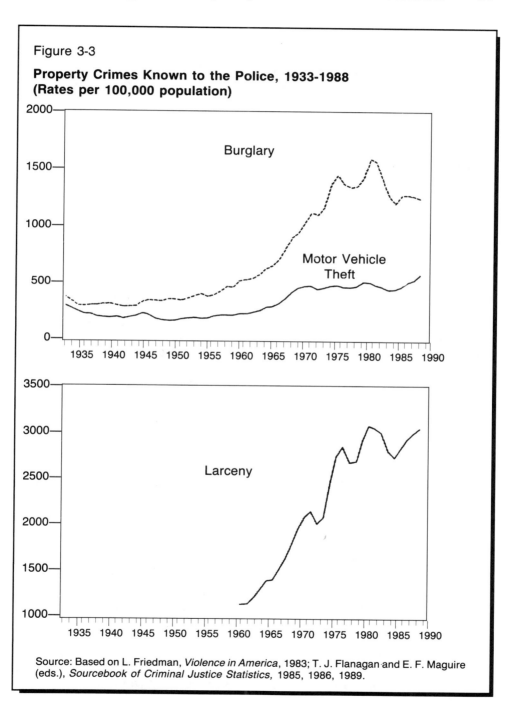

Figure 3-3

**Property Crimes Known to the Police, 1933-1988
(Rates per 100,000 population)**

Source: Based on L. Friedman, *Violence in America*, 1983; T. J. Flanagan and E. F. Maguire (eds.), *Sourcebook of Criminal Justice Statistics,* 1985, 1986, 1989.

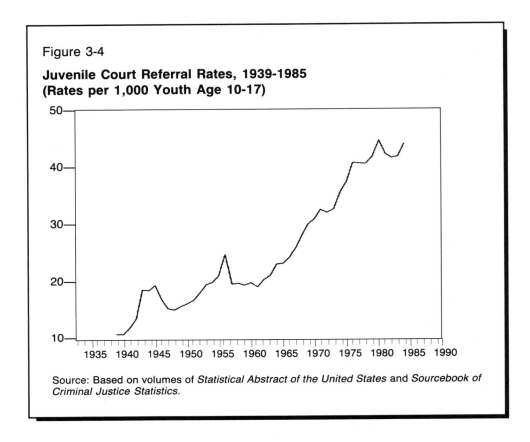

Figure 3-4

Juvenile Court Referral Rates, 1939-1985
(Rates per 1,000 Youth Age 10-17)

Source: Based on volumes of *Statistical Abstract of the United States* and *Sourcebook of Criminal Justice Statistics*.

FBI's *Uniform Crime Reports* (see Chapter 1). Referral rates increased most steadily from the early 1960s through the early 1980s.

Tracy et al., (1985) have compiled data on two "birth cohorts" in Philadelphia (males born in 1945 and 1958) and examined the *prevalence* and *incidence* of recorded trouble with the police. Their data show that minority or white youths born in Philadelphia in 1958 are *less* likely to have acquired a police record by their 18th birthdays than those born in 1945. Of boys born in 1958, 23 percent of whites had acquired a record (i.e. the prevalence rate was 23 percent) as compared to 29 percent among those born in 1945. For minority youths (predominantly blacks), 42 percent had acquired a record by 18 years of age as compared to 50 percent of boys born in 1945. However, while a smaller percentage of boys acquired a record in 1958, they were responsible for more offenses than the earlier cohort. Their offense rate was 1,159 offenses per 1,000 youths as compared to 1,027 per 1,000 in the 1945 cohort. In other words, the 1958 cohort had a higher *incidence* rate but a lower *prevalence* rate.

The fact that the prevalence rates were not greater for youths growing up in that city from 1958 through 1975 than for those growing up from 1945 through 1962 is consistent with evaluations of official statistics in England and Wales. After examining data for those societies, Rutter and Giller (1984:88) conclude that "the increase in *acts* of delinquency has been greater than that in the number of *people* committing such acts."

In considering the official statistics on juvenile delinquency and their changes over time, we should recognize that the rate may have been higher in the years before nationwide estimates were first compiled in the 1930s. It appears, for example, that the 1870s—the reconstruction period following the American Civil War—may have been the most violent period in American history (National Commission on the Causes and Prevention of Violence, 1969). Even after the development of the *Uniform Crime Reports* we find that the homicide rate in 1988 (8.4 per 100,000 population) is less than in 1933 (9.6 per 100,000 population). The rate declined during the 1930s, leveled out in the late 1940s and 1950s at about 5 per 100,000 and began increasing in the early 1960s. On the other hand, a study of juvenile cases in an Ohio county found a rate of 66 per 100,000 in 1919, as compared to 21 in 1939 and 34 in 1957 (Teeters and Matza, 1959). Thus, juvenile court referral and arrest rates may have been higher at points in time when nationwide data were not available.

We should also note that an increase in the national delinquency rate does not mean that the rate is increasing in every jurisdiction and in every state. Increases in referral rates nationwide could be due to the expansion of juvenile referral facilities. Changes in police practices can also play a role in increasing referral and arrest rates. In a study of the processing of juveniles in two California communities—one with a *professional* police force and the other with a *fraternalistic* police force—James Wilson (1968) compared police contacts with juveniles that resulted in arrest. The professional force was one in which there were formally stated guidelines for handling cases, centralized control of the police, and close supervision and record keeping. On the other hand, the fraternalistic force was decentralized and had little supervision, few formally stated procedures, and little emphasis on record keeping. Of cases processed by the professional police force, 47 percent resulted in arrests or citations. Of cases processed by the fraternalistic department, 30 percent resulted in an arrest or citation. Thus, in the one jurisdiction there was a greater probability of a case resulting in arrest. As police jurisdictions move increasingly in the direction of the professional model, we would expect some increase in arrests because of changes in procedure. Similarly, as people move to urban centers with professionally run police departments, their behavior may become subject to a higher risk of official labeling.

Box 3-1

Misconceptions About Youth Crime

In October 1988 the Field Institute conducted a telephone poll of 1,109 adults in California for the National Council on Crime and Delinquency (NCCD). One of the questions asked was "Do you think the rate of juvenile crime in California has been going up in the last five years, going down, or staying about the same?" Respondents answered as follows:

Going up	82.2%
Staying the same	8.3%
Going down	1.6%
No opinion	7.4%

David Steinhart, Director of Policy Development for NCCD reports that this public perception bears little relationship to the facts about juvenile arrests in California. From 1981 through 1986 juvenile arrests declined by 11.3 percent with an apparent upturn between 1985 and 1986. Juvenile arrests for violent crimes (murder, assault, rape, and robbery) fell by 25.2 percent during that time. The *rates* of juvenile arrests per 100,000 juveniles age 12 to 17 as well as the number of arrests declined.

Why do people believe that the rate of juvenile crime is always getting worse whether or not it actually is?

Source: David Steinhart, "California Opinion Poll: Public Attitudes on Youth Crime," *NCCD FOCUS*. National Council on Crime and Delinquency, December 1988.

Changes at other points in the juvenile justice system can affect delinquency statistics as well. For example, in a study of delinquency statistics in Florida, Chilton and Spielberger (1971) found that a "meteoric" rise in delinquency in one county coincided with the construction of a new court building and increases in staff. If referral facilities do not exist, then police and the public may be more inclined to handle cases informally; inadequate facilities may have the same effect.

Changes in police practices seem to affect delinquency rates in other societies as well. In England, for example, police forces established specialized bureaus to deal with juvenile cases with the intention of diverting youths from official processing. Children were to be "cautioned" when possible rather than arrested. However, a study in London by Farrington and Bennett (1981) found that the arrest rate increased 85 percent in a two-year period following the establishment of the cautioning option. More youths were being arrested rather than fewer. This "widening of the net" when new programs and policies are attempted has also been reported for diversion programs in the United States (see Chapter 11). Thus, the chance of becoming an official statistic may increase as police and communities develop special programs and procedures to handle the delinquency problem.

Space. Variation in delinquency rates within different areas of a city was the subject matter of some of the earliest theories of delinquency in the United States. As a result of studies begun in the 1920s, Clifford Shaw and Henry McKay (1942) observed that rates of officially recorded delinquency in the city of Chicago were characterized by a *gradient tendency*: with the greatest rates occurring in the "transitional" (or "interstitial") zone surrounding the central business district. Successively lower rates occurred in areas more removed from that transitional zone. It did not appear that any unique property of particular racial or ethnic minorities accounted for such a gradient: the high-rate areas tended to remain high-rate areas even though different groups occupied the transitional zone over time. Thus, Shaw and McKay concluded that the causes of delinquency must be found in characteristics of communities and social settings:

> The high degree of consistency in the association between delinquency and other characteristics of the community not only sustains the conclusion that delinquent behavior is related dynamically to the community but also appears to establish that all community characteristics, including delinquency, are products of the operation of general processes more or less common to American cities. Moreover, the fact that in Chicago the rates of delinquents for many years have remained relatively constant in the areas adjacent to centers of commerce and heavy industry, despite successive changes in the nativity and nationality composition of the population, supports emphatically the conclusion that the delinquency-producing factors are inherent in the community. (1942:435)

Of course, we must remember that official statistics reflect the behavior of victims and officials, as well as of offenders. Thus, variations by area of the city may reflect variations in reactions to delinquency as well as variations in delinquent behavior.

Reporting on these same areas several decades later, McKay (1967) found that there had been a rather dramatic decline in delinquency rates in areas where the population had remained sufficiently stable to "make an adjustment to urban life." The areas of Chicago with the greatest decrease were the very areas that had had the highest rates in the earlier studies. The areas of the city characterized by increasing rates were areas that were experiencing the same sort of population changes and transitions associated with the high rates in the 1930s. Thus, the spatial distribution of officially recognized crime may change as the conditions associated with high rates change and redistribute themselves. Bursik (1986) suggests that the Shaw and McKay thesis may not be totally applicable to post-World War II communities, but the process of community stabilization and delinquency rates still appear to be amazingly robust (1986:40).

Other spatial patterns of interest to criminologists are the urban-rural difference and differences by community size. Based on an analysis of FBI statistics for 1980, Howard Snyder and Ellen Nimick (1983) conclude that "juveniles in urban areas accounted for a larger proportion of the community's serious crime problem, committed serious crimes at a greater rate, and comprised a larger proportion of arrests than those in suburban and rural areas." The rate of property crimes cleared by a juvenile arrest was 2,216 (per 100,000 youth 10 through 17) for youths in cities compared to 1,297 for suburban youth and only 625 for youth in rural areas. There were especially dramatic variations for robbery, with a rate of 88 for city youth and only 7 for rural youth. City youth had a rate over twice that of rural youth for rape and about four times greater for assault.

Differences by area are not as great using juvenile court referrals (rather than crimes cleared by an arrest) as a yardstick. Nevertheless, Snyder and Nimick's analysis (1983) shows that the variation is substantial for violent offenses when comparing courts in metropolitan areas (4.5 per 1,000) to courts in nonmetropolitan areas (2.0 per 1,000). Juvenile referral rates for property offenses are greater in metropolitan (23.5) versus nonmetropolitan courts (17.7) as well. In sum, police and court data both suggest that delinquency is more of an urban than a rural problem.

While there is a general correlation between crime rates and such variables as city size and population density, there are exceptions. In short, it is not a perfect relationship. For example, in his study of rural Oregon teenagers, Kenneth Polk (1974) found that his subjects got into trouble with the police just about as often as a similar cohort of urban boys in Philadelphia (Wolfgang et al., 1972). Polk noted:

> In the days when the United States was primarily a country of farms and small towns, it was generally believed that teenage delinquency was almost entirely confined to cities. Even today many people think that teenage boys who live outside metropolitan areas get into substantially less trouble than their city cousins, and that when they do, their scrapes are usually minor.
>
> Perhaps surprisingly, studies made in recent years have shown that there is no basis for this common assumption—nonmetropolitan youth have just about as many run-ins with the law as metropolitan youths, and the causes of these confrontations are often of roughly equal seriousness in both towns and cities. (1974:1)

Sutherland and Cressey (1974:176-180) have observed that the crime rates in urban areas may be exceeded by crime rates in some types of rural or small-town settings. Crime rates appear to have been high in frontier cities, resort towns, and logging communities. The Bureau of Justice Statistics (1983) reports that counties with extremely high crime rates are usually highly urbanized or include resort areas with a large number of tourists and transients. In short, while crime rates do vary by size of community, other characteristics of communities can affect them as well.

Variations Among Categories of Youth

Official statistics on recorded crime and delinquency have also been used to discern variations among different categories of youth. We have already reported in Chapter 1 that people under 18 contribute disproportionately to arrest statistics. Since people 10 through 17 years of age comprise only 12 percent of the population but account for 40 percent of motor vehicle thefts, they are overrepresented in such statistics. Several characteristics of youth affect the degree to which they are overrepresented in crime and delinquency statistics.

Two cautions are important when examining variations among categories of youth. First, a category of youth can be greatly overrepresented in such statistics but be a small dimension of the problem in numerical terms. For example, native American or Indian American youth may have a high rate of trouble with the law but constitute a small number of the officially recognized cases. The crime problem is often viewed as a "minority" problem because minority groups are overrepresented in crime and delinquency statistics. Yet, in most jurisdictions in the United States the majority of offenders will be members of the majority population.

Second, while certain categories of youth are overrepresented in crime and delinquency statistics, no characteristic or combination of characteristics of youth enable us to determine who will get into trouble. Many youths in the overrepresented categories will not get into trouble while many in the underrepresented categories will do so. Moreover, knowledge of a person's gender, age, and race might increase the "odds" of a correct prediction if we were predicting for a large number of youth but we would not be able to predict for any specific person in the category. When we discuss probabilities of trouble among different categories of youth we are discussing probabilities for those aggregate categories, not for individuals.

Gender Differences. Crime and delinquency are commonly thought of as male problems, and we have noted that FBI arrest statistics often support such an image. For instance, if we consider 17-year-olds, the FBI arrest rate for males is nearly 15 times greater than that for females. Robbery rates for juvenile males are eight to fifteen times higher than that for juvenile females. According to FBI arrest data, the arrest rates for males exceed the rates for females for every offense except running away from home and prostitution. Differences are especially large for major property offenses and violent offenses involving the use of weapons.

The predominance of males in crime and delinquency statistics appears to be both a historical and an international regularity. The gender difference has been noted since statistics were first compiled and has been found in every society for which such statistics are available. In India, where juveniles account for only 3 percent of arrests, male arrests outnumber female arrests about 32 to 1 (Priyadarsini and Hartjen, 1981). In Papua, New Guinea, the ratio of male to female arrests is close to 50 to 1 (Sundeen, 1981). A study of Kampala, Uganda, Africa, found a male-female arrest ratio of about 23 to 1 (Clinard and Abbott, 1973). The ratios in those nations appear to be much larger than in the United Kingdom (5:1 in 1977), Japan (6:1 in 1972) or the United States (about 3.5:1 for all offenses in 1984).

While the gender difference is persistent, it has also been declining in most societies, including the United States. In Figure 3-5 we have summarized arrest rates at the beginning of the last three decades and for the latest FBI report. In 1960 girls had extremely low rates relative to boys, ranging from about 6 to 1 for larceny to nearly 32 to 1 for burglary. By 1988, however, the ratio for larceny was about 3 to 1 with a ratio of about 12 to 1 for burglary. The lower ratios reflect greater increases in arrest rates for girls than for boys. The major declines in male predominance occurred

Figure 3-5

Ratios of Male to Female Arrest Rates for Persons Under Age 18

	1960	1970	1980	1988
Murder	13.5	13.1	11.3	13.2
Robbery	19.9	12.6	12.6	11.9
Assault	8.5	5.7	5.5	5.6
Burglary	31.7	21.0	13.6	12.3
Larceny	5.7	2.7	2.6	2.7
Motor Vehicle Theft	24.6	17.5	8.3	8.3

Note: Numbers indicate male arrests per 1 female arrest.

Source: Based on FBI, *Uniform Crime Reports* for 1960, 1970, 1980, and 1988 and U.S. Census data for those years.

during the period of dramatically increasing rates of juvenile arrest from the early 1960s through the mid-1970s.

Juvenile court cases also disproportionately involve males, but this distinction is less prominent in recent statistics than it was during the 1950s and early 1960s. In 1957 male cases nationwide outnumbered female cases by about 4.4 to 1. By 1960 the ratio was 4 to 1. By 1965 it was 3.9 to 1, and by 1970 it was down to 3.2 to 1. During the 1970s the ratio dropped to 2.8 to 1. Currently, the ratio is about 3 male referrals to each female referral. This pattern is consistent with computations of arrest rates for all offenses in the FBI reports. The gender ratio for total offenses of juveniles in the *Uniform Crime Reports* has been relatively stable for the last ten years.

Besides prostitution, two particular types of offenses are often depicted as the domain of females—shoplifting and status offenses. For example, Edwin Schur (1969:177) noted that "women shoplifters greatly outnumber men." In *Sisters in Crime* (1975:89), Freda Adler expressed another common claim when she observed that "while boys tend to be arrested for offenses involving stealing and various sorts of mischief, girls are typically charged with sex offenses which are euphemistically described as 'delinquent tendencies,' 'incorrigibility,' or 'running away'."

Such claims can be misleading. For example, the research cited to reach such conclusions about shoplifting was done over three decades ago in stores frequented primarily by women. National and local studies of juvenile delinquency suggest that shoplifting rates are actually greater for males than females. National Center for Juvenile Justice data on shoplifting cases in jurisdictions encompassing about 35 percent of youth in the United States for 1985 (the latest available report) include 36,617 cases of male shoplifting compared to 20,274 cases for females. The ratio is about 1.8 male cases for each female case. Similarly, a study of court records in one Arizona county found that male juveniles accounted for 55 percent of referrals for shoplifting in 1975 (Jensen and Rojek, 1980).

Shoplifting stands out for females *not* because of a greater incidence of female shoplifting, but because females are so unlikely to appear in court statistics for the wider range of offenses dominated by males. Shoplifting accounts for a greater proportion of female arrests and referrals *not because they have a high rate relative to males, but because they have low rates for so many other types of offenses.*

A profile of runaway cases in twelve states (National Center for Juvenile Statistics for 1985) shows a greater number of female runaways (13,678) than male runaways (8,121). However, males accounted for 74 percent of liquor violations among juveniles, 55 percent of truancies, and 51 percent of referrals for being "ungovernable." When all status offenses are added together, males account for 55 percent. Again, status offenses (and especially runaways) stand out when discussing delinquency among females because males so greatly outnumber females for other types of offenses (see Figure 3-6).

Age. In an analysis of data on age and crime in several societies, Travis Hirschi and Michael Gottfredson (1983:581) conclude that "age is everywhere correlated with crime." By "everywhere" they mean that similar differences by age are found at different times, in different societies, and in different subgroups (blacks, whites, males, females, and so on).

Official statistics on criminal offenders in England and Wales in the 1840s have been summarized by Hirschi and Gottfredson and are represented in Figure 3-7. We have also summarized FBI arrest rates in 1986 for males and females in different age categories. Both graphs show a comparable pattern by age and gender. Officially recorded crime increases rapidly during the teenage years, peaks in the young adult years, and rapidly declines after the mid-20s.

In Figure 3-8 we have listed the peak years for arrest rates by gender for each offense in the FBI data. While every offense peaks sometime between 13 years of age and the late 20s, it is direct theft of, and attacks on, property which peak among juveniles, together with status offenses. Offenses involving interpersonal violence or conflict as well as more sophisticated forms of theft peak in the young adult years. For males, seven offenses peak before 18 and eleven peak at age 18. For males, 19 of 29 offenses peak at the three significant points of legal transition for American youth—ages 16, 18, and 21. Offense peaks are less concentrated for females with ten offenses peaking in the juvenile years, three peaking at 18 and other peaks spread throughout young adulthood.

National statistics on juvenile delinquency referrals show patterns by age and gender from age 10 through 17 similar to those found in FBI data. For boys, delinquency accelerates rapidly and peaks at 17. For girls, delinquency levels out at age 15.

In contrast to the pattern for developed Western nations, young people appear to be underrepresented in arrest data for India. For example, Priyadarsini and Hartjen (1981:111) report that as of 1974, only 3 percent of crimes were attributed to juveniles even though about 50 percent of the population is under 21 years of age. Like youth in other nations, their offenses were predominantly property crimes. Clinard and Abbott (1973) report similar results for Kampala, Africa.

Hence, while there is a strong tendency for teenagers and young adults to have high arrest rates, there are some exceptions to the general pattern. We do know whether these exceptions reflect idiosyncracies of police or reporting procedures in those settings, or real differences in patterns by age in underdeveloped nations. However, it is important to note that offenses against property characterize juvenile delinquency even in those instances where juveniles do not have exceptionally high arrest rates.

Figure 3-6

Offense by Gender and Race, 1985

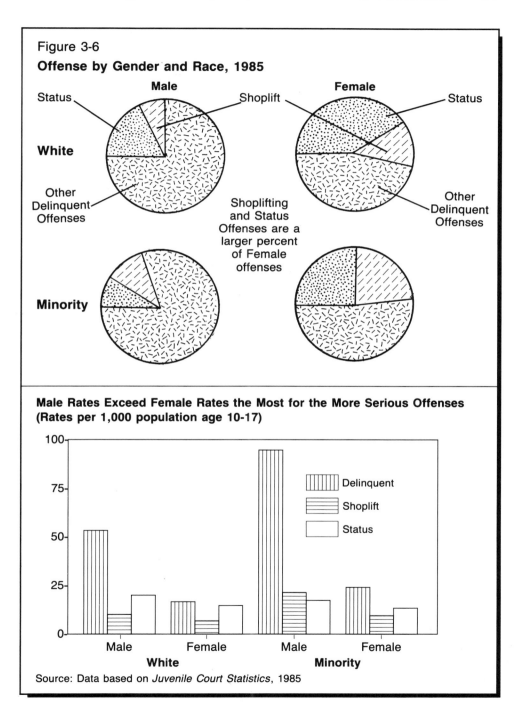

Shoplifting and Status Offenses are a larger percent of Female offenses

Male Rates Exceed Female Rates the Most for the More Serious Offenses (Rates per 1,000 population age 10-17)

Source: Data based on *Juvenile Court Statistics*, 1985

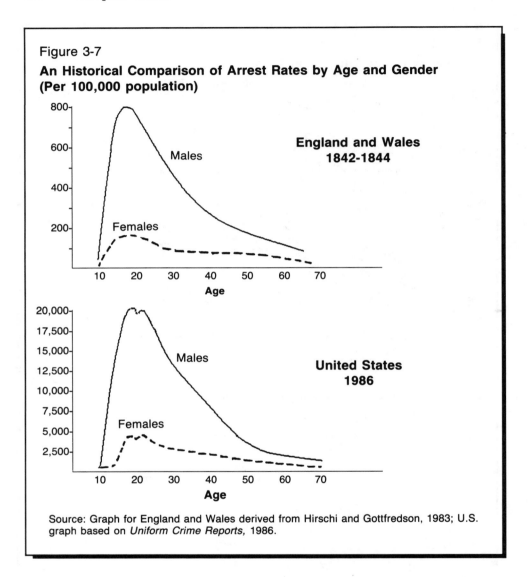

Figure 3-7

An Historical Comparison of Arrest Rates by Age and Gender (Per 100,000 population)

Source: Graph for England and Wales derived from Hirschi and Gottfredson, 1983; U.S. graph based on *Uniform Crime Reports,* 1986.

Race and Ethnicity. A third characteristic of youth which is typically recorded when they get into trouble with police is racial or ethnic status. The *Uniform Crime Reports* provide a breakdown into four categories: white, black, Indian or Eskimo, and Asian or Pacific Islander. Arrest rates for 1989 showed Asian Americans to have the lowest rates followed by whites and Indians, with black American youth exhibiting the highest rates.

Figure 3-8

Peak Ages for Arrest Rates

Age	Female	Male
13-14	Arson Curfew/Loitering Runaway Suspicion	Arson
15	Burglary Motor Vehicle Theft Simple Assault Vandalism	
16	Larceny	Motor Vehicle Theft Curfew/Loitering Runaway Suspicion Vandalism
17		Larceny
18	Stolen Property Liquor Laws Vagrancy	Murder Robbery Burglary Forcible Rape Stolen Property Weapons Sex Offenses Drug Offenses Liquor Laws Disorderly Conduct Vagrancy
19	Forgery/Counterfeiting	Embezzlement
20	Embezzlement All Other	
21	Family and Children	Aggravated Assault Forgery/Counterfeiting Drunkenness All Other
22	Aggravated Assault Sex Offenses Disorderly Conduct	Simple Assault Fraud Prostitution/Vice D.U.I.
23	Robbery Weapons Prostitution/Vice	
24	Murder Fraud Drug Offenses D.U.I. Drunkenness	Gambling Family and Children
25-29	Gambling	

Source: Based on FBI data for 1988.

If we compare arrest rates for 1989, black youth (under 18 years of age) exceed white youth most dramatically for robbery (10.1 to 1), murder (8.4 to 1) and rape (5 to 1). Other offenses where the ratio is at least 3 to 1 include assaults, motor vehicle theft, fraud, receiving or possessing stolen property, weapons violations, prostitution and vice, drug offenses, and gambling. The ratios are smaller for property crimes such as burglary (1.6 to 1) and larceny (1.9 to 1) and for sex offenses other than rape (2.0 to 1). Blacks and whites have comparable rates for arson, forgery and counterfeiting, vandalism, and curfew violations. Whites exceed blacks for runaway, suspicion, drunkenness, liquor law violations, and driving under the influence. Further analysis of the 1989 report reveals that the difference in arrest rates between blacks and whites is even greater among adults than among juveniles.

The National Center for Juvenile Justice report for 1984 presented data on white, black, hispanic and "other" youth for states providing such data. It reports actual referral rates for blacks, whites, and all other youth. For index crimes against persons the referral rate for blacks is about 3.1 times greater than the white rate. For property crimes the ratio is about 1.6 to 1. Whites exceed blacks for "public order" offenses and have about the same rates for status offenses.

Combining these Center reports with census estimates of the Hispanic population under age 18, we can estimate the referral rates for Hispanic youth. However, these figures are only crude estimates since only 21 percent of U.S. jurisdictions provided data relevant to that breakdown. For all referrals the rate for black males was 38 per 1,000 as compared to 26 for Hispanic males and 18 for white males. Among females the comparable rates were 11, 6, and 5 respectively. For crimes against persons, the rate for Hispanic males ages 10 through 17 (3.1 per 1,000) falls between black males (7.9) and white males (1.8). Among girls, blacks exceed both Hispanic and white females (2.0 compared to .5 per 1,000 for both Hispanics and whites). These figures suggest that gender differences may be greater among Hispanic youth than either white or black youth and that the overrepresentation of Hispanic youth is limited to males.

The Center's report for 1985 provides data comparing "white" and "nonwhite" youth. In Figure 3-9 their data on delinquency cases by age and race are represented for four types of offenses. Nonwhites exceed whites for each offense category but the differences are especially prominent for offenses against persons.

The studies of cohorts of youth in Philadelphia show differences in both the prevalence of delinquency and the incidence of delinquency by race. Among boys born in 1945, 50 percent of nonwhites had acquired a record by age 18, as compared to 29 percent of whites. In the 1958 cohort, 42 percent of nonwhites were delinquent compared to 23 percent of whites.

Figure 3-9

**Delinquency Case Rates by Age and Race
(Per 1,000 Youth in Age Group)**

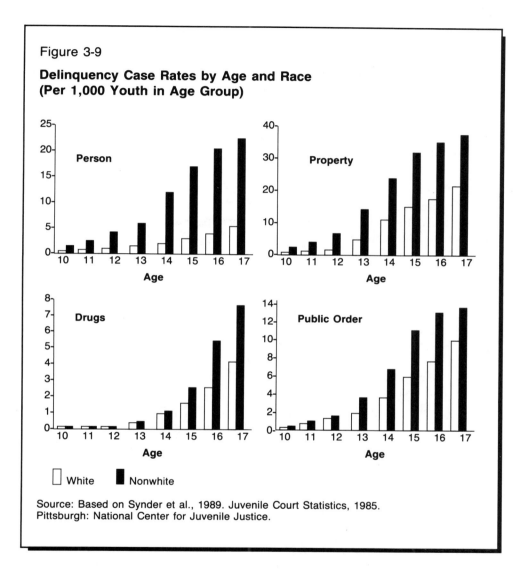

White   Nonwhite

Source: Based on Synder et al., 1989. Juvenile Court Statistics, 1985.
Pittsburgh: National Center for Juvenile Justice.

Data on girls were collected for the 1958 cohort and nonwhites were about twice as likely as whites to acquire a police record.

The offense rates based on acts or incidents of delinquency as recorded by police were 15 times higher among nonwhites than whites for violent offenses for the 1945 cohort and about 6 times greater in the 1958 cohort. For property theft, nonwhites born in 1945 were about four times as likely as whites to acquire a record, while for the 1958 cohort, nonwhites had a rate about twice that of whites. Again, racial differences appear most prominent for crimes involving interpersonal violence.

Differences among racial or ethnic groups have been obtained comparing white, black, and Asian youth in the United Kingdom as well. Summarizing a number of studies, Rutter and Giller (1983) conclude that Asian youth tend to have a delinquency rate lower than whites but that black youth had a rate substantially greater than white youth. Moreover, the high rates for blacks were most prominent for violent behavior. All three of these conclusions are consistent with research in the United States.

Social Status and Social Class. Popular stereotypes, as well as scholarly works, have depicted delinquency (or, at a minimum, the most serious forms of delinquency) as a problem of "lower- or working-class" youth. However, while the *Uniform Crime Reports* provides breakdowns by race, sex, age, and community setting, it provides no nationwide data on crime by social class.

Even sociologists, who are most familiar with the concepts of social status and class, have been unable to agree on their meaning or measurement. For example, Richard Centers (1949) argued that the terms *social class* and *social status* are not synonymous. He maintained that a social class is subjective in character and emerges from a feeling of group membership or class consciousness. As such, "class" is a psychological phenomenon and may not necessarily conform to objective lines of cleavage, such as income, occupation, or education. In contrast, the concept of social status *is* based on objective criteria, including income, occupation, education, and place of residence. For ease of discussion, we will use the terms *social class* and *social status* interchangeably here.

Even if we agree that income is relevant to the measurement of social class, we still have problems of setting boundaries. What amount of money shall we establish as the maximum that a lower-class person can earn? If we use poverty level criteria to define social class, we would place approximately 10 percent of all families in the lowest category and somehow divide the other 90 percent between middle and upper classes. Changes in the cost of living make it difficult to specify what income levels "middle-class" should represent and, finally, defining "upper-class" may be the most illusory of all. It may incorporate moderately successful business persons or professionals earning upwards of $25,000 per year, as well as heads of corporations, eminently successful medical specialists, and popular entertainers whose annual earnings exceed $250,000.

While major sources of national data do not bear on the topic, there are numerous limited studies relating indexes of parental income, education, and occupation to officially recorded crime and delinquency in specific samples or settings. A review of twenty-three such studies (Tittle et al., 1978) reported that 65 percent of them found that crime or delinquency were disproportionately common among persons categorized as of low status or class but that the differences between classes were not very great.

A study of sons of blue-collar and white-collar fathers (Frease, 1973) involving over 1,000 high school students in Marion County, Oregon, in 1964, could find no significant differences between the two groups in juvenile court referrals, referrals for serious offenses, or number of referrals. Similarly, a study based on a national survey of 847 teenagers, age 13 to 16, found: 1) a "negligible" relationship between social status and police contacts among both males and females, and 2) a significant relationship between social status and a police record only among white girls (Williams and Gold, 1972).

In contrast, the study of all boys born in Philadelphia in 1945 that we mentioned earlier (Wolfgang et al., 1972) found that among both blacks and whites, boys of lower socioeconomic status (SES) 1) had a greater likelihood of having acquired a delinquent record, 2) had a greater likelihood of having committed more than one offense, and 3) had a tendency to commit more serious offenses. The differences between SES categories were not huge. For example, 36 percent of the whites of lower SES had delinquent records by the time they were 18, as compared to 26 percent of the whites of higher SES. For blacks, the comparable percentages were 53 percent and 36 percent. In the subsequent study of a cohort of Philadelphia youth born in 1958, the results of the earlier cohort study were replicated with a difference of about 18 percent between low SES and high SES youth.

A study of official statistics in the San Francisco Bay area (Hirschi, 1969:74-75) reported similar results: the average number of officially recorded offenses for high school students of lower status was greater than the average number for students of higher social standing.

The controversy about social class and delinquency continues and we will return to it in the next chapter when we examine self-report measures of delinquency. Researchers are still exploring different ways to measure social class or status which might yield more consistent and meaningful results. However, as matters stand right now, we can neither state with complete confidence that there is a definite relationship between social status and officially recorded delinquency nor can we claim that there is no such relationship. There are studies to support both conclusions. The safest conclusion is that there appears to be a *slightly disproportionate tendency* for youths of lower status to appear in police and court records more often than youths of higher status (Tittle et al., 1978). Moreover, it also appears safe to conclude that differences by social class are neither as prominent nor as consistently observed as are differences by gender, age, and race. Given this latter observation, it is surprising that so much attention is paid to explaining small and inconsistent differences when there are more prominent and consistent differences to address.

Drug and Alcohol Offenses

Given the amount of media, public, and political attention devoted to the problems of drug and alcohol use among the young in American society, it is important to consider patterns over time and among different categories of youth based on arrest and referral statistics for those specific offenses. When we do so, the results are somewhat surprising to most people.

While the media, political, and public imagery is one of skyrocketing use, the trend exhibited in juvenile court statistics and FBI arrest data is comparable to that noted for other offenses. During the ten-year span covered by the National Center for Juvenile Justice (1975-1984), the referral rate for drug offenses actually declined from 3.7 per 1,000 youth at risk in 1975 to 2.3 per 1,000 in 1984. Referrals for drug offenses did not account for an increasing proportion of referrals during that time.

Since that report covers a limited span of years, we should also consider FBI data. However, some comparisons reflect changing definitions of the drug problem rather than illegal drug use. For example, in 1960 when the FBI category was called "Narcotic Drug Law Violations," the rate for persons under age 18 was only 2.6 per 100,000 youth. There were likely some major increases in drug use during the 1960s, but the shift in definitions to the more encompassing "Drug Abuse Violations" likely accounts for much of the increase to 78.4 per 100,000 by 1970. By 1980 the rate for drug abuse arrests was 108.2. However, consistent with trends for a variety of offenses, the rate had declined to 92.3 by 1984. The rate in 1988 was 119 per 100,000 youth under 18. Arrest rates are on the upswing again but research to be summarized in Chapter 4 suggests that this may reflect changes in enforcement rather than changes in drug use.

The variations in alcohol case rates by age and gender are similar to other offenses. Drug and alcohol offense rates increase with age and are greater for males than females. However, white youth have a juvenile court case rate several times greater than that of nonwhites for alcohol offenses. Moreover, whites and nonwhites have similar rates for drug possession and use offenses. Nonwhites have a case rate greater than whites for drug trafficking. Thus, while the drug problem is typically depicted as a minority problem that view is not justified overall when juvenile court referrals are considered (Office of Juvenile Justice and Delinquency Prevention, 1989).

We must once again reiterate the fact that official statistics do not necessarily reflect actual behavior, and this point may be all the more relevant when dealing with behavior where there are few complaining victims to report such activity. Fortunately, survey researchers have been studying drug use by other means for several years now, and in the next chapter we will examine patterns suggested by techniques for measuring drug use which do not depend on complainants or police response.

Discretion and Discrimination

Many critics of the justice system in the United States charge that the lower classes and minority groups are sanctioned more frequently and more severely than middle- or upper-class white Americans and that their overrepresentation in statistics on crime and delinquency reflects enduring prejudice and discrimination. Indeed, as argued in Chapter 1, the conception of delinquency and street crime as the nation's major crime problem reflects a biased image of the costs and consequences of crime. Differential enforcement of different types of laws and regulations can favor certain categories of potential offenders.

When the discussion is limited to the control of street crime and common delinquency, the issue is whether characteristics of people that are not supposed to disadvantage them before the law *do* have such consequences. It is a foregone conclusion to many people that black, Chicano, Puerto Rican and other readily identifiable minority groups are harassed and intimidated by the police and that serious miscarriages of justice are inflicted upon the poor. While debate on this subject is prolific, the research evidence to date is extremely complex and hard to summarize. No one simple conclusion can be stated concerning overt bias in enforcement that would apply in all jurisdictions at all times and to all stages.

There are a number of points at which discretionary decisions are being made that determine whether potential delinquencies and delinquents are identified and processed through official agencies. Figure 3-10 from the National Center's report for 1987 summarizes the processing of referrals to the juvenile courts in the United States. We have seen already that most possible cases do not make their way to the first stage of this process. Of those that do, most are referred by law enforcement officials but a sizeable minority are referred by "other sources" such as parents, schools, and victims. Status offenses are less likely to be referred by law enforcement than other delinquent offenses.

Most cases (54 percent) are "adjusted" short of a petition being filed. Such adjustments can take several forms, including dismissal for lack of evidence, voluntary referrals to social agencies, agreement that the juvenile make restitution or some other "informal" response. The most important characteristic of an adjustment is that further legal action stops and a juvenile does not acquire a record.

Formal steps are taken by filing petitions. A petition requests that the court take further action and is much like an indictment in the adult system in that the juvenile has been judged by the screening or intake officer as warranting adjudication. Of those petitioned, about 63 percent are "adjudicated" (a procedure much like a trial). Most of those cases result in probation, where a juvenile is allowed to live at home but must abide by restrictions set down by a judge. Very few cases result in some form

Figure 3-10

Juvenile Court Processing of Delinquency Cases, 1987

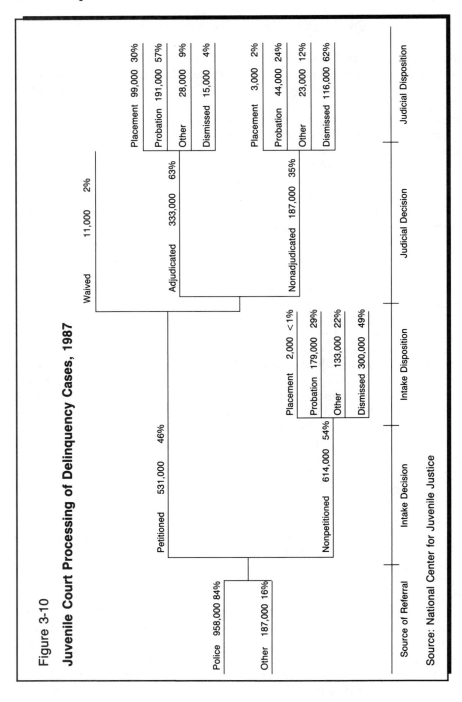

Source: National Center for Juvenile Justice

of confinement (about 9 percent of the 1.1 million cases initially referred). Numerous characteristics other than the offense alone are considered at each stage in the system and, understandably, such discretion generates concerns about the appropriate or "just" standards at each filtering point.

Police and the courts are obviously making decisions and exercising discretion and, in that sense, are "discriminating" among juveniles in the processing of offenders. Moreover, the basic philosophy of juvenile justice has been that the disposition or treatment of a case *should* vary depending on factors other than the specific legalities of the case. In terms of the philosophy invoked to justify a separate system for children, the juvenile court is *supposed* to take a juvenile's background and home life into account in deciding what action to take.

The controversy concerning discrimination centers around *acceptable* criteria for that differential processing of cases. The most attention has been devoted to discrimination on the basis of race, but there has been increasing concern over the influence of social class, gender, age, and other attributes on decision making. For example, coming from a broken home may affect a juvenile court disposition, and the way a youth interacts with the police — his or her demeanor — may affect the probability of arrest. To the police and the court, such considerations may seem completely legitimate, while to others they may appear completely arbitrary and unfair. That the law should treat girls differently than boys may seem mandatory to some and totally discriminatory to others.

Use of the word *discrimination* implies differential treatment of people on the basis of characteristics that are defined by law or interest groups as inappropriate as a basis for differential discretion. Our review of discrimination against juveniles will concentrate on three particular background characteristics that have been studied as sources of unfair bias — race, social class, and gender.

Differential Processing by Race

There is a long history of research on discrimination by race in the criminal justice system and a growing number of studies of bias in the processing of juveniles. Patterns suggesting racial bias are found often enough to justify continuing concern about discrimination. In one review of the research on racial bias, Marjorie Zatz (1987) identifies four "waves" of research since the 1950s. The first wave of research published from the 1950s through the mid-1960s reported clear and consistent biases. A second wave of research published between the mid-1960s and into the 1970s found little evidence of discrimination. The next wave of research (conducted in the 1970s and 1980s) reported complex findings which stressed the indirect and cumulative ways in which racial bias could operate. Finally, some of the most recent research has reported evidence of bias. A sample of such studies is summarized in the following discussion to illustrate the complexity and range of findings on the topic.

One of the earliest studies illustrating evidence of discrimination was reported in the 1960s but based on data from the 1940s. Nathan Goldman (1963) conducted a study on police decisions to refer apprehended juvenile delinquents to court in Allegheny County, Pennsylvania, in the late 1940s. Goldman's study did point toward racial bias in processing. He found that 65 percent of black juveniles were referred to court, whereas only 34 percent of white juveniles were referred. Although for more serious offenses there was no evidence of a race differential, black offenders were more likely to be referred to juvenile court for such minor offenses as property damage, status offenses, and malicious mischief.

Other studies have also reported evidence of bias by race. In tracking boys in Philadelphia who were 10 years old in 1955 until they reached 18, Terence Thornberry (1973) found significant racial differences in processing. Seriousness of the offense was positively related to severity of disposition by the police, court intake procedures, and final disposition by the juvenile court. However, even with seriousness of the offense and prior juvenile record taken into account, racial differences were still very apparent. A greater proportion of black youths than whites were sent to court and more were committed to institutions.

Theodore Ferdinand and Elmer Luchterhand (1970), using a random sample of 1,525 teenagers in six inner-city neighborhoods in a city they called "Easton," found that black youths who were first offenders were referred to the juvenile court disproportionately more often than their white counterparts. The harsher dispositions received by black youths could not be explained by type of offense, age, or gender. Although Ferdinand and Luchterhand concluded that black offenders are more likely to be arrested or referred to court, they did not find evidence that black youths are more rejecting of public authority. That factor might have precipitated a greater number of police arrests.

Irving Piliavin and Scott Briar (1964) examined juvenile encounters with the police and found that the police had a wide latitude of discretion in dealing with minor offenses. Approximately 10 percent of the offenses studied were serious crimes, such as robbery, aggravated assault, rape and auto theft, and these cases were dealt with uniformly for both black and white youth. In the 90 percent of police encounters which involved minor offenses, however, the police searched for "clues" to the personal character of the offender, defining some offenders as "good boys" and others as "bad boys." The character assessment made a difference in whether the disposition was an arrest, informal reprimand, or outright release. Thus, in addition to previous record, the youth's demeanor affected the probability of arrest. When the youth's demeanor was assessed as being uncooperative, the probability of an arrest was extremely high. On the other hand, when a youth was seen as a cooperative "good guy," he was very likely released. Black youths were typically seen as "would-be tough guys," or "punks," who fully deserved the sanction of arrest because of their hostile demeanor toward the police. Piliavin and Briar noted that police routinely patrolled the inner-city areas to a greater extent than other areas. This may have produced resentment, leading to low respect for the police, and ultimately culminating in higher arrest rates.

There is not only considerable evidence that young blacks are less likely to respect the police than other categories of youth (Wilson, 1975:111-16), but there is also evidence that such attitudes may account for a higher risk of arrest. In his research on the social organization of arrest, Donald Black (1971) found that a black youth had a higher probability of being arrested than a white youth. However, Black found that this difference reflected the suspect's conduct in interacting with the police. Rather than responding specifically to race, the police appear to respond to indications of disrespect, which are in turn associated with race. The end result may be the same (that is, higher arrest rates for black), but the interpretation is different (that is, the police respond more severely to a hostile suspect, whether black or white, and more blacks are hostile toward police).

The observational studies of police interactions with the public have introduced some complicating considerations for understanding the differential risks in official processing. For example, a study by Black and Reiss (1970) delineated the social circumstances surrounding an arrest and showed the probability of a juvenile arrest to be very low: only about 15 percent of contacts with juvenile suspects resulted in an arrest. However, the probability of arrest was found to increase with the legal seriousness of the juvenile's offense. This finding may appear to be a fairly obvious point, but it tends to be discarded far too quickly when arrest statistics reflect a racial bias. Black and Reiss also found that the presence of a complainant greatly enhanced the chances of a black youth's being arrested. When the police officer acted on his own initiative without the presence of a complainant, the black-white arrest rates were quite similar: 14 percent of black youths and 10 percent of white youths were arrested. However, when a complainant participated in the arrest process, the differentials were considerably greater—21 percent for black youths and only 8 percent for white youths. Moreover, black complainants were more likely than white complainants to press for police action.

While the police in this study did not appear to be blatantly biased in their decisions, it should be noted that a slightly higher rate for blacks than whites (14 vs 10 percent) can be compounded over time. That is, because prior record is a major determinant of severity of enforcement, small differences by race in the acquisition of a record compound the bias based on race alone.

Yet another study has suggested that the organization of police departments can play a major role in facilitating or inhibiting arbitrary discretion against black juveniles. James Q. Wilson (1968) examined police departments in two California cities, which he called "Western City" and "Eastern City." Western City had a highly bureaucratic, professional police department, while Eastern City had an informal, fraternal police department. The standards and procedures in Western City resulted in the recruitment of officers who were better educated, less moralistic, and more rule-oriented than officers in Eastern City. The difference in organizational milieu was associated with dramatically different results in the handling of juveniles. Western City processed more than twice as many juvenile offenders as Eastern City, indicating that the greater the aura of professionalism and formalized procedure, the greater the arrest rate and the less discretion exercised by the police officer. On the other hand, in Eastern City, where the police force was highly decentralized and the opportunity for police discretion much greater, discriminatory arrest practices were apparent. Wilson found that approximately three times as many black as whites were taken to court, whereas in Western City the black-white differentials were very small.

Since cohort studies have been conducted for youth born in Philadelphia at two points in time, we can consider whether the differences in official processing observed for youth born in 1945 are still relevant among youth born in 1958. Tracy, Wolfgang and Figlio report that the race and social class differentials in the 1958 cohort were not as prominent as in the earlier cohort. Sixty percent of nonwhites were arrested as compared to 51 percent of whites. For the 1945 cohort, 44 percent of nonwhites were officially arrested as compared to 23 percent of whites. A greater proportion of youth were arrested in 1958 than 1945 but there was less differentiation based on race. This change may reflect the process observed in Wilson's study. As police adopt uniform and standardized procedures, characteristics such as race make less difference for processing and decisions become more "legalistic." However, this change may result in increases in official processing, particularly of categories of youth who in earlier times were being dealt with informally.

One of the most recent and largest (in terms of number of cases) studies of juvenile justice processing was carried out in Florida by Donna Bishop and Charles Frazier (1988). They collected data on a cohort of 54,266 youths processed in the late 1970s and early 1980s. They report that what might appear to be small differences at various stages do accumulate and result in "sizeable incremental differences that place black youth at a substantial disadvantage relative to whites (258)." Black youth were at a disadvantage at most stages of juvenile processing.

The study referred to earlier by Smith et al., (1984) also reported a greater probability that black suspects would be arrested than white suspects—

but this was the case only when complainants were involved in the encounter and was limited to female suspects. In encounters where no complainant was present, researchers found that what initially appeared to be a racial bias instead reflected a greater probability of arrest in poor neighborhoods whether the suspects were black or white.

Overall, no single conclusion is justified by the research on racial bias. However, findings which suggest bias are sufficiently common to justify continual examination of the issue. It is difficult to "add up" the research but it does appear that in more jurisdictions than not, black youth are treated more harshly than their offenses or history would lead us to expect.

Differential Processing by Social Class

In our review of the relationship between social class and delinquency, we noted that several studies found no relationship between social class and the probability of appearing in police or court statistics. We also noted that in those studies that did suggest a bias, the differential was generally small. Nevertheless, since nearly two-thirds of the studies did report some differences by social class, the issue of discrimination by class merits our consideration.

The situation involving bias by social class is as complex as that involving race. Terry (1967) found no class differences when prior offense record and seriousness of offense were taken into account. Arnold (1971) reported racial bias but no class differences in the southern city he studied. In contrast, Thornberry (1973) found racial differences in the severity of treatment, as well as harsher treatment of lower-class males.

In an attempt to resolve such inconsistencies, Lawrence Cohen and James Kluegel (1978) studied the dispositions of juvenile cases in Denver and Memphis. Since these two jurisdictions differed in regional location and operating philosophies, the researchers felt that the comparison might yield different findings concerning bias. However, they concluded that their analysis "uncovered no evidence of race or class bias" working to the disadvantage of minority youth or youth from low-income families. In fact, they found that the effect of parental income was contrary to common predictions. Although the differences were small, Cohen and Kluegel's findings showed that the higher the income of a youth's parents, the more severe the treatment. In keeping with most research findings, the seriousness of the offense and the existence of a prior record were found to be the major determinants of dispositions. Cohen and Kluegel concluded that their findings challenge the view that racial bias and class discrimination "permeate the juvenile justice system" (1978: 174).

The situation is even more complex when the Smith et al., (1984) study is considered. As already noted, they found that what appeared to be a racial bias in some police encounters was generated by neighborhood character-istics. People in poor neighborhoods were more likely to be arrested than people in advantaged neighborhoods. It was the fact that more blacks lived in the poorer neighborhoods that accounted for their greater susceptibility to arrest. The researchers point out that it was not individual status or class that determined the greater risk but the properties of neighborhoods them-selves. Living in the wrong place resulted in higher probabilities of arrest. Thus, economic well-being was a relevant consideration but it was at the neighborhood level that it operated to generate a bias in law enforcement.

Differential Processing by Gender

In a classic work on female criminality published in 1950, *The Criminal-ity of Women*, Otto Pollak challenged the assumption that women commit fewer crimes than men and argued that women merely get away with more because 1) the types of crimes they commit are less likely to be reported than male crimes (e.g., shoplifting), 2) their roles allow crimes to go undetected (e.g., poisoning), or 3) they are treated more protectively by the criminal justice system. Women were depicted as receiving preferential treatment as a product of "chivalry," or as more clever at avoiding detection.

This "chivalry" perspective has been countered in more recent years by claims that girls are treated more harshly for some offenses than boys because of a "double standard" which allows "boys to be boys" but defines similar behavior among girls as immoral. In 1975, Rita Simon noted that an alternative to the preferential treatment model is the view that women receive more punitive treatment than males because their criminal behavior is more "out of line" with social expectations than male crime. In other words, involvement in crime and delinquency is a greater departure from ideals of how a woman *should* act than it is from ideals of how a man should act. If we were to accept this hypothesis, we would assume that girls who violate the law and are caught receive harsher treatment than their male counterparts.

On examining data on the conviction of adult female offenders, Simon found some support for the argument that females receive preferential treatment. She concluded that "women as recently as 1972 seem to be receiving some preferential treatment at the bar of justice" (1975:67). On the other hand, a report by the Female Offender Resource Center (1977) cited evidence of discriminatory treatment of female juveniles when they are arrested. This report noted that female status offenders were more likely to be confined than male status offenders and that a disproportionate number were sent to training schools.

In his study of discrimination in the handling of juvenile offenders, Terry

(1967) reported that the police released 85 percent of the females and 90 percent of the males. The biggest disparity in release rates stemmed from the fact that police referred about 7 percent of the females to social or welfare agencies, rather than releasing them outright. In general, boys who were not released were referred to the county probation department; they were rarely (0.8 percent) referred to social or welfare agencies. Over 70 percent of referrals to such agencies were for status offenses; hence, female offenders had a lesser chance of outright release because of the inclination of police to refer female status offenders to social and welfare agencies.

Terry found that a greater proportion of males than females was referred to juvenile court or criminal court by the probation department, largely because the males' offenses were more serious. On the other hand, once a female reached the point of a juvenile court disposition, her chances of being committed to an institution were actually greater. Terry reported that females were more likely to be severely sanctioned even though males had more extensive previous records. One of the reasons for this was the harsh punishment given for offenses concerning relations with the opposite sex and involvements with adult offenders, both of which were more common among female juvenile offenders than among males.

Other studies have also suggested differential treatment of *some* female versus male offenders. For instance, in a study of police dispositions in Philadelphia, Thomas Monahan (1970) found that police treated girls somewhat more leniently than boys in cases involving acts that would be criminal for adults, but more harshly when sexual offenses were involved. In a similar study in Honolulu, Meda Chesney-Lind (1974) found that girls accused of their first status offense were actually more likely to be referred to the juvenile court than girls charged with their first criminal offense. In a study using Los Angeles police records, A.W. McEachern and Reva Bauzer (1967) observed that in cases involving what they called "juvenile offenses," boys were less likely than girls to have petitions requested; but were more likely to have them requested in cases involving acts that would be crimes if committed by adults.

The most comprehensive study of gender bias in juvenile justice was conducted by Katherine Teilman and Pierre Landry (1981) using data from eight different sites (one southern and one northern California county, an Arizona county, two Illinois counties, two counties in Washington state, and one in Delaware). Taking into account type of offense and prior records, they report:

> There seems to be little gender bias once youngsters are in the system. However, where it does exist, it is more often against boys than girls. Boys are at particular risk for delinquent offenses. Status offenses sometimes yield gender-biased decisions, but this bias is sporadic and not uniform in direction (76).

They also note that girls appear to be "overarrested" for runaway and incorrigibility relative to actual involvement in such activity, based on self-reports (see Chapter 4). They speculate that parents get more alarmed when their daughters leave home than when sons do so and that police are responding to parental preferences.

In another study, Marvin Krohn, James Curry and Shirley Nelson-Kilger (1983) explore the question, "Is chivalry dead?" Based on police contacts for three cohorts of youth in a Midwestern city (those born in 1942, 1949, and 1955), they found a trend toward egalitarian (equal) treatment of males and females for misdemeanors. However, males were more likely than females to be referred to the juvenile court when a comparable felony was involved, while females were more likely than males to be referred when a status offense was involved. The gender differences were small but they were more prominent than differences by minority status. A youth's minority status was not found to make a difference for police response when other characteristics such as prior contacts and complainants were controlled.

Overall, there does appear to be a tendency for boys and girls to be treated differently for different offenses. When a girl runs away, it appears to be taken more seriously than when a boy does so, possibly because parents call the police or the juvenile court more quickly. On the other hand, there is a tendency to respond more severely to males than females who commit nonstatus offenses. Of course, this disparity may reflect greater harm or loss for male offenses that cannot be taken into account by merely considering comparable "types" of offenses broadly defined, such as "property" offenses or "violent offenses."

Summary

Proclamations about the problem of juvenile delinquency typically cite a body of "facts" about youth crime or "facts" about delinquency. It is more appropriate to discuss "images" of delinquency since there are multiple sources of information that may or may not yield divergent observations. Many criminologists have questioned whether police and court statistics can give us the real or true facts about delinquency in that these statistics are the outcome of numerous behaviors and decisions by the public and by agents of the law. Thus, such data are influenced by a wide range of factors other than the behavior of juveniles. Whether an event is recorded as a crime is a product of both public and police action and the interaction between the two.

Whether suspects become statistics as criminals or delinquents depends on such contingencies as the offense committed, offense history, complainant preference, the way suspects and complainants interact with the police and the organization and operational practices of police departments. Despite these complexities, the image of delinquency suggested by police and court data is in many ways consistent with public stereotyping, but with numerous qualifications. The major observations suggested by the research and statistics examined in this chapter, together with important qualifications, are summarized below:

1. Crime and delinquency as recorded in police and court statistics increased rapidly from the 1960s through the mid-1970s, *but* the rates may have been much higher before the collection of statistics nationwide. Moreover, the United States entered a period of stable or declining rates in the late 1970s through the mid-1980s with some upward movement in the late 1980s.

2. For several decades, juveniles accounted for a growing proportion of arrests in national crime data, *but* their contribution seems to have stabilized or declined for some offense categories beginning in the mid-1970s.

3. Rates of crime and delinquency appear to be high in areas experiencing population changes and transitions, and in cities as compared to rural settings, *but* the differences between rural and urban settings appear to be declining. Moreover, some small towns and nonmetropolitan areas have rates greater than or comparable to those of large metropolitan communities.

4. Males are more likely than females to appear in arrest and court statistics in every nation collecting such data, *but* the disparity was much greater in past decades than it is now (although the disparity has been relatively stable in the last several years in the United States); the disparity is not as great for shoplifting and status offenses as for more serious offenses; and females actually outnumber males for some status offenses, such as running away from home.

5. In the United States and other developed nations, people aged 10 through 17 are disproportionately represented in arrest statistics, *but* the highest arrest rates for such people are for crimes against property. Juveniles are not overrepresented in arrest statistics in some studies of Third World settings.

6. Of those racial categories used by the FBI, black Americans have the highest overall arrest rates, followed by Hispanic Americans and whites, with Asian Americans exhibiting the lowest rates. Similar results have been noted for Asian, white and black youth in the United Kingdom.

7. Lower-class youths disproportionately contribute to police and court statistics, *but* numerous studies have found no relationship between

social class and officially recorded delinquency. In studies that have noted such a relationship, the differences observed were small.

8. Official statistics suggest relatively stable rates of arrest and referral for drug offenses with racial differences variable, depending on type of drug activity involved.

9. No simple conclusion can be reached concerning discrimination against black American youth by police and courts. There is evidence that differentials in arrest and processing are generated 1) by the seriousness of the offense committed and the offense history of the suspect; 2) by the preferences of complainants who, if black, are more likely to press for police action; and 3) by the nature of the suspect's interaction with police. Several studies have indicated greater risk of arrest and more severe dispositions for blacks than whites even when prior record and nature of the offense are taken into account, but a recent cohort study suggests that disparity may be declining.

10. Studies of the processing of lower-class youths suggest that legal criteria (offense seriousness and prior record) explain disproportionate representations in police and court statistics, *but* there is not always a disproportionate representation to explain.

11. Females *may* receive either preferential or harsher treatment than males, depending on the offense and the stage of processing. When studies do find differentials, males appear to be treated more severely than females for offenses that are crimes for adults, *but* this differential may reflect the more serious nature of male offenses. On the other hand, several studies suggest that female status offenses are responded to more severely than male status offenses (especially runaways).

The tendency of social scientists to "qualify everything" is upsetting to politicians, students, and the general public. People like simple, direct, unambiguous, and straightforward answers. One of the authors of this book was once interviewed for a local news program and asked: "Why is the crime rate increasing?" The answer was supposed to fit in a twenty-second spot on the six o'clock news. Such questions cannot and, we would argue, *should not* be answered in twenty seconds. The observations and qualifications that we have made in this chapter may have to be revised on the basis of further evidence and challenges by other criminologists. We have attempted to simplify a wealth of complex data and to provide the type of supporting detail that a questioning student should demand of anyone who makes observations about delinquency. When such detail is provided, we learn something new and end up with observations that often challenge everyday beliefs and proclamations about juvenile delinquency.

Since so many factors other than offense activity alone can affect the chances of becoming an official statistic, some criminologists choose to view such data as a reflection of stereotypes and biases rather than "real" behavioral variations among categories of youth. However, the more common contemporary approach to such data is to study delinquent behavior as a product of a variety of influences and to gather data by other means as well. In the next chapter we will look at alternatives to official statistics, some of which are thought to more directly tap the real behavior of offenders. But, as we shall see, those methods have their shortcomings as well and critics challenge whether any technique short of direct observation could can give us an accurate or valid picture of delinquency.

References

Adler, F. 1975. *Sisters in Crime*. New York: McGraw-Hill.

Arnold, W. R. 1971. "Race and Ethnicity Relative to Other Factors in Juvenile Court Dispositions." *American Journal of Sociology* 77 (September):211-17.

Bishop, Donna M., and Charles E. Frazier. 1988. "The Influence of Race in Juvenile Justice Processing." *Journal of Research in Crime and Delinquency* 25 (August):242-63.

Black, D. J. 1970. "Production of Crime Rates." *American Sociological Review* 35 (August):733-48.

_____. 1971. "The Social Organization of Arrest." *Stanford Law Review* 23 (June):1087-111.

Black, D. J., and A. J. Reiss, Jr. 1970. "Police Control of Juveniles." *American Sociological Review* 35 (February):63-77.

Bureau of Justice Statistics. 1983. *Report to the Nation on Crime and Justice*. U.S. Department of Justice.

Bursik, R. J., Jr. 1986. "Ecological Stability and the Dynamics of Delinquency." Pp. 35-66 in Albert J. Reiss, Jr. and Michael Tonry (eds.), *Communities and Change*. Chicago: University of Chicago Press.

Centers, R. 1949. *The Psychology of Social Class*. Princeton, NJ: Princeton University Press.

Chesney-Lind, M. 1974. "Juvenile Delinquency: The Sexualization of Female Crime." *Psychology Today* (July):44-46.

Chilton, R., and A. Spielberger. 1971. "Is Delinquency Increasing? Age Structure and the Crime Rate." *Social Forces* 47:487-93.

Clinard, M., and J. Abbott. 1973. *Crime in Developing Countries: A Comparative Perspective*. New York: John Wiley.

Cohen, L. E., and J. E. Kluegel. 1978. "Determinants of Juvenile Court Dispositions: Ascriptive and Achieved Factors in Two Metropolitan Courts." *American Sociological Review* 43 (April):162-76.

Farrington, D. P., and T. Bennett. 1981. "Police Cautioning of Juveniles in London." *British Journal of Criminology* 21:123-35.

Federal Bureau of Investigation. 1989. *Crime in the United States*. Washington, DC: U.S. Government Printing Office.

Female Offender Resource Center. 1977. *Little Sisters and the Law*. Washington, DC: American Bar Association.

Ferdinand, T. N., and E. G. Luchterhand. 1970. "Inner-City Youths, the Police, the Juvenile Court, and Justice." *Social Problems* 17 (Spring):510-27.

Flanagan, T. J., and E. F. Maguire (eds.). 1989, 1986, 1985. *Sourcebook of Criminal Justice Statistics*. U.S. Department of Justice: Bureau of Justice Statistics.

Frease, D. E. 1973. "Delinquency, Social Class, and the Schools." *Sociology and Social Research* 57 (July):443-59.

Friedman, L. 1983. *Violence in America*. Vol. 3. New York: Chelsea House.

Goldman, N. 1963. *The Differential Selection of Juvenile Offenders for Court Appearance*. New York: National Council on Crime and Delinquency.

Hirschi, T. 1969. *Causes of Delinquency*. Berkeley: University of California Press.

Hirschi, T., and M. Gottfredson. 1983. "Age and the Explanation of Crime." *American Journal of Sociology* 89:552-84.

Jensen, G. F., and D. G. Rojek. 1980. *Delinquency: A Sociological View*. Lexington, MA: D. C. Heath and Company.

Krohn, M. D., J. P. Curry, and S. Nelson-Kilger. 1983. "Is Chivalry Dead?" *Criminology* 21 (August):417-38.

Lundman, R. J., R. E. Sykes, and J. P. Clark. 1978. "Police Control of Juveniles." In R. Lundman (ed.), *Police Behavior: A Sociological Perspective*. New York: Oxford Press, 1980.

McEachern, A. W., and R. Bauzer. 1967. "Factors Related to Disposition in Juvenile Police Contacts." In M. W. Klein (ed.), *Juvenile Gangs in Context*. Englewood Cliffs, NJ: Prentice-Hall.

McKay, H. D. 1967. "A Note on Trends and Rates of Delinquency in Certain Areas in Chicago." In President's Commission on Law Enforcement and Administration of Justice. *Task Force Report: Juvenile Delinquency and Youth Crime*. Washington, DC: U.S. Government Printing Office.

Monahan, T. 1970. "Police Dispositions of Juvenile Offenders in Philadelphia 1955 to 1966." *Phylon* 31 (2):134.

National Commission on the Causes and Prevention of Violence. 1969. *To Establish Justice to Ensure Domestic Tranquility: Final Report*. Washington, DC: U.S. Government Printing Office.

Office of Juvenile Justice and Delinquency Prevention. 1989. "Juvenile Courts Vary Greatly in How They Handle Drug and Alcohol Cases." *Juvenile Justice Bulletin* (July/August). Washington, DC: U.S. Government Printing Office.

Piliavin, I., and S. Briar. 1964. "Police Encounters with Juveniles." *American Journal of Sociology* 70 (September):206-14.

Polk, K. 1974. *Teenage Delinquency in Small Town America*. Research Report 5. Center for Studies of Crime and Delinquency. Rockville, MD: National Institute of Mental Health.

Pollak, Otto. 1950. *The Criminality of Women*. Philadelphia: University of Pennsylvania Press.

Priyadarsini, S., and C. A. Hartjen. 1981. "Delinquency and Corrections in India." Pp. 109-23 in G. F. Jensen (ed.), *The Sociology of Delinquency*. Beverly Hills, CA: Sage Publications.

Rutter, M., and H. Giller. 1984. *Juvenile Delinquency: Trends and Perspectives*. New York: The Guilford Press.

Schur, E. M. 1969. *Our Criminal Society*. Englewood Cliffs, NJ: Prentice-Hall.

Shannon, L. W. 1978. "Predicting Adult Criminal Careers." Iowa Urban Community Research Center, University of Iowa. Mimeographed.

Shaw, C. R., and H. D. McKay. 1942. *Juvenile Delinquency and Urban Areas*. Chicago: University of Chicago Press.

Simon, R. J. 1975. *Women and Crime*. Lexington, MA: D. C. Heath.

Smith, D., and L. Davidson. 1986. "Interfacing Indicators and Constructs in Criminological Research: A Note on the Compatibility of Self-Report and Violence Data for Race and for Groups." *Criminology* 24:473-87.

Smith, D., C. A. Visher, and L. A. Davidson. 1984. "Equity and Discretionary Justice: The Influence of Race on Police Arrest Decisions." *The Journal of Criminal Law and Criminology* 75 (Spring):234-59.

Snyder, H. N., and E. H. Nimick. 1983. "City Delinquents and Their Country Cousins." *Today's Delinquent* 2:45-69.

Snyder, H. N., J. L. Hutzler, and T. A. Finnegan. 1985. *Delinquency in the United States, 1984*. Pittsburgh: National Center for Juvenile Justice.

Snyder, H. N., T. Finnegan, E. H. Nimick, M. H. Sickmund, D. P. Sullivan, and N. J. Tierney. 1989. *Juvenile Court Statistics, 1985*. Pittsburgh: National Center for Juvenile Justice.

Sparks, R. F., H. Genn, and D. J. Dodd. 1977. *Surveying Victims*. London: John Wiley.

Sundeen, R. A. 1981. "Juvenile Arrests in Papua, New Guinea." Pp. 124-42 in G. F. Jensen (ed.), *The Sociology of Delinquency*. Beverly Hills, CA: Sage Publications.

Sutherland, E. H., and D. R. Cressey. 1974. *Criminology*. Philadelphia: J.B. Lippincott.

Teeters, N., and D. Matza. 1959. "The Extent of Delinquency in the United States." *Journal of Negro Education* 28 (Summer):200-13.

Teilman, K. S., and P. H. Landry, Jr. 1981. "Gender Bias in Juvenile Justice." *Journal of Research in Crime and Delinquency* 18 (January):47-80.

Terry, R. M. 1967. "Discrimination in the Handling of Juvenile Offenders by Social Control Agencies." *Journal of Research in Crime and Delinquency* 4 (July):218-30.

Thornberry, T. 1973. "Race, Socioeconomic Status, and Sentencing in the Juvenile Justice System." *Journal of Criminal Law and Criminology* 64 (March):90-98.

Tittle, C. R., W. J. Villemez, and D. A. Smith. 1978. "The Myth of Social Class and Criminality." *American Sociological Review* 43 (October):643-56.

Tracy, P. E., M. E. Wolfgang, and R. M. Figlio. 1985. *Delinquency in Two Birth Cohorts: Executive Summary*. U.S. Department of Justice: Office of Juvenile Justice and Delinquency Prevention.

Williams, J. R., and M. Gold. 1972. "From Delinquent Behavior to Official Delinquency." *Social Problems* 20 (Fall):209-29.

Wilson, J. Q. 1968. "The Police and the Delinquent in Two Cities." In S. Wheeler, (ed.), *Controlling Delinquents*. New York: John Wiley.

_____. 1975. *Thinking About Crime*. New York: Vintage Books.

Wolfgang, M. E., R. Figlio, and T. Sellin. 1972. *Delinquency in a Birth Cohort.* Chicago: University of Chicago Press.
Zatz, Marjorie. 1987. "The Changing Forms of Racial/Ethnic Biases in Sentencing." *Journal of Research in Crime and Delinquency* 24 (February):69-92.

chapter 4

Images of Delinquency
Survey Data

The juvenile delinquent leans against the lamppost, cigarette in hand and leer on face. His gang controls this part of the black ghetto, so he is, for the moment, safe. He and his buddies plan their crimes carefully, for crime gives them kicks and macho points. The boy's parents don't know or care what he does out on the street; his father ran out years ago, and his weary mother has lost control of the boy.

We all know this juvenile delinquent. His image has been drummed into us from Hollywood movies, Government commissions, scholarly reports. In one sense it is handy to have a commonly accepted image: it provides a symbol for people to hurl accusations at or to rally around. There is only one thing wrong. Despite all the care and ink lavished on him by so many for so long, the delinquent is a myth.

—Bill Haney and Martin Gold, "The Juvenile Delinquent Nobody Knows."

The Delinquent As Myth

Some years ago a national magazine ran a feature story entitled "The Youth Crime Plague." In their report, the authors dramatically portrayed an image of the juvenile delinquent as a unrepentant terrorist threatening to take over America. "Many youngsters appear to be robbing and raping, maiming and murdering as casually as they go to a movie or join a pickup baseball game. A new, remorseless, mutant juvenile seems to have been born, and there is no more terrifying figure in America today" (*Time*, 1977: 18). More recently, *Time* Magazine devoted a special issue to gangs, emphasizing the link between drug dealing and violence: "Gang warfare has bedeviled Los Angeles for more than three decades, but the burgeoning crack trade has lately made such groups as the Crips even more willing to kill for the sake of greater profits. Children of the underclass, weaned on violence and despair, have become bloodthirsty entrepreneurs" (*Time*, 1988: 32). Similarly, George Will writes, "Fifteen-year olds drive BMW's and make bail from pocket cash. Young teenagers have been arrested with $10,000 in their jeans. No wonder young dealers wear phone beepers in school" (Will, 1988). According to Will, "What is new is the killing for commerce and crack business" (Will, 1988:76).

We are continually bombarded with editorials and dramatic depictions of the delinquency problem designed to intensify concern and to reinforce the view that crimes of the young have reached alarming levels. As noted in Chapter 1, "The world's always in the worst mess it's ever been in." But are such dramatic images a valid reflection of delinquency as a dimension of the crime problem?

In the brief excerpt given at the beginning of this chapter, Haney and Gold suggest that portrayals of delinquency are embellished to draw public attention to the topic. They also argue that such portrayals do not accurately represent the distribution of serious delinquency and exaggerate the degree to which crime is primarily attributable to specific categories of youth. However, as with many media dramatizations of the delinquency problem, there are some elements of truth to the stereotype. The media image is an exaggeration of those characteristics related to crime and delinquency. The more serious and violent the offense, the more likely offenders are to be urban, male, young, lower-class, and members of disadvantaged groups. In the popular image of these characteristics, features are combined to construct a crystal-clear image of "the delinquent," thus isolating and defining the "enemy." In the process of over-generalizing patterns suggested by official data, Haney and Gold believe that a "myth" is created.

As we noted in Chapter 3, statistics about persons who are caught reflect the behavior of the public, police, prosecutors, judges, and attorneys as well as characteristics of offenses, offenders, and victims. Criminologists have long recognized that those people who are caught are not necessarily representative of the total population of people who have done things for which they could have been arrested and punished. In scientific terms the issue is one of *sampling bias*: Are the cases that appear in police and court statistics representative of all lawbreakers or are they a biased sample? Are comparison groups of people who do not have records representative samples of noncriminals and nondelinquents?

While Haney and Gold are concerned about the delinquent nobody knows, there is also a growing concern about "the victim nobody knows." The statistics on crime rates discussed in Chapter 3 can be viewed from two different perspectives. First, for all the "serious" crimes in the FBI's crime index, there are both offenders and victims. Thus, the crime rate in those instances can be viewed as both an offense rate and a victimization rate. Second, just as police and court data do not measure the total amount of offenses committed, neither do they accurately measure the total extent of victimization. We noted in Chapter 3 that a large proportion of offenses or victimizations is never reported to the police, that police do not respond to some victimizations as criminal events, and that the probability that victimizations will become an officially recognized crime is contingent on the seriousness of the offense and a variety of aspects of the relationships and interaction among complainants, suspects, and the police. Hence, those events or victimizations that make their way into police and court statistics may not be representative of all the events that could be included.

Because official statistics may be affected by more than criminal or delinquent activity (e.g., race, gender, social status, and criminal justice processing), sociologists and other researchers have tried to develop alternative sources of data. Two alternative sources of information are currently used: *self-report surveys* and *victimization surveys*. Self-report surveys attempt to measure offense behavior through interviews or questionnaires by asking individuals about the extent of their criminal or delinquent involvement. Victimization surveys attempt to measure the extent of certain types of crime through interviews or questionnaires dealing with the individual's experiences as the victim of a crime. Although both of these techniques for assessing the extent and correlates of crime and delinquency have been criticized, they do overcome some of the criticisms of police and court statistics. By considering several different sources of information, even though each has its own limitations, we can begin to formulate a fuller, more accurate image of delinquency. In some instances we will find a convergence of police, self-report, and victimization findings, in other instances we will find a marked divergence. However, the inconsistencies associated with using different methods have helped generate new ideas about the nature of crime and delinquency in our society.

Self-Reports of Delinquency

The most widely used alternative to police and court statistics in the study of delinquency is the self-report survey in which people are asked to report on their own delinquent activity. Such surveys date back to the 1940s (Porterfield, 1946; Murphy et al., 1946), but the technique gained popularity in the late 1950s with the work of F. Ivan Nye and James F. Short, Jr. (1957). Not only did Nye and Short show the feasibility of the self-report method in the study of delinquency, but their findings immediately challenged conventional assumptions about social class in relation to delinquency. The self-report technique became the dominant method of studying delinquency in the 1960s and 1970s, and *UCR* data or police statistics were nearly totally avoided. As we shall discuss later in this chapter, difficulties arose with the exclusive use of self-reports and this research strategy is not without its own problems.

Self-report surveys have taken two basic forms, each with its own advantages and disadvantages. One form is the interview, in which the subject is questioned about his or her background, opinions, and delinquent activities. The second is a checklist or questionnaire that the subject fills in or completes. The interview method is thought to reduce error since the interviewer can explore a respondent's answers and gather more detail when needed. On the other hand, the interview makes it more difficult to assure the respondent of anonymity since he or she can be identified by the interviewer. Interviews are also more costly than surveys because surveys can be administered to large groups of people all at once. The questionnaire method is useful both for gathering information from large samples and for assuring anonymity, but it does not allow for detailed elaboration of answers or the ability to clarify certain questions. Questionnaires also assume that subjects can read reasonably well and can follow written directions. However, the anonymous questionnaire has been the more common of the two self-report procedures in recent years. An example is presented in Figure 4-1.

Criticism of Self-Report Surveys

Although the self-report method emerged in an attempt to find measures of criminal and delinquent behavior that would be more valid and reliable than police and court statistics, the validity and reliability of self-reports have, in turn, been challenged. The issues of validity and reliability are very complex, and we cannot deal with all of the complexities here. Rather, we will concentrate on the most central issues.

When questioning the *reliability* of a measurement technique, the basic issue is whether repeated measurements would yield consistent results. If repeated measures using a particular technique yield inconsistent results (when there is no reason to believe that the phenomena being measured have changed), then that technique is likely to be viewed as unreliable. The basic issue in assessing *validity* is whether the technique or instrument being used measures what it claims to measure. Even though the self-report technique has been extremely popular, several critics of the method feel that its reliability and validity are not certain enough to justify such popularity (Reiss, 1975; Bidwell, 1975). As noted in Box 4-1, the subjects of such surveys have raised similar criticisms.

A number of studies have tested the reliability of the self-report technique by comparing the results of measurements at different points in time, by examining the results of different ways of measuring the same thing, and by scrutinizing the consistency of responses to different questions in the same survey. Such tests suggest that in terms of prevailing standards for assessing reliability, self-reports yield consistent, reliable data on delinquency (Hindelang et al., 1981). Some researchers argue, however, that interviews provide more reliable data than questionnaires (Elliott and Ageton, 1980). However, while it may appear that the matter of interview verses questionnaire format is extremely controversial, the evidence to date suggests that the differences are minor (Krohn et al., 1975). Regarding the overall reliability of self-report data, Hindelang, Hirschi and Weis conclude:

> Even with a relatively small number of items, self-report instruments are able to achieve reasonable reliability as defined by the consistency of results across independent sets of items. Furthermore, with a large number of items, the self-report split-half reliability appears to approach

Figure 4-1

Sample Self-Report Survey

For each act, mark on the answer sheet how often **you** have done it **during the past year.**

	Never	Once or Twice	About Once a Month	About Once a Week	Nearly Every Day
During the past year have you ever:					
1. Used beer	A	B	C	D	E
2. Used hard liquor (whiskey, vodka, gin)	A	B	C	D	E
3. Used marijuana	A	B	C	D	E
4. Used stimulants (pep pills, speed, uppers)	A	B	C	D	E
5. Used depressants (downers, sleeping pills)	A	B	C	D	E
6. Used narcotics (heroin, morphine)	A	B	C	D	E
7. Used cocaine	A	B	C	D	E
8. Used psychedelics or mind-altering drugs (LSD, PCP, MDA)	A	B	C	D	E
9. Used cigarettes	A	B	C	D	E
10. Inhaled glue, spray or fumes	A	B	C	D	E
11. Experimented with unknown drugs	A	B	C	D	E
12. Broken into a place to steal something	A	B	C	D	E
13. Used wine	A	B	C	D	E
14. Taken a car without permission (not parents' car)	A	B	C	D	E
15. Run away from home	A	B	C	D	E
16. Beat up or physically attacked another (including brothers or sisters)	A	B	C	D	E
17. Sold drugs (except liquor, beer or wine)	A	B	C	D	E
18. Been suspended, sent to an alternative school or kicked out of school	A	B	C	D	E
19. Used chewing tobacco	A	B	C	D	E
20. Used dip or snuff	A	B	C	D	E
21. Gotten really drunk	A	B	C	D	E

Source: Dean G. Rojek, ''Georgia Youth Survey,'' Department of Sociology, University of Georgia.

Box 4-1

Patagonia High students decry drug survey, story

Protesters boycott classes for 3½ hours

By Dan Huff
The Arizona Daily Star

Nearly half the students at Patagonia Union High School walked out of classes for about 3½ hours yesterday to protest what they said was an inaccurate state survey and what some called an unfair newspaper story about drug use.

Sunday's Arizona Daily Star reported the results of an Arizona Criminal Justice Commission survey on drug use among students at Patagonia Union and roughly 18,000 students at 20 other Arizona high schools.

State officials promised anonymity to students who took the survey last fall, but Patagonia education officials recently revealed the results for their high school. It showed that more than 70 percent of the seniors there admitted that they have attended class while high on alcohol or illegal drugs.

Only 35.8 percent of seniors surveyed statewide said they had done so.

Yesterday, some Patagonia students and parents said perhaps some of those who answered the survey did not take it as seriously as they should have—a possibility noted in the story.

Debbie Hill, the mother of a Patagonia High student, said, "Ninety percent of the kids did not treat the survey with the respect they should have. A couple of boys I talked to put on there that they went to school high, and they were only joking."

The story quoted several teachers and Patagonia Union Superintendent Dennis Adams as saying there is a problem with drugs and alcohol among students.

Yesterday, Adams' secretary said he would have no comment on the demonstration or anything else.

Students were talking, though. Sophomore Lainie Johnstone, 15, a straight-A student, said the demonstration by about 50 students was their

way of saying, "We feel the article gave the school a bad name unfairly. A lot of the interviews were one-sided and nobody put any good points in there."

Johnstone said students feel the story will make it more difficult for them to find jobs or get into college. She, too, said she thought some of those who answered the questions about drug and alcohol use were joking.

"I took it seriously, but I guess a lot of other people didn't, and I'm pretty sure they're sorry about it now," she said.

Johnstone added: "We are a good school, a small school that's above average in academics. It's sad to see everything ruined because of this survey and this article."

Star Managing Editor John Peck said, "We noted their concerns in the original story. The impetus for doing the story and basic data were taken directly from a flier published by the school.

"We further checked up on that information. We stand by the story as reported."

Johnstone noted that the school football team has won the state Class B football championship two years running.

"I know my friends on the football team are all straight," she said. "You can't do that and be on drugs."

James Green, 18, a junior, said, "There's no way that 70 percent of the seniors went drunk to school. No way." He said Patagonia Union has about 15 seniors.

"I certainly haven't noticed that much usage among my friends," he said.

Shelagh Banks, Johnstone's mother, said "Maybe Mr. Adams was too naive about how the kids answered the survey. This thing was a big shock to everybody here. The kids really flipped out. They had a fit."

Do you think students answer self-report questions about their behavior honestly?

Source: *Arizona Daily Star*, May 17, 1989

that of the best psychometric instruments. Test-retest reliabilities for full delinquency instruments are impressively large, even after the passage of a considerable amount of time . . . If self-report measurement is flawed, it is not here, but in the area of validity. (1981:84)

The validity of self-reports as measures of delinquent behavior has been a more controversial issue than their reliability. Do people give accurate, honest answers to questions about their involvement in delinquency? This question is very difficult to answer for the simple reason that if we had the information needed to assess whether self-reports "really" measure delinquent behavior, we would not need self-reports. In other words, other information would itself be providing us with valid, reliable data.

Direct observation or measurement of phenomena is preferred in all of the sciences but is rarely achieved. Instruments are designed to measure the unobservable or to measure more precisely and systematically those phenomena that we can observe. Self-report methods represent an effort to measure the occurrence of events that are not recorded or observed in police and court statistics, as well as those that are, and to measure both "hidden" and public events. In their attempts to provide accurate, valid measures of delinquent behavior, self-report methods assume: 1) that the behavior in question can be clearly and precisely described, 2) that people will remember their transgressions, 3) that they will give honest answers to queries about their behavior, and 4) that they can follow directions, read, and understand the questions. Grave doubts have been expressed regarding all four assumptions.

Researchers concerned with measuring behavior that is in violation of the law are confronted with the fact that laws are imprecise and ambiguous. For example, question 14 in Figure 4-1 asks "During the past year have you ever taken a car without permission (not parents' car)?" The question was intended to measure events that could end up in police statistics as motor vehicle theft. However, circumstances of "who took it from whom, for what reason, and for how long" would affect which events made their way into motor vehicle theft statistics and which did not. Similarly, question 15, "During the past year have you ever run away from home?" could be labeled as an act of incorrigibility, truancy, curfew, or run-away. Once again, depending on the circumstances, a single event could be handled officially in numerous ways. In short, while behavioral events described in self-reports are often imprecise and may encompass activities that have little chance of causing police or court action, the laws defining activities that can result in legal action are also broad and imprecise.

People may not remember their transgressions and may therefore under-report delinquency; or they may remember activities that occurred before the period in question and may over report crime for that time period. They may also conceal their activities or exaggerate them, depending on the image they want to project. Interviews are viewed as superior to questionnaires for accurate recall since answers can be probed during the interview. However, given the potentially sensitive nature of information being requested in self-report studies, it might seem logical to argue that the use of an anonymous questionnaire is advantageous.

Since most researchers cannot validate their measurement of delinquency by direct observation of the delinquent behavior, how can the validity of self-reports be assessed? In his study of delinquency in Flint, Michigan, Martin Gold (1970:19-24) assessed the validity of his self-report survey by interviewing the teenaged acquaintances of his respondents who were most likely to have information about the respondents' delinquent behavior. Thus, Gold could compare what the respondents in his study admitted with what the informants said about them. He found that his self-report interviews underestimated delinquent behavior by about 30 percent, but that there were no marked differences in concealment across categories of sex, race, and social status. Although the self-reports underestimated delinquency, they did so to such comparable degrees for different groups that differences among groups could be plausibly interpreted as reflecting real differences in delinquent behavior rather than differences in honesty or memory.

Numerous studies have shown involvement in delinquency as measured by self-reports to be highly correlated with police, court, and institutional statistics (Nye, 1958; Erickson and Empey, 1963; Hirschi, 1969; Elliott and Voss, 1974; Hindelang et al., 1981). We have already noted that memory, honesty, and understanding may preclude a perfect match between self-reports and police statistics but it is also important to recognize that what appears to be the "same" event may have quite different meanings to the offender and the police. Rojek (1983) found that when youths' reports and police reports of offenses over a six-month period were compared that they matched only 46 percent of the time. Mismatches were due to errors in youths' recollections of when events took place, differences in what they remembered being arrested for and what the police recorded, and uncertainties about arrests in situations with multiple arrests. In some instances the events were interpreted differently:

> A field encounter between a police officer and a juvenile may not have resulted in an arrest but perceived through the eyes of a juvenile, he or she was "busted" by the police. Further, the categorization of the deviant act may be unduly complex because of multiple offenses and differing levels of seriousness for each offense. The juvenile may perceive a police encounter in terms of an arrest for a particular behavior, while the police officer may view the encounter as a "police contact" for a different act of deviance (Rojek, 1983: 73).

Thus, the issue is not necessarily a matter of one body of data being the correct standard against which to judge the validity of another. The police officer sees "reality" from one perspective in defining delinquent events and it does not necessarily correspond with the adolescent's perspective.

While the issue of validity hinges on the correspondence between delinquent events and their measurement, self-reports have also been criticized for concentrating on relatively common and trivial events. Leonard Savitz, Michael Lalli, and Lawrence Rosen (1977) argue that:

> . . . the more widely used standardized scales have, for the most part, been concerned with the incidence of rather trivial behaviors (talking back to parents, stealing items of small value, smoking cigarettes, drinking wine, etc.) and as a result usually fail to distinguish between the serious delinquent (those committing acts involving serious physical harm and property loss) and the mildly errant boy. (1977:4)

It is true that self-report studies have not dealt with offenses such as murder and rape or even concentrated on serious offenses such as robbery. Such events are sufficiently rare that they just do not show up often enough in surveys for specific analysis. In the entire United States in 1988, there were 16,326 arrests for murder but only 1,765 or 10.8 percent of these were juveniles. Similarly there were 28,482 arrests in 1988 for rape, but only 4,118 or 14.4 percent were juveniles. While 1.6 million juveniles were arrested, only 4.3 percent were apprehended for serious violent crimes. Unless one used a huge national sample, it is unlikely that there would be enough cases involving the most serious offenses to do any meaningful analysis.

Since the more serious delinquent events are more likely to make their way into police and court statistics, and self-reports do not reveal many serious events, the two bodies of data reflect different "domains" (Hindelang et al., 1979). This difference in domain has led some self-report researchers to refer to the domain they are measuring as "common delinquency" (see Hagan et al., 1985, 1987). Moreover, self-report researchers have worked to overcome such problems by differentiating between relatively serious offenses and trivial ones in their analysis. It is quite common for self-report researchers to do offense-specific analysis when sample size and frequencies allow such detail.

Patterns Based on Self-Reports

Both police or court statistics and self-reports have their limitations, and we will encounter different people accepting or rejecting the "facts" suggested by each method, depending on the weight that they assign to those limitations and the fit of the facts with their own preconceptions. "Experts" committed to the assumption that social status is an important correlate of delinquency are more likely to doubt the results of self-report research than are those committed to theories that do not assume such a correlation. Those who argue that the justice system discriminates against minorities are more likely to accept results that seemingly minimize real behavioral differences among groups.

In certain areas, both self-report data and police data are typically less disparate than they seem, and data produced by both types of studies yield a surprising number of comparable findings. When different ways of measuring a phenomena yield similar patterns, then we tend to have greater confidence that the patterns are real and not merely artifacts of our methodology. We will now examine self-report surveys in terms of the same variations or patterns over time, space, and among various socio-demographic categories that we considered in relation to police and court statistics in Chapter 3.

Frequency of Delinquent Behavior. Self-report surveys have been conducted in a number of different nations with literally hundreds having been carried out in the United States. In Figure 4-2 we have summarized the results of a survey conducted among a representative sample of high school seniors in the United States in 1985 (Johnston et al., 1986). A similar survey carried out in India among high school boys in 1978 and another carried out in 1979 among high school students in Ontario, Canada are summarized in Figure 4-3. Differences in wording, ages included, and year preclude straightforward comparison among countries but the frequencies for seniors in the United States seem particularly large when we consider that the questions asked referred to the previous twelve months while the questions for Canadian and Indian youths asked if they had "ever" committed such an offense. It is very likely the case that youths in the United States are more involved in delinquency than Canadian youth and that youths in India have very low rates compared to the United States and Canada.

The reports of high school seniors in the United States provide considerable detail on drug use and the overall impression suggested by the data is that drug use is a particularly prominent activity among United States youth. Only about 6 percent of boys in the India study report any alcohol use in their lifetime as compared to about 67 percent of Canadian boys. In the United States, 85 percent of male high school seniors report alcohol use in the preceding twelve months alone.

Since there is some evidence that offenses such as vandalism, theft, and burglary peak at ages 15 or 16, the reports of high school seniors likely underestimate twelve-month involvement by juveniles in the United States. Yet, even an underestimate suggests that involvement of United States youth in property offenses definitely exceeds that of youths in India and very probably exceeds involvement of Canadian youth. Without international research using similar instruments and samples from similar settings

Figure 4-2

High School Seniors Self-Reported Delinquent Involvement in Last Twelve Months (Percent Admitting Activity)

Delinquent Activity	Male	Female	White	Black
Argued or had a fight with parents				
Not at all	14.0	8.2	7.5	30.1
Once	11.2	7.4	7.2	16.7
Twice or more	74.8	84.5	84.4	53.1
Gotten into a serious fight				
Not at all	76.3	87.3	81.5	83.7
Once	13.8	8.6	11.5	11.5
Twice or more	9.9	4.2	7.0	5.0
Taken something not belonging to you worth under $50				
Not at all	61.4	78.5	68.8	78.3
Once	16.7	11.4	14.5	9.8
Twice or more	21.9	10.2	16.7	11.9
Taken something from a store				
Not at all	68.2	79.2	73.7	79.2
Once	12.6	10.5	11.8	9.7
Twice or more	19.1	10.3	14.9	11.2
Taken a car that didn't belong to you				
Not at all	92.2	96.6	94.9	94.7
Once	3.9	2.3	3.0	3.9
Twice or more	3.9	1.1	2.1	1.4
Gone into a building when you weren't supposed to be there				
Not at all	65.5	82.0	72.9	80.7
Once	17.5	9.2	13.9	9.8
Twice or more	16.9	8.7	13.1	9.5
Damaged school property on purpose				
Not at all	81.1	91.5	86.0	91.7
Once	8.5	4.8	6.8	5.3
Twice or more	10.3	3.7	7.2	2.9
Gotten into trouble with the police				
Not at all	68.6	87.1	76.5	86.4
Once	18.2	10.1	14.5	10.6
Twice or more	13.3	2.9	9.1	3.0
Traffic ticket or warning				
None	62.6	81.5	69.8	86.7
Once	21.3	13.5	19.0	9.1
Twice or more	16.1	5.0	11.2	4.2

Traffic ticket or warning while under the influence of alcohol				
None	82.2	87.7	83.2	94.3
Once	13.3	10.1	12.8	3.6
Twice or more	4.5	2.2	3.9	2.0
Drank alcohol (beer, wine or liquor)				
Never	13.8	15.0	11.2	30.9
Once or twice	11.7	17.8	13.3	23.6
Three or more	73.7	67.2	75.4	45.5
Used marijuana				
Never	56.9	62.2	57.8	67.6
Once or twice	11.3	11.9	11.9	11.2
Three or more	31.8	26.0	30.4	21.2
Used LSD				
Never	94.1	97.2	95.1	99.1
Once or twice	3.4	2.0	3.0	0.6
Three or more	2.6	0.7	2.0	0.3
Amphetamines				
Never	85.1	83.6	82.3	95.7
Once or twice	5.9	6.9	7.3	2.1
Three or more	9.1	9.5	10.4	2.3
Barbiturates				
Never	84.8	96.1	95.2	98.5
Once or twice	2.4	2.0	2.4	0.6
Three or more	2.8	1.8	2.5	0.8
Cocaine				
Never	98.6	99.2	98.9	99.0
Once or twice	0.8	0.6	0.7	0.5
Three or more	0.5	0.3	0.3	0.6
Heroin				
Never	98.6	99.2	98.9	99.0
Once or twice	0.8	0.6	0.7	0.5
Three or more	0.5	0.3	0.3	0.6
Cigarettes (during the past 30 days)				
Never	71.8	68.6	68.3	81.3
One to five per day	15.9	19.3	18.3	14.6
More than five per day	12.4	12.1	13.6	4.1

Source: Johnston, L. D., J. G. Bachman, and P. M. O'Malley, *Monitoring the Future*, 1986.

Figure 4-3

Comparison of Self-Reported Delinquency Among Males in Canada and India (Percent Admitting Activity)

	Ontario, Canada	Tamil Nadu, India
Vandalism	39.4	11.2
Breaking and Entering	21.8	8.3
Car Theft	14.5	4.1
Major Theft	9.5	2.1
Medium Theft	20.2	3.9
Minor Theft	63.1	17.4
Used Alcohol	67.2	6.4
Runaway	10.7	8.1
Truancy	54.3	27.9

Source: Priyadarsini, S., and C. Hartjen, "Delinquency and Corrections in India," 1981; Gomme, et al., "Rates, Types, and Patterns of Delinquency in an Ontario County," 1984.

(e.g., similar sizes of communities, etc.), we cannot say a great deal about international variations.

Not only has self-report research shown the extent of involvement of youth to be greater than many people might anticipate but research encompassing junior as well as senior high school students suggests that a surprising proportion of pre-adolescent youths are involved. For example, in a study of drug use among junior and senior high school students in Georgia (Rojek, 1986), students have asked "Have you ever gotten really drunk in the past twelve months?" More than 8 percent of 6th graders, 16 percent of 7th graders, and about 26 percent of 8th graders report being intoxicated at least once in the preceding twelve months. When one considers that 6th grade students are about 12 years old, these results are quite startling. The percentage increases steadily by grade to the point that close to 55 percent of seniors report getting really drunk in a twelve-month period. As we will see in the next section, alcohol use is the number one drug problem among youth and a problem which has remained relatively constant over time, even during periods when other forms of drug use have declined.

In sum, while certain aspects of media images of the delinquent may be a myth, delinquent activity is certainly not a myth. Among youth in Western nations it is quite common and among youth in the United States it is the juvenile who has not broken the law who is the exception. The prominence of delinquency does not mean that the typical youth is a chronic offender, repetitively involved in serious crimes. However, it does mean that delinquency is a problem that is not easily compartmentalized and attributed to a select few. The occasional acts of many can be as costly to society as the repetitive acts of a few. It is in that sense that "the delinquent nobody knows" is often someone we knew all along, perhaps even a friend or relative.

Changes over Time. Unlike the FBI's *Uniform Crime Reports* or the Juvenile Court's statistics that are nationwide and released annually, self-report studies tend to be sporadic and regionally specific. That is, the bulk of self-report findings come from research administered in different parts of the country, with different age groups and different questions. It is very difficult to assess what precise type of changes in delinquent behavior are occurring over time with the smattering of self-report data that currently exists. The only reliable self-report research that has been conducted over an extended period of time is administered by the Institute for Social Research at the University of Michigan. That project, entitled "Monitoring the Future," was designed to explore changes in values, behaviors, and attitudes of American youth. It began in 1975, and involves sampling some 16,000 high school seniors from approximately 125 schools. The sampling is done in such a way that the results are representative of the nation as a whole. This annual survey is a valuable source of information for change over time.

In an earlier version of this survey conducted in 1967 and again in 1972, Gold and Reimer found that the 1972 male respondents reported more frequent use of illicit drugs—mostly marijuana—than the 1967 respondents did, and less larceny, threatened assault, trespassing, forcible and non-forcible entry, and gang fighting. The girls in 1972 also reported greater use of drugs—mostly marijuana but including alcohol—than girls did in 1967, while reporting less larceny, property destruction, and breaking and entering. But the decline of the latter kinds of offenses among the girls in 1972 does not balance their greater use of drugs, so the girls in 1972 reported more delinquent behavior overall (1974:43).

More recent findings from the Institute for Social Research's surveys from 1975 through 1989 suggest declines in percentage admitting shoplifting through 1984 with some upward movement after that time. Thefts involving less than fifty dollars have been relatively stable between 1975 and 1989, exhibiting no significant trend. There has been some upward movement in thefts greater than fifty dollars, robbery, fights and group fights (see Figure 4-4).

Figure 4-4

Percent of High School Seniors Admitting Delinquent Acts in 12-Month Period

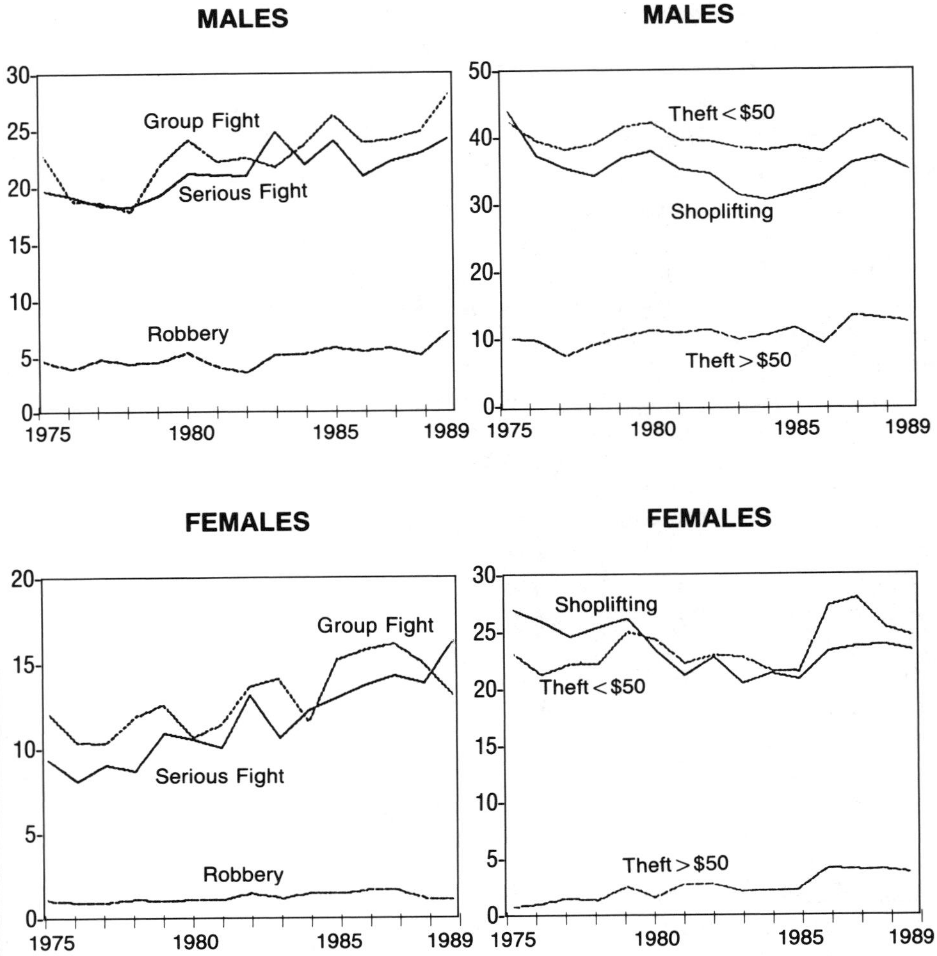

Source: Based on surveys by L. Johnston, J. Bachman, and P. O'Malley, summarized in *Sourcebook of Criminal Justice Statistics*, 1985, 1989.

Since shoplifting and thefts involving less than fifty dollars loss are much more common than more serious thefts, the data on property offenses is fairly consistent with police data. Data on larceny summarized in Chapter 3 indicate a decline in the early 1980s followed by increases in the late 1980s. After a brief period of stable or declining rates of aggravated assault in the early 1980s, aggravated assault increased considerably. While the self-report data do not correspond in each year the overall upward movement in aggravated assault during this span is paralleled by serious fights and group fights. The trend in robbery is relatively flat in the self-report data and has fluctuated with a general overall increase in *Uniform Crime Reports*. In sum, there are not glaring disparities between the trends exhibited in the reports of high school seniors over time and overall trends in police data.

Figures 4-5 and 4-6 summarize data on drug use encompassing the years 1975 through 1990. After prompting concern of an epidemic in the early 1980s and rising sharply in the mid-1980s, cocaine use has declined each year since 1986. There have been declines in the use of marijuana, stimulants, tranquilizers, and sedatives as well. Marijuana use peaked in 1979 and has declined fairly steadily since that year. After fourteen years of stability (1975-1988) alcohol use has shown some recent declines in 1989-1990. Low frequency drug activities have not changed very much but do shown some downward movement on the average.

An exception to the pattern for most drugs is prevalence of inhalant use. While stable in the last several years, use in recent years is at an all time high. In the survey of Georgia youth (Rojek, 1986), nearly 30 percent of 7th graders used inhalants while the percentage steadily declined to 14 percent in the 12th grade. While inhalants are incredibly dangerous, causing damage to the nasal passages, trachea, and lungs as well as oxygen deficiency to the brain, these substances are cheap and readily available to younger adolescents. Older adolescents have the social contacts and the money to procure more "traditional" drugs like alcohol and marijuana.

Johnston, Bachman, and O'Malley suggest that one factor contributing to declines in drug use is changing attitudes about the health hazards of these drugs. Perceived risk of harm, perceptions of availability, and reported use are summarized in Figures 4-7 and 4-8. Perceptions of harm have increased for a variety of drugs but the change in perception is particularly prominent for cocaine. A sudden shift in cocaine use can be noted beginning in 1986. In 1986, Len Bias, a college basketball player headed for the professional ranks, died of complications attributed to cocaine and the national publicity surrounding this case may have helped generate this sudden shift. The data do suggest that changes in drug use are affected more by changes in demand than by changes in availability.

It is important to recognize that some downward trends have been relatively long-term. The first official "drug czar," William Bennett, often

Figure 4-5

Percent of High School Seniors Admitting Drug Use in 12-Month Period

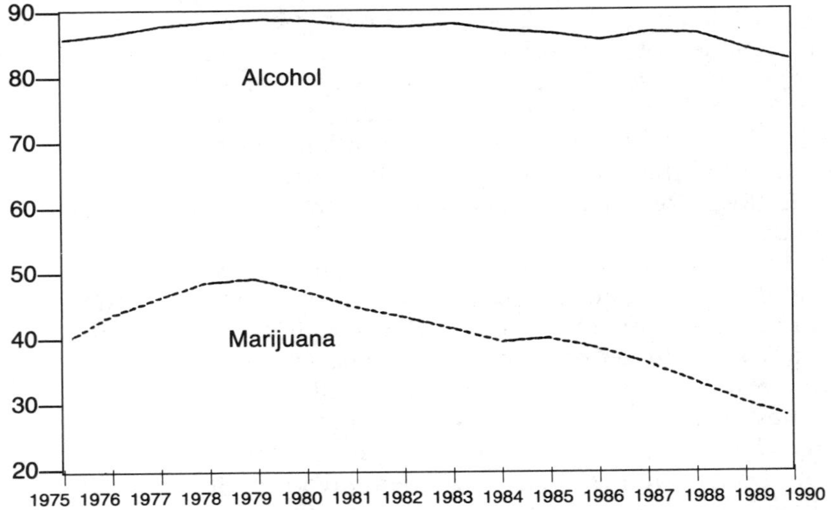

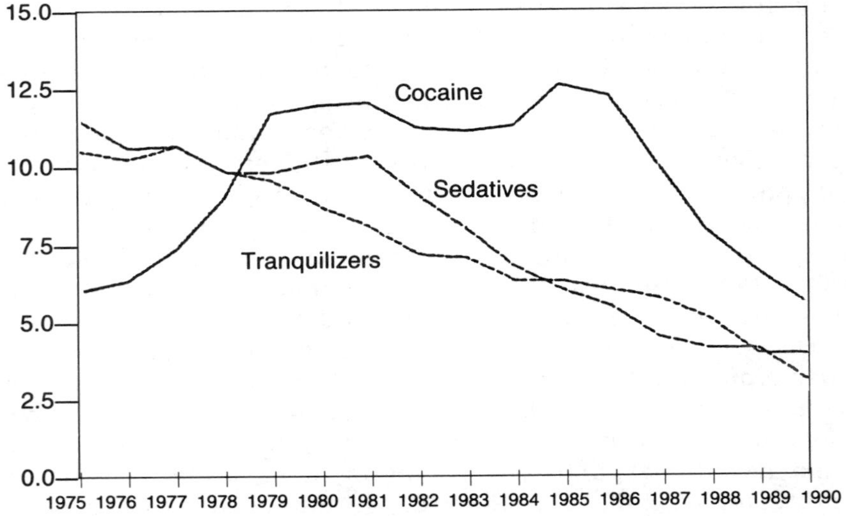

Source: From L. Johnston, J. Bachman, and P. O'Malley, 1991. *Monitoring the Future.* Ann Arbor: Institute for Social Research.

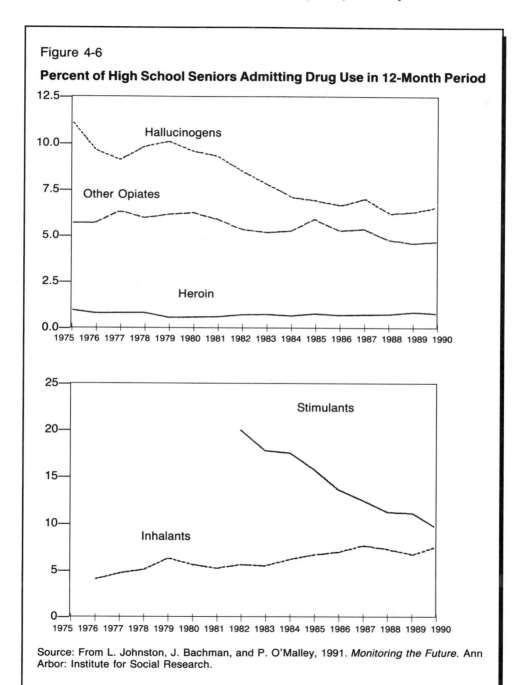

Figure 4-6

Percent of High School Seniors Admitting Drug Use in 12-Month Period

Source: From L. Johnston, J. Bachman, and P. O'Malley, 1991. *Monitoring the Future.* Ann Arbor: Institute for Social Research.

cited intensive patrol efforts and law enforcement crackdowns as the explanation for the types of decreases reported above. Yet, some forms of drug use had been declining for a decade prior to the establishment of Bennett's position as Director of the Drug Enforcement Administration in 1989 and President George Bush's "war on drugs." In addition, the very data taken as evidence of a decline also shows that perceived availability (supply) did not change and that the decline in demand reflected a concern for the harm that drugs caused. Highly publicized tragic events such as Bias' death likely had more to do with turning the corner on cocaine use than any activities under the auspices of the drug czar. This critical observation does not mean that laws and their enforcement are ineffective.

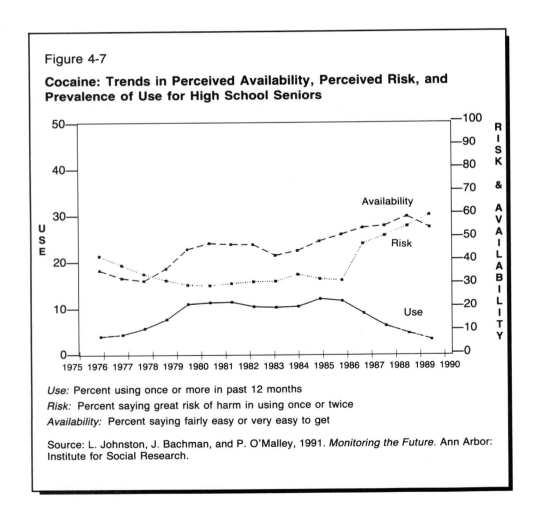

Figure 4-7

Cocaine: Trends in Perceived Availability, Perceived Risk, and Prevalence of Use for High School Seniors

Use: Percent using once or more in past 12 months

Risk: Percent saying great risk of harm in using once or twice

Availability: Percent saying fairly easy or very easy to get

Source: L. Johnston, J. Bachman, and P. O'Malley, 1991. *Monitoring the Future.* Ann Arbor: Institute for Social Research.

Laws and risks of punishment probably do affect choices (see Chapter 9). However, in this instance, the data suggest that changes in assessments of harm were the key changes. Thus, efforts at drug education may be more beneficial than periodic law enforcement crackdowns.

Spatial Distribution. In our discussion of official rates in Chapter 3, we noted two aspects of the spatial distribution of delinquency that are of interest to criminologists: the distribution of delinquency in areas of cities and variations among communities of different size. We also noted that in their explanation of variation in official delinquency rates, Shaw and McKay argued that rapid change or succession in the racial or ethnic composition of a neighborhood prevented or disrupted the development

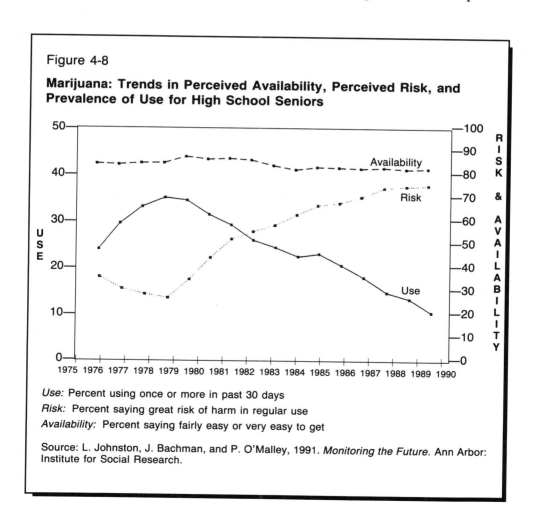

Figure 4-8

Marijuana: Trends in Perceived Availability, Perceived Risk, and Prevalence of Use for High School Seniors

Use: Percent using once or more in past 30 days
Risk: Percent saying great risk of harm in regular use
Availability: Percent saying fairly easy or very easy to get

Source: L. Johnston, J. Bachman, and P. O'Malley, 1991. *Monitoring the Future.* Ann Arbor: Institute for Social Research.

of conventional institutions or organizations in the area. This resulted in social disorganization that led to a high delinquency rate. This explanation fit their information on the distribution of officially recorded delinquency.

Although no self-report exactly parallels studies of the spatial distribution of delinquency that are based on police and court data, there are some studies examining characteristics of neighborhoods in relation to self-reported delinquency. Focusing on black adolescent males in the San Francisco-Oakland and metropolitan region, Robert Kapsis (1978) examined rates of self-reported and official delinquency in three neighborhoods that were at varying stages of racial change. Kapsis found that according to both measures of delinquency, the delinquency rate was highest for males living in neighborhoods with the highest racial succession and lowest in the most stable neighborhoods. Moreover, this pattern held true even when measures of socioeconomic status, family structure, and educational performance and commitment were taken into account.

A more recent study of "Neighborhood and Delinquency" (Simcha-Fagin and Schwartz, 1986) collected data from 553 urban adolescent males between 11 and 18 years of age and from their mothers or female guardians. They also collected census data on neighborhoods. After several preliminary stages of analysis they examined the relation between measures of self-reported delinquency and residential stability, community economic well-being, level of organizational participation, and a measure of community disorder and criminal subcultures. The level of organizational participation in a neighborhood was found to affect adolescent delinquent behavior while the extent of disorder and the existence of criminal subcultures was more relevant to official reactions to delinquency. Residential stability affected delinquency as well but indirectly through their relation to attachment to school. In neighborhoods with a lot of turnover, children were less likely to form bonds in school and more likely to engage in delinquency as a result.

Self-report studies bearing on rural-urban differences have been conducted as well. Clark and Wenninger (1962) found that although the rural farm community they studied tended to rank lowest in self-reported delinquency, there was actually very little overall difference between adolescents in a rural farm community and adolescents in urban settings. Compared with 1) youth in an industrial city of 35,000, 2) youth in a lower-class urban neighborhood, and 3) youth in a wealthy Chicago suburb, rural youth ranked fourth for fourteen of thirty-eight offenses studied. However, for those fourteen offenses, the average percentage difference between the rural youth and each of the three urban samples was only 4.7 percent. The greatest urban-rural differences involved sneaking into theaters, curfew violations, major theft, borrowing money without intending to pay it back, drinking, using slugs in vending machines, and truancy. Major theft was the only serious offense for which the average difference between the rural youth and the three urban samples exceeded 10 percent. For violent offenses, arson, many forms of vandalism, trespassing, breaking and entering, and hanging around or entering adult-only establishments, the rural sample ranked first or second.

In their 1967 national survey of youth, Gold and Reimer (1974) found that central-city youths reported an average of 8.6 delinquent offenses during the three years preceding the interview, as compared to 7.5 for suburban youths. In 1972 the comparable rate was 7.8 for central-city youths, 6.0 for suburban youths, 7.1 for youths in small cities and towns, and 4.5 for rural youths. Overall, the differences by residence were small and varied between the two years of Gold and Reimer's study. However, the differences did show higher average delinquent involvement among central-city youths than among youths in smaller communities.

The longitudinal study of high school seniors conducted by the University of Michigan reveals some fairly consistent regional differences. On virtually every single measure of property crime, crimes against persons, and drug involvement, students from the Northeast (New England and Middle Atlantic states) scored higher than students from any other region of the country. Conversely, high school seniors from the South were consistently lower on all forms of delinquent behavior than students from other parts of the country. In comparing rural with urban delinquency rates, there again is agreement that urban youth are more involved in most forms of delinquency (Napier and Pratt, 1982; Napier et al., 1983; Goe et al., 1985). However, as we will discover later, it is not merely the non-urban nature or Southern mystique that accounts for lower delinquency rates, but rather a host of other characteristics such as a community's economic position, stability, resources, racial mix and educational levels that affect its rates.

Gender Differences. One of the most studied topics in criminology since the mid-1970s has been the gender difference in delinquency. Whether the data base is police, court, or self-report data, the general conclusion is that males are more involved in delinquency than females. Beyond that observation there is considerable disagreement. Some criminologists argue that self-report data show less dramatic differences than official statistics and give the impression that the sex difference is quite small. For example, based on her analysis of self-report data on middle-class youth, Pamela Richards (1981:453) argues "there is little evidence that there are marked differences in the delinquent activities reported by girls and boys." Yet, in another self-report study, Hagan, Gillis, and Simpson tell us that "gender is a strong and consistent correlate" (1985:1151). In short, scholars do not agree on the magnitude and importance of the gender difference, although they do agree that males are more delinquent.

Part of the problem in arriving at agreement stems from the fact that most self-report studies are carried out on urban samples which makes comparisons of the sex ratio using official statistics and self-reports misleading. Official statistics show more prominent gender differences for youths in rural than urban settings. Self-report surveys carried out in urban settings should show less prominent sex differences than do national data lumping all sorts of settings together.

Moreover, some self-reported acts are so common (e.g., petty theft, shoplifting, defying parents, and so on) that the sex difference will appear smaller in self-report studies because the measures used are heavily weighted with those offenses where sex differences are the least prominent. In fact, one analysis (Jensen, 1985) has shown that when acts that rarely enter into official statistics are eliminated and the samples matched for jurisdiction, age, and setting, that estimates of the sex difference based on official statistics are remarkably similar to estimates based on self-reports. The ratio of male to female delinquency for FBI Index crimes in a 1976 survey in Tucson, Arizona was 2.5 to 1 for juvenile court statistics, 2.6 to 1 when youths were asked to report on arrests and referrals, and 2.4 to 1 when self-reports were used with smoking, drinking, and disobedience or defiance of parents excluded from the measure of total delinquency. Data from a nationwide survey (Elliott et al., 1985) yield similar results. When only FBI Index crimes are counted, the 1978 National Survey of Youth yields a male to female ratio of about 3.9 to 1. The ratio using FBI data on arrests of persons under 18 for that same year is 3.2 to 1 and the ratio using national Juvenile Court statistics is 3.2 to 1. Whether ratios of this magnitude are evidence of strong or marked differences is simply a matter of judgment. Compared to social class, broken homes, time spent watching television, and all sorts of other variables to be reviewed in this and subsequent chapters, the differences observed by gender are impressive.

Gender differences in the prevalence of delinquency can be noted in Figures 4-2 and 4-4. Analyses of estimated *average offenses* for males and females among high school seniors in the United States yield ratios for major theft and hurting someone badly of between 5 and 6 to 1. For shoplifting and thefts under $50, the ratios are between 1.5 and 2.0 to 1. In sum, consistent with police and court data, the sex difference is most prominent for the most damaging and harmful offenses whether against people or property.

Another topic where different impressions abound is the magnitude of gender differences over time. As we noted in Chapter 3, the differences between the sexes narrowed most dramatically during the 1960s through the mid-1970s, but has been relatively stable since then. The lack of nationally representative self-report data precludes definitive conclusions about gender differences during the 1960s but we can refer to such data for a 1967-1972 comparison and to the data on high school seniors for the 1975 through 1989 period. We can also draw on a study of surveys carried out between 1940 and 1975. All of these data sources suggest similar conclusions.

Smith and Visher (1980) have examined forty-four self-report studies carried out between 1940 and 1975. They conclude that for the time period covered, the gender gap narrowed for all offense categories but narrowed the most for drug and status offenses. Moreover, it appears to have narrowed more for younger people than older people and for blacks than whites.

Gold and Reimer's (1974) "National Survey of Youth" provided comparative data for girls and boys in 1967 and 1972, and their data suggest a decline in the sex difference in most settings during that five-year period as well. The disparity between male and female delinquency was lower in terms of both frequency and seriousness in 1972 among central city, suburban, and rural youth. The disparity was actually greater in 1972 than in 1967 for small town youth due to an unusual increase in reported delinquency among boys.

Analyses of the *Monitoring the Future* surveys from 1975 through 1989 reveal variations in the gender ratio for prevalence of delinquency suggesting a general decline but some of the declines are quite recent (see Figure 4-4). For example, the male-female ratio for reports of serious fights hovered close to 2.0 to 1 for the 1975 through 1984 but declined to between 1.5 and 1.6 to 1 in the most recent years (1986-89). While shoplifting exhibits a curvilinear trend, the trend is similar for males and females with the gender ratio close to 1.5 to 1 since 1975. The ratio changed little between 1975 and 1985 for thefts involving less than $50 but reached an historic low in 1986 and has not returned to its previous high. For thefts involving more than $50 the ratio was 10.6 to 1 in 1975 but declined to about 5 to 1 in 1976. After a period of stability between 1976 and 1985 the ratio dropped to between 2.5 and 3.5 to 1. Overall, data on admitted delinquency among high school seniors suggest a decline in the gender ratio. For several offenses the most prominent declines are very recent.

Criminologists have suggested that males and females engage in different types of delinquency because of learned gender differences or sex role socialization. Haskell and Yablonsky (1974) assert that more masculine people are more involved in delinquent behavior. They summarize this masculinity and delinquency perspective as follows: "Since men are expected to be aggressive, males are more likely to be delinquent than females who are expected to adopt a more passive role" (1974: 67). Norland, Wessel, and Shover (1981) tested this masculinity hypothesis and found no direct, positive relationship between masculinity and various types of offenses for females. In fact, they found the opposite: females with more masculine characteristics were actually less involved in delinquency than those with less masculine traits.

Jensen and Eve (1976) draw on a number of sociological theories to explain the sex difference in delinquency, using data gathered from junior and senior high school students in the San Francisco Bay area in 1964-65. They found that to a considerable degree, the difference could be attributed to greater parental supervision and control, greater attachment to parents, more favorable attitudes towards and success at school, greater acceptance of the law and lesser involvement with deviant peers for girls than for boys. Boys and girls with similar experiences and subject to similar controls still differ (with boys exhibiting slightly higher delinquency but they are far more similar than when such information is not considered).

There is mounting evidence supporting the view that much of the difference in delinquency between the sexes is a product of variations in the freedom, beliefs, opportunities, and social relationships of males and females (see Hagan et al., 1985, 1987; Duke and Duke, 1978; Thorton and James, 1979). In fact, one study concludes that "In general, the findings show that the sex-school deviance relationship is completely explained by differences in social controls and pressures that are structured by sex . . ." (Felson and Liska, 1984:1). While we do not know if the decline in the gender difference during the 1960s and early 1970s was a product of changes in these same social variables, an explanation in terms of such social change is quite plausible.

Racial Differences. Whether or not there are racial differences in delinquency rates is a complex and extremely volatile issue. There has been repeated accusations that the criminal justice system is racist and discriminatory. While 12 percent of the U.S. population is black, 23 percent of those arrested and 52 percent of those arrested for violent crimes are black. Further, of the total number of people in correctional institutions, 47 percent are black. Forty-two percent of persons under the death sentence and 53 percent of those executed were black. The high disproportion of blacks arrested, imprisoned, and executed have led to accusations that "extra-legal" factors play a major role in explaining these racial differences. Indeed, some early self-report findings found race to be of little relevance to delinquency compared to police and court data. However, as discussed earlier, these self-report studies have been criticized for focusing too heavily on petty offenses and ignoring serious offenses.

More recent self-report studies find black youth to be more heavily involved in some forms of delinquency behavior than white youth. For example, the Illinois Institute for Juvenile Research found that black youths are approximately twice as likely to report a violent act as white youths (1973). Gold found black youth to be far more involved in assaults, burglary, and theft than white youths (Williams and Gold, 1972; Gold and Reimer, 1974). Perhaps the best evidence for a race differential is found in the National Youth Study (Elliott and Ageton, 1980). For petty offenses like status offenses or public disorder, the black-white rates are essentially the same. However, when one examines serious property offenses and crimes against persons, black youths are more involved than white youths. Elliott and Ageton found that black youths report twice as many property offenses (burglary, larceny, vandalism) as white youths, and for crimes against persons (robbery and assault), blacks report three offenses for every two reported by whites.

As noted earlier, Hindelang, Hirschi, and Weis (1981) found blacks to be only slightly more delinquent than whites using self-report data. When juvenile court records were searched to verify the accuracy of the respondents' answers, they found that their white respondents reported 90 percent of the offenses on their records, while blacks reported only 67 percent of their official record. Further, they found that the black-white difference was related to the seriousness of the offense, with blacks tending to underreport such offenses as burglary, vehicle theft, and weapons offenses. The precise reason for this underreporting is not clear. The researchers suggested it might be attributable to intentional lying, poor reading ability, social desirability, lower saliency of events or higher rates of forgetting. However, they were unable to arrive at any precise explanation.

If we accept the fact that racial differences do exist, how are they to be explained? Differences in crime rates between blacks and whites are likely a function of group differences in a host of social characteristics, such as education, occupation, income, family background, and social status. But beyond these social characteristics are centuries of discrimination that have had painful consequences for blacks in America. It is not simply that blacks are lower class, since comparing lower-class blacks and lower-class whites still shows blacks to be more involved in crime. Comparing black Africans with black Americans show a much higher crime rate for black Americans (Bohannan, 1960). What is unique among blacks in America has been simply termed the "black experience." The institution of slavery disrupted the entire social system of the pre-slave West African, producing an Afro-American that had been relegated from the status of person to property. Generations of social chaos as well as social and economic deprivation have had a significant impact on black Americans. The black community in America is still struggling more than 100 years after the abolition of slavery, as evidenced by anger, frustration and powerlessness, all of which can contribute to the high involvement of blacks in crime (Comer, 1985).

Very few studies have differentiated minority groups other than blacks and very little is known about the self-reported delinquency of Asian, Chicano or Indian American youth. One survey in Seattle (Chambliss and Nagasawa, 1969) reports that 36 percent of Japanese youths admitted to some delinquent activity as compared to 52 percent of whites and 53 percent of blacks. Only 2 percent of Japanese youth had been arrested as compared to 36 percent of blacks and 11 percent of whites. Leroy Gould

(1969) also reports lower rates for Asian Americans than for black or white youths.

An Arizona survey of high school students (Jensen et al., 1977) found that Indian youths attending public high schools had higher rates than Anglo or Chicano youths, and further analysis (Jensen et al., 1978; Jensen, 1985) indicated a slightly higher overall involvement in delinquency for Chicanos than for Anglos. However, the differences between Anglos and Chicanos are quite small and more prominent for fighting and assault than for property offenses. These results are similar to those reported for black youths in the National Survey of Youth. Crimes involving interpersonal conflict are indicated more often by black and Chicano youths than white youths.

Age. In our summary of police and court records in Chapter 3, we noted that arrest rates for the types of offenses that disproportionately involve juveniles tend to peak during middle adolescence and that the more serious offenses tend to peak somewhat later, between 18 to 22. The drop in arrest rates for the over-25 age group is quite dramatic.

Self-report studies of delinquency have tended to suggest a similar pattern with regard to overall involvement. Hirschi (1969) found the greatest proportion of youths self-reporting delinquent acts in grades nine and ten. In a national survey of youth that encompassed only those aged 13 through 16, self-reported delinquency was found to be more frequent and more serious the older the age category of the respondent (Williams and Gold, 1972).

On the other hand, Fors and Rojek (1983) found that in examining sixth-through twelfth-graders, property offenses and "traditional" drug involvement increased with age but certain activities were more prevalent in younger age categories. For example, running away, assault, inhalant use, and school suspension were significantly higher in the middle school grades (grades 6 through 8) than in high school.

In their study of self-reported criminality in a sample of persons aged 15 and older residing in three different states, Tittle and Villemez (1977) presented data that are essentially consistent with the view that young persons account for a disproportionate share of most offenses. Data from that study show the highest rates reported among persons 15 through 24 years of age for four offenses (minor and major theft, assault, and marijuana use) out of the six examined. Gambling and cheating on one's income tax were most common among persons aged 25 through 44. For all six offenses, persons over 65 had the lowest rates. Finally, for all age groups and offenses, males tended to report more criminality than females.

Social Status and Social Class. Since the advent of self-report surveys some thirty years ago, the relationship between social status and delinquent behavior has been the most studied relationship in delinquency research.

In the mid-1930s Sophia M. Robison (1963) investigated "hidden" delinquency in New York City. On the basis of self-reported data, Robison argued that juvenile court statistics were unduly biased toward lower-class children; that the differentials between lower-class youths and middle- and upper-class youths reflected the greater availability of noncourt resources for more affluent children. A few years later Edward Schwartz (1945) conducted a similar study in Washington, D.C., and found far more delinquency in the middle- and upper-classes than was recorded in official statistics.

In his pioneering study of college students in Fort Worth, Texas, Porterfield (1946) found that despite the self-reports of a great number of delinquent offenses, virtually none of them had been brought to the attention of the police or the court. Porterfield interpreted his findings as the result of a differential application of the law that works against lower-class youths. He suggested that adolescents from economically deprived areas or families are observed more closely than juveniles from higher status backgrounds. Porterfield also concluded that juveniles from lower socioeconomic strata are dealt with in a more punitive manner than upper-class youth.

The research conducted by James Short, Jr. and F. Ivan Nye in the late 1950s was a major contribution to the study of hidden delinquency. These investigators measured delinquency by using a list of twenty-three delinquent behaviors, with offenses ranging from driving without a license to grand larceny and drug use. The data were gathered with anonymous questionnaires in high schools and in correctional training institutions in several Western and Midwestern communities. Short and Nye found that nearly all of the institutionalized youths were from the lower socioeconomic strata, in contrast to only 53 percent of the total high school population. However, when the high school samples were analyzed, the overall results showed essentially no consistent relationship between delinquency and social class. In a few instances some differences were found to be significant but, out of a total of 756 tests for differences by socioeconomic status, only 33 were found to be significant. The researchers concluded that juvenile delinquency is not linked to class and that much middle and upper class delinquent behavior goes undetected.

These early studies examining the relationship between social class and delinquency challenged the popular notion that lower-class adolescents were more deviant than middle- or upper-class youth. During the decades of the 1960s and 1970s, a plethora of studies were conducted on the issue of social class and delinquency that seemed to suggest that there was either no association, or, at best, a very weak relationship. However, the debate has never been settled, and presently, there is renewed interest in this controversial topic.

From a methodological perspective, two questions have been asked: how does the way in which delinquency is measured affect the class-delinquency relationship? And, how does the way that class is measured affect the relationship? The measurement of delinquency was discussed earlier. In far too many instances, self-report research tended to focus predominantly on petty acts of vandalism and property theft, while ignoring serious criminal acts. Serious law-breaking is relatively rare, and unless the sampling frame is very large, it is not inconceivable that serious delinquent acts will not be detected. Previous research on social class and delinquency may be problematic because of an undersampling of serious acts.

Similarly, the measurement of social status may be flawed. Some measures are very crude: for example, placing people in a threefold class category, such as high, middle, or low. Other measures may mask important distinctions within their ranking scheme. Johnson (1980) argues that the crux of the issue is not the lower class per se, but a particular range of the lower class called the "underclass." This underclass is distinguished from what Johnson calls the "earning class" in terms of unemployment, poverty level, and welfare eligibility. "When the truly lower-class adolescents are sampled, they are usually not identifiable as a distinct group when respondents are stratified by socioeconomic status of fathers' occupations" (Johnson, 1980: 87). The lower class can contain a wide range of blue-collar or manual trade categories that are economically secure as well as those who are destitute or impoverished because of underemployment.

It is generally agreed that in the area of relatively minor misbehavior, which is extremely commonplace, there is no evidence of a class-linked relationship (Tittle et al., 1971). But when attention is focused on serious and repetitive delinquency, there is some evidence that it is class-linked (Hindelang et al., 1979). Elliott and Huizinga examined the results from the National Youth Survey administered from 1976 through 1979 to youths age 11 to 17 and concluded that middle-class youth commit fewer offenses than do working- or lower-class youth. "Not only are these class differences statistically significant, they are also substantial, with lower- and working-class male rates ranging between two and ten times those of middle-class males" (Elliott and Huizinga, 1983:164). Once again, it needs to be emphasized that the bulk of delinquent behavior involves petty property offenses which are equally common to all social classes. But in those instances where serious offenses, such as felony assault and robbery, are differentiated, there are significant class differences. Moreover, while the ratio between middle-class and lower-class delinquency may be two to ten times greater for lower-class youth, these ratios are based on very small numbers of lower- or working-class youths involved in serious delinquency.

Because of the methodological difficulties associated with the measurement of social class and delinquency, it is reasonable to assume this controversy will continue. Even if there are differences between the lower class and upper class, it may be that in terms of explaining crime, these class differences are still not crucial. Johnson (1979) went through great effort to examine the relationship between social class and delinquency only to find that there are other more critical forces at work, such as delinquent associates, success in school, perceived risk of apprehension, and susceptibility to peer influence.

Axenroth (1983) suggests that there might be a link between social class and delinquency but only in economically developing societies where there is a rigid division between the classes and when educational opportunity is lacking. Indeed, one of the most recent works on the class-delinquency relationship argues that advantaged youth in capitalist societies have higher rates of delinquency than disadvantaged youth. Others suggest that inflation and the unemployment rate have an impact on crime (Devine et al., 1988) and racial change in adjoining communities can impact local communities (Heitgerd and Bursik, 1987). These latter studies introduce the notion of destabilizing forces that have a certain ebb and flow in influencing the crime rate, producing a stronger relationship between class and delinquency at one point in time than another

Thus, the relationship between class and delinquency is still unclear. There will continue to be research findings that presumably show a relationship; others will "conclusively" demonstrate the lack of a relationship. However, all available research seems to suggest that delinquency is the result of multiple problems and multiple processes. In the complex equation that eventually explains delinquency, it may very well be that for certain types of deviant behaviors, social class plays a role. However, to assume that social class plays a dominant role in the overall equation is extremely doubtful.

Victimization Surveys

The victimization survey is another alternative to using police and court statistics for measuring the extent and nature of crime in the United States. Whereas self-report surveys ask people to report their own involvement in criminal and delinquent activity, the victimization survey asks people to report on their experiences as victims of such activity (see Figure 4-9). Following exploratory efforts in the mid-1960s to measure victimization in a national sample of households in a few cities (Ennis, 1967), the technique grew rapidly in popularity. Beginning in 1972, the Bureau of the Census conducted two sets of national crime surveys for the Bureau of Justice Statistics (formerly the Law Enforcement Assistance Administration). In one set of studies, entitled "The National Crime Survey" (NCS), the Bureau of the Census selected a national sample of approximately 60,000 households and interviewed and re-interviewed

Figure 4-9

Sample Questions from Victim Survey

	116
37a. (Other than the . . . business) does anyone in this household operate a business from this address?	1 ☐Yes—Ask b
b. What kind of business is that? _____	2 ☐No—SKIP to
▶INTERVIEWER: *Enter unrecognizable business only*	38

HOUSEHOLD SCREEN QUESTIONS

38. Now I'd like to ask some questions about crime. They refer only to the last 6 months—between____1, 19____ and ____, 19____. During the last 6 months, did anyone break into or somehow illegally get into your (apartment/home), garage, or another building on your property?	☐Yes—How many times? ☐No _____	41. Did anyone take something belonging to you or to any members of this household, from a place where you or they were temporarily staying, such as a friend's or relative's home, a hotel or motel, or a vacation home?	☐Yes—How many times? ☐No _____
39. (Other than the incident(s) just mentioned) Did you find a door jimmied, a lock forced, or any other signs of an *attempted* break in?	☐Yes—How many times ☐No _____	42. How many *different* motor vehicles (cars, trucks, motorcycles, etc.) were owned by you or any other member of this household during the last 6 months?	a☐None— *Skip* to 45 1☐1 2☐2 3☐3 4☐4 or more
		43. Did anyone steal, *try* to steal, or use (it/any of them) without permission?	☐Yes—How many times? ☐No _____
40. Was anything at all stolen that is kept outside your home, or happened to be left out, such as a bicycle, a garden hose, or lawn furniture? (other than any incidents already mentioned)	☐Yes—How many times ☐No _____	44. Did anyone steal or *try* to steal parts attached to (it/any of them), such as a battery, hubcaps, tape-deck, etc.)	☐Yes—How many times? ☐No _____

INDIVIDUAL SCREEN QUESTIONS

45. The following questions refer only to things that happened to *you* during the last 6 months— between ____1, 19____ and ____, 19____. Did you have your (pocket picked/purse snatched)?	☐Yes—How many times? ☐No _____	55. Did you find any evidence that someone *attempted* to steal something that belonged to you? (other than any incidents already mentioned)	☐Yes —How many times? ☐No _____
46. Did anyone take something (else) directly from you by using force, such as by a stickup, mugging or threat?	☐Yes—How many times? ☐No _____	56. Did you call the police during the last 6 months to report something that happened to *you* which you thought was a crime? (Do not count any calls made to the police concerning the incidents you have just told me about.) ☐No—*Skip* to 57 ☐Yes—What happened? _____	118 ☐☐ ☐☐ ☐☐
47. Did anyone *try* to rob you by using force or threatening to harm you? (other than any incidents already mentioned)	☐Yes—How many times? ☐No _____	Check Item D ▶ Look at 56, was HHLD member 12 + attacked or threatened, or was something stolen or an attempt made to steal something that belonged to him/her?	☐Yes—How many times? ☐No _____
48. Did anyone beat you up, attack you or hit you with something, such as a rock or bottle? (other than any incidents alrady mentioned)	☐Yes—How many times? ☐No _____	57. Did anything happen to *you* during the last 6 months which you thought was a crime, but did *not* report to the police? (other than any incidents already mentioned) ☐No—*Skip* to check Item F ☐Yes—What happened?	
49. Were you knifed, shot at, or attacked with some other weapon by anyone at all? (other than any incidents already mentioned)	☐Yes—How many times? ☐No	_____	119 ☐☐

respondents at six-month intervals. The Bureau of the Census had also conducted a number of city surveys aimed at estimating the nature and extent of victimizations against persons, households, and commercial establishments during the twelve months preceding the interview (Garofalo, 1977). Unfortunately, commercial robbery and burglary were dropped from the program in 1977 for economic reasons. In 1984 the NCS study was reduced by 20 percent from its previous funding level.

Whereas the anonymous, self-response questionnaire has been the most common technique in self-report research on delinquency, the most common technique in victimization surveys has been the in-person interview. This technique is preferred because 1) it yields a high response rate from representative samples of households and commercial establishments, 2) victimization surveys seek a great deal of specific information from victims, and 3) interviewers can probe answers and clarify questions (Garofalo, 1977:20-21). Each housing unit selected for the National Crime Survey is in the sample for three years with a total of seven interviews taking place at six-month intervals. The first contact is in person, with the following interviews by telephone. Individuals aged 12 and over living in the selected house are eligible to be interviewed.

Because the in-person interview technique is quite costly (about $30 per household in the NCS city surveys), telephone interviews and mail questionnaires have been considered as alternatives. Since over 90 percent of households have telephones, it is possible to obtain a fairly representative sample of households by means of "random-digit" dialing. Using this method, the interviewer or a machine dials the three-digit prefixes listed for a given area and dials the remaining four digits at random. Thus, all possible numbers for a particular area become the population from which a sample is drawn. This method also eliminates the problems caused by unlisted numbers. In his review of different techniques, Garofalo concluded that the results of exploratory efforts show random-digit telephone interviewing to be "a promising, relatively low-cost technique for conducting victim surveys" (1977:23).

The mail questionnaire is less expensive than the in-person interview and may have some advantages, such as greater privacy and greater time for responding. However, victimization researchers feel the mail questionnaire technique results in less reliable and less valid information than the interview because it produces lower response rates and because it does not allow for probing and clarification of questions.

We have noted that self-report surveys have several limitations; most apply to victimization surveys as well. Savitz, Lalli, and Rosen (1977:11) have summarized the problems of victimization surveys as follows:

1. Memory decay. The respondent forgets personal or familial victimization

experiences or thinks that they occurred before or after the study year, while in fact they occurred within the research period.

2. Lack of knowledge by respondent. Head-of-household respondent never knew of some or all of the victimizations experienced by other household members.

3. Deliberate exaggeration and deliberate failure to admit victimization. The respondent, in effect, lies and recites events that did not take place or consciously fails to reveal victimization which had occurred.

4. Telescoping of criminal events into the study period. The respondent states that a specific crime took place within the research year when, in fact, it occurred before or after the period being investigated. Brantingham and Brantingham (1984) suggest that the problem of telescoping may inflate victimization rates by as much as 20 percent, leading to higher estimates of crime than actual rates.

5. Victimization not a criminal event. The act thought to be, and described as a crime, but upon close examination, it is found not to be a legal offense.

Victimization researchers have tried to cope with these problems by limiting the time period covered by the survey (for example, the NCS chose the preceding six months to help avoid memory decay and telescoping), by carefully describing criminal victimizations, and by cross-checking reports by different members of households.

Limitations of Victimization Survey Data

As with police and court data and self-report studies, victimization surveys have certain drawbacks. If we wish to focus exclusively on juvenile delinquency, victimization surveys are quite limiting. While the age of the victim can be ascertained, the age of the offender can only be estimated where there was face-to-face contact. Of course, in those instances where knowledge of the offender is a complete unknown, such as in most property theft, there is no way of determining the age of the offender.

A second major problem with NCS data is that it focuses exclusively on Part I offenses (with the obvious exclusion of homicide). That is, questions deal only with rape, robbery, assault, burglary, personal and household larceny, and motor vehicle theft. Murder and kidnapping are not covered, and commercial robbery and burglary were dropped in 1977. Victimless crimes, such as drug abuse, prostitution, and gambling are excluded. Similarly, all Part II offenses such as fraud, embezzlement, forgery, and driving under the influence of drugs are excluded. Thus, NCS offenses are heavily geared toward those offenses that are perceived by the FBI to be "serious." Conversely, white-collar offenses, such as income tax evasion, price-fixing, or shoddy business ethics are completely ignored.

Penick and Owens (1976) mention several environmental factors that are not studied by NCS but that contribute to victimization, such as racial composition in the surrounding area, crime rates, median income of the community, and location of the victimization in relation to the center of town. Other critics have suggested that NCS data are too focused on the description of the victimization and show little concern for the explanation of the victimization (O'Brien, 1985). Sparks (1981) suggested that more educated respondents are more cooperative and more at ease in interview situations, and thus able to recall more victimizations. Hence, while NCS data offer a new and innovative way to study crime, they have their shortcomings just as *UCR* and self-report data do.

Patterns Based on Victimization Data

Volume. Most researchers agree that NCS data record fewer victimizations than actually occur. Memory decay, embarrassment in reporting crimes, coding errors, and other limitations mean that NCS data do not provide a totally accurate picture of crime. Despite these limitations, NCS data suggest that only 37 percent of all victimizations and less than half of violent crimes are reported to the police. A comparison between the amount of crime reported in the *Uniform Crime Reports* for 1989 and for the National Crime Survey for the same year are given in Figure 4-10. For comparable offenses, the *UCR* data show over 14 million crimes while NCS show nearly 33 million, more than twice as many offenses.

According to the 1989 NCS findings, 56 percent of all violent crime victimizations were reported to the police, but only 29 percent of personal theft victimizations (purse snatchings, pocket picking and larceny, without contact) were reported, as were 41 percent of household crimes (burglary, household larceny and motor vehicle theft). NCS victims indicated that they were most likely to report a completed motor vehicle theft (76 percent). Even in instances of extremely serious crimes, some victims are reluctant to report these to the police. For example, only 51 percent of completed rapes and 51 percent of robberies were reported.

There has been a slight upward trend in the percent of all victimizations reported to the police from a low of 32 percent in 1973 to a high of 37 percent in 1989. However, their has been no significant upward trend for the percent of rapes reported with a smaller percentage (51 percent) the last five years of the NCS reporting than in the first five years of the survey (54 percent). Because the percentage reporting in 1985 reached a high of 61 percent it appeared that rape was being increasingly reported but that high was not maintained and there has been no overall upward trend.

Figure 4-10

Amount of Crime Reported in *UCR* and NCS Data for 1989

	UCR	NCS	Ratio NCS/*UCR*
Rape	94,500	135,000	1.4:1
Robbery	578,330	1,092,000	1.9:1
Aggravated Assault	951,710	1,665,000	1.8:1
Burglary	3,168,200	5,352,000	1.7:1
Larceny-Theft	7,872,400	22,784,000	2.9:1
Motor Vehicle Theft	1,564,800	1,820,000	1.2:1
Total	14,229,940	32,848,000	2.3:1

Source: *Uniform Crime Reports,* 1989; U.S. Department of Justice, *Criminal Victimization in the United States,* 1989.

The major reasons people give for not reporting crimes to the police are 1) the object was recovered without calling them (26 percent), 2) the crime was reported to some official other than police (15.5 percent), 3) "lack of proof" (11 percent), 4) the crime was a private matter (7.3 percent), or 5) that police would not want to be bothered or could do nothing anyway (6.5 percent). About 15 percent respond that it was a "private matter" as an explanation for their failure to report rape victimizations to the police (Bureau of Justice Statistics, 1988).

Time. Since victimization survey data have been collected systematically on a national scale only since 1972, such data are not available for those time periods during which police data indicate sizable increases in crime in the United States (see Chapter 3). However, in 1974 the Law Enforcement Assistance Administration began publishing comparisons of victimization survey results over time. The most recent data from the Bureau of Justice Statistics shows the extent of criminal victimizations between 1973 and 1989 (U.S. Department of Justice, 1990). Figure 4-11 shows the trends in victimization rates for select crimes between 1973 and 1989. Household larceny, personal larceny and household burglary have shown rather substantial declines in recent years. In contrast, there has

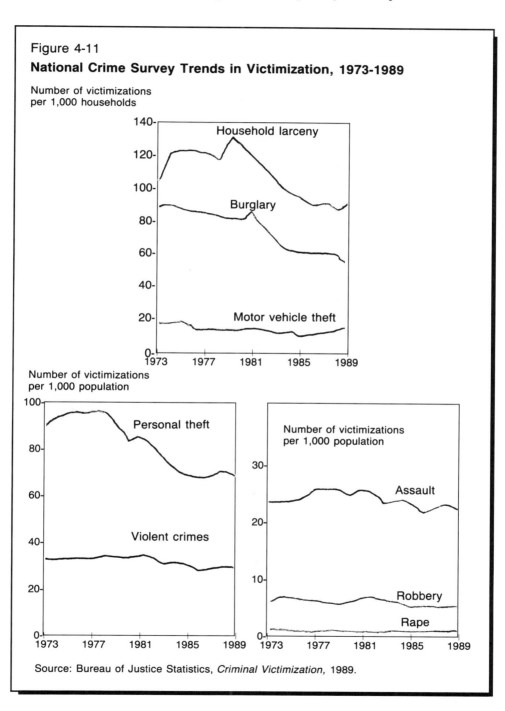

Figure 4-11

National Crime Survey Trends in Victimization, 1973-1989

Number of victimizations
per 1,000 households

Number of victimizations
per 1,000 population

Source: Bureau of Justice Statistics, *Criminal Victimization,* 1989.

been little change in violent crimes or motor vehicle theft during that same period. Looking more specifically at violent crimes for 1973 to 1989, assaults increased slightly in the 1970s and then declined in the 1980s. When graphed with other crimes robbery and rape look particularly flat with no appreciable change in the 17-year reporting period, although 1981 was a peak year for both offenses.

In Figure 4-12 we have graphed the NCS rape victimization rate and the *UCR* victimization rate together to illustrate a major disparity in the image of crime suggested by the two bodies of data. The trend in *UCR* rape rates is upward while the trend in NCS rates is downward! Such disparate patterns are often attributed to changes in propensities to report crimes to the police but we have already seen that there has been no comparable upward trend in the percent of rape victimizations allegedly reported. A more likely explanation for the disparity would be a change in official processing of rape cases with fewer cases dismissed as "unfounded" by police (LaFree, 1989). More cases might appear in police statistics as recorded crimes over

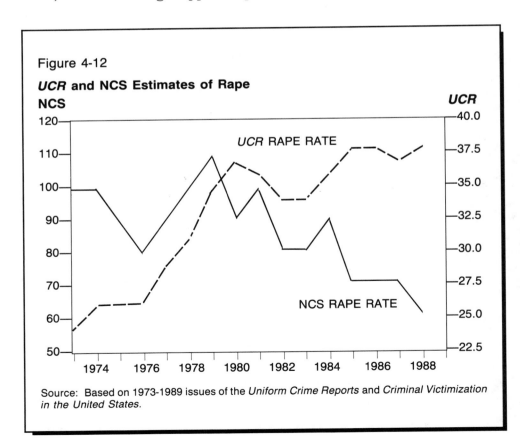

Figure 4-12

UCR and NCS Estimates of Rape

Source: Based on 1973-1989 issues of the *Uniform Crime Reports* and *Criminal Victimization in the United States.*

time even if victimizations were declining. Moreover, the fact that women seem to be less afraid of walking alone at night near their homes (according to national opinion surveys) suggests that the NCS data may more closely approximate trends in actual rapes than the police data (Jensen, 1991). At any rate, the different bodies of data are not perfectly consistent.

The Bureau of Justice Statistics does not offer any suggestions why the victimization rate is declining in the 1980s for property offenses but undoubtedly the declining birth rate and proportion of people under age 30 is a major factor. This declining crime rate found in NCS data mirrors the declining crime rate since 1980 found in *UCR* data. The declining birth rate means fewer persons under the age of 18 and a concomitantly older population. In the United States the median age has increased from 27.9 years in 1970 to 32.3 years in 1989; the percent of the population under age 18 has declined from 34.1 percent in 1970 to less than 26 percent in 1989. These dramatic population changes can exert a significant impact on the crime rate.

Space. Victimization survey data have been collected on a nationwide scale, and victimization rates have been computed for central-city, suburban, and nonmetropolitan areas. As summarized in Figure 4-13, the risk of personal and household victimization is greatest for central-city

Figure 4-13
Criminal Victimization by Setting (Per 1,000 population)

Crimes of violence (rape, robbery, assault)
Central cities	40.3
Suburban areas	23.0
Nonmetropolitan areas	24.5
All areas	28.6

Crimes of theft (personal larceny)
Central cities	79.7
Suburban areas	69.9
Nonmetropolitan areas	50.1
All areas	67.5

Household crimes (burglary, larceny, motor vehicle theft)
Central cities	223.7
Suburban areas	154.8
Nonmetropolitan areas	134.9
All areas	171.4

Source: U.S. Department of Justice. 1987. *Criminal Victimization in the United States.* Washington, D.C.: Bureau of Justice Statistics.

residents, followed by suburbanites, with nonmetropolitan residents having the lowest risks of victimization. The variation in these data is consistent with the *Uniform Crime Reports*. This consistency extends to variations by type of offenses as well. The biggest differences in victimization rates between metropolitan and nonmetropolitan settings are found for robbery and motor vehicle theft.

Perceived Gender, Age, and Race of Offenders. The National Crime Surveys have gathered data on perceived characteristics of the offender(s), but since such information depends on victims' perceptions, it is subject to greater error and distortion than other victimization survey findings. Such perceptions do, however, provide another source of data in constructing an image of crime and delinquency. Needless to say, no information can be gathered on property offenses where the victim is unknown.

Consistent with police statistics and self-report survey data, victimization data show the vast majority of offenders in personal crimes of violence to be male. For lone offenders in 1988, males were perceived to be the offender in 85.6 percent of the crimes and females 13.7 percent of the time (with 0.7 percent unknown). For multiple offenders the offenders were all male in about 80 percent of victimizations.

John Laub (1983) has plotted the rates of personal offending based on the estimated age of the offender using National Crime Survey data for 1973 through 1980, and those data are quite consistent with both official statistics and self-report studies. According to Laub, the rate was stable or declining for offenders estimated to be 12 to 17 years of age. In fact, the biggest decline is for the most recent years in the analysis. The rate of personal offending was estimated to be 5,121 per 100,000 persons in the 12 through 17 age group in 1979 as compared to 4,388 in 1980. "Personal" offending includes those victimizations where there was contact or observation of the offender, and age of offender was based on victim estimates for lone offenders and estimates for the oldest offender when there were multiple offenders. Hence, despite the amount of attention devoted to the problem of youth violence and youth crime, Laub's analysis was contrary to the tendency to view juvenile offenders as a growing dimension of the crime problem in the 1970s.

We could not update Laub's analysis exactly because the NCS data available for 1980-87 provide detail on estimated age of offender for crimes of violence only and do not include a breakdown for the juvenile age group. An approximation where offense rates are presented for persons aged 12 through 20 and for persons 21 and over seems to support Laub's overall assessment that the rates have been relatively flat over time for both age groups.

Victimization data on the perceived race of offenders show blacks to be disproportionately identified as offenders. Although in 1987 only 12 percent of the population was black, Hindelang's analysis of NCS data for that year showed that in 30 percent of rape victimizations, 49 percent of robberies, 27 percent of aggravated assaults, and 20 percent of simple assaults, the offender was identified as black. NCS data also show that crimes of violence are predominantly intraracial; that is, blacks tend to victimize blacks, and whites victimize whites. Figure 4-14 shows the percent distribution of single-offender victimizations, based on race of victims, by type of crime, and perceived race of offenders. In those instances where a white person was raped, 78.4 percent of the time the offender was white and in only 14.4 percent of the cases was the offender black. Conversely, when a black person was raped, 70.4 percent of the time the offender was black and in 11.1 percent of the instances the offender was white. For robbery, white-on-white accounted for 53.4 percent and black-on-black 86.0 percent. Finally, for assault, white-on-white amounted to 81.8 percent and black-on-black was 81.7 percent. Thus, crime is essentially an intraracial phenomenon and instances where it is interracial are relatively rare. The possible exception to this pattern is the robbery of a white victim, but even in this instance a majority of the time the offender is also white.

Figure 4-14

Single-Offender Victimization: Perceived Race of Offender by Type of Crime and Race of Victim

Type of crime and race of victim	Perceived race of offenders			
	White	Black	Other-not known	Total
Rape				
White	78.4%	14.4%	7.2%	100.0%
Black	11.1%	70.4%	18.5%	100.0%
Robbery				
White	53.4%	37.9%	8.7%	100.0%
Black	8.1%	86.0%	5.9%	100.0%
Assault				
White	81.8%	12.2%	6.0%	100.0%
Black	13.0%	81.7%	5.3%	100.0%

Source: U.S. Department of Justice. 1987. *Criminal Victimization in the United States.* Washington, D.C.: Bureau of Justice Statistics.

Who Are the Victims?

In addition to providing another source of information on the distribution of crime and delinquency and a means of assessing the perceived characteristics of offenders, victimization data have been central to the growth of interest in *victimology*, that is, the study of victims. A considerable amount of descriptive detail is now available on the characteristics of victims. In fact, so much detailed information is available that it is not possible to summarize all of it in this text. The information provided by the U.S. Department of Justice suggests that victims of crime tend to be young, rather than old, male rather than female, black rather than white, poor rather than rich, and of low educational status rather than high educational status. For example, the male victimization rate for crimes of violence (rape, robbery, and assault) was 37 victims per 1,000 males while for females it was nearly half, 21.8 per 1,000 females. For crimes of theft, the male rate was 72.6 victims out of 1,000 males, while for females it was 65 per 1,000 females. For individuals aged 16 to 19, the victimization rate for crimes of violence was 73.8 per 1,000, while for those 65 or older it was only 3.9 per 1,000. Similarly, for crimes of theft, the 16-19 age category recorded 115.3 victimizations per 1,000, and the 65 or older group, 19.6 per 1,000. For blacks the victimization rate was 36 per 1,000 for violent crimes, for whites it was 28.2 per 1,000. In terms of income, those earning less than $7,500 per year had a victimization rate of 50.2 per 1,000 for violent crimes and 71.2 per 1,000 for crimes of theft, while those earning $50,000 or more had a violence victimization rate of 20.5 per 1,000 and a theft victimization rate of 78.1 per 1,000. Finally, those who had five to seven years of schooling had a violence victimization rate of 38.1 per 1,000, while those with four or more years of college had a victimization rate of 17.6 per 1,000.

While the tendency is to view teenagers as the "offenders" when depicting the crime problem, they also have the highest rates of victimization. The Bureau of Justice Statistics has issued two reports on "Teenage Victims" (1986, 1991) based on National Crime Survey data. The 1986 report showed the victimization of teenagers to parallel the nation as a whole between 1973 and 1984 with rates of violent victimization stable and rates of larceny victimization declining. The exception to stable or declining rates was simple assault, which rose about 21 percent from 1973 through 1984. This exception is interesting because "fights" increased in the study of high school seniors summarized earlier while aggravated assault ("hurting someone badly") did not. The pattern is similar in victimization data.

The 1991 report reveals a major disparity between the trends over time for teenagers as compared to persons aged 20 or older. While rates of violent victimization remain relatively stable for older age groups, they have been increasing since the mid-1980s for juveniles (see Figure 4-15). Thus, the increase in violence noted since the mid-1980s in police data is paralleled by an increase in violence in victimization data. However, it is teenagers who are the victims of the increase, not adults. Other interesting facts about teenage victims are listed below:

1. About one-half of violent teenage victimizations and 63 percent of theft victimizations occur at school.

2. Crimes against teenagers are less likely to be reported to law enforcement authorities than crimes against adults. A major reason for this disparity is that other authorities were told (school officials, parents, etc.).

3. Black teenagers had homicide rates several times higher than the rates for white teenagers. A much greater proportion of black victims were killed by a gun than white victims.

4. Blacks, males, and teenagers living in central cities were more likely to experience violence than their white, female, or suburban and rural counterparts.

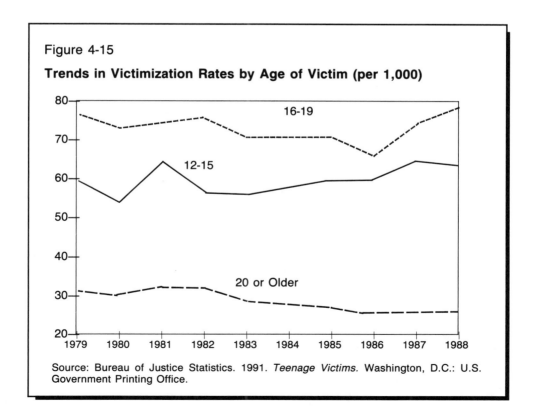

Figure 4-15

Trends in Victimization Rates by Age of Victim (per 1,000)

Source: Bureau of Justice Statistics. 1991. *Teenage Victims.* Washington, D.C.: U.S. Government Printing Office.

Analyses of victimization data have noted the similarity or "homogeneity" in the backgrounds of victims and offenders. The most highly victimized groups (the young, blacks, males, people of low income and with little education) tend to be the same groups with high offense rates. Conversely, the least victimized categories (older, white, female, high income and education) tend to have the lowest offense rates as well. Some theorists have argued that this similarity reflects the tendency of people with certain characteristics to come into close proximity with offenders (Cohen et al., 1981). A recent analysis of the "Monitoring the Future" data (Jensen and Brownfield, 1986) found that much of the sex difference in victimization reflects sex differences in delinquent activities. Self-admitted involvement in delinquent activities is one of the strongest correlates of victimization. The high risk of victimization encountered by males appears to be associated with high male involvement in risky and deviant routines. The types of situations providing the opportunities and situational pressures and pulls conducive to offense activity also provide a high risk of victimization. That study suggests that the explanation of victimization involves some of the same circumstances and variables as explanations of offending.

The 1991 Bureau of Justice report on teenage victims suggests that homogeneity is even greater for teenagers than for adults. Violence with teenage victims is more likely than violence with adult victims to involve offenders of the same race, sex or age. Moreover, the offender is more likely to be at least a casual acquaintance of the victim when a teenager is victimized than when an adult is victimized.

Summary

We began this chapter with Haney and Gold's statement that "the delinquent is a myth." When characteristics that tend to be associated with delinquency are abstracted and assigned to a "typical" delinquent as if they were the identifying properties of a distinct type of person, the depictions that result take on a mythical quality. Such attempts to summarize and generalize are oversimplifications of complex situations. Tentative generalizations about probable relationships are often transformed into "facts" about the definitive and unquestionable nature of delinquency in American society. In this chapter and Chapter 3, we have attempted to summarize very complex situations at the risk of some oversimplification. However, the images we have constructed are far less simplistic than those that abound in most proclamations about the "facts" of delinquency.

In this chapter we have tried to summarize a body of self-report survey research, as well as a body of research based on a more recently developed technique for studying crime — the victimization survey. Some conclusions suggested by the data produced by these two research methods conflict with patterns suggested by police and juvenile court statistics. However, there is also a surprising amount of consistency in some of the patterns of variation suggested by different bodies of data. Below are several statements that are consistent with at least two types of data. We deem these statements to be "consistent with the data" rather than "supported" or "demonstrated by the data" because they often go beyond the specific information available. For example, victimization survey data do not bear directly on statements about delinquency; this is often the case for national crime statistics as well. Thus these statements are not statements of fact but, rather, tentative generalizations that appear at this time to be justified:

1. Offense rates are higher among central-city youths than among youths in smaller communities and rural settings.
2. Offense rates are higher among youths living in changing or unstable neighborhoods and communities than in more stable settings.
3. Offense rates are higher for males than females, with the greatest disparities involving the most serious offenses.
4. The gender difference was far greater in the past than it is now.
5. Offense rates are higher for blacks than whites for offenses involving violence or major theft. Asian Americans have the lowest rates and Hispanics fall between Anglo and black youth.
6. Young adults and juveniles account for a disproportionate amount of crime, but offenses involving theft tend to peak in younger age groups than offenses involving interpersonal violence (rape, assault, robbery).
7. Offense rates for juveniles have been stable or declining in "recent" years, but the self-report data suggest such a pattern for an earlier time period than do victimization or police data.

We present these statements with the warning that further research may negate or further qualify each and every one of them. However, these patterns or images have been suggested in enough studies using different methods to qualify as some of the strongest candidates for "facts" about juvenile delinquency.

References

Axenroth, J. B. 1983. "Social Class and Delinquency in Cross-Cultural Perspective." *Journal of Research* in Crime and Delinquency 20 (July):164-182.
Bidwell, C. E. 1975. "Commentary." In N. J. Demerath III, et al., (eds.), *Social Policy and Sociology*. New York: Academic Press.

Bohannan, P. (ed.) 1960. *African Homicide and Suicide*. Princeton: Princeton University Press.

Brantingham, P., and P. Brantingham. 1984. *Patterns In Crime*. New York: Macmillan.

Bureau of Justice Statistics. 1986, 1991. *Teenage Victims*. Washington, DC: U.S. Government Printing Office.

_____. 1990. *Criminal Victimization 1988, 1989*. Washington, DC: U.S. Government Printing Office.

Chambliss, W. J., and R. H. Nagasawa. 1969. "On the Validity of Official Statistics: A Comparative Study of White, Black and Japanese High School Boys." *Journal of Research in Crime and Delinquency* 6 (January): 71-77.

Clark, J. P., and E. P. Wenninger. 1962. "Socioeconomic Class and Area as Correlates of Illegal Behavior among Juveniles." *American Sociological Review* 27 (December):826-34.

Cohen, L. E., J. R. Kluegal, and K. C. Land. 1981. "Social Inequality and Criminal Victimization." *American Sociological Review* 46 (October): 505-24.

Comer, J. P. 1985. "Black Violence and Public Policy." In L.A. Curtis (ed.) *American Violence and Public Policy*. New Haven: Yale University Press.

Devine, J. A., J. F. Sheley, and M. D. Smith. 1988. "Macroeconomic and Social Control Policy Influence on Crime Rate Changes, 1948-1985." *American Sociological Review* 53:407-20.

Duke, D. L., and P. M. Duke. 1978. "The Prediction of Delinquency in Girls." *Journal of Research and Development in Education* 11:18-33.

Elliott, D. S., and H. L. Voss. 1974. *Delinquency and Dropout*. Lexington, MA: DC Heath.

Elliott, D. S., and S. Ageton. 1980. "Reconciling Race and Class Differences in Self-Reported and Official Estimates of Delinquency." *American Sociological Review* 45(February):95-110.

Elliott, D. S., and D. Huizinga. 1983. "Social Class and Delinquent Behavior in a National Youth Panel, 1976-1980." *Criminology* 21:149-77.

Elliott, D. S., D. Huizinga, and S. Ageton. 1985. *Explaining Delinquency and Drug Use*. Beverly Hills: Sage.

Ennis, P. H. 1967. *Criminal Victimization in the United States: A Report of a National Survey*. Washington, DC: U.S. Government Printing Office.

Erickson, M. L., and L. T. Empey. 1963. "Court Records, Undetected Delinquency and Decision-Making." *Journal of Criminal Law, Criminology and Police Science* 54 (December): 456-69.

Felson, R. B., and A. E. Liska. 1984. *Deviant Behavior* 5: 1-10.

Flanagan, T. J., and K. Maguire. 1989. *Sourcebook of Criminal Justice Statistics*. Washington, DC: U.S. Government Printing Office.

Fors, S. W., and D. G. Rojek. 1983. "The Social and Demographic Correlates of Adolescent Drug Use Patterns." *Journal of Drug Education*. 13:205-22.

Garofalo, J. 1977. *Local Victim Surveys: A Review of the Issues*. U.S. Department of Justice. Washington, DC: U.S. Government Printing Office.

Goe, W. R., T. L. Napier, and D. C. Bachtel. 1985. "Use of Marijuana Among High School Students." *Rural Sociology* 50 (Fall):409-26.

Gold, M. 1970. *Delinquency Behavior in an American City*. Belmont, CA: Wadsworth.

Gold, M., and D. J. Reimer. 1974. "Changing Patterns of Delinquent Behavior Among Americans 13 to 16 Years Old, 1967-1972." Ann Arbor: Institute For Social Research.

Gomme, I. M., M. E. Morton, and W. G. West. 1984. "Rates, Types, and Patterns of Male and Female Delinquency in an Ontario County." *Canadian Journal of Criminology* 26 (July): 313-44.

Gould, Leroy. 1969. "Who Defines Delinquency: A Comparison of Self-Reported and Officially-Reported Indices of Delinquency in Three Racial Groups." *Social Problems* 16 (Winter): 325-36.

Hagan, J., A. R. Gillis, and J. Simpson. 1985. "The Class Structure of Gender and Delinquency: Toward a Power-Control Theory of Common Delinquent Behavior." *American Journal of Sociology.* 90: 1151-78.

_____. 1987. "Class in the Household: A Power Control Theory of Gender and Delinquency." *American Journal of Sociology* 92 (January): 788-816.

Haney, B., and M. Gold. 1973. "The Juvenile Delinquent Nobody Knows." *Psychology Today* (September):49-55.

Haskell, M. R., and L. Yablonsky. 1974. *Crime and Delinquency.* Chicago: Rand McNally.

Heitgerd, J. L. and R. J. Bursik, Jr. 1987. "Extracommunity Dynamics and the Ecology of Delinquency." *American Journal of Sociology* 92:775-87

Hindelang, M. J., T. Hirschi, and J. Weis. 1979. "Correlates of Delinquency: The Illusion of Discrepancy Between Self-Report and Official Measures." *American Sociological Review* 44:995-1014.

Hindelang, M. J., T. Hirschi, and J.G. Weis. 1981. *Measuring Delinquency.* Beverly Hills, CA: Sage.

Hirschi, T. 1969. *Causes of Delinquency.* Berkeley: University of California Press.

Illinois Institute for Juvenile Research. 1973. *Juvenile Delinquency in Illinois.* Chicago, IL. Department of Mental Health.

Jamieson, K. M., and T. Flanagan. 1986. *Sourcebook of Criminal Justice Statistics.* Washington, DC: U.S. Government Printing Office.

Jensen, G. F. 1985. "The Truth About Sex and Crime." Paper presented at the Annual Meeting of Arizona Justice Educators, Arizona State University, Tempe.

_____. 1991. "Disparities between Uniform Crime Report and Victim Survey Data on Rape: Alternative Interpretations." Paper presented at the 1991 Convention of The Academy of Criminal Justice Sciences, Nashville, Tennessee.

Jensen, G. F., M. L. Erickson, and J. P. Gibbs. 1978. "Perceived Risk of Punishment and Self-Reported Delinquency." *Social Forces* 57 (September): 57-78.

Jensen, G. F., and R. Eve. 1976. "Sex Differences in Delinquency: An Examination of Popular Sociological Explanations." *Criminology* 13: 427-48.

Jensen, G. F., and D. Brownfield. 1986. "Gender Lifestyles and Victimization: Beyond Routine Activity." *Victims and Violence* 1 (Number 2): 85-99.

Jensen, G. F., J. H. Stauss, and V. W. Harris. 1977. "Crime, Delinquency, and the American Indian." *Human Organization* 36: 252-57.

Johnson, R.E. 1979. *Juvenile Delinquency and Its Origins.* New York: Cambridge Union Press.

_____. 1980. "Social Class and Delinquent Behavior: A New Test." *Criminology* 18:86-93.

Johnston, L. D., J. G. Bachman, and P. M. O'Malley. 1986. *Monitoring the Future*. Ann Arbor: Institute for Social Research-University of Michigan.

_____. 1991. *Monitoring the Future*. Ann Arbor: Institute for Social Research.

Kapsis, R. E. 1978. "Residential Succession and Delinquency: A Test of Shaw and McKay's Theory of Cultural Transmission." *Criminology* 15 (February):459-86.

Krohn, M., G. Waldo, and T. Chiricos. 1975. "Self-reported Delinquency: A Comparison of Structural Interviews and Self-administered Checklists." *Journal of Criminal Law and Criminology* 65:545-55.

LaFree, G. 1989. *Rape and Criminal Justice*. Belmont, CA: Wadsworth.

Laub, J. H. 1983. "Trends in Serious Juvenile Crime." *Criminal Justice and Behavior* 10:485-506.

Murphy, F. J., M. M. Shirley, and H. L. Witmer. 1946. "The Incidence of Hidden Delinquency." *American Journal of Orthopsychiatry* 16 (October):686-95.

Napier, T., D. Bachtel, and M. Carter. 1983. "Factors Associated with Illegal Drug Use in Rural Georgia." *Journal of Drug Education* 13(2):119-40.4

Napier, T., and M. Pratt. 1982. "Frequency of Drug Use Among Rural High School Students." Pp. 104-23 in T. Carter, G. Phillips, J. Donnermeyer, T. Wurschmidt (eds.) *Rural Crime: Integrating Research and Prevention*. Totowa, NJ: Allenheld Osmun Publishing Co.

Norland, S., R. C. Wessel, and N. Shover. 1981. "Masculinity and Delinquency." *Criminology* 19:421-33.

Nye, F. I. 1958. *Family Relationships and Delinquent Behavior*. New York: John Wiley.

Nye, F. I., and J. F. Short, Jr. 1957. "Scaling Delinquent Behavior." *American Sociological Review* 22 (June):326-31.

O'Brien, R. M. 1985. *Crime and Victimization Data*. Beverly Hills, CA: Sage.

Penick, B. K. E. and M. Owens. 1976. *Surveying Crime*. Washington, DC: National Academy of Sciences.

Porterfield, A. L. 1946. *Youth in Trouble*. Fort Worth: Leo Potishman Foundation.

Priyadarsini, S., and C. Hartjen. 1981. "Delinquency and Corrections in India." Pp. 109-23 in G. F. Jensen (ed.), *Sociology of Delinquency*. Beverly Hills, CA: Sage.

Reiss, A. J. 1975. "Inappropriate Theories and Inadequate Methods as Policy Plagues: Self-reported Delinquency and the Law." In N. J. Demerath III, et al., (eds.), *Social Policy and Sociology*. New York: Academic.

Richards, P. 1981. "Quantitative and Qualitative Sex Differences in Middle-Class Delinquency." *Criminology* 18:453-70.

Robison, S.M. 1936. *Can Delinquency Be Measured*? New York: Columbia University Press.

Rojek, D.G. 1983. "Social Status and Delinquency: Do Self-Reports and Official Reports Match?" In G.P. Waldo (ed.), *Measurement Issues in Criminal Justice*. Beverly Hills, CA: Sage Publications.

_____. 1986. A Longitudinal Analysis of Attitudes and Behaviors Related to Drug Involvement. Department of Sociology, University of Georgia.

Rojek, D. G., and S. Fors. 1983. "The Social and Demographic Correlates of Adolescent Drug Use Patterns." *Journal of Drug Education* 13:205-22.

Savitz, L. D., M. Lalli, and L. Rosen. 1977. *City Life and Delinquency-Victimization, Fear of Crime and Gang Membership.* Washington, DC: Office of Juvenile Justice and Delinquency Prevention.

Schwartz, E. E. 1945. "A Community Experiment in the Measurement of Juvenile Delinquency." In *Yearbook, National Probation Association, 1945.* New York: National Probation Association.

Short, J. F., Jr., and F. I. Nye. 1958. "Extent of Unrecorded Juvenile Delinquency: Tentative Conclusions." *Journal of Criminal Law, Criminology and Police Science* 49 (November- December):246-302.

Simcha-Fagin, O., and J. E. Schwartz. 1986. "Neighborhood and Delinquency: An Assessment of Contextual Effects." *Criminology* 24 (November):667-704.

Smith, D. A., and C. A. Visher. 1980. "Sex and Involvement in Deviance/Crime: A Quantitative Review of the Empirical Literature." *American Sociological Review* 45(August):691-701.

Sparks, R. F. 1981. "Surveys of Victimization: An Optimistic Assessment." *Crime and Justice: An Annual Review of Research* 3:1-60.

Thorton, W. E., and J. James. 1979. "Masculinity and Delinquency Revisited." *British Journal of Criminology* 19:225-41.

Time. 1977. "The Youth Crime Plague" (July 11):18-20, 25-28.

Tittle, C. R., and W. J. Villemez. 1977. "Social Class and Criminality." *Social Forces* 56(December):474-502.

Tittle, C. R., W. J. Villemez, and D. Smith. 1978. "The Myth of Social Class and Criminality." *American Sociological Review* 43: 643-56.

U.S. Department of Justice. 1977. *Criminal Victimization in the United States: A Comparison of 1975 and 1976 Findings.* Washington, DC: U.S. Government Printing Office.

_____. 1988. *Criminal Victimization in the United States.* Bureau of Justice Statistics: Washington, DC.

_____. 1990. *Criminal Victimization in the United States.* Bureau of Justice Statistics: Washington, DC.

Weis, J.G. 1983. "Crime Statistics: Reporting Systems and Methods," Pp. 378-91 in Sanford H. Kadish, (ed.), *Encyclopedia of Crime and Justice.* Vol. 1. New York: Free Press.

Will, George. 1988. "Essay." *Time* 111(April):76.

Williams, J. R., and M. Gold. 1972. "From Delinquent Behavior to Official Delinquency." *Social Problems* 20 (Fall):209-29.

chapter 5

Explanations of Delinquency
Body, Mind, and Learning

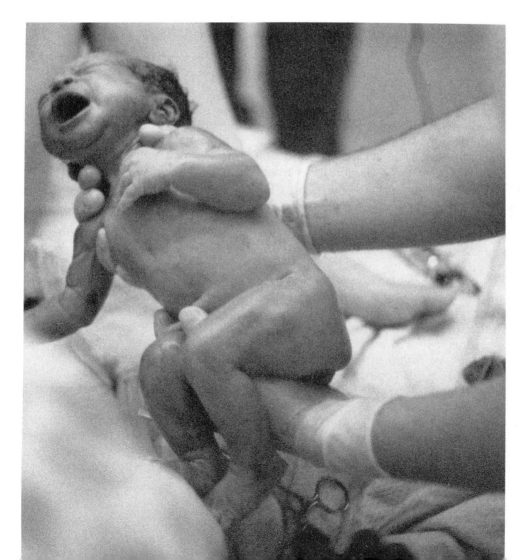

> *At the sight of that skull, I seemed to see all of a sudden, lighted up as a vast plain under a flaming sky, the problem of the nature of the criminal—an atavistic being who reproduces in his person the ferocious instincts of primitive humanity and the inferior animals. Thus were explained anatomically the enormous jaws, high cheek bones, prominent superciliary arches, solitary lines in the palms, extreme size of the orbits, handle-shaped or sessile ears found in criminals, savages and apes, insensibility to pain, extremely acute sight, tattooing, excessive idleness, love of orgies, and the irresistible craving of evil for its own sake, the desire not only to extinguish life in the victim, but to mutilate the corpse, tear its flesh and drink its blood.*
>
> —Cesare Lombroso, *Crime, Its Causes and Remedies*, 1911

Few people would want to encounter the primitive, inhuman, atavistic creature described by Cesare Lombroso. However, such atavistic criminals would be hard to avoid since Lombroso estimated some 40 percent of the criminal population to be evolutionary throwbacks exhibiting some combination of atavistic characteristics. Of course, we have learned a great deal about crime since Lombroso's observations were published in 1911 and few of his conclusions have stood the test of time.

Yet, the image of the criminal as fundamentally inhuman, biologically, psychologically, and socially, is still a common theme in popular culture. Any fan of old horror movies is familiar with the notion that the body parts of a criminal are so infused with evil that even a transplanted hand can compel an otherwise law-abiding concert pianist to murder and mayhem. Notions such as "the criminal mind," "compulsion," "psychopath," "depravity," and "disease" often conjure up the same sort of images. The explanation of criminality is found in characteristics of offenders so terrible as to disqualify them from civilized society and the human race.

Is such an image correct? Is there something fundamentally different about people who commit crimes which compels them to break laws? Do juvenile offenders differ from nonoffenders in their biological or psychological makeup? In this chapter we consider attempts to explain criminality and delinquency in terms of biological and psychological characteristics of individuals as well as attempts to identify the learning mechanisms resulting in delinquent behavior. We concentrate primarily on theories that have been advanced as "scientific"—that is, anchored in fact and verifiable by means of observation.

Searching for Answers

In order to evaluate theory and research on delinquency effectively, we must first consider points of view on how we should go about finding answers. Some people believe we can arrive at the answers by asking other people their opinions or by "discussing" the issues. Some believe we can find answers by asking those practitioners who deal with delinquents every day. Others believe that such questions can only be answered through carefully conducted, systematic research. Moreover, in seeking answers people have different expectations about what constitutes a satisfactory explanation, and understanding those expectations will help us to understand different ways of seeking answers. Lombroso was seeking answers in a manner he considered to be scientific and objective when he had his flash of insight into "criminal atavism." Yet, in terms of the standards for good research in contemporary criminology his work has not withstood critical evaluation.

Public Opinion

Most of us are familiar with public opinion polls that attempt to assess the beliefs, attitudes, and values of the American populace. One such poll in 1989 by George Gallup asked a representative sample of American adults (twenty-one years of age and older), "In your opinion, what factors are most responsible for crime in the U.S. today?" The most chosen factors were drugs, unemployment, and breakdown of family values. Similarly, another public opinion survey focusing on juvenile crime found that 87 percent agreed that there was a steady and alarming increase in serious juvenile crime; 57 percent agreed that sending juveniles to a correctional institution serves as a deterrent; and 89 percent felt that increasing employment opportunities would prevent a lot of serious crime. These polls give us perspective on public beliefs but do not necessarily correspond with reality measured in other ways. Public opinion is often wrong. For example, in a survey conducted by the Hearst Corporation, over half of the respondents felt a district attorney's job is to defend those who cannot afford a lawyer, some 55 percent felt a person must prove his or her innocence in criminal court, and over two-thirds felt if you are found innocent of a crime, the state can appeal the case for a new trial. Obviously, in the Hearst survey, the majority were wrong!

While public opinion polls are informative in assessing the mood or the pulse of the country, they do not necessarily reflect what is true or accurate. Particularly in the area of crime and delinquency, public opinion can be strongly influenced by such social background characteristics as age, occupation, religion, and race.

Expert Testimony and Practical Experience

When a news reporter sets out to get information on a topic, the opinion of "experts" is likely to be a major source. Some people are considered experts because of the positions they occupy, regardless of any additional qualifications based on experience. For example, a nominee for Director of the Office of Juvenile Justice and Delinquency Prevention under President Reagan was unable to define the word delinquency when questioned by a Congressional committee but was ultimately approved for the position (Cerf and Navasky, 1984).

A second rationale for according legitimacy to some people as experts is the amount of "practical experience" they have had in working with criminals and delinquents. The assumption that experience will provide the answers has its shortcomings as well. For example, J. Edgar Hoover was the first Director of the FBI, serving in that position for much of its history. While there was mounting evidence that organized crime and Mafia activities were a major dimension of the crime problem in the United States, Hoover viewed such beliefs as "baloney" and claimed that the conception of organized crime as a national problem was the invention of imaginative crime writers. One crime historian contends that when faced with mounting evidence of mob activities on a national scale the FBI started referring to organized crime as "La Cosa Nostra" in order "to get Hoover off the hook" (Hammer, 1989).

Government commissions often seek information on topics by soliciting expert testimony but such solicitations can be stacked for or against a particular "explanation" to arrive at the desired conclusion. For example, the 1986 report on pornography issued by the United States Attorney General came to a very different conclusion than an earlier 1970 Commission on Obscenity and Pornography. The 1986 Commission, unlike the 1970 Commission, saw pornography as inherently harmful and called for the vigorous enforcement of pornography laws. While the 1970 Commission had a budget of 2 million dollars and spent two years on its report, the 1986 Commission had a budget of only $500,000 (sixteen times less than the 1970 Commission expressed in 1970 dollars) and spent one year gathering data. The 1986 Commission pointed with pride to the fact that they obtained their information from "experienced" authorities in public hearings as well as written statements. This 1986 Commission was criticized for "stacking the deck" by selecting eleven commission members whose opinions coincided with the administration's views and for soliciting written statements from individuals and organizations who were staunchly opposed to pornography. The meaning of being "experienced" is highly subjective and, as exemplified by the two different pornography commissions, the conclusions reached by experts and experienced professionals can be radically different.

Requirements for Answering Causal Questions

If public opinion, expert testimony, and practical experience are not sufficient for identifying causes of crime and delinquency, then how do we decide between conflicting points of view? While there is considerable debate and controversy over the whole issue of causation, there does seem to be some agreement in the social sciences and criminology that certain minimum requirements must be met before any argument that some condition causes some other condition can be accepted as convincing (Hirschi and Selvin, 1967). These minimum requirements involve the determination of association, nonspuriousness, and causal order.

Association

The first requirement in trying to establish causality is that the conditions must be correlated, or associated, with one another in a probabilistic sense. For example, if divorce is seen as a cause of delinquency, then it needs to be shown that children of divorced parents have a higher tendency to violate the law than the children of parents who are not divorced. It would not be enough merely to show that a large proportion of teenagers who come to the attention of the court happen to come from "broken" families. Further, is it a bias in the juvenile justice system that inadvertently results in more children of divorced parents appearing in juvenile court, or are there in fact behavioral differences in children of divorced and non-divorced parents? The issue in demonstrating an association is whether the probability is greater in one circumstance than in the other. For example, the Journal of the American Medical Association (JAMA) published an article in 1971 written by two physicians, Harold Kolansky and William Moore on the adverse effects of marijuana. This 1971 article cited an earlier article focusing on twelve heavy marijuana smokers. All twelve of these marijuana users showed signs of "acute toxic psychosis." Kolansky and Moore expanded their study to thirty-eight patients. What they found was nothing less than terrifying: psychosis, suicidal attempts, ego decomposition, and sexual promiscuity. The authors concluded that: "there is, in our patients, a demonstration of an interruption of normal psychological adolescent growth processes following the use of marijuana; as a consequence the adolescent may reach chronological adulthood without achieving adult mental functioning or emotional responsiveness" (Kolansky and Moore, 1971:492).

Kolansky and Moore did not demonstrate that there was an *association* between marijuana and psychosis. Rather, they had a sample of thirty-eight individuals who were experiencing psychological problems, many had used multiple drugs, and no attempt was made to measure the amount of marijuana consumed, other than asserting that "most of the 38 patients in this study smoked marijuana two or more times weekly" (p. 487). This study was seriously flawed in numerous ways (see Goode, 1972), and from a scientific perspective, it did not demonstrate any basic relationship between marijuana use and psychiatric impairment. However, this study has been cited repeatedly as demonstrating the dangers of marijuana use (which is not to imply that marijuana is not harmful).

We used the word "probability" previously when discussing the search for causes because researchers generally search for variations in the probability of crime or delinquency in a large number of cases. If we focus on specific individuals we can find a wide range of statements about why particular individuals broke the law. In fact, our legal system is based on an ideology of individual motivational causes. An important factor in the search for suspects is the establishment of a motive, or reason, why a particular individual might have committed a crime, and the determination of guilt is supposed to be based on standards more definite than mere probabilities (for example, guilt beyond a reasonable doubt). In contrast, criminologists are generally interested in identifying factors or conditions that increase the probability of crime or delinquency in a population. Such factors or conditions may not always result in delinquency, and delinquency may not always follow from those factors or conditions. In short, as contemporary sociological criminologists, we do not presume to be searching for what are called "necessary and sufficient" causes. If we found some characteristic or circumstance that always resulted in delinquency and if we determined that delinquency never occurred unless that characteristic or circumstance was present, then we would have identified a necessary and sufficient cause. That is, we would have found *the* explanation and would have absolute certainty of the presence or absence of delinquency. However, no one has done so yet, and it would be safe to predict that no one is likely to do so in the future. Rather, we are likely to find conditions that "tend" to generate delinquency — that is, that increase the probability of delinquency. It might be scientifically exciting to find necessary and sufficient causes, but we do not expect such a discovery in examining human behavior.

For some people this is rather unsettling. Those who study the physical sciences often deal with laws that result in predictions that hover close to 100 percent accuracy. An apple will always fall to the ground with a precise acceleration, and water will boil at the same number of degrees Fahrenheit at the same altitude every time. But the world of the social scientist is not so precise. Political scientists can study election candidates carefully and often arrive at an election result that is "too close to call." Similarly, psychologists can observe and evaluate a person for an extended period of time and still not predict when a suicide will occur. In dealing with human behavior we are dealing with many unknowns and we cannot (and in a Democratic society should not) control all of the social forces that are impinging on a person as if we were physicists studying the law of gravity.

Nonspuriousness

A second requirement in advancing a causal argument is to assess the possibility that two conditions are only *spuriously* (superficially) related. Even when we can empirically demonstrate some measure of association between event A and event B, it is conceivable that the relationship is coincidental or misleading for one reason or another.

Some spurious relationships are totally due to changing coincidences, with no causal or logical connection between the variables under consideraion. For example, it might be possible to show some degree of statistical association between the volume of smoke in German steel mills and the number of cloistered nuns in Australia. There is no logical reason for there to be any connection between these two variables, but if by some coincidence there is, we may dismiss it as a random, spurious relationship.

Another type of spuriousness arises when two conditions are associated because of a connection with some third condition. Two variables, X and Y, may be related only because of some association with a third variable, Z. For example, the finding that adolescents with delinquent records watch more violent programs on television than adolescents without delinquent records does not demonstrate a causal connection between violent TV programs and delinquency. What an adolescent watches on TV and what he or she does may coincide without being causally related. Both could reflect the operation of other influences, such as parental supervision, peer group pressure, or success in school. Although it is difficult to anticipate all arguments of spuriousness, a careful thinker will anticipate as many as possible.

Once again, we should note that a concern for identifying spurious relationships is not an esoteric concern of "nit-picking" scientists. If two variables are only spuriously related, then changing one will not have any effect on the other. If other conditions are accounting for both, then it is those other conditions that will make a difference.

Causal Order

A theorist or researcher must also confront the issue of causal order. If two conditions, characteristics, or phenomena are associated, and the relationship is nonspurious, then we will want to know which caused which—that is, the causal order, or the sequence of interrelations. In everyday terms this is the issue of which comes first, the chicken or the egg. For example, if incarcerated offenders were found to be anxious,

---

Box 5-1

What kind of cause of delinquency is the band director assuming?

The following data are based on a survey of high school students. Is the probability of delinquency affected by band membership? Is band membership a causal force inhibiting delinquency in this high school?

Percent of Band and Non-Band High School Students Reporting At Least One Delinquent Offense

	Band	Non-Band
Theft	37%	52%
Vandalism, fights, joyriding	37%	52%
Hard drugs	13%	21%
Marijuana	40%	57%
Drunk	40%	56%
Smoking	41%	49%
	(N = 67)	(N = 161)

---

fearful, and depressed, someone might argue that anxiety, fear, and depression cause or facilitate involvement in crime and delinquency. Someone else might argue that anxiety, fear, and depression are caused by the labeling or sanctioning experience itself. The mere fact that the two conditions are related does not by itself allow a determination of causal order. In many instances it makes sense to think about processes of *reciprocal causation*, wherein both conditions feed upon each other. For example, failure in school may contribute to delinquency, and delinquent behavior may produce reactions and experiences that further contribute to problems at school. Many theorists implicitly assume a certain causal order without considering alternatives or mustering any evidence that their assumption is correct.

Intervening Processes

While the minimum requirements outlined above are important for assessing claims about causation, another crucial question concerning causal relationships involves the processes that intervene and in essence explain how or why a connection between two conditions or characteristics comes to exist. Different theorists may agree that a causal characteristic or circumstance has been found but may disagree on the way it exerts causal influence. For example, we noted in Chapters 3 and 4 that females are less likely to be delinquent than males. Some biologically oriented theorists have attempted to attribute this difference to chromosomes or the presence or absence of testosterone. Other theorists have attributed the difference to a greater risk of official labeling for boys than for girls. Still others have attributed this difference between males and females to variation in parental supervision, variation in status problems, variation in cultural and subcultural values, or combinations of such conditions. Thus, even with a convincing demonstration of association, nonspurious-ness, and causal order, the difference between a valid and an invalid theory may hinge on the successful identification of intervening or explanatory processes. Hence, it may be necessary to develop a complex theoretical model with "billiard ball" effects whereby one variable or characteristic affects another, which in turn affects another, ultimately increasing the probability or odds of delinquency.

Specification

An additional concern in contemporary criminological research is the specification of circumstances of time, setting and samples studied that may affect research outcomes. We noted in Chapter 4 that the results of research on social class and delinquency might vary over time. In Chapter 7 we suggest that the impact of the broken home on delinquency may be different when it is a common experience as compared to when it is an unusual experience. In Chapter 8 we summarize disparate results from research on religion and delinquency and the attempts to reconcile those disparities by focusing on the specific samples, settings, and behaviors studied.

Our Methodological Toolbox

In Chapters 3 and 4 we discussed notions of validity, reliability, and repre-sentative versus biased samples. If claims are made about characteristics of youth that affect the odds that they will engage in delinquent behavior, then we should expect valid, reliable measures of "delinquent behavior" and a reasonably representative sample of "youth." To expectations that researchers will use valid, reliable measures of their concepts and gather data from cases that are representative of the populations under study, we can add expectations that they demonstrate nonspurious associations, address the issue of causal order, consider the mechanisms generating observed relationships, and attempt to specify the circumstances that might limit the generalizability of their results. All of these issues constitute a critical methodological "toolbox" that we can draw on in our review of criminological research and in our search for possible "causes" of delinquency. We should have greater confidence in claims advanced after attending to such issues than claims advanced with blatant disregard for such expectations.

Biological Schools of Thought

For much of the history of Western civilization, people have been viewed as occupying a special, unique niche in the universe by virtue of a soul, free will, and reason. Some of the earliest systematic thought about crime and criminal justice was based on such a premise. The *classical school* of criminology (prominent during the 1700s and represented by such philosophers as Montesquieu, Voltaire, Marat, Beccaria, and Bentham) believed that the law and criminal justice should be predicated on the view of people as rational, thinking beings. This school argued that human behavior is based on hedonism and that the pleasure-pain principle should serve as the guide for social control. Individuals choose actions that give pleasure and avoid those that give pain. Punishment should fit the crime and be certain, severe, and swift enough to deter a rational human being. According to the classical school of criminology, lawbreaking is due to free and rational decision making, therefore laws need to be clear and simple. Deterrence comes not from severe punishment but from punishment that is appropriate, prompt, and inevitable.

By the mid-1800s, however, with the development of biology and theories of natural selection and evolution, the "uniqueness" of humankind was being called into question. If Charles Darwin's theories of evolution were correct, human beings could be viewed as one stage in the evolution of organic life and, as such, humans were neither perfect nor complete but were evolving into higher organic forms. The most famous criminological work along this line was carried out in Italy in the late 1800s and early 1900s and is referred to as *Italian positivism.* The name positivism is derived from the Latin word positivus which means that which is laid down and can be found by rational insight and observation. That is, explanations for criminal behavior can be discovered by gathering facts and using the scientific method to discover clues about relationships.

Cesare Lombroso (1835-1909)

The name most prominently associated with the positivistic school is that of the Italian physician Cesare Lombroso. Using data from government agencies, anthropological measurements, and tools of the medical sciences, Lombroso sought to discover the "causes" of crime. While Lombroso considered a wide range of social and societal forces that might contribute to crime (for example, population density, the price of bread, wealth, education, unemployment, newspaper crime coverage, and so on), he is best known for his view of the "born" criminal, or "innate" criminal types. Lombroso argued that a large proportion of criminals (he estimated 40 percent) were *atavistic*—that is, genetic throwbacks. He reached this conclusion on the basis of observations of the physical and biological characteristics of criminals. The preface to this chapter is a statement from Lombroso after he examined the skull of a notorious Italian criminal. Lombroso believed his observations revealed an unusual number of criminals to be more akin to lower forms of life and to primitive humans than to "civilized" people (see Box 5-2).

Lombroso was inclined to advocate biological interpretations of differences that could be given sociological interpretations. For example, when confronted with the fact that women had lower rates of crime than men, Lombroso argued as follows:

> That women less often engaged in highway robbery, murder, homicide, and assault is due to the very nature of the feminine constitution. To conceive an assassination, to make ready for it, to put it into execution demands, in a great number of cases at least, not only physical force, but a certain energy and a certain combination of intellectual functions. In this sort of development women almost always fall short of men. It seems on the other hand that the crimes that are habitual to them are those which require a smaller degree of physical and intellectual force, and such especially are receipt of stolen goods, poisoning, abortion, and infanticide. (1911:184-85)

Lombroso depicted women as inferior to men, lacking the intellectual and constitutional ability to carry out the same acts as men. If women did commit crimes, it was because they had "masculine" characteristics. He typically proceeded by discovering a fact based on available statistics and then provided an interpretation that made the fact fit his theory. Since no predictions or hypotheses were ever presented before assessing the facts, Lombroso's theory could be bent to explain anything.

There are good grounds for criticizing the "savage" image of primitive

---

Box 5-2
"Criminal Man"

Applying Lombrosian methods, Gina Lombroso-Ferrero (1911, reissued 1972) described the physical characteristics of male criminals:

Eyes. The eyebrows are generally bushy in murderers and violators of women. Ptosis, a paralysis of the upper lid, which gives the eye a half-closed appearance, is common in all criminals.

Nose. In thieves the base of the nose often slants upwards, and this characteristic of rogues is so common in Italy that it has given rise to a number of proverbs.

Jaws. Enormous maximillary development is one of the most frequent anomalies in criminals and is related to the greater size of the zygomae and teeth.

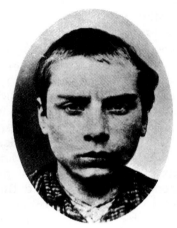

HEAD OF CRIMINAL

Chin. This part of the face, which in Europeans is generally prominent, round and proportioned to the size of the face, in degenerates as in apes is frequently receding, flat, too long or too short.

Height. Criminals are rarely tall. Like all degenerates, they are under medium height.

Can you describe what you think the "typical" delinquent looks like? What sort of image comes to mind? Where do you think such images originate? Can you look around your classroom and spot offenders using these descriptions?

---

humanity and "lower" forms of life in Lombroso's comparisons as well. For example, most aggression in animals takes the form of "posturing" and "bluffing" with the winner scaring off the loser. The ultimate outcome of animal aggression is rarely lethal. The nearest biological kin to humans, gorillas, orangutans, and other apes rarely engage in the behavior credited to them by Lombroso.

Lombroso's work also can be criticized in terms of the criteria of causality that we discussed earlier in this chapter. For one, Lombroso did not establish an association between physical attributes ("biological inferiority," or "degeneracy") and the probability of criminal activity. The most he could say (and even that is debatable) is that he found some physical differences between incarcerated or dead Italian convicts and a sample of Italian soldiers. Moreover, once Lombroso had developed his working hypothesis that criminals tended to be atavistic, he selectively searched for and highlighted slight differences. He did not state in advance of his search any criteria for identifying atavism or biological inferiority but, rather, defined atavism in terms of whatever differences he found.

Lombroso did not conduct his research in a manner that would be acceptable in modern criminology. He did not use a control group from the general population to make comparisons between criminals and noncriminals. Moreover, many of the traits he assumed to be inherited are not necessarily genetically determined — for example, heads too small or too large, short legs, sloping shoulders, flat feet, distinctive hair, eyes, nose, ears, lips, or jaw. Many of these traits could be caused by diet or the environment; circumstances that resulted in poor health care. While the list of problems with Lombroso's work is long, he is still considered "the father of scientific criminology." His most important contribution to modern criminology was his advocacy of a scientific approach to the study of crime.

As a result of his positivistic or scientific approach, his ideas on crime causation underwent revision, and by the time of his death in 1909 he increasingly took social and environmental factors into account. He argued that scientists should remain neutral to societal values and maintain total objectivity by sticking to the facts. Finally, Lombroso suggested that crime was determined by causal forces often beyond the awareness of individuals involved and that it was not the expression of free will as depicted by the classical theorists. Since crime was caused rather than freely committed, it would not deserve punishment. The Lombrosian outlook allied itself with the reformatory movement of the nineteenth century which favored rehabilitation rather than retribution. Indeterminate sentences, probation, and prisons with educational or vocational programs became the norm.

Charles Goring (1870-1919)

In *The English Convict*, published in 1913, Charles Goring, an English physician, delivered a devastating critique of Lombroso's work. Goring argued that Lombroso had not provided adequate statistical evidence of the differences claimed and that his theoretical biases had colored his interpretation of the data. Rather than merely criticize, however, Goring gathered data on 3,000 convicts and compared types of offenders within that sample. He then compared those findings to data available for the general population on ninety-six traits. Goring could find no evidence of Lombroso's criminal types. However, he did find differences between convicts and nonconvicts in the English population in terms of stature and measures of intelligence. Convicts were shorter, weighed less, and were classified as lower in intelligence than the general population. While Goring concluded that "There is no such thing as a physical criminal type" (1913:173), his findings led him to conclude that convicts were "inferior" to nonconvicts.

E. A. Hooton (1887-1954)

Although Goring's work has been described as dealing a "crucial blow to Lombrosian theory" (Quinney, 1970:69), the controversy over Lombroso's work did not end there. In a work entitled *Crime and the Man* (1939), E.A. Hooton attacked Goring on much the same grounds as Goring had attacked Lombroso. Hooton was a Harvard anthropologist who felt that Goring had been biased against Lombrosian theory and had interpreted his data in the manner least favorable to Lombrosian notions. After comparing data from more than seventeen thousand individuals, including convicts, college students, police officers, and mental patients, Hooton concluded that criminals are organically inferior and that this inferiority is genetically inheritable.

Hooton argued that "our information definitely proves that it is from the physically inferior element of the population that native born criminals from native parentage are mainly derived" (1939:309). Taking elaborate measurements of his subjects, he concluded that in nineteen out of thirty-five measurements there were significant differences between offenders and nonoffenders. According to Hooton, criminals had low foreheads, crooked noses, thin lips, long thin necks, narrow jaws, and several other distinctive features.

Hooton's work met with severe criticism because of his lack of representative control groups, blatant deficiencies in his methodology, and his failure to demonstrate how physical deviations are in any way indicative of inferiority. A reviewer of Hooton's book called it "the funniest academic performance that has appeared since the invention of movable type" (Reuter, 1939). Hooton's research is now only of historical importance.

William Sheldon (1898-1977)

Drawing on earlier work by Ernst Kretschmer, a German psychiatrist, William Sheldon, a physician and professor of psychology, proposed a *constitutional psychology* in which the body is the starting point for understanding personality and behavior (*Varieties of Delinquent Youth*, 1949). Sheldon's focus was on body type, or *somatotype*, which he defined as "a quantification of the primary components determining the morphological structure of the individual." A person's type was determined by the predominance of structures associated with digestion and assimilation of food (endomorphy), by the predominance of bone, muscle, and connective tissue (mesomorphy), or by the predominance of skin, appendages, and the nervous system (ectomorphy).

Sheldon's hypothesis was that there would be differences between the somatotypes of delinquent boys and the somatotypes of the rest of the population, although he could not predict in advance what those differences might be. Bodies were somatotyped by measuring the intermixture of the three types of structures. According to Sheldon every physique can be calibrated into three components on seven-point scales, with 1 as the lowest value and 7 as the highest. A three-digit number based on the estimate of endomorphy, mesomorphy, and ectomorphy was created. Sheldon's data were based on two hundred youths who were wards of a home for delinquent boys in Boston between 1939 and 1942. The measurements for the delinquent youths were compared with measurements for four thousand college students drawn primarily from Harvard University, the University of Chicago, and Oberlin College. Compared to the college sample, the sample of delinquent youths tended to be mesomorphic. Sheldon concluded, "So far as the somatotype is concerned our sample of delinquents, far from being weaklings, are a little on the hefty and meaty side" (1949:730). In contrast to Hooton's criminal sample, Sheldon's delinquents were not shorter than the general population.

Although Sheldon showed, at best, a difference in body build between some delinquent youths and a college sample, he presumed that such data are relevant to understanding delinquent behavior in general. In fact, he claimed that further exploration of constitutional differences could "cure the lust for war and delinquency" and proposed a nationwide compilation of biological profiles in order to "find out who are the biological best" (1949:879). He did not examine the possibility that the differences between his two samples might have been related to differential selection by the institutions from which the samples were drawn. He also did not address the social meaning or cultural relativity of "inferiority," the social meaning of different body builds, and the differences in social experiences that might result from differences in physical appearance. Rather, he argued that different body types are reflected in different personality types and, ultimately, in behavior. Sheldon's data are inadequate for substantiating his more grandiose arguments for unique temperamental traits that were ascribed to the three somatotypes.

Sheldon Glueck (1896-1980) and Eleanor Glueck (1898-1972)

The last of the classic works dealing with bodily constitution and delinquency that we will review here is a study by Sheldon and Eleanor Glueck (*Unraveling Juvenile Delinquency*, 1950). This study involved five hundred delinquent youths and five hundred relatively nondelinquent youths in the Boston area. The groups were matched as well as possible in terms of age, general intelligence, ethnicity, and residence in an underprivileged neighborhood. The study gathered data on a wide variety of social, psychological, and physical characteristics.

The Gluecks found no significant differences in health between their two samples but did report that a greater proportion of delinquent youths than of nondelinquent youths had been "restless" children. They also reported that the delinquents were "superior" to nondelinquents in body size and conformity to a "masculine" physical type. As in William Sheldon's research, delinquent boys were found to be more mesomorphic than the control group of nondelinquents.

No one has explained why there is an unexpected proportion of mesomorphic boys among official delinquents. It may be that boys with such builds are reacted to as dangerous or threatening. If the "masculine" build is overrepresented because of reactions rather than some temperamental, neurological, or physiological difference, then body build should not be related to self-reports of delinquency. There has been one study of body type in relation to self-reports of delinquency and that study reports no significant correlation (McCandless et al., 1972). Thus, even if other criticisms of the Glueck's research are ignored (see Cortes and Gatti, 1972), a persistent finding about body type among boys in institutions tells us little about differences in behavior.

Chromosomal, Glandular, and Neurological Variables

While early research focused on physical characteristics of people and observable external characteristics that were thought to correlate with variations in internal processes of some kind, more contemporary research has examined variations in chromosomal abnormalities and in glandular and neurological functioning. Some of the traits studied have been found to be too uncommon to explain much crime and the causal role of others has not yet been established.

Chromosomal Abnormality

There are twenty-three pairs of chromosomes in humans which carry the biological structures responsible for the transmission, development, and determination of inherited characteristics. Of these twenty-three pairs or forty-six chromosomes, two determine the sex of the person. The male chromosome configuration is recorded as 46, XY and the female as 46, XX. In the process of human conception, the female contributes 23 chromosomes and the male also 23 chromosomes. If the male contributes an X chromosome, this unites with the X of the female and a female offspring will ensue. Conversely, if the male contributes a Y chromosome, this unites with the X of the female and a male offspring is created. Thus, the male determines the sex of the child.

In 1961 it was discovered that there are instances of chromosome abnormalities. For example, males can have an additional chromosome (47, XXY) which results in Klinefelter's syndrome, a condition in males that causes certain female characteristics such as diminished facial hair, increased breast tissue, and lower testosterone levels. The converse of this abnormality is the 47, XYY syndrome, which results in males who are tall and "presumably" unusually prone to violence. Such cases were suspected of being "supermale."

In 1965 a British research team headed by Patricia Jacobs (1965) reported that 7 out of 197 mentally abnormal males in a prison hospital had an extra Y chromosome. Through the use of the *buccal mucosa smear technique*, in which cells are scraped from the inside of the cheek to determine chromosomal content, it has been found that only 1 out of every 1,000 males are XYY. Thus, 7 out of 197 is unexpectedly high. However, the characteristic is sufficiently rare among inmates that it can explain very little. Moreover, the trait appeared to be associated with an unexpectedly high probability of property crime, not violence (Price and Whatmore, 1967). The popular assumption was that the trait would be associated with inclinations towards violence (see Figure 5-1).

Figure 5-1

Percent of Males with XYY for Criminals and General Population

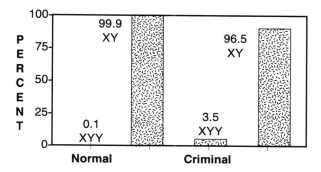

Source: Based on data in Jacobs et al., "Aggressive Behavior, Mental Subnormality, and the XYY Male," *Nature*, 1965.

In 1977, more than 31,000 Danish men who were tall were checked for chromosome composition (Witkin et al., 1976; Mednick and Volavka, 1977). While researchers found only twelve men with the XYY abnormality, five of the twelve had records. If the probability of acquiring a record were the same as for XY males (9 percent), only one should have been found to have a record. Moreover, consistent with the British study, it was property crime that was overrepresented.

The infrequency of this chromosomal abnormality suggests that even if a connection could be established between the XYY syndrome and crime, it could only account for a small fraction of crime that is committed. Certain chromosomal abnormalities can affect physical and mental functioning and, hence, it is plausible that they might also affect probabilities of criminality. However, the XYY syndrome cannot take us very far in the explanation of crime and delinquency (Trasler, 1987).

Endocrinology

Another possible source of some variations in human behavior is the functioning of the endocrine glands. These glands include the pituitary, adrenals, thyroid, and gonads which secrete hormones that affect such body functions as metabolism, emotions, and sexual processes. Secretions by the endocrine glands have been shown to affect emotional states, but the connection between endocrine abnormalities and criminal behavior are not clearly established.

For example, abnormal secretions of testosterone, a male steroid hormone, have been hypothesized as a possible cause of criminal aggression. Some research has shown that testosterone levels are higher among offenders who have committed violent crimes than among those committing nonviolent crimes. However, research on testosterone levels and aggressiveness is quite contradictory on this point (Mednick and Volavka, 1980).

Some work is also being conducted on the female menstrual cycle. According to Shah and Roth (1974), the four premenstrual days and the four days of menstruation itself account for 29 percent of the days in the typical lunar month. However, during these eight days, some 50 to 80 percent of female suicide, violence, depression, crime, and admittance to mental institutions occurs. Recently, significant attention has been given to premenstrual syndrome or PMS, which manifests itself in *some* women in terms of tension, fatigue, headaches, cramps, and depressed moods. PMS has been introduced in the British courts as mitigating circumstances in reducing the sentences of some female offenders. Shah and Roth (1974) suggest that some 25 percent of the female population suffer from PMS or some type of imbalance between estrogen and progesterone. However, while variable moods can be associated with the menstrual cycle, this does not mean that such moods increase the probability of criminal conduct.

Hypoglycemic Disorders

The brain obtains its energy from carbohydrates which are measured in terms of *glucose* or blood sugar. When the pancreas is unable to secrete enough insulin to maintain a normal concentration of glucose in the blood, the brain is malnourished and symptoms of anxiety, irritability, nervousness, and depression can occur. If the condition is permanent, this is called sugar diabetes and is treated with insulin. What is of more interest in understanding antisocial behavior is the state of spontaneous hypoglycemia which is a temporary state caused by overexertion, fatigue, or illness. During these temporary hypoglycemic episodes, explosive personality changes can take place resulting in assault, rape, and homicide. Some studies of prison inmate populations have found a higher than normal amount of hypoglycemia (Yaryura-Tobias and Neziroglu, 1975).

Autonomic Nervous System

The Autonomic Nervous System (ANS) controls the physiological activity associated with emotions and is often referred to as the involuntary nervous system. There are two systems involved, the *sympathetic* nervous system and the *parasympathetic* nervous system. The sympathetic nervous system is activated when anger, fear, or anxiety is being experienced and it influences heart rate, blood pressure, sweating, and changes in galvanic skin response (changes in the saline content of perspiration). The parasympathetic nervous system is activated after the sympathetic and induces a state of quiescence and relaxation. For normal individuals, encountering a stressful situation activates the sympathetic nervous system and the arousal of human emotions can be detected with the use of the polygraph or "lie" detector which measures changes in the ANS. However, there are some individuals who cannot experience an ANS arousal and for these people polygraph results are meaningless. Individuals who are referred to as sociopaths are alleged to be incapable of experiencing fear or anxiety. The notion of a "cool and calculating killer" may be indicative of a person who has a sympathetic nervous system that has a high threshold for fear or anxiety. For some of these individuals, adrenalin injections lowers the threshold of the sympathetic nervous system and they can experience anger, guilt, or fear.

The basis of biosocial theory in explaining antisocial behavior is that individuals who cannot experience the dissipation of fear or anxiety have difficulties learning (Mednick and Volavka, 1980). Mednick et al. (1982) describes this process as follows:

1) Child A contemplates aggressive action.
2) Because of previous punishment or the threat of punishment he suffers fear.
3) Because of fear he inhibits aggressive response.
4) Because he no longer entertains the aggressive impulse, the fear will begin to dissipate, to be reduced. Fear reduction is the most powerful, naturally occurring reinforcement that psychologists have discovered. The reduction of fear (which immediately follows the inhibition of the aggression) can act as a reinforcement of this inhibition and will result in learning inhibition of aggression (1982:39-40).

The faster that fear can be reduced, the faster the delivery of the reinforcement. A person who has an ANS that recovers quickly from fear or anxiety will receive immediate rewards from inhibiting the aggression and in the process learn socially approved behavior quickly. On the other hand, the slower the ANS recovery, the less the reward factor from the parasympathetic system and hence, the less learning that takes place. Trasler (1987), in reviewing the work done by Mednick, finds his results to be "excessively optimistic" but concludes that "the research which has been stimulated by Mednick's work promises major gains" (1987:205).

It is also important to remember that the initial connection between fear and rule-breaking may not be established because no aversive consequences were experienced. A youth with a responsive ANS in an environment where parents are unaware or unresponsive to initial rule-breaking or where rule-breaking is more rewarding than alternatives will not be inhibited by autonomic reactions. The types of conditioning that establish fear reactions may never have occurred. At present no one has untangled the effects of learning environments and contingencies from the responsiveness of individuals to learning in those environments.

Genetics and Inherited Dispositions

A common observation in the history of criminology has been that the criminality of one member of a family is related to the criminality of other members of a family. Early research focused on "criminal families" (Dugdale, 1877; Estabrook, 1916) while more recent research examines the behavior of twins, siblings, and the correlation between the criminality of adopted children and their adoptive and biological parents' criminality. Some of the most recent research uses measures of self-reported delinquency and attempts to estimate the "heritability" of criminality by controlling for social relationships.

Twin Studies

One way of examining the possible impact of biological factors on human behavior is the study of identical or *monozygotic* twins. Identical twins develop from a single female egg and have no hereditary differences. Fraternal or *dizygotic* twins are produced when two eggs are fertilized and have only half of their genes in common. If heredity plays a role in explaining criminal behavior, then monozygotic twins should have a higher concordance rate, or similarity of deviant behavior, than dizygotic twins. The earliest of these studies conducted in the United States, Europe, and Japan between 1929 and 1962 found concordance rates for identical twins to be as high as 70 percent, while those for fraternal twins were between 15 to 20 percent. However, because of numerous methodological problems in these early studies (such as the use of official definitions of crime, the nonrepresentativeness of the samples, and the higher probability that identical twins are more likely to be treated similarly than fraternal twins), these studies are suspect (Pollock et al., 1983).

Some of the best twin studies focusing on recorded criminality were conducted by Karl O. Christiansen (1977) in Denmark. He tried to overcome some of the methodological shortcomings of the earlier studies by examining all twins, not just those found in institutions, and by taking into consideration more background variables. His studies support the notion of a higher concordance rate between identical than fraternal twins. He found that if one identical twin had a criminal conviction, the other twin also had a conviction in 35 percent of the cases. The concordance rate for fraternal twins was only 12 percent. While these results have been criticized (Dalgaard and Kringlen, 1977), these twin studies do suggest a role of inherited traits in the causation of crime.

David Rowe (1986, 1987, 1990) has used complex forms of statistical analysis in studying antisocial behavior in twins and his research suggests a genetic basis for delinquent behavior (see Box 5-3). Using self-reports of delinquency from twins in high schools throughout Ohio, Rowe compared the similarity in delinquency of identical twins and nontwin siblings from a single high school in Ohio. Since he also measured respondents' perceptions of family environment and associations with delinquent peers, he was able to examine the similarity in behavior of twins when controlling for environmental sources of delinquency. The greater similarity in the behavior of identical twins than in fraternal twins or nontwin siblings persists despite controls for other variables when using self-report measures. The correlations are similar for fraternal twins and nontwin siblings. Rowe argues that it is not that genetic factors directly cause delinquent behavior, but rather than there is a genetic basis for temperamental traits such as aggressiveness, anger, impulsivity, and dishonesty or genetic variation in capacities to learn. His work suggests some form of "heritability" of individual characteristics that correlate with delinquency.

Box 5-3

Self-Report Studies of Twins
(MZ = Monozygotic, DZ = Dizygotic)

Hypothesis: If the greater similarity is due to social variables, then controlling for those variables will eliminate the effect of the twin factor.

If it does not do so, then we have to conclude that being identical twins has an impact of its own above and beyond shared social experiences. That direct effect may be the "heritability" or genetic factor working through other mechanisms such as ANS, intelligence, learning disabilities, temperament, etc. (ANS = autonomic nervous system).

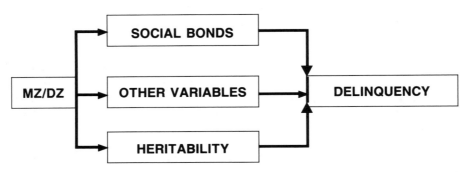

Research Conclusion: The greater similarity in MZ behavior cannot be explained by social variables and persists despite controls for a wide range of such measures.

Plausible Explanation: There is a hereditary factor involved.

Source: Derived from research by David Rowe (1986).

Adoption Studies

Because of the difficulty in differentiating between social and genetic influences in twin studies (see Walters and White, 1989), some researchers have turned to the study of adoptees as a more meaningful way of assessing the impact of biological factors on human behavior. By comparing the criminal behavior of adopted children with their biological parents and their adoptive parents researchers can arrive at better estimates of the impact of inheritance. Mednick and Volavka (1977) conducted such a study in Denmark for all adoptions between 1924 and 1947. Denmark is often the site of such adoption studies because Danish records of vital statistics including adoptions have been meticulously kept since the 1890s. In a study of more than 14,000 adoptions, Mednick and Volavka found that children who had biological parents with criminal convictions had a far greater chance of being involved in deviant behavior than those who had noncriminal biological parents. Figure 5-2 shows the percentage of adoptees who had a criminal conviction in the four possible combinations of adoptive and biological parents with or without criminal convictions.

Among adoptees whose adoptive and biological parents had no criminal convictions, only 13.5 percent of these had a criminal conviction. Similarly, of those whose adoptive and biological parents had a criminal conviction, 24.5 percent had a criminal conviction. A biological influence is suggested by the two off-diagonal cells. About 15 percent of sons had a criminal record when their adoptive parent had a criminal conviction and the biological parent did not. In contrast, 20 percent of those with a convicted

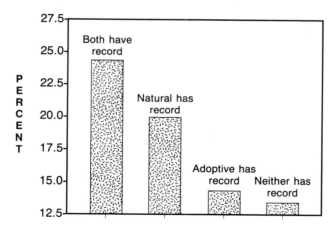

Figure 5-2

Percent of Sons with Criminal Records by Natural and Adoptive Parents' Criminality

Source: Based on S. Mednick et al., 1984. "Genetic Influences in Criminal Convictions: Evidence from an Adoption Cohort." *Science* 224: 891-94.

biological parent and a crime-free adoptive parent had a conviction. While the percent difference is not dramatic, having parents who have had a criminal conviction increases the chances that a child will also have a criminal conviction.

Biology and Delinquency: An Overview

In a review of the literature on genetic influence on human behavior, Ellis concludes that "significant amounts of the observed variation in human tendencies to behave criminally appear to be the result of some genetic factors" (1982:57). Again, the evidence is not conclusive but certainly suggestive of an association between some genetic factors and criminal or delinquent behavior.

C.R. Jeffrey is one of the most vocal criminologists to support a "biosocial" approach. He argues that the evidence from biology and behavioral genetics is so overwhelming that it is about to become the foundation for an interdisciplinary model in the study of crime and delinquency. "We cannot separate man's ethical and social systems from his brain and biological system" (Jeffrey, 1979:17).

More recently, James Q. Wilson and Richard J. Herrnstein (1985) published a book entitled *Crime and Human Nature* that strongly endorses a biosocial approach. They argue that the causes of crime lie in a combination of predisposing biological traits that temper social influences into criminal behavior.

> The average offender tends to be constitutionally distinctive, though not extremely or abnormally so. The biological factors whose traces we see in faces, physiques, and correlations with the behavior of parents and siblings are predispositions toward crime that are expressed as psychological traits and activated by circumstances. It is likely that the psychological traits involve intelligence and personality, and that the activating events include certain experiences within the family, in school, and in the community at large . . . (Wilson and Herrnstein, 1985:102-103).

These assessments are unduly positive given the fact that the vast majority of studies are based on official measures of criminality and that only a few attempt to separate the impact of environmental variables from individual biological characteristics. The twin research by David Rowe and colleagues is the most promising for estimating the impact of genetics on criminality and, at present, that research justifies the tentative conclusion that there are inherited characteristics that affect the probability of crime. However, whether "traces" of these characteristics are visible in faces and physiques which correlate with criminal or delinquent behavior has not been established.

Psychological Schools of Thought

In our review of biological perspectives, we noted the gradual shift away from the assumption that lawbreakers are born criminals to the notion that there are biological factors which can predispose one to antisocial behavior when certain environmental conditions exist. Beginning with the work of Sigmund Freud, a new perspective for understanding human behavior emerged. This perspective attributed troublesome behavior to psychological problems anyone could encounter in the course of human development. Leading further away from the notion of born criminal types, the new perspective emphasized experiences that anyone might have and learning processes that anyone might experience.

We cannot deal here with all psychological perspectives that might be relevant to understanding crime and delinquency. Rather we will consider four lines of inquiry that have specifically addressed crime and delinquency: 1) the psychoanalytic approach, 2) the concept of psychopathology, 3) personality research, and 4) social learning theories.

The Psychoanalytic Approach

The shift away from the assumption that people who break the law are biologically or constitutionally different from others is reflected in the work of Sigmund Freud and other psychoanalysts. Freud was not particularly concerned with explaining criminal behavior but, rather, with advancing his ideas on mental illness. However, the Freudian psychoanalytic approach opened a new dimension to the study of deviant behavior by proposing that problem behavior reflects problems in personality development.

Freud postulated that the human personality can be conceived of in terms of three basic forces. At birth the only force that functions is the *id*. The id is concerned with immediate gratification and is concerned only with pleasure. As the child grows, an *ego* develops that is in close contact with social reality. The ego attempts to curb the drives and urges of the id and to direct behavior in a way that is consistent with physical and social reality. The *superego*, the last element of the personality to develop, captures the idea of a conscience that attempts to restrain the id. Freud introduced the concept of the unconscious by describing the id and superego as basically unconscious elements of the personality and the ego as the conscious part.

From the Freudian perspective, the human personality is characterized by a struggle between the creative urges of the id and the constraining force of the superego. The ''healthy'' personality achieves a balance between these two forces. Personality disorders arise when one of the other forces is too dominant. For example, domination of the id could be reflected in criminal activities, and an overdeveloped superego could result in anxiety neurosis. Normal socialization processes are conducive to healthy personality development, but if the socializing agents are punitive, inconsistent, or arbitrary, the child's personality may get out of balance. Thus, from the psychoanalytic view, delinquent behavior can be symptomatic of deep emotional conflicts and unconscious motivations. All people are seen as antisocial by nature but through balanced, proper socialization people become law-abiding citizens.

August Aichhorn, a Viennese psychoanalyst, was one of the first scholars to approach the issue of delinquency from a Freudian perspective. In *Wayward Youth* (1936), Aichhorn argued that although there are "dissocial" types with inborn defects, individuals constitutionally predisposed to crime at birth are rare. He believed that such behavior as delinquency is a symptom of one of a variety of psychic problems or conflicts experienced by children as they are transformed from organisms dominated solely by instinctive needs into social beings. In Aichhorn's view, anyone could experience the problems that result in delinquency; social and dissocial persons differ merely in the degree to which they encounter problems in personality development.

From a psychoanalytic perspective, what are the problems that can result in delinquency? An almost endless list of specific problems could be compiled. There are, however, some basic categories of problems that psychoanalysts stress. One set of problems centers around the development of the superego. Normal personality development supposedly entails incorporation of ego ideals—that is, identification with the social and ethical standards of conduct of "significant others" in one's environment. If experiences or circumstances interfere with superego development, or if ego ideals are themselves criminal, then delinquency can result.

Another cause of delinquency from the psychoanalytic perspective is inadequate ego development. The infant is depicted as guided by the pleasure principle in seeking gratification of instinctive needs. However, normal personality development involves learning to take "reality" into account (the reality principle). To achieve normal development, the ego must learn to sacrifice immediate pleasures in order to achieve pleasure in the future. Thus, from the psychoanalytic perspective, the inability to defer gratification is indicative of disturbed ego development and is a potential source of delinquency.

The normal personality is characterized by harmony, or balance, between instinctive needs, reality, and the conscience. If the ego and superego are unable to control instinctive needs, the individual is likely to get into trouble with others in his or her environment. On the other hand, if such needs are denied or repressed by an overly rigid ego or superego, the individual may develop mental and behavioral problems that are a reflection of the inner tension or conflict. In Kate Friedlander's words, "Generally speaking, delinquent behavior is the result of a disturbance in the relative strength of the three domains of the mind, the Id, the Ego, and the Super-Ego" (1947:185).

The proof that psychoanalysts offer for these theories is very different from that demanded by social scientists. Psychoanalysts support their arguments with case histories of individuals who come to their attention. If a person is experiencing some sort of mental, emotional, or behavioral difficulty, analysts attempt to identify the source of the problem by encouraging the person to talk freely about past experiences that may have caused unconscious conflicts. Thus, causes are discovered "after the fact." Rather than identifying those conditions thought to generate delinquency, measuring them, and assessing whether or not such conditions increase the probability of delinquency, psychoanalysts point to cases that support their notions. It is unlikely that psychoanalytic theories will ever be tested in terms of the standards of causation that are central to the social sciences. In the psychoanalytic view, causes are unknown to the subject and can only be discovered with the help of experts who have special psychoanalytic training. Thus, there is no way for an outsider to prove or disprove the validity of psychoanalytic explanations. The "data" that support psychoanalytic theories are events and experiences that only the expert is qualified to interpret. The inference of unconscious motives is often made through techniques that are largely subjective and susceptible to multiple interpretations.

On the other hand, some basic psychoanalytic notions are quite compatible with the sociological explanations that we will consider in the next chapter. The assumption that the attempt to maximize pleasure can lead to conflict with the law if not checked by socialization is quite compatible with a brand of sociological theory known as social control theory. The emphasis in psychoanalytic theory on relationships with parents and identification with adult ego ideals is quite compatible with the emphasis of some sociological theories on the family in delinquency causation. However, sociological theorists are at odds with psychoanalytic explanations that attribute crime and delinquency to hidden mental conflicts. The focus in sociological explanations is on more observable and more readily measurable aspects of the external social environment and the groups to which an individual belongs. Moreover, although the psychoanalytic approach acknowledges that human social adaptation is a continuous, lifelong process, it focuses extensively on early childhood experiences and maternal relationships. Both may be important for understanding delinquency, but sociologists tend to focus more extensively on institutions that a child enters in later childhood and adolescence, such as the school and adolescent society. The sociological focus includes forces that are not likely to be recognized when the focus is on early childhood — for example, limited economic opportunity, legitimacy of the law, and social standing.

Sociologists also question the cultural biases that tend to be implicit in psychoanalytic notions. What is "normal" personality development? The answers depend on the norms or standards of the system being studied. Psychoanalytic theory maintains that learning to defer gratification in the short run for the sake of gratification in the long run is a normal, healthy stage in human social adaptation. But what if a child is born into an environment where the likelihood of gratification in the long run is extremely uncertain? Children in economically secure, predictable environments where parents and other agents insure future gratification, have reason to follow such a pattern of adaptation. Under different circumstances, focusing on immediate gratification may be normal. Such sayings as "Live for today and let tomorrow take care of itself" were not necessarily invented by people with "abnormal" personalities.

Psychopathology

Psychiatrists, psychologists, and some sociologists have used the concept of the *psychopath* in dealing with criminality. This concept grew out of the notion that some criminals are so depraved, so bad, or so "morally insane" that they stand out from the ordinary criminal population. The psychopath has been depicted as having a complex of character traits that supposedly makes him unique among criminals. Sociologists William and Joan McCord have described the psychopath as follows:

> The psychopath is asocial. His conduct often brings him into conflict with society. The psychopath is driven by primitive desires and an exaggerated craving for excitement. In his self-centered search for pleasure, he ignores restrictions of his culture. The psychopath is highly impulsive. He is a man for whom the moment is a segment of time detached for all others. His actions are unplanned and guided by his whims. The psychopath is aggressive. He has learned few socialized ways of coping with frustration. The psychopath feels little, if any, guilt. He can commit the most appalling acts, yet view them without remorse. The psychopath has a warped capacity for love. His emotional relationships, when they exist, are meager, fleeting, and destined to satisfy his own desires. These last two traits, guiltlessness and lovelessness, conspicuously make the psychopath as different from other men. (1964:16)

The term *psychopath* is used interchangeably with the more recent terms of *sociopath* and *antisocial personality*. Collectively, the three terms are used by various psychiatrists in describing individuals who are unsocialized, irresponsible, unable to feel guilt, or incapable of significant loyalty as defined in the *Diagnostic and Statistical Manual of Mental Disorders*.

Attempts to use this concept to explain the behavior of the psychopath can easily result in a circular argument. Illegal behavior is taken as "symptomatic" of some deeper psychopathology but the evidence for that pathology is the very behavior to be explained. If a person commits "irresponsible" acts, then is the behavior explained by deeming that person to be "irresponsible?" To argue that a person commits antisocial, aggressive, and impulsive acts because he or she is antisocial, aggressive, and impulsive is hardly a satisfactory explanation.

Diagnoses as psychopathic have been criticized as a basis for predicting future dangerousness. William McCord and Jose Sanchez (1983) followed children over a twenty-five year period who were diagnosed as psychopathic at two juvenile institutions. He found very little evidence to suggest that these children were any more crime prone than other delinquents who were not considered to be psychopaths.

In 1966 the Supreme Court required that 967 patients who were considered dangerous and institutionalized in a mental hospital for the criminally insane be transferred to regular mental hospitals (Steadman, 1973). The court found that the procedures for labeling individuals "dangerous" were quite arbitrary. Of the 967 patients, only 26 (2.7 percent) were ever returned to a hospital for the criminally insane. One-half of the original group were eventually discharged within a relatively short period of time and of those released, over 80 percent had no further arrests.

Hakeem's (1958) statement, dating back some three decades, still seems appropriate when assessing the significance of the concept of psychopathology for explaining or predicting criminal or delinquent behavior: "Psychiatrists are in disagreement on whether they are in agreement or in disagreement on the subject" (1958:669).

Personality Research

Some psychological researchers have attempted to provide empirical support for the notion that certain personality types are unusually prone to delinquency. Two popular personality tests used in the study of delinquency are the *Minnesota Multiphasic Personality Inventory* (MMPI), a self-administered inventory of 550 items with several subscales to measure different personality traits, and the *California Personality Inventory* (CPI).

Reviews of personality research have concluded that the MMPI has consistently differentiated delinquents from nondelinquents. For example, Waldo and Dinitz (1967) reported that of ninety-four studies using the MMPI between 1950 and 1965, 81 percent found significant differences between delinquents and nondelinquents. However, the MMPI as a whole has not yielded consistent results; its most consistent findings have been produced with a subscale known as the *psychopathic deviate scale* (Pd scale).

But what does the difference indicated by such personality research mean? Can we conclude that delinquents differ from nondelinquents in psychopathic personality traits? A partial answer to this question can be found by considering the items in the MMPI and Pd scale. At least fourteen items in the MMPI inventory actually measure self-reported delinquency, and one item in the Pd scale calls for a response to the statement "I have never been in trouble with the law." We have already seen that the concept of psychopath does not get us very far in explaining delinquency since the definition of psychopath includes reference to the very behaviors that the concept is meant to explain. Similarly, the Pd scale itself includes measures of the very behavior that the scale is introduced to explain. In other words, the scale may show nothing more than that adolescents who have been in trouble with the law are more likely than those who have not been in trouble with the law to indicate they have been in trouble with the law! We have to conclude that such tests do not tell us much about the causes of delinquency.

Tennenbaum reviewed personality studies during a ten-year period and concluded that "the data do not reveal any significant differences between criminal and noncriminal psychology because most results are based on tautological argument" (1977:228). Specifically, these tests fail to distinguish between the causes and effects of personality traits. Is criminal behavior the result of a certain personality trait or is the trait the result of criminal experience? Further, along with the problems of cause and effect, a major shortcoming of these personality studies is that they are based on officially defined delinquents, who have been arrested and referred to the juvenile court. Thus, it is possible that whatever personality differences that have been found between delinquents and nondelinquents such as maturity, aggressiveness, or irresponsibility, may have more to do with getting "caught" than being delinquent.

The California Personality Inventory, consisting of some 480 true-false items, has also been found to differentiate between offenders and nonoffenders in a variety of societies (Gough, 1965). The inventory focuses on normal variations in traits such as "socialization," "self-control," and "responsibility" and, thus, is less prone to the reification of pejorative concepts like psychopathic deviance in the MMPI. Moreover, it has been studied in relation to self-reported delinquency in a high school sample (Hindelang, 1972). Scores on the inventory correlate with self-reported delinquency regardless of gender, age or social status. However, the same problems of circularity remain. Hindelang concludes that those who engage in a wide range of delinquent activities are "impulsive, shrewd, uninhibited, aggressive and pleasure-seeking" and have "a disregard for social mores" (1972:81). If the task is to explain why some people are more aggressive, uninhibited, impulsive, and unconcerned with social mores than others, then such statements do not take us very far.

Learning Theories

Much of the biological theory and research as well as most psychological theories previously summarized assume that delinquents and criminals are somehow deficient in ways which affect their ability to learn—whether that deficiency is a result of temperament, irritability, mental ability, or conditionability. However, there are several different learning processes which can affect behavior and several learning mechanisms have been introduced in the explanation of delinquency. The emphasis in some theories is on how delinquency and crime can result from normal learning processes rather than deficiencies in learning.

Classical Conditioning. Most college students have heard of Russian physiologist Ivan Pavlov and of "Pavlov's dogs." Pavlov conducted experiments in which he rang a bell before giving a dog a piece of meat. Pavlov found that after he had repeated this procedure thirty or forty times, the dog began to salivate at the sound of the bell even when it was not given meat. The dog's salivation was a *conditioned response* to a stimulus (the bell) that had come to signal, or cue, the presentation of food. Over time, if the bell was not followed by food, the response gradually faded (*extinction*), although it could reappear (*spontaneous recovery*). Pavlov also found that such learned associations or conditioned responses could be transferred to new but similar situations and stimuli (*generalization*).

Building on the work of psychologist Hans Eysenck, Gordon Trasler applied some of Pavlov's classic principles of learning to the explanation of criminality. Trasler (1962) argued that learning experiences when we are very young affect the probability of delinquency and crime later in life. For example, when parents respond negatively to a child's breaking rules at home, the child will experience anxiety, an involuntary reaction like the salivation of Pavlov's dogs. Such anxiety can become a conditioned response to a variety of similar situations. Since anxiety is viewed as a state that people like to avoid, people supposedly avoid or escape situations that cause anxiety. Thus, Trasler's theory is that conformity is *escape-avoidance behavior* and that the inhibition of criminality is a learned, conditioned response that is strongly resistant to extinction because it functions to reduce anxiety. Trasler did introduce personality notions into his theory in that he argued that some people are more resistant to such conditioning than others—specifically, that people who are outgoing and crave excitement (extroverts) are resistant to escape-avoidance conditioning, while people who are quiet, self-controlled, and introspective (introverts) readily subject to such conditioning. The most central principle in Trasler's theory, however, is the idea that cues in learning situations come to be coupled with reactions of the involuntary nervous and glandular system and that these conditioned reactions come to act as a barrier to crime.

Fundamental to Trasler's theory is the idea that through a training procedure, the individual learns not to become a criminal. Trasler illustrated his concept of *passive avoidance conditioning* with experiments in which rats were given an unpleasant stimulus when they touched a lever that normally released food pellets. Even after the negative reinforcement was removed, the rats still would not touch the lever. The "anxiety" that the rats had acquired in anticipation of punishment continued, even though the punishment no longer existed. Similarly, if an individual is conditioned to experience punishment for wrongdoing during early years of socialization and thereby acquires anxiety, the individual will experience anxiety in contemplating delinquent behavior, even when the actual probability of punishment is remote. In this fashion, deviant behavior is avoided.

Operant Conditioning. Operant theory is another brand of learning theory that has been applied to the study of crime and delinquency. Operant theory draws on the theoretical formulations of B.F. Skinner, a well-known Harvard psychologist. Rather than focusing on ill-defined concepts of personality or on involuntary conditioned reactions, operant theorists focus on behaviors that are considered to be voluntary and controlled by the central nervous system. For example, when a child touches a candle flame, the behavior results in pain. The withdrawal of the child's hand may be a reflex action, but the future inhibition of the behavior (touching flames) can be viewed in operant terms. *Operant behavior* is behavior that is controlled by its consequences. Stimuli that increase or strengthen the behavior are called *reinforcers*, and stimuli that decrease or weaken the behavior are known as *punishers*. Stimuli that become learned cues associated with reinforcement or punishment are called *discriminative stimuli*. In classical conditioning, as with Pavlov's dogs, the organism is passive and simply learns what to expect from the environment, that is, a stimulus leads to a response. However, in operant conditioning, the organism is active and learns how to get what it wants from the environment.

The emphasis in operant theory is on behavior and the explanation of behavior in terms of observable aspects of the individual's environment. Radical behaviorists feel that such concepts as personality are unobservable artifacts that contribute nothing to the explanation of behavior but, rather, hinder scientific progress. Skinner (1971) was particularly adamant in attacking theories that assume the existence of autonomous human beings who act of their own free will. Skinner believed that a science of behavior will be achieved only if such notions as free will and personality are abandoned. Of course, proponents of other psychological schools of thought do not agree. This disagreement is reflected in divergent definitions of psychology as the science of the "mind" and as the science of "behavior."

Differential Association Theory. We noted in Chapter 1 that as early as 1896 American sociologists had postulated that criminal or delinquent behavior is learned behavior. A formal statement of this position — known as the *differential association theory* of criminal behavior — was first presented by Edwin Sutherland in 1939. Sutherland's basic premise was that deviant behavior was not the product of some sort of Freudian unconscious drives or Lombrosian biological factors but simply was behavior that was the product of social interaction. His first edition of *Criminology*, published in 1924, was a modest attempt to refute the theories of heredity. The second edition appeared in 1934 but it was in his third edition in 1939 that the concept of differential association appeared. Sutherland further modified his theory in 1947 and the theory has remained unchanged since that edition. He named the perspective "differential association theory" because delinquency was attributed to the balance of associations with people who defined lawbreaking in favorable and unfavorable terms. The most central learning process was normative — delinquency was a product of an excess of "definitions" favorable to lawbreaking as compared to definitions unfavorable to lawbreaking. Such definitions were learned in social interaction with others.

From this perspective delinquency did not result from deficiencies in learning but, rather, reflected the successful learning of values, norms, and beliefs which encouraged delinquency. Fundamental to differential association theory is the view that deviant behavior is learned in much the same way as conforming behavior. Sutherland stated that "criminal behavior as human behavior, has much in common with noncriminal behavior, and must be explained within the same general framework used to explain other human behavior" (Sutherland and Cressey, 1970:73). In other words, delinquency was not an inherited trait but like any other behavior, it involved socialization. A person must be taught how to commit a delinquent act and must acquire the necessary attitudes, motives, and rationalizations conducive to the violation of legal norms. Sutherland's conception of crime as conformity to deviant norms rather than abnormality, directed attention away from pathological conditions to more normal and natural factors. It provided an explanation of crime and delinquency in diverse social settings and cultures. For his contribution, Sutherland is referred to as the "Dean of American criminology."

Differential Reinforcement Theory. In an effort to provide a more precise specification of learning theory, Robert Burgess and Ronald Akers formulated what they called *differential association-reinforcement theory.* Their purpose was to reformulate Sutherland's approach in terms of general principles of behaviorism. In their original formulation of the theory the emphasis was on delinquency as "operant" behavior; that is, involvement in delinquency could be explained by the reinforcing or punishing consequences in the environment. In some instances, the behavior could be explained by its nonsocial reinforcement. If a person were hungry and alleviated that hunger by stealing food and eating it and experienced few negative consequences for doing so, then that behavior is likely to be repeated. Its frequency is affected by its nonsocial outcomes.

While incorporating nonsocial reinforcement, greater emphasis is placed on variations in the reactions of others and the theory has come to be referred to as a "social learning" theory of delinquency. As summarized by Akers and his colleagues:

> The primary learning mechanism in social behavior is operant (instrumental conditioning in which behavior is shaped by the stimuli which follow, or are consequences of the behavior). Social behavior is acquired both through direct conditioning and through imitation or modelling of others' behavior. Behavior is strengthened through reward (positive reinforcement) and avoidance of punishment (negative reinforcement) or weakened by averse stimuli (positive punishment) and loss of reward (negative punishment). [Akers et al, 1979:637]

The person first learns the behavior in question through processes of imitation or through observing consequences experienced by others (vicarious reinforcement) and then the behavior is maintained by rewards and punishments from the group. The family, peers, and other "significant others" such as teachers are especially important for both imitation and differential reinforcement of behaviors. This theory has been tested in dozens of articles dealing with drug use and delinquency and has fared quite well. It appears safe to conclude that the probability of delinquency for any given individual is affected by the behavior and reactions of significant others and that imitation, differential reinforcement, and the values, norms, and beliefs that people learn in the process each seem to play a role in explaining delinquency. Since this theory has been elaborated by sociologists as well as psychologists we will return to some issues involving the theory in Chapter 6.

Social learning theory focuses on the mechanisms that explain how individuals learn deviant and conforming behavior. Social learning theories tell us little about the specific social environments where these processes generate one or the other form of behavior. Explicitly or implicitly, the sociological perspectives that we will consider in the following chapter make assumptions about the conditions affecting the differential reinforcement of criminal and conforming behavior. For example, "social disorganization" perspectives attribute variation in crime to variation in the vitality of certain institutions that have traditionally rewarded conformity and punished deviance (such as the family, the neighborhood, the church, and the school). If these social institutions are "disorganized" because of such factors as population change, urbanization, and industrialization, the probability that crime will be punished and conformity rewarded may be quite low. Similarly, the "strain" theorists whom we will discuss in the next chapter argue that when people find that the legitimate opportunity to obtain certain goals or rewards is limited, they are likely to explore or invent illegitimate alternatives. If specific social groups come to approve illegitimate avenues for achieving success, or if new standards of conduct and order emerge where conventional institutions have failed, crime and delinquency may then become subculturally acceptable ways of behaving. Thus, variable crime rates may reflect normative conflict, which is the central tenet of the "cultural conflict" theories we will consider later.

Social learning theories are quite compatible with sociological perspectives since they postulate that other people play a major role in the process through which individuals learn delinquent behavior. They also attempt to delineate the nature of learning processes, which sociologists have taken for granted. On the other hand, sociologists have been more concerned than psychologists and learning theorists with identifying the social conditions that structure the distribution of differential learning processes. As Akers has noted:

> The general culture and structure of society and the particular groups, subcultures, and social situations in which the individual participates provide learning environments in which the norms define what is approved and disapproved and the reactions of others (for example, in applying social sanctions) attach different reinforcing or punishing consequences to this behavior. In a sense, then, social structure is an arrangement of sets and schedules of reinforcement contingencies. (1977:64)

We turn to such perspectives in the next chapter where we consider theory and research that attempt to explain delinquency by focusing on the structural, cultural, and group characteristics that shape learning processes.

Summary

We began this chapter by outlining the different sources people rely on in seeking answers to questions about the causes of delinquency — public opinion and expert testimony and experience. As an alternative to these sources, social scientists have attempted to gather and analyze data on crime and criminals and on delinquency and delinquents, with the aim of identifying characteristics of people or their environments that increase the probability of crime and delinquency. In the course of these efforts, scientists have developed a set of standards for assessing claims that some characteristic or condition is a cause of crime or delinquency. Such standards require that causal claims be backed up with evidence that 1) shows an association, 2) eliminates possibilities of spuriousness, and 3) establishes a causal order. Causal claims should also be preceded by a concerted effort to acquire data representative of the populations under study and to create valid, reliable measures of variables. Even when these standards have been taken into account, there may be divergent views concerning the mechanisms or processes through which the causal relationship is established. Different theorists may identify different intervening variables. Finally, it is also vital to specify the circumstances of sample, setting, and time that may affect the relationships observed. It is important to have a rudimentary understanding of these issues because most criticisms of research focus on failures to take one or more of them into account.

In terms of those standards for assessing causal claims, assessment of biological research on the causes of crime and delinquency have resulted in such conclusions as "biological explanations of crime have repeatedly failed to withstand critical examination" and "most criminologists today believe that in light of the available evidence, such explanations are of little use in understanding criminal behavior" (Sykes, 1978:231). The biological research we reviewed was often characterized by sampling bias, ill-defined or undefined concepts, possibilities of spuriousness, alternative causal orders, and failure to consider nonbiological interpretations. The shortcomings of these studies mean that we cannot accept their results as conclusive.

On the other hand, studies that have overcome many of these criticisms have yielded results suggesting a genetic basis for behavior. Several studies have found differences in body build between delinquent and nondelinquent youth, and more than one study has found higher than expected proportions of property offenders among men with chromosomal abnormalities. In addition, several studies have reported that identical twins are more similar in their criminal behavior than are fraternal twins. These findings do not demonstrate that tendencies toward crime are inherited, but neither do methodological shortcomings allow us to reject such possibilities.

The development of psychoanalytic and psychological schools of thought represented a shift away from the assumption that criminals and delinquents are basically different types of organisms to the view that they are simply people who have encountered problems while in the process of developing into social beings. The standards of proof for such theories are very different from those expected in the social sciences. We cannot judge whether psychoanalytic perspectives are correct or incorrect explanations of delinquency since they have not been tested in terms of the standards of causation that are central to the social sciences.

The concept of the psychopath and attempts to measure the dimensions of the psychopathic personality have not advanced our understanding of crime and delinquency. Definitions of the concept, as well as scales that are presumed to measure it, actually include reference to the very phenomenon to be explained. We certainly do not doubt that people's feelings, attitudes, and beliefs are correlated with their behavior, but we do question whether the search for personality differences has in any way provided scientifically adequate or consistent evidence about such correlations.

One issue on which sociological and psychological theories are likely to agree is that delinquent behavior is primarily learned behavior. Psychologists and social psychologists vary in the learning processes that they emphasize and in the degree in which they incorporate notions of personality into their theories. Some focus on principles of classic conditioning and involuntary anxiety reactions, while others focus on operant conditioning that involves voluntary behavior and on the interplay between behavior and its consequences. Sociologists have actually used principles of operant conditioning to restate sociological theory. Such efforts show lines of convergence between sociological and psychological perspectives, with the latter identifying learning processes and the former identifying characteristics of society, culture, or groups that structure distribution of those learning processes.

References

Aichhorn, A. 1936. *Wayward Youth*. New York: Viking Press.

Akers, R. L. 1977. *Deviant Behavior*. Belmont, CA: Wadsworth.

Akers, R. L., M. D. Krohn, L. Lanza-Kaduce, and M. Radosevich. 1979. "Social Learning and Deviant Behavior: A Specific Test of a General Theory." *American Sociological Review* 44: 636-55.

Burgess, R. L., and R. L. Akers. 1966. "A Differential Association-Reinforcement Theory of Criminal Behavior." *Social Problems* 14 (Fall):128-47.

Cerf, C., and V. Navasky. 1984. *The Experts Speak*. New York: Pantheon Books.

Christiansen, K. O. 1977. "A Preliminary Study of Criminology Among Twins." In Sarnoff Mednick and Karl Christiansen (eds.), *Biosocial Bases of Criminal Behavior*. New York: Gardner Press.

Cortes, J. B., and F. M. Gatti. 1972. *Delinquency and Crime*. New York: Seminar Press.

Dalgaard, O. S., and E. Kringlen. 1977. "A Norwegian Twin Study of Criminality." *British Journal of Criminology* 16 (July):213-32.

Dugdale, R. L. 1877. "The Jukes: A Study in Crime." In *Pauperism, Disease, and Heredity*, 4th ed. New York: Putnam.

Ellis, L. 1982. "Genetics and Criminal Behavior." *Criminology* 20: 43-66.

Estabrook, A. H. 1916. *The Jukes in 1915*. Washington, DC: Carnegie Institute.

Friedlander, K. 1947. *The Psycho-Analytic Approach to Juvenile Delinquency*. New York: International Universities Press.

Glueck, S., and E. Glueck. 1950. *Unraveling Juvenile Delinquency*. New York: Commonwealth Fund.

Goode, E. 1972. *Drugs in American Society*. New York: Alfred A. Knopf, Inc.

Goring, C. 1913. *The English Convict*. London: His Majesty's Stationery Office.

Gough, H. G. 1965. "Cross-Cultural Validation of a Measure of Asocial Behavior." *Psychological Reports* 17: 379-87.

Hakeem, M. A. 1958. "A Critique of the Psychiatric Approach to Crime and Corrections." *Law and Contemporary Problems* 23:650-82.

Hammer, R. 1989. *The Illustrated History of Organized Crime*. Philadelphia: Running Press Book Publishers.

Hindelang, M. J. 1972. "The Relationship of Self-Reported Delinquency to Scales of the CPI and MMPI." *Journal of Criminal Law, Criminology and Police Sciences* 63(1):75-81.

Hirschi, T., and H. C. Selvin. 1967. *Delinquency Research: An Appraisal of Analytic Methods*. New York: Free Press.

Hooton, E. A. 1939. *Crime and the Man*. Cambridge, MA: Harvard University Press.

Jacobs, P. A., M. Brunton, M. M. Melville, R. P. Brittain, and W. F. McClemont. 1965. "Aggressive Behavior, Mental Subnormality, and the XYY Male." *Nature* 208 (December):1351.

Jeffrey, C. R. 1979. "Biology and Crime: The New Neo-Lombrosians." In C. R. Jeffrey (ed.), *Biology and Crime*. Beverly Hills: Sage Publications.

Kolansky, H., and W. T. Moore. 1971. "Effects of Marijuana on Adolescents and Young Adults." *The Journal of the American Medical Association* 216: 486-92.

Kozol, H. L., R. J. Boucher, and R. F. Garofalo. 1972. "The Diagnosis and Treatment of Dangerousness." *Crime and Delinquency* 18:371-92.

Lombroso, C. 1911. *Crime, Its Causes and Remedies*. Boston: Little, Brown.

Lombroso-Ferrero, G. 1972. *Criminal Man*. Montclair, NJ: Patterson Smith.

McCandless, B. R., W. S. Persons, and A. Roberts. 1972. "Perceived Opportunity, Delinquency, Race and Body Build Among Delinquent Youth." *Journal of Consulting and Clinical Psychology* 38:281-91.

McCord, W., and J. McCord. 1964. *The Psychopath: An Essay on the Criminal Mind*. Princeton, NJ: Van Nostrand.

McCord, W., and J. Sanchez. 1983. "The Treatment of Deviant Children: A Twenty-five Year Follow-Up Study." *Crime and Delinquency* 29:238-53.

Mednick, S. A., W. F. Gabrielli, and B. Hutchings. 1984. "Genetic Influences in Criminal Convictions: Evidence from an Adoption Cohort." *Science* 224:891-94.

Mednick, S. A., V. Pollock, J. Volavka, and W. F. Gabrielli. 1982. "Biology and Violence." In M. E. Wolfgang and N. A. Weiner (eds.), *Criminal Violence*. Beverly Hills: Sage.

Mednick, S. A., and J. Volavka. 1977. "Biology and Crime." In *Biosocial Bases of Criminal Behavior*. New York: Gardner Press.

_____. 1980. "Biology and Crime." In N. Morris and M. Tonry (eds.), *Crime and Justice: An Annual Review of Research*. Chicago: University of Chicago Press.

Pollock, V., S. Mednick, and W. Gabrielli, Jr. 1983. "Crime Causation: Biological Theories." In Sanford H. Hadish (ed.), *Encyclopedia of Crime and Justice*. Vol 1. New York: Free Press.

Price, W. H., and P. B. Whatmore. 1967. "Behavior Disorders and Patterns of Crime among XYY Males Identified at a Maximum Security Hospital." *British Medical Journal* 1:533-37.

Quinney, R. 1970. *The Problem of Crime*. New York: Dodd, Mead.

Reuter, E. B. 1939. "Review of E. A. Hooton, *Crime and the Man*." *American Journal of Sociology* 45:123-26.

Rowe, D. C. 1986. "Genetic and Environmental Components of Anti-social Behavior: A Study of 265 Twin Pairs." *Criminology* 24:513-32.

_____. 1987. "Resolving the Person-Situation Debate: Invitation to an Interdisciplinary Dialogue." *American Psychologist* 42:218-27.

_____. 1990. "Inherited Dispositions for Learning Delinquent and Criminal Behavior: New Evidence." In L. Ellis and H. Hoffman (eds.), *Evolution, the Brain, and Criminal Behavior: A Reader in Biosocial Criminology*. New York: Praeger.

Shah, S. A., and L. H. Roth. 1974. "Biological and Psychophysiological Factors in Criminology." In D. Glaser (ed.), *Handbook of Criminology*. Chicago: Rand McNally.

Sheldon, W. H. 1949. *The Varieties of Delinquent Youth*. New York: Harper.

Skinner, B. F. 1971. *Beyond Freedom and Dignity*. New York: Alfred A. Knopf.

Steadman, H. J. 1973. "The Psychiatric As a Conservative Agent of Social Control." *Social Problems* 20:263-71.

Sutherland, E. H. 1939. *Principles of Criminology*, 3rd ed. Philadelphia: J.B. Lippincott.

_____. 1947. *Principles of Criminology*, 4th ed. Philadelphia: J.B.Lippincott.

Sutherland, E. H., and D. Cressey. 1970. *Criminology*, 8th ed. Philadelphia: J.B. Lippincott.

Sykes, G.M. 1978. *Criminology*. New York: Harcourt Brace Jovanovich.

Tennenbaum. D. J. 1977. "Research Studies of Personality and Criminality: A Summary and Implications of the Literature." *Journal of Criminal Justice* 5 (3):1-19.

Trasler, G. 1962. *The Explanation of Criminality*. London: Routledge & Kegan Paul.

_____. 1987. "Biogenetic Factors." In H. C. Quay (ed.), *Handbook of Juvenile Delinquency*. New York: John Wiley

Waldo, G. P., and S. Dinitz. 1967. "Personality Attributes of the Criminal: An Analysis of Research Studies, 1950-1965." *Journal of Research in Crime and Delinquency* 4 (July):185-202.

Walters, G., and T. White. 1989. "Heredity and Crime: Bad Genes or Bad Research?" *Criminology* 27:455-85.

Wilson, J. Q., and R. J. Herrnstein. 1985. *Crime and Human Nature*. New York: Simon and Schuster.

Witkin, H., et. al. 1976. "Criminality in XYY and XXY Men." *Science* 193 (August):547-55.

Yaryura-Tobias, J. A., and F. Neziroglu. 1975. "Violent Behavior, Brain Dysrhythmia and Glucose Dysfunction, A New Syndrome." *Journal of Orthopsychiatry* 4:182-88.

chapter 6

Explanations of Delinquency

Structure, Culture, and Interaction

> *The way men behave is largely determined by their relations with each other and by their membership in groups. Social relations are at the foundation of both motivation and control. The goals and aspirations that set people into motion are greatly influenced by their social relations. Social relations are also instruments of control, for they limit action and restrain impulses that might threaten the orderly arrangement of independent lives.*
>
> —L. Broom and P. Selznick, *Sociology,* 1968

Sociology and The Study of Delinquency

In the last chapter we considered the ideas and research of a variety of physicians, biologists, psychologists, and learning theorists attempting to explain how and why individuals come to be involved in crime and delinquency. To some, the answers could be found in properties of the body or physiological processes. To others, the answers could be found in properties of the individual mind or personality. And, to yet other scholars, the behavior of individuals could be explained by contingencies of reward and punishment in the external world. In each instance, the focus was on the behavior of individuals. One academic tradition, sociology, stresses ways of thinking about delinquency which focus our attention on aspects other than the individual or individual behavior.

For much of this century, the scientific study of crime and delinquency has been dominated by scholars who are identified as "sociologists." Sociology is typically defined as the scientific study of social systems, and such systems can range from small groups of interacting individuals to nations and international systems. In the attempt to understand delinquency, one of the central premises characterizing a sociological approach has been that delinquency is "more" than the behavior of individuals. As noted in Chapter 1, delinquency is "group behavior." In fact, some prominent early sociologists specifically excluded the explanation of individual lawbreaking from their theories. For example, Clifford Shaw and Henry McKay (1942) developed a theory of delinquency during the 1920s and 1930s that they intended to apply "primarily to those delinquent activities which become embodied in groups and social organization."

Moreover, many of the terms used in Chapters 3 and 4, such as the "incidence" and "prevalence" of delinquency, refer to characteristics of populations, territories, communities, or socially differentiated categories of people. Such measures involve the behavior of individuals but are viewed by sociologists as characteristics of social systems to be examined in relation to other properties of those systems. For instance, when we ask why the delinquency rate is lower in rural than urban settings and consider such possibilities as the proportion of strangers in a setting or strength of communal bonds, we are thinking in sociological terms. When we ask questions about variations in delinquency rates over time and social space, and begin to think of other characteristics of social systems which might make sense of such variations, then we are asking distinctively sociological questions (see Box 6-1).

Conceptions of Delinquency

The focus of many sociologists on the social nature of delinquency does not mean that such scholars have no interest in behavior or individuals. In fact, a review of the sociological literature would show at least three distinct treatments of the subject matter. For one, delinquency can be conceived of as an activity involving a type of group—*the delinquent gang.* For much of the 1950s and 1960s, the nature and origins of delinquent gangs was the dominant focus among sociologists studying delinquency, and gangs were viewed as a particularly serious dimension of the urban and inner-city crime problem. The focus on gangs was associated with a second conception of delinquency which stressed *subcultures or contracultures.* Such subcultures or contracultures consisted of values, norms, and beliefs passed on from one generation of youth to another and which facilitated trouble with the law. Such subcultural traditions were the subject matter of theories of gang delinquency since one of the distinct defining characteristics of such groups was, presumably, the criminogenic perspective shared or created by members of such groups. Different types of subcultures were thought to emerge in different types of urban settings.

In the 1970s sociological theory and research shifted away from the study of gangs and the presumption of subcultural traditions to conceptions of delinquency which were thought to be more applicable to delinquency as a common and pervasive activity among youth. Thus, delinquency came to be viewed simply as *behavior in violation of the law.* Such behavior can occur in gangs but most of it involves casual groups of youth who do not fit the image of delinquent gangs. Rather than treating the subject matter as the explanation of the origin and perpetuation of certain types of groups or subcultures, the focus shifted to the contribution of group processes and variable values to delinquent activity in a wide range of social settings.

Box 6-1

County Crime Rates

Sociologists and sociologically-oriented criminologists are interested in crime and delinquency as individual and group behavior, as labels applied to individuals and groups, and as rates characteristic of territories and time periods.

In the graph below each dot represents a county. In this instance, the state is Tennessee. The vertical axis (the "Y" axis) is the crime rate per 100,000 population for 1985 for each county and the horizontal axis (the "X" axis) is the percent of households in the county with only one family. The straight line in the graph is called a regression line and gives you an idea of the nature of the relationship. Criminologists typically compute a variety of statistics that convey information about the nature and the magnitude of relationships.

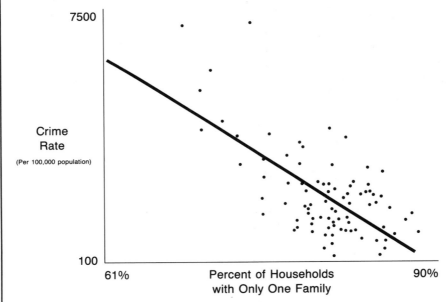

Crime Rate
(Per 100,000 population)

Describe the relationship between percent of one-family households and county crime rates? Can you think of any reasons why these two variables should be related to one another as they are?

The Subject Matter of Theories

Sociologists continue to debate over the "best," "most sociological," and "most comprehensive" concept of delinquency. For purposes of this text, we are merely concerned that the reader recognize the distinctions and the possibility that a theory which explains "delinquent behavior" does not necessarily explain the phenomenon of delinquent gangs. Moreover, a theory relevant to delinquent behavior in general may not incorporate exactly the same explanatory variables as a theory focusing on group delinquency or on specific types of delinquency (e.g., drug use). On the other hand, most theories have been applied explicitly or implicitly to the concept of delinquency as a gang phenomenon and to the concept of delinquency as behavior that is in violation of the law. Similarly, most theories have been applied to explaining how individuals come to be involved in delinquency, as well as to explaining variations in delinquency rates among different groups or settings.

One concept over which sociological theories differ considerably is that of the delinquent subculture. Many theorists take it for granted that subcultures *do* exist and have developed theories to explain their development, content, or form. However, the specific meaning of the word "subculture" when dealing with delinquency is vague. If we accept the cultural referent of the concept, then we are assuming the existence of values, norms, beliefs, and techniques (supposedly held by identifiable groups) that call for or facilitate delinquency. While there is consensus that gangs and groups that engage in delinquent behavior do exist, there is little consensus that these groups are the embodiment of such a distinct culture. In fact, contemporary sociological explanations of delinquency are at odds over whether there are group-linked systems of values, norms, beliefs, and techniques that can explain gang delinquency, let alone delinquent behavior. These controversies will be examined further when dealing with specific theories.

Sociological Schools of Thought

There are several different ways to summarize the body of theory in a field. We could present the field in historical sequence—in terms of specific contributions of specific theorists—or in terms of schools of thought. At the risk of oversimplification, we will take the latter approach and attempt to summarize three systems of ideas that have dominated sociological theory and research on juvenile delinquency. No one theorist necessarily addresses all the issues or assumptions characteristic of a particular perspective, but certain similarities in fundamental assumptions tend to locate theorists in one or another school of thought. Moreover, theorists may draw on more than one system of ideas to explain delinquency. By approaching sociological perspectives on delinquency as schools of thought, we will discover areas where the theories are in marked conflict, as well as areas where they are in agreement.

Shared Assumptions

Since the views that we will consider are all "sociological," they do share certain basic sociological assumptions. One basic assumption (shared by several psychological perspectives as well) is that delinquency can be best understood if it is approached as *learned*, rather than biologically determined, behavior. This assumption is closely linked to a second assumption, which is that as learned behavior, delinquency is not totally random or unpredictable, but is instead more common in some circumstances than in others. What those exact circumstances are varies from one sociological theory to another, but all such theories share the view that it is dimensions of the *social environment* which explain the distribution of delinquency and the probability that individuals will learn delinquent behavior. Important aspects of the social environment are its values, norms, beliefs, and techniques. These cultural patterns are variably learned, depending on the nature and operations of such socializing forces as the family, school, church, community, and peer groups (each of these will be dealt with in Chapters 7 and 8). Learning also depends on the *structure of opportunities* for engaging in delinquent and nondelinquent activities.

Thus, the basic sources of delinquency are viewed as *originally external* to the individual. People are not born delinquent but are born into circumstances or have experiences that are conducive to delinquency. Individual values, beliefs, and conceptions of right and wrong become part of the individuals' personal makeup, or self, through processes of social learning and socialization. This argument does not mean that genetic or biological factors are totally irrelevant to explaining delinquency. Instead, it reflects a belief that delinquency can be more adequately predicted and explained by considering the influences of relationships with other people and institutions, as well as the values, norms, beliefs, and techniques learned as a product of such relationships. The research summarized in this and the following chapter provides considerable support for such a position.

In the sections to follow we will concentrate on three basic systems of ideas which have been applied to explaining variations in the distribution of delinquency in different settings and categories of people, as well as to explaining individual behavior and the development of delinquent gangs. Those three systems of ideas or "schools of thought" will be referred to as *Social Disorganization-Social Control*, *Structural Strain-Status Frustration*, and *Normative Conflict-Differential Association* theories. Our discussion of each system will be organized around the following topics: 1) causal forces relevant to explaining the distribution of delinquency, 2) causal forces relevant to explaining individual involvement, 3) the emergence and persistence of gangs, 4) views on the relevance of culture,

5) views of the socialization process, 6) views on motivation, and 7) the "image" of the delinquent.

It is important to note here that there are more than three theories of delinquency and that our discussion of the three basic perspectives will be followed by consideration of theories referred to as *social learning theory, integrated theory*, and *Marxist theory*. Such theories are currently more limited in the scope of issues encompassed than the first three. Social disorganization-social control, structural strain-status frustration, and normative conflict-differential association perspectives have dominated the literature in criminology in the United States and can be compared and contrasted on a wide range of topics. Moreover, since these more recent theories draw on and incorporate ideas from prior perspectives, it is vital that we have a thorough understanding of traditional perspectives before moving on to more specialized or less developed systems of ideas.

Social Disorganization—Social Control Theory

The concept of *social disorganization* was widely used in early American sociology and criminology to refer to unsettled conditions of urban life generated by growth and change. This theoretical perspective is based on the seminal work of Emile Durkheim who suggested that when societies undergo significant social change the common bonds that tie people together can weaken, facilitating various forms of deviance. It is not surprising that the notion came into use among sociologists at the University of Chicago in the early 1900s, since Chicago was a booming industrial city increasingly populated by recent immigrants of diverse racial and ethnic backgrounds. Such conditions were viewed as contributing to a breakdown in the teaching and learning of prior "social rules" which had inhibited crime and delinquency (Thomas and Znaniecki, 1918). Robert Park argued that city life is characterized by a breakdown in the "traditional" schemes of control that have always depended on intimate personal relationships, such as occur in "the home, neighborhood, and other communal institutions" (1952: 58).

Clifford Shaw (1929) and Edwin Sutherland (1939), both Chicago sociologists, used the concept of social disorganization and social control to develop theories of delinquency. Shaw argued:

> Under the pressure of the disintegrative forces which act when business and industry invade a community, the community thus invaded ceases to function effectively as a means of social control. Traditional norms and standards of the conventional community weaken and disappear. Resistance on the part of the community to delinquent and criminal behavior is low, and such behavior is tolerated and may even become accepted and approved. (1929: 204-205)

Thus, the expansion of business and industry, coupled with immigration, growth, mobility, and cultural diversity, was seen to weaken or inhibit certain traditional forms of control, which, in turn, facilitated high rates of delinquency.

Sutherland's view of social disorganization was very similar to Shaw's in that he believed the disorganization of institutions that have traditionally reinforced the law facilitates the development and persistence of "systematic" crime and delinquency. He also believed that such disorganization fosters cultural traditions that support such activity. Sutherland wrote that "if the society is organized with reference to the values expressed in the law, the crime is eliminated; if it is not organized, crime persists and develops" (1939:8).

The value of the concept of social disorganization for explaining crime and delinquency has been challenged on grounds of *circularity*: crime and delinquency have often been cited as indexes of social disorganization, as well as phenomena to be explained by social disorganization. It is meaningless to argue that crime and delinquency rates are high because of some condition referred to as "social disorganization" and, then, to turn around and cite high crime rates as a measure of such disorganization. Moreover, since there is generally some order to social life even under the most dire circumstances and even when it is organized around illegal activities, the concept of social disorganization can be misleading. As we have noted before, delinquency itself has social qualities to it.

Although the concept itself may be vague and difficult to use in a noncircular fashion, it does tie together a variety of explanations of crime and delinquency that focus on the social conditions that affect conventional social institutions, as well as the bonds between people and those institutions. Moreover, some theorists (see Chapter 8) have recently reintroduced the central ideas of social disorganization theory but use the term "social integration" in its place. Others (Simcha-Fagin and Schwartz, 1986; Taylor and Covington, 1988; Bursik, 1988) have used or proposed a variety of measures of the concept that are distinct from crime and delinquency, including measures of informal neighboring, organizational involvement, and social networks. In addition, social-psychological versions of social disorganization theory are currently among the most popular explanations of delinquent behavior. Such contemporary versions of the social disorganization perspective are referred to as *social control, containment, commitment,* or *social bond theories.*

Like social disorganization theory, social control theory focuses our attention on the strength of the individual's bonds to conventional institutions, persons, goals, and values. The focus is on barriers to delinquent behavior rather than the causes that propel an individual into delinquent activities.

Social control theory, like social disorganization theory, has been criticized for circularity. In one of the first systematic presentations of a social control theory of delinquency, A.J. Reiss, Jr., wrote:

> Delinquency may be defined as the behavior consequent to the failure of personal and social controls to produce behavior in conformity with the norms of the social system to which legal penalties are attached. Personal control may be defined as the ability of the individual to refrain from meeting needs in ways which conflict with the norms and rules of the community. Social control may be defined as the ability of social groups or institutions to make norms or rules effective. (1951: 196)

The difficulty with such statements is that delinquency is by definition behavior that does not conform with certain norms. Thus, the statement can appear circular: "Failure to abide by norms occurs when people fail to abide by norms." However, when we consider the specific conditions cited or measured in the development of social control theories, we find that they are not necessarily circular. For example, Reiss went on to identify the failure of such primary groups as the family to provide reinforcement for nondelinquent roles and values as a crucial variable in the explanation of delinquency. Such conditions can be defined and measured in different terms than the delinquent behavior they are supposed to explain.

Another theory emphasizing the lack of constraints is drift theory, which derives from David Matza's work on *Delinquency and Drift* (1964). Matza saw the delinquent as an "actor neither compelled nor committed to deeds nor freely choosing them: neither different in any simple or fundamental sense from the law-abiding, nor the same; conforming to certain traditions in American life while partially unreceptive to other more conventional traditions" (1964: 28). The word "drift" does convey some of the distinctive characteristics of social control theory. According to Matza the delinquent "flirts" with criminal and conventional behavior. It is essentially an "amotivational" perspective — that is, rather than seeking an answer to the question "What *motivates* adolescents to commit delinquent acts?", it seeks to answer "What *prevents* an adolescent from committing such acts?". If an adolescent has few stakes in conformity, then she or he is freer to break rules than the adolescent who has high stakes in conformity.

Social control theorists use several different tactics in dealing with the issue of motivation. Some control theorists argue that a focus on motives does not tell us much about who will commit criminal and delinquent acts since most of us have been "motivated" to do so repeatedly in our lives (Briar and Piliavin, 1965). Moreover, rather than being generated by one or a few dominant forces, the motives for delinquency are quite diverse, ranging from instrumental needs (for example, stealing when one is poor and hungry) to emotional rage, frustration, and sheer thrill and excitement. Other control theorists merely acknowledge that human beings are active, flexible organisms who will engage in a wide range of activities unless the range is limited by processes of socialization and social learning. Thus, although several control theorists address the issue of motivation, social control theory views the search for mechanisms that prevent or deter crime and delinquency as far more fruitful than the search for underlying motivation.

We noted in Chapter 1 that different sociological theories take quite different stands on the role that values and norms play in the explanation of crime and delinquency. Social disorganization-social control theorists have taken a variety of positions on the issue. According to Travis Hirschi (1969), there is a general consensus in American society that criminal and delinquent activities involving personal harm and loss or damage to property are improper or immoral. By "consensus," Hirschi did not mean that everyone feels equally strong about the impropriety of lawbreaking. Some people accept the law as more morally binding than other people do and are therefore less likely to break it. Rather, Hirschi argued against the notion that any sizable racial, ethnic, or status groups in America have subcultural systems of values and norms that require criminal or delinquent behavior.

Matza and Gresham Sykes (1961) have observed that although "official" proclamations and conventional institutions stress the importance of obeying the law, "subterranean" traditions are conducive to crime. Supposedly law-abiding citizens accord respect and admiration to the person who "pulls off the big con," who takes risks and successfully engages in exciting, dangerous activities, whether legal or illegal. Movies and television programs about this type of risk-taker or maverick are popular among all groups and classes of people, which reflects a widespread ambivalence toward the law. Sykes and Matza (1957) have also pointed out that although conventional institutions prevail upon us not to break the law, other social norms tell us that breaking the law is not so bad under certain circumstances: when the victim "had it coming" (denial of an innocent victim); when those supporting the law are not morally pure themselves (condemnation of the condemners); when the offender "had no choice" (denial of responsibility); when "no one was hurt" (denial of injury); or when the offense was motivated by social purposes more important than the law (appeal to higher loyalties). Such beliefs, or techniques of neutralization, can be learned in quite conventional contexts. They are reflected in legal codes as "extenuating circumstances" and in the public's reaction to certain types of crime. In this view, then, delinquency is not a response to different, "subcultural" values but, rather, is facilitated by specific beliefs that reduce the impact of more general moral commitments or by sporadic endorsement of deviant values hidden beneath the surface of society's traditional normative order.

Thus, some social control theorists view delinquency as a reflection of rather pervasive beliefs that encourage illegal and immoral activities. For them, delinquency reflects an ambivalence about lawbreaking or the lack of a consistent moral stance against lawbreaking. Other social control theorists merely emphasize the lack of commitment to the law: the person who is not morally bound to the law is freer to violate the law.

In sum, social disorganization-social control theorists generally believe that social conditions that attenuate or inhibit bonds to conventional institutions are the cause of individual and gang delinquency. To paraphrase Jackson Toby (1957), "the uncommitted adolescent is a candidate for gang socialization." Harold Finestone (1976:10) has characterized this view of the delinquent as a "dissatisfied" drifter. This image of the individual delinquent is consistent with the social control perspective on the nature of delinquent gangs; uncommitted or disaffiliated adolescents are seen as drifting together to form tenuous, unstable aggregates, which Yablonsky (1959) has labeled "near groups." Gangs, or "near groups," are held together by lack of alternatives and conflict with authority. In contrast to other sociological schools of thought, the social control perspective views the gang delinquent as "committed to neither delinquent nor conventional enterprise" (Matza, 1964: 1).

Structural Strain-Status Frustration Theory

A second major perspective on delinquency first emerged in the late 1930s and grew in popularity during the 1950s through the mid-1960s. It is referred to as *structural strain theory* because it relates crime and delinquency to a combination of cultural emphases on "success" with social structures in which the realistic possibilities of attaining success are limited. Four sociologists have been especially prominent in the development of this perspective: Robert Merton, Albert Cohen, Richard Cloward, and Lloyd Ohlin.

According to the French sociologist Emile Durkheim, "No living being can be happy or even exist unless his needs are sufficiently proportioned to his means" (1951: 246). Writing in the late 1800s and early 1900s, Durkheim argued that some forms of suicide occurred when needs and means were badly out of alignment. Extending Durkheim's ideas, Robert Merton (1957) believed that deviance of various kinds could be attributed to the disparity between the cultural emphasis on success (leading to cultural "needs" or "goals") and the actual opportunity to achieve success (means). When people learn that they should strive for certain goals and there is not equal opportunity to realize them, then some portion of people are going to be frustrated. This disparity, coupled with a weakening of norms defining acceptable means of achieving success, prompts people to "innovate" and consider illicit means of obtaining their goals. Merton viewed crime and delinquency as "innovative" behavior that is most characteristic of lower-class people. The lower-class concentration of crime allegedly reflected the combination of limited opportunity, coupled with a commitment to success and weak acceptance of the norms embodied in the law. People who are strongly bound to norms precluding criminal or delinquent behavior can respond to disparities between valued goals and limited opportunity by giving up their aspirations and conforming in a "ritualistic" fashion. Merton viewed ritualism as a common lower-middle-class adaptation to problems that generate crime and delinquency in the lower classes. He also argued that some people give up the pursuit of success and reject conventional norms. Their behavior is characterized by drug use, alcoholism, and vagrancy. Merton referred to this type of adaptation as "retreatism." Finally, other people may adopt new goals and norms and rebel against the existing system.

The disparity between success and opportunity can have consequences for people of every social standing. However, in Merton's view, criminal and delinquent behavior is a lower-class response to this type of social disorganization because the lower-class youth is more thoroughly socialized to aspire toward success than to abide by legal norms. Under such circumstances, conventional norms are likely to be ignored, and new ways of getting ahead considered.

In his classic work *Delinquent Boys* (1955), Albert Cohen's explanation of delinquency is strongly influenced by Merton's version of strain theory. However, Cohen believes that Merton's conception of the process does not explain the emotion involved in many delinquent activities. Cohen concluded that delinquent behavior represents a collective effort by juveniles to resolve adjustment problems caused by their loss of social status in American society. The lower-class child is constantly measured by the "middle-class measuring rod," which is discriminatory because socialization experiences differ according to class. Lower-class youth are not adequately socialized to fulfill the status requirements of middle-class society. Differential socialization experiences result in what Cohen referred to as "status frustration." Status frustration is supposedly most common among boys from lower- or working-class families, since the middle-class measuring rod stresses characteristics that working-class socialization does not (for example, thrift, neatness, the ability to defer gratification, and good manners).

When status problems are experienced collectively — that is, by a number of adolescents who interact with one another — one outcome may be the creation of an alternative set of criteria for determining status. According to Cohen, delinquents create a new set of standards *contrary* to those emphasized in middle-class institutions. Thus, Cohen viewed delinquent gangs as a "contracultural" phenomenon. The concept of contraculture refers to a system of values that are in opposition to dominant standards and that are the result of problems experienced in trying to obtain status while abiding by such standards. Thus, delinquent activities are supposedly marked by a repudiation of middle-class standards and the adoption of nonutilitarian, malicious, rebellious attitudes. Although Cohen refers to a delinquent "subculture," the term "contraculture" conveys the sense of his explanation much better (Yinger, 1960).

Another elaboration of structural strain theory is found in Richard Cloward and Lloyd Ohlin's *Delinquency and Opportunity* (1960). Cloward and Ohlin argued that the motivation to deviate is provided when one accepts culturally prescribed goals of success and finds that legitimate avenues for achieving such goals are limited. However, Cloward and Ohlin attempted to merge Merton's strain theory with approaches that emphasize illegal opportunity and criminal traditions. They argue that the consequences of strain depend on the availability of the illegitimate opportunities in a given setting. If status problems are experienced in a setting in which criminal activities are well organized, then involvement in a criminal subculture characterized by instrumental acts of theft is a likely resolution to such problems. If no such well-organized illegitimate activities are available, then gang life centered around conflict, fighting, or violence may be the collective resolution to status problems. Finally, boys who are ill-equipped for organized criminal activity or for a gang life oriented toward conflict may withdraw into a "retreatist" subculture organized around drug use.

Although the structural strain-status frustration theorists reviewed are at odds on a number of points (for example, whether delinquent behavior is irrational and malicious or rational and utilitarian), they all emphasize a particular type of motivation in their explanations of crime and delinquency: status problems induced by discrepancies between conventional culture and limits imposed by our social structure. Strain theorists argue that rates of crime and delinquency are highest in those categories of the population in which such discrepancies are most likely to occur. Delinquency is viewed as a form of social behavior that functions to solve the status problems induced by these discrepancies. Thus, strain theorists introduce a special motivation to explain delinquency: structurally-induced status frustration.

Strain theorists also share the view that persons born into our society *at least initially* want to conform to the conventional standards that are reflected in the law. According to Cohen, before they hit upon delinquent alternatives, lower-class boys try to live up to the standards of middle-class adults but are unable to do so. Alternatives are explored after status problems are experienced. Strain theorists depict people as basically "moral" in the sense that they are always trying to be honorable, whether by adhering to conventional norms and values or by elaborating new norms that define delinquency and crime as good and acceptable.

In describing the delinquent as a "frustrated social climber," Harold

Finestone (1976:2) summed up the strain theorists' image of delinquent youth. Delinquency, especially gang delinquency, is viewed as a solution to status problems. The gang delinquent is a "problem solver" who is involved in a problem-solving contracultural or subcultural system. As Cohen (1955) expressed it, "The same value system, impinging upon children differently equipped to meet it, is instrumental in generating both delinquency and respectability." The strain theorists' image of the delinquent, then, is that of an essentially moral, striving human being who has been forced by circumstances beyond his or her control to explore new ways of attaining respect and self-esteem. Group delinquency is depicted as problem-solving behavior.

Normative Conflict-Differential Association Theory

Thus far we have considered theories that view delinquency as a product of 1) freedom from or inconsistencies in conventional socialization and control, and 2) status problems generated by disparities between cultural aspirations and social reality. A third perspective is characterized by the argument that in certain social contexts, delinquency and crime are approved, required, or expected behavior. Some advocates of this last position have specifically repudiated the basic assumptions of strain theory. For example, Walter Miller (1958) has argued that the strain theorists' image of a "delinquent subculture" is erroneous. Miller does not believe that the value systems of lower-class gangs are "contracultural" (that is, a rejection of dominant middle-class values). Rather, Miller has argued, the values, or "focal concerns," of gang members are a product of "the lower class community itself—a long established, distinctively patterned tradition with an integrity of its own" (1958: 5-6). According to Miller, the gang boy conforms to the values or standards of a larger subculture that is generally linked to regional, racial, or social status. Thus, delinquency is supposedly a reflection of the values, norms and beliefs of large, but distinct, segments of the population.

From the normative conflict perspective, the basic source of variation in delinquency rates is subcultural diversity in standards of right and wrong. When a region of the nation, particular sections of a city, or particular groups or categories of people have high crime rates, cultural conflict theorists posit that the values, norms, and beliefs of those particular segments of the population differ from the standards embodied in the law. Contrary to the strain and control theorists, normative conflict theorists view society as characterized by quite diverse standards of right and wrong, with some standards more likely than others to be expressed in the law. Groups or segments of the population whose cultures are in conflict with the law are more likely to come into actual conflict with the law. Sutherland

and Cressey have noted that the "principle of normative conflict . . . makes sense out of variations in crime rates by observing that modern societies are organized for crime as well as against it, and then observing further that crime rates are unequally distributed because of differences in the degree to which various categories of persons participate in this normative conflict" (1974: 89). This concept of normative conflict differs from the concept of "subterranean" values in that it attributes the values that are conducive to delinquency to disadvantaged groups whose cultures are in conflict with the dominant middle class. In contrast, the type of inconsistency or conflict that Matza and Sykes have described as "subterranean" characterized the value systems of the dominant groups in society.

Once such cultural conflict, or diversity in standards of right and wrong, is assumed, then the process of learning delinquency becomes one of "differential association" with different standards. Hence, the basic principle of Sutherland and Cressey's differential association theory is that "a person becomes delinquent because of an excess of definitions favorable to violation of law over definitions unfavorable to violation of law" (1974:75-77). The emphasis is on the learning of normative or cultural standards, some of which define lawbreaking in favorable terms while others define it in unfavorable terms. The principle of normative conflict at the collective level sets the stage for differential exposure to different standards at the individual level.

From a cultural conflict perspective, delinquency is explained by the same processes as is lawfulness. The motivation for delinquency, like the motivation for lawfulness, is quite natural—the human tendency to live up to the expectations of significant others. Children ultimately become involved in delinquency because the standards they learn are in conflict with the standards reflected in the law. As John DeLamater (1968:447) has noted, cultural deviance (in this case delinquency) "occurs through the normal process of social learning." Thus, cultural conflict theorists view deviance as a product of successful subcultural socialization; strain theorists view it as a product of "resocialization" through the collective development of contracultural standards; and control theorists view it as a product of failures or inconsistencies in conventional socialization. Because they see delinquency behavior as conforming behavior that is only deviant from some other group's perspective, normative conflict-differential association theorists need posit no special motivation for deviance.

Since this school of thought defines delinquency as conforming behavior that is shaped by normative standards and the expectations of others, its image of the delinquent differs from the images of the other two perspectives that we have reviewed. Delinquents tend to be depicted as among the most able, persevering, and gregarious members of their particular communities. For example, Walter Miller (1958) has argued that to become a gang member, a boy must be able to subordinate individual preference to group interest and that lower-class gang members "possess to an unusually high degree both the capacity and motivation to conform to perceived cultural norms." From such a perspective, it is the best products of a "lower-class culture," rather than the worst, who are likely to become delinquent. Those most sensitive to the opinions and expectations of members of their subculture are those most likely to become involved in delinquency. To borrow Hirschi's (1969) term, the image of the delinquent is one of "hypermorality." The delinquent is a conformist in a subculture whose standards are in conflict with the law.

Sociological Theories and Delinquency: An Overview

Several sociologists have summarized different perspectives on deviance, crime, and delinquency, and we can get a good overview of the three approaches outlined above by drawing on their works. Figure 6-1 describes these three approaches in terms of causal forces, socialization processes emphasized by each, their images of the delinquent and of the law and moral standards, and their views of culture and motivation.

Referring to Figure 6-1, we see that the three causal perspectives on delinquent behavior envision a causal process that operates on a macro, or societal, level, as well as a causal process that operates on a micro, or individual, level. On the societal level, disorganization-control theory attributes variation in crime and delinquency to variations in the collective ties to traditional institutions of social control. Strain theory attributes variation in crime among and within societies to the malintegration of cultured ambitions and opportunity. Cultural conflict theory assumes the presence of multiple cultures or subcultures within a particular society that inadvertently produces a clash among the cultural prescriptions of these varying groups.

At the individual level, control theory focuses on barriers to delinquency in the form of investments or stakes in conformity. Strain theory translates social strain into "status frustration," which occurs when individuals cannot attain prescribed goals. Finally, cultural conflict theory introduces the concept of differential association to explain how members of differing subcultures acquire and maintain attitudes and behaviors that nonmembers of the subcultural groups view as deviant.

DeLamater (1968) has delineated three perspectives on the deviant "socialization" process. Becoming deviant may reflect: 1) inadequate socialization into conventional norms, 2) initial socialization into deviant subcultural norms, or 3) problem-solving resocialization. Each of these perspectives is associated with one or another of the three theories of delinquency. Control theorists tend to emphasize failures or inconsistencies of socialization, cultural theorists focus on successful subcultural

Figure 6-1

Characteristics of Major Causal Theories

	Control	**Strain**	**Cultural Conflict**
Causal Factor: Societal Level	Social disorganization	Structural strain	Normative conflict
Causal Factor: Individual Level	Weak conventional bonds	Status frustration	Differential association
Role of Socialization	Failures or inconsistencies	Resocialization	Successful subcultural socialization
Image of Delinquent	Drifter	Problem solver	Conformist
View of law and morality	Consensus but variable acceptance	Initial consensus Strain-induced rejection	Conflicting definitions
View of Culture	Infraculture	Contraculture	Subculture
Motivation	Natural Diverse Situational	Special status problems	Natural Social Cultural

socialization, and strain theorists focus on processes of deviant resocialization. The last process is "resocialization" because it is assumed that the individual initially learns conventional standards and tries to abide by them. If such attempts lead to frustration, then the individual may turn to delinquency and the creation of alternative standards.

Hirschi (1969) and Finestone (1976) have dealt with the general image of the delinquent suggested by different theories. In the social control perspective, the delinquent is "dissatisfied" (Finestone) or "amoral" (Hirschi). By "amoral," Hirschi means that the delinquent is less bound to conventional moral standards and can therefore deviate more freely, with fewer moral complications and less guilt. According to this view, delinquent youth are also "uncommitted" (Matza, 1964). From a cultural conflict perspective, delinquent youth are actually "hypermoral" (Hirschi) in the sense that they make the greatest effort to live up to expectations in their subcultural environment. They are conformers. Finally, from the perspective of strain theory, those youths who initially try to adhere to conventional standards, but fail to get ahead by doing so, seek moral solutions to their status problems. Finestone has depicted this image as one of "frustrated social climber." Group delinquency can become a solution for youths who lack conventional status resources.

Each theoretical approach is also characterized by a particular image of the law and moral standards. Cultural conflict theorists stress normative conflict in society and a view of the law as representative of the standards of certain powerful segments of society. In this view, society is characterized by dissention and conflict between the standards of some sizable subcultures and the standards that are reflected in the law. In contrast, both control and strain theorist view society as characterized by consensus regarding the impropriety of most types of crime and delinquency. Hirschi has noted that control theory assumes "a common value system within the society whose norms are being violated" and that "deviance is not a question of one group imposing its rules on the members of another group" (1969). Control theory does not deny that traces of deviant values are buried or embedded within our culture. These "subterranean" values occasionally serve as convenient rationalizations for delinquent behavior. Strain theorists also assume that there is a common value system, as well as basic agreement on the impropriety of criminal and delinquent activity, but that those who experience frustration may construct an alternative moral order (contraculture) to cope with such problems.

Cultural concepts are used differently in each of these theories as well. For example, Yinger (1960) has noted that the concept of the delinquent subculture characteristic of Cohen's strain theory is really that of a contraculture—a system of values, norms, and beliefs that specifically develops in reaction to problems in coping with the dominant system. In contrast, the cultural conflict theorists use the concept of subculture in a more conventional way. Their focus is on a system of values, norms, and beliefs that is in conflict with standards reflected in the law but that exists as an enduring set of traditions characteristic not merely of delinquent gangs but of whole subpopulations, communities, or neighborhoods. Finally, for control theorists like Hirschi, such concepts as contraculture or subculture are not necessary for understanding delinquency, since an overall cultural consensus regarding moral standards is assumed and delinquency is seen as resulting from freedom from moral constraints.

Empey (1967) has noted that control theorists have advanced a third concept of American culture—that of an infraculture, the system of "subterranean" values, norms, and beliefs that we discussed earlier. According to this concept, certain values, norms, and beliefs are conducive to delinquency but are part and parcel of the dominant system rather than the standards of specific subgroups. Such infracultural aspects of American culture are not viewed as requiring crime but as tending to neutralize abstract moral commitments to the law. However, this concept has not been incorporated specifically into any explanatory theory. To be relevant to explaining variation in delinquent activity, subterranean beliefs would have to be viewed as "variably" learned aspects of American culture and some effort made to identify the circumstances associated with such learning. On the other hand, to the degree that subterranean beliefs are viewed as "neutralizing" the moral constraints of the dominant system and "freeing" the individual to deviate, the concept seems to fit better with control theory than with strain or cultural conflict theory. Both strain and cultural conflict theory point to norms among gangs or minority populations that require delinquency.

Finally, the three perspectives differ in their approaches to the motivational issue. Cultural conflict theory and control theory focus on quite "natural" motives, while strain theory is characterized by a "special motivation" (Hirschi, 1969). Cultural conflict theory focuses on the natural tendency of people to abide by the cultural expectations and normative standards prominent in their own social environments. (In other words, delinquents learn the delinquent standards of their particular subcultural environments.) For control theorists, motives are natural in a very different sense. Hirschi did not feel that control theory need pay any attention to the motivational issue (1969:33), while control theorists who have focused on motivation have merely outlined short-term, situationally-induced desires experienced by all youths. The motives for delinquency are diverse, situational, and so common that they have little explanatory power. In contrast, the strain theorist identifies a very special, structurally-induced type of motive: status frustration. People have to be forced to deviate by circumstances largely beyond their control. The introduction of a special force is necessary in neither cultural conflict theory nor in control theory.

Theory-Related Research

Each of the three sociological schools of thought that we have reviewed developed in an attempt to make sense out of presumed "facts" about delinquency and crime. Arrest rates were highest in the areas surrounding the central business district of cities and decreased in zones outside of the city centers. Why did rates vary in such a fashion? Social disorganization-control theorists attributed such variation to the deleterious effect of growth and change on conventional institutions. Structural strain-status frustration theorists argued that people living in areas with the highest arrest rates are those most likely to experience a disparity between aspiration and reality. Cultural conflict theorists argued that such areas are characterized by cultural traditions that define lawbreaking in favorable terms. In short, all three perspectives explain commonly believed "facts" about delinquency.

Each of the major theories of delinquency can make sense out of variations in delinquency by setting, social class, age, and gender. However, each does so using different concepts and assumptions about people, culture, and society. Hence, tests of sociological theories have come to concentrate directly on the causal mechanisms generating delinquency. If high delinquency rates are attributable to subcultural normative traditions passed on through socialization in specific territories or collectivities of people, then research should uncover systematic differences in such traditions by territory or collectivity. If gang delinquency grows out of failure in the conventional system and repudiation of conventional values and norms, then there should be evidence of an oppositional value system among gang youths as compared to other youth. If delinquency is most probably when youth develop few stakes in conventional institutions and lines of action, then we should expect that youths who are relatively free of conventional entanglements will be freer to violate rules of all sorts. Theory-oriented research concentrates on bringing evidence to bear as directly as possible on the specific causal mechanisms and assumptions of one or more theories of delinquency.

It is not a simple matter to do such research since theorists are typically quite vague on the exact meaning of concepts and only rarely provide guidelines for actually measuring them. Moreover, scholars disagree on the actual significance or meaning of findings for the validity of a theory. A piece of research viewed as contrary to a theory by one scholar may be viewed as irrelevant or even supportive evidence by another. In addition, "delinquency" can be conceived of and measured in several different ways, and an explanation of delinquency conceived in one fashion may not adequately explain delinquency conceived of in a different fashion. Thus, any review of research bearing on theory is open to challenge and based on the judgment of the reviewer. With those cautions in mind, we will attempt a summary of research which we consider relevant to strain, cultural conflict, and disorganization-control theories.

Strain Theory

There have been numerous efforts to test one or more assumptions characterizing strain theories of delinquency, most of them focusing on the explanation of delinquent behavior as reported by junior and senior high school students. The focus on delinquent behavior has been a source of criticism of such research (e.g., see Vold and Bernard, 1986), since several strain theorists sought to explain the emergence of urban lower-class gangs or the negativistic and malicious nature of gang activities. However, strain theorists typically cited the preponderance of lower-class male youths in police and court statistics as "facts" to be explained by a theory. If such data are relevant to the utility of a theory when they are thought to be supportive, then contrary facts conceiving of delinquency as behavior cannot be dismissed as totally irrelevant when they conflict with a theory. Moreover, since most delinquent activity takes the form of a spontaneous pick-up game, the limitation of strain theory to gangs would mean that the theory cannot compete as a general theory of delinquency. Moreover, even when limited to the explanation of gangs, research has generated problems for strain theory.

As we have noted, strain theorists attribute the nature and distribution of delinquent gangs to the existence of delinquent subcultures that have distinctive values, norms and beliefs. Thus, Cohen claimed to be explaining the "content" of a delinquent gang subculture, or contraculture. However, actual research on the values of gang delinquents has not supported the notion of a delinquent contraculture. Several studies (Gordon et al., 1963; Lerman, 1968; Gold, 1963) have found that gang boys evaluate deviant and conventional behaviors in terms of their "goodness" much the same as do nondelinquents. For example, Short and Strodtbeck (1965) compared gang boys in Chicago with lower-class and middle-class nongang boys in terms of their evaluations of conventional images (for example, "someone who works for good grades at school," "someone who saves his/her money") and deviant images (for example, "someone who is a good fighter with a tough reputation," "someone who knows where to sell what he/she steals"). They found that all of their samples evaluated middle-class, conventional images in equally high terms. Moreover, each sample ranked conventional images more highly than any of the unconventional images. Gang boys did tend to "tolerate" deviant lifestyles or images more than nongang boys, but there was no evidence of a reversal in evaluations of different lifestyles. Hyman Rodman (1963) has suggested the notion of the "lower-class value stretch," which is an adaptive mechanism that enables lower-class people to share the general values of society but stretch them to fit their particular circumstances. Similarly, Lee Rainwater (1970) has argued that certain groups may develop a "set of survival techniques for functioning in the world of the disinherited." However, Rainwater's argument does not incorporate the negation of conventional norms.

Some theorists have argued that strain theory is not challenged by the lack of evidence of reversal or repudiation of conventional values among gang boys. Cohen and Short (1958) claim that evidence of ambivalence is consistent with strain theory. They argue that since delinquent boys initially learned conventional values, they should continue to exhibit some commitment to them. They also suggest that lingering commitments to conventional values is what necessitates the psychological defense mechanism of "reaction formation." If delinquent youths did not care about conventional values, they would not have to reject them.

The problem with such defenses of strain theory is that they make the theory intestable. For example, according to Cohen's version of strain theory, certain forms of delinquency allegedly reflect a value system in which status is accorded for behavior which opposes conventional values. Since such a subcultural status system is a collective creation which comes to sustain oppositional behavior after it has been invented, there should be evidence that delinquent gang boys are committed to an oppositional value system. If opposition is not exhibited in evaluations of conventional and deviant lines of action, then what evidence is there that an oppositional subculture exists other than the behavior which it is supposed to explain? The empirical reality of such a collective value system has not been established, and data from the individuals thought to share that subculture show them to be ambivalent. If an oppositional value system exists but is not reflected in the personal evaluations of the youths thought to be committed to it, then strain theorists must tell us how to measure it.

Moreover, if Cohen's version of strain theory implies ambivalence, then what provides the motive force for malicious and negativistic behavior? Ambivalence does not seem to be a likely source of hostility. Yet, it was the oppositional nature of collective delinquency which this version of strain theory sought to explain. If the behavior to be explained is an emotionally charged form of opposition, then findings of valuational ambivalence are a problem for the theory.

Strain theory explains variations in delinquency rates by variations in the distribution of blocked ambitions. Those categories of youth with the highest collective levels of strain are predicted to have the highest rates of delinquency. Some researchers have assumed that this argument can be tested by measuring perceived opportunities for success, and have reported that rates of delinquency are higher for youths who perceive their opportunities as limited than among those who anticipate no barriers to success (Cernkovich, 1978; Aultman, 1979). However, while these findings are consistent with strain theory, they do not provide "crucial" support in that they are consistent with other theories as well. Youths who do not anticipate achieving certain success goals may not be committed to such goals and experience little or no frustration. A social control theorist could argue that they merely have less to lose by involvement in delinquency. A cultural deviance theorist could argue that deviant routes to success are accorded respect in the wider subcultural community and that youths who perceive conventional opportunity as limited are not frustrated.

It is blocked opportunity *coupled* with commitment to certain success goals which characterizes the logic of a strain explanation of delinquency. "Strain" is defined in terms of a discrepancy between a person's ambitions and opportunity; not opportunity alone. Because a disparity between ambition and reality is central to strain theories of delinquency, some researchers have predicted that the highest rates of delinquency should be found among youths who have high ambitions but do not expect to realize them. Their rates should be higher than those for youths who neither expect to achieve nor care about such conventional goals. The latter youth should not be frustrated since they do not have blocked ambitions. In actual research, the highest delinquency rates are found among boys who have both low aspirations *and* low expectations (Hirschi 1969; Short et al., 1965). Reanalysis of one of these studies (Jensen, 1986) indicates that boys low in both aspirations and expectations are not significantly higher in delinquency than boys in the high strain category (i.e. high aspirations, low expectations). Such a finding is contrary to strain theory predictions that the highest delinquency rates should be found among boys experiencing frustrated ambitions (see Box 6-2).

Several scholars have suggested that an adequate test of strain theory requires consideration of goals that are important and meaningful in the everyday lives of teenagers. While an initial examination of such a possibility suggested that anticipated failure in the achievement of immediate goals was related to delinquency (Quicker, 1974), reanalysis of such data (Greenberg, 1979a, 1979b) and two additional studies (Elliott and Voss, 1974; Agnew, 1984) have failed to provide support for strain theory. Robert Agnew (1984:446) argues that there is a sufficient range of goals for adolescents to allow them to achieve at least some of them, and, hence, strain theory may be unable to explain delinquency because "very few adolescents are strained." Rather than doggedly contemplating failure in the pursuit of unrealistic goals, teenagers are likely to shift goals and concentrate on those they can achieve.

When applied to the explanation of delinquency, all strain theories imply that, given the right circumstances, such activities are part of a solution to the problems generating them. For example, Albert Cohen depicts a delinquent contraculture as a collective solution to status problems:

> The delinquent subculture we suggest, is a way of dealing with the problems of adjustment we have described. These problems are chiefly status problems: certain children are denied status in respectable society because they cannot meet the criteria of the respectable status system. The delinquent subculture deals with these problems by providing criteria of status which these children *can* meet. (1955:121)

Other theorists have expressed similar arguments in which the specific problem prompting a search for a solution is "damaged self-esteem." Howard Kaplan (1975) argues that a wide variety of deviant behaviors are "defenses of self," prompted initially by social rejection. Sociologists advancing such arguments have focused specifically on participation in

---

Box 6-2

Strain Theories vs Control or Bond Theories

Strain theories are so-called because they introduce some form of a discrepancy between what people have learned to aspire towards and what they expect to be able to realize. This discrepancy generates status frustration which provides the motivating force for breaking laws.

Social control or bond theories view aspirations and conventional ambitions as barriers to delinquency. Even unrealistic aspirations constitute stakes in or commitments to conformity that inhibit delinquency.

Aspirations

	High	Low
High		
Low		

Expectations

In which categories above should the probability of delinquency be greatest according to the two different theories?

---

delinquent groups as a means of acquiring status and self-respect (see Rosenberg and Rosenberg, 1978).

Research on status problems and delinquency has yielded mixed results with regard to the role delinquency plays in solving those problems. Two studies (Kaplan, 1980; Bynner et al., 1981) have found that when youths are followed over time, those who initially have low self-esteem have a subsequently higher probability of delinquency, and that self-esteem appears to increase after such involvement. In contrast, two studies (McCarthy and Hoge 1984; Wells and Rankin, 1983) report no significant enhancement of self-esteem following participation in delinquency. One of the studies supporting the problem-solving argument (Kaplan, 1980) also reports that it applies only to certain categories of boys who lack other means of coping with or mitigating rejection. As matters stand today, we cannot say for certain that delinquency solves status problems, but neither can such a possibility be dismissed. Moreover, none of these studies specifically examines group delinquency, and it is the allocation of status by other similarly-situated youth which helps solve status problems, according to sociological brands of strain theory.

It is also important to ask whether strain theory can explain variations in delinquency rates in different categories of youth. While delinquency is supposed to be problem-solving, the fact that it is generated by structural-cultural problems means that categories of youth with high delinquency rates should be categories characterized by status problems. Such problems should be continually generated for minority youth and boys, as compared to white youth and girls. Some of them may solve their problems, but the forces generating such problems should continually reproduce them anew for others. Yet, studies of minority youth have not shown them to be lower in self-esteem than white youth (Rosenberg and Simmons, 1972; Harris and Stokes, 1978; Taylor and Walsh, 1979; Jensen et al., 1982). Studies of males and females have shown no difference, or slightly lower self-esteem, for females than for males (F. Rosenberg and Simmons, 1975; Jensen and Wiltfang, 1987). There is no evidence that males experience greater status frustration than females. Hence, if status problems are reflected in low self-esteem, then there is little evidence that such problems are more characteristic of those categories of youth with high delinquency rates than those with low rates.

One study has specifically addressed the relevance of perceptions of gender-based barriers to achievement on female delinquency. Stephen Cernkovich and Peggy Giordano (1979) analyzed self-report data from 1,355 male and female high school students and found perception of blocked opportunity based on gender to be unrelated to delinquency among girls. General perceptions of blocked opportunity were also unrelated to delinquency among girls. In contrast, such general perceptions were a significant correlate of delinquency for boys. Thus, strain-theory notions may be more relevant for boys than girls (as Cohen originally proposed). However, it is important to remember that without data on the aspirations or ambitions of youth, the perception of limited opportunities is not necessarily indicative of frustration. Those who perceive limited opportunity may or may not be ambitious and may or may not be frustrated. At any rate, there is little evidence that strain theory applies to girls and, currently, there is a lack of crucial support among boys.

Normative Conflict Theory

Normative or cultural conflict theory assumes that society is characterized by socially differentiated groups who have conflicting definitions of right and wrong, and that delinquency is the product of differential learning of conflicting definitions. Paul Lerman has captured the essence of cultural conflict theory, noting that "in a traditional conflict of conduct codes, it appears that one of the codes prescribes explicitly illegal behavior while the other proscribes it" (1968: 235). Research, however, has failed to reveal the types of class-linked definitions that cultural conflict theorists posit.

In his study of white youths in California, Hirschi (1969) compared the sons of fathers in lower-class occupations with the sons of semi-skilled, white-collar fathers, and those of professional fathers. He found no significant differences among these groups in attitudes that supposedly characterize lower-class youths (for example, an expedient attitude toward the law, admiration of "sharp" operators, or sensitivity to adult criticism). He did find that the sons of professionals were less likely to feel fatalistic (that is, that "there is no sense looking ahead since no one knows what the future will be like") than sons of fathers in other occupations. However, when Hirschi took measures of academic success or failure into account, he also found that the academically incompetent middle-class child was much more likely than the academically incompetent lower-class child to exhibit fatalistic attitudes. Thus, Hirschi suggested that fatalistic attitudes, rather than being an enduring aspect of a class culture, are anchored in experiences that may be more common in the lower than in the middle classes. In short, even the minimal differences in attitudes that Hirschi observed may be produced and reproduced through socially structured experiences rather than through cultural transmission.

Another set of research findings tends to contradict the argument that the "focal concerns" of lower-class culture automatically lead to lawbreaking. Studies of attachment to or identification with parents have consistently shown that children attached to their parents are less likely to be delinquent in a variety of different samples and settings (Glueck and Glueck, 1950; Hindelang, 1973; Elliott and Voss, 1974) and regardless of social class (Hirschi, 1969). If lower-class focal concerns are conducive to delinquency, then adolescents who are most sensitive to the opinions of lower-class adults should be most likely to violate the law. Research has yet to support this argument.

The finding providing the most support for differential- association theory has been the observed relationship between delinquent peers and involvement in delinquency. Adolescents with delinquent friends are themselves more likely to get into trouble with the law or report involvement in delinquency than are adolescents without delinquent friends (Glueck and Glueck, 1950; Short, 1957; Voss, 1964; Erickson and Empey, 1965; Hirschi, 1969; Linden and Hackler, 1973; Akers et al., 1978). The relationship is one of the strongest and most persistent in delinquency research.

For most of the history of research on delinquent peers and delinquency, it was not possible to claim that association with delinquent peers actually preceded involvement in delinquency, since it was also conceivable that youths involved in delinquency drifted together (i.e. "birds of a feather flock together"). It was also possible that the relationship was due to some common connection with circumstances affecting both the nature of one's friends and one's behavior. For example, youths with poor grades might be more prone to trouble and more prone to drift into delinquent groups. However, research studying sets or "panels" of youths over time have shown that association with delinquent peers does affect a youth's subsequent probabilities of delinquency (Elliott et al., 1985; Paternoster and Triplett, 1988).

The image of the gang delinquent as one of the most able, persevering, and gregarious members of the community has also been challenged. Several researchers have argued that internal sources of gang solidarity or cohesiveness are weak and that it is conflict with authority that holds delinquent gangs together. Lewis Yablonsky has depicted gang members and gang life as far from gregarious:

> A prime function of the gang is to provide a channel to act out hostility and aggression to satisfy the continuing and momentary emotional needs of its members. The gang is a convenient and malleable structure quickly adaptable to the needs of emotionally disturbed youths, who are unable to fulfill the responsibility and demands required for participation in constructive groups. A boy belongs to the gang because he lacks the social ability to relate to others and to assume responsibility for the relationship, not because the gang gives him a "feeling of belonging." Because of the gang youth's limited "social ability," he constructs a social organization which enables him to relate and to function at his limited level of performance. In this structure, norms are adjusted so that the gang youth can function and achieve despite his limited ability to relate to others. (1959:116)

Yablonsky's description is consistent with Short and Strodtbeck's findings that gang boys are less "self-assertive," less gregarious, and "slightly more neurotic and anxious" than nongang boys (1965:230). It is also consistent with Hirschi's (1969) study of high school students in California and with several other studies (Rothstein, 1962; Bandura and Walters, 1959).

A final issue in cultural conflict theory involves its emphasis on "definitions" as the most crucial variable in the explanation of delinquency. While delinquent peers are central to learning delinquency, it is the values, norms, and beliefs acquired through such associations which explain such group influences. When people break the law, it must be because they have learned a set of moral standards that require lawbreaking or because they have learned an "excess of definitions favorable to the violation of the law." Definitions control behavior to such a degree that what appears to be deviant behavior is really conforming behavior. People are always doing what they believe to be morally correct. This characteristic of cultural-deviance-differential association theory sets it off from social learning theory (see Chapter 5). According to social learning theorists, delinquency can be learned through imitation, differential reward and punishment, and "normative" socialization. Cultural deviance theorists stress the last process.

It does appear that variations in moral beliefs about the law and the impropriety of lawbreaking are affected by delinquent friends, and one study reports that such friends have their impact through such normative or definitional learning processes (Matsueda, 1982). Other studies (Akers et al., 1978; Elliott et al., 1985; Paternoster and Triplett, 1988) suggest that while definitions and delinquent associations are key to understanding delinquency, delinquent friends may affect delinquency through group processes and pressures other than normative learning. Youths who "go along with their friends" may be rewarded by others for such conformity and do what their friends are doing even though they define such activity as wrong. However, there is a general tendency for people to seek consistency between their moral beliefs and behavior as well. It may be that youths become involved in delinquency due to friendships, conflict at home and school, and a variety of circumstances, and subsequently develop a moral code which legitimizes their behavior. At present, the cultural deviance theorists' emphasis on normative learning is a plausible hypothesis but remains a subject for further investigation.

While cultural-deviance-differential-association theorists have claimed that such a perspective "explains" the gender difference in delinquency, there has been very little research on that topic and what research there is causes some difficulty for the theory. For example, while most sociologists would agree that there are differences in the "socialization" of males and females it is not clear that there is a difference in the *content* of male and female roles which explains the gender difference in delinquency. For example, one study (Jensen, 1983) found that youths' responses to statements such as "It's worse for girls to break the law than boys" or "Girls need more protection and care than boys" were unrelated to delinquency for either girls or boys. However, responses to questions about the law and the impropriety of lawbreaking in general showed girls to be more "conventionally" socialized than boys. Variation in such attitudes were relevant to both male and female delinquency and partially explained the gender difference in delinquency. Thus, there appear to be differences between boys and girls in degrees of conventional socialization but little evidence that there is a specific value-orientation and set of norms for boys that set them apart in marked contrast to girls.

Girls are subject to greater restrictions than boys (Jensen and Eve, 1976; Hagan et al., 1985), less likely to express positive attitudes towards risk and danger (Hagan et al., 1985; Jensen, 1983) and are more likely to express commitment to the law (Jensen and Eve, 1976). Such variations have been shown to explain much of the sex difference in delinquency. However, such data are as consistent with social control theory as with cultural deviance theory and may even be more consistent in that for both males and females it is those youths who are most attached to and involved with parents who are least likely to get into trouble. If boys were being taught one set of norms and girls another within the family, we would expect positive familial relationships to inhibit delinquency for girls but not boys. Indeed, we might even expect that if the content taught boys encourages crime then the most socialized boys should be the most delinquent. Research has tended to show just the opposite. Interaction with parents seems to have the same inhibiting consequences for males and females (Jensen and Eve, 1976; Canter, 1982). The sex difference is more likely to reflect differences in the degree of "conventional" socialization than conflicting norms for each sex. Boys appear to be "freer" to violate the law but there is little evidence that they do so because it is somehow "moral" for them to do so and "immoral" for girls to do so. Boys do spend more time free from adult control and engage in both conventional and unconventional activities where risk-taking and danger are more common. Such freedom and risk-taking may be viewed as more appropriate for boys than girls but such variations are not indicative of a normative conflict structured by gender.

Social Control Theory

While the cultural conflict theorist attributes the motivation for lawbreaking to subcultural socialization, and the strain theorist attributes it to structurally-induced status problems, the social control theorist makes few claims about motivation. The important variables for the control theorists are those that act as *barriers* to crime and delinquency. Hence, research relevant to control theory has focused on attitudes toward the law and its agents, commitments to conventional goals, involvement in conventional activities, or relationships with parents, the school, and the church. Much of this research is summarized in Chapter 7, where we consider several key sources of adolescent socialization. However, here we will outline research relevant to some of the crucial issues that differentiate control theory from cultural conflict and strain theory.

Control theorists focus on barriers to involvement in delinquency and have argued that the search for underlying motivation will not get us very far in understanding delinquency. The most important question becomes "Why don't youths commit offenses?" rather than why they do. Briar and Piliavin challenge the view that there are measurable, long-term motives of the sort emphasized when structural strains or subcultural value systems are introduced to explain delinquency:

> Because delinquency behavior is typically episodic, purposive, and confined to certain situations, we assume that the motives for such behavior are frequently episodic, oriented to short-term ends, and confined to certain situations. That is, rather than considering delinquency acts as solely the product of long-term motives, deriving

from conflicts or frustrations whose genesis is far removed from the arenas in which the illegal behavior occurs, we assume these acts are prompted by short-term situationally-induced desires experienced by all boys to obtain valued goods, to portray courage in the presence of, or be loyal to, peers, to strike out at someone who is disliked, or simply to "get kicks". (1965:36)

The support for the social control view of motivation has been rather indirect. For one thing, the *lack of* research to support arguments that emphasize structurally and culturally-induced motives has been interpreted as an indication that the motives must be much more diverse and difficult to predict than motivational theories suggest. Second, the fact that delinquency *itself* is episodic and sporadic, occupying very little time (even among gang delinquents), has been cited as support for the idea that the motives are similarly sporadic and episodic. Finally, the fact that delinquent activity is so common has suggested that the motives are quite commonly experienced and not concentrated in any one social class or social setting.

Martin Gold's research into the degree of premeditation involved in delinquent behavior, as well as the intensity of delinquent participation, led him to compare delinquency to a "pickup game" of basketball or football (1970). Such games are casual, unplanned, and short-term. Some youngsters are strongly committed to the game, but many are indifferent or unwilling to play. With the proper "ingredients" of time and place, a game can be organized, but in many instances sufficient catalyzing forces do not emerge. If and when the stage is set and the game begins, performance becomes an important aspect. The fact that a group of friends is present is not so important as the notion of the performance. In other words, Gold sees delinquency as a spontaneous, unplanned event with certain members of the group performing as players and others being more passive and performing as the audience. Gold believes that the image of delinquency as an impromptu performance is closer to the truth than the image of the delinquent as chronic offender or disturbed adolescent. Thus, Gold's findings support social control theory's downplaying of motivational factors and strong emphasis on the situational nature of delinquent behavior.

Research studies have shown significant relationships between involvement in delinquency and attachment to conventional others, values, and institutions. Youths who identify with their parents, care what their teachers think about them, aspire toward high occupational or educational status, and respect the law and its agents are significantly less likely to commit delinquent acts than are youths with fewer "stakes in conformity" (Hirschi, 1969; Hindelang, 1973; Jensen, 1972; Hepburn, 1976). However, the most recent studies following youth over a period of time suggest that the impact of such stakes in conformity may have been exaggerated in research examining such relationships at single points in time (see Agnew, 1985; Elliott et al., 1985; Liska and Reed, 1985). Since youths' relationships with conventional people, values, and institutions can be affected by their past misbehavior some of the association between such variables and delinquency may be a product of the impact of misbehavior on such relationships rather than the inhibiting impact of those relationships. Those studies suggest that delinquent peers and variation in conventional and unconventional beliefs may have the greatest impact on delinquency and that other circumstances such as family and school relationships have an impact on delinquency through their impact on association with such peers and beliefs.

The studies following youths over time involve a relatively short period of their lives and tend to involve youths at or past the peak ages for delinquency. Such characteristics of the studies are relevant to our interpretation of results because the relevance of such variables as relationships with parents to delinquency may rest with responses to behavior in childhood socialization. Youths who do not care about their parents' reactions or whose parents do not detect or react to misbehavior in early childhood are likely to get into difficulties at school and in the community. Research to be summarized in Chapter 10 shows that changes in parental response to behavior can impressively alter their children's behavior as well. In sum, while some studies are challenging the relevance of social control variables to delinquency, there is considerable counter evidence that parental attempts at control and socialization are relevant to the behavior of children.

Control theory is at odds with strain theory over the relationship between conventional aspirations and delinquency. As already noted, strain theorists argue that high aspirations, coupled with limited opportunity, generate status problems and that such problems are concentrated in the lower or working classes. On the other hand, some control theorists (Hirschi, 1969) believe that conventional aspirations constitute a "stake" in conformity and therefore act as a barrier to delinquency.

As noted in the discussion of strain theory, ambitious youth who anticipate failure do not appear to be significantly more delinquent than unambitious youth. However, neither has it been conclusively shown that high conventional aspirations inhibit delinquency regardless of realistic expectations. For example, some of the findings that Hirschi (1969:172) uses to challenge strain theory also show that it is youths who do not expect to achieve high status who have high delinquency rates, whether or not they aspire to such status. Some of these youths may have abandoned any commitment to conventional success as a result of anticipated failure, and many of them may never have had such aspirations. However, such findings constitute a problem for the control theorists' argument that aspirations act as a barrier to delinquency, regardless of youths' expectations.

The scope of factors that control theory presents as barriers to delinquency is quite broad. For example, Briar and Piliavin (1965) have cited the following barriers: 1) fear of material deprivations and punishments, 2) protection of self-image, 3) maintenance of valued relationships, and 4) preservation of future status and activities. Hirschi has differentiated four dimensions of the "social bond" between youths and conventional society that act as a barrier to delinquency: 1) attachment or identification (for example, with parents), 2) commitment to conventional goals (such as high occupational status), 3) belief in the legitimacy of conventional norms, and 4) involvement in conventional activities.

Several studies of involvement in conventional activities have failed to support the predictions of control theory. Hirschi found that participation in work, sports, recreation, and hobbies were unrelated to delinquency (1969:189-90). Robin reported that involvement in antipoverty job corps or neighborhood youth corps programs had no significant impact on delinquent behavior during or after participation in the programs (1969:323-31). Schaefer found no significant relationship between participation in interscholastic athletics and delinquency when controlling for grade point average and social class (1969:40-47). Even amount of time under direct parental control or surveillance has been found to be only weakly related to delinquency. On the other hand, involvement in some academic activities has been shown to be negatively related to delinquency (Hirschi, 1969:191-92; Hindelang, 1973: 481-83). In short, although control theory predicts that participation in conventional activity should deter delinquency, many forms of participation do not. There is little overall support for the folk belief that "idle hands are the devil's workshop." Those forms of participation that are related to delinquency (for example, time spent on homework) are those that are likely to reflect real commitment and valued relationships. Control theorists have not been able to predict what forms of participation are important barriers to delinquency.

Research has also failed to support some control theorists' claims that attachment to others is a barrier to delinquency even if those others are involved in delinquency. One of the most prominent control theorists has argued that "we honor those we admire not by imitation, but by adherence to conventional standards" (Hirschi, 1969:152). This argument represents an extreme version of control theory in which it does not matter to whom a person is attached. The actual support for that argument is very weak, and there are several studies whose findings are to the contrary. Hirschi reported a weak negative correlation between "wanting to be like one's friends" and delinquency, even for youths with several delinquent friends. However, further analysis of the same body of data (Jensen and Erickson, 1977) showed no significant association between peer commitment and delinquency among black youths. Moreover, at least four studies have reported positive associations—that is, the greater the attachment to peers, the greater the delinquency (Empey and Lubeck, 1971; Hindelang, 1973; Erickson and Empey, 1965; Elliott and Voss, 1974). Linden and Hackler (1973: 43) report that the characteristics of the peers to which a youth is attached do affect the relevance of peer attachment to delinquency. Boys with weak ties to conventional associates but with moderate or strong ties to deviant peers are more involved in delinquency than are boys who are not tied to their delinquent peers.

Giordano, Cernkovich, and Pugh (1986) argue that delinquents are not lone wolves whose only personal relationships are manipulative and exploitative. Rather, they argue that the friendship patterns of delinquent youth are quite like those of nondelinquent youth. The bulk of the research at present is consistent with this view, suggesting that there are weak but positive associations between attachment to peers and delinquency, and that boys who are "tied," "committed," or "attached" to their delinquent peers are more likely to be involved in delinquency than those who are not so committed. However, contrary findings have yet to be explained and will no doubt be the subject of further research.

Control theory variables have been introduced in the attempt to explain the gender difference in delinquency with some success. Boys and girls do differ in the strength of familial bonds, in degrees of parental control, school performance, endorsement of conventional beliefs, and in their perceptions of risk of punishment. In that sense girls have more stakes in conformity than boys. Furthermore, variations in such variables have been shown to explain much of the gender difference in delinquency (Jensen and Eve, 1976; Hagan et al., 1985, 1987). However, association with delinquent peers has been found to be relevant to the sex difference as well and such associations are not central to some versions of control theory.

Combinations and Reformulations

As we noted earlier, Cloward and Ohlin attempted to combine notions of strain theory with some aspects of cultural conflict theory. Similarly, other theorists have attempted to combine notions derived from cultural conflict and social control theory. Linden and Hackler (1973) have developed an *affective ties* theory that focuses on ties to delinquent peers as a source of delinquent activity, and on ties to conventional people in one's environment (parents, teachers, and some peers) as barriers to delinquency. This theory combines many of the basic elements of control theory with differential association theory. However, in contrast to cultural conflict theorists, Linden and Hackler do not assume that all factors that might influence delinquency do so through their influence on cultural "definitions." Such definitions are viewed as relevant to explaining delinquency but not as mediating the impact of all other influences. According to this theory, ties to conventional and unconventional people are relevant to explaining delinquency, regardless of what an adolescent feels to be right or wrong.

Social learning theorists (Conger 1976; Akers 1985; Akers, et al., 1979) take a similar stand in that they view delinquent peers as a source of reinforcement for delinquent action and bonds to conventional institutions as barriers to delinquency. In addition, social learning theorists believe that although "definitions" play a role in the learning of conventional and unconventional behavior, such definitions do not mediate all other influences. Peer pressures to "go along" can, it is argued, increase the odds of delinquency even when a youth defines the activity as wrong. Concern about parental reaction can inhibit delinquency even when a youth does not define the activity involved as wrong. In short, social learning theory, in contrast to differential association and cultural deviance theory, stresses nonnormative as well as normative learning mechanisms that can lead to delinquency. While social control and social learning theories are compatible with one another, social learning theory attempts to identify the processes and motivational forces involved in the initiation and reinforcement of delinquent behavior whereas social control theory focuses on processes and forces which inhibit delinquent behavior. Moreover, social control theory is linked theoretically to the social disorganization perspective while social learning theory is not clearly linked to any of the epidemiological theories. Its developers viewed it as a reformulation of the differential association perspective but, as noted above, the social learning theorists acceptance of nonnormative learning mechanisms sets it apart from the cultural deviance-differential association tradition.

Both affective ties theory and social learning theory deal with the immediate social influences which facilitate and inhibit delinquency among individuals. It is important to note that most recent attempts at "integration" focus on such proximate influences as they affect individuals and do not deal with the macro-level contrasts among theories. For example, a demonstration of the importance of delinquent peers in the generation of individual delinquency has little bearing on divergent images of the role of subcultural, contracultural or infracultural values or the distribution of such values among territories or categories of people.

Two of the most recent efforts to draw on ideas from several theories have added strain theory to the explanation of delinquency, either by introducing it as a factor affecting bonds to conventional people and institutions or by introducing new conceptions of strain. Elliott, Huizinga, and Ageton (1985) attempt to integrate the strongest features of social learning, social control, and strain theories into a single model. They argue that high levels of strain and weak conventional bonds lead youth to seek out and imitate deviant peers. Moreover, high levels of strain can actually weaken conventional bonds in their theory.

In another attempt to integrate strain, differential association, and control theories, David Greenberg (1979a) proposes that it is the disparity between the everyday, immediate needs for cash and resources to participate in youth culture and access to such funds which generates motivational pressure towards delinquency. Other variables stressed by control and differential association theorists can inhibit or facilitate acting on such motives.

Neither of these proposals have been based on any new evidence clearly justifying the inclusion of strains in some specific sequence or as defined by a disparity between needs for cash and access to it (Jensen, 1986). Critics (Hirschi and Gottfredson, 1983) of Greenberg's efforts have pointed to research indicating that the more money a youth has, through work or allowance, the greater the odds of delinquency (Cullen et al., 1985; Hirschi, 1969). Greenberg's response has been that since needs may be greater for those with more resources, those with more money may experience more strain than the relatively disadvantaged. Of course, if that argument were correct, then strain should be greater for adults than adolescents and, contrary to Greenberg's argument about age differences, crime rates should be greater for adults than teenagers. "Strain," like other vague, unmeasured concepts in criminology, is shifted around to coincide with high rates of crime and delinquency with little evidence to justify its reality.

An even more recent approach has been to define strain not in terms of blockage in the pursuit of valued goals, but blockage in the avoidance of painful or "aversive" situations. Robert Agnew (1985) argues that children are legally compelled to stay in situations which may generate anger and frustration for many of them. For example, they may have punitive or abusive parents, feel trapped at school, or be disliked by their teachers. Such circumstances allegedly generate anger, which increases the probability of delinquency. Using data from a national survey of 3,213 adolescent boys, Agnew found support for such an argument. However, it is important to note that although the term "strain" is used, Agnew's reformulation is so different from the original versions of strain theory that support for his argument is not support for those earlier formulations. In fact, elsewhere (Agnew, 1984) presents data contrary to the major formulations of strain theory.

The notion of integration is very popular in criminology and scholars will no doubt continue to propose integrated theories, borrowing elements from diverse perspectives. It does, in fact, appear that the motivational forces provided by deviant peers must be combined with the inhibiting forces provided by conventional institutions to adequately explain delinquency. If those forces affect delinquency only through normative learning, then no integrated theory is required since that was the central thrust of differential association as originally formulated. If other nonnormative processes are at work, then no integrated theory is needed, since social learning theory proposes such processes. However, unlike social control theory and differential association theory, social learning theory has not been linked with a macro or epidemiological parallel. Since social learning theory has worked so well at the individual level, the most promising line of theoretical integration in the future will be to build such links. The current emphasis on integrating theories by salvaging strain has gotten us nowhere.

Marxist Theories

The combinations and reformulations we have just summarized focus on the learning mechanisms, immediate frustrations, and variations in intimate social relationships which facilitate or inhibit delinquent behavior among individuals. With the exception of Greenberg's theory, they do not make claims to explain variations among societies or take stands on the role of culture, structure, and social organization in generating variations among collectivities and territories within society. In contrast, several theorists, including Greenberg, Herman and Julia Schwendinger, Richard Quinney, Jock Young, and others propose perspectives which draw on or reformulate prior theoretical notions in terms of ideas developed by the German social philosopher, Karl Marx (1818-1883).

In Marxist perspectives the economic system is central to understanding all other aspects of society and culture and people's lives revolve around economic production. Marxist theorists focus on the control of economic production and work in societies, and locate the origins of social problems in the "contradictions" characterizing capitalism as a particular form of political-economic organization. For example, in capitalist societies and societies colonized or under development by capitalist societies, it is to the advantage of those who own or control economic development to have a large, readily available, surplus labor force. Cheap, available labor helps keep costs down and profits up. Moreover, to generate profits, the products of economic production must be sold. There must be a market for them. People must "want" both the necessities and luxuries produced. Of course, the generation of a large surplus labor force which is often unemployed and underemployed, combined with the emphasis on consumption, creates the same condition emphasized by strain theory—sizeable segments of society with needs that cannot be realized.

When applied to the explanation of delinquency, young people are viewed as particularly likely to experience such a strain or contradiction. In fact, as noted in Chapter 2, Marxist theorists argue that the category of delinquency itself was invented to cope with the problem behaviors generated as the marginal period of life (between childhood and incorporation into the economy) grew.

A central concept in some Marxist perspectives on delinquency is marginality. Categories of people who exist on the periphery of the economic system as an unemployed or underemployed surplus population or labor force are "marginal" categories. Youth as a whole are a "marginal" category, although many will move into the mainstream economy with age. Marxists attribute the high crime rate of youth to their status as a marginal category, and variations within the adolescent world reflect variations in marginality as well (see Schwendinger and Schwendinger, 1976; Greenberg, 1979a). The Schwendingers (1985) claim that it is in the best interest of the state and dominant economic classes to maintain such marginal categories as a ready pool for low-paid manual labor.

The exact nature of variations among adolescents and the processes operating at the individual level in the determination of delinquency have not been clearly specified by Marxist theorists and scholars claiming a Marxist heritage for their theories make contradictory claims. For example, the emphasis on marginality implies that among young people, the most marginal and those with the least hope of escaping marginality with age, will have the highest delinquency rates. Yet, John Hagan and colleagues (1985) predict that children whose parents control other workers will be raised to take risks and to believe that they are relatively free from the control of others and, hence, will engage in more delinquency than lower status youth. In their work, it is those youth who are least marginal in terms of potential dominance of others and occupational power who are predicted to have the highest rates, rather than those on the periphery. Those youth are posited as "freer" to break laws with impunity. Hagan, Gillis, and Simpson (1985) hypothesize that power decreases the probability of being caught and punished and, hence, increases rather than decreases most common types of delinquency.

In contrast, Mark Colvin and John Pauley (1983) propose a *structural Marxist* approach to delinquency, predicting an inverse relationship between parent's occupational power and children's delinquency. According to their theory parents tend to reproduce the authority relations they experience at the work place in the home and the coercive social milieu that most workers find themselves in leads to authoritarian relationships at home. Coercive and authoritarian family relationships allegedly undermine affection and intimate bonds to parents, leading to a higher probability of delinquency than nonauthoritarian and noncoercive familial relationships. Thus, while Hagan, Gillis, and Simpson predict that those parents who are most controlled and dominated in the work place will have children who are controlled and, hence, less likely to break laws, Colvin and Pauley predict that such control undermines social bonds and increases the odds of delinquency. The predictions are the exact opposite in each case although they both propose to be structural Marxist theories.

In their award-winning book on *Adolescent Subcultures and Delinquency* (1985), the Schwendingers propose a different approach that combines notions of symbolic interactionism with Marxist theory in the explanation of delinquency. The focus in *symbolic interaction theory* is on the formation and selection of symbolic identities which occurs in interaction with other people. In their theory adolescent subcultures are organized around certain common identities that youths can take on and those identities are more important for understanding delinquency than parental class. Indeed, the Schwendingers predict small but negative relationships between parental status and delinquency. In contrast, youths who belong to certain stradoms (stratified peer group domains) are predicted to vary in delinquency and school misconduct. Data on delinquency and membership in different stradoms support their argument. They found the lowest rates of delinquency among "brains" and "athletes" and the highest rates among streetcorner types of youth referred to as "Hodads" or "Greasers." "Socialites" and "Surfers" were more likely to be involved in delinquency than brains or jocks as well. The stradom a youth falls in is affected by parental status but determined by other variables as well such that the relationship between parental status and delinquency may be quite weak while the relationship between stradom membership and delinquency may be quite strong. In this theory it is stratification and lifestyles in the adolescent social world that are central to understanding delinquency (see Box 6-3).

At the individual level, Marxist theorists introduce variables much like those stressed in other criminological theories. Why don't people break laws more often than they do when the economic system is not serving their interests? Some Marxists will emphasize fear of legal punishment in answering this question. Powerful groups determine the nature of laws defining crime and law enforcement serves to control marginal groups (see Quinney, 1980; Chambliss and Mankoff, 1976; Taylor et al., 1973). Fear of punishment is central to explaining crime and delinquency in deterrence theory, a classical criminological perspective which we will discuss in Chapter 9.

In his presentation of a "Working Class Criminology" (1975), English criminologist Jock Young argues that people are inhibited by a conservative "ideology" of law and order which is maintained through educational institutions and which does, to some degree, appeal to working class and marginal groups who need protection from crime. Compulsory education helps insure a common exposure to a belief system stressing the virtue of conformity to law, patience in the pursuit of material and social success, and the horrendous personal and social costs of lawbreaking. Thus, variations in crime and delinquency can reflect variations in acceptance

---

Box 6-3
High School Social Types and Delinquency

Herman and Julia Schwendinger (1985) have conducted research on adolescent subcultures in Southern California. Rather than focusing on the social class of parents as the primary indicator of the social categorization of youth, they focused on the "social types" that predominate in teenage society—such as surfers, athletes, socialites, brains, clods, and hodads (street corner youth). The categories and names differ among locales. Other names of social types used by teenagers and others are "nerds," "bops," "jocks," and "punkers." Youth may not fall into a single category.

In terms of delinquent behavior, a partial listing of categories ranked approximately as follows:

HIGH DELINQUENCY   Hodads
                        Surfers
                        Socialites
                        Athletes
                        Brains
LOW DELINQUENCY   Clods

What social types were you aware of as a teenager and how do you think they would have ranked in terms of delinquency?

---

or "internalization" of beliefs which inhibit lawbreaking, a notion consistent with several traditional theories.

Another variable introduced in the discussion of capitalism and social problems is *alienation*. This concept is widely used by sociologists and has been used in a variety of studies of delinquency (see Menard and Morse, 1984; Engstad and Hackler, 1971; and Stinchcombe, 1964). The *Dictionary of the Social Sciences* (1964:19) defines alienation as "an estrangement or separation between the parts or whole of the personality and significant aspects of the world of experience." The concept originally referred to aspects of economic production under capitalism wherein people became "estranged" from the products of their labor (e.g., mass assembly lines where each worker performs a repetitive, specialized task and neither owns nor controls the final product). However, it is widely used to refer to estrangement from society in general or specific institutions such as the school. For example, modern mass education is often depicted as "alienating" and those youths who are most alienated from such institutions are predicted to be the most likely to get into trouble. There are several studies supporting such arguments (e.g., Stinchcombe, 1964; Engstad and Hackler, 1971). Moreover, research taken as support for social control theory is also consistent with this argument in the sense that youths who are not attached to conventional people and institutions can also be considered to be estranged or alienated from those institutions.

Another individual cause of delinquency and crime emphasized by the Marxist theorist William Bonger (1916) was *egoism*. According to Bonger, people in a capitalist society are encouraged to pursue satisfaction of ever-expanding desires for wealth and status with little regard for the well-being of others. Such egoism is viewed as common to most people in such societies and even more common among the relatively advantaged classes than among the disadvantaged. However, while egoism provides a motive force for delinquency, Bonger argues that the children of the well-to-do are watched more closely and prevented from associating with "bad society" and, thus, are less likely to commit delinquent acts.

In sum, it is difficult to discern one consistent set of specific predictions about such basic issues as the relation between social class and delinquency which could be considered *the* Marxist perspective. Furthermore, the processes operating at the individual level are similar to those characterizing strain, cultural deviance, control, and deterrence theories of criminality. The most distinctive claim is that societies characterized by capitalism or capitalist colonization should have higher rates of delinquency than societies characterized by socialist or communist forms of economic organization (Chambliss, 1976). Due to international variations in crime statistics and the lack of comparative data on actual rates of delinquent activity among distinctive societies, that claim is still a hypothesis to be tested. Moreover, some Marxist theorists (Quinney) would not necessarily accept that variations in crime and delinquency among *existing* societies are relevant to the view that a "true" socialist society would have low crime rates, for the simple reason that the principles of a true socialist state have not been realized in existing societies. Hence, the fact that advanced capitalist economies do not have invariably high delinquency rates (e.g. Japan, Switzerland) may be irrelevant to such theories. As we will note in Chapter 12, such theories make claims about the future which are not necessarily anchored in existing variations. That fact does not make them wrong, but puts the verification of the theory in the future realization of alternative forms of economic organization.

Directions for Future Theoretical Development

Several major advances in the physical sciences have involved specification of the circumstances affecting the validity of a theory. For example, the shift from Newtonian physics to Einsteinian physics entailed the specification of the conditions under which traditional Newtonian ideas were relatively accurate. Similarly, the reconciliation of diverse theories of delinquency may require the specification of the circumstances affecting the validity of a theory. Since the major theories are in fundamental conflict on several issues, efforts to synthesize them shift to issues where the theories are not in as marked conflict (i.e. learning mechanisms or individual level correlates).

There are ways of reconciling theories which do not require that they be combined, synthesized, or integrated. Rather, theories can apply under specific circumstances that need to be more precisely specified. It is conceivable that theories are differentially applicable at different times in history. For example, there is some evidence that attachment to parents inhibits childrens' drug use when their parents are "straight" but has little or no impact among children of drug-using parents (Jensen and Brownfield, 1983). Thus, at a time in history when parents are extremely conventional in their own behavior and attitudes, attachment will operate as an important barrier to deviance. If parental behavior and attitudes change, the impact of attachment may change. The impact of other variables may vary over time as well. Variables such as mother's employment and presence of the father in the home may have been more relevant to understanding delinquency when they were rare than when they are commonplace. Differences among territories and ethnic groups may have declined over time. In short, to the degree that social change reflects change in social and cultural circumstances shaping behavior, a theory may apply better at one time than another.

Different theories may apply to different types of offenses as well. As we will note in Chapter 8, variables such as church membership may affect drug use more than offenses against persons and property. Measures of community integration may affect property crime more than crimes of interpersonal violence. As noted in Chapter 4, race and social class variations may be greater for interpersonal violence than property crimes. Furthermore, there is some evidence that drug use may take on a more "subcultural" quality than other forms of offense activity. Based on an analysis of serious forms of drug use, Smeja and Rojek (1986:1047) report that "The cultural milieu of illicit drug users is more rigorously defined and isolated from the dominant culture" than is the case for marijuana users. They also suggest that "Perhaps there was a time when marijuana use reflected a counterculture, but it has gradually acquired a sense of conventionality, and in time may lose its subcultural underpinnings." Thus, another direction for making sense out of divergent theories may be specification of their relevance to different types of crime.

Finally, the importance of different variables and, hence, the applicability of different theories, may vary among settings and groups as well. As will be elaborated in Chapter 8, it is quite common now to argue that religious involvement is more relevant to delinquency in some types of communities than others or in some types of religious denominations than others. Similarly, Kaplan's (1984) finding that delinquency enhances self-esteem and satisfaction of needs only among boys lacking other status resources suggests that some versions of strain theory apply only in limited circumstances and not to girls. In contrast, there is evidence that social control theory applies to both girls and boys (Canter, 1982; Jensen and Eve, 1976) although there is still disagreement over whether family variables are more important for understanding female delinquency than male delinquency (cf. Canter, 1982; Rodman and Grams, 1967).

Krohn and Massey (1980) have suggested that social control theory may be better able to explain female than male delinquency, and less serious forms of delinquency than more serious delinquent acts. Both Krohn and Massey and LaGrange and White (1985) suggest that Hirschi's social control model may be more applicable to youths in their mid-teens than to older adolescents. Agnew (1985) reports that as an adolescent matures the effect of social bonds diminishes.

In sum, progress in understanding delinquency may require specification of those times, settings, circumstances, groups and offenses affecting the relevance of certain barriers and motivating forces. Despite decades of research on correlates of delinquency there has been little attention paid to the systematic specification of the conditions affecting the applicability of a theory to social reality. However, there are sufficient hints in recent research to prompt more precise attention to such issues.

Summary

This chapter outlined theories developed by sociologists to explain the distribution of delinquency as well as much of the research carried out to test such theories. Such approaches have been most distinct from psychological or biological perspectives when treating delinquency as a type of group, a distinctive subcultural orientation, or as a characteristic of neighborhoods, communities or territories. Moreover, years of research have shown delinquency to be an eminently sociological subject matter in that it is generally a "social activity." The fact that most delinquency occurs among youths interacting with other youths has been established in numerous studies and is true for both boys and girls and in a variety of different settings.

While much of the chapter concentrated on the contrasts among theories it is important to remember that the theories do share certain broad assumptions in common, enabling us to classify them as sociological in orientation. They all assume that delinquency is acquired or *learned* behavior and that the probability that such behavior will be acquired varies depending on cultural patterns, social institutions and groups, and the structure of legal and illegal opportunities. Different sociological theories are characterized by different ideas about the exact nature and relative importance of different environmental circumstances. Three theories that differ sufficiently to be considered unique schools of thought are 1) social disorganization-social control theory, 2) structural strain-status frustration theory, and 3) normative conflict-differential association theory. Other perspectives can be identified as well, including proposed *integrations*, that is, theories focusing on learning processes and Marxist theories. However, such theories cannot yet be presented as a system of consistent ideas about the individual and societal level aspects of delinquency causation. As new research is generated and conflicting predictions are discussed and resolved, these recent perspectives may develop into coherent macro-micro-theories incorporating elements of the old with the new.

Social disorganization-social control theories emphasize the failure of social systems or agencies of conventional socialization to give juveniles personal, social, or moral stakes in conformity. As a result, a sizeable proportion of the juvenile population has little to lose by making delinquent choices and are free to drift into delinquency. *Structural strain-status frustration* perspectives emphasize difficulties experienced by some segments of society in achieving learned success goals. The disparity between goals and opportunity at the societal level generates status problems and, if enough similarly situated juveniles interact with one another, one outcome may be the development of an oppositional group culture, or a "contraculture." *Normative conflict-differential association* theory assumes that there are certain segments of society or social settings characterized by values, norms and beliefs that require or encourage delinquency. Differential exposure to such subcultural values is thought to explain variations in delinquency rates as well as variable individual involvement in delinquency.

Research relevant to strain theory has failed to substantiate a number of assumptions central to the perspective. There is little evidence that gang boys are characterized by a contracultural value system. High aspirations appear to act as a barrier to delinquency even in groups or among youths whose probabilities of failure are high. Most research suggests that delinquency does not solve status problems although there is one study suggesting that delinquency may help reenhance self-esteem among a small category of boys who have very few conventional status resources. Delinquency rates and status problems do not vary among categories of youth in a manner consistent with the theory when gender and race are considered either. The one issue where data are consistent with the theory involves perceived opportunity in that males who perceive limited opportunity have higher probabilities of delinquency. However, such findings can be explained by other theories and do not appear to apply to girls. Hence, there may be some specific groups and or circumstances to which strain theory applies but its unique applicability has not been demonstrated.

The variations in subcultural definitions of lawbreaking that normative conflict theory posits have not been substantiated in actual research. Studies of public evaluations of the seriousness of criminal or delinquent activities, of public disapproval of such activity, and of adolescent attitudes toward lawbreaking have not supported the notion of a class subculture that requires, encourages, or tolerates crime and delinquency. Researchers have presented evidence that questions the assumption that delinquent youths are among the most able, persevering, and gregarious members in their particular social setting. In contrast, the importance of delinquent companions for understanding delinquency has been well substantiated and there are definite associations between peoples' definitions of proper conduct and their own reported conduct. Whether all group and institutional influences operate through definitions or "normative" learning is a subject of debate with some evidence for that argument but some evidence against it as well.

Research has been consistent with social disorganization-social control theory in a number of key areas but inconsistent in others. Research suggests that the focus on barriers to delinquency is of greater utility in explaining variable involvement in delinquency than is the search for motives. Relationships with conventional persons and institutions as well as commitments to conventional goals and acceptance of conventional beliefs about lawbreaking appear to act as barriers to delinquency. Recent studies following youth over time have suggested that the impact of social control variables has been exaggerated. Control theorists have not been able to predict what forms of involvement in conventional activities are important as barriers to delinquency although the theory assumes that such involvements should decrease delinquency. Moreover, contrary to the view that attachment inhibits delinquency regardless of the behavior of those to which a youth is attached, the impact of attachment is the greatest when the objects of attachment are conventional themselves.

Other theories have been proposed that reformulate or combine ideas from different theories, that focus on learning processes, or that apply notions suggested by the German philosopher, Karl Marx, to the explanation of delinquency. Social learning theory details the learning processes involved in the initiation and persistence of delinquent behavior but does not deal with broader issues relevant to the distribution of delinquency within or among societies. Similarly, integrated theory focuses on individual level variables and has not been characterized by positions on structural and cultural issues. Marxist theories potentially apply at both the individual and the structural-cultural level but proponents have advanced quite contrary predictions about some key issues and have only recently attempted to provide quantitative data relevant to such theories.

Further progress in the explanation of delinquency is likely to require that more attention be paid to several issues that have been raised repeatedly over the decades but have rarely been investigated in a systematic fashion. Specifically, we need to learn far more about the relevance of different variables at different times in history, for specific groups and settings, for different types of offenses, and for group as opposed to individual delinquent activities. This issue will become even more obvious in the chapters to follow which deal with the relevance of family, school, peers, religion, media, and community to the explanation of delinquency. The same limitations characterizing tests of theory apply to seemingly straightforward studies of the relevance of specific social variables to the explanation of delinquency.

References

Agnew, R. 1985. "A Revised Strain Theory of Delinquency." *Social Forces* 64 (Number 1):151-67.

_____. 1985. "Social Control Theory and Delinquency: A Longitudinal Test." *Criminology* 23:47-61.

_____. 1984. "Goal Achievement and Delinquency." *Sociology and Social Research*. 68 (No. 4):435-51.

Akers, R. L. 1985. *Deviant Behavior: A Social Learning Approach*, 3rd ed. Belmont, CA: Wadsworth.

Akers, R. L., M. D. Krohn, L. Lanza-Kaduce, and M. Radosevich. 1978. "Social Learning and Deviant Behavior." *American Sociological Review* 44 (August): 636-55.

Aultman, M. 1979. "Delinquency Causation: Typological Comparisons of Path Models." *Journal of Criminal Law and Criminology* 70:152-63.

Bandura, A., and R. H. Walters. 1959. *Adolescent Aggression*. New York: Ronald Press.

Bonger, W. 1916. *Criminality and Economic Conditions*. Boston: Little, Brown.

Briar, S., and I. Piliavin. 1965. "Delinquency, Situational Inducements, and Commitments to Conformity." *Social Problems* 13 (1):35-45.

Broom, L., and P. Selznick. 1968. *Sociology*. New York: Harper & Row.

Bursik, R. J., Jr. 1988. "Social Disorganization and Theories of Crime and Delinquency: Problems and Prospects." *Criminology* 26 (November):519-51.

Bynner, S. M., P. M. O'Malley, and J. G. Bachman. 1981. "Self-Esteem and Delinquency Revisited." *Journal of Youth and Adolescence* 10:407-44.

Canter, R. J. 1982. "Family Correlates of Male and Female Delinquency." *Criminology* 20 (August):149-67.

Cernkovich, S. A. 1978. "Evaluating Two Models of Delinquency Causation." *Criminology* 16: 335-52.

Cernkovich, S. A., and P. C. Giordano. 1979. "Delinquency, Opportunity and Gender." *Journal of Criminal Law and Criminology* 70 (Summer):145-51.

Chambliss, W. J., and M. Mankoff (eds.). 1976. *Whose Law? What Order?* New York: John Wiley and Sons, Inc.

Cloward, R. A., and L. E. Ohlin. 1960. *Delinquency and Opportunity.* New York: Free Press.

Cohen, A. K. 1956. *Delinquent Boys.* New York: Free Press.

Cohen, A. K., and J. F. Short. 1958. "Research in Delinquent Subcultures." *Journal of Social Issues* 14:20-37.

Colvin, M., and J. Pauley. 1983. "A Critique of Criminology: Toward an Integrated Structural Marxist Theory of Delinquency Production." *American Journal of Sociology* 89:513-55.

Conger, R. D. 1976. "Social Control and Social Learning Models of Delinquent Behavior: A Synthesis." *Criminology* 14 (May):17-40.

Cullen, F. T., M. T. Larson, and R. A. Mathers. 1985. "Having Money and Delinquency Involvement." *Criminal Justice and Behavior* 12 (June):171-92.

DeLamater, J. 1968. "On the Nature of Deviance." *Social Forces* 46 (June):445-55.

Durkheim, E. 1951. *Suicide.* Translated by J.A. Spaulding and G. Simpson. New York: Free Press.

Elliott, D. S., and H. L. Voss. 1974. *Delinquency and Dropout.* Lexington, MA: Lexington Books.

Elliott, D. S., D. Huizinga, and S. S. Ageton. 1985. *Explaining Delinquency and Drug Use.* Beverly Hills, CA: Sage Publications.

Empey, L. T. 1967. "Delinquency Theory and Recent Research." *Journal of Research in Crime and Delinquency* 4 (January):32-42.

Empey, L. T., and S. G. Lubeck. 1971. *Explaining Delinquency.* Lexington, MA: Lexington Books.

Engstad, P., and J. C. Hackler. 1971. "The Impact of Alienation on Delinquency Rates." *Canadian Journal of Criminology and Corrections* 13 (April):1-8.

Erickson, M. L., and L. T. Empey. 1965. "Class Position, Peers and Delinquency." *Sociology and Social Research* 49 (April):268-82.

Finestone, H. 1976. *Victims of Change: Juvenile Delinquents in American Society.* Westport, CT: Greenwood Press.

Giordano, P., S. Cernkovich, and M. Pugh. 1986. "Friendships and Delinquency." *American Journal of Sociology* 91:1170-1202.

Glueck, S., and E. Glueck. 1950. *Unraveling Juvenile Delinquency.* Cambridge, MA: Harvard University Press.

Gold, M. 1963. *Status Forces in Delinquent Boys.* Ann Arbor, MI: Institute for Social Research, University of Michigan.

_____. 1970. *Delinquent Behavior in an American City.* Monterey, CA: Brooks/Cole.

Gordon, R. A., J. F. Short, Jr., D. S. Cartwright, and F. L. Strodtbeck. 1963. "Values and Gang Delinquency." *American Journal of Sociology* 69 (September): 109-28.

Greenberg, D. 1979a. "Delinquency and the Age Structure of Society." In S. Messinger, and E. Bittner (eds.), *Criminology Review Yearbook.* Beverly Hills, CA: Sage Publications.

Greenberg, D. 1979b. *Mathematical Criminology,* New Brunswick: Rutgers.

Hagan, J., A. R. Gillis, and J. Simpson. 1985. "The Class Structure of Gender and Delinquency: Toward a Power-Control Theory of Common Delinquent Behavior." *American Journal of Sociology* 90: 1151-1178.

Hagan, J., A. R. Gillis, and J. Simpson. 1987. "Class in the Household: A Power Control Theory of Gender and Delinquency." *American Journal of Sociology* 92 (January):788-816.

Harris, A. R., and R. Stokes. 1978. "Race, Self-evaluation and the Protestant Ethic." *Social Problems* 26:71-85.

Hepburn, J. R. 1976. "Casting Alternative Models of Delinquency Causation." *Journal of Criminal Law and Criminology* 67 (December): 450-60.

Hindelang, M. J. 1973. "Causes of Delinquency: A Partial Replication and Extension." *Social Problems* 21 (Spring):471-87.

Hirschi, T. 1969. *Causes of Delinquency*. Berkeley: University of California Press.

Hirschi, T., and M. Gottfredson. 1983. "Age and the Explanation of Crime." *American Journal of Sociology* 89:552-84.

Jensen, G. F. 1969. "Crime Doesn't Pay: Correlates of a Shared Misunderstanding." *Social Problems* 17 (Fall):189-201.

_____. 1972. "Parents, Peers and Delinquent Action: A Test of the Differential Association Hypothesis." *American Journal of Sociology* 78 (November):562-75.

_____. 1979. "The Religious Factor and Delinquency." In Robert Wuthnow, (ed.), *The Religious Dimension: New Directions in Quantitative Research*. New York: Academic Press.

_____. 1983. "The Truth About Sex and Crime." Paper presented at the 1983 Conference of Arizona Justice Educators, Tempe, Arizona.

_____. 1986. "Dis-Integrating Integrated Theory." Paper presented at the Annual Convention of the American Society of Criminology, Atlanta, Georgia.

Jensen, G. F., and R. Eve. 1976. "Sex Differences in Delinquency." *Criminology* 13 (February):427-48.

Jensen, G. F., and M. L. Erickson. 1977. "Peer Commitment and Delinquency: New Tests of Old Hypotheses." Unpublished manuscript.

Jensen, G. F., M. L. Erickson, and J.P. Gibbs. 1978. "Perceived Risk of Punishment and Self-Reported Delinquency." *Social Forces* 57 (September):57-78.

Jensen, G. F., C. S. White, and J. M. Galliher. 1982. "Ethnic Status and Adolescent Self-Evaluations." *Social Problems* 30 (December):226-239.

Jensen, G. F., and D. Brownfield. 1983. "Parents and Drugs: Specifying the Consequences of Attachment." *Criminology* 21 (November):543-54.

Jensen, G. F., and G. Wiltfang. 1987. "Gender and Adolescent Self-Evaluations." Unpublished manuscript.

Kaplan, H. 1975. *Self-Attitudes and Deviant Behavior*. Pacific Palisades, CA: Goodyear.

_____. 1980. *Deviant Behavior in Defense of Self*. New York: Academic Press.

_____. 1984. *Patterns of Juvenile Delinquency*. Beverly Hills, CA: Sage Publications.

Krohn, M., and J. Massey. 1980. "Social Control and Delinquent Behavior: An Examination of the Elements of the Social Bond." *Sociological Quarterly*. 21:529-43.

LaGrange, R., and H. White. 1985. "Age Differences in Delinquency: A Test of Theory." *Criminology*. 23:19-45.

Lerman, P. 1968. "Individual Values, Peer Values and Subcultural Delinquency."
American Sociological Review 33 (April):219-35.

Linden, E., and J. C. Hackler. 1973. "Affective Ties and Delinquency." *Pacific Sociological Review* 16 (January):27-46.

Liska, A. E., and M. D. Reed. 1985. "Ties to Conventional Institutions and Delinquency." *American Sociological Review* 50:547-60.

Matsueda, R. 1982. "Testing Control Theory and Differential Association." *American Sociological Review* 47:489-504.

Matza, D. 1964. *Delinquency and Drift.* New York: John Wiley.

Matza, D., and G. M. Sykes. 1961. "Juvenile Delinquency and Subterranean Values." *American Sociological Review* 26 (October):712-17.

McCarthy, J. D., and D. R. Hoge. 1984. "The Dynamics of Self-Esteem and Delinquency." *American Journal of Sociology* 90 (Number 2):396-410.

Menard, S., and B. J. Morse. 1984. "A Structural Critique of the IQ- Delinquency Hypothesis: Theory and Evidence." *American Journal of Sociology* 89:1347-78.

Merton, R. K. 1957. *Social Theory and Social Structure.* New York: Free Press.

Miller, W. 1958. "Lower Class Culture as a Generating Milieu of Gang Delinquency." *Journal of Social Issues* 14:5-19.

Paternoster, J., and R. Triplett. 1988. "Neighborhood Changes in Ecology and Violence." *Criminology* 26 (November): 591-620.

Park, R. E. 1952. "Community Organization and Juvenile Delinquency." In Everett C. Hughes, et al., (eds.), *Human Communities: The City and Human Ecology.* Glencoe, IL:Free Press.

Quicker, J. C. 1974. "The Effect of Goal Discrepancy on Delinquency." *Social Problems* 22 (October):76-86.

Quinney, R. 1977. *Class, State and Crime.* New York: David McKay.

———. 1980. *Class, State and Crime* (Second Edition). New York: Longman.

Rainwater, L. 1970. "The Problem of Lower Class Culture." *Journal of Social Issues* 26 (Winter):133-48.

Reiss, A. J., Jr. 1951. "Delinquency as the Failure of Personal and Social Controls." *American Sociological Review* 16:196-207.

Robin, G. D. 1969. "Anti-poverty Programs and Delinquency." *Journal of Criminal Law, Criminology and Police Science* 60 (Fall):323-31.

Rodman, H. 1963. "The Lower Class Value Stretch." *Social Forces* 42:205-15.

Rodman, H., and P. Grams. 1967. "Juvenile Delinquency and the Family: A Review and Discussion." In President's Commission on Law Enforcement and Administration of Justice, *Task Force Report: Juvenile Delinquency and Youth Crime.* Appendix L. Washington, DC: U.S. Government Printing Office.

Rosenberg, F. R., and M. Rosenberg. 1978. "Self-Esteem and Delinquency." *Journal of Youth and Adolescence* 7:279-91.

Rosenberg, F. R., and R. G. Simmons. 1975. "Sex Differences in the Self-Concept in Adolescence." *Sex Roles* 1:147-59.

Rosenberg, M., and R. G. Simmons. 1972. *Black and White Self-Esteem: The Urban School Child.* Washington, DC: The American Sociological Association.

Rothstein, E. 1962. "Attributes Related to High Social Status: A Comparison of the Perceptions of Delinquent and Non-delinquent Boys." *Social Problems* 10:75-83.

Schaefer, W. E. 1969. "Participation in Interscholastic Athletics and Delinquency: A Preliminary Study." *Social Problems* 17 (Summer):40-47.

Schwendinger, H., and J. S. Schwendinger. 1976. "Marginal Youth and Social Policy." *Social Problems* (December):84-91.

———. 1985. *Adolescent Subcultures and Delinquency.* New York: Praeger.

Shaw, Clifford. 1929. *Delinquency Areas.* Chicago: University of Chicago Press.

———. 1969. *Juvenile Delinquency and Urban Areas, Revised Edition.* Chicago: University of Chicago Press.

Shaw, C., and H. McKay. 1942. *Juvenile Delinquency and Urban Areas.* Chicago: University of Chicago Press.

Short, J. F. 1957. "Differential Association and Delinquency." *Social Problems* 4:233-39.

Short, J. F., R. Rivera, and R. A. Tennyson. 1965. "Perceived Opportunities, Gang Membership and Delinquency." *American Sociological Review* 30 (February):56-67.

Short, J. F., and F. L. Strodtbeck. 1965. *Group Processes and Gang Delinquency.* Chicago: University of Chicago Press.

Simcha-Fagan, O., and J. E. Schwartz. 1986. "Neighborhood and Delinquency: An Assessment of Contextual Effects."*Criminology* 24 (November):667-703.

Smeja, C. M., and D. G. Rojek. 1986. "Youthful Drug Use and Drug Subcultures." *The International Journal of Addictions* 21:1031-1050.

Stinchcombe, A. L. 1964. *Rebellion in a High School.* Chicago: Quadrangle Books.

Sutherland, E. H. 1939. *Principles of Criminology.* Philadelphia: J. B. Lippincott.

Sutherland, E. H., and D. R. Cressey. 1974. *Criminology.* 9th ed. Philadelphia: J. B. Lippincott.

Sykes, G. M., and D. Matza. 1957. "Techniques of Neutralization: A Theory of Delinquency." *American Journal of Sociology* 22 (December):664-70.

Taylor, I., P. Walton, and J. Young. 1973. *The New Criminology.* New York: Harper and Row.

Taylor, M. C., and E. J. Walsh. 1979. "Explanations of Black Self-Esteem: Some Empirical Tests." *Special Psychology Quarterly* 42 (September):242-53.

Taylor, R. B., and J. Covington. 1988. "Neighborhood Changes in Ecology and Violence." *Criminology* 26 (November):553-89.

Thomas, W. I., and F. Znaniecki. 1918. *The Polish Peasant in Europe and America.* New York: Alfred A. Knopf.

Toby, J. 1957. "Social Disorganization and Stake in Conformity: Complementary Factors in the Predatory Behavior of Hoodlums." *Journal of Criminal Law, Criminology and Police Science* 48:12-17.

Vold, G., and T. J. Bernard. 1986. *Theoretical Criminology.* New York: Oxford University Press.

Voss, H. L. 1964. "Differential Association and Delinquent Behavior: A Replication." *Social Problems* 12:78-85.

Wells, L. E., and J. H. Rankin. 1983. "Self-Concept as a Mediating Factor in Delinquency." *Social Psychology Quarterly* 46:11-22.

Yablonsky, L., and M. Haskell. 1988. *Juvenile Delinquency.* 4th ed. New York: Harper & Row.

Yablonsky, L. 1959. "The Delinquent Gang as Near-Group." *Social Problems* 7: 108-17.

Yinger, M. 1960. "Contraculture and Subculture." *American Sociological Review* 25: 625-35.

Young, J. 1975. "Working-Class Criminology." In I. Taylor, P. Walton, and J. Young (eds.), *Critical Criminology*. London: Rutledge and Kegan Paul.

chapter 7

Contexts for Socialization
Family, School, and Peer Groups

> *Violence seems as typical of family relationships as love; and it would be hard to find a group or institution in American society in which violence is more of an everyday occurrence than it is within the family. Family members physically abuse each other far more often than do nonrelated individuals. Starting with slaps and going on to torture and murder, the family provides a prime setting for every degree of physical violence. So universal is the phenomenon that it is probable that some form of violence will occur in almost every family.*
>
> —Suzanne K. Steinmetz and Murray A. Straus, 1973

Major Socializing Forces

In Chapter 6 we outlined the similarities and differences among the major sociological theories examining the causes of delinquency. One of the common themes characterizing those theories is that most human behavior, including delinquent behavior, is *learned* and that the major source of human learning involves interaction with other people. People become human beings through processes of social interaction and social learning that are referred to as *socialization*. Socialization takes place in a variety of settings. For the child growing up in a developed, industrial society, the family, school, and peer groups are viewed as particularly crucial to the process. Although there is disagreement over their relative importance, parents, teachers, and peers are considered the most significant or consequential people in the child's environment. These three social institutions or groups have received the bulk of attention in criminological theory and research, and we will summarize the relevant literature in this chapter. In Chapter 8 we will consider the state of research on religion, mass media, and community.

The Family

The family has typically been viewed as the most crucial institution in our society for shaping a child's personality, attitudes, and behavior. At the same time, however, many social commentators have noted a decline in the range of functions performed by the family. Some fifty years ago, William Ogburn (1938) observed that of seven functions served by the family throughout history (economic production, status allocation, education, religious training, recreation, protection, and provision of affection), only the family's role in providing affection was not declining. Although the family may have been a more important social institution at earlier points in history, most scholars are still willing to accept that it remains a major setting for socialization in American society.

Harry Harlow's (1962) classic work with the rhesus monkey dramatically illustrates the importance of parents to young infants. Harlow raised monkeys in isolation from their parents and replaced the parents with a variety of surrogates made of wire or terrycloth, and some with a bottle for feeding and others with none. Harlow found that infant monkeys preferred the cloth surrogate mother over the regular feeding provided by the bare-wire surrogate. Infant monkeys appeared to have an innate need for warmth and closeness rather than simply food. Harlow also found that infant monkeys raised in isolation were aggressive and unsociable in the presence of other monkeys. These isolated and orphaned monkeys did not know how to play, how to interact, or even how to mate. Perhaps what was most significant was that their poor social development could not be easily remedied by placing them back into a normal social environment.

If generalized to humans, the monkey experiments suggest that normal behavior is dependent on meaningful parent-child relationships and that inadequacies in early childhood socialization can have ramifications later during the period of adolescence and adulthood. Similarly, the discovery of *feral children*, children who were isolated from human contact, analogous to Harlow's monkeys, attest to the critical need of meaningful social interaction at an early age. Feral children are often the result of an illegitimate birth, and are hidden from public view. One such child called "Anna" was kept in an attic for her first six years. When discovered, she was unable to walk, talk, or display normal human emotions. Despite intensive care and attention, "Anna" could not attain the status of a normal child, and in fact died at the age of ten (Davis, 1947). While Harlow's monkey experiments and the few cases of feral children are extreme cases of defective parental socialization, they do point to the critical need of a warm and meaningful parent-child interaction. When this is absent, the child may suffer permanent deficiencies.

Variation in Emphasis on the Family

The centrality of the family to delinquency theory and research has varied over the years, with most of the emphasis on the family occurring in the past twenty years. In 1974, Karen Wilkinson classified the ebb and flow of attention given the family into three periods: 1900-1931, 1933-1950, and 1950-1972. The first period was one of acceptance of the theme by sociologists and criminologists that the family was a basic social institution. Social reformers and "child savers" emphasized the importance of stable family life in the prevention of delinquency. In fact, as noted in Chapter 2, the invention of the juvenile court was coupled with a correctional ideology that emphasized the home and family as targets of treatment.

Wilkinson characterizes the second period (1933-1950) as one of rejection of the importance of the family setting. During this time, the decline of family functions and the role of other institutions in the socialization and control of children were being emphasized. The popular sociological theories of the time focused on social class standing and the learning of delinquent behavior in interaction with peers. Thus, the emphasis had shifted from social disorganization and the breakdown of traditional institutions to "differential social organization"—that is, the development of new patterns of cooperative relationships among neighbors, relatives, and peers. These new patterns were viewed as more suitable to urban living. Delinquent behavior was considered either a normal response to limited opportunity or a product of normal learning in stable, but subcultural, environments.

Wilkinson argues that beginning in the 1950s interest in the family revived. Along with a concern for the broken home, there emerged a renewed interest in the effect of family relationships on delinquency. Rather than concentrating on the structure of the home, researchers began considering the nature of interaction between parents and children, styles of parental discipline and supervision, and such variables as "family integration" and "cohesion." This trend in research is exemplified in the work of Reiss (1951), Glueck and Glueck (1950), Nye (1958), Hirschi (1969), and Larson and Myerhoff (1967), and more recently in the family violence research of Richard Gelles and Murray Straus (1979). The quote at the beginning of this chapter reflects a growing concern that family experiences can facilitate as well as inhibit crime and delinquency.

The Family in Major Theories

The ebb and flow of concern about the family is associated with the popularity of the various theories of delinquency that we summarized in Chapter 6. For example, strain theory emphasizes such variables as aspirations, limited opportunities for success, status frustration, and delinquent subcultures. The family plays a role in the strain theory of delinquency insofar as it determines a youth's social standing, his or her chances of getting ahead by legitimate means, and, hence, the probability of status problems. In Merton's version of strain theory (1957), the family is also important in that working-class children are depicted as more thoroughly socialized to aspire toward culturally prescribed goals of success than to accept norms limiting the means to do so. In short, the family is important as the determinant of social class position.

The role of the family in cultural conflict perspectives varies from one theorist to another. Sutherland and Cressey (1974) have argued that the family is important to the degree that it affects the chances of exposure to definitions favorable and unfavorable to lawbreaking. In cultural conflict theory, such definitions are always intervening to explain the effects of various institutions on delinquency. Walter Miller's (1958) emphasis on lower-class "focal concerns" suggests that the lower-class family facilitates delinquency insofar as the values conveyed by adults lead to trouble with the law. However, like Sutherland and Cressey, Miller contended that it is the "one-sex peer unit" and not the two-parent family unit that is most relevant to understanding the behavior of members of the lower-class community. Miller argued that such peer units are especially salient for understanding adolescent males who come from female-based households since it is within peer groups that they solve problems of sex-role identification and learn the "male" role.

Social control theory accords relationships with parents a central role in the explanation of delinquency. If parents keep track of their children and parent-child ties are strong, then the probability of delinquency is greatly reduced. Children refrain from delinquency not only to avoid their parents' ire, but also because of the values, aspirations, and beliefs learned in interaction with their parents (Hirschi, 1985). This inhibiting effect is presumed to occur in all social categories and settings—among males and females, minority and nonminority, rural and urban youth.

Social learning theory also accords a major role to parents and the family in the explanation of delinquency. The processes of imitation, differential reinforcement, and normative learning so central to this theory, all involve parents and other members of the family. In most instances it is assumed that parents will try to shape their children's behavior and beliefs in ways which will keep them out of serious trouble and that it is in the world of their peers that contrary behavior is likely to be rewarded. However, children can also learn to violate rules from their parents either directly or indirectly. If parents smoke, drink, or use drugs, then the probability that their children will do so is significantly greater than if they do none of these (Jensen and Brownfield, 1983). In fact, strong ties to parents are not likely to discourage deviance in children if parents themselves are known to engage in the same behavior. Admonishments to "Do as I say, not as I do!" are often used by parents in the attempt to overcome imitation effects, but it is doubtful that they can be totally effective considering the contradictory messages communicated (see Box 7-1).

One of the most recent attempts to incorporate family variables into the explanation of delinquency is the *power-control* theory posited by Hagan, Simpson, and Gillis (1985, 1987). Power-control theory specifically addresses the gender difference in delinquency and links the gender difference to the class status of mothers and fathers in the household. The

Box 7-1

Conflicting Messages

What does this cartoon suggest about parental values and childrearing? Thinking back to Chapter 6, how does it illustrate the notion of "subterranean" or "infracultural" values? What assumption about parents as a barrier to delinquency might be challenged by Snuffy Smith's behavior?

difference between girls and boys is predicted to be greatest in households where 1) fathers are in occupations where they dominate or control others, and 2) mothers are either housewives or in occupations where they are controlled by others. Such households are classified as high in *patriarchy* (i.e. father rule). In such households girls are thought to be treated very differently than boys. Girls are closely supervised and raised to avoid taking risks while, allegedly, boys are raised to take risks and are relatively free to do what they want. In contrast, households where mothers and fathers are in similar occupational categories are classified as *egalitarian* or balanced in terms of male-female power. In such households girls and boys, it is argued, are subject to more nearly comparable degrees of adult control and encouragement of risk-taking.

Hagan, Simpson, and Gillis provide some research support for their theory (1987) but, at present, their power-control explanation of the gender difference has not been shown to be superior to other sociological explanations of the gender difference (Jensen and Eve, 1976). However, their theory reflects the continuing centrality of the family in sociological theories of delinquency.

Research on the Family and Delinquency

There are literally hundreds of studies dealing with various aspects of family life and delinquency. We have organized our presentation around certain aspects of the family that have been the subject of considerable research. First, we will consider certain structural characteristics of the family and a child's place in the family: the broken home, ordinal position, and family size. Then we will turn to research concerning actual relationships among family members, that is, affective relationships between parents, and between parents and child, methods of parental control, and parental supervision. Our conclusion will be in accord with that of Gove and Crutchfield who stated, ''The evidence that the family plays a critical role in juvenile delinquency is one of the strongest and most frequently replicated findings among studies of deviance'' (1982:302).

The Broken Home

A very common claim about juvenile delinquency is that it is the result of a ''broken'' home. The departure of a parent, typically the father, is assumed to disrupt the life of the child and hamper the effective socialization and supervision of children. In fact, the belief in the deleterious effect of a broken home on children is so firmly entrenched in many quarters of the juvenile court system that it would be surprising not to find the juvenile system producing ''facts'' to support this assertion. The conviction that family disruption is a cause of delinquent conduct can act as a self-fulfilling prophecy: a juvenile from a broken home who is in trouble may have a greater chance of juvenile court intervention than a similar case from an intact home. In Figure 7-1 we have summarized data on the living arrangements of Tennessee youths compared to the living arrangements of juvenile court referrals in Tennessee. Juveniles referred to the court are twice as likely to come from single-parent households as the population as a whole.

In his classic work, *Causes of Delinquency* (1969), Hirschi found that both black and white boys from broken homes were more likely to have police records than boys from intact homes but when their self-reported

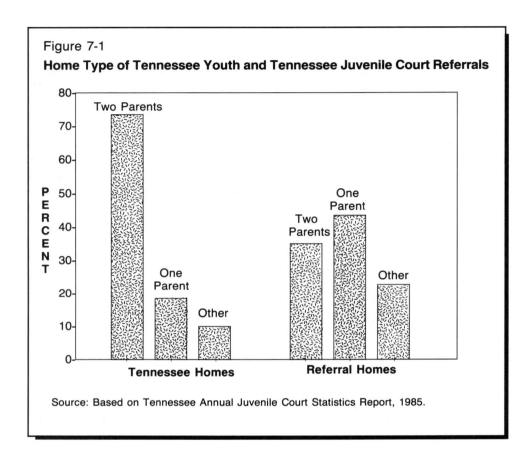

Figure 7-1

Home Type of Tennessee Youth and Tennessee Juvenile Court Referrals

Source: Based on Tennessee Annual Juvenile Court Statistics Report, 1985.

delinquent acts were considered he could find no significant differences. More recent research has echoed similar findings, prompting Johnson (1986) to conclude, "It is very tempting to conclude that the official system is indeed responding differently to similar behavior by adolescents from different types of families—families which do not otherwise differ in expected ways along several dimensions presumed to relate to delinquent behavior" (1986:77). As we examine the issue of the family and delinquency, it is critical that we bear in mind the data source we are using to measure delinquency.

The relevance of the broken home to delinquency has varied in research depending on whether other characteristics of families have been taken into account, how the concept of "broken/nonbroken" is calibrated, as well as on the way delinquency is measured. For example, Chilton and Markle (1972) found that children living in something other than an intact family were disproportionately represented in juvenile court statistics. However, when classified according to income, it appeared that economics had more to do with the referral rate than family composition. Furthermore, when self-report techniques are used to measure delinquency the differences in delinquency between broken and intact homes is quite small (Gove and Crutchfield, 1982; Rosen and Neilson, 1982). Rachelle Canter (1982b) reports the results summarized in Figure 7-2 based on interviews of self-reported delinquent behavior conducted with 1,725 youths between ages 11 and 17. Youths from broken homes reported more delinquent acts than youths in intact homes, but when comparing averages the differences are far from striking.

A study of black and white youths living in Philadelphia (Rosen, 1985) suggested that structural variables such as the father's presence or absence from the home are more consequential for white youths than black youths. This finding is consistent with speculation by Alan Berger and William Simon (1974) that the broken home is least consequential in settings where it has been a common experience. Moreover, it may very well be the case that the impact of broken homes has declined over the years as divorce has become an increasingly common experience. Not only might it lose any stigmatic consequences it might have had but the development of a variety of alternatives to family care could also attenuate the consequences of divorce.

Figure 7-2

Average Number of Delinquent Acts Reported by Youths in Broken and Intact Homes (from sample of 1,725 youths)

Type of Act	Intact Homes	Broken Homes
Felony theft	4.18	4.30*
Minor theft	3.36	3.46
Status offenses	7.31	8.00*
Against persons	10.23	10.83*

* For felony theft, status offenses, and crimes against persons the differences were small but statistically significant.

Source: Based on Canter, R. J., 1982, "Family Correlates of Male and Female Delinquency," *Criminology* 20: 149-67.

One hundred years ago, less than 5 percent of marriages ended in divorce. Currently about 50 percent of marriages end in divorce, and about one-third of white children and three-fourths of black children can expect to live in a "non-intact" family. Hence, it is no longer an easy matter to define the "normal" or "typical" family, and variations in family structure may lose whatever small differentiating impact they had in the past. At the present time there is little conclusive evidence to suggest that the broken home is a critical variable in the understanding of delinquency (Cernkovich and Giordano, 1987; Rosen, 1985; Laub and Sampson, 1988; Loeber and Stouthamer-Loeber, 1986). Richard Johnson (1986) asserts that the broken home may be related to official delinquency (police data) because the juvenile system perceives the broken home as a critical background characteristic, but it is not related to delinquent behavior (self-report data).

Others feel that studies totally dismissing the broken home as a correlate of delinquency have not adequately considered variations by offense and type of broken home. Joseph Rankin (1983) reports that "When family context is operationalized as a simple dichotomy (broken versus intact homes), broken homes are more closely associated with "family" offenses such as running away and truancy than with other types of juvenile misconduct." More specific breakdowns into homes where a parent is absent due to death versus divorce and consideration of the gender of the missing parent did not appear to matter.

Ordinal Position

While the broken home has historically been a dominant focus in relating family characteristics to delinquency, there has been periodic interest in the impact of *ordinal position*, or birth order, in relation to juvenile delinquency. For example, an early study in England by Lees and Newson (1954) found that intermediate children who had older and younger siblings (that is, brothers and/or sisters) tended to be overrepresented among delinquents. The explanation posited for this finding is that the firstborn sibling lives the first years as an only child and receives the undivided attention and affection of his or her parents. The child born last enters into a firmly established family situation with parents who are experienced in raising children and older siblings function as role models. The intermediate sibling may get "squeezed out" of affection and may gravitate into delinquent behavior for attention.

Research in England and the United States suggests that the higher delinquency rates for middle children may actually be an artifact of family size (Loeber and Stouthamer-Loeber, 1986). Obviously, families with only one or two children have no middle children and small families have lower delinquency rates than large families. Hence, any study of ordinal position must examine the impact of birth order in families with three or more children and exclude smaller families from the analysis. When Hirschi took family size into account in his research on youth in the San Francisco Bay area he could find no evidence that middle children are more likely to commit delinquent acts than youngest or oldest children. West and Farrington (1973) report the same results for British youth. Ordinal position was not associated with delinquency when family size was taken into account.

Wilkinson, Stitt, and Erickson (1982) suggested that the relevance of birth order may depend on the sex of the siblings in a family. In three-child families middle boys and girls with older and younger sisters were found to be the most delinquent. Girls with older and younger brothers did not have high rates while middle boys in such situations did. Such specific analysis of sibling structure suggests that the issue is far more complex than implied by the simple notion that middle children are more delinquent. Further, with the shrinking size of families any discussion of birth order effects may be moot. For example, the median size of families in the United States is 3.24. Furthermore, only 15 percent of families have more than five members, 6 percent have more than six members, and 2 percent have more than seven members.

Family Size

While variations by birth order may be the product of family size, several issues involving family size and delinquency have not been settled. For one, to isolate the independent relevance of family size other variables which correlate with family size and delinquency have to be taken into account (e.g. racial/ethnic status, unemployment, social class). Not only might family size be confounded with other variables but the relevance of family size may vary depending on other circumstances such as economic advantage. For example, British research suggests that family size is related to delinquency but that the connection is quite weak for middle-class families as compared to lower-class families (Rutter and Giller, 1984:185-86). It may be that the number of children does not affect delinquency when families have sufficient economic resources to manage a large household.

Hirschi (1969) examined the relationship between family size and delinquency using self-report data and controlling measures of academic performance, parental supervision, and emotional attachment. Regardless of such controls, family size appears related to delinquency. He notes, however, that the mechanisms generating a family size effect have not been identified. Loeber and Stouthamer-Loeber (1986) suggest that it is not family size that contributes to delinquency but rather having delinquent siblings. In other words, in large families there are more siblings and if one sibling is delinquent, there is a higher probability that another sibling would be delinquent. However, as with birth order effects, with the gradual demise of large families due to a declining birth rate, the relevance of family size to delinquency is not likely to be a major research topic in coming years.

Family Relationships

During the blitzkrieg of London in World War II, British officials built large nurseries in the rural countryside where infants and young children could be safely cared for by nannies and child care personnel, while their parents continued the war effort in the urban areas. Despite the professional care that was ministered to these children, many of them appeared to have physical and psychological difficulties. Listlessness, emotional outbursts, and mental aberrations seemed to be the result of maternal deprivation. Elaborating on this observation, Bowlby (1951) attempted to determine the importance of the maternal relationship for juvenile delinquency. Studying a group of juvenile delinquents drawn from patients at a child guidance center, Bowlby found a relationship between the absence of the mother and delinquent behavior. He concluded that "on the basis of this varied evidence it appears that there is a very strong case indeed for believing that prolonged separation of a child from his mother (mother-substitute) during the first five years of life stands foremost among the causes of delinquent character development and persistent misbehavior" (1951:11).

Despite the popular acceptance of this observation, Bowlby's findings have been severely criticized, and no supporting evidence has been provided to substantiate his theory of maternal deprivation. Research has suggested that it is not the absence of a parent per se that results in delinquency, but the quality of the relationship that exists between the child and the remaining parent. In recent years, the maternal deprivation hypothesis was altered to suggest that working mothers contribute to their children's chances of becoming delinquent. The concept of "latchkey children" (the child carries the key to the house on a string around his or her neck) has become a popular phrase. However, rather than being a case of neglect, Hill and Stafford (1979) reported that some working mothers compensate for being away from home by reducing their leisure time in order to spend time with their children. Generally, studies examining the effects of mothers' employment and delinquency find little evidence of any type of an impact (Hayes and Kamerman, 1983; Loeber and Stouthamer-Loeber, 1986). Hirschi (1985) suggests that supervision is the key explanatory variable, and when working mothers can provide supervision for the child, there is no increased likelihood of delinquency.

The percent of women in the labor force who have children under six years of age and the divorce rate in the United States are plotted together with juvenile referral rates in Figure 7-3. There is a much better correspondence in trends over time between divorce rates and juvenile court referrals than between working mothers and referrals. Delinquency rates leveled out somewhat in the 1980s as did the divorce rate while the percent of working mothers with small children has increased regularly for many decades. A mere "eyeballing" of trends will not provide conclusive answers about the causal importance of different dimensions of family life for delinquency. However, the lack of correspondence for many spans of time should lead to some skepticism about claims attributing the delinquency problem to working mothers.

It is also important to note that unemployment of fathers is typically viewed as a cause of delinquency because of its presumed consequences for family well-being. In the past, when fathers were supposed to be the sole "breadwinners," deviations from that standard were viewed as problematic. When women's roles were linked primarily to the home, working mothers were a source of problems. To the degree that working mothers can contribute to the well-being of families, their employment might lower the odds of delinquency. To the degree that unemployed fathers might help supervise children, their unemployment might reduce the odds of delinquency. In sum, the relationship between parental employment outside of the home and delinquency may be weak or nonexistent either because such circumstances make no difference or because of counterbalancing consequences.

Research has consistently shown that children who feel unwanted by their parents are more likely to report involvement in delinquency (McCord, 1984; Pulkkinen, 1982). These results appear to hold whether the rejection was by a mother or a father. Several studies also showed that if children rejected their parents that this can be related to delinquency (Loeber and Stouthamer-Loeber, 1986). Patterson (1980) found in comparing parents of children who steal with the parents of law abiding children that the former set of parents lacked basic parenting skills. These parents failed to be assertive, failed to punish, and perhaps most importantly failed to interact and show concern.

A considerable volume of research suggests that actual relationships within the family are more relevant to understanding delinquency than are the structural variables such as number of parents, ordinal position, or family size. Current research findings strongly suggest that quarrelsome and negligent homes are more conducive to delinquent behavior than parental presence or absence (Loeber and Stouthamer-Loeber, 1986).

Many intact families are in fact "broken" in terms of the actual relationships among family members. Rutter (1977) found that family tensions and parental discord greatly contribute to delinquent behavior. Long-term tension supposedly reduces family cohesiveness and impairs

Figure 7-3

Juvenile Referrals, Divorce Rates, and Percent of Mothers Working

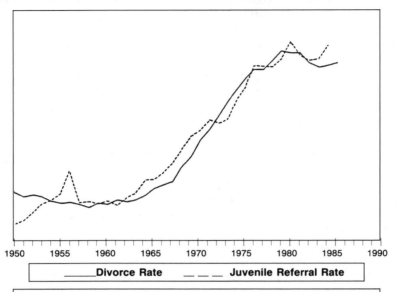

**Referral rates follow a pattern more similar
to divorce rates than to mothers in the labor force.**

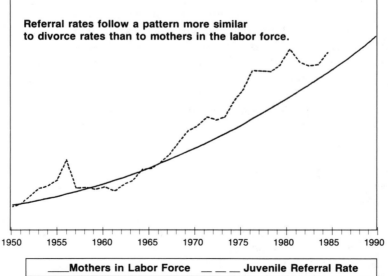

Source: Based on data from 1950-1989 issues of *Statistical Abstracts of the United States.*

the parents' ability to provide an atmosphere conducive to meaningful adolescent growth and development. If the family environment is disruptive and unstable, and parents display constant hostility toward one another, it is doubtful whether they will be able to exert a positive influence on their children.

Some research has focused on the parental relationship in terms of its impact on delinquency rates. Nye (1958) found a strong association between the reported marital happiness of parents and delinquent behavior. Power et al., (1974) showed that more delinquents from unhappy homes became *recidivists* (habitual offenders) than did delinquents from broken homes. Finally, Stouthamer-Loeber et al., (1984) found that unhappily married mothers supervised their children significantly less well than did happily married mothers. Results from one of the oldest but still one of the best family studies are summarized in Figure 7-4. Youth from unhappy unbroken homes have been found to admit to more delinquency than youth from broken but happy homes.

Hirschi (1969) has argued that an affective tie between parent and child is one of the strongest convention-inducing variables in delinquency research. The weaker the bond between parent and child, the greater the probability of delinquent behavior. Hirschi found a consistent pattern of a lack of attachment and poor communication between delinquent children and their parents. For example, among boys reporting little intimate communication with their fathers, 43 percent reported committing at least two delinquent offenses. On the other hand, only 5 percent of boys with a high level of communication with their fathers reported such delinquent behavior.

Utilizing a social learning perspective, Rand Conger argued that "willingness to respond positively to one's children will raise the reinforcement value of the home and increase the rate of interaction from juvenile to parents as well as increase the probability that a juvenile will emulate conventional parental patterns of behavior" (1976:31). Conger found that communication between parent and child acts as a barrier to delinquency only if the interaction is positive. Thus, communication in an excessively punitive home does not act as a barrier to delinquency. In a similar vein, Jensen and Brownfield (1983) reported that attachment to nondrug-using parents inhibits children's drug use, while attachment to drug-using parents either makes no difference or encourages children's drug use. Dembo et al., (1986) also found that parents who use drugs serve as poor role models and can affect children's drug use. No matter how strong the degree of attachment between parent and child, if parents are involved with drugs the chance that the child may also use drugs is enhanced.

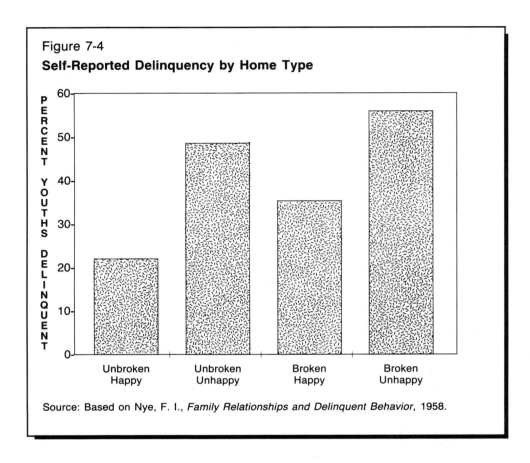

Figure 7-4

Self-Reported Delinquency by Home Type

Source: Based on Nye, F. I., *Family Relationships and Delinquent Behavior*, 1958.

Parental Control, Discipline, and Punishment

Parental methods of control, discipline, and punishment are also related to delinquency. Extremely strict discipline appears to affect adolescents in their relationships with peer groups by hindering normal interaction (Nye, 1958). Laub and Sampson (1988) found that permissiveness, lax discipline, poor supervision, and a lack of attachment were associated with a high probability of delinquency. Similarly, the McCords and Zola (1959) found a relationship between lax and erratic discipline and delinquency. Nye also found that discipline that could be categorized as "fair" or "equitable" tended to be associated with low involvement in delinquent behavior. In summary, discipline and the way it is administered appear to be important variables in understanding the relevance of the family environment to delinquency.

Most parents have spanked their children at some time, believing that pain will help to deter further misbehavior. Such a belief is certainly consistent with various learning theories and deterrence theory (see Chapter 9). Anticipated pain can lower the odds of behavior that has elicited such a response in the past. However, social learning theories also imply that physical punishment can have consequences that increase the odds of future misbehavior through processes of imitation. For example, if family problems are dealt with through some form of physical violence, then a child may learn to deal with daily problems in other settings through force and violence. Thus, while potentially inhibiting some forms of misbehavior, physical punishment might increase other forms through processes of imitation. Moreover, if punishment is administered in a manner that weakens bonds to parents, the net impact could be an increase rather than a decrease in misbehavior. Thus, while the use of physical means of punishment may be common and widely accepted as necessary by parents, there are reasons to be concerned about its possible negative consequences.

As Robert Agnew (1983) points out, criminological research on the topic has not been perfectly consistent. The most common finding has been that physical punishment by parents is positively associated with both official and self-reported measures of delinquency. However, some research has also suggested that physical punishment can reduce the odds of delinquency (McCord et al., 1961) or has no effect (Nye, 1958) *if it is consistently applied.* All studies agree that inconsistent or erratic discipline are positively associated with delinquency and that the association of physical punishment with these two properties of discipline may make physical punishment appear to be positively related to delinquency.

Agnew provides some further support for the argument that the impact of physical punishment depends on consistency of discipline. Using data from a nationally representative sample of over 2,000 10th-grade boys, Agnew found that physical punishment, intermittent (erratic) discipline, and inconsistent demands by parents as perceived by youth each increased the odds of self-reported delinquency. However, physical punishment increased delinquency the most among parents whose children perceived inconsistent demands. Physical punishment slightly decreased delinquency for children whose parents were perceived to be consistent in their demands. Since few parents fell in the highly consistent category, physical punishment increased the odds of delinquency for most youth. These results suggest that parents should worry about the messages communicated through physical punishment and that the relationship is much more complex than implied by common sense beliefs and folklore.

Family Violence

The family is typically studied as an agency of conventional socialization and control, inhibiting delinquency. Yet, the family can also be "a cradle of violence" (Steinmetz and Straus, 1973). After an extensive review of the literature on the family, Snyder and Patterson (1987) conclude that family conflict manifested in terms of anger, less communication, less problem solving, more defensiveness, more blaming, and less friendly talk are strongly related to delinquent behavior and recidivism. Even beatings, stabbings, burnings, and chokings are surprisingly common events within some families. According to a survey by Murray Straus, Richard Gelles, and Suzanne Steinmetz (1980), victims of family violence in the United States total about 8 million people a year. This survey found that during the span of one year, 16 out of every 100 couples have violent confrontations; 3 out of every 100 children are punched, kicked, or bitten by their parents, and more than one-third of all brothers and sisters severely attack each other. While it is commonly thought that the home is synonymous with safety, security, and love, in some instances it is far more dangerous than walking the streets in a "tough" neighborhood. In fact, Straus and his colleagues suggest that "the family is society's preeminent violent institution" (1980:16).

One particular type of violence that has received increasing publicity and concern is parental violence against children. Gelles (1974) estimated that somewhere between one and a half to two million children are subjected to physical injury in a given year. Gil (1970) conducted a nationwide survey and estimated between two and a half to four million children were abused each year. Clearly, accurate statistics on child abuse are simply not available because the act of child abuse can be easily disguised as "falling down the stairs" or because medical personnel are reluctant to report suspected abuse. But what is currently known is quite disturbing. For example, homicide is one of the five leading causes of death for children between one and eighteen years of age. It is estimated that about 2,000 children are killed each year, but the actual number is most likely higher because of misrecording homicides as accidents. Nearly 75 percent of these children are infants under the age of one year. In addition to child abuse (which refers to any type of physical or psychological harm, ranging from bruises and welts to poisoning), there are various forms of child neglect which can include abandonment for long periods of time; lack of supervision; nutritional, medical, or educational neglect; insufficient clothing or shelter; and moral or ethical neglect where children are not provided any guidance.

An early report on child abuse gives the medical details of such abuse:

Seven out of ten battered children are under 5, and many are less than a year old. Most often the child suffers injury to the head from repeated blows, as well as broken arms and legs from violent pulling or shaking. The commonest serious injury is a skull fracture accompanied by the formation of a hematoma, or blood clot, on the brain. X-rays of the limbs often show multiple breaks in various stages of healing, indicating that the child has been subjected to repeated assaults. (Helfer and Kempe, 1974)

Child abuse cuts across all categories of race, sex, social class, religion, and ethnicity but it does appear that lower-class families are subjected to more stress and have fewer coping techniques than higher classes, resulting in higher rates of child abuse. Abusive parents are often experiencing stress and one method of coping with it is to take it out on others, including children. If children of abusive parents grow up to be abusive parents themselves, then we may be faced with a perpetual cycle of violence (Gelles and Cornell, 1985).

The legacy of child abuse is not just the physical scars that children carry with them. The consequences of violence and abuse produce innumerable problems. Some researchers feel that abused children have a higher probability of growing up to be delinquents and have less respect for the conventional order (Schmitt and Kempe, 1975). There is also some evidence that adults who were abused children have higher rates of drug and alcohol problems as well as psychiatric disturbances (Gelles and Cornell, 1985). Finally, there is also research evidence to suggest that abused children have developmental delays, developmental difficulties, and experience problems entering into intimate relationships (Goldston, 1975). The notion of a cycle of violence (today's abused children are tomorrow's murderers or violent offenders) has significantly tempered (Widom, 1989), but the evidence does suggest that being an abused child does increase one's risk of having an adult criminal record.

In 1974, Congress passed the Child Abuse Prevention and Treatment Act which served as an impetus for states to implement legislation to deal with this problem. In most states it is required that school or medical personnel who suspect child abuse must report this to the proper authorities. Unfortunately there is a marked reluctance to report child abuse, particularly if it is a middle- or upper-class family, and thus the problem may continue without detection or intervention.

Fortunately, there is some evidence that family violence may be on the decline. Figure 7-5 summarizes rates of parent-child violence in surveys conducted in 1975 and 1985 and reported on by Murray Straus and Richard Gelles (1986). The data suggest that parents are less violent towards children in 1985 than in 1975. The declines in severe and very severe violence directed toward children are particularly notable and statistically significant. This same study also surveyed rates of marital violence and

Figure 7-5

Parent-to-Child Violence, 1975 and 1985

Type of Violence	Rate per 1,000 Children Aged 3 through 17[a]		*t* for 1975–1985 Difference
	1975 *n* = 1,146[b]	1985 *n* = 1,428[c]	
A. Minor Violence Acts			
1. Threw something	54	27	3.41**
2. Pushed/grabbed/shoved	318	307	0.54
3. Slapped or spanked	582	549	1.68
B. Severe Violent Acts			
4. Kicked/bit/hit with something	32	13	3.17**
5. HIt, tried to hit with something	134	97	1.41
6. Beat up	13	6	0.26
7. Threatened with gun or knife	1	2	0.69
8. Used gun or knife	1	2	0.69
C. Violence Indexes			
Overall Violence (1-8)	630	620	0.52
Severe Violence (4-8)	140	107	2.56*
Very Severe Violence (4, 6, 8)	36	19	4.25**
("child abuse" for this article)			

[a] For two-caretaker households with at least one child 3 to 17 years of age at home.
[c] A few respondents were omitted because of missing data on some items, but the *n* is never less than 1,140.
[c] A few respondents were omitted because of missing data on some items, but the *n* is never less than 1,418.
*$p < .01$l **$p < .00$ (two-tailed tests).

Source: From Straus, M. A. and R. J. Gelles, "Societal Change and Change in Family Violence from 1975 to 1985 as revealed by Two National Surveys," 1990, 1986. *Journal of Marriage and the Family* 48 (August): 465–79. Copyrighted 1986 by the National Council on Family Relations. Reprinted by permission.

the data suggest that husbands are less violent toward their wives in 1985 than in 1975, although the differences were small enough that only the difference for wife-beating approaches statistical significance. Violence directed at husbands has declined the least of all the forms of family violence. Straus and Gelles suggest that the greatest declines are found for those forms of domestic violence that have received the greatest attention and where the most change in law enforcement has occurred.

The School

While the range of functions served by the family has been declining, the importance of the school as a context for socialization has been growing. What was viewed as a luxury for the affluent during the seventeenth and eighteenth centuries has grown to encompass a greater and greater proportion of the entire population. For example, in 1870, 57 percent of the youth in the 5 to 17 age category were enrolled in school, and only 1.2 percent were in high school. By the mid-1980s, 95 percent of 5 and 6 year olds, 99.2 percent of 7 to 13 years olds, 98.5 percent of 14 and 15 year olds, and 90.6 percent of 16 and 17 year olds were enrolled in school. Not too many years ago, completion of elementary school was considered a significant educational attainment. Today, completion of high school is seen as virtually mandatory for even the most menial of jobs, and it is becoming increasingly expected that a college degree is the appropriate level of educational attainment for many entry level positions (see Figure 7-6).

Since so much of the average American's teenage life is encompassed by school, it is hardly surprising that the schools should be viewed as central to an understanding of delinquency. According to some versions of strain theory (see Chapter 6), adolescents are driven to delinquency as a way of rebelling against school authority (Stinchcombe, 1964) or as a way of solving status problems generated by school experiences. The school is also central in social control theory, which generally views the school as an institution designed to encourage conventional attitudes and behavior. Hirschi views the role of the school in the following manner:

> Between the conventional family and the conventional world of work and marriage lies the school, an eminently conventional institution. Insofar as this institution is able to command his attachment, involvement and commitment, the adolescent is presumably able to move from childhood to adulthood with a minimum of delinquent acts. (1969:110)

While the strain theorist views school experiences as a source of frustration and rebellion, the control theorist views school experiences as important in the sense that they represent bonds to an eminently conventional institution. The person who is not attached, involved, or committed to school or concerned about the teachers' opinions is "freer" to drift into delinquency.

From a cultural deviance-differential association perspective, the school is a source of definitions "unfavorable" to lawbreaking and from a social learning perspective it is a major setting for the reinforcement of rule-abiding conduct. In short, while they may differ in the specific mechanisms

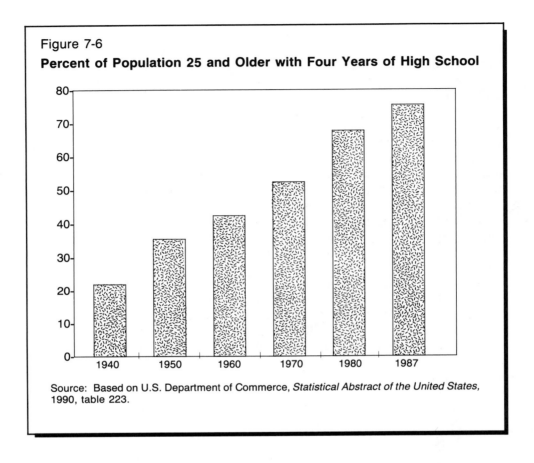

Figure 7-6

Percent of Population 25 and Older with Four Years of High School

Source: Based on U.S. Department of Commerce, *Statistical Abstract of the United States,* 1990, table 223.

involved, the major theories of delinquency all accord experiences at school a critical role in the explanation of delinquency.

Research on the School and Delinquency

A special task force was established during the administration of President Lyndon Johnson in the late 1960s to investigate the link between the school and juvenile delinquency. The authors of the resulting report, Walter Schaefer and Kenneth Polk, listed the following as "defects in the schools that heighten educational failure and deterioration, and hence delinquency": 1) belief in the limited potential of disadvantaged pupils, 2) irrelevant instruction, 3) inappropriate teaching methods, 4) testing, grouping, and "tracking," 5) inadequate compensatory and remedial education, 6) inferior teachers and facilities in low-income schools, 7) school-community distance, and 8) racial and economic segregation (President's Commission on Law Enforcement and Administration of Justice, 1967:236-46). While plausible arguments concerning the contributory influence of each condition to the advent of delinquency have been advanced, there is not a large body of research that relates specifically to each of these points. Some studies have, however, dealt with delinquency in specific relation to school achievement, attachment to teachers and school, dropping out of school, tracking, and intelligence tests. In addition to reviewing those studies, we will consider some research on the association between characteristics of schools, victimization rates, and violence in schools.

Achievement

One of the most persistent findings concerning the school and delinquency is that students who are not doing well in school have higher rates of delinquency than those who are faring better. For example, Johnson (1979) in examining the causal connection between parents, school, and delinquent associates as primary agents in explaining delinquent behavior, found success in school and attachment to school to be of utmost importance. Students who experience success in school have higher occupational expectations, fewer delinquent associates, and become more attached to school. Stronger attachment to school means fewer delinquent values, which ultimately means less delinquent involvement. Johnson's model of the relationships among these variables is summarized in Figure 7-7.

School achievement serves as a crucial background variable in the long causal chain affecting delinquency. As we shall see in the section on peers, delinquent associates appear to be the most critical factor in the understanding of delinquency, but school achievement and attachment to school serve as counter forces in the development of delinquent associates. Johnson argues that schools become "the central arena for the shifting and sorting of adolescent companionships, which prove to be so relevant to delinquent behavior" (1979:109).

Jensen (1976) found that achievement level is significantly related to delinquency status and that the relationship persists regardless of socioeconomic status and racial classification. Among whites and nonwhites, the higher the achievement, the lower the odds that a youth will acquire a delinquent record before his or her eighteenth birthday. The findings also suggested that differences in delinquency status occur only when we move beyond the lowest levels of achievement. Similarly Frease (1973) reported that no student with a grade-point average of 3.0 (B) or better had a police record, but that the arrest rate was as high as 75 percent among boys with

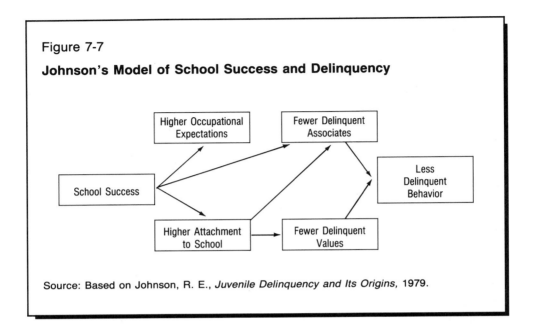

Figure 7-7

Johnson's Model of School Success and Delinquency

Source: Based on Johnson, R. E., *Juvenile Delinquency and Its Origins,* 1979.

the lowest grades. In sum, research thus far is consistent with the notion that academic success and achievement at school act as a barrier to delinquency.

Attachment to Teachers and School

As we noted earlier, control theory emphasizes the strength of the bond between students and their school and teachers as an important barrier to involvement in delinquency. Further, as discussed in the previous section, students who do not achieve good grades in school do not develop strong emotional ties or a sense of attachment to school. There is, in fact, persistent evidence that students who do not like school or who do not like their teachers are more likely to report delinquency than those who are more strongly attached to their teachers and school (Jensen et al., 1978; Hirschi, 1969; Hindelang, 1973). Students who disrupt class and upset teachers at an early age are more likely to get into trouble with the law in later years (Spivack and Cianci, 1987). Goldman (1961) found that schools that manifest a close relationship between teachers and students have low levels of school vandalism, whereas schools that are cold and institutional are continually plagued with broken windows, graffiti, and "trashings." The evidence to date strongly suggests that students who are not bonded to their school tend to have higher rates of delinquent behavior than those who see their school as a warm and meaningful part of their lives.

School Dropouts

Schools play a significant role in channeling youth into the higher-status positions in society. Conversely, school performance also sorts out those who will occupy the lower rungs on the occupational ladder. The chances of "making it" in American society without the proper educational credentials are remote. For example, according to U.S. Bureau of Census statistics, people with less than eight years of education earned $12,395 a year, four years of high school produced an income of $23,705, and college graduates (four years or more of college) earned $38,896. Individuals who do not complete at least high school will be severely disadvantaged. In the United States nearly 25 percent of current grade school cohorts will drop out of school without obtaining a high school diploma. While some dropouts will return to school and others will obtain a high school graduate equivalency degree (GED), there is still a disturbing number of school dropouts who will not have completed four years of high school.

Overall, 30 percent of the U.S. population has less than four years of high school education. Some 60 percent of those aged 65 or older did not graduate from high school compared to only 15 percent of the 25-34 age group. However, as recent as 1985, 1.7 million whites between the ages of 18 and 21 dropped out of school (13.6 percent of that age group) and 376,000 blacks between the ages of 18 and 21 dropped out (17.5 percent of that age group). What is even more disconcerting is that dropout rates are now increasing for blacks, Hispanics, and American Indians. Sternberg and his associates (1984) conclude that the overall dropout rate for blacks is approaching 25 percent, for Hispanics nearly 40 percent, and for American Indians in excess of 70 percent. Clearly, dropouts are going to be seriously disadvantaged in terms of socioeconomic status. But what about their crime potential while in school and out of school?

Elliott (1966) followed several cohorts of boys over a period of time and kept track of the delinquency referral rates of boys who eventually graduated from high school and of those who dropped out. Data on the dropouts included delinquency rates while in school and afterward. Elliott found that lower-status youths who eventually dropped out had a higher rate of delinquent referrals than lower-status youths who eventually graduated. Lower-status dropouts who were still in school had the highest delinquency referral rate of all groups studied. However, after dropping out, the referral rate for lower-status dropouts was actually the lowest of all the groups studied. This finding is contrary to the expectation that school dropouts will continue or perhaps escalate delinquent activities once they are out of school. Elaborating on these findings, Elliott and Voss (1974) found that over the time that future dropouts will continue or perhaps escalate delinquent activities once they are out of school. Elaborating on these findings, Elliott and Voss (1974) found that over the time that future dropouts were in school, there was a progressive escalation of their delinquency rates: before they dropped out, their police contact rate was anywhere from four to nine times greater than the rate of those who graduated. However, after dropping out, their referral rates fell off dramatically.

Elliott and Voss interpreted this pattern as support for a strain-frustration-delinquency argument. They suggested that students who eventually drop out of school grow increasingly frustrated the longer they are in school and that their increasing referral rate reflects their increasing frustration. Dropping out alleviates their school-generated frustrations, and (so the argument goes) their involvement in delinquency falls off. Of course, there are other possible interpretations that do not require that the potential dropout be viewed as frustrated. We could argue that the school experiences that weaken the student's bond to the school and lead to dropping out progressively "free" the student to violate the law. After dropping out, new bonds (for example, marriage, a job) are formed, and the delinquency rate therefore drops. However, whether delinquency and school dropout are viewed as results of frustration or progressive detachment, Elliott and Voss's findings support the argument that school experiences are important in explaining involvement in delinquency. This also raises the complex issue of the efficacy of compulsory school attendance. If a 14- or 15-year-old is experiencing nothing but failure in school, and finds school to be not only meaningless but perhaps stress-inducing, should this student be compelled to attend school? Elliott and Voss's findings would suggest that compulsory education laws can exacerbate delinquent behavior.

A more recent study of the issue suggests that, rather than decreasing the probabilities of future crime, dropping out increases the chances of future trouble. In a study of a 10 percent sample of the 1945 Philadelphia cohort discussed in Chapter 1 and throughout this text, Thornberry, Moore, and Christenson (1985) found that both the short-term and long-term effects of dropping out were higher probabilities of further criminality. This finding applied to both minority and majority groups and to youths from blue-collar backgrounds. The odds of greater crime were increased regardless of later marital or employment status. They note that the results are consistent with social control theory and contrary to Elliott and Voss's strain theory predictions. Until more convincing data are presented to the contrary, the safest conclusion appears to be that dropping out is associated with greater chances of future crime.

Tracking

One educational technique that has received a significant amount of attention as a potential contributor to delinquency is the use of educational "tracks" or ability groups for students of varying intellectual capabilities. In general, tracking refers to a method of curriculum assignment that places students in an educational program according to scores on intelligence tests and levels of academic achievement. The criticism of such an educational classification scheme is that students assigned to the lower track are accorded second-class status. It may also be the case that students who are not placed in higher tracks are denied opportunities for achievement and success and that slow bloomers are not given the opportunity of being transferred to the upper track.

Schaefer, Olexa, and Polk (1972) gathered data on the impact of track placement on academic achievement and delinquency. They found that students in the college-bound track achieved far better grades than those in the noncollege track. While 37 percent of the students in the college track fell in the top quarter of their class and only 11 percent in the bottom quarter, students in the noncollege track achieved significantly lower grades: only 2 percent in the top quarter and 52 percent in the bottom quarter. If students who are not in college tracks are simply less intelligent than those who are, the results of this study are not particularly disturbing.

However, Schaefer and associates analyzed their data controlling or holding constant father's occupation, IQ scores, and grade-point average for the last semester of junior high school. They found that significant differences still persisted between the two tracks. Of the students in the college track, 30 percent fell in the top quarter and only 12 percent in the bottom quarter, whereas 4 percent of students in the noncollege track fell in the top quarter and 35 percent in the bottom quarter. The researchers concluded that assignment to the noncollege track has a pronounced negative effect on grades.

Schaefer, Olexa, and Polk found that track assignment was also associated with dropout, lack of participation in school activities, and delinquency. Students in the noncollege track tended to be less involved in extracurricular activities during high school than students in the college track, and far more of them dropped out of high school. Finally, track position appeared to be a powerful explanatory variable in predicting deviant behavior. The researchers found that although students in the noncollege track comprised 29 percent of their sample, they accounted for 53 percent of all students disciplined once, 70 percent disciplined three or more times, and 51 percent of those who were suspended from school. Similarly, they were more than twice as likely as students in the college track to have a juvenile court record. The researchers argued that the alienation, frustration, and stigma caused by this second-class citizenship may have been partly to blame for the marginality of this group.

Other research on tracking has supported the notion that school status is a far more important determinant of delinquent behavior than the traditional variable of parental social class. David Hargreaves (1968) studied an English secondary school and found that boys in the lowest "stream" tended to be social isolates and were more involved in delinquent activities than were those in higher "streams." Kelly and Balch (1971) put forth a "school status" theory of delinquency, arguing that one's location in the reward structure of the school is an important predictor of delinquent involvement. In further analysis, Kelly (1974) found that track position, compared to gender and social class, emerged as the strongest predictor of some twenty-five different forms of delinquent activity.

Such findings have been interpreted as the results of a self-fulfilling prophecy. According to this interpretation, students in the low or basic tracks do not do as well in school as they should because school personnel expect them to do poorly. In one of the several experiments that have explored self-fulfilling prophecies, Rosenthal and Jacobson (1968) gave three kinds of IQ tests to 650 elementary school students. They told the teachers that these tests would predict which children were about to "bloom" or "spurt" intellectually. After administering the tests, the researchers merely selected at random a certain proportion of students as intellectual bloomers regardless of their IQ scores. The teachers assigned to these students were told to expect them to make marked intellectual gains. The remaining children constituted a control group, with no purported intellectual superiority. At the end of the first year, the IQ gains of the "specially gifted" students greatly exceeded the gains of the control group; the same results occurred at the end of the second year. Rosenthal and Jacobson published their findings in a book entitled *Pygmalion in the Classroom*, borrowing from the story of a Greek king named Pygmalion who brought to life a statue of a beautiful woman. Hence, the phrase "Pygmalion effect" became associated with this work.

As engaging as these findings are for delinquency research, there have been numerous criticisms of the Rosenthal and Jacobson study (Thorndike, 1968; Snow, 1969) and not all studies of teacher expectations have obtained the same results (Boocock, 1978). However, a large number of studies with various methodologies have obtained results similar to Rosenthal and Jacobson's indicating that the process they identified seems to occur. Subsequent studies suggest that teachers' expectations as well as those of parents and peers have dramatic effects on how much students learn (Rist, 1970; Eder, 1981). Oakes (1985), in a highly acclaimed study entitled *Keeping Track: How Schools Structure Inequality*, suggests that low track students are being exposed to material that is qualitatively different from the educational material presented to high track students. Tracking retards the academic progress of certain students, lowers self-esteem and career aspirations, and encourages racial and economic segregation. Oakes found that low track students are being taught how to fill out forms and write checks while high track students are reading Shakespeare and learning analytic geometry. She asks:

> Could it be that we are teaching kids at the bottom of the educational hierarchy — who are more likely to be from poor and minority groups — behaviors that will prepare them to fit in at the lowest levels of the social and economic hierarchy? And, at the other extreme, are we teaching kids at the top of the schooling stratification system behaviors that are most important for professional and leadership roles? In essence, are we teaching kids at the bottom how to stay there and kids at the top how to get ahead? (1985:91)

Intelligence Tests

"Intelligence tests" of one kind or another are used in schools to channel youth into different educational programs. They are accorded significance by educational institutions and, in general, those youth who do poorly on such tests also have high rates of delinquency.

Albert Binet, the creator of the first IQ test, wrote in 1905 that an IQ score should only be used as a rough guide for identifying mildly retarded and learning disabled children who needed extra help in school. He emphatically stated that the test "does not permit the measure of intelligence because intelligence is not a single scalable thing like height" (quoted in Gould, 1981:151). Binet argued that the IQ score was intended to be a rough guide, constructed for a limited, practical purpose.

A popular movement known as *eugenics* claimed that one's IQ was inherited and that by allowing individuals with low IQs to reproduce, we were weakening our "human stock." In 1927 the U.S. Supreme Court supported this view by upholding Virginia's compulsory sterilization law in the *Buck v. Bell* case. More than 30 states enacted such laws, with Virginia ordering over 7,500 compulsory sterilizations. Carrie Buck was reexamined by psychologists in 1980 and was found to be of normal intelligence. However, based on her test scores in 1927 she was labelled feeble-minded and had an operation supposedly for a ruptured appendix. She never was informed that her fallopian tubes were severed until it was discovered in 1980 (Gould, 1981). Thus, IQ tests have been used in highly questionable ways, and for many, the deification of the IQ score is quite unpalpable.

No test can measure native intelligence, because "IQs always are based on the individual's interactions with the environment" (Sattler, 1982:64) and no matter how carefully the questions are written, there is always a cultural bias to such tests. It is generally agreed that IQ tests are a better indicator of a child's background and learning environment than of his or her natural intelligence. Further, it has been shown that test scores can be influenced by test readiness, test anxiety, motivation, perceived test payoff, and even the race of the test administrator. However, for all the negative points of IQ tests, they still do predict academic success better than anything else. What they do measure is a combination of factors including intelligence, knowledge, middle-class language patterns and experiences, motivation, and test readiness, to name but a few of the test dimensions.

While not a perfect measure and clearly culturally biased towards white, middle-class standards, IQ tests do give some indication of how well a student will perform in school. Immigrants typically score low on IQ tests but their descendants score considerably higher—not because of a change in innate ability but because of familiarity with white middle-class norms, behaviors, and values.

No matter what our interpretation of IQ tests, we should expect a relationship between IQ test performance and delinquency. Wolfgang, Figlio, and Sellin's (1972) study in Philadelphia found that the average IQ of boys who had been stopped by the police was 101, compared to 108 for those not stopped. An English study also found that the average IQ of boys age 8 to 10 who would later become delinquent was 95, while it was 101 for those who did not become delinquent (West, 1982). Hirschi and Hindelang (1977) also pointed to the small but consistent difference of about nine points between the IQs of delinquents and nondelinquents. It is quite reasonable from a sociological perspective to expect that all sorts of measures of ability, achievement, and intelligence may be related to delinquency. Students who do not fare well in terms of the criteria that a particular institution uses to evaluate people are likely to be less sensitive to the emphases and concerns of that institution. The reason that they do not do well in terms of those criteria can be debated. However, it would be surprising to find anything other than lower test scores among delinquents since school experiences are important in the explanation of delinquency. And, as Hirschi and Hindelang concluded in their review of the literature, the relationship between IQ test performance and measures of official delinquency is at least as strong as relationships found for social class and race. Hirschi and Hindelang's research indicated that IQ affects delinquency through its association with school performance—that is, students who do not score well on IQ tests tend not to score well in terms of grades and academic achievement and, hence, have a higher probability of involvement in delinquency.

Menard and Morse (1984) are highly critical of any attempt to suggest that IQ is an important variable in explaining delinquency. They argue that delinquent behavior is a consequence of social institutional practices rather than individual characteristics. Thus:

> Access to desirable social roles and positive labeling in the school, the home, and society in general mutually reinforce one another and lead to commitment to the legal and social norms of society. Commitment, in turn, leads to nondelinquent, conforming, or prosocial behavior. Negatively, the absence of access to desirable social roles plus premature and/or inappropriate negative labeling mutually reinforce one another and lead to alienation, a rejection of rejectors. Alienation, in turn, leads to delinquent behavior. The behavior generated by institutional structures through opportunity and labeling may then feed back into the institutional structure, generating responses which reinforce that behavior. (Menard and Morse, 1984:1349)

In other words, rather than suggesting that IQ exerts any direct causal impact on delinquency, these authors argue that differences in IQ may lead to differences in institutional responses, and these responses may stimulate delinquency. While they are critical of Hirschi and Hindelang's research, their conclusion is basically the same: IQ tests gain their significance from the meaning accorded them by educational institutions and through their correlation with other measures of achievement and academic success at school.

Crime in School

In the past few years a great deal of attention has been given to the problem of order and personal safety within the American school system. Reports of rapes, assaults, and robberies of students as well as teachers have been reported and congressional hearings have been held on the problem of maintaining order and discipline in the school system. In 1974 Congress required the Department of Health, Education and Welfare to study the extent of crime in American schools and in 1978, a report entitled "Violent Schools—Safe Schools" was published (National Institute of Education, 1978). In this study, thousands of teachers and students reported their experiences in school and how their lives and property are in jeopardy. While this study sensitized the nation to the problem of crime in the school, it has been highly criticized for being too slipshod in its analysis and too unsophisticated (Baker and Rubel, 1980; Gottfredson and Gottfredson, 1985). Sensationalized accounts of murder and mayhem reached such a crescendo in California that the Attorney General sued the Los Angeles city school district for not providing a safe environment for students. The suit, based on the shaky legal ground that requiring students to attend schools that were unsafe constituted cruel and unusual punishment, was dismissed by the trial judge. In 1982 the state of California amended its constitution to read:

> Right to Safe Schools. All students and staff of public primary, elementary, junior high and senior high schools have the inalienable right to attend campuses which are safe, secure and peaceful. (Article I, section 28C)

Precisely what this amendment has accomplished is not clear, but it has dramatized the concern over this issue.

The evidence to date indicates that school crime, like crime in the community, is fairly widespread but at the same time is essentially nonviolent (Short, 1990). Teachers and students are in much greater danger of losing their property through theft than of being assaulted or robbed. However, while the victimization of teachers is predominately for larceny and only rarely for assaults or robberies, student victimization was not so skewed in the direction of property crime. For example, in communities of 500,000 or more, 31 percent of junior high teachers reported being the victim of a larceny over a two-month period but only 2.1 percent of these same teachers reported being assaulted and 1.4 percent robbed. For teachers in senior high schools, 21.6 percent reported a larceny, 1.4 percent reported an assault and 1.1 percent a robbery (Boesel, 1978). On the other hand, students in these same size communities reported a 14.8 percent larceny rate in junior high, 8.5 percent assault rate, and 5.7 percent robbery rate. For students in senior high schools, the larceny rate was 14.9 percent, assault was 3.7 percent, and the robbery rate was 2.8 percent.

Jackson Toby (1983) suggests that the teacher and student victimization rate may not be as dramatic as the perception of fear of crime in school. In the largest of cities, 7 percent of senior high school students said they stayed home from school out of fear *at least once in the month before the survey* as did 8 percent of the junior high students. Among the teachers in the largest of cities, 28 percent said they hesitated to confront misbehaving students in the month preceding the survey out of fear for their own safety.

Toby suggests that schools mirror the local community or neighborhood in the volume and type of crime. "Some schools become virtual jungles from the point of view of student and staff safety and wastelands from the point of view of education" (Toby, 1983:76). Toby sees the major problem of crime in school to be compulsory attendance. He suggests that a uniform age of compulsory attendance be set at 15 years, and disruptive or unruly students who are 15 years of age or older would simply be expelled from school.

Gottfredson and Gottfredson (1985) are not convinced by Toby's argument. They argue that the average school is not "the hotbed of violence and disorder that popular accounts suggest" (1985:1). Teachers are exposed to a wide variety of personal indignities, the least frequent being rape or assault and the most common being verbal abuse. Students are rarely robbed or assaulted but do experience a fair amount of petty theft. Hence, the major problem in schools according to Gottfredson and Gottfredson is the frequency of minor victimizations and personal indignities. They see school size as the critical variable. When teachers have extensive contact with a limited number of students, social control is at the optimum level. In exceedingly large schools, the educational climate becomes impersonal and disruptive as teachers are exposed to large numbers of different students who are rotated through an endless series of classes. Secondly, the Gottfredsons suggest that rules must be clear and enforced, not with an emphasis on authoritarian rule but fair and predictable school policies. Thirdly, schools that are located in areas characterized by high poverty, unemployment, and female-headed households will manifest high crime rate in the school. Policies calling for more integration than segregation in the community itself are imperative. Finally, the Gottfredsons are not convinced that if compulsory education laws were uniformly lowered to age 15 that the crime rate in school would be improved in any significant way.

Peer Groups

We noted in Chapter 6 that several sociological theories attempt to explain the emergence and persistence of delinquency in terms of gangs rather than individual delinquent behavior. In fact, one of the reasons that sociology was prominent in the academic foundation of American criminology was that it focused on social systems or social "organizations" — everything from groups to nations. Some criminal activities were clearly "organized" whether that organization took the form of an adult syndicate such as the Mafia or attempts to maximize corporate profits through price-fixing. Similarly, while thought of as "antisocial" behavior, delinquency was also "social" behavior in the sense that it typically occurred in groups of youths of similar age and social characteristics. Delinquent behavior was and remains an activity that tends to occur in groups and that is true in all settings and categories of youth studied.

The term "gang" is likely to be used in everyday depictions of the peer group nature of delinquency. Since that term evokes images of an identifiable set of youths with a common identity as members of a named group controlling a certain territory or "turf," other terms have been used as well to convey other senses in which delinquency is peer group behavior — for example, delinquency as "a pickup game," "law-violating youth groups," and "near groups." Even the term "gang" can be qualified based on the degree of organization involved. Some researchers believe that the focus on gangs characterizing criminology in the 1960s helped perpetuate a "gang myth" and ignored the essentially spontaneous and casual nature of delinquency in very loosely organized play groups. To fully understand the group nature of delinquency requires recognition of its most common form as well as its more dramatic, but less common, form — the street gang.

Peer Group Delinquency as a Pickup Game

Many sociologists have criticized an exclusive focus on gangs because it limits the study of delinquency to one type of group which accounts for a small amount of the total volume of delinquency in America (Hirschi, 1969:52-53). This point of view is expressed by Martin Gold, based on research on delinquency in Flint, Michigan:

> The "gang" image seldom fit the teen-age groups involved in delinquent behavior. That is, the groups did not regularly and frequently commit delinquent acts together; their members did not characterize themselves as especially delinquent compared with other teen-agers; and their behavior together was not usually delinquent. Rather, the groups of teen-agers who committed delinquent acts consisted usually of two or three youngsters who often hung around together, and from time to time engaged in delinquent behavior. From the point of view of even the most delinquent boys, their companions in crime were drawn from the ranks of the many fellows they knew and spent time with; seldom were any particular boys ever consistent fellow offenders. More important than the particular company was the presence of an opportunity for delinquency at a time when everyone's mood was ripe for the action.
>
> Perhaps gang delinquency, not much a part of the Flint (Michigan) scene, is more characteristic of the hearts of great cities where teen-agers may stick closer together with fewer friends than they do in Flint, and where the delinquent opportunity and the daring-defiant mood are more often coincident. Yet observers of delinquency in the inner-city slums of London and New York report that the gang image is much overblown even there.
>
> Delinquent behavior, as our data describe it, is more casual, spontaneous, and loosely organized than the gang myth would lead us to believe. We have suggested that delinquent activity more closely resembles the pickup games of ball we used to get into at the park or on the street, when someone showed up with a bat and ball, the environment provided an adequate setting, and we had the spirit for the game. (1970).

The image of delinquency presented by Gold and others emphasizes spontaneity. When the stage is set and the right combination of youth get together, the odds of delinquency may be enhanced but such activity is not the premeditated aim of such groups. Moreover, most such collections of youth lack the features that would justify calling them a gang. Gold's research supports the conclusion that delinquency is most often a spontaneous activity in ordinary peer groups.

Gender and the Group Nature of Delinquency

When conceived of as spontaneous peer group activity, delinquency is a social event for both girls and boys. The fact that true delinquent gangs are rare among girls has led some scholars (see Cloward and Piven, 1978) to depict female delinquency as "individualistic" and lacking in the social solidarity of male delinquency. However, at least three studies have examined the relation between gender and peer delinquency and all three report the same results (see Erickson and Jensen, 1977). Girls are just as likely or even more likely than boys to indicate that they were with others when they engaged in delinquent action. This finding should not be surprising since no one has ever demonstrated greater sociability, solidarity, or engrossment in intimate peer group relationships for boys than girls. As summarized in Chapters 3 and 4, girls are less likely than boys to be engaged in most forms of delinquency and have especially low rates for the most serious offenses. However, when they do commit delinquent acts, they are as likely to commit them with company as are boys (see Figure 7-8).

The fact that delinquency is as likely to be a social activity for girls as for boys does not mean that there are no differences in the group nature or organizational nature of crime and delinquency by gender. Darrell Steffensmeier (1983) has studied "institutional sexism" in the underworld of crime and proposes that sex segregation is particularly prominent for organized, professional, and high-risk-high-gain criminal activity. Since most juvenile delinquency is spontaneous, nonprofessional, and low in profit, the gender difference in delinquency should not be as distinct as it is for more highly structured crime. Moreover, the gender difference in structural gang membership should be greater than the difference in more casual and spontaneous peer group activity. The gender difference should also be lower for the least dangerous and lowest risk group activities. Thus, the difference between males and females varies depending on the organization of the activity but, in general, both male and female delinquency are forms of "social" action.

Gangs, Near Groups, and Law-Violating Youth Groups

Some peer groups involved in delinquency are more structured and have features that justify the term "gang." However, there is great variation in the features of groups thought of as gangs and the degree to which gangs are responsible for serious crime and delinquency depends on the definition used. As a reflection of this diversity criminologists have used a variety of terms to refer to "gang-like" peer groups.

In a study of youths in Philadelphia, Savitz, Lalli, and Rosen (1977:49)

Figure 7-8

Group and Lone Offenses by Gender

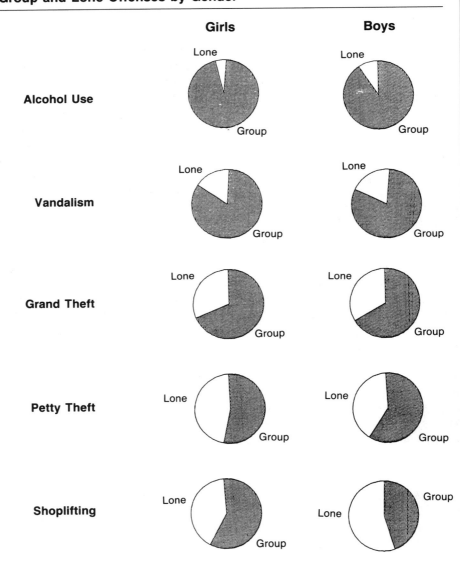

Source: Derived from Erickson, M. L., and G. F. Jensen, "Delinquency Is Still Group Behavior,"*Journal of Criminal Law and Criminology,* 1977.

found that police records of gang membership were not adequate for assessing the extent of gang delinquency. Thus, they chose to gather information on delinquent gangs through interviews. They defined the gangs in two different senses. Drawing on William Arnold's work, they classified youths as either structural gang members or as functional gang members. A structural gang member belonged to a group with "acknowledged leadership, common gang meeting place, and a territory or 'turf' within which the group feels safe and where entry by others can provoke the group to violence." Such gangs were defined solely on the basis of their structural characteristics and not according to whether they actually engaged in aggressive behavior. A functional gang member was one who belonged to a group that did get into fights with other groups and that expected fighting of its members.

Among males with delinquent records, structural gang membership was quite rare. Of blacks with delinquent records, 16 percent were classified as structural gang members, as were 22 percent of whites. While few youths belonged to structural gangs, a greater proportion indicated that their group of friends fought with other groups and that they were expected to join in the fighting. This type of functional gang membership was true of 44 percent of the blacks with records and 68 percent of the whites. In short, the territorially-based gang with acknowledged leadership was relatively rare, even among youths with records. It was even rarer among Philadelphia youths who did not have official records (11 percent of blacks and 14 percent of whites).

The Philadelphia data are essentially consistent with the arguments of Lewis Yablonsky that gangs are misconceived as having a measurable number of members, clearly defined membership, specific roles for different members to play, a set of norms that are mutually agreed upon, and a definite leadership structure. Yablonsky (1959) argued that a more accurate image is that of a "near group." Such a group is characterized by 1) diffuse role definitions, 2) limited cohesion, 3) impermanence, 4) minimal consensus of norms, 5) shifting membership, 6) disturbed leadership, and 7) limited definition of membership expectations. From this perspective, even identifiable gangs in large cities would be viewed as falling somewhere between the structural gang, a true social group, and a totally unorganized, unstructured mob. Hence, Yablonsky uses the term "near group" to emphasize the point that the typical juvenile gang is more than a disorganized mob but less than an highly organized social group.

Walter Miller (1980) has attempted to delineate "gangs" as just one type of "law-violating youth group." He defines youth gangs as ". . . a self-formed association of peers, bound together by mutual interests, with identifiable leadership, well-developed lines of authority, and other organizational features, who act in concert to achieve a specific purpose or purposes which generally include the conduct of illegal activity and control over a particular territory, facility or type of enterprise.''

Such gangs are viewed by criminal justice, youth service, and other local officials as a serious problem in most major cities in the United States. In a later study, Miller (1982) found that gang problems were unexpectedly high in many smaller cities, some with populations of less than 20,000. According to Miller's estimate, 2,300 youth gangs were found in 300 cities with membership exceeding 100,000. All evidence suggests that gang activity increased in the 1980s, but national data is more impressionistic than factual. What is known about gang activity is localized. For example, law enforcement authorities in Los Angeles claim 400 separate gangs in that city, with 40,000 to 50,000 members. In Chicago, estimates indicate 135 gangs with some 14,000 members. It is estimated that the gang problem has doubled or tripled in those two cities, while the youth population has declined. It does appear that gang members account for far more than their share of violent offenses and that they are a significant dimension of the crime-delinquency problem in certain settings. However, it is also important to remember that most delinquency is a peer group activity more akin to Gold's ''pickup game'' than the routine activities of identifiable and structured gangs.

Perhaps some of the best documented evidence on gangs was provided by Short and Strodtbeck's Chicago studies in the mid-1960s. Detailed records were maintained of the day-to-day activities of gangs. The researchers found little evidence of tightly structured gangs with narrowly focused behavioral patterns. Rather, they concluded that gangs were loosely organized with enormous behavioral versatility. The major offense for many of the gangs involved drinking and disturbing the peace.

Gangs and Drug Trafficking

The movement of gangs into organized drug trafficking has brought renewed attention to the ''gang problem.'' While most group delinquency is casual and spontaneous, some gangs are sufficiently structured and organized that they approach the status of what one criminologist refers to as ''corporate'' gangs (Taylor, 1990). Enduring structured gangs have been particularly notable in Chicago (e.g. the Cobras, El Rukns, Vice Lords) and Los Angeles. Two of the largest gangs in Los Angeles, the Bloods and the Crips, are estimated to have 25,000 members collectively. Each consists of distinct ''sets'' who often draw their names from their geographical area or turf. The Crips are estimated to have 190 such sets compared to 65 sets for the Bloods. An additional 50,000 youths are thought to belong to around 400 other sets in the Los Angeles area (Attorney General of the United States, 1989). While clearly the province of the young, the proportion of gang members who are juveniles is estimated to be about 35 percent. The "Original Gang Members" (known as OGs in the gangs) are now adults in their late 20s and early 30s. The hard core members, "Gangsters" range from 16 to 22. While the gangs include "baby" and "tiny" gangsters, it is important to remember that the types of offenses that are drawing national attention are the same ones that have peaked in the young adult years among nongang offenders.

There have been some changes in gang activity in terms of frequency, characteristics of participants, and in targets. There were an estimated 200 gang-related deaths in Los Angeles County in 1978, 351 in 1980, and 600 in 1987. Moreover, the participants are thought to be older than they were two or three decades ago (Maxson et al., 1985). While the targets of gang violence in the past were typically other gang members who had impugned the honor or invaded the territory of rival gangs, the killings in recent years have been less direct. Most victims were members of rival gangs, but were not targeted specifically because of an affront or personal vendetta. Rather, they were casualties of increased competition among gangs for control of the drug market. Based on their study of gang homicides in Los Angeles, Maxson and associates conclude that 54 percent of gang homicides show no evidence of a prior personal contact: "In these gang homicides, the relationship between opponents appears to be based on gang affiliation rather than enmity between familiar individuals." They also report that "In spite of rising public concern about innocent bystander victims, we found mention of only four such cases (all gang-related)" (1985). Gang homicides dealt with by Los Angeles county sheriffs disproportionately involved Hispanic subjects as compared to nongang homicides, while gang homicides dealt with by the city police department disproportionately involved black suspects. Out of a total of nearly 700 gang homicides less than 1 percent involved white suspects. In contrast, about one-quarter of nongang homicides involved whites. Only 3 percent of gang homicide suspects were female as compared to about 15 percent of nongang homicides. Gang violence appears to be more distinctively a minority group and male activity than is nongang violence.

In his discussion of inner-city gangs, Jeffrey Fagan suggests that gangs may have become "quasi-institutionalized" in some inner cities, ghettos, and barrios. By "quasi-institutionalized" he means that they compete for status and authority with other social institutions in an area such as church, school, and family. "If schools, families, and legal institutions are weak in inner cities, gangs have a near monopoly on status-conferring activities" (Fagan, 1990). Moreover, in areas where they control some portion of the drug market, they can become the most lucrative "employer" as well.

The movement of gangs into the drug trade has been accompanied by an escalation of violence as rival groups and dealers battle for control of a market. Guns are vital to gaining and maintaining that control. The use of guns escalates and spreads to younger members and peripheral youth both for self-protection and as a source of status. A shift to more and more lethal weapons transforms fights and assaults into homicides. While constituting a small fraction of homicides in the United States, the involvement of juveniles in murders with firearms increased 43 percent between 1984 and 1988 (Witkin, 1991).

There is reason to believe that the violence associated with gang drug wars might stabilize and decline in future years. Violence is particularly likely when rival gangs are attempting to gain control over the same market. When rival criminal syndicates were battling for control of bootlegging, prostitution or other illegal markets in American cities in the 1920s and 1930s, mob violence was quite common. In a sense, it was when "organized" crime was "disorganized" that violence was most likely. Profits are likely to be maximized when illicit goods and services are provided in an organized manner and when criminal organizations operate in a businesslike manner. Excessive violence draws attention and is likely to lead to crackdowns that increase the cost of doing business.

To some degree gang violence may reflect the effect of successful law enforcement efforts to disrupt the leadership of criminal organizations such as the Mafia. Disruption of traditional syndicates, the expansion of trade routes for drugs, and the availability of cheap crack-cocaine has increased the number of competitors for control of the drug market. When the market is "divided up" (organized) and original gang members and leaders begin operating as a business, the overall extent of violence associated with the drug trade may decline. There are already reports that some of the identifying characteristics of gang membership have been abandoned because they make gang members too visible (Attorney General, 1989). Crime generates the greatest profits when it can be carried out with a low profile and when it is organized. Violence associated with such activities will never disappear but the history of criminal organizations suggests that overall violence could very well decline.

Adolescent Society

It is widely accepted that delinquency is a peer group activity and that the odds of a youth engaging in delinquency are much greater for youth with delinquent friends than those with only conventional friends. Youths asked to report on how they initially got involved in delinquency are likely to mention friends just as peer pressure is acknowledged as a source of initial experimentation with drugs. The characteristics and activities of a youth's peers are important for understanding her or his own behavior.

Some theorists dealing with the world of adolescent peer groups present an image of adolescent society *in general* as essentially unconventional and in conflict with the norms and laws of parents (see Box 7-2). Some years back, Ralph England (1967) suggested that rapid urbanization and industrialization in the nineteenth century resulted in the marginalization of youth. That is, they were neither adult nor child, but an isolated group of individuals who became extremely hedonistic and materialistic. It is alleged that in the twentieth century teenagers began to express their independence from adult society by adopting distinctive and faddish dress and hair styles, entertainment idols, dance steps, musical tastes, and even a distinctive language (VanderZanden, 1986). These external symbols were suggestive of what many perceived to be a definitive break from the larger culture and the inculcation of a distinct youth culture (Richards, 1988).

In one of the best-known works on adolescent society, James Coleman wrote:

> Our adolescents today are cut off, probably more than ever before, from the adult society. They are still oriented toward fulfilling their parents desires, but they look very much to their peers for approval as well. Consequently, our society has within its midst a set of small teen-age societies which focus teen-age interests and attitudes on things far removed from adult responsibilities, and which may develop standards that lead away from these goals established by the larger society. (1961:9)

The fact that teenage groups have emerged does not necessarily mean that involvement in such groups is conducive to delinquency, but the imagery of pursuing goals "different from" those of the larger society suggests such a possibility. Bell (1983) indicated that a distinctive style and taste develop within a youth culture such that they share more with each other than with their parents or other adults. Covington (1982) takes the youth culture argument directly into the realm of delinquency. She states that because adolescence is a transitional stage between childhood and adulthood, it must have its own set of norms, values, and expectations. Parents create conflict by expecting adolescents to subscribe to the same set of standards and values as when the youth was a child. The adolescent finds such norms and values to be unfulfilling and unchallenging. The adolescent begins to question parental norms and values, turns to his or her peers for guidance and meaning, and in the process an adolescent deviant subculture arises.

The emphasis on the unconventional aspects of youth culture has not gone unchallenged. For example, in an article entitled "The Myth of Adolescent Culture" (1955), Frederick Elkin and William A. Westley argued that the "distinctiveness" of youth culture has been over exaggerated. They suggested that adolescents are far more conventional than the "youth culture" stereotype allows. Other scholars have attacked the emphasis on the distinctiveness of youth culture by arguing that the adult world is not

Box 7-2

Peers and Delinquency

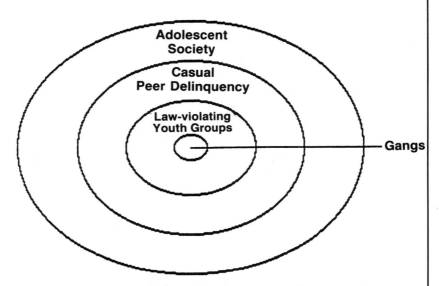

Some scholars writing about "adolescent society" view involvement in ordinary peer group activities as conducive to delinquency. Adolescents are viewed as committed to a subcultural value system that leads to trouble. For others it is a smaller category of youth who are free from adult control and have relatively little to lose by involvement in casual, spontaneous, delinquent episodes that typify delinquency. Delinquent peer groups that take on the more stable characteristics that would justify calling them "gangs" account for a disproportionately high share of serious delinquency but are a small part of the overall problem.

Do you think that teenagers in general are inclined to break laws?

as prudish and square as it is commonly depicted. Bennett Berger (1963) pointed out that many adults share the values and interests of adolescents regarding cars, sports, and romance, as well as their emphasis on status, popularity, and anti-intellectualism. John Coleman (1980) suggests that when conflict occurs between parents and teenagers, it is usually over trivial matters, not debates over morality or ideology. Coleman also points out that teenagers in his study saw their parents more positively than they saw themselves in terms of honesty, reliability, unselfishness, and patience. Finally, Cohen (1980) found that early adolescents do gravitate away from their parents but as the adolescent moves through high school peer acceptance becomes less salient and the importance of the family becomes more apparent.

Compared to the amount of research on the family, school, and gangs we actually know very little about the distinctiveness of adolescent society in comparison to the adult world. Moreover, there is relatively little research on variations within the adolescent world. Race, socioeconomic status, age, sex, and educational attainment most likely cut across adolescent society creating a plurality of group memberships, values, and attitudes. Several questions have not been asked about adolescent subcultures. For example, do adolescents in general 1) repudiate the dominant culture of their parents and create a "contraculture," 2) differ in degree as to basic values and ideals and constitute a "subculture," or 3) merely differ in some respects, ultimately subscribing to the same value system. Raymond Eve (1975) found support for the third view. He reported statistically significant differences between students and teachers for drinking, but in other areas both groups were quite similar. Eve concluded that students' values differ only in a small degree from the adult value system. Similarly Smeja and Rojek (1986) found that college students who use marijuana but not hard drugs like barbiturates, amphetamines, cocaine, or narcotics were eminently conventional. They exhibited respect for and endorsement of the social order in every way except for the regulation of marijuana. On the other hand, nonusers of drugs and marijuana-only users were quite distinct from regular users of hard-core illicit drugs like narcotics, barbiturates, and amphetamines. The fact that adolescents behave somewhat differently or are somewhat rebellious does not mean that they subscribe to a value system that is radically different from their parents. There is marked heterogeneity in American society on a number of dimensions but there can still be a basic endorsement of a common set of values and beliefs.

The importance of peers in the lives of adolescents and the existence of a youth culture are two quite distinct issues. At present, there is little support for the argument that adolescents in general share values, norms, or beliefs that conflict with or cut them off from the adult world. Nonetheless, there are ways in which participation in peer group activities can facilitate delinquency. For one, although the majority of adolescents may express quite conventional values and beliefs, their structural position in modern America gives them considerable leisure time and freedom from many types of conventional social bonds. They are not children, but neither are they adults. This marginality, coupled with the age-grading of schools, sets the stage for a high level of peer group interaction and considerable free time. While the popular literature would suggest that adolescents become involved in a tug-of-war between the values of their parents and the values of their friends, the truth lies somewhere in between. Recall Matza and Syke's (1964) concept of subterranean values. There is a certain allurement or excitement associated with deviant activities but that does not require rejection of the dominant culture. Adolescents, like adults, can appear entrenched on the side of law and order and still transgress the law.

Jensen and Erickson (1978) attempted to assess the impact of incorporating elements of conflict into questions about peers. Students were asked whether they would "go along with their friends" or join their families if their families were planning to go to a show. There was no significant relationship between a student's answer to this question and self-reported delinquency (although a slightly greater proportion of those who indicated they would go along with friends did report delinquent activities). On the other hand, when an element of conflict was introduced by asking them whether they would go riding around with friends after school if their parents had told them never to do that, there was a sizable relationship: students who indicated they would disregard parental authority reported significantly more delinquency. Similarly, students who indicated they would go along with peers in situations of conflict with the law reported significantly more delinquency than did those who indicated they would not go along. Several different variables are confounded together in these types of measures (peer commitment, attachment to the law, attachment to parents), precluding any simple conclusion that peer commitment encourages delinquency.

In considering socialization within the context of adolescent society, it is important to ask the following questions: How often do adolescents experience conflict between peers and conventional authority? What are the general tendencies of adolescents in making such choices? In general, research suggests that adolescents and parents tend to get along reasonably well. Hill states that:

> The psychoanalytic position that rebelliousness is normal during adolescence enjoys considerable support from those who work with troubled and troublesome young people. Studies of more representative samples of the population, however, do not support this position. Adolescence is not, in general, a period of overt rebelliousness and familial conflict in industrial societies according to representative samples of parents and their adolescent offspring. (1980:38)

In those situations where there is a question of peers versus parents, Brittain (1963) found that parents have more influence in those issues that involve future plans such as education or occupation, while peers have more influence in the more mundane aspects of daily life such as dress, grooming, and music. Jensen and Erickson (1978) found that the tendency of the adolescent to go along with peers is highly variable and depends on the choice. In general adolescents chose to go along with their friends when the degree of conflict with their parents was minimal.

Overall, it does not appear that adolescent society *in general* is characterized by values, norms and beliefs that clearly cut them off from the adult world or that facilitate delinquency. However, as a leisure class or as a large segment of the population with time to bide, adolescents have considerable freedom to commit delinquent acts. Moreover, those most involved in the activities that, in the eyes of adults, characterize adolescent society are those most likely to become involved in delinquency. When adolescents choose to please their peers despite the possibilities of conflict with authority, the probability of their involvement in delinquency is very high.

A major study dealing with diversity among adolescents was conducted by Herman and Julia Schwendinger (1985) and, as summarized in Chapter 6, they were able to differentiate among adolescents in terms of a set of identities that correlated with different life styles and different probabilities of delinquency. Youth could be differentiated into what they called "stratified domains" or "stradoms" based on the membership in groups or subcultures. The probability of belonging to different groups was affected by social class of parents but it was membership in a stradom which correlated most strongly with variations in delinquency. Their study suggests new directions for research on the adolescent world but actually tells us little about variations by race and gender and the determinants of membership in various groups. Moreover, if membership in different stradoms is shaped by characteristics of parents, then these stradoms may be parallels of similar stradoms in the adult world. In short, we still do not know if these subcultures are truly subcultures in relation to the adult world. It is also important to remember that the research was based on California and, as the researchers acknowledge, research in other regions may yield different categories and distinctions.

Mutual Interdependence, Independence, and Causal Sequences

Although we have dealt with family, school, and peers individually, it is important to recognize that social reality involves an interrelated web of influences. At several points in the discussion, we commented on the difficulty of isolating the impact of one specific characteristic of a situation that intertwines many other characteristics. Experiences and relationships in one setting are shaped and influenced by experiences and relationships in other settings. The complexity of these interrelationships is what makes it so difficult to differentiate causal relationships from spurious relationships and to decide between causes and effects.

Consider, for example, the relationship between conditions of family life and experiences at school. The stronger the bond between parents and child, the stronger the bond between the child and teachers. Of course, there are numerous exceptions to that observation, but there is definitely an association between the two variables. Similarly, the stronger the bond between a youth and school, or between a youth and parents, the weaker the chances that he or she will acquire delinquent friends or choose to go along with peers in situations of conflict with authority.

While most scholars would agree that experiences in different settings are interrelated, there are several different positions taken in the literature on a number of other issues. For example, Hirschi (1969) reports that experiences within school and the family as well as associations with delinquent peers *each* help explain delinquency; that is, experiences in a variety of settings are each *independently* relevant to explaining delinquency. Other scholars posit causal sequences where the influence of some experiences are *indirect* through their association with other experiences. Some of these models borrow from several different theories and put the variables in a specific sequence.

For example, Johnson (1979) constructed a general model to explain delinquent behavior by starting with parental affection for the child, which leads to parental attachment, then attachment to school. These variables then influence the selection of delinquent friends, which ultimately impacts delinquent behavior. Moreover, delinquent values are strengthened by having delinquent associates but weakened by strong attachment to school. Finally, delinquent behavior is positively influenced by having delinquent associates and acquiring delinquent values. Marcos, Bahr, and Johnson (1986) developed a similar model to examine the causal forces leading up to adolescent drug use. They found as did Johnson (1979) that friends are the most influential factor in delinquent behavior but the acquisition of delinquent friends is influenced by parental attachment and school attachment.

The exact causal sequence among these forces is still a subject of debate as is the simple question of cause versus effect. While social scientists tend to think of family life, school experiences, and peer relationships as sources or causes of delinquency, it is widely recognized that experiences in each can be *affected by* delinquency and trouble-making as well. Youths who get into trouble may be judged more harshly at school and be disliked by teachers. They may upset their parents and break down family bonds. They may come to associate with other kids in trouble and come to define law-breaking in favorable terms. In sum, delinquency might precede and account for the circumstances presumed to generate it.

In one recent study Liska and Reed (1985) used data from a large sample of boys gathered at two points in time and found that involvement in delinquency affected how attached they were to teachers and school, but that relations at school did not have much relevance to predicting delinquency. They concluded that "Delinquency appears to be more of a cause than a consequence of school attachment" (1985). Of course, findings on attachment to school do not necessarily apply to school performance and there are research results supporting the view that school failure precedes delinquency (Phillips and Kelly, 1979). Moreover, while low school attachment did not appear to precede delinquency, attachment to parents did. Liska and Reed conclude that their findings "suggest that parents, not school, are the major institutional sources of delinquency control" (1985). At present there are conflicting points of view about the relevance of each of these institutions to delinquency and their direct independent effects versus indirect effects as well as whether they follow or precede delinquency. Some of the results summarized in subsequent chapters do suggest that parents can affect their children's troublemaking by changing their own behavior and that school programs can influence student behavior as well. Thus, it is still reasonable to conclude that the modification of family life and school experiences hold some promise for addressing delinquency even if the exact causal sequences in everyday life have yet to be untangled.

Not only are there debates about causal sequences, but there is mounting concern that explanations of delinquency may vary for different categories of youth. We have already noted the view that broken homes may be more consequential for whites than blacks and that as the unusual becomes typical it may no longer differentiate among youth. Liska and Reed, in the study mentioned previously, report results suggesting that school attachment does affect delinquency in the black sample but not the white sample. Similarly, Matsueda and Heimer (1987) report that the effect of a nonintact home is much greater for blacks than for whites because blacks have fewer coping resources than whites. Both Johnson (1986) and Dornbusch et al. (1985) suggest strong evidence that the presence of a stepfather seems to engender delinquency. Thus, it may be necessary to consider intact, nonintact, and "restructured" families. Likewise Hansell and Wiatrowski (1981) present evidence regarding the nature of delinquent group relationships. Some delinquent associates are close friends, with average social and interpersonal skills. These youths belong to what is labelled a *social ability model*, whereas social isolates with below average interpersonal skills may band together in what Hansell and Wiatrowski call a *social disability model*.

It also remains to be seen whether variables important in one society are comparably important in others. For example, there is some evidence that social class may differentiate between delinquents and nondelinquents in Korea better than in the United States (Axenroth, 1983). Yet, most variables emphasized in research in the United States have also been found to be relevant to the explanation of delinquency in Canada (see Hagan et al., 1985, 1987) and in the United Kingdom (see Rutter and Giller, 1984). Theories that were developed to explain delinquency in the United States when it was growing, urbanizing, and industrializing may apply to developing nations at similar stages of development. Hopefully, as criminologists around the world begin using similar techniques to study similar issues we will be able to distinguish between factors which lead to the development of delinquent behavior among humans in general and characteristics that are unique and of variable relevance in different societies.

Summary

Social scientists have long regarded the influences of family, school, and peer group as particularly crucial to understanding delinquency. However, theories vary on the importance of each and the specific ways these three variables influence delinquency. There is a growing concern with identifying the specific contribution of family, school, and peers to understanding delinquency among different groups and within different settings.

Studies of family structure and interaction in relation to delinquency suggest a number of generalizations, all of which must be tempered with the recognition that cause and effect have not been conclusively established.

1. Children from broken homes are disproportionately likely to appear in police, court, and institutional statistics, but studies using self-report data indicate at the most a weak association with delinquency.

2. The nature of relationships between children and parents is more relevant to explaining delinquency than is the broken or intact nature of the home.

3. The greater the reciprocal communication and mutual bonds between parent and child, the less the involvement in delinquency.

4. The extremes of permissiveness and overly strict discipline are more often associated with higher rates of delinquency than is a mild emphasis on discipline administered according to standards that appear fair and equitable to children.

5. The quantity of time a parent spends with a child is not as critical as the quality of the interaction between parent and child.

6. While violence is a significant aspect of American family life it appears to be declining.

7. Experiences of family violence are correlated with violence outside of the family and increase the odds that a youth will acquire a record in the future.

There has been far more speculation than actual research on the specific aspects of school that are relevant to an understanding of delinquency. The following observations seem justified in view of the research to date with the same reservations about cause and effect expressed for family influences:

1. The higher a student's academic achievement or performance, the lower the involvement in delinquency.
2. The stronger the bond between students and teachers and the more favorable the attitudes of students toward school, the less the involvement in delinquency.
3. Students in remedial or noncollege "tracks" have higher probabilities of delinquent involvement than students in college "tracks," regardless of IQ scores, father's occupation, or grade-point average.
4. The lower the performance on IQ tests, the poorer a student's school performance, and the poorer the school performance, the greater the probability of delinquent involvement.

We have noted that there is some controversy over the nature of the relationship between delinquent peers and a youth's involvement in delinquency. There seems to be common agreement that the acquisition of delinquent companions has a strong impact on involvement in delinquency. However, the view that teenagers have interests and attitudes that set them apart from the adult world and the view that a general orientation toward peers is conducive to delinquency are both subject to debate. The following observations are consistent with research findings:

1. Delinquent friends consistently emerge as critical in the explanation of delinquency but the acquisition of delinquent associates is influenced by the degree of attachment to the family and success in or attachment to school.
2. Delinquency is most often a form of group behavior and typically occurs spontaneously in ordinary teenage peer groups.
3. While girls are less likely to engage in delinquency than boys, when they do so it is at least as likely to occur while with peers.
4. Peer groups with gang characteristics account for a disproportionate share of crime and delinquency but are not the typical form of peer group delinquency.
5. Peer groups with gang characteristics range in degree of organization

and structure from loosely structured "near groups" to more enduring institutionalized gangs ("corporate" gangs).

6. The attitudes of teenagers in general toward the law, delinquent activities, and goals are primarily conventional, differing according to degrees of approval and disapproval from adults.

7. Teenagers are quite commonly concerned about maintaining autonomy and resisting adult control, and those most involved in activities that facilitate such freedom have higher probabilities of involvement in delinquency.

Experiences in each setting—family, school, and peer groups—are interrelated and affect one another. The exact sequence of events differs among theorists but most research suggests that family and school experiences increase the odds of delinquency among youth by increasing their involvement with similarly situated peers.

References

Agnew, R. 1983. "Physical Punishment and Delinquency: A Research Note." *Youth and Society* 15 (December):225-36.

Attorney General of the United States. 1989. *Drug Trafficking*. U.S. Department of Justice: Office of the Attorney General.

Axenroth, J. B. 1983. "Social Class and Delinquency in Cross-cultural Perspective." *Journal of Research in Crime and Delinquency* 20:164-176.

Baker, K., and R. J. Rubel. 1980. *Violence and Crime in the Schools*. Lexington, MA: Lexington Books.

Bell, R. R. 1983. *Marriage and Family Interaction* (6th ed.). Homewood, IL: Dorsey.

Berger, A. S., and W. Simon. 1974. "Black Families and the Moynihan Report: A Research Evaluation." *Social Problems* 22 (December):145-61.

Berger, B. M. 1963. "Adolescence and Beyond." *Social Problems* 10 (Spring): 394-408.

Boocock, S. S. 1978. "The Social Organization of the Classroom." In R. H. Turner, J. Coleman, and R. C. Fox (eds.), *Annual Review of Sociology — 1978*. Palo Alto, CA: Annual Reviews.

Bowlby, J. 1951. *Maternal Care and Mental Health*. Geneva: World Health Organization.

Brittain, C. V. 1963. "Adolescent Choices and Parent-peer Cross Pressures." *American Sociological Review* 28:385-91.

Canter, R. J. 1982a. "Sex Differences in Self-report Delinquency." *Criminology* 20:373-93.

_____. 1982b. "Family Correlates of Male and Female Delinquency." *Criminology* 20 (Number 2):149-67.

Cernkovich, S. A., and P. C. Giordano. 1987. "Family Relationships and Delinquency." *Criminology* 25:295-321.

Chilton, R. J., and G. E. Markle. 1972. "Family Disruption, Delinquent Conduct and the Effect of Subclassification." *American Sociological Review* 37 (February):93-99.

Cloward, R. A., and F. F. Piven. 1979. "Hidden Protest: The Channelling of Female Innovation and Resistance." *Signs* 4 (November):651-69.

Cohen, J. 1980. "Adolescent Independence and Adolescent Change." *Youth and Society* 12:107-14.

Coleman, J. C. 1980. "Friendship and the Peer Group in Adolescence." In J. Adelson (ed.), *Handbook of Adolescent Society.* New York: Wiley.

Coleman, J. S. 1961. *The Adolescent Society.* New York: Free Press of Glencoe.

Conger, R. D. 1976. "Social Control and Social Learning Models of Delinquent Behavior." *Criminology* 14 (May):17-40.

Covington, J. 1982. "Adolescent Deviation and Age." *Journal of Youth and Adolescence* 11:329-44.

Davis, K. 1947. "Final Note on a Case of Extreme Isolation." *American Journal of Sociology* 52:432-37.

Dembo, R., G. Grandon, L. LaVoie, J. Schmeidler, and W. Burgas. 1986. "Parents and Drugs Revisited: Some Further Evidence in Support of Social Learning Theory." *Criminology* 24:85-104.

Dornbusch, S. M., J. M. Carlsmith, S. J. Buschwall, P. L. Ritter, H. Leiderman, C. Hastorf, and R. T. Gross. 1985. "Single Parents, Extend Households, and the Control of Adolescents." *Child Development* 56:326-41.

Eder, D. 1981. "Ability Grouping as a Self-Fulfilling Prophecy: A Micro-Analysis of Teacher-Student Interaction." *Sociology of Education* 54:151-62.

Elkin, F., and W. Westley. 1955. "The Myth of Adolescent Culture." *American Sociological Review* 20 (December):680-86.

Elliott, D. S. 1966. "Delinquency, School Attendance and Dropout." *Social Problems* 13 (Winter):306-18.

Elliott, D. S., and H. L. Voss. 1974. *Delinquency and Dropout.* Lexington, MA: Lexington Books.

England, R. 1960. "A Theory of Middle Class Juvenile Delinquency." *Journal of Criminal Law, Criminology, and Police Science* 50:535-40.

Erickson, M. L., and L. Empey. 1965. "Class Position, Peers and Delinquency." *Sociology and Social Research* 49 (April):268-82.

Erickson, M. L., and G. F. Jensen. 1977. "Delinquency Is Still Group Behavior!" *Journal of Criminal Law and Criminology* 68 (No. 2):262-73.

Eve, R. 1975. "Adolescent Culture: Convenient Myth or Reality? A Comparison of Students and Their Teachers." *Sociology of Education* 48 (Spring):152-67.

Fagan, J. 1990. "Social Processes of Delinquency and Drug Use Among Urban Gangs." In C. Ronald Huff (ed.), *Gangs in America.* Newbury Park, CA: Sage.

Frease, D. E. 1973. "Delinquency, Social Class, and the Schools." *Sociology and Social Research* 57 (July):443-59.

Gelles, R. J. 1974. *The Violent Home.* Beverly Hills, CA: Sage.

Gelles, R. J., and M. A. Straus. 1979. "Determinants of Violence in the Family: Toward a Theoretical Integration." In W. R. Burr, R. Hill, F. I. Nye, and I. L. Reiss (eds.), *Contemporary Theories about the Family.* New York: The Free Press.

Gelles, R. J., and C. P. Cornell. 1985. *Intimate Violence in Families*. Beverly Hills, CA: Sage.

Gil, D. 1970. *Violence Against Children: Physical Child Abuse in the United States*. Cambridge, MA: Harvard University Press.

Glueck, S., and E. Glueck. 1950. *Unraveling Juvenile Delinquency*. Cambridge, MA: Harvard University Press.

Gold, M. 1970. *Delinquent Behavior in an American City*. Monterrey, CA: Brooks/Cole.

Goldman, N. 1961. "A Socio-Psychological Study of School Vandalism." *Crime and Delinquency* 7:221-30.

Goldston, R. 1975. "Preventing Abuse of Little Children." *American Journal of Orthopsychiatry* 45:372-81.

Gottfredson, G. D., and D. C. Gottfredson. 1985. *Victimization in Schools*. New York: Plenum Press.

Gould, S. J. 1981. *The Mismeasure of Man*. New York: W. W. Norton.

Gove, W., and R. Crutchfield. 1982. "The Family and Juvenile Delinquency." *The Sociological Quarterly* 23 (Summer):301-19.

Hagan, J., J. Simpson, and A. R. Gillis. 1985. "The Class Structure of Gender and Delinquency: Toward a Power-control Theory of Common Delinquent Behavior." *American Journal of Sociology* 90:1151-78.

_____. 1987. "Class in the Household: A Power-control Theory of Gender and Delinquency." *American Journal of Sociology* 92:788-816.

Hansell, S., and M. D. Wiatrowski. 1981. "Competing Conceptions of Delinquent Peer Relations." In G. F. Jensen (ed.), *Sociology of Deviance: Current Issues*. Beverly Hills, CA: Sage.

Hargreaves, D. 1968. *Social Relations in a Secondary School*. New York: Humanities Press.

Harlow, H., and M. Harlow. 1962. "Social Deprivation in Monkeys." *Scientific American* 207:137-47.

Hayes, C. D., and S. B. Kamerman (eds.) 1983. *Children of Working Parents*. Washington: National Academy Press.

Helfer, R. E., and C. H. Kempe. 1974. *The Battered Child*. Chicago: University of Chicago Press.

Hill, C. R., and F. P. Stafford. 1979. "Parental Care of Children." *Journal of Human Resources* 15:219-39.

Hill, J. P. 1980. "The Family." In M. Johnson (ed.), *Toward Adolescence*. Chicago: University of Chicago Press.

Hindelang, M. J. 1973. "Causes of Delinquency: A Partial Replication." *Social Problems* 21 (Spring):471-87.

Hirschi, T. 1969. *Causes of Delinquency*. Berkeley: University of California Press.

_____. 1985. "Crime and Family Policy." In R. A. Weisheit and R. G. Culbertson (eds.), *Juvenile Delinquency: A Justice Perspective*. Prospect Heights, IL: Waveland Press.

Hirschi, T., and M. J. Hindelang. 1977. "Intelligence and Delinquency: A Revisionist Review." *American Sociological Review* 42 (August):571-87.

Jensen, G. F. 1976. "Race, Achievement and Delinquency: A Further Look at Delinquency in a Birth Cohort." *American Journal of Sociology* 82 (September):370-87.

Jensen, G. F., and R. Eve. 1976. "Sex Differences in Delinquency." *Criminology* 13:427-48.

Jensen, G. F., and D. Brownfield. 1983. "Parents and Drugs: Specifying the Consequences of Attachment." *Criminology* 21:543-54.

Jensen, G. F., and M. L. Erickson. 1978. "Peer Commitment and Delinquent Conduct." Unpublished manuscript.

Jensen, G. F., M. L. Erickson, and J. P. Gibbs. 1978. "Perceived Risk of Punishment and Self-Reported Delinquency." *Social Forces* 57(September):57-78.

Johnson, R. E. 1979. *Juvenile Delinquency and Its Origins*. London: Cambridge University Press.

———. 1986. "Family Structure and Delinquency: General Patterns and Gender Differences." *Criminology* 24:65-84.

Kelly, D. H. 1974. "Track Position and Delinquency Involvement: A Preliminary Analysis." *Sociology and Social Research* 58 (July):380-86.

Kelly, D. H., and R. W. Balch. 1971. "Social Origins and School Failure." *Pacific Sociological Review* 14 (October):413-30.

Larson, W. R., and B. G. Myerhoff. 1967. "Family Integration and Police Contact." In M. Klein (ed.), *Juvenile Gangs in Context: Theory, Research and Action*. Englewood Cliffs, NJ: Prentice-Hall.

Laub, J. H., and R. J. Sampson. 1988. "Unraveling Families and Delinquency: A Reanalysis of the Gluecks' Data." *Criminology* 26:355-80.

Lees, J. P., and L. J. Newson. 1954. "Family or Sibship Position and Some Aspects of Juvenile Delinquency." *British Journal of Delinquency* 5:46-65.

Liska, A. E., and M. D. Reed. 1985. "Institutions and Delinquency." *American Sociological Review* 50 (August):547-60.

Loeber, R., and M. Stouthamer-Loeber. 1986. "Family Factors as Correlates and Predictors of Juvenile Conduct Problems and Delinquency." In M. Tonry and N. Morris (eds.), *Crime and Justice: An Annual Review of Research* Vol. 7. Chicago: University of Chicago Press.

Marcos, A. C., S. J. Bahr, and R. E. Johnson. 1986. "Test of a Bonding/Association Theory of Adolescent Drug Use." *Social Forces* 65:135-61.

Matsueda, R. L., and K. Heimer. 1987. "Race, Family Structure, and Delinquency." *American Sociological Review* 52:826-40.

Matza, D., and G. M. Sykes. 1964. "Juvenile Delinquency and Subterranean Values." *American Sociological Review* 26 (October):712-17.

Maxson, C. L., M. A. Gordon, and M. W. Klein. 1985. "Differences Between Gang and Non-Gang Homicides." *Criminology* 23 (May):209-22.

McCord, W., J. McCord, and A. Howard. 1961. "Familial Correlates of Aggression in Nondelinquent Male Children." *Journal of Abnormal Social Psychology* 62:79-93.

McCord, J. 1984. "Family Sources of Crime." Paper presented at the meeting of the International Society for Research on Aggression, Turku, Finland.

McCord, W., J. McCord, and I. Zola. 1959. *Origins of Crime*. New York: Columbia University Press.

Menard, S., and B. J. Morse. 1984. "A Structuralist Critique of the IQ-Delinquency Hypothesis: Theory and Evidence." *American Journal of Sociology* 89:1347-78.

Merton, R. K. 1957. *Social Theory and Social Structure.* Rev. ed. New York: Free Press of Glencoe.

Miller, W. G. 1958. "Lower Class Culture as a Generating Milieu of Gang Delinquency." *Journal of Social Issues* 14:5-19.

_____. 1980. "Gangs, Groups and Serious Youth Crime." In D. Schicor and D. H. Kelley (eds.), *Critical Issues in Juvenile Delinquency.* Lexington, MA: Lexington Books.

Nye, F. I. 1958. *Family Relationships and Delinquent Behavior.* New York: John Wiley.

Oakes, J. 1985. *Keeping Track: How Schools Structure Inequality.* New Haven: Yale University Press.

Ogburn, W. F. 1938. "The Changing Family." *Family* 19 (July):139-43.

_____. 1964. "Youth in the Context of American society." In T. Parsons (ed.), *Social Structure and Personality.* Glencoe, IL: Free Press of Glencoe.

Patterson, G. R. 1980. *Mothers: The Unacknowledged Victims.* Monograph of the Society for Research in Child Development, Vol. 45. Chicago: University of Chicago Press.

_____. 1980. "Children Who Steal." In T. Hirschi and M. Gottfredson (eds.), *Understanding Crime: Current Theory and Research.* Beverly Hills, CA: Sage.

Phillips, J. C., and D. H. Kelly. 1979. "School Failure and Delinquency: What Causes Which?" *Criminology* 17 (August):194-207.

Power, M. J., P. M. Ash, E. Schoenberg, and E. C. Sirey. 1974. "Delinquency and the Family." *British Journal of Social Work* 4:13-28.

President's Commission on Law Enforcement and Administration of Justice. 1967. *Juvenile Delinquency and Youth Crime.* Washington, DC: U.S. Government Printing Office.

Pulkkinen, L. 1982. "Self-control and Continuity from Childhood to Late Adolescence." In P. B. Baltes and O. G. Brim (eds.), *Life-Span Development,* Vol. 4. New York: Academic Press.

Rankin, J. 1983. "The Family Context of Delinquency." *Social Problems* 30 (April):466-79.

Reiss, A. J., Jr. 1951. "Delinquency as the Failure of Personal and Social Controls." *American Sociological Review* 16 (April):196-207.

Richards, L. 1988. "The Appearance of Youth Subculture: A Theoretical Perspective on Deviance." *Clothing and Textiles Research Journal* 6:56-64.

Rist, R. 1970. "Social Class and Teacher Expectations: The Self-Fulfilling Prophecy in Ghetto Education."

Rosen, L. 1985. "Family and Delinquency: Structure or Function." *Criminology* 23 (August):553-73.

Rosen, L., and K. Neilson. 1982. "Broken Homes." In L. Savitz and N. Johnston (eds.), *Crime in Society.* New York: John Wiley.

Rosenthal, R., and L. Jacobson. 1968. *Pygmalion in the Classroom.* New York: Holt, Rinehart, and Winston.

Rutter, M. 1977. "Separation, Loss and Family Relations." In M. Rutter and L. Herson (eds.), *Child Psychiatry: Modern Approaches.* Oxford: Blackwell.

Rutter, M., and H. Giller. 1984. *Juvenile Delinquency: Trends and Perspectives.* New York: Gilford Press.

Sattler, J. M. 1982. *Assessment of Children's Intelligence and Special Abilities.* Boston: Allyn & Bacon.

Savitz, L. D., M. Lalli, and L. Rosen. 1977. *City Life and Delinquency-Victimization, Fear of Crime and Gang Membership.* Washington, DC: Law Enforcement Assistance Administration.

Schaefer, W. E., C. Olexa, and K. Polk. 1972. "Programmed for Social Class Tracking in High School." In K. Polk and W. E. Schaefer (eds.), *Schools and Delinquency.* Englewood Cliffs, NJ: Prentice-Hall.

Schmitt, B., and C. H. Kempe. 1975. "Neglect and Abuse of Children." In V. Vaughan and R. McKay (eds.), *Nelson Textbook of Pediatrics.* Philadelphia: W. B. Saunders.

Schwendinger, H., and J. R. Schwendinger. 1985. *Adolescent Subcultures and Delinquency.* New York: Praeger

Short, J. F. 1990. *Delinquency and Society.* Englewood Cliffs, NJ: Prentice-Hall.

Short, J. F., and F. L. Strodtbeck. 1965. *Group Process and Gang Delinquency.* Chicago: University of Chicago Press.

Smeja, C. M., and D. G. Rojek. 1986. "Youthful Drug Use and Drug Subcultures." *The International Journal of Addictions* 21:1031-50.

Snow, R. 1969. "Unfinished Pygmalion." *Contemporary Psychology* 14:197-99.

Snyder, and G. Patterson. 1987. "Family Interaction and Delinquent Behavior." In Herbert C. Quay (ed.), *Handbook of Juvenile Delinquency.* New York: Wiley.

Spivack, G., and N. Cianci. 1987. "High-risk Early Behavior Pattern and Later Delinquency." In J. D. Burchard and S. N. Burchard (eds.), *Prevention of Delinquent Behavior.* Beverly Hills, CA: Sage.

Stafford, M. 1984. "Gang Delinquency." In R. F. Meier (ed.), *Major Forms of Crime.* Beverly Hills, CA: Sage.

Steffensmeier, D. J. 1983. "Organizational Properties and Sex-segregation in the Underworld: Building a Sociological Theory of Sex Differences in Crime." *Social Forces* 61 (June):1010-32.

Steinmetz, S. K., and M. A. Straus. 1973. "The Family as Cradle of Violence." *Society* 10:119-28.

Sternberg, L., P. L. Blinde, and K. S. Chan. 1984. "Dropping Out Among Language Minority Youth." *Review of Educational Research* 54:113-32.

Stinchcombe, A. 1964. *Rebellion in a High School.* Chicago: Quadrangle Books.

Stouthamer-Loeber, M., K. B. Schmaling, and R. Loeber. 1984. "The Relationship of Single Parent Family Status and Marital Discord to Antisocial Child Behavior." Unpublished manuscript. Department of Psychiatry. University of Pittsburgh.

Straus, M. A., R. J. Gelles, and S. K. Steinmetz. 1980. *Behind Closed Doors: Violence in the American Family.* Garden City, NY: Anchor.

Straus, M. A., and R. J. Gelles. 1990. "Societal Change and Change in Family Violence from 1975 to 1985 as Revealed by Two National Surveys." In N. A. Weiner, M. A. Zahn, and R. J. Sagi (eds.), *Violence: Patterns, Causes and Public Policy.* San Diego: Harcourt Brace Jovanovich.

Sutherland, E. H., and D. R. Cressey. 1970. *Criminology.* 8th ed. Philadelphia: J.B. Lippincott.

_____. 1974. *Criminology.* 9th ed. Philadelphia: J. B. Lippincott.

Taylor, C. S. 1990. "Gang Imperialism." In C. Ronald Huff (ed.), *Gangs in America.* Newbury Park, CA: Sage.

Thornberry, T. P., M. Moore, and R. L. Christenson. 1985. "The Effect of Dropping Out of High School on Subsequent Criminal Behavior." *Criminology* 23:3-18.

Thorndike, R.L. 1968. "Review of R. Rosenthal and L. Jacobson, 'Pygmalion in the Classroom'." *American Educational Research* 5:708-11.

Toby, J. 1983. "Crime in the Schools." In J.Q. Wilson (ed.), *Crime and Public Policy.* San Francisco: Institute for Contemporary Studies.

VanderZanden, J. 1986. *Core Sociology.* New York: Alfred A. Knopf.

West, D. J. 1982. *Delinquency: Its Roots, Careers and Prospects.* Cambridge, MA: Harvard University Press.

West, D. J., and D. P. Farrington. 1973. *Who Becomes Delinquent?* London: Heinemann Educational.

Widom, C. S. 1989. "Child Abuse, Neglect, and Violent Criminal Behavior." *Criminology* 27: 251-71.

Wilkinson, K. 1974. "The Broken Family and Juvenile Delinquency: Scientific Explanation or Ideology." *Social Problems* 21 (June): 726-39.

Wilkinson, K., G. Stitt, and M. L. Erickson. 1982. "Siblings and Delinquent Behavior: An Exploratory Study of a Neglected Family Variable." *Criminology* 20 (2): 223-38.

Wolfgang, M., R. M. Figlio, and T. Sellin. 1972. *Delinquency in a Birth Cohort.* Chicago: University of Chicago Press.

Yablonsky, L. 1959. "The Delinquent Gang as a Near Group." *Social Problems* 7: 108-17.

chapter **8**

Contexts for Socialization

Religion, Media, and Community

> *Hasn't anyone noticed that the worst criminals have been corrupted, since their infancy, by injurious reading? Hasn't anyone beheld them, in the course of their trials, confessing that it was sordid literature that dragged them onto the road which ended fatally at prison and at the gallows?*
> —E. Caron, Director of Education for the City of Paris, 1864
>
> *Not only are crime comics a contributing factor to many delinquent acts, but the type of juvenile delinquency of our time cannot be understood unless you know what has been put into the minds of these children.*
> —Frederic Wertham, *Ladies Home Journal*, November, 1953
>
> *Long-term television viewing is one cause of violent or aggressive behavior in children and contributes substantially to childhood obesity,* the American Academy of Pediatrics said yesterday.
> —Chicago—Associated Press, 1990

The family, school, and peer group have been the most central contexts for childhood and adolescent socialization in modern criminological theory and research. As we found in the last chapter, relationships within these settings are important for understanding variable involvement in juvenile delinquency. A child's parents, friends, and teachers are *the* major sources of differential reinforcement and normative socialization and the major models for imitation. However, there are a number of other social institutions and forces that have been viewed as relevant to understanding delinquency at one time or another and have often dominated popular discourse and public debate about the causes of delinquency—the church, mass media, and community or neighborhood.

"Give Me That Old-Time Religion"

In the 1970s and 1980s various religious groups were a major force in politics in the United States. Conservative religious groups lamented the alleged demise of religion in educational institutions and the spread of an alternative nonreligious philosophy called *secular humanism*. Secular humanism was characterized by the assumption that social problems could be addressed by learning about and appreciating diversity and variation in the real world and through policies and programs that changed circumstances of everyday life for the better. The answers were not to be found in any particular religion.

The elimination of specifically Christian practices and beliefs from public institutions was viewed by conservative Christian groups as the major cause of social ills. Any solutions to such problems as crime and drug abuse would require a return to that "old-time religion."

While neither advocating its desirability nor endorsing any particular religion as necessary for social order, the most prominent general theorists in the historical development of sociology were all concerned with the nature and consequences of religion. Emile Durkheim viewed religion as a basic integrative mechanism in human society and felt that social order could be maintained only if people had common beliefs in something greater than themselves. He saw the basic problem in the Western civilization of his time to be a trend toward "individualism" and the demise of shared values, norms, and beliefs. Karl Marx accorded religion a role in the prevention of crime, unrest, and revolution. For Marx, religion was the "opium of the masses" in that it directed their attention away from repressive, alienating economic systems. The powerless could find an illusion of happiness through religion and look to a future life filled with meaning and satisfaction. Religion was a force maintaining a status quo that Marx believed inevitably had to be brought down by a revolution of alienated human beings. Finally, a third "grand master" of sociology — Max Weber — felt religious institutions were intertwined with other institutions and with the economic development of society. Weber stimulated considerable sociological research on the role that Protestantism, Catholicism, and other religious beliefs play in facilitating or inhibiting economic development and achievement.

The "sociology of religion" has been and remains a major specialty in sociology. However, with some recent exceptions, those specializing in the sociology of religion pay little attention to its relationship to crime or delinquency. Similarly, while every delinquency text discusses the relevance of the family, school, and peers for understanding delinquency, it is quite rare to find a text that gives any consideration to religion. This neglect reflects the fact that religious variables were dismissed as irrelevant or unnecessary by some prominent criminologists (see Sutherland and Cressey, 1978) or were not specifically incorporated into other types of theories until quite recently. It has also been argued that religiosity was ignored because of irreligious or anti-religious attitudes among sociologists (Stark et al., 1982).

Religious variables could have been incorporated quite readily into all major theories. For example, bonds to the church, a faith, or most sets of religious beliefs can be viewed as barriers to crime and delinquency since most religions encourage law-abiding conduct and respect for authority. In fact, recent research on religious variables has included them as a type of social bond within a social control theory framework.

Strain theories could encompass religious variables as well. For example, if religion directs attention away from the pursuit of worldly success, it would alleviate strain. Thus, theoretically, religion might inhibit delinquency by attenuating strain. It is also conceivable that involvement in religion could be an alternative response to strain or social rejection. In either case, religious variables would be relevant to explaining delinquency. As already noted, Karl Marx viewed religion as one force in the maintenance of social order and its role in directing attention away from the contradictions and strains of capitalism was emphasized.

Historically, religion has also been a source of some degree of lawlessness. Some Mormons still believe in polygamy and a few have been arrested in recent years for practicing their beliefs. Some faiths do not believe in medical intervention to deal with health problems and proponents of that view have been prosecuted for neglect or abuse. The bombing of abortion clinics and the trashing of adult bookstores attest to the ways in which commitments to certain religious beliefs can produce lawlessness. The protection and transportation of political refugees in violation of immigration laws is another example. Acts considered criminal have been carried out in the name of religion throughout human history.

Box 8-1
The Many Faces of Religion in the United States

The *Yearbook of American and Canadian Churches* lists 156 different religious groups in the United States, plus another 600 religious sects or cults. While over 95 percent of the United States population professes a belief in God, how this belief is manifested and the actual content of this belief can differ dramatically. For example, the Church of Jesus Christ Christian-Aryan Nations endorses white supremacy and the Ku Klux Klan. Many other religious organizations in the United States would undoubtedly oppose this group for being "un-Christian." Religion can manifest many different dimensions, beliefs, and creeds, making the study of religion fascinating but at the same time exceedingly difficult. Trying to find the relationship between religion and delinquency is fraught with problems and ambiguities because there is no simple definition of religion. For some, being religious means nothing more than belonging to a social organization like the Elks or the Moose, while for others it has profound implications.

Do you believe that organized religion is an important force discouraging youth from involvement in delinquency?

One of the most prominent cultural deviance theorists, Donald Cressey, argues that "there is no specific evidence regarding the effect of religion, considered as something different from anti-criminal values, on crime" (Sutherland and Cressey, 1978:234). Of course, if participation in or commitment to a religion were found to encourage commitment to anti-criminal values, then it would have relevance to delinquency. The relevance would be indirect; that is, anti-criminal values would be the intervening mechanism explaining the relevance of religion to delinquency. However, that is also the case for family, school, and peer group influences in a cultural deviance perspective. It is the impact of social institutions and arrangements on normative learning that distinguishes cultural deviance theory from other theories. The church is one context in which normative learning can occur.

Research on Religion and Delinquency

An examination of references to religion in studies of labeled delinquents reveals a hodgepodge of results: 1) delinquents are more religious than non-delinquents (Middleton and Fay, 1941), 2) delinquents do not differ from nondelinquents in their attitudes toward religion (Kvaraceus, 1944; Mursell, 1930; Hightower, 1930; Hartshorne and May, 1930), and 3) non-delinquents are more religious than delinquents (Healy and Bronner, 1936; Glueck and Glueck, 1950; Miller, 1965). Moreover, no matter which of the three patterns researchers have found, the actual differences they have reported are small.

Self-report research has also yielded seemingly divergent findings. Rhodes and Reiss (1970) and Nye (1958) concluded that church attendance is associated with lower rates of delinquency, while Hirschi and Stark (1969) reported no significant relationships. We will consider Hirschi and Stark's research here in some detail for two reasons. First, their study reinforced the common sociological opinion of the 1960s that organized religion was irrelevant to understanding delinquency. Second, their research stimulated a whole new line of inquiry, as evidenced by the flourish of research on religion and delinquency that began in the mid-1970s.

Using data gathered from junior and senior high school students in Richmond, California, Hirschi and Stark investigated the relationship between church attendance and attitudes toward the law, the police, people in general, and supernatural beliefs (that is, a life after death and the existence of the devil). They found no significant relationship between church attendance and attitudes toward people and some weak, but significant relationships between church attendance and positive attitudes toward police and the law. The strongest relationship was between church attendance and belief in supernatural sanctions. In turn, Hirschi and Stark found that positive attitudes toward people, the law, and the police were associated with low involvement in delinquency, while belief in the supernatural was unrelated to delinquency. In short, those attitudes that were *unrelated* or weakly related to church attendance were the most relevant for delinquency, and those beliefs that *were related* to church attendance were not related to delinquent behavior. In view of these findings, it is not surprising that Hirschi and Stark found no relationship between church attendance and delinquency. The results of this study appeared to further substantiate Glock and Stark's earlier observation in *Religion and Society in Tension:* "Looking at American society as a whole . . . organized religion at present is neither a prominent witness to its own value system nor a major focal point around which ultimate commitments to norms, values, and beliefs are formed" (1965:184). While the vast majority of Americans will confess to being religious or to a belief in a deity, such beliefs may not be reflected in actual behavior as compared to the irreligious. Moreover, our everyday secular life is so infused with religious notions (e.g. the salute to the flag, "in God we trust," etc.) paralleling traditional religious beliefs that even the irreligious may be committed to a type of "civil religion" (Bellah, 1967). The pervasiveness of religious notions in everyday life may keep formal religion from distinguishing people.

Variations by Type of Offense

Five years after the publication of Hirschi and Stark's study, Burkett and White's "Hellfire and Delinquency: Another Look" appeared (1974). Burkett and White argued that when secular values do not clearly define certain criminal or delinquent activities as wrong, then religious participation or beliefs may be relevant to understanding delinquent behavior. They suggested that offenses about which there is moral ambiguity in everyday life and offenses that run counter to religious traditions of self-control and self-denial might be inhibited by religiosity. Thus, they hypothesized that activities such as alcohol and marijuana use should be less common among the religiously active than among the inactive and less common among those who believe in the supernatural than among those who do not. Their findings were in large part consistent with their expectations. After analyzing questionnaire data from high school students in a city of about 170,500 in the Pacific Northwest, Burkett and White concluded that belief in the supernatural is only "slightly" related to the use of alcohol and marijuana, but that "a very definite relationship" exists between religious participation and the use of those substances. In comparison to Hirschi and Stark, Burkett and White reported stronger associations between religious participation and attitudes toward worldly authority and endorsement of conventional moral positions.

It should also be noted that before Burkett and White's study, Bruce Johnson (1972) had concluded that among college students, religious participation is one of four variables (the others being sex, political liberalism, and cigarette smoking) that are good predictors of marijuana use. In Johnson's study, 77 percent of regular church attenders reported never having used marijuana, while only 26 percent of nonattenders were complete abstainers. Church attenders were also less likely to be "regular" users. Similarly, in even earlier research, Middleton and Putney (1962) had proposed that the relation between religion and delinquency was stronger for "anti-ascetic" offenses than "anti-social" offenses; that is, religion should be more consequential for actions which violate religious expectations for disciplined and sober conduct than actions which violate widely shared social norms.

Since the Burkett and White study, additional studies dealing with the relevance of religiosity to delinquency have appeared. Using self-report data from tenth graders in Atlanta, Georgia, Paul Higgins and Stan Albrecht (1977) found a "moderate" relationship between church attendance and a wide variety of delinquent activities. They suggested that "church attendance in Atlanta might indicate a stronger commitment to general ethical and moral values than does church attendance in California." Albrecht, Bruce Chadwick, and David Alcorn (1977) collected data from Mormon teenagers in three western states and found that religious variables were greater inhibitors of victimless deviance (for example, drug use) than of deviance involving victims, and that a good prediction of deviance was possible when religious variables were combined with measures of peer and family relationships. In yet another study, Rick Linden and Raymond Currie (1978) reported that among their sample of youths aged 15 to 24 in Calgary, Canada, the greater the ties to the church, the lower the probability of drug use.

Gary Jensen and Maynard Erickson (1979) attempted a reconciliation of divergent findings by analyzing aspects of Hirschi and Stark's data, as well as data gathered from high school students in southern Arizona. The analysis of Hirschi and Stark's data on students in Richmond, California, showed that as church attendance increases, smoking, drinking, and truancy decline (the only victimless offenses on which data were available from the Richmond youths). This finding is consistent with the findings of the other five studies we've summarized and was replicated in the analysis of the southern Arizona data.

Finally, in a more recent study, Burkett and Warren (1987) showed that the impact of religion on marijuana use was mediated by involvement with other users. Specifically, they found that "youth with lowered religious commitment are vulnerable to progressive and more exclusive involvement with other users, and with that they are more likely to use marijuana. Religious youth, on the other hand, are likely to select as companions those who are similarly inclined both in attitude and behavior" (1987: 127). In other words, religion operates as a critical variable in the creation of peer groups and those peer groups have a vital impact on the use or nonuse of marijuana.

Variations by Measures of Religiosity

In addition to the elaboration of research to encompass different types of offenses, researchers have proposed that some measures of religiosity are more likely to correlate with delinquency as well. Scholars studying religion have noted that there are multiple dimensions to what they refer to as "religiosity" (Glock and Stark, 1965), and church or Sunday school attendance is only one way in which a person can be religious. People vary in terms of more personal and private aspects of religiosity as well. For instance, people who attend church regularly may vary considerably in the extent to which their religious beliefs influence their everyday life. People who never attend church may have deeply felt religious beliefs. Variations in these personal measures of religiosity have been argued to be more relevant for delinquency than behaviors (such as regular church attendance) which may only reflect parental coercion. This argument has been substantiated in several recent studies (Hadaway et al., 1984; Stark et al., 1982; Elifson et al., 1983).

Variations by Denomination and Moral Climate

While all recent studies indicate that religious participation is associated with some types of delinquency, there is no comparably consistent observation concerning religious affiliation and delinquency. Some studies have indicated lower delinquency rates for Jews than for Protestants and higher rates for Catholics than for Protestants (Goldscheider and Simpson, 1967; Rhodes and Reiss, 1970). In an analysis of arrest statistics, Roy Austin (1977) found that Jews had significantly lower rates than Catholics and this difference could not be explained solely by the social-class composition of the samples. Austin found no significant differences between Catholics and Protestants. In comparing Catholics, Protestants, and all "other" denominations, Burkett and White found no significant differences in self-reported delinquency. Similarly, Hirschi and Stark reported no significant differences by denomination.

Rather than considering denomination and church attendance as totally separate variables, Jensen and Erickson (1979) proposed that the "meaning," or relevance, of religious involvement for behavior should be *variable* by denomination. Higgins and Albrecht (1977) suggested a similar possibility when they argued that religious variables appear more relevant to understanding delinquency in the South because of regional variation in the meaning of religion. Jensen and Erickson hypothesized that the denominational composition, rather than the regional composition, of the samples studied may have accounted for some of the variation in research findings.

Jensen and Erickson's findings were consistent with their hypothesis. In analyzing Hirschi and Stark's data, they found that church attendance was more relevant to delinquency in "fundamentalistic" or highly "ascetic" denominations (such as Church of Christ, Church of God, and Disciples of Christ). Among Baptists, the overall relationships turned out to be quite comparable to those reported in Higgins and Albrecht's study of Atlanta youth. Further evidence of the intertwining relevance for delinquency of denomination and church attendance was found in Jensen and Erickson's analysis of southern Arizona data. Catholic, Protestant, and Mormon differences in delinquency were most prominent among regular church attenders (see Figure 8-1). Attendance made the greatest difference among Mormons, particularly with regard to those activities strongly and distinctively prohibited by the Mormon church (smoking, drinking, and drug use). In sum, it appears that there is considerable similarity in research results when analyzed in terms of similar offenses for similar groups and settings. Given the research available, the most plausible explanation of divergent findings and complicated inconsistencies may rest with the variable and complicated nature of our society.

Another line of theoretical development in the study of religion and crime stresses the importance of the "religious climate" for explaining the impact of religiosity on delinquency. Rodney Stark, Lori Kent, and David Doyle (1982) argue that religious variables are most likely to be relevant to variations in delinquent behavior in communities or contexts where religion is a salient feature of everyday life. In contrast, Stark and his colleagues argue that in "secular" communities, variations in religiosity make little difference for behavior. They support this interpretation with data for youths in schools which varied in the salience of religion in youths' lives, as well as through a comparison of studies in Seattle, Richmond, California and Provo, Utah. While they do not address the possibility that variations in the relevance of religiosity for delinquency are due to denominational differences, subsequent analyses by other researchers (see Thompson and Brownfield, 1986) show that the variations in the relevance of religiosity between moral and secular school settings remains even when denomination is taken into account.

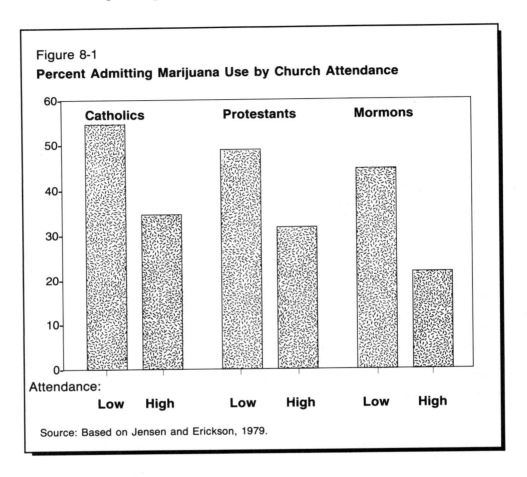

Figure 8-1
Percent Admitting Marijuana Use by Church Attendance

Catholics   Protestants   Mormons

Attendance:
Low   High   Low   High   Low   High

Source: Based on Jensen and Erickson, 1979.

Other Issues

Researchers studying religion and delinquency have also considered whether the association between measures of religiosity and some types of delinquency are due to other circumstances in youths' lives. The fact that measures of religiosity have been found to correlate with delinquency in a variety of studies does not necessarily mean that those variables inhibit delinquency, since variations in religiosity often go hand-in-hand with other variations as well. Youths who are religious also tend to have strong familial bonds and to do well in school (Elifson et al., 1983). Efforts to untangle the potential relevance of distinct but correlated characteristics of youth have not yielded any one simple generalization about the independent relevance of religion. A study by Jensen and Erickson (1979) reports that church attendance is associated with lower rates of drug use even when other characteristics of youth are taken into account. In contrast, Elifson and colleagues (1983) found that the relation between religiosity and delinquency appeared to be due to other characteristics of the youths studied and conclude that "It appears that the relationship of religion to delinquency is so closely tied to the family and other influences that it has little influence that is statistically independent of other predictor variables" (1983: 521). As noted earlier, Burkett and Warren (1987) found peer groups to be the key mediating force accounting for the relationship between religiosity and marijuana use. In short, while researchers have not yet fully untangled the relationships, religion may turn out to be consequential only because of its impact on other social relationships.

While most research focuses on the inhibiting influence of religion for involvement in delinquency, there has been some interest in the effects of strong norms of prohibition on those who do engage in prohibited activity. Ephraim Mizruchi and Robert Perrucci (1968) have argued that when groups are characterized by norms of abstinence, there are no "directives" to regulate or limit the prohibited activity when it does occur. Such groups have low rates of the prohibited behavior overall but the minority of youths who do violate such norms may do so excessively. This argument is supported by two studies of drinking among college students (Straus and Bacon, 1954; Snyder, 1958). Both studies found the intoxication rate much higher for ascetic Protestant and Mormon groups than for nonascetic Jewish students. In Jensen and Erickson's study (1977), a similar pattern was noted among Mormon high school students. Overall, Mormon youth had low rates of smoking, drinking, and marijuana use. However, Mormon students who did not attend church had higher rates of smoking, drunkenness, and marijuana use than Catholics or Protestants, while regularly attending Mormon youth ranked well below Protestants and Catholics for every drug-related offense studied. When a faith is characterized by a "hard line" on certain forms of behavior, those on the fringes may have a higher incidence of those behaviors than those on the fringes of more liberal denominations, possibly as a result of rebellion, stigmatization, or the lack of norms regulating prohibited behavior when it does occur.

The Media

In his study of adolescent society almost thirty years ago, James Coleman reported that nearly one-half of the students he studied spent two hours or more per day watching television (1961: 18-23). More than one-half went to movies at least twice a month. Over 20 percent spent three hours or more per day watching television, and more than 25 percent went to movies once a week. By the mid-1970s, people were spending more time watching television than any activity except working and sleeping. Children actually spent more of their free time watching television than they spent playing (Comstock et al., 1978). By the late 1980s, pre-school children were viewing television nearly 30 hours per week, children aged 6 to 11 were spending 28 hours per week watching television, and teenagers were averaging about 24 hours per week (*The World Almanac*, 1990). Many researchers think these estimates are low and that time spent watching television exceeds time spent in school.

Recent studies indicate that by the age of 16 children will have seen about 20,000 murders and by the age of 65 the average American will have spent nine years in front of the television set. More homes have television sets (98 percent) than have telephones or indoor toilets and 60 percent of homes now have two or more sets. Obviously, in addition to the family, school, peers, and religion, the media constitute another force with the potential to influence behavior.

As the quotations at the beginning of this chapter suggest, the idea that exposure to the media contributes directly to crime and delinquency has been advanced with considerable emotional fervor for close to 150 years. Referring to the impact of newspaper publicity of crime, Lombroso leaves little doubt as to where he stood on the issue:

> This morbid stimulation is increased a hundred-fold by the prodigious increase of really criminal newspapers, which spread abroad the virus of the most loathsome social plagues, simply for sordid gain, and excite the morbid appetite and still more morbid curiosity of the lower social classes. They may be likened to those maggots which, sprung from putrefaction, increase it by their presence. (1911: 211)

Despite the alleged influence of the media, the major theories of delinquency do not accord mass media a major role. There are, however, ways in which the media could be specifically incorporated into these theories. For example, control theorists could argue that media content fosters values, norms, and beliefs that "free" a youth to commit delinquent acts, or that the media convey the "subterranean" aspects of American culture that facilitate delinquency. Some forms of media activity might actually constitute involvement in a "conventional" activity as well (e.g., going to movies or watching television with the family). From a strain perspective, the media emphasis on advertising could be seen as facilitating strain by raising wishes and aspirations that cannot be met. On the other hand, television, films, and other media might constitute escape mechanisms and means of attenuating frustrations. Cultural conflict theorists might argue that the media present "definitions favorable to lawbreaking." Marxist theorists might argue that media constitute an "opium of the masses" or a means of control which serves the interests of ruling elites. Movies such as *Rollerball* and *The Running Man* are based on the theme that violence in the media can be used to occupy and control the masses. However, sociologists have relegated the media to the category of "questionable crime theories" (Schur, 1969:73-82) and stress more personal, intimate social relationships in their explanations of delinquency.

Research on Media and Delinquency

The particular targets of concern regarding the effects of the media on crime and delinquency have varied over the years. For example, a major concern from the 1930s through the early 1950s was the impact of comic books on the young. Comic book sales were reported at over 60 million copies per month. Frederic Werthman (1954), a psychiatrist, argued that comic books were seducing the innocent and contributing to crime and delinquency by exposing the young to violence, sex, and sadism. These assertions were based on his own clinical experience and were not based on any rigorous scientific analysis. However, the idea that reading comic books may be associated with certain attitudes or behaviors has also been supported by more systematic research. In a study of 374 schoolboys in grades six through eight, S. H. Lovibond (1967) reported that the more a youth read comic books, watched television, or attended movies, the more likely he was "to endorse an ideology which makes the use of force in the interest of egocentric needs the essential content of human relationships." Whereas Lovibond could only suggest that such media exposure may be associated with delinquency, Thomas Hoult (1949) and Travis Hirschi (1969) did, in fact, report such an association. Hirschi noted that "the more time a boy spends watching television, reading romance magazines and comic books, or playing games, the *more* likely he is to have committed delinquent acts" (1969:190). However, Hirschi added that such relationships are "*very* weak."

We should also note that showing an association is only one step in reaching conclusions about the causal impact of exposure to media. Pfuhl (1956) and Lovibond (1967) suggest that the relationship between media exposure and children's attitudes might be *spurious*—that is, that children's preferences in reading and viewing material and their attitudes could both be products of other personal and social characteristics. Moreover, it is difficult to untangle the *causal ordering* of this relationship: children who commit delinquent acts or share attitudes favorable to violence may, *as a result* of those behaviors and attitudes, be media-oriented or choose certain forms of programming. It is also very difficult to isolate the impact of one set of experiences from a host of others. Consider, for example, going to the movies. For many, if not most, teenagers, this activity combines "exposure to movies," interaction with peers, freedom from adult surveillance, and a range of interests (cars, drive-in restaurants) common in the adolescent social world. Thus, a study showing that going to the movies is correlated with delinquency may tell us nothing about the impact of the media.

Much of the scholarly debate over television violence centers around the issues of causation outlined in Chapter 5. For example, in a 1972 issue of the *American Psychologist*, L. D. Eron and his colleagues claimed to have "demonstrated that there is a probable causative influence of watching violent television programs in early formative years on later aggression" (Eron et al., 1972:263). This claim immediately (and quite legitimately) drew criticism. Kay Herbert argued that the relationship described by Eron and colleagues was spurious and that the important factor in shaping both viewing preferences and aggressive behavior is parental responses to aggression in a child's early years (1972). Dennis Howitt presented a similar argument, positing that media exposure is part of a subculture and that participating in such a subculture accounts for relationships between media preferences and behavior (1972). A methodological critique by Gary Becker suggested not only that the relationship could be spurious but also that (given possibilities too complex to be discussed here) the study by Eron and associates could actually support conclusions directly contrary to its authors' claims (1972). In a more recent publication Eron is even more convinced of the detrimental effect of television violence: "A youngster who is continually bombarded with violence on television may well come to think that aggressive behavior is typical and therefore an appropriate way to solve life's problems" (1980:247).

Eron made reference to a three-year, $1 million research project by the Surgeon General's Scientific Advisory Committee on Television and Social Behavior (1971). The conclusion of that research was that violence on television can induce mimicking in children shortly after exposure and that *under certain circumstances* television violence can lead to an increase in aggressive acts. The committee acknowledged that it had been unable to determine either the size of the population of susceptible children or the exact reason why some children imitate media content and others do not. The committee did suggest that those most responsive to television violence are those who are prone to aggression to begin with, or those who respond with pleasure to violent content.

Experimental Studies

The Surgeon General's Scientific Advisory Committee paid considerable attention to experimental work since it avoids many of the criticisms that have been directed at survey studies. By manipulating exposure and content, measuring the subsequent outcome, and randomly assigning subjects to different conditions or experiences, experimental researchers can avoid problems of spuriousness and causal order. However, such research has *not* consistently demonstrated a relationship between media exposure to violence and subsequent aggression. For example, Stein and Friedrich (1971) observed a group of preschoolers who had been exposed to "aggressive" programming, "neutral" programming, and "pro-social" programming, and found no significant behavioral differences overall. On the other hand, a study by Liebert and Baron (1971) found that children who viewed aggressive episodes on television were more willing to engage in interpersonal aggression than a control group. One review has summed up the complex situation as follows:

> Robert D. Singer and I recently have completed a comprehensive review of the television and aggression literature. We have found that the majority of the experimental studies showed that witnessing violence can instigate "aggressive" behavior. These experiments, however, most frequently gained their effectiveness through the intentional arousal of subjects and the use of dependent measures that removed ordinary sanctions against aggression. Instigation effects were rarely found in studies or experimental conditions in which the subjects were not aroused intentionally. When the measure of aggression has been some naturally occurring behavior, it has been shown that television violence either has no effect . . . or only affects children who were initially highly aggressive . . . Thus we would argue that the link between televised violence and aggression has not been established clearly. (Kaplan, 1972:969)

The Surgeon General's Committee released another comprehensive report a decade later (1982) and concluded that the studies "strongly suggest" that viewing violent television programs contribute to aggressive behavior.

Survey Data

A study by Hartnagel, Teevan, and McIntyre (1975) is one of the better examples of survey research on the relationship between television violence and violent behavior. The study was based on questionnaires administered to junior and senior high school students in one county in Maryland. Students were asked to specify their favorite television shows, total amount of time they spent watching television, and their perceptions of violent content in their favorite shows. Other questions asked about the students' involvement in violence (fights and assaults) and their background characteristics. Hartnagel, Teevan, and McIntyre found that when other characteristics of youth (e.g., age, grades, social class) which could affect rates of violence were taken into account, that television violence made no difference for violence among males but was slightly correlated for females. In comparison to background characteristics of youth, they deemed the impact of television violence to be "unimportant." Their final interpretation of the results was consistent with the reservations expressed by Kaplan (1972). They noted that because laboratory studies use stimuli that elicit aggression, create situations where the opportunity for aggression is specifically provided, and assess immediate effects, the possibility of generalizing from these studies is limited. They also noted that laboratory studies use young children, whereas their own study focused on junior and senior high school students. Moreover, their study dealt with violent offense behavior rather than with the types of aggression studied in a laboratory setting. Although the researchers found only a slight relationship between individual exposure, preference for violent programming, and self-reports of violence, they did not rule out the possibility that television violence might have subtle and indirect effects on attitudes toward violence in our society as a whole. However, any such effects are merely speculative and have not been established through research.

Trends in Violent Content

Comstock et al. (1978) and Comstock (1980) have reviewed the many studies of the association between television violence and violent activity and conclude that most of the evidence is "consistent with but cannot, by itself, be said to unambiguously support the view that violent entertainment contributes to crime and violence against others" (1980:109). In fact, Comstock and colleagues (1978) found no positive relationship between trends in violent television programming over time with trends in violent crime statistics for the United States (see Figure 8-2). If we refer to Chapters 1 and 3, we can add that violent programming was *declining* during the 1960s while during that same period delinquency was *increasing* dramatically in the United States. Violent programming started to climb again in the mid-1970s while the juvenile crime rate was stable or declining.

Panel Studies

Aimee Dorr has recently reviewed research on the impact of television on children, including panel studies carried out in 1972 (Lefkowitz et al.) and 1982 (Milavsky et al.). The 1972 study found some relationships between viewing in the third grade and aggression at age 19 among boys but no relationship among girls. The 1982 study found television viewing at one point in time made little or no difference for aggression at subsequent

Figure 8-2

Violence in the Media

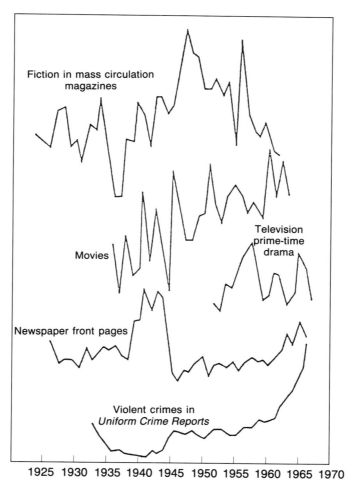

Fiction in mass circulation magazines

Television prime-time drama

Movies

Newspaper front pages

Violent crimes in *Uniform Crime Reports*

1925 1930 1935 1940 1945 1950 1955 1960 1965 1970

NOTE: Fiction in mass-circulation magazine: percent stories in *Saturday Evening Post* with a violent incident; Movies: percent synopses in *Movies on TV* with violent incident, coded by year of production; Television prime-time drama: percent synopses in *TV Guide* with violent incident; Newspaper front pages: percent stories of violent events for ten days each year on front pages of four urban dailies; Violent crimes in *Uniform Crime Reports*: rate per 100,000 of murder, forcible rape, robbery, and aggravated assault.

Source: Based on Comstock et al., *Television and Human Behavior,* 1978. Copyright © 1978. Columbia University Press. Used by permission.

points in time for either boys or girls. Dorr concludes that studies of television and aggression "suggest that the effects of exposure to television violence are attenuated in everyday life as compared to the laboratory" and that effects on the individual over time "are particularly weak or even nonexistent" (1986:78). The most that could be concluded at the present time is that there appears to be a small correlation between watching television and later aggression but that tells us very little about the causes of crime and delinquency.

Pornography

Another heated debate involving the media and delinquency centers on the effects of pornography. This topic was the subject of considerable review and research by the President's Commission on Obscenity and Pornography (1970). Like the Surgeon General's report, the report of this commission generated considerable controversy, yet failed to resolve the issue that it addressed. For example, in response to the Commission's final report, one of the commissioners, Charles Keating, took the position that the public has "enough common sense to know that one who wallows in filth is going to get dirty. This is intuitive knowledge. Those who spend millions of dollars to tell us otherwise must be malicious or misguided, or both" (President's Commission on Obscenity and Pornography, 1970:ix). Others called the report a "Magna Carta for the pornographers."

Some of the conclusions that generated such a reaction concern the relationship between pornography and criminal or delinquent behavior. One of the Commission's conclusions was that there was "no evidence to date that exposure to explicit sexual materials plays a significant role in the causation of delinquent or criminal behavior among youths or adults" (1970: 32). Support for this observation came from 1) studies comparing delinquent and nondelinquent youth, 2) statistical studies of the relationship between availability of erotic materials and rates of sex crimes in both Denmark and the United States, and 3) comparisons of sex offenders with other adults.

In 1985 a second government study was undertaken under the auspices of Attorney General Edwin Meese. The formal mandate to the new commission was to "determine the nature, extent, and impact on society of pornography in the United States, and to make specific recommendations to the Attorney General concerning more effective ways in which the spread of pornography could be contained, consistent with constitutional guarantees" (*Final Report*, 1986:215). The commission had a budget of $500,000 and one year to complete its task. In comparison, the 1970 Commission on Obscenity and Pornography had a budget of $2 million (sixteen times larger in terms of the value of the dollar at that time) and two years to complete the task.

Many of the members appointed to the 1985-1986 commission were already on record as opposing the conclusions of the previous commission and advocating stiffer obscenity laws. They did not fund any research program and did not conduct a serious review of the scientific literature. Rather, they sponsored a series of public hearings in major cities and their report is essentially a compilation of the testimony of private individuals. The 1986 *Final Report* states "We have found a causal relationship between sexually explicit materials featuring violence and these consequences, and thus conclude that the class of such materials, although not necessarily every individual member of that class, is on the whole harmful to society" (1986: 329). The 1986 report emphatically undercut the 1970 report, suggesting that times had changed and that "There can be no doubt that we confront a different world than that confronted by the 1970 Commission" (1986:286). However, a major difference was the composition of the two commissions and the cautious scientific approach of the 1970 panel.

Several studies were carried out between the two commission reports. A study by Harold S. Kant and Michael Goldstein (1976) led them to conclusions similar to those reached by the 1970 commission. After comparing 60 molestation cases, 52 cases of "users of pornography," and 63 supposedly normal males, Kant and Goldstein concluded that sexual deviates have little exposure to erotica during adolescence. In fact, these researchers suggested that such adolescent exposure is associated with "adult patterns of acceptable heterosexual interest and practice." They noted that exposure to erotica appeared to be a quite common aspect of adolescence and that there was no evidence in their study that such exposure was associated with sex crimes. Their findings seemed to suggest the opposite—that is, that such exposure may be associated with acceptable sexual patterns.

There is very little research on the possible impact of pornographic and erotic media material on juveniles, whether coupled with violence or not. In contrast, there is mounting research on the possible consequences of such material among adult males. Pornography which depicts violent sexual activity and abuse of women has been of particular concern, as has the use of children in pornographic media. And, as might be anticipated, given the uncertainty encountered in other areas of research, the picture is not altogether clear on this topic. For example, Malamuth and Check (1981) reported that college men who viewed pornography that coupled sex with violence reported being aroused by the idea of rape and showed less sympathy for rape victims than men not shown such material. However, in a review of this research, Susan Gray (1982) notes that research on sexual arousal which measures activity in male sex organs does not show that such material is sexually arousing. After a review of relevant research, Gray concludes that "there is little evidence that

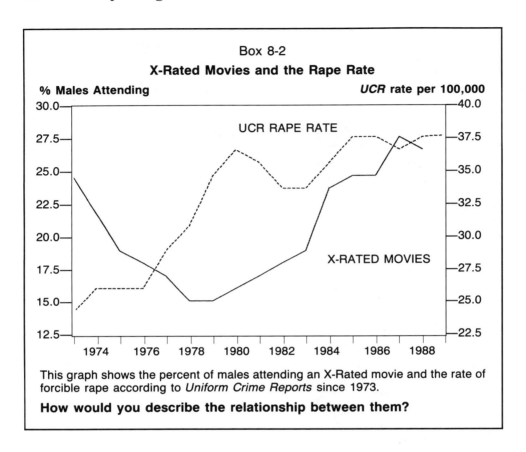

This graph shows the percent of males attending an X-Rated movie and the rate of forcible rape according to *Uniform Crime Reports* since 1973.

How would you describe the relationship between them?

exposure to hard-core pornography produces aggressive behavior in men." She also concludes that there is evidence that "levels of aggression in already angered men are increased by exposure to hard-core materials" (387).

Of course, whether there is conclusive evidence of a link between pornography and violence may be quite irrelevant to opposition to such material. Many people oppose pornography on moral or religious grounds while others oppose it for the images of men and women conveyed. Moreover, most of the research just summarized focuses on either the *immediate impact* of various media and media content or differences *among individuals* who have been variably exposed. Thus, the research findings are largely irrelevant to some of the larger issues concerning the impact of mass media in the long run or on society as a whole. The Danish experience with pornography indicated that increased availability of sexual materials was accompanied by a decrease in sex offenses (President's

Commission on Obscenity and Pornography, 1970:31). In the United States during a period characterized by a marked increase in pornography, the juvenile arrest rate for sex crimes decreased, while the rate for nonsexual crimes increased. Furthermore, juveniles are not disproportionately represented in murder and rape statistics, yet are disproportionately involved with the media. John Conklin observed that although there was a 50 percent increase in robbery incidents between 1967 and 1969, the amount of television violence remained constant during that time (1972). The age groups supposedly most susceptible to violence in the media actually account for very few robberies. Conklin's conclusion was that available data do not show a connection between violence in the media and increased robbery rates in the 1960s.

It is highly unlikely that there will ever be research providing clear-cut evidence on the subtle or long-term influences of the media. Current emphases and popular theory focus on negative consequences, which have not been clearly demonstrated. The various government investigations into the media have focused on such negative consequences because they are of concern to many people and organizations. However, the content and messages conveyed in the media are very complex, and negative outcomes may be balanced by positive outcomes. For example, the 1970 President's Commission on Obscenity and Pornography developed a list of "presumed consequences of exposure to erotica" (see Figure 8-3). The list of consequences, some of which are regarded as "beneficial," was compiled on the basis of all the arguments presented by various theorists and parties to the pornography issue.

Similarly, although numerous television programs have violent content, the actual meaning of that content can be complex, and arguments can be advanced listing beneficial consequences as well (for example, television's "bad guys" tend to lose in the end). We have to note that some of the presumed negative consequences of violence in the media are actually traits that are accorded considerable admiration in the United States. There are probably as many parents concerned that their children are not sufficiently aggressive and "do not stand up for themselves" as there are parents concerned about violence and crime.

Crime As Entertainment

Crime has been a theme of the American entertainment industry since its beginning and is a common feature of tourist attractions around the United States. A city in Kansas stages an annual "Jesse James festival." Tombstone, Arizona, publicizes itself as "The Town Too Tough to Die!" and celebrates "Helldorado Days." Visitors to Disneyland's "Pirates of the Caribbean" sail through the sacking of a harbor town, complete with

Figure 8-3

Presumed Consequences of Exposure to Erotica

	Sexual	Nonsexual
Criminal or generally regarded as harmful:	1. Sexually aggressive acts of a criminal nature. 2. Unlawful sexual practice. 3. Nonconsensual sex acts. 4. Incest. 5. Sexually perverse behavior. 6. Adultery. 7. Illegal sexual activities. 8. Socially disapproved sexual behavior 9. Sexual practices harmful to self. 10. Deadly serious pursuit of sexual satisfaction. 11. Dehumanized sexual acts. 12. Preoccupation (obsession) with sex. 13. Change in direction of sexual development from natural pathway. 14. Blocking psychosexual maturation. 15. Misinformation about sex. 16. Moral breakdown.	17. Homicide. 18. Suicide. 19. Delinquency. 20. Criminal acts. 21. Indecent personal habits. 22. Unhealthy habits. 23. Unhealthy thoughts. 24. Rejection of reality. 25. Ennui. 26. Submission to authoritarianism.
Neutral:	27. Sex attitudes. 28. Sex values. 29. Sex information. 30. Sex habits.	
Beneficial/ helpful:	31. Draining off of illegitimate sexual drives. 32. Outlet for otherwise frustrated sex drives. 33. Release of strong sexual urges without harming others. 34. Pleasure. 35. Discharge of ''antisocial'' sexual appetites. 36. Consummation of legitimate sexual responsibilities.	

Source: President's Commission on Obscenity and Pornography. *The Report of the Commission on Obscenity and Pornography.* New York: Bantam Books, 1970.

shooting, hanging, and the rape and sale of female victims. By presenting rape in a humorous fashion such exhibits can be charged with perpetuating rape myths.

David Matza and Gresham Syke's (1961) notion of subterranean values (see Chapter 6) applies to the tendency to be fascinated by some forms of crime. While most of us endorse law and order, we still admire a good "con" act, are intrigued by the professional thief, and find ourselves rooting for the bad guys in numerous instances. Our folklore is filled with people who broke laws but still became folk heroes. The use of crime in the media endures because it is popular, entertaining, and profitable. The presentation of crime for fun and profit *may* reinforce crime and delinquency, but it is extremely difficult to isolate those enterprises that merely reflect preferences and those that shape them. Thus, the relationship between the media and crime and delinquency will no doubt continue as a source of debate and controversy.

Community and Delinquency

A common lament about American society has been focused on the demise of a "sense of community" or common bonds among people living in a certain territory. In his introduction to Shaw and McKay's classic work on juvenile delinquency in urban areas (1942:xi), Ernest Burgess wrote that "the common element" explaining the distribution of delinquency was "social disorganization or the lack of organized community effort to deal with these conditions." Shaw and McKay's solution to the delinquency problem rested with establishing neighborhood organizations (see Chapter 12).

In *A Nation of Strangers*, Vance Packard (1972) argued along similar lines. He wrote that "great numbers" of Americans "feel unconnected" to people or places as a result of mobility. Moreover, Packard continued, not only are the "rootless" viewed as prime candidates for mental problems, aggression, alcoholism, and crime, but in addition the turnover of people in a community "demoralizes" those who remain behind. Packard felt we needed more stability in neighborhoods, limits on population growth and density, and "settings small enough in scale to meet people's needs for social interaction and a sense of significant citizenship" (1972:302). He listed the following as the characteristics of communities that would reduce fragmentation and reestablish a sense of community:

1. The natural human community is one that is small enough to be in scale to man.
2. It provides a natural way for people to come together if they wish to do so.

3. It offers a natural setting for individuals to achieve personal recognition, to share experiences, to find assurance of emotional and other support, and to develop some enduring friendships.

4. Its stability and diversity provide a sense of wholeness and coherence to a participant's life, a sense that what is happening today is part of an ongoing process.

5. It provides people with a sense that they have some control over events about to happen that can affect their lives.

6. And it offers people a special group and a special place that they can think of as their own. They have a living environment they can seek to improve and one in which they can come to feel a proprietary pride. (1972:334-35)

The emphasis on community and neighborhood controls is reiterated in James Q. Wilson's *Thinking About Crime* (1975). Wilson argued that the population of the central city consists disproportionately of childless, affluent whites, the elderly, the poor, and the transient, who either have no interest in maintaining a sense of community or lack the ability to work actively to maintain one. The failure to develop communal bonds is viewed as facilitating crime and delinquency, which in turn contribute to further suspicion, isolation, and withdrawal. Wilson describes the process as a vicious cycle, with community disorganization contributing to crime and delinquency, which lead to further disorganization.

Such claims about the role of community stability, organization and communal bonds in relation to crime and delinquency are not only common in contemporary literature but were among the earliest sociological arguments about deviance and social problems. Emile Durkheim, writing in 1897, argued that the lack or breakdown of communal bonds was a major cause of suicide and that idea has been extended to other forms of deviance (see Faris and Dunham, 1939; Hirschi, 1969). One of the most recent statements integrates the study of religion with the study of community characteristics in the following propositions:

1. Social integration of communities is undercut by substantial population turnover. To the degree that a community consists of newcomers and transients, deviance rates will be high.

2. Religion *as such* tends to support conformity. Communities with higher rates of church membership will have lower rates of deviance.

3. Elements of social control do not restrain *all* forms of deviance. For example, population turnover and church membership are highly related to burglary and larceny rates, but they are virtually unrelated to homicide and assault. (Stark et al., 1983)

This perspective is similar to the social disorganization perspective summarized in Chapter 6. However, rather than referring to the lack of social and moral bonds as indicative of social disorganization, the emphasis is on the *presence* of such bonds, and the term used to refer to degrees of social organization is social *integration*. The criticisms of the concept of social disorganization summarized in Chapter 6 have led scholars to avoid the term. Yet, a low level of integration is conceptually the same as a high level of social disorganization, and the new research in that area can be viewed as evidence of the validity of some of the basic notions of social disorganization theory.

Of course, other major theories also make claims about the experiences of people inhabiting communities or specific territories as well. Both strain and Marxist theories focus on levels of poverty and inequality in societies, specific collectivities, and communities as determinants of crime and delinquency. For such theorists, a high level of social integration or bonding is unlikely when there are sizeable "marginal" groups in a social setting. In circumstances where people do not share strong common interests in the maintenance of social bonds, more coercive means of maintaining social order prevail.

Cultural deviance theorists attribute communal variations to variations in systems of values, norms, and beliefs. In its most extreme form, behavior which is defined as illegal by the law is defined favorably by people in a subculture. In fact, circumstances deemed to be indicative of a low level of social integration by social disorganization theorists were attacked by cultural deviance theorists as indicative of "differential" social organization or integration. In other words, high crime rates reflected the existence of multiple, socially and culturally integrated subcultural communities.

Research on Community and Delinquency

A major problem with early research on community and delinquency was that the characteristics of communities that were actually measured and correlated with crime or delinquency did not bear directly on the conditions (e.g. disorganization, normative conflict, anomie, etc.) thought to generate high rates. For example, Karl Schuessler and Gerald Slatin examined the characteristics of major American cities and found substantial intercorrelations among offense rates, divorce rates, and suicide rates. They concluded that their findings were "suggestive of a social process which leads to demoralization in the person and consequent abandonment or denial of generally recognized social obligations" (1964:147). This observation is consistent with earlier research by Shaw and McKay (1931) that showed delinquency rates of urban neighborhoods to be related to population change, poor housing, tuberculosis, mental disorders, and adult crime. The general underlying condition that Shaw and McKay identified was "neighborhood disorganization," which was facilitated by population change and economic deprivation. Other studies have yielded similar results, indicating that the delinquency rate in areas of cities is related to overcrowding, transiency, poor housing, and a variety of economic indicators. However, as Roland Chilton (1964) has noted, the relationship of these conditions to delinquency rates does not directly demonstrate that neighborhood disorganization or lack of communal bonds generates high rates. Gresham Sykes reached a similar conclusion about city size and crime rates, noting that variations *may* reflect anonymity, depersonalization, and social disorganization, but that a good deal more research is needed before such arguments can be viewed as something more than interpretation (1978:153).

In his comparison of crime and delinquency in Swiss, American, Scandinavian, and German societies, Marshall Clinard (1978) suggested that the very low offense rates in Swiss society may be due (among other things) to the importance of *cantons* and political *communes* in that society. While Switzerland is an affluent, urban country with a heterogeneous population, its government is decentralized into twenty-five federated states, or cantons, with each of these divided into smaller political communes. Clinard noted that the Swiss maintain "both a physical and a social psychological tie to the cantons and communes from which they come." Since there are several characteristics of Swiss society that might account for its low crime rate, Clinard could not be certain which specific feature is responsible. He did feel that his findings support recommendations to limit city size, to develop small governmental units operating on a neighborhood or "commune" level, and to encourage more direct citizen participation at such a level.

Research on crime and delinquency in China and Japan suggests that in those societies where the needs of the community are placed before the individual, the crime rate is very low. Particularly under the quasi-religious ethic of Confucianism, where the individual is taught to pursue self-perfection and self-control, the community can become much like an extended family. Moreover, despite the large population in these societies, there are relatively clear and widely accepted lines of authority and considerable cooperation in supporting and enforcing rules.

Individual Mobility

Some studies of individuals have attempted to test the argument that mobility inhibits the development of communal bonds, which in turn facilitates delinquency. Sheldon and Eleanor Glueck posited that "frequent moving about means relative anonymity and the likelihood of failure to develop a feeling of loyalty and responsibility to neighborhoods; it tends rather to develop a sense of instability" (1950:155). They contrasted the instability of neighborhoods in recent times to earlier times when "people were born, reared, and lived their lives in one small community, and everyone was known to his neighbors." In comparing 500 delinquent youths and 500 nondelinquent youths, the Gluecks found no significant difference between these groups in length of residence in a neighborhood. However, they did find that the delinquent boys had moved from one house to another significantly more often than the nondelinquent boys. They concluded that "whatever the effect of greater mobility may be upon the tendency to disregard neighborhood opinion as a guide to behavior, it must have operated more excessively upon the delinquents than the nondelinquents" (1950:156). However, as in the studies of cities and urban areas, lack of neighborhood bonds is only one possible interpretation of the relationship. It may be that family circumstances associated with frequency of moves are also associated with delinquency. In short, the relationship could easily be spurious.

Studies of mobility and its consequences for children have not shown mobility to be particularly detrimental. For example, one study found that length of time spent in a particular school did not appear to affect a student's degree of acceptability into peer groups (Miller, 1952). Other studies have indicated that school moves do not affect students' reading achievement (Bollenbacher, 1962) or their performance on IQ tests (Downie, 1953; Evans, 1966). In a study of the effect of student mobility on academic achievement, John Evans concluded that "if moving must be considered a 'handicap,' as we have traditionally thought it is, then this study shows definite ability on the part of the mobile students to adjust" (1966:22).

In a more recent study, Butler and colleagues (1973) found that moving had "little effect" upon informal social relations, alienation, unhappiness, and mental disturbance. Yet another study found that children who had moved did not differ from a sample of their peers who had not moved in terms of mothers' perceptions of disability, aggression, or measures of inhibition (Barrett and Noble, 1973).

In sum, the overall body of research suggests that school changes, frequency of moves, and long-distance moves do not make much difference for a variety of factors that are typically associated with delinquency. On the other hand, the Gluecks' study, which dealt directly with delinquency, suggested that frequency of moves and delinquency are related. Since there are numerous interpretations of that relationship, we cannot reach any one conclusion concerning the interrelationships among mobility and communal ties in relation to individual delinquency.

However, arguments based on the idea that transiency inhibits the development of community or neighborhood bonds and facilitates delinquency can be presented at several different levels. For instance, Packard argued that transiency demoralizes those left behind *as well as* those who move and thus fosters crime and delinquency, even among long-term residents. If that is so, then we would expect no significant differences in crime and delinquency between movers and nonmovers. Rather, the greater the transiency of an *area*, the greater the crime rate should be for that area. In other words, it is at the neighborhood or communal level that transiency should facilitate delinquency since transiency supposedly affects the bonds among people whether they are long-time residents or frequent movers. As will be noted later, the recent revival of interest in social integration and the social "ecology" on crime has shown turnover and transiency of population to be an important correlate of crime.

Defensible Space

Another line of argument concerning the relevance of characteristics of community, neighborhood, or residential environments for crime focuses on architecture and architectural arrangements. The term used by Oscar Newman (1972) to refer to the characteristics of neighborhoods or residential environments that make them safe and secure is *defensible space*. By defensible space, Newman did not mean armed camps or vigilante defense of areas but, rather, architectural arrangements that reinforce a sense of "territoriality" and a "sense of community." In a comparison of two housing projects, Newman found that the crime rate was lowest in the project that was divided into small, manageable zones where residents could maintain surveillance over commonly shared space (see Figure 8-4). Vandalism was lower than in less defensible arrangements, as was the rate of persons vacating the projects. Newman has warned us not to take this comparison as proof that such architectural arrangements reduce crime; however, the analysis is basically consistent with the recommendations outlined by Packard. Whether defensible space reduces vandalism among inhabitants by reinforcing communal bonds or merely keeps outsiders under control is not known.

Researchers have also attempted to measure defensible space by studying types of dwellings. The results have been mixed and the research has not directly measured visibility or the sense of responsibility which defensible space is supposed to facilitate (see Gillis, 1974; Hagan, 1978; Waller and Ohikiro, 1978; Baldwin and Bottoms, 1976; Mawby, 1977; Reppetto, 1974). A major critique of the defensible space model has been the lack of precision in specifying what makes space "defensible" (Taylor et al., 1980). However, a study by Alan Booth (1981) attempted to measure the degree to which space is defensible in terms of access by strangers and opportunities of residents in households or apartments to observe public areas. He found no correlation between outdoor features of built environments and burglary or vandalism, but did find that easy access and limited opportunity to observe facilitated crime for public areas inside apartment

Figure 8-4
Brownsville Houses from Street

The buildings' dispositions at Brownsville create triangular buffer areas that are used for play, sitting, and parking. These areas are easily observed from the street and from apartment windows. Entry to buildings is typically from the street through these buffer zones. Residents regard these areas as an extension of their own buildings and maintain active surveillance over them.

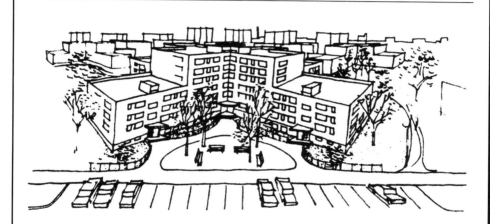

Source: Used with permission of Macmillan Publishing Co., Inc. From *Defensible Space* by Oscar Newman. Copyright © 1972, 1973 by Oscar Newman.

buildings. He also reports that architectural arrangements were related, although not strongly, to people's "sense of responsibility" for an area. In sum, we actually know very little about the types of architectural or physical arrangements which might inhibit crime and delinquency. While there is some support for the theory there appear to be only small differences in some circumstances.

The Revival of Ecological Research

In the first edition of this textbook (Jensen and Rojek, 1980:248) we predicted that criminological research "is likely to return to the same issues which dominated criminology earlier in this century — the variable degrees and types of organization or disorganization that inhibit or facilitate crime and delinquency among people inhabiting a common territory." There has been just such a revival of interest in characteristics of territories or the people inhabiting them in relation to crime and delinquency. This revival is reflected in the works of the new *social integration* theorists and in recent works by theorists interested in the distribution or *ecology* of crime in communities. Indeed, concepts such as social disorganization have been revived in the literature and, as noted in Chapter 6, researchers have attempted to more directly measure the extent of bonds and ties within neighborhoods.

We have already listed some of the propositions advanced by social integration theorists. These propositions have been anchored in research by a variety of scholars (see Crutchfield et al., 1982; Stark et al., 1980; Bainbridge and Stark, 1981; Stark et al., 1983). Foremost in this revival are Robert Crutchfield and Rodney Stark. Stark, Crutchfield, and colleagues have found that crime rates by state correlate with both church membership by state as well as population turnover. More specifically, it appears to be rates of certain property crimes which vary most with these state characteristics. Stark and his colleagues attribute this finding to the impulsive nature of offenses such as homicides as compared to the more intentional and calculative nature of property crimes. They believe that impulsive crimes are not as sensitive to inhibiting forces as more rational crimes. We would like to add that people are freer to steal from one another when there are few bonds tying them together and they are also more likely to avoid detection. In contrast, offenses such as homicide and assault typically involve people who are acquainted with one another or, at least, people who tend to recognize one another.

While the social integration theorists focus on interpersonal ties or bonds in a territory, other researchers have focused on the "opportunity" to commit offenses. Opportunities to commit crime are enhanced when targets are readily available and unguarded. This approach is also known as the *routine activities* approach because variations in the everyday routines of people in a given territory affect the opportunity for crime (Cohen and Felsen, 1979; Cohen et al., 1981). For example, variations in the presence of people in their homes affect the availability of homes as targets. The more unprotected the household, the greater the opportunity for burglary. Similarly, the movement of people affects their availability as targets. Notions such as "defensible space" are also relevant to this perspective since defensible space is more likely to be "guarded." People and property are more likely to be guarded in circumstances where people know and can protect one another. In that sense, social integration should be relevant to the opportunity for crime. The greater the interpersonal ties, the greater the degree to which property is guarded.

Robert Sampson (1985a, 1985b) has examined a wide range of "structural" characteristics of large cities in the United States using both arrest statistics and victimization data. The word "structural" is important because the focus is on characteristics of cities which are not specific characteristics of individuals. For example, the number of people per square mile or the number of multiple dwelling units are characteristics of the cities. Such characteristics are part of the structural context in which people carry out their lives but they are not relevant as a measurable property of the individual.

Sampson (1985a) examined the associations between arrest rates and measures of the density of housing, percent black, location in the South, income inequality, black poverty, white poverty, police per capita, and arrest probability. Some of these variables are relevant to theories emphasizing economic causes of crime and delinquency (e.g., poverty and income inequality) and cultural deviance theories (location in the South, percent black) as well as opportunity theories (density).

Sampson looked at arrest statistics for adults and juveniles for violent crimes (murder, rape, and aggravated assault), robbery, and burglary. For crimes of violence, he found that income inequality affected black juvenile offending and poverty affected white offending. These results are consistent with theories emphasizing structural-economic determinants of delinquency. He found little support for theories which would attribute high rates of juvenile violence to location in the South or to percent black. In fact, location in the South lowered both the black and white juvenile arrest rates relative to other locations. Income inequality was correlated with both black and white arrest rates for robbery. Moreover, for robbery the greater the percent of a city that is black, the lower the black juvenile arrest rate. Location in the South decreased robbery arrest rates as well.

The results for burglary were quite different. Economic variables had little impact on juvenile arrest rates by city. In contrast, measures of "structural density" did increase burglary arrest rates for both black and white youth. The greater the proportion of a city's housing made up of multiple dwelling structures, the higher the city's juvenile burglary rate. Sampson cites this result as support for opportunity theories of victimization in that "high building density decreases the defensible space and guardianship potential of an area while increasing the actual and perceived opportunities for household crimes" (1985a:668).

Since Sampson's analysis was based on arrest statistics, it is subject to the criticisms discussed in Chapters 3 and 4. However, he has also carried out analyses using victimization data. While these data avoid some of the problems of arrest data, they do not allow a specific examination of juvenile offending. Hence, the results may or may not apply specifically to juveniles. Using victimization data, Sampson found that variables measuring social integration and opportunity were the strongest correlates of victimization, and that economic variables and racial composition had only small effects when mobility, family structure, and structural density were considered (1985b). These results are consistent with Stark and Crutchfield's arguments about social integration, in that mobility and family breakdown can be viewed as conditions inhibiting the development or maintenance of interpersonal bonds. They also suggest that economic variables may have relevance to crime through their association with variable social integration.

Summary

Religion and the media have not been central to major sociological perspectives or to research on delinquency during the last several decades. Although the grand masters of sociology in the late 1800s and early 1900s accorded a significant role to religion in the maintenance of social order, contemporary criminologists and specialists in the sociology of religion have only recently devoted much attention to the relationship between religious variables and delinquency or crime. Since the mid-1970s, however, there has been a revival of interest in this relationship, and a tentative set of generalizations has been suggested by pertinent studies:

1. Religiosity is more likely to be related to illegal drug use than to other delinquent offenses.
2. Religiosity is most relevant to drug use in denominations that prohibit such activity and is more relevant to delinquent offenses in general among ascetic or fundamentalistic denominations than among liberal denominations.
3. Religiosity is more relevant to delinquency in moral than in secular settings.
4. Measures of personal religiosity are more relevant to delinquency than such measures as church attendance.
5. Religiosity explains relatively little about delinquency when compared to the impact of more intimate social relationships and social bonds.
6. When religious groups are characterized by norms of abstinence, peripheral or fringe members appear to violate those norms to a greater degree than fringe members of other religious groups.

We are reluctant to state any other tentative conclusions because, typically, new issues and possible reconciliations of divergent findings have been explored in single pieces of research. There are promising indications that further research on the relationship between dimensions of religiosity and delinquency will find relevance for this relationship in some social contexts but not in others.

The impact of the media on delinquency and crime has been examined in a considerable body of research. However, most of it has been criticized as either irrelevant or inadequate for assessing such relationships. The following observations reflect the current state of research and the qualifications that the criticisms demand:

1. Experimental studies have shown that exposure to televised content intended to arouse aggressive behavior increases the probability of interpersonal aggression in controlled situations where the opportunity for aggression is provided following exposure. However, these findings cannot be automatically generalized to the relationship between delinquent behavior and exposure to television outside the laboratory setting.

2. The more time a person spends watching television, reading comic books, or reading romance magazines, the greater the probability of involvement in delinquency, but arguments concerning the causal order and spuriousness of this relationship have not been eliminated. Moreover, research specifically examining preferences for violent programming in relation to self-reports of violence have found such programming to be only weakly correlated, if at all.

3. The conclusion of the 1970 President's Commission on Obscenity and Pornography still stands: Scientific studies have not shown exposure to erotica to increase the probability of sex crimes or delinquent behavior.

4. Reactions to mass media are conditioned by other characteristics of consumers such that no simple, definitive conclusion about the impact (or lack thereof) of violence and/or pornography is possible at this time.

Once again we will state that we are focusing on regularities. There are undoubtedly people who are incited to commit a crime by something they have seen or read, but there are also people who may refrain from crimes as a result of such stimuli. *On balance*, there is no basis for concluding that television violence or erotic literature enhances the probability of delinquency.

One of the oldest sociological notions about crime and delinquency attributes such problems to urbanization and mobility. Urbanization and mobility are seen as inhibiting the development of bonds among people in communities, or neighborhoods. This idea has been revitalized in recent years and is reflected in new research on *social integration* and the *social ecology* of crime and delinquency. Our review of the literature on the topic justifies the following observations:

1. Characteristics of states, communities or neighborhoods which are assumed to measure the density and strength of social

bonds (e.g., church members, intact families, population stability) appear to inhibit crimes, especially property offenses.

2. Several studies have shown physical mobility among students to be unrelated to school achievement and social relationships. One study did show that the number of residential changes for delinquents was greater than the number for nondelinquents, but there are several possible interpretations for that finding.

3. There is some evidence that physical and architectural arrangements can affect the sense of responsibility residents have for public areas and thus inhibit crime, but no simple generalizations about those arrangements are possible at this point.

Research on religion and mass media as forces relevant to juvenile delinquency has not shown them to be as important for understanding the behavior of individuals as family, school, and peers. In that sense, the tendency to ignore media and religion in criminology and delinquency texts is somewhat justified. However, the recent revival of interest in religiosity and delinquency has yielded insights into the circumstances affecting the relevance of religiosity. Moreover, while research concerning media and delinquency is not conclusive, it does suggest possible relationships which may be as complicated and qualified as those now being generated in the study of religiosity.

Social scientists are limited in what they can do in analyzing the relevance of community characteristics to delinquency, since they rely on statistics which bear on only a few variables. Direct research on variations in the strength and density of social ties in a large sample of communities and their relation to variations in actual rates of lawbreaking activity in communities would be invaluable for assessing theories that stress social integration or organization in the explanation of crime and delinquency.

References

Albrecht, S. L., B. A. Chadwick, and D. S. Alcorn. 1977. "Religiosity and Deviance: Application of an Attitude-Behavior Contingent Consistency Model." *Journal for the Scientific Study of Religion* 16 (3):236-74.

Attorney General's Commission on Pornography. 1986. *Final Report*. Washington, DC: U.S. Department of Justice.

Austin, R. 1977. "Religion and Crime Control." Paper presented at American Society of Criminology convention, Atlanta, Ga.

Bainbridge, W. S., and R. Stark. 1981. "Homicide, Suicide and Religion." *The Annual Review of the Social Sciences of Religion*, Vol. 5. The Hague, The Netherlands: Mowton.

Baldwin, J., and A. Bottoms. 1976. *The Urban Criminal: A Study of Sheffield.* London: Tavistock.

Barrett, C. L., and H. Noble. 1973. "Mother's Anxieties Versus the Effects of Long Distance Moves on Children." *Journal of Marriage and the Family* 35 (May):181-88.

Becker, G. 1972. "Causal Analysis in R-R Studies: Television and Aggression." *American Psychologist* 27: 967-68.

Bellah, R. 1967. "Civil Religion in America." *Daedalus* 96: 1-21.

Bollenbacher, J. 1962. "A Study of the Effect of Mobility on Reading Achievement." *Reading Teacher* 15 (March): 356-60.

Booth, A. 1981. "The Built Environment as a Crime Deterrent." *Criminology* 18 (February):557-75.

Burkett, S., and B. Warren. 1987. "Religiosity, Peer Association and Adolescent Marijuana Use: A Panel Study of Underlying Causal Structures." *Criminology* 25: 109-25.

Burkett, S.,and M. White. 1974. "Hellfire and Delinquency: Another Look." *Journal for the Scientific Study of Religion* 13 (December): 455-62.

Butler, E. W., R. J. McAllister, and E. J. Kaiser. 1973. "The Effects of Voluntary and Involuntary Residential Mobility of Females and Males." *Journal of Marriage and the Family* 35 (May):219-27.

Chilton, R. J. 1964. "Continuity in Delinquency Area Research: A Comparison of Studies for Baltimore, Detroit, and Indianapolis." *American Sociological Review* 29 (February):71-83.

Clinard, M. B. 1978. *Cities with Little Crime: The Case of Switzerland.* Cambridge: Cambridge University Press.

Cohen, L., and M. Felson. 1979. "Social Changes and Crime Rate Trends: A Routine Activity Approach." *American Sociological Review* 46 (October): 505-24.

Cohen, L., J. Kluegal, and K. Land. 1981. "Social Inequality and Predatory Criminal Victimization: An Exposition and Test of a Formal Theory." *American Sociological Review* 46 (October):505-24.

Coleman, J. S. 1961. *The Adolescent Society.* New York: Free Press of Glencoe.

Comstock, G. 1980. *Television in America.* Beverly Hills: Sage Publications.

Comstock, G., S. Chaffee, N. Katzman, M. McCombs, and O. Roberts. 1978. *Television and Human Behavior.* New York: Columbia University Press.

Conklin, J. 1972. *Robbery and the Criminal Justice System.* Philadelphia: J. B. Lippincott.

Crutchfield, R., M. Geerken, and W. Gove. 1982. "Crime Rates and Social Integration: The Impact of Metropolitan Mobility." *Criminology* 20:467-78.

Dorr, Aimee. 1986. *Television and Children.* Beverly Hills: Sage Publications.

Downie, N. M. 1953. "A Comparison Between Children Who Have Moved from School with Those Who Have Been in Continuous Residence on Various Factors of Adjustment." *Journal of Educational Psychology* 44 (January): 50-53.

Durkheim, Emile. 1897. *Suicide.* Glencoe, IL: Free Press.

Elifson, K. W., D. M. Petersen, and C. K. Hadaway. 1983. "Religiosity and Delinquency: A Contextual Analysis." *Criminology* 21 (November): 505-27.

Empey, L. T. 1978. *American Delinquency.* Homewood, IL: Dorsey Press.

Eron, L. D., L.R. Huesmann, M.M. Lefkowitz, and L. O. Walder. 1972. "Does Television Violence Cause Aggression?" *American Psychologist* 27: 253-63.

Eron, L. D. 1980. "Prescription for Reducing Aggression." *American Psychologist* 35: 244-52.

Evans, J. W., Jr. 1966. "The Effect of Pupil Mobility upon Academic Achievement." *National Elementary Principal* 45 (April): 18-22.

Faris, R. E. L., and H. Warren Dunham. 1939. *Mental Disorders in Urban Areas.* Chicago: University of Chicago Press.

Gillis, A. R. 1974. "Population Density and Social Pathology: The Case of Building Type, Social Allowance and Juvenile Delinquency." *Social Forces* 53 (December): 306-14.

Glock, C. Y., and R. Stark. 1965. *Religion and Society in Tension.* Chicago: Rand McNally.

Glueck, S., and E. Glueck. 1950. *Unraveling Juvenile Delinquency.* Cambridge, MA: Harvard University Press.

Goldscheider, C., and J. E. Simpson. 1967. "Religious Affiliation and Juvenile Delinquency." *Sociological Inquiry* 37 (Spring): 297-310.

Gray, S. H. 1982. "Exposure to Pornography and Aggression Towards Women: The Case of the Angry Male." *Social Problems* 29 (April): 387-98.

Hadaway, C. K., K. W. Elifson, and D. M. Petersen. 1984. "Religious Involvement and Drug Use Among Urban Adolescents." *Journal for the Scientific Study of Religion* 23 (No. 2): 109-28.

Hagan, J., A. Gillis, and J. Chan. 1978. "Explaining Official Delinquency: A Spatial Study of Class, Conflict and Control." *Sociological Quarterly* 19: 386-98.

Hartnagel, T. F., J. J. Teevan, and J. J. McIntyre. 1975. "Television Violence and Violent Behavior." *Social Forces* 54 (December): 341-51.

Hartshorne, H., and M. A. May. 1930. *Studies in Deceit,* vol. 1. New York: Macmillan.

Haskell, M. R., and L. Yablonsky. 1978. *Juvenile Delinquency.* Chicago: Rand McNally.

Healy, W., and A. J. Bronner. 1936. *New Light on Delinquency and Its Treatment.* New Haven, CT: Yale University Press.

Herbert, K. 1972. "Weaknesses in the Television Causes Aggression Analysis by Eron et al." *American Psychologist* 27 (October): 970-73.

Higgins, P. C., and G. L. Albrecht. 1977. "Hellfire and Delinquency Revisited." *Social Forces* 55 (June): 952-58.

Hightower, P. R. 1930. "Biblical Information in Relation to Character and Conduct." *University of Iowa Studies in Character* 3: 33-34.

Hirschi, T. 1969. *Causes of Delinquency.* Berkeley: University of California Press.

Hirschi, T., and R. Stark. 1969. "Hellfire and Delinquency." *Social Problems* 17 (Fall): 202-13.

Hoult, T. F. 1949. "Comic Books and Juvenile Delinquency." *Sociology and Social Research* 33: 279-84.

Howitt, D. 1972. "Television and Aggression: A Counter Argument." *American Psychologist* 27 (October): 969-70.

Jensen G. F., and M. L. Erickson. 1977. "Delinquency and Damnation." Paper presented at Pacific Sociological Association convention. San Francisco, California.

Jensen G. F., and M. L. Erickson. 1979. "The Religious Factor and Delinquency: Another Look at the Hellfire Hypothesis." In R. Wuthnow (ed.), *The Religious Dimension: New Directions in Quantitative Research*. New York: Academic Press.

Jensen, G. F., and D. G. Rojek. 1980. *Delinquency: A Sociological View*. Lexington, MA: D. C. Heath and Company.

Johnson, B. 1972. *Social Determinants of the Use of Dangerous Drugs by College Students*. New York: John Wiley.

Kant, H. S., and M. J. Goldstein. 1976. "Pornography." *Psychology Today* 4 (7): 61-64.

Kaplan, R. M. 1972. "On Television as a Cause of Aggression." *American Psychologist* 27: 968-69.

Kvaraceus, W. 1944. "Delinquent Behavior and Church Attendance." *Sociology and Social Research* 28: 284-89.

Lefkowitz, M. M., L. D. Eron, L. O. Walder, and L. R. Huesmann. 1972. "Television Violence and Child Aggression: A Followup Study." In G. A. Comstock and E. A. Rubinstein (eds.), *Television and Social Behavior*, Vol. 3. Washington, DC: U.S. Government Printing Office.

Liebert, R. M., and R. A. Baron. 1971. "Short-Term Effects of Televised Aggression on Children's Aggressive Behavior." In J. P. Murray, E. A. Rubenstein, and G. A. Comstock (eds.), *Television and Social Behavior*. Washington, DC: U.S. Government Printing Office.

Linden, R., and R. Currie. 1978. "Religiosity and Drug Use: A Test of Social Control Theory." *Canadian Review of Anthropology and Sociology* 15: 346-55.

Lombroso, C. 1911. *Crime, Its Causes and Remedies*. Boston: Little, Brown.

Lovibond, S. H. 1967. "The Effect of Media Stressing Crime and Violence upon Children's Attitudes." *Social Problems* 15 (Summer): 91-100.

Malamuth, N., and J. Check. 1981. "The Effects of Mass Media Exposure on Acceptance of Violence Against Women: A Field Experiment." *Journal of Research in Personality* 15: 436-46.

Matza, D., and G. Sykes. 1961. "Juvenile Delinquency and Subterranean Values." *American Sociological Review* 26: 712-19.

Mawby, R. I. 1977. "Defensible Space: A Theoretical and Empirical Appraisal." *Urban Studies* 14: 169-79.

Middleton, R., and S. Putney. 1962. "Religion, Normative Standards, and Behavior." *Sociometry* 25: 141-52.

Middleton, W., and P. Fay. 1941. "Attitudes of Delinquent and Non-Delinquent Girls toward Sunday Observance, the Bible and War." *Journal of Educational Psychology* 32: 555-58.

Milavsky, J. R., R. C. Kessler, H. Stipp, and W. S. Rubens. 1982. *Television and Aggression: A Panel Study*. New York: Academic Press.

Miller, L. R. 1952. "Identifying the Outsider." *National Elementary Principal* 32 (September): 156-61.

Miller, M. 1965. "The Place of Religion in the Lives of Juvenile Offenders." *Federal Probation* 29: 50-54.

Mizruchi, E., and R. Perrucci. 1968. "Prescription, Proscription and Permissiveness: Aspects of Norms and Deviant Drinking Behavior." In M. Lefton, J. K. Skipper, Jr., and C. H. McGaghy (eds.), *Approaches to Deviance*. New York: Appleton-Century-Crofts.

Mursell, G. R. 1930. "A Study of Religious Training as a Psychological Factor in Delinquency." Ph.D. dissertation, Ohio State University.

Newman, O. 1972. *Defensible Space*. New York: Macmillan.

Nye, F. I. 1958. *Family Relationships and Delinquent Behavior*. New York: John Wiley.

Packard, V. 1972. *A Nation of Strangers*. New York: David McKay.

Pfuhl, E. H. 1956. "The Relationship of Comic and Horror Comics to Juvenile Delinquency." *Research Studies of the State College of Washington* 2: 170-77.

President's Commission on Obscenity and Pornography. 1970. *The Report of the Commission on Obscenity and Pornography*. New York: Bantam Books.

Reppetto, T. 1976. "Crime Prevention Through Environmental Policy: A Critique." *American Behavioral Scientist* 20: 275-88.

Rhodes, A., and A. Reiss, Jr. 1970. "The Religious Factor and Delinquent Behavior." *Journal of Research in Crime and Delinquency* 7: 83-98.

Sampson, R. J. 1985a. "Structural Sources of Variation in Race-Age-Specific Rates of Offending Across Major U.S. Cities." *Criminology* 23 (November): 647-73.

_____. 1985b. "Neighborhood and Crime: The Structural Determinants of Personal Victimization." *Journal of Research in Crime and Delinquency* 22 (February): 7-40.

Sanders, W. B. 1976. *Juvenile Delinquency*. New York: Praeger.

Schuessler, K., and G. Slatin. 1964. "Sources of Variation in U.S. City Crime, 1950 and 1960." *Journal of Research in Crime and Delinquency* 1 (July): 127-48.

Schur, E. M. 1969. *Our Criminal Society*. Englewood Cliffs, NJ: Prentice-Hall.

Shaw, C. R., and H. D. McKay. 1931. *Social Factors in Juvenile Delinquency*, vol. 2. Report no. 13 of the National Commission on Law Observance and Enforcement. Washington, DC: U.S. Government Printing Office.

_____. 1942. *Juvenile Delinquency and Urban Areas*. Chicago: University of Chicago Press.

Snyder, C. R. 1958. *Alcohol and the Jews*. Glencoe, IL: Free Press.

Stark, R., L. Kent, and D. P. Doyle. 1980. "Religion and Delinquency: The Ecology of a 'Lost' Relationship." *Journal of Research in Crime and Delinquency* 18 (No. 2): 4-24.

Stark, R., W. S. Bainbridge, R. D. Crutchfield, D. P. Doyle, and R. Finke. 1983. "Crime and Delinquency in the Roaring Twenties." *Journal of Research in Crime and Delinquency* 20 (January): 4-23.

Stein, A. H., and L. K. Friedrich. 1971. "Television Content and Young Children's Behavior." In J. P. Murray, E. A. Rubinstein, and G. A. Comstock, (eds.), *Television and Social Behavior*. Washington, DC: U.S. Government Printing Office.

Straus, R., and S. D. Bacon. 1954. *Drinking in College*. New Haven, CT: Yale University Press.

Surgeon General's Scientific Advisory Committee on Television and Social Behavior. 1971. *Television and Growing Up: The Impact of Televised Violence.* Washington, DC: National Institute of Mental Health.

Sutherland, E. H., and D. R. Cressey. 1978. *Criminology.* 10th ed. Philadelphia: J. B. Lippincott.

Sykes, G. M. 1978. *Criminology.* New York: Harcourt Brace Jovanovich.

Taylor, R.B., S.D. Gottfredson, and S. Browder. 1980 "The Defensibility of Defensible Space." In Travis Hirschi and Michael Gottfredson (eds.), *Understanding Crime: Current Theory and Research.* Beverly Hills: Sage Publications.

Thompson, K., and D. Brownfield. 1986. "Religiosity and Delinquency in Moral and Secular Communities." Paper presented at the 1986 meetings of American Society of Criminology, Atlanta, Ga.

Thrasher, F. M. 1927. *The Gang.* Chicago: University of Chicago Press.

Waller, I., and N. Ohikiro. 1978. *Burglary: The Victim and the Public.* Toronto: University of Toronto Press.

Werthman, F. 1954. *Seduction of the Innocent.* New York: Holt, Rinehart and Winston.

Wilson, J. Q. 1975. *Thinking about Crime.* New York: Vintage Books.

World Almanac and Book of Facts. 1990. New York: Pharos Books.

chapter 9

Deterrence and Labeling

> *People are governed in their daily lives by rewards and penalties of every sort. We shop for bargain prices, praise our children for good behavior and scold them for bad, expect lower interest rates to stimulate home building and fear that higher ones will depress it, and conduct ourselves in public in ways that lead our friends and neighbors to form good opinions of us. To assert that "deterrence doesn't work" is tantamount to either denying the plainest of facts of everyday life or claiming that would-be criminals are utterly different from the rest of us.*
>
> —James Q. Wilson, *Thinking About Crime*, 1983

Getting Tough

A common suggestion for dealing with problems of crime and delinquency is to "get tough"—to do something more punitive and threatening than is currently being done. Declarations that the juvenile court is a "kiddies court" and that it is "soft" on crime reflect the view that the court ought to be a punitive agency assigning penalties with sufficient certainty, severity, and speed (celerity) to scare real and potential offenders straight. To many people this *deterrence doctrine* is so unquestionably true that only the naive and misguided would challenge it.

The idea that a primary aim of legal sanctioning or punishment is to deter offenders, as well as the general public, from future transgressions developed in the eighteenth century. It is associated with such philosophers as Cesare Beccaria (1738-1794) and Jeremy Bentham (1748-1832), who formulated a perspective on crime which came to be called the *classical school* of criminology. The classical view was rational and utilitarian, emphasizing that a punishment is "just" only if it contributes to the greatest happiness for the greatest number. The major justification for legal sanctioning was its presumed inhibiting effect on the extent of crime. For a punishment to serve such a purpose and contribute to the social good, there had to be (so it was argued) a measure of equality between the crime and the punishment. Thus, Beccaria maintained that "for a punishment to attain its end, the evil which it inflicts has only to exceed the advantage derivable from the crime" (1767). For Beccaria, punishment should be as certain as possible and as harsh as necessary to deter potential offenders. Bentham, basing his approach on "utilitarian" principles, argued that criminal activities were a product of free choices made by rational beings on the basis of a consideration of profit and cost. Consistent with this view, the function of criminal law and criminal justice was to design punishments that would *deter*, but that would do so without inflicting more pain than was necessary. Classical theorists attacked arbitrary and cruel practices found in many countries in Europe and focused instead on human reason and the perfectibility of social institutions as rational agencies dealing with rational beings.

Although the classical school's principles of deterrence became the philosophical foundation for our criminal justice system, they were attacked while the juvenile justice system was developing. The optimism of the classical school during the eighteenth century gave way to the reformatory movement of the nineteenth century, which sought to save youthful offenders from the perils of contemporary society. The function of the juvenile court, according to nineteenth century reformers, was not to punish, nor was it to design and implement penalties that would deter. Rather the court was to find appropriate techniques for "treating" or "helping" troubled youths. The juvenile justice system was supposed to emphasize rehabilitation rather than deterrence.

In Chapter 2 we summarized the arguments of social historians who assert that the primary motives behind the creation of the juvenile justice system were not so benevolent and that punishment and control of dangerous youth were central to the practices of the juvenile court. Indeed, the Supreme Court critique of the juvenile justice system that led to the extension of several rights of due process to juveniles in the 1960s emphasized the punitive nature of the system and its failure to serve the interests of children. The dominant orientation among sociologists at that time emphasized the failure of the system to rehabilitate or deter. Rather, the juvenile justice system was accused of turning youth into career offenders by labeling and stigmatizing them and treating temporary problems of youth as if they were criminal activities (see Schur, 1969b).

While the dominant mood of politicians, the public, and numerous criminologists in recent years has been to "get tough" there are strong advocates for a less punitive approach as well. For example, Ira Schwartz, administrator of the Office of Juvenile Justice and Delinquency Prevention under President Carter, advocates an "action agenda" for the future that is in marked contrast to deterrence-based arguments. Among other things, he proposes 1) enacting laws which would prohibit the confinement of juveniles in adult jails, 2) closing all large training schools, 3) reducing predispositional detention, 4) raising the maximum age of juvenile court jurisdiction to 18 in all states, and 5) ending the use of detention as a "short, sharp shock" (1989). Schwartz's book is titled *(In)justice for Juveniles* to convey his view that a recent return to a deterrence orientation is a step backward rather than progress. Schwartz's views are in marked contrast to the administrator of the Office of Juvenile Justice and Delinquency Prevention under President Reagan, Alfred Regnery, who argued that juveniles are "Getting Away with Murder" (1985) and that "the deterrent approach should be the main focus of the justice system." There are strong advocates on both sides of the issue, just as there were when the system was being developed.

In this chapter we will review theory and research relevant to two contrasting positions on law enforcement and delinquency—deterrence theory and labeling theory. While they have varied in popularity, ideas central to both underlie continuing debate about how the problem of juvenile delinquency should be addressed. In Chapter 11 we will examine programs that implement or reflect these different theories. In this chapter we will concentrate on social scientific research relevant to the basic tenets of the two general perspectives.

Deterrence Theory and Explanations of Delinquency

For much of the twentieth century social scientists either ignored deterrence or deemed it irrelevant to understanding crime or delinquency.

Box 9-1
Be Tough With Delinquents

The view that we should get tough with juveniles is advocated by numerous politicians and commentators on contemporary American society. For example, in a 1989 article in *The New York Times*, Rita Kramer argues that:

"Youthful offenders have no reason to fear the system. In Family Court, one hears again and again the mugger of old men, sodomizer of young children, victimizer of decent neighbors, laughing at a system that 'can't do nothing to me—I ain't sixteen yet.'. . .

We owe it to victims, past and future, and to the law-abiding everywhere in the city, to restructure our juvenile justice system and redefine our attitude toward it so that the chronically violent young predator knows he has reason to fear the consequences of his acts."

In contrast, Ira Schwartz, Director of the Office of Juvenile Justice and Delinquency Prevention under President Carter argues that "there is reason to believe that the 'get tough' movement is waning and that we may be entering another new era of reform" (1989:61). Schwartz does not believe that increasing rates of incarceration would lower the delinquency rate. He claims that there is "little or no relationship between rates of serious juvenile crime and the rates of youth incarceration" (1989:29).

Do you believe that juveniles are deterred from committing offenses by fear of imprisonment?

In his influential *Principles of Criminology*, Edwin Sutherland wrote that "control . . . lies in the group pressure, the recognition and response secured by lawful conduct rather than fear of punishment. Not the fear of legal penalties but the fear of loss of status in the group is the effective deterrent" (1924:374). Sutherland argued that the whole psychology underlying the classical school, with its emphasis on free will and the calculations of pleasures and pains, was questionable.

Of the three dominant sociological theories of delinquency examined in Chapter 6, none originally included deterrence in its explanation of delinquency. The most popular sociological theories have been motivational theories which focus on the social, cultural, and interactional forces that encourage or discourage lawbreaking. The emphasis has been on people as social and moral beings who make decisions on the basis of values, norms, and beliefs, rather than on the basis of rational calculations of losses and gains. Although social control theory, as an amotivational theory, could readily encompass legal sanctions as a potential barrier to crime and delinquency, only some formulations incorporated such notions (Minor, 1977). Social control theorists have instead focused on what are referred to as "informal" control mechanisms and "positive" social bonds (such as attachment, commitment, involvement, and acceptance of conventional beliefs).

Fear of punishment is a major source of social order in Marxist theory, but it is not viewed as an enduring or healthy basis of order in the long run. From a Marxist perspective, a true socialist order would not have to be maintained by force. However, when social and economic arrangements are not serving the interests and needs of sizeable segments of society, control over legal punishment is one means of keeping the masses in line. Hence, while the classical school and social control theories are often viewed as ideologically contrary to Marxist theory (the latter attacking the status quo and the former defending it) they share in common the belief that people can be constrained, at least in the short run, by actual and anticipated punishment.

Although it had generally been ignored in major theories and had been questioned repeatedly by prominent criminologists, the study of deterrence emerged as a major research topic in the late 1960s and continued to grow in prominence in the 1970s. This growth in interest was stimulated in part by the development of the labeling perspective, which focused on the role that laws, law enforcement, and sanctioning played in magnifying, rather than reducing, social problems. From the labeling perspective, not only was deterrence questionable, but criminalization, stigmatization, and legal sanctioning were potential *sources* of the very problems they were supposed to solve. On the other hand, deterrence theory argued that reacting to deviance by imposing sanctions deterred individuals from deviance and helped solve problems. The two perspectives stressed contrasting outcomes. However, the development of the labeling perspective had the effect of shifting the emphasis from deviant behavior to *reactions* to deviance and, especially, the *consequences* of reactions to deviance. Thus, although labeling theorists attacked deterrence, the very fact that they did so (coupled with the surge of interest in reactions to deviance) helped to generate new interest in deterrence.

Distinctions in Deterrence Theory

Before we can examine the research literature on deterrence, we must deal with several conceptual matters. First, some deterrence theorists insist that a distinction be made between "deterrence" and the "general preventive effects of punishment." Jack Gibbs, one of the most prominent deterrence theorists, has defined deterrence as "the omission of an act as a response to the perceived risk and fear of punishment for *contrary* behavior" (1975:2). The omission of an act must be linked to assessments of risk and fear before a valid claim can be made that deterrence has occurred. Moreover, other circumstances or conditions may inhibit delinquency but not be instances of deterrence. For example, moral commitments and fear of social disapproval can inhibit delinquency (Grasmick and Green, 1980) but they are not directly relevant to deterrence theory.

From Gibb's perspective, certain ways of preventing or inhibiting lawbreaking do *not* involve fear of punishment and therefore should be viewed as "preventive consequences of legal punishment" rather than deterrence. For example, locking people up may prevent certain forms of crime (such as auto theft) while those people are locked away, but this preventive consequence is called *incapacitation* rather than deterrence. In addition, people may refrain from lawbreaking because they know and respect the law. If that knowledge and respect were influenced by punishment, it would be called an *enculturation* or *socialization* consequence of punishment. In this case, punishment would prevent crime through socialization rather than fear of punishment. Gibbs listed a total of ten preventive effects of punishment other than deterrence, but the important point here is that some theorists restrict the term *deterrence* specifically to the inhibiting effects of *fear of punishment*. On the other hand, Gibbs himself noted that we may never be able to isolate the effect of fear of punishment from other preventive effects of punishment (see Box 9-2). Thus, the research we will summarize in the next section deals with the preventive effects of punishment but is generally phrased in terms of the study of deterrence.

Another very important conceptual matter in examining the research literature on deterrence (or preventive effects) is the distinction between

---

Box 9-2
The Preventive Effects of Law and Law Enforcement

Drinking-related deaths among young drivers fall

Federal safety researchers for the Centers for Disease Control (CDC) recently reported that fewer than one in five 15-17 year-old drivers involved in fatal crashes in 1989 had been drinking. Nineteen percent had been drinking as compared to 22 percent in 1988 and 32 percent in 1982. The decline was attributed to an increase in the legal drinking age during the 1980s, stricter laws, and education (*The Tennessean,* Friday, March 22, 1991, p. 11-A).

Assuming that raising the drinking age and stricter laws and law enforcement did make a difference, use Gibb's notions about general preventive effects to explain that decline. Which of the mechanisms do you think is most important?

---

specific deterrence and *general deterrence.* Specific deterrence refers to the omission of *further* criminal or delinquent acts *by the individual who was punished.* For instance, if a juvenile refrains from shoplifting because he or she was caught and fears being caught again, this would be an instance of specific deterrence. In contrast, general deterrence refers to the omission of criminal or delinquent acts as a result of *anticipated or feared punishment* among those who have not been punished. The two types of deterrence are distinct, and in this chapter we will focus most extensively on the general deterrence literature.

Another distinction of some importance for understanding the research literature on deterrence is the difference between two types of general deterrence: *absolute deterrence* and *restrictive deterrence.* Jack Gibbs has defined the two as follows:

> The term "absolute deterrence" denotes instances where an individual has refrained throughout life from a particular type of criminal act because in whole or in part he or she perceived some risk of someone suffering a punishment as a response to the crime. Defined explicitly,

"restrictive deterrence" is the curtailment of a certain type of criminal activity by an individual during some period because in whole or in part the curtailment is perceived by the individual as reducing the risk that someone will be punished as a response to the activity, even though no one has suffered a punishment as a consequence of that individual's criminal activity. (1975:32-33)

In short, if people never break the law as a result of fear of punishment, the deterrence process would be "absolute." If people merely restrain themselves to some degree, then the process would be "restrictive."

These conceptual distinctions are important for assessing the arguments for and against deterrence because parties to the debate may be referring to quite different issues. For example, someone might advance the following argument: "Sending people to prison does not deter crime but, instead, increases it. Look at the high recidivism rate among convicts. Obviously the prisons are not deterring." This particular argument focuses on *specific* deterrence. It has no bearing on whether the threat of imprisonment deters the *general* public. It would be possible for imprisonment to increase crime among the imprisoned and yet decrease crime among potential offenders. The net effect of an increase in the use of imprisonment might be a decrease in the crime rate (via general deterrence), even given an increase in recidivism (that is, a failure of specific deterrence). The main point is that we make certain we are talking about the same phenomenon when debating the issue of deterrence.

Another possible critique of deterrence might take the following form: "Most Americans drank during the Prohibition. Most adolescents have tried marijuana. Virtually all people break the law sometime during their lives. Obviously people are not deterred by the law." This type of statement focuses on *absolute* deterrence. It has no necessary bearing on whether people *restrict* their involvement in crime or delinquency as a result of threat or fear of punishment. If everyone in a population violates a law sometime, then absolute deterrence does not exist. However, even then, the threat of punishment might restrict people's involvement to one or two transgressions on the average, rather than ten or twelve.

Debates about capital punishment can often confuse different "preventive consequences" of execution with deterrence as well. The central issue in the debate has been whether capital punishment has a deterrent effect on capital crimes. The grounds for advocating such a response shift whenever someone argues that capital punishment is effective because the people executed are no longer able to commit crimes. Execution is the ultimate form of *incapacitation* and arguing for it on those grounds is irrelevant to deterrence theory. Similarly, while execution might have an effect on crime through the message communicated about the moral gravity of certain crimes, this would be a socialization effect rather than deterrence.

Research on General Deterrence

Much of the research on deterrence does not deal directly with juveniles since it is based on crime rates for the general population and focuses on punishments that are more commonly meted out to adults than to juveniles. For example, many studies have attempted to measure the deterrent effect of capital punishment by analyzing homicide rates for states or for the total United States population. Homicide is actually quite rare among juveniles, as is the probability of being executed or sentenced to death. Prisoners under sentence of death tend to be young adults, and only a small percent of those prisoners are under the age of twenty.

Since the first hanging in Plymouth colony in 1642 a total of 281 juveniles have been executed and, given the 1989 Supreme Court decision (*Penry v. Lynaugh*) allowing states to execute nonadults, the number is likely to increase significantly. Fourteen states allow persons under the age of 18 to be executed and both the federal system and fourteen additional states have no minimum age. Twenty-five juveniles in 13 states were under sentence of death in 1989 (Scanian, 1989). Thus, arguments about the deterrent effects of capital punishment are relevant to juveniles.

Capital Punishment

Several types of evidence have been brought to bear on the general deterrent effects of capital punishment. One type of evidence has been based on comparisons of capital crime rates for states with and without the statutory possibility of capital punishment. Such comparisons have shown that states without the death penalty do not have higher capital crime rates than states with the death penalty. Similarly, rates in individual states before and after abolishment of the death penalty, as well as comparisons of those before and after statistics with data for states retaining capital punishment, have failed to show a deterrent effect. These findings hold true even when comparing similar or contiguous states (Bowers, 1974; Schuessler, 1952; Sellin, 1967).

Such research has been criticized, however, in that the statutory possibility of the death penalty does not mean that it is actually used or that those so sentenced are executed. Actually, during the period for which national statistics are available, the peak year for executions was 1938 when 190 prisoners were executed. By the 1950s the number had declined to less than 100 per year, and by 1960 there were 56. From 1968 to 1976 there were none. Between 1977 and 1983 only eleven prisoners were executed; however, beginning in 1984, there have been approximately 20 executions per year.

Does the actual occurrence of executions reduce capital crime rates? The safest answer to that question is that there is no consistent evidence of a deterrent effect. For example, Leonard Savitz (1958) examined the frequency of felony murders in Philadelphia (that is, murders committed in the act of committing another felony) several weeks before and after well-publicized executions and found no evidence of a deterrent effect. In contrast, research by Isaac Ehrlich (1975) claimed to show that executions had a deterrent effect on homicide rates. After analyzing homicide rates and executions from 1933 to 1969, Ehrlich concluded that each additional execution per year may have prevented seven or eight murders. The reason we indicate that he "claimed" to show a deterrent effect is because subsequent evaluations and replications of Ehrlich's analysis have challenged his conclusions. One of the problems is that after 1962 the homicide rate climbed rapidly, while the number of executions continued to decline as it had been doing for several decades (see Figure 9-1). These factors accounted for most of the association that Ehrlich observed. Moreover,

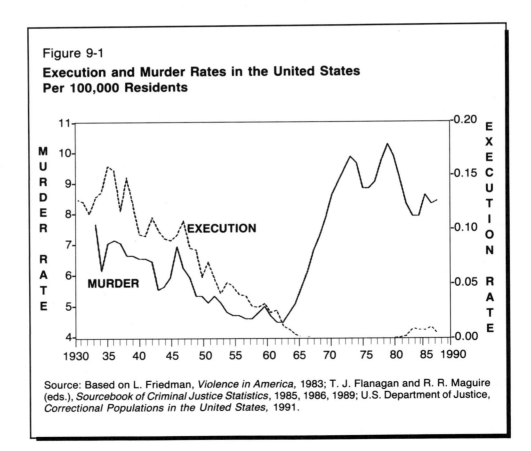

Figure 9-1

Execution and Murder Rates in the United States Per 100,000 Residents

Source: Based on L. Friedman, *Violence in America*, 1983; T. J. Flanagan and R. R. Maguire (eds.), *Sourcebook of Criminal Justice Statistics*, 1985, 1986, 1989; U.S. Department of Justice, *Correctional Populations in the United States*, 1991.

further analysis of data from the 1960s (Forst, 1976) led to the same old conclusion: There is at present no scientifically acceptable support for the view that capital punishment is any more of a deterrent to capital crime than is imprisonment (Zeisel, 1976).

Bowers, Pierce, and McDevitt (1984) find some evidence which suggests that executions may increase the homicide rate. They suggest that the state's use of lethal violence can have a "brutalization effect," facilitating homicide rather than deterring it. One of the most recent studies examined the impact of the resumption of executions on the homicide rate and concluded that the resumption had no significant impact on homicide nationwide (Peterson and Bailey, 1988).

Another approach to the capital punishment issue has been to propose that the amount of publicity and drama surrounding executions might make a difference for the detection of deterrent effects. Initial studies suggested that publicity did make a difference. Steven Stack (1987) reported that executions that were publicized sufficiently to be reported in national information sources were followed by reductions in homicide rates. However, a more recent analysis of these same data found several errors in measuring the publicity of executions and reanalyzed the data in different ways. William Bailey and Ruth Peterson (1989:722) conclude that "the cumulative effect of capital punishment on homicides during the execution and subsequent months is essentially zero."

In an even more recent analysis Bailey (1990) examined publicity about executions in television news from 1976 through 1987 in relation to monthly homicide rates. This research may be particularly important in the debate over capital punishment since television news services have been pressing for permission to televise executions. The possibility of televised executions has generated considerable controversy with encouragement coming from both supporters and opponents of capital punishment (see Box 9-3). Bailey found that the amount and nature of television publicity neither reduced (deterrence) nor increased (brutalization) homicide rates. Thus, while some advocates of televised executions cite Stack's research on the topic as empirical support for a possible deterrent effect, more recent analyses do not show publicity to enhance the deterrent effect of executions. Of course, the results of research on publicity cannot necessarily be generalized to preclude deterrent or brutalization effects from televised executions. All we can state is that there is no support for such a prospect in existing data.

Certainty and Severity of Punishment

The issue of capital punishment was central to research on deterrence from the 1930s through the 1960s with a renewed interest in the 1980s.

Box 9-3

Should Executions Be Televised?

Ernest van den Haag (1986), John Ohlin Professor of Jurisprudence and Public Policy at Fordham University, defends the use of the death penalty as "the ultimate punishment" available to society. However, he opposes televised executions because "The death even of a murderer, however well-deserved, should not serve as public entertainment . . . Further, television unavoidably would trivialize executions, wedged in, as they would be, between game shows, situation comedies and the like." He also argues that televised executions would shift the focus from "the nature of the crime and the suffering of the victim" to the murderer as the victim. He states, "Far from communicating the moral significance of the execution, television would shift the focus to the pitiable fear of the murderer."

A person can oppose the death penalty and still advocate televised executions. For example, opponents of the death penalty might support televised executions on the grounds that the public should not be able to hide from state violence. Moreover, those who believe that the death penalty is justified only if it has a deterrent effect might support televised executions as a means to enhance deterrence. Richard Moran (1990), a sociologist at Mount Holyoke College, proposes that executions be televised on the grounds that it would 1) provide a test of the deterrence argument, 2) ignite public debate and 3) allow a better evaluation of "the moral foundation of the death penalty." Of course, if Ernest van den Haag is correct, then the death penalty would lose its deterrent effect through such drama. If brutalization theorists are correct, then televised executions would backfire and Moran's proposed test would cost lives rather than save them.

Based on your own opinions in which of the following categories do you belong? What are your reasons for that choice?

Do you favor execution over life in prison for murder?

	No	Yes
No		
Yes		

Do you favor televised executions?

Beginning in the late 1960s, social scientists turned to the more general issue of whether variations in the certainty and severity of arrest and imprisonment had a deterrent effect on crime rates. Since its inauguration in a study by Jack Gibbs (1968), a common procedure in United States research has been to create measures of the certainty of punishment (for example, the number of admissions to prison for a certain offense relative to the number of such offenses known) and the severity of punishment (for example, the number of months served in prison for a certain type of offense) within the different states. If deterrence notions are to be supported, then states that have a higher degree of certainty and severity of punishment for a certain offense should have a lower incidence of that offense than states in which the punishment is less certain and less severe. In general, the data have supported that hypothesis (although, as always, with some controversy). Research has also indicated some variations in deterrence by type of offense.

Atunes and Hunt (1973) noted that research results have been consistent with the conclusion that certainty of punishment "has a mild deterrent impact," but that severity of punishment appears to be relevant only to homicide. Their own analysis led them to similar conclusions. They found that the greater a state's certainty of punishment, the lower that state's crime rates, but that severity of punishment only made a difference for crime rates when certainty of punishment was high. If the chances of being punished are quite low, then it appears that the severity of the punishment does not matter.

Research by Tittle and Rowe (1974) also suggests that the effect of certainty of arrest on crime rates is strongest when a "threshold" in terms of probability of arrest is passed. Thus, certainty of arrest had its greatest impact after the probability of arrest exceeded 30 percent. When the certainty of arrest is very low, variations within that range do not appear to be important for explaining crime rates.

There are several major problems with deterrence research that uses official statistics. Two of them are the same problems we have dealt with throughout this text: causal order and spuriousness. It is conceivable that states with high crime rates have low rates of certainty of punishment because of the "overload" on the criminal justice system. Hence, a relationship between low certainty and high crime rates could reflect the overload rather than deterrence. Moreover, any such relationship could be due to other factors, such as the moral climate or degree of social condemnation regarding particular types of offenses. When the populace is relatively intolerant of a certain crime, that crime may have both a high certainty of punishment and a low crime rate because of moral and social condemnation rather than because of deterrence (Erickson et al., 1977). Finally, a third major problem confronting such research is separating incapacitation effects from deterrence effects. If a state has a high rate of certainty of imprisonment, then the crime rate for that state may be low because heavy contributors to the crime rate are locked away. This would be an incapacitation effect, rather than a deterrence effect.

A study by Michael Geerken and Walter Gove (1977) attempted to assess which interpretation of the relationship between certainty of punishment and crime rates was most plausible—deterrence, overload, or incapacitation. Through an analysis of data for all cities with a population of 500,000 or more they concluded that predictions derived from deterrence theory receive more support than do those derived from interpretations of the relationship as the result of overload or incapacitation. To reach this conclusion, Geerken and Gove tested the argument advanced by numerous deterrence theorists (for example, Chambliss, 1967; Andenaes, 1971; Zimring and Hawkins, 1973) that rational, "instrumental" crimes (such as stealing) are more readily deterred than emotional, "expressive" crimes (such as most murders). They posited that the deterrence model, being a rational model, should be most applicable to rational, property-oriented offenses directed at profit and least applicable to emotional crimes of interpersonal violence, such as murder and assault. Their findings (as well as some earlier research) were consistent with this hypothesis. They found that certainty of arrest had a strong effect on property crimes, a moderate association with rape, and little or no relationship to homicide or assault.

Research during the 1980s examining variations in crime and punishment over time has shown the support for the deterrence doctrine to be much weaker than earlier research using official statistics suggested. For example, research on clearance rates in relation to crime rates over time for 1964 to 1970 failed to support deterrence theory; that is, changes in clearance rates did not explain variation in crime rates (Greenberg and Kessler, 1982). An analysis of rates of imprisonment and crime rates between 1941 and 1978 (Bowker, 1981) also concluded that changes in imprisonment rates did not lead to changes in crime rates. Both of these studies dealt with variations over time and, thus, attempted to address the issue of causal order.

Experimental Research on Deterrence

The ideal procedure for dealing with problems of causal order and spuriousness is an experimental model. By manipulating the certainty and severity of punishment and measuring the subsequent effects, the problem of causal order is solved, and by controlling other conditions, problems of spuriousness can be minimized. However, controlled experiments relevant to many deterrence issues are ethically impossible. To illustrate these problems, Hans Zeisel outlined some possible experiments with the death penalty:

How morally and legally impossible such an experiment is can easily be seen if its details are sketched out. In one conceivable version a state would have to decree that citizens convicted of a capital crime and born on odd-numbered days of the month would be subject to the death penalty; citizens born on even-numbered days would face life in prison. A significantly lower number of capital crimes committed by persons born on uneven days would confirm the deterrent effect. The date of birth here is a device of randomly dividing the population into halves by a criterion that we will assume cannot be manipulated.

The equally impossible experiment that would test the effect of differential frequencies of execution would require at least three randomly selected groups. In the first group everybody convicted of a capital crime would be executed. In the second, only every other such convict (again selected by lot) would be executed. In the third, nobody would be executed. (1976)

The deterrence experiments that have been done have been limited to such activities as classroom cheating, income tax evasion, and illegal hook-ups to television cable services. For instance, Charles Tittle and Allan Rowe (1973) carried out an experiment in which college students were allowed to grade their own exams. Students were initially reminded of their moral obligation to grade their exams honestly. Such an appeal had no effect. Later the students were told that spot checks of their accuracy in grading would be made and offenders punished. The threat of sanction did reduce cheating. It was less effective for males than for females and less effective for those experiencing disparity between earned grades and expected grades. Those who were dissatisfied with their grades were less likely to be deterred than those who were content with their grades.

With the cooperation of the Internal Revenue Service, Richard Schwartz and Sonja Orleans (1967) designed a field experiment in which sets of people were randomly assigned 1) to be interviewed and made aware of the penalties for income tax evasion, 2) to be interviewed and reminded of their moral obligation to pay taxes, 3) to be interviewed with neither of these messages, and 4) not to be interviewed at all. Subjects in both the moral-appeal and sanction-threat groups paid more taxes than either of the other two groups, with the moral appeal apparently making the biggest difference.

Mark Stafford and colleagues (1986) designed a deterrence experiment in which college students could cheat in a computer-simulated game. However, they informed subjects about the chances of getting caught and the consequences in terms of points fined. They report that certainty and severity of punishment each made a difference for cheating but that they magnified the effect of each other as well; that is, certainty of punishment had a much stronger effect at high levels of severity, and severity had a stronger effect at high levels of certainty. Since the same pattern was found in their analysis of homicide data, they believe that their results reflect processes that occur outside the laboratory setting.

Another experiment carried out in the field involved illegal hookups to Home Box Office services through unauthorized descramblers (Green, 1985). Cable thieves were sent a written legal threat and their reaction measured by reexamining cable hookups after the warning. The main reaction was an attempt to hide the violation. Two-thirds of violators removed descramblers and a few others reacted in other ways. Males, the youngest, and the richest were least likely to heed the warning.

In another study by Block, Nold, and Sidak (1981), the government filed a complaint for price-fixing against bakeries. While the government threatened to take action, no litigation actually took place. Yet, the price of bread began to drop. Braithwaite and Geis (1982) suggest that deterrence is most evident for activities that are profit-oriented and where there is little commitment to the activity.

Although experimental studies can avoid the problems confronting statistical studies, experimental research has its own shortcomings. Cheating is not a crime, and the way people behave in regard to paying taxes and cable-t.v. crime may not be generalizable to other types of behavior. Moreover, in the real world people may not perceive the threat of sanctions, whereas in experimental research the threat can be directly communicated. However, experimental research overcomes many of the limitations of other types of research and has consistently supported deterrence theory.

Survey Research on Deterrence

Several deterrence theorists have noted that deterrence theory is a psychological theory in that it makes certain assumptions about the *perception* of risk of apprehension or punishment (Jensen, 1969; Waldo and Chiricos, 1972; Erickson et al., 1977). As a "perceptual" theory, deterrence theory presumes some public knowledge and awareness of legal sanctions. In fact, Jensen, Erickson, and Gibbs have argued that the central assertion of the deterrence doctrine is that "the more members of a population perceive the punishment for a type of offense as being certain, severe and celeritous (swift), the lower the rate for that population" (1978:58). Thus, subjective or perceptual estimates of risk of punishment are viewed as more directly relevant to testing deterrence hypotheses than the probabilities reflected in official statistics. Moreover, by focusing on perceptions of the nonincarcerated public, the problem of incapacitation effects is solved.

Although most of the research on perceptions of risk has been consistent with the deterrence doctrine, such research has not yielded a perfectly consistent set of conclusions. For example, in interviews with a sample of youths aged 13 to 16, Martin Gold (1970) asked: "Out of every ten kids who commit an offense, how many get caught?" Gold found very little difference between the delinquents and nondelinquents in such perceptions and concluded that his findings cast considerable doubt on deterrence theory.

A study of college students by Bailey and Lott (1976) also failed to support deterrence notions. Bailey and Lott gathered data from 268 college students enrolled in sociology courses and found no significant relationships between number of reported criminal offenses and perceived certainty of punishment (likelihood of arrest and conviction) or between number of reported criminal offenses and perceived severity of punishment.

In contrast to these two studies, numerous others have reported some degree of support for the deterrence theory when studying perceived certainty of punishment (Jensen, 1969; Waldo and Chiricos, 1972; Grasmick and Milligan, 1976; Kraut, 1976; Minor, 1977; Silberman, 1976; Tittle, 1977; Jensen et al., 1978; Jensen and Stitt, 1982; Montmarquette and Nerlove, 1985). Like objective deterrence research, survey research is more likely to support arguments regarding certainty of punishment than it is to support those regarding severity of punishment. There is some evidence that the more socially intolerable property-oriented offenses may be the most deterrable (Jensen et al., 1978).

The key issue confronting perceptual research on deterrence is causal order. It has not been demonstrated that the perceived threat or fear of punishment *precedes* involvement in delinquency. Those who perceive low risk may be those who have violated the law already and have not been caught. Beliefs about punishment and delinquent behavior may be interrelated. Environmental responses to behavior may shape perceptions or beliefs about risk, and those beliefs in turn may affect the probability of future delinquency. Perceptual studies have only shown an association between perception of risk and delinquent behavior.

There have been some studies of people at different points in time and such research suggests greater support for the view that perceptions of risk are affected by successful deviance than for the view that perceived risk has deterrent consequences (Minor and Harry, 1982; Saltzman et al., 1982). However, such research has been based on undergraduates followed over a relatively short period of time and has focused on drug use and minor forms of theft. As one of those studies concludes, ". . . even after a decade of intensified perceptual deterrence research, very little is known about the relationship between perceptions and behavior" (Paternoster et al., 1985:430).

Although each type of deterrence research has its shortcomings, the shortcomings vary from one type to another. Thus, perceptual research has not demonstrated causal order, but it has suggested an association between perceived risk and criminal or delinquent behavior in many different samples of the population. Experimental work solves the problem of causal order, but it has been limited to a narrow range of lawbreaking activities and its findings may not be generalizable to everyday situations. Deterrence research has been confronted with issues of spuriousness, incapacitation, overload, and all the problems stemming from the use of official statistics. At present, the whole body of research supports the *tentative* conclusion that stiffer law enforcement would likely reduce the extent of several forms of crime and delinquency. Although this hypothesis has not been proven conclusively, there appears to be more compatible than contrary evidence.

It is important to remember that such a statement does not require nor necessitate a "get tough" approach to delinquency prevention (see Chapter 12). The school, family, peer groups, beliefs about proper and improper conduct, and a variety of other social forces exert greater influences on behavior than fears or beliefs about legal punishment. Programs attempting to change experiences within these settings can be advocated as potentially more consequential. However, that view does not mean that legal sanctions make no difference for behavior.

Labeling Theory

Our criminal and juvenile justice systems are based on the assumption that laws that accord the state the right to regulate certain types of conduct are necessary for the prevention and control of undesirable or injurious behavior. Moreover, the enforcement of those laws is presumed to be necessary if they are to have their intended effects. Such assumptions, at one time taken for granted, have been challenged for several decades now by *labeling theorists*, who advocate examining the unanticipated, hidden, and negative consequences of law and law enforcement.

Labeling theorists have focused on three issues involving the law and law enforcement: 1) the creation of and changes in the legal categories applied to people and their behavior, 2) circumstances affecting the actual application of legal labels, and 3) the individual and societal effects of the labeling process. One of the most quoted statements in the sociology of deviance is Howard Becker's observation that:

> Social groups create deviance by making rules whose infractions constitute deviance, and by applying those rules to particular people and labeling them as outsiders. From this point of view, deviance is not a quality of the act a person commits, but rather a consequence of the application of rules and sanctions to an "offender." The deviant is one to whom the label has successfully been applied; deviant behavior is behavior that people so label. (1963:9)

In labeling theory the focus is not on the causes and correlates of deviant acts but on the social and political construction of the rules defining acts as deviant and the labeling process involved in applying and enforcing those rules.

The basic thesis with regard to the laws defining criminal and delinquent conduct is that they represent the values and interests of those groups, organizations, and entrepreneurs who are able to organize resources and influence legislation. Whenever a new category of people or conduct is "criminalized" or an old one "decriminalized" we should expect, according to labeling theorists, that certain groups, organizations, or individuals were at work providing the moral entrepreneurship leading to changes in the law.

Labeling theorists challenge us to ask questions like the following: "Why is marijuana use illegal but tobacco legally available to most members of society?" "Why is alcohol use acceptable but other, less serious, forms of drug use criminalized?" "Why were status offenses included in definitions of delinquency and why are they now being separated from that category?" "Why is youth crime dramatized when the most profitable crimes involve adults?" The answers to such questions can be found by studying the people, groups, and organizations involved in the creation and change of legal categories.

Labeling theorists also direct our attention to the application of labels and argue that those who are most likely to be labeled are those who lack the resources necessary to avoid such processes. They presume that since most people have engaged in activities for which they could have been caught and processed, it is not really the offense that determines reactions but other characteristics of the offender such as race, gender, and social status.

Just as the nature of laws reflects the values and interests of people with the resources to shape legislation, the enforcement and application of laws is viewed as a reflection of power. Punishment is most certain and severe among those who lack the resources to avoid it. Thus, the labeling perspective approaches the explanation of laws and their application in much the same manner as Marxist and conflict theories (see Chapter 2).

The most unique feature of labeling theory is its emphasis on the role that legislation and law enforcement can play in perpetuating or magnifying problems at both the societal and individual levels. In considering the deviance of individuals, labeling theorists emphasize the role that organizational processing plays in *engulfment* in deviant careers. In considering deviance on a societal level, they focus on the *secondary expansion* of social problems as a result of the legal reaction to them. Arguments that processing children as delinquent has the self-fulfilling consequence of encouraging further delinquency reflect the approach of labeling theorists to individual deviance, while arguments concerning the

consequences of overcriminalization or overlegislation reflect their societal
concern. In both instances, the emphasis is on the role that law and law
enforcement can play in compounding the problems that they are intended
to solve. We will consider arguments about the general consequences of
criminalization (general labeling effects) first and then turn to arguments
and research relevant to the effects of labeling on offenders (specific labeling
effects).

Drug Legislation

An area in which labeling arguments have been particularly forceful is
with regard to the prohibition of various kinds of drugs. The view that the
criminalization of drugs contributes to the crime problem rather than
reducing it was a popular argument in the late 1960s and early 1970s and
has been revived in political debates of the late 1980s. While associated
with liberal and radical politics in the first wave, the position has been
embraced by a broad range of scholars and politicians in more recent times
(see Trebach, 1988; Inciardi, 1986). The "war on drugs" mounted by
President George Bush and Drug Czar William Bennett in the late 1980s
prompted several counterproposals to decriminalize the activity as a means
of lowering its profitability.

With regard to drug laws, Erich Goode has written that "ironically and
tragically, it is the law and its enforcement that is principally responsible
for the size of the addict population, for the recent increase in addiction,
and for a majority of the most harmful features of drug use and the drug
scene" (1972:181). However, in supporting such labeling arguments the
emphasis tends to be on the way laws and their enforcement transform
the "drug problem" *in general*, rather than on the way they affect the
specifically targeted behavior. For example, Goode summarized data that
suggested that the number of heroin addicts decreased but that addiction
in general was transformed, following the passage of the Harrison Act in
1914 and the establishment of the Bureau of Narcotics in 1930. With the
passage of the Harrison Act, over-the-counter sale of narcotic preparations
was outlawed. A deterrence theorist could legitimately argue that legislation had a general deterrent effect on heroin addiction. However, in
attacking deterrence arguments, Goode shifted the focus to addiction in
general. After noting the apparent deterrent impact of outlawing heroin,
Goode argued:

> Clearly, then, what happened as a result of the Harrison Act was not
> a diminution of a once large addict population but the appearance of
> a totally different population altogether. Far from reducing a problem,
> legislation and enforcement practices on drugs appear to have *created
> a problem* out of whole cloth. The federal laws outlawing the sale of

narcotics seem to have created three distinct groups from the existing addict population. The first of these represents the majority of the middle-class addicts, mostly women; when the supply of opium and morphine was discontinued for the nervous, distressed housewife, she eventually turned to the use of barbiturates, under the care of her physician. What the law did for this segment of the population of addicts was to take the over-the-counter narcotics away and replace them with sedatives, by prescription. *Exactly the same types of people who used narcotics in 1900 are now using barbiturates*—middle-aged, middle-class white women with various quasi-medical, largely emotional problems that (they feel) can be solved by taking a drug. The laws did absolutely nothing to terminate this class of addicts, who certainly were in the majority in 1900—they simply changed the drug to which people were addicted.

The second group created by the narcotic laws consists of those addicts who discontinued use altogether. But it is likely that this segment comprised the least addicted of the turn-of-the-century addict population. Thus the legislation probably "helped" only those who were most capable of being helped, and who constituted the least troublesome problem anyway. The third segment of the addict population constitutes the present group of "street" addicts. A certain proportion of the earlier addicts refused to discontinue the use of narcotics, and since they did not, or could not, obtain legally available drugs, they became dependent on an illegal supply and thus automatically joined the ranks of the criminal underworld.

It is obvious then, that the first half of the 1920s witnessed the dramatic emergence of a criminal class of addicts—*a criminal class that had not existed previously*. The link between addiction and crime—the view that the addict was by definition a criminal—was forged. The law itself created a new class of criminals. (1972:193-94)

In sum, the evidence mustered is not directly contrary to deterrence arguments. No data indicate that the outlawing of heroin led to an overall increase in the extent of heroin addiction. The arguments and evidence presented are more relevant to the *shaping* or *transformation* of the drug problem than to the inability of the legislation to deter the prohibited activity.

Even arguments concerning some of the secondary problems generated by the outlawing of heroin have been challenged. For instance, both Schur and Goode believed that drug legislation and law enforcement contributed to the creation of an addict subculture. Goode argued that before the passage of the Harrison Act there was "no addict subculture of any significance" and that "it was the criminalization of addiction that created addicts as a special and distinctive group" (1972:195). On the other hand, William McAuliffe argued that "there can be no doubt that there was . . . a substantial subculture of drug users" before the outlawing of heroin (1975:

225). In analyzing research published in 1928, McAuliffe found what he considered to be all the major features of a "criminal-addict subculture" *before punitive laws came into effect.* According to McAuliffe, the legislation did not cause the problem; rather, the problem developed because of the absence of controls. Thus, punitive drug laws were a response to an already existing problem. Moreover, following the passage of the Harrison Act, the prevalence of heroin addiction in some settings declined (O'Donnell, 1967).

The argument that addicts are driven to commit *secondary* forms of crime as a result of the law has been criticized as well. McAuliffe claimed that "almost all heroin addicts are deviant prior to drug dependence and are not mere victims of an innocently acquired habit and unreasonable laws" (1975: 228). James Q. Wilson argued along similar lines. He noted that we really do not know the extent to which other crimes would be affected if heroin were legalized because as many as three-fourths of known addicts have been found to have records for delinquent acts before their drug dependence. However, Wilson also noted that "heroin addiction does necessitate some degree of involvement in crime beyond that which would occur without addiction" (1975). In contrast, Greenberg and Adler (1974) have argued that criminal activity in general would be about the same regardless of addiction.

In a study of narcotic addicts admitted to the California Civil Addict Program, McGlothlin, Anglin, and Wilson (1978) found that addicts had a higher rate of property crime (both in terms of arrests and self-reports) during periods of addiction than at times when they were not using narcotics daily. In short, criminal activity does seem to be reinforced by addiction even though many addicts would have been involved in criminal activity despite their addiction. McGlothlin and his colleagues concluded that although policies that *limit* daily use of narcotics may not lead to total abstinence, they show promise of minimizing the social costs of addiction.

The Prohibition of Alcohol

Labeling theorists view laws as the outcome of activities by moral entrepreneurs and interest groups to get their point of view embodied in the law. The 1919 Volstead Act that prohibited the manufacture, sale, or transportation of liquor in the United States has been attributed to the activities of such groups as the "Anti-Saloon" League and the Women's Christian Temperance Union who were defending the values of small-town and rural Protestants against the growing urban, Catholic population. Joseph Gusfield (1963) argues that Prohibition was a "symbolic crusade" in the sense that the prohibitionist legislation symbolically reaffirmed the points of view of a threatened group of people. It did not matter whether it would work or not in addressing alcohol problems. What was important was the symbolic victory of native Protestants threatened by immigration, urbanization, and industrialization.

It is commonly believed that Prohibition failed or actually made the alcohol problem worse. This conclusion is perpetuated in criminology texts with virtually no discussion of historical evidence on the topic (e.g. Siegel, 1989: 378-79). The fact that this period is called "The Roaring Twenties" conveys the wild, carefree image of America during that time. Organized crime gained control over the supply of liquor. People made liquor at home. Illegal bars, or "speakeasies," flourished. Prohibition certainly did not stop alcohol use and transformed it in several ways.

However, it is not altogether clear that the prohibition of alcohol failed to affect the activity toward which it was directed. And, we can actually turn to a labeling theorist, Erich Goode, for a summary of evidence that Prohibition did attenuate some aspects of the "alcohol problem." Goode argues that the repeal of Prohibition was not a result of clear evidence of its failure to reduce alcohol consumption and related problems but, rather, reflected gains in political, organizational, and economic power by groups opposed to Prohibition. In short, the repeal of Prohibition was the product of yet another symbolic crusade with groups pursuing their interests and values regardless of actual evidence. Ironically, to strengthen the case for the repeal of Prohibition as a symbolic event, Goode argues that there was considerable evidence that the legislation had worked! It is ironic because in the course of defending one labeling argument, Goode supports the deterrent effects of prohibitionist legislation. He notes that estimates of alcohol consumption were lower for the Prohibition period, that alcohol-related traffic fatalities dropped, and that cirrhosis of the liver declined as well (see Figure 9-2).

While the deterrent effects of Prohibition may seem only remotely related to juvenile delinquency, it is analogies to the failures of legislation that have provided the fuel for labeling arguments. The general emphasis is on how attempts at legal control "backfire" or "boomerang." Yet, to argue that Prohibition was repealed because it did not work would imply a rational, reasonable response to reality—a position contrary to the emphasis on the symbolic, value-laden sources of legislative change. The most dramatic evidence of the "irrationality" of its repeal would be evidence that it worked. Hence, to support one labeling argument Goode inadvertently defended deterrence theory. In subsequent editions of his work Goode has recognized the implications of those findings and actually opposes legalization of many forms of illicit drugs on the grounds that the law does constrain use to some degree.

Evidence of legislation's deterrent effect on some aspects of the alcohol problem does not mean that the overall consequences of Prohibition were positive. It may have contributed to other sorts of problems. It may have

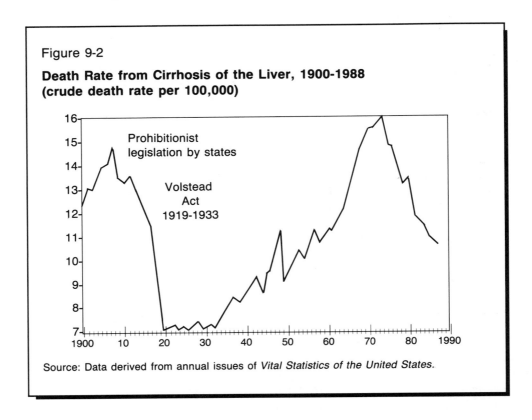

Figure 9-2

**Death Rate from Cirrhosis of the Liver, 1900-1988
(crude death rate per 100,000)**

Source: Data derived from annual issues of *Vital Statistics of the United States.*

given organized crime an economic boost. It may have led to a black market and necessitated association with all sorts of undesirable characters in order to get a drink. As we noted for drug legislation, labeling theorists require a consideration of a wide range of secondary problems that may be generated in attempts to deal with the primary one. Yet, the development of secondary problems and the transformation of the nature of problems as a result of legislation does not rule out deterrent consequences.

Specific Labeling Effects

Although it was rooted in earlier theories and some early works on crime, labeling theory emerged in the 1960s as a critique of the official processing of several forms of deviance. According to labeling theorists, socio-legal categories or "typifications" such as "delinquent," "retarded," or "mentally ill" are applied to only a fraction of the people to whom they could be applied (generally, those without the resources to resist such labeling). Those to whom such labels are applied are reacted to by others in terms of the label and are gradually "engulfed" in deviant roles. In the words of one of the earliest labeling theorists, "the person becomes the thing he is described as being" (1938:20).

Edwin Lemert (1967), one of the major figures in the development of the labeling perspective, introduced a distinction between *primary deviance* and *secondary deviance* to distinguish between the initial acts of rule-breaking which can result in labeling and acts which reflect acceptance of a deviant role, identity, or career. One means by which primary deviance is transformed into secondary deviance is through labeling. While initially a youth might engage in a series of deviant acts which have little meaning ("I was just having fun," "We were just fooling around," etc.), the process of being caught and labeled can dramatize those events and the "roles" or "identities" associated with them. When those activities become a reflection of a career or acceptance of a particular role, then future rule-breaking takes on new meaning and is called secondary deviance. Labeling theorists have been interested primarily in describing and explaining the creation of secondary deviance and the labeling process is central to their explanation. The emphasis in the study of juvenile delinquency has been on the consequences of labeling for youth who are labeled.

Juvenile Justice and Labeling

The earliest statement of a labeling argument specifically relating to juvenile delinquency appeared in Frank Tannenbaum's *Crime and the Community* (1938). Tannenbaum argued that the tagging and processing of the young delinquent was a "dramatization of evil" that had self-fulfilling consequences:

> The process of making the criminal, therefore, is a process of tagging, defining, identifying, segregating, describing, emphasizing, making conscious and self-conscious; it becomes a way of stimulating, suggesting, emphasizing, and evoking the very traits that are complained of. If the theory of relation of responses to stimulus has any meaning, the entire process of dealing with the young delinquent is mischievous in so far as it identifies him to himself or to the environment as a delinquent person.

> The person becomes the thing he is described as being. Nor does it seem to matter whether the valuation is made by those who would punish or by those who would reform. In either case the emphasis is upon the conduct that is disapproved of. The parents or the policemen, the older brother or the court, the probation officer or the juvenile institution, in so far as they rest upon the thing complained of, rest upon a false ground. Their very enthusiasm defeats their aim. The harder they work to reform the evil, the greater the evil grows under their hands. The persistent

suggestion, with whatever good intentions, works mischief, because it leads to bringing out the bad behavior that it would suppress. The way out is through a refusal to dramatize the evil. The less said about it the better. The more said about something else, still better. (1938:19-20)

This line of argument has been extended to deviance in general (see Lemert, 1967) and to a variety of specific types of deviance (for example, mental illness). However, the basic logic is the same in each instance: official processing results in the application of labels to which others react in such a manner that they propel those so labeled into careers of crime and delinquency.

Since the juvenile court does not adjudicate criminal matters, discussions of criminal labeling do not technically concern juvenile delinquents. Nonetheless, it has been the labeling theorists who have mounted the most vociferous criticisms of juvenile justice in the United States. Although the juvenile court was initially conceived as an experiment in the decriminalization of juvenile lawbreaking, labeling theorists tend to view the actual changes that the court has wrought as minimal. Schur has argued that despite the terminology employed in juvenile justice, the "adjudicated delinquent is in fact stigmatized, punished, and potentially criminalized" (1973:87). The focus in this statement, however, is on how being processed through the juvenile justice system affects the individual juvenile. This specific focus is in contrast to the labeling theorists' concern over the more general effects of drug legislation and consensual crimes. The labeling theorists' major criticism of the juvenile court has been the alleged impact of adjudication on those processed through the system, or what we call *specific labeling* (in contrast to *specific deterrence*).

Ideas about the general labeling effects of juvenile law and its enforcement are only hinted at in the literature. For example, the broad scope of juvenile delinquency statutes might promote a view among adolescents in general that laws are totally arbitrary and deserving of little respect. This possibility is suggested by Schur's argument that increased clarity, precision, and limits on the legal compass of juvenile law and juvenile court jurisdiction "would probably generate among young people greater respect for the legal system" (1973: 169). An implicit assumption underlying such a statement is that juvenile law and its enforcement may have consequences for the attitudes of the juvenile population in general and not just for those who directly experience the system.

Research on the Specific Effects of Labeling

As we have just noted, the labeling theorists' major criticism of juvenile justice has been the possible deleterious consequences of official processing and adjudication for those juveniles who are netted by the system. In this view, juvenile processing does not deter further delinquency through fear of further apprehension and processing, nor does it prevent additional delinquency through rehabilitation of the offender. Rather, the labeling critique has emphasized the role that the juvenile justice system may play in facilitating further delinquent or criminal behavior.

In this section we will consider research that has focused on the consequences of official processing for future behavior and adolescent self-images. The latter topic is of most significance to the labeling theorists since they are interested in deviant behavior that represents or reflects a person's identity or self-image. A behaviorist would be most interested in the consequences of official processing for future *behavior* and would not feel it necessary to consider the effects of labeling on identity or self-image (see Chapter 5). These topics would be viewed by the behaviorist as hypothetical mental constructs that contribute little or nothing to understanding actual behavior. Most labeling theorists would find the focus on the consequences of official processing for subsequent rates of crime and delinquency as *relevant* to labeling theory but not necessarily *crucial*. From a labeling perspective, Edwin Schur has argued that sociologists have been challenged to study the self-concept of the deviating individual as a crucial dependent variable "to which we should pay more attention than to the deviating behavior itself" (1969b:311). Of course, the value of such a viewpoint depends on the theoretical inclinations of different publics, and certainly a behaviorist would not find such an emphasis crucial. Recognizing that there are divergent points of view, we will consider research on attitudes and self-conceptions, as well as future behavior. First, however, we will consider research that has attempted to determine whether official processing of juveniles has a specific deterrent or a specific labeling effect.

Specific Deterrence vs. Specific Labeling

How can we tell if official processing by the juvenile justice system increases involvement in crime and delinquency? One answer might be to determine the relationship between adult crime and juvenile delinquency. Why not just look at the proportion of juveniles with a records who go on to acquire a record as adults? For instance, in a study of males and females born in 1949, Shannon (1976) reported the following progression of contacts with the police: of 677 white males, about 61 percent (414) acquired a record between the ages of six and eighteen. Of those 414, 326 acquired a record after age eighteen. In sum, of those white males labeled as juveniles, around 78 percent acquired a subsequent record. In contrast, of the white males who did *not* acquire a juvenile record, about 50 percent acquired a record as an adult. Thus, those labeled as delinquent as youths were more likely than those not so labeled to acquire records when they were older. *One* possible conclusion based on such a difference is that labeling when young increases the chances that further delinquent or criminal acts will be committed in the future.

However, there are other possible explanations. We have already encountered a number of social characteristics, experiences, and attitudes that are correlated with juvenile delinquency. These characteristics may account for involvement in lawbreaking activity over a period of time. Thus, a high-risk youth at age thirteen may remain a high-risk person at eighteen, twenty-one, and beyond, whether or not he or she is caught and labeled. In short, such a finding does not tell us whether the *labeling experience* increases the probability of future crime.

The scientifically ideal methodological procedure for assessing whether official processing of juveniles increases involvement in crime or delinquency would be an experiment in which youths were ignored or processed on a random basis. Under the right circumstances, the groups would be nearly the same on every conceivable characteristic *except* the one under experimental control (that is, being processed or labeled). Since such experiments are legitimately challenged on ethical grounds, the alternative is to examine the relationship between labeling and future delinquency among youths who are as similar as possible in terms of other characteristics. This procedure involves comparing "matched pairs" and was the basis for Martin Gold and Jay William's study of "the aftermath of apprehension" (1969). Gold and William's data included self-reports of delinquent activity, as well as police and court records. On this basis, they were able to compare youths involved in delinquency who had been caught with youths who had not been caught. Out of 847 cases, 74 youths had been apprehended. Gold and Williams were able to match 35 of these cases with boys who had committed similar offenses and who had other similar characteristics, but who had not been apprehended. Of the 35 pairs, apprehended youth had a higher subsequent delinquent involvement than the nonapprehended youth in 20 comparisons. On the other hand, in 10 comparisons the youth who had been apprehended reported *less* involvement than the nonapprehended youth, and 5 pairs exhibited comparable involvement. The data are contrary to the view that apprehension reduces the chances of further delinquency and suggest that the opposite may be a more likely occurrence.

David Farrington reports similar results for working-class boys in London (1977). Farrington studied boys with similar degrees of involvement in delinquency at age 14 and examined the delinquency scores at age 18 for youths who had been determined guilty in court compared to youths who had not appeared in court. The delinquency of those labeled was greater by age 18 while delinquency had decreased for those not labeled. He could not find any other characteristic that would account for this difference other than the labeling experience itself.

Lloyd Klemke (1978) attempted to determine whether apprehension for shoplifting amplified shoplifting, as suggested by labeling theory, or terminated shoplifting, as suggested by deterrence theory. Among high school students he found that there were very few significant relationships between apprehension by store personnel or parents and shoplifting activity, although relationships were consistently in the direction suggesting higher rates for those caught than those not caught. Similarly, youth who were referred to the police had higher rates than those who were dealt with less formally. However, these results were statistically insignificant as well. Moreover, Klemke acknowledges that some of the shoplifting activity he measured could have occurred before youths were apprehended. There were also no controls for variables that might make the relationship spurious (i.e. variables related to the frequency of shoplifting and the chances of getting caught).

While these studies are typically cited as support for the labeling perspective, their meaning is actually quite ambiguous. For example, if the reason the youths who were caught had a higher subsequent rate of involvement in delinquency was because they realized that nothing much happened after being caught, then the results could support deterrence theory. In contrast, if the experience increased subsequent delinquency by decreasing other opportunities, increasing association with other labeled youth, stigmatizing the youth, or leading to further social rejection, then the results could support labeling theory. Without evidence concerning the mediating processes or mechanisms affecting future behavior, the results could support either point of view.

In contrast to research in which one set of youths had experienced a legal reaction and the other set had experienced none, most of the research cited as relevant to labeling focuses on the effects of *different reactions* to crime. For example, comparisons have been made between juveniles who received a court hearing and those who were released short of any formal procedure (Meade, 1974). Other studies have compared youths who became wards of the court with youths who did not (McEachern, 1968). Thornberry (1971) analyzed the subsequent offense records of youths in terms of the degree of severity of the dispositions they originally had received. In the study of deterrence, these comparisons would be viewed as relevant to establishing the *marginal deterrent efficacy* of a reaction to delinquency since the comparison is between or among *different possible reactions* (Gibbs, 1975:33). When assessing marginal deterrent effects, the question is what "margin" of delinquency is deterred by a particular reaction beyond that which would occur given an alternative reaction. Similarly, studies of different reactions cited as relevant to labeling theory are really dealing with *marginal labeling effects* (in that these studies attempt to determine the extent to which a more severe reaction leads to a higher subsequent rate of delinquency). Actually, the topics dealt with in the next two chapters (alternative reactions, imprisonment, "scared straight," diversion, and restitution) are all potentially relevant to issues of labeling effects and specific deterrence. In the remainder of this section, we will deal with research that has been cited or presented as relevant to labeling theory or that has been couched in labeling terms.

Labeling and Future Behavior

The three studies of marginal labeling effects previously mentioned (Meade, McEachern, and Thornberry) have generated findings that are both consistent and inconsistent with labeling arguments. For example, in a study of over two thousand youths in eight California counties, McEachern (1968) reported that those who were made wards of the court showed *less* subsequent involvement in delinquency than those dealt with less severely, but those probationers who had the most contact with their probation officers had the highest rates of subsequently detected offenses. The latter finding could mean that the risk of *detection* increases as contact with probation officers increases. Thus, the finding may not be evidence of a labeling effect. Thornberry's study (1971) of the delinquent careers of all boys born in Philadelphia in 1945 yielded similar equivocal results. He found that youth who had been institutionalized had a lower subsequent volume of delinquency and lesser involvement in terms of seriousness of the offenses committed than youth who had not been institutionalized. On the other hand, measures of the severity of disposition were associated with a *higher* volume of delinquency for *some* offenders. It was among the white youths and the less serious offenders that severity of reaction was associated with higher subsequent delinquency. Finally, Meade's research (1974) indicated that youths who faced a court hearing had higher subsequent rates of detected delinquency than those dealt with less formally.

These results are so variable that we cannot reach a firm conclusion about the effect of labeling. Moreover, the findings are not clearly relevant to labeling theory to begin with, since they focus on alternative reactions *after* initial apprehension and labeling. In addition, studies that focus on subsequent delinquent activity *that is detected* (that is, "recidivism" rates derived from police data) do not have a clear bearing on the effects of labeling on *actual* subsequent behavior. As we will discover in Chapter 10, some experimental programs appear to have low recidivism rates compared to the recidivism rates of available alternatives. The lower rates may reflect the unwillingness of more tolerant probation officers to officially recognize a subsequent offense for youths in an experimental program.

Recidivism rates may therefore not be accurate reflections of actual delinquent behavior. Thus, the results of recidivism research can be given a number of alternative interpretations that have little to do with either labeling or deterrence effects.

Labeling and Adolescent Attitudes and Self-Images

Another line of research relevant to labeling and delinquency has focused on the consequences of labeling in a youth's social environment or the potential impact of labeling on values, commitments, or self-images. The results of this type of research have been both consistent and inconsistent with labeling notions. For example, Foster, Dinitz, and Reckless (1972) interviewed boys in trouble with the law and found that very few perceived that their predicaments had generated any difficulties with family or friends. Sethard Fisher (1972) examined the school grade-point averages of probationers before and after being processed and found no demonstrable effect of that experience on school grades. Probationers were found to have lower grades on the average than other students both *before and after* acquiring that legal status.

David Matza (1964) has argued that violation of the commonly held expectations of adjudication gives rise to a "sense of injustice" and that sense of injustice in turn weakens "the bind of the law." In Matza's view, the actual operation of the juvenile court regularly violates "norms of fairness" or "due process," which confirms the delinquent's "conception of irresponsibility and feeds his sense of injustice."

Peggy Giordano (1976) has attempted to test such arguments in a study of juvenile reactions to the justice system. She interviewed youths who had 1) been reprimanded by the police and released, 2) proceeded as far as an intake hearing, 3) been placed on probation, 4) been placed on probation at least twice, or 5) had not been processed by the justice system at all. She found no significant difference in attitudes or behavior between the group with no contact and the contact groups. Among youths who had had some contact, the extent of system contact made no difference for attitudes toward police but was associated with positive attitudes toward probation officers and judges. Youths with more extensive contact judged police, probation officers, and judges as less "effective" than did those with less contact. However, there was no evidence that contact or adjudication generated a sense of injustice.

In contrast, in the study of working-class boys in London, Farrington and his colleagues (1978) found that hostility towards the police increased after conviction. Since they were able to examine attitudes before and after conviction as well as compare these boys with the nonlabeled youths at different points in time, their results are more meaningful than studies that compare youths with different degrees of labeling using data gathered after the experience alone (e.g. Giordano's study). The British research supports Matza's argument.

Jensen (1972) examined the self-images of youths with police records and those without and found that the relationship was quite variable in different categories of junior and senior high school students. Among black males who had police records for one offense or two or more offenses, about 47 percent at least sometimes thought of themselves as delinquent, compared to 56 percent of the white males with a record for one offense and 72 percent of the white males with a record for two or more offenses. Among both blacks and whites, about one-third of those without records at least sometimes thought of themselves as delinquent. Thus, in both groups, those with a record were more likely to think of themselves in terms of the label. However, the biggest differences between the labeled and unlabeled occurred among whites. Jensen also found that labeling differentiated most among youths who held fairly positive attitudes toward the law. His analysis was consistent with an earlier study by Leroy Gould (1969) in which he argued that if the label "delinquent" or "troublemaker" is commonly applied to a particular group, then the labeling process may have little personal relevance.

Ageton and Elliott (1974) improved upon Jensen's study by examining changes in attitudes over time and by limiting their analysis to subjects who had no contacts with the police or court at the beginning of the study. They found that respondents with subsequent police contacts demonstrated "substantial" gains in measures of delinquent orientations as compared to respondents who had no such subsequent contacts. Moreover, neither controls for self-reported delinquency nor controls for delinquent friends altered this finding. However, further analysis revealed that police contact was related to increased delinquent orientations only for white youth. Thus, two separate studies based on large random samples of populations have yielded quite similar observations: labeling may be more consequential for whites than for blacks.

John Hepburn (1977) gathered data from two samples: 1) 105 white males (aged 14 to 17) with no record of police contact who were randomly selected from school enrollments, and 2) 96 white males (aged 14 to 17) who had had formal contact with the municipal police. Hepburn found that official intervention was not significantly related to self-concept variables when other variables, such as self-reported delinquency, were taken into account. On the other hand, some measures of official intervention did have an impact on respondents' predictions of future delinquency, measures of "commitment to delinquent others," and attitudes toward the police. Hepburn suggested that the relationships between official intervention and measures of "self-satisfaction" or "delinquent identification" are spurious. He argued that the greater the involvement in delinquency, the greater the chances of being labeled and of developing a delinquent identity. However, according to Hepburn, official labeling or intervention itself has no impact on delinquent identity.

Once again, we are confronted with some consistent and some divergent findings. Data from Hepburn's study, as well as from Ageton and Elliott's, suggest that labeling affects the development of delinquent value orientations. The studies by Jensen, Ageton and Elliott, and Thornberry (1971) suggest that labeling effects are more prominent for whites than for blacks. However, Hepburn found a spurious relationship between official intervention and measures of delinquent identity, whereas Jensen implied that official intervention did affect the degree to which an adolescent viewed himself in terms of the label.

The inconsistency may reflect differences in the samples studied by the researchers. Jensen (1980) found that youths who acquired a record were more likely to express delinquent self-evaluations than those without police records, even when the variable of self-reported delinquent behavior was controlled. Hepburn found that official intervention had no impact when self-reported delinquency was taken into account. However, Hepburn's sample was purposely designed to overrepresent delinquents with records. Jensen's sample included only those officially recorded delinquents who happened to be included in a representative sample of the junior and senior high school populations in the area studied. In short, Hepburn's sample included more labeled delinquents than Jensen's, and possibly more heavily involved delinquents as well. If labeling has different consequences depending on the extent to which the sample is involved in delinquency, then the apparently disparate findings of these two studies could be reconciled. In a further analysis of the issue, Jensen found that the differences in delinquent self-evaluations between the labeled and unlabeled are very slight among youths who report having committed several delinquent acts. However, among adolescents who are less involved in delinquency, differences between the labeled and unlabeled are more prominent. Along similar lines, Farrington (1977) reports that while convictions prior to age 14 increased delinquency, subsequent convictions did not intensify the difference. In view of such findings and those outlined previously, it appears that the effects of labeling may be quite variable from one group or setting to another.

Strengths and Weaknesses of Labeling Theory

Throughout this summary we have referred to labeling as a "theory" and discussed it in contrast to deterrence theory. Deterrence theorists argue that variations and changes in the perceived risks of legal punishment will affect the probabilities of subsequent criminal and delinquent behavior.

In contrast, labeling theorists generally claim that official reactions intended to inhibit delinquency "may" have the opposite effect. It is virtually impossible to falsify a claim that official reactions "may" propel youths into delinquent careers. Conceivably, the vast majority of youths might go straight the remainder of their lives after being caught, processed, and labeled, and the statement would not be falsified. If translated into a more definitive claim such as "youths who spend time in detention will engage in more delinquent activity after that experience than they did prior to it," then the findings that would falsify or support the statement are clearer. Thus, while labeling theory helped "sensitize" the justice system to the potential harm of certain types of negative labeling, it did not develop into a set of testable propositions to be pitted against deterrence theory or other sociological theories.

Labeling theory stimulated study of the invention, application, and consequences of legal labels and sanctions. However, it did not pay much attention to variations in primary deviance. In fact, that is why we did not deal with it as a theory of delinquent behavior in Chapter 6. All of the theories in that chapter assume that there are real variations in behavior that are not mere artifacts of discrimination in labeling. All assume that rates of primary and secondary deviance are patterned and that there are significant behavioral differences between delinquent and nondelinquent youth both before and after labeling and the research summarized in Chapters 6, 7, and 8 support that view.

In Chapter 3 we summarized the literature on the role of extra-legal variables on official labeling. That literature suggests that the frequency and seriousness of delinquent activity are primary determinants of labeling but that there are some differences by social background. Thus, labeling is not as arbitrary and discriminatory as claimed by labeling theorists. On the other hand, the data do not allow the dismissal of charges of bias. Unexplained differences by social background appear often enough to warrant continued investigation.

Finally, the labeling theorist's arguments may no longer apply to juvenile justice in numerous jurisdictions, partly because practitioners have become sensitive to negative labeling. Many of the treatment and prevention programs we will consider in subsequent chapters attempt to build positive self-images and to counter the types of negative labeling stressed by the theory. Some programs for treating drug and alcohol abuse actually include acceptance of a label as a first step in treatment. For example, in Alcoholics Anonymous admission that one is an alcoholic is viewed as a crucial step toward rehabilitation. However, in the process the meaning of the label is changed and it carries with it group beliefs that the individual can gain control of the problem. Such programs are actually trying to change the meaning of labels in positive directions. However, labeling theory suggests that even programs which attempt to avoid dramatizing evil have to be wary of self-fulfilling prophecies and to assess whether acceptance of modified labels has positive or negative consequences. Enough programs have "boomeranged" to warrant continued concern about such prospects.

The Social Meaning of Sanctions

The observation that labeling and sanctions may reinforce, deter, or make no difference for subsequent behavior or self-images has stimulated theoretical attempts to specify the conditions under which sanctions or labels may have different consequences. For instance, Bernard Thorsell and Lloyd Klemke (1972) argued that the labeling process may be both a reinforcement and a deterrent. Its positive and negative consequences for future behavior depend upon several conditions that have yet to be studied. In addition to the stage in a person's deviant career when labels are applied, these conditions include: 1) whether the label is confidential, 2) whether the person labeled cares about or acknowledges the legitimacy or authority of the labeler, 3) whether the label can be easily removed, and 4) whether official labels generate a negative social response.

Other theorists (for example, Tittle, 1975) have attempted to develop comparable lists of factors that might improve our knowledge of the conditions under which sanctions have different effects. However, very little research has been done in this area. We have seen evidence that perceived threat of punishment may deter some types of offenses more than it does others, but that observation is the only specification suggested thus far in research literature. The fact of the matter is that we know very little about such seemingly simple (but, in reality, complex) issues as the actual meaning of the labeling process or the threat of labeling to juveniles.

Eckland-Olson, Lieb, and Zurcher report that the relationship between perceived threat and behavior is exceedingly complex and depends on interpersonal relationships and a host of situational factors. For example, they propose that "persons rich in associations will fear sanctions more than loners, and those who expect that after a sanction their friends and associates will treat them as before will fear that sanction less than those who expect to be shunned" (1984: 160). Based on field observations and interviews of drug dealers, the researchers found that fear of sanctions led drug dealers to restrict their network of relationships. This closure also decreased their opportunities to supply drugs. In this instance, fear of punishment inhibited criminal activity but not directly through fear-related avoidance of the behavior. Rather, restricted interpersonal relationships limited the market for drug dealing. The impact of feared sanctions was mediated by social relationships.

In research carried out among high school students in southern Arizona (Jensen and Erickson, 1978), students were asked to imagine that they had been caught and taken to juvenile court. They were then asked how much each of the following would worry them (to which response categories were "definitely yes," "probably yes," "uncertain," "probably not," and "definitely not"): 1) the police might hurt you, 2) the judge might send you to a reformatory, 3) the judge might put you on probation, 4) how your parents might react, 5) a delinquent record might keep you out of college, 6) a record might keep you from getting a good job, 7) other teenagers might think badly of you, 8) your teachers might think badly of you, 9) you might think badly of yourself.

Figure 9-3 reports the average percentage of students in six Arizona high schools who indicated they would probably or definitely worry about each of these nine potential consequences. Nearly all the students indicated they would worry about their parents' reaction, and 83 percent indicated they would worry about a record keeping them from getting a good job. Sixty-nine percent would worry about a record keeping them out of college. It

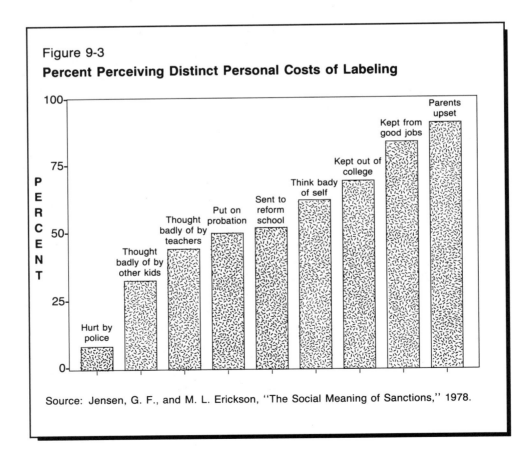

Figure 9-3
Percent Perceiving Distinct Personal Costs of Labeling

Source: Jensen, G. F., and M. L. Erickson, "The Social Meaning of Sanctions," 1978.

was quite common for students to indicate they might "think badly" of themselves. Relatively few students (34 percent) worried about the reactions of peers, and the least concern was expressed over the possibility of being hurt by the police. With regard to the reactions of significant reference persons or groups, parental reaction was of more concern than either teacher reaction or the reactions of other teenagers.

Jensen and Erickson report some interesting variations in these perceived ramifications of labeling. For each of the nine concerns, females were found to be significantly more concerned than males. Girls were especially more concerned than boys over parental reaction and over the possibility that they might think badly of themselves. Similarly, youths who wanted to go to college were obviously more concerned about jeopardizing their plans than were those who did not plan to go to college. Students who were doing well in school worried more about teacher reaction than students who were not faring well. Students with delinquent friends worried less about the reactions of other teenagers than did students with no delinquent friends. In short, the nature and degree of concern about the possible ramifications of labeling is related to a person's attachments, commitments, and beliefs. Furthermore, the study indicated that those who are not worried about such costs are the most likely to commit delinquent acts.

What relevance do such observations have for labeling and deterrence among juveniles? For one thing, it appears that those who anticipate stigmatic consequences as a result of official labeling are the least likely to engage in behavior that is liable to labeling. In contrast, those most likely to commit delinquent acts are those for whom labeling may be socially meaningless. Similarly, those most likely to be *persistently* or *repeatedly* involved in delinquency are the very youths for whom labeling or official processing generates relatively little concern. If this interpretation is correct, then we would expect that official labeling would *neither* specifically deter *nor* reinforce involvement in delinquency but would instead be a rather meaningless experience. Labeling does not constitute a "dramatization of evil" when there is no audience, no drama, and no shared definition of evil. Thus, if a study of the effects of labeling is based on a sample that includes a sizable proportion of youths who accord little significance to official labels, the application of labels is likely to be of little consequence in the study. On the other hand, a sample that includes youths who accord legitimacy to official labels might find the experience traumatic and stigmatizing. Moreover, those who find the experience stigmatizing might actually be deterred from further delinquency to avoid further stigmatization.

The study of the social meaning of sanctions suggests a possible labeling paradox: those most likely to be affected by labels are those least likely to do things that make them liable to labeling; those who do accord stigmatic significance to labels but become the victims of labeling are likely to refrain from further acts to avoid further stigmatization. Such speculation does not rule out the possibility of labeling effects. For example, if a delinquent record is a source of status or reputation in a particular group or social setting, then labeling could lead to an increase in delinquent behavior through processes of social reinforcement. Similarly, if the labeling experience undermines tenuous "stakes in conformity," or becomes the "last straw" for already shaky bonds between a youth and parents or school, then it could increase the chances of further violations.

The study of the social meaning of sanctions may provide clues as to why some categories of youth are less likely than others to go on to adult crime. For example, the study of delinquent and criminal careers mentioned earlier (Shannon, 1976) revealed that 78 percent of white males who acquired records before age 18 acquired a record after that age. About 48 percent of the white females who had been labeled as juveniles subsequently acquired records as adults. Thus, the majority of white girls who were labeled did *not* go on to acquire records as adults. Why are girls less likely to acquire subsequent records than boys? As we noted earlier, the answer may have nothing to do with labeling or deterrent effects, but the hypothesis that females are more likely than males to be deterred by labeling is at least tenable. At the very minimum, we should be studying the variable meaning of sanctions or labels in different groups as the possible source of answers concerning the effects of different reactions to delinquency.

Jensen and Erickson's findings regarding the meaning of the labeling process for high school students are also relevant to the study of general deterrence and to some of the sociological positions taken on that issue. At the beginning of this chapter, we cited Edwin Sutherland's claim from more than half a century ago that "not the fear of legal penalties but the fear of loss of status in the group is the effective deterrent." For adolescents, that statement should be revised: Apprehension, adjudication, and legal penalties are feared most when they are perceived to entail loss of status, opportunity, and self-respect. Fear of loss of status and loss of opportunity are important barriers to delinquency. It is when such losses are perceived to result from being caught and labeled that the justice system may have its greatest impact.

Summary

In this chapter we examined labeling theory and deterrence theory — two divergent points of view about the impact of the law on the social problems that the law is intended to solve. From a deterrence perspective, the criminalization of an activity is supposed to reduce the involvement of those punished (specific deterrence) and inhibit involvement in the rest of the populace (general deterrence). Labeling theorists have challenged such notions, arguing that criminalization can transform minor problems into major ones by creating new dimensions of the problem (general labeling effects) and by increasing the criminal involvement of those labeled or punished (specific labeling effects).

Research on issues of general deterrence has progressed from the study of capital punishment to the study of the relationship between perceived risk of punishment and self-reported delinquent behavior to field observation and experiments. At present, there is still no evidence that capital punishment has a general deterrent impact on criminal homicide or on other capital crimes. However, research of several different types (laboratory, field, and natural experiments; analysis of police, court, and corrections statistics for states; and survey studies) has tended to support the conclusion that the greater the threat of punishment for crime and delinquency, the lower the involvement in crime and delinquency. Several issues concerning that relationship (causal order, spuriousness, variations by offense, mediating or intervening processes) have yet to be resolved. However, there is evidence of an *association* of the type predicted by the deterrence perspective.

Labeling theorists are often unclear about whether the law and its enforcement increase the magnitude of the specific activity toward which they are directed or add new dimensions to the total problem. Their arguments seem to apply best to the latter possibility, although even arguments about the secondary effects of drug legislation have been challenged by critics of the labeling perspective. Since arguments about secondary effects are often matters of historical conjecture based on impressionistic evidence, we may never arrive at a resolution to the debate. We can say that there is evidence that property crime is greater for narcotic addicts than for nonaddicts and that it is greater during periods of daily narcotics use than at other times. It appears that addiction reinforces criminal involvement, although many addicts would have been involved despite their addiction. However, the larger issues of the impact of the law and its enforcement on the total crime problem, the delinquency problem, and even problems involving so-called victimless crimes are still subject to debate.

The situation is comparably complex and confusing when we consider issues of specific deterrence versus specific labeling effects. There are bits and pieces of research consistent with both arguments. Clarification of the impact of labeling may evolve from greater attention to a variety of issues concerning the social meaning of sanctions. Both labeling theorists and deterrence theorists have suggested that the consequences of labeling vary depending on characteristics of the authority applying labels, the meaning of such experiences in the social world of different youths, and a variety of other circumstances that shape the relevance of legal sanctions in different environments.

References

Ageton, S. S., and D. S. Elliott. 1974. "The Effects of Legal Processing on Delinquent Orientations." *Social Problems* 22 (October):87-100.

Andenaes, J. 1971. "Deterrence and Specific Offenses." *University of Chicago Law Review* 38:537-53.

Atunes, G., and L. Hunt. 1973. "The Impact of Certainty and Severity of Punishment on Levels of Crime in American States: An Extended Analysis." *Journal of Criminal Law and Criminology* 64 (4):486-93.

Bailey, W. C., and R. P. Lott. 1976. "Crime, Punishment and Personality: An Examination of the Deterrence Question." *Journal of Criminal Law and Criminology* 67 (March):99-109.

Bailey, W. C., and R. Peterson. 1989. "Murder and Capital Punishment: A Monthly Time-Series Analysis of Execution Publicity." *American Sociological Review* 54 (October): 722-43.

Bailey, W. C. 1990. "Murder, Capital Punishment, and Television: Execution Publicity and Homicide Rates." *American Sociological Review* 55: 628-33.

Beccaria, C. 1767. *On Crimes and Punishments.* Translated (1963) by Henry Paolucci. Indianapolis, IN: Bobbs-Merrill.

Becker, H. 1963. *Outsiders.* New York: Macmillan.

Block, M., F. Nold, and J. Sidak. 1981. "The Deterrent Effect of Anti-Trust Enforcement." *Journal of Political Economy* 89: 429-45.

Bowers, W. J. 1974. *Executions in America.* Lexington, MA: D.C. Heath.

Bowers, W. J., G. Pierce, and J. McDevitt. 1984. *Legal Homicide: Death as Punishment in America, 1864-1982.* Boston: Northeastern University Press.

Bowker, L. 1981. "Crime and the Use of Prisons in the United States: A Times Series Analysis." *Crime and Delinquency* 27(2): 206-12.

Braithwaite, J., and G. Geis. 1982. "On Theory and Action for Corporate Crime Control." *Crime and Delinquency* 28: 292-314.

Chambliss, W. T. 1967. "Types of Deviance and Effectiveness of Legal Sanctions." *Wisconsin Law Review* (Summer):703-19.

Davis, E. 1973. "Victimless Crime: The Case for Continued Enforcement." *Police Science and Administration* 1:11-20.

Eckland-Olson, S., J. Lieb, and L. Zurcher. 1984. "The Paradoxical Impact of Criminal Sanctions: Some Microstructural Findings." *Law and Society Review* 18: 159-78.

Ehrlich, I. 1975. "The Deterrent Effect of Capital Punishment: A Question of Life and Death." *American Economic Review* 65:397

Erickson, M. L., J. P. Gibbs, and G. F. Jensen. 1977. "Deterrence and the Perceived Certainty of Legal Punishment." *American Sociological Review* 42 (April):305-17.

Farrington, D. P. 1977. "The Effects of Public Labelling." *British Journal of Criminology* 17: 112-25.

Fisher, S. 1972. "Stigma and Deviant Careers in School." *Social Problems* 20 (Summer):78-83.

Forst, B. 1976. "The Deterrent Effect of Capital Punishment: A Cross-State Analysis of the 1960s." Mimeographed.

Foster, J. D., S. Dinitz, and W. C. Reckless. 1972. "Perceptions of Stigma Following Public Intervention for Delinquent Behavior." *Social Problems* 20 (Fall):202-09.

Geerken, M., and W.R. Gove. 1977. "Deterrence, Overload and Incapacitation: An Empirical Evaluation." *Social Forces* 56 (December):424-47.

Gibbs, J. P. 1968. "Crime, Punishment and Deterrence." *Southwestern Social Science Quarterly* 48 (March):515-30.

_____. 1975. *Crime, Punishment and Deterrence.* New York: Elsevier.

_____. 1986. "Deterrence Theory and Research." In G. Metton (ed.), *Law as a Behavioral Instrument.* Lincoln, NE: University of Nebraska Press.

Giordano, P. C. 1976. "The Sense of Injustice: An Analysis of Juveniles' Reactions to the Justice System." *Criminology* 14 (May):93-112.

Gold, M. 1970. *Delinquent Behavior in an American City.* Belmont, CA: Brooks/Cole.

Gold, M., and J. R. Williams. 1969. "National Study of the Aftermath of Apprehension." *Prospectus* 3:3.

Goode, E. 1972. *Drugs in American Society.* New York: Alfred A. Knopf.

_____. 1978. *Deviant Behavior: An Interactionist Approach.* Engelwood Cliffs, NJ: Prentice-Hall.

_____. 1989. *Deviant Behavior: An Interactionist Approach.* Engelwood Cliffs, NJ: Prentice-Hall.

Gould, L. C. 1969. "Who Defines Delinquency?: A Comparison of Self-Reported and Officially Reported Indices of Delinquency for Three Racial Groups." *Social Problems* 16 (Winter):325-36.

Grasmick, H. G., and H. Milligan, Jr. 1976. "Deterrence Theory Approach to Socioeconomic Demographic Correlates of Crime." *Social Science Quarterly* 57 (December):608-17

Grasmick, H. G., and D. Green. 1980. "Legal Punishment, Social Disapproval and Internalization as Inhibitors of Illegal Behavior." *Journal of Criminal Law and Criminology.* 71: 325-335.

Green, G. S. 1985. "General Deterrence and Television Cable Crime: A Field Experiment in Social Control." *Criminology* 23 (November): 629-45.

Greenberg, D. F., and R. C. Kessler. 1982. "The Effects of Arrest on Crime: A Multivariate Panel Analysis." *Social Problems* 60 (March): 771-90.

Greenberg, S. W., and F. Adler. 1974. "Crime and Addiction: An Empirical Analysis of the Literature, 1920-1973." *Contemporary Drug Problems* 3:221-69.

Gusfield, J. R. 1963. *Symbolic Crusade: Status Politics and the American Temperance Movement.* Urbana: University of Illinois.

Hepburn, J. R. 1977. "The Impact of Police Intervention upon Juvenile Delinquents." *Criminology* 15 (August):235-62.

Inciardi, J. 1986. *The War on Drugs.* Palo Alto, CA: Mayfield Publishing Company.

Jensen, G. F. 1969. "'Crime Doesn't Pay': Correlates of a Shared Misunderstanding." *Social Problems* 17 (Fall):189-201.

_____. 1972. "Delinquency and Adolescent Self-Conceptions: A Study of the Personal Relevance of Infraction." *Social Problems* 20 (Summer):84-103.

_____. 1980. "Labeling and Identity: Toward a Reconciliation of Divergent Findings." *Criminology* 18: 121-29.

Jensen, G. F., and M. L. Erickson. 1978. "The Social Meaning of Sanctions." In M. Krohn and R. Akers (eds.), *Crime, Law and Sanctions: Theoretical Perspectives*. Beverly Hills, CA: Sage.

Jensen, G. F., M. L. Erickson, and J. P. Gibbs. 1978. "Perceived Risk of Punishment and Self-Reported Delinquency." *Social Forces* 57 (September):57-78.

Jensen, G. F., and B. G. Stitt. 1982. "Words and Misdeeds." In J. Hagan (ed.), *Deterrence Reconsidered*. Beverly Hills, CA: Sage Publications.

Klemke, L. W. 1978. "Does Apprehension for Shoplifting Amplify or Terminate Shoplifting Activity?" *Law and Society Review* 12 (Spring): 391-403.

Kramer, R. 1989. "Be Tough with Delinquents." *Arizona Daily Star*, A-9.

Kraut, R. E. 1976. "Deterrent and Definitional Influences on Shoplifting." *Social Problems* 23 (February): 358-68.

Law Enforcement Assistance Administration, National Criminal Justice Information and Statistics Services. 1977. *Capital Punishment*. Washington, DC: U.S. Government Printing Office.

Lemert, E. M. 1967. *Human Deviance, Social Problems, and Social Control*. Englewood Cliffs, NJ: Prentice-Hall.

Matza, D. 1964. *Delinquency and Drift*. New York: John Wiley.

McAuliffe, W. 1975. "Beyond Secondary Deviance: Negative Labeling and Its Effects on the Heroin Addict." In W. Gove (ed.), *The Labeling of Deviance*. New York: John Wiley.

McEachern, A. W. 1968. "The Juvenile Probation System." *American Behavioral Scientist* 11 (3):1.

McGlothlin, W. H., M. D. Anglin, and B. D. Wilson. 1978. "Narcotic Addiction and Crime." *Criminology* 16 (November):293-315.

Meade, A. C. 1974. "The Labeling Approach to Delinquency: State of the Theory as a Function of Method." *Social Forces* 53 (September):83-91.

Minor, W. 1977. "A Deterrence-Control Theory of Crime." In R. F. Meier (ed.), *Theory in Criminology: Contemporary Issues*. Beverly Hills, CA: Sage.

Minor, W., and J. Harry. 1982. "Deterrent and Experiential Effects in Perceptual Deterrence Research: A Replication and Extension." *Journal of Research in Crime and Delinquency* 19 (July): 190-215.

Montmarquette, C., and M. Nerlove. 1985. "Deterrence and Delinquency: An Analysis of Individual Data." *Journal of Quantitative Criminology* 1: 37-58.

Moran, R. 1990. "The Case for Public Executions." Newsletter of the Crime, Law and Deviance Section of the American Sociological Association (Spring).

O'Donnell, J. A. 1967. "The Rise and Decline of a Subculture." *Social Problems* 15 (1):73-84.

Paternoster, R., L. Saltzman, G. P. Waldo, and T. Chiricos. 1985. "Assessments of Risk and Behavioral Experience: An Exploratory Study of Change." *Criminology* 23 (August): 417-36.

Peterson, R., and W. C. Bailey. 1988. "Murder and Capital Punishment in the Evolving Context of the Post-*Furman* Era." *Social Forces* 66 (March): 1973-1984.

President's Commission on Law Enforcement and Administration of Justice. 1967. *Task Force Report: Delinquency and Youth Crime.* Washington, DC: U.S. Government Printing Office.

Regnery, A. S. 1985. "Getting Away with Murder: Why the Juvenile Justice System Needs an Overhaul." *Policy Review* 34 (Fall):65-68.

Rose, A. 1968. "Law and the Causation of Social Problems." *Social Problems* 16 (1):33-43.

Saltzman, L., R. Paternoster, G. P. Waldo, and T. G. Chiricos. 1982. "Deterrent and Experiential Effects: The Problem of Causal Order in Perceptual Deterrence Research." *Journal of Research in Crime and Delinquency* 19 (July): 172-89.

Savitz, L. 1958. "A Study of Capital Punishment." *Journal of Criminal Law, Criminology and Police Science* 49:338.

Scanian, C. 1989. "Death Penalty Ruling Rekindles Emotional Debate Over Executing Teens." *Arizona Daily Star*, June 27.

Schuessler, K. F. 1952. "The Deterrent Influence of the Death Penalty." *Annals of the American Academy of Political and Social Science* 284 (November): 54-62.

Schur, E. 1965. *Crimes Without Victims: Deviant Behavior and Public Policy.* Englewood Cliffs, NJ: Prentice-Hall.

_____. 1969a. *Our Criminal Society.* Englewood Cliffs, NJ: Prentice-Hall.

_____. 1969b. "Reactions to Deviance: A Critical Assessment." *American Journal of Sociology* 75 (November):309-22.

_____. 1973. *Radical Non-Intervention: Rethinking the Delinquency Problem.* Englewood Cliffs, NJ: Prentice-Hall.

Schwartz, I. M. 1989. *(In)justice for Juveniles.* Lexington, MA: D.C. Heath.

Schwartz, R. D., and S. Orleans. 1967. "On Legal Sanctions." *University of Chicago Law Review* 34 (Winter):274-300.

Sellin, T. 1967. *Capital Punishment.* New York: Harper & Row.

Shannon, L. 1976. "Predicting Adult Careers from Juvenile Careers." Paper presented at Pacific Sociological Association annual meeting, San Diego, CA.

Siegel, L. 1989. *Criminology.* Third Edition. St. Paul: West Publishing Company.

Silberman, M. 1976. "Toward a Theory of Criminal Deterrence." *American Sociological Review* 41 (June):442-61.

Stack, S. 1987. "Publicized Executions and Homicide, 1950-1980." *American Sociological Review* 52: 532-40.

Stafford, M. C., L.N. Gray, B. A. Menke, and D. A. Ward. 1986. "Modeling the Deterrent Effects of Punishment." *Social Psychology Quarterly* 49: 338-47.

Sutherland, E. 1924. *Principles of Criminology.* Philadelphia: J. B. Lippincott.

Tannenbaum, F. 1938. *Crime and the Community.* New York: Columbia University Press.

Thornberry, T. P. 1971. "Punishment and Crime: The Effect of Legal Dispositions on Subsequent Criminal Behavior." Ph.D. Dissertation, University of Pennsylvania.

Thorsell, B. A., and L. W. Klemke. 1972. "The Labeling Process: Reinforcement and Deterrent?" *Law and Society Review* 7 (Spring):372-92.

Tittle, C. R. 1975. "Deterrents or Labeling?" *Social Forces* 53 (March):399-410.

———. 1977. "Sanctions Fear and the Maintenance of Social Order." *Social Forces* 55 (March):579-96.

Tittle, C. R., and A. R. Rowe. 1973. "Moral Appeal, Sanction Threat and Deviance: An Experimental Test." *Social Problems* 20 (Spring):488-98.

Tittle, C. R., and A. R. Rowe. 1974. "Certainty of Arrest and Crime Rates: A Further Test of the Deterrence Hypothesis." *Social Forces* 52: 455-62.

Trebach, A. S. 1988. *Law Enforcement News*. April 30.

Van den Haag, E. 1986. "The Ultimate Punishment: A Defense." *Harvard Law Review* 7 (May): 99.

Waldo, G. P., and T. G. Chiricos. 1972. "Perceived Penal Sanction and Self-Reported Criminality: A Neglected Approach to Deterrence Research." *Social Problems* 19 (Spring):522-40.

Wilson, J. Q. 1975. *Thinking about Crime*. New York: Basic Books.

———. 1983. *Thinking about Crime*. Revised Edition. New York: Basic Books.

Zeisel, H. 1976. "The Deterrent Effect of the Death Penalty: Facts V. Faiths." In P. Kurland (ed.), *The Supreme Court Review*. Chicago: University of Chicago Press.

Zimring, F.E., and G. Hawkins. 1973. *Deterrence: The Legal Threat in Crime Control*. Chicago: University of Chicago Press.

chapter 10

Imprisonment and Alternatives

> *If it were the wish and aim of magistrates to effect the destruction . . . of young delinquents, they could not devise a more effectual method than to confine them so long in our prisons, those seats and seminaries . . . of idleness and every vice.*
>
> —John Howard, *The State of Prisons in England and Wales*, 1780:13

Imprisonment: The Continuing Controversy

The comparison of criminal and juvenile justice processing summarized in Chapter 2 showed that adult violent offenders were more likely than juveniles committing similar offenses to be sentenced to some form of confinement. In fact, the United States has more adults in prison relative to its population (426 per 100,000 population) than any other nation for which statistics are available, including South Africa (333 per 100,000) and the Soviet Union (268 per 100,000). The imprisonment rate for black men in the United States is 3,109 per 100,000—four times the rate for black men in South Africa (Mauer, 1991). Moreover, both the number of prisoners and rates of imprisonment are at all time highs, generating serious problems of prison crowding and renewed calls for the development of alternatives to imprisonment (see Figure 10-1).

Juveniles are less likely than adults to be sentenced to secure confinement and serve less time when they are confined. However, like adults, an increasing proportion of the juvenile population and of juvenile offenders are being "held in custody." As we noted in earlier chapters, national juvenile justice statistics are more difficult to compile and summarize than statistics on adults and are less up-to-date as a result. The latest comprehensive national report reveals that close to 92,000 juveniles were confined in 3,299 public or private juvenile justice facilities in the United States in 1987 (U.S. Department of Justice, 1987). The average cost per day was close to $75 per resident which translates into $27,375 per resident year. More recent statistics (1989) are limited to public facilities but indicate operating costs ranging from $17,600 to $78,800 (Allen-Hagen, 1991). It is expensive to imprison or detain juveniles and the costs have nearly doubled in a decade.

While growing awareness of the high cost of imprisonment is likely to generate renewed discussions and debates about imprisonment and

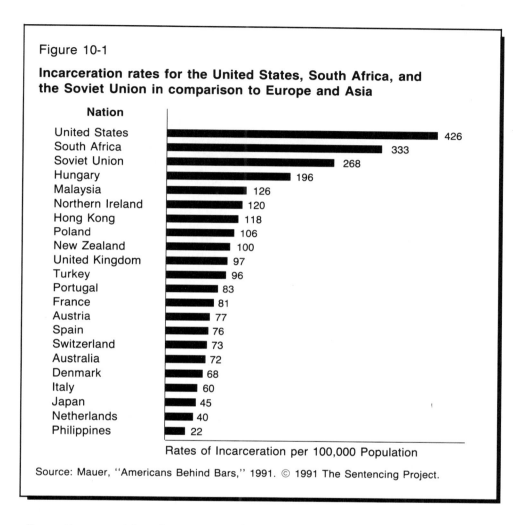

Figure 10-1

Incarceration rates for the United States, South Africa, and the Soviet Union in comparison to Europe and Asia

Rates of Incarceration per 100,000 Population

Source: Mauer, "Americans Behind Bars," 1991. © 1991 The Sentencing Project.

alternatives, cost is only one consideration. The debate over imprisonment as a means of deterrence, retribution, and/or rehabilitation has been on-going for centuries, as is reflected in the quote by John Howard at the beginning of this chapter. The advocates of a "get tough" policy (see Regnery, 1985) typically favor expanded confinement of juveniles while others (see Schwartz, 1989) favor community-based treatment programs and the dismantling of prisons for juveniles.

The original rationale for the creation of a separate justice system for juveniles was to remove them from the presumably corrupting influence of adult criminal courts and the horrors of prisons and jails. Children were not to be punished or imprisoned; rather, they were to be placed in a therapeutic setting that would foster positive, constructive change. However, secure confinement or "imprisonment" persisted as a feature of the juvenile justice system in the form of detention centers and training or reform schools and, as you might expect, controversy over their use has persisted as well. To some critics the only changes brought about by the creation of the juvenile justice system was the substitution of words such as "detention center" for jail, "training school" for prison and "treatment" for punishment. One of the major themes in reform efforts of the 1960s and 1970s was to minimize the use of imprisonment and to provide alternatives which were less punitive.

In a review of public opinion polls Jim Galvin and Ken Polk conclude that "the public's views on the juvenile court are in conflict, seeing too much leniency but supporting rehabilitation" (1983). Seventy-eight percent of adults polled agreed that the main purpose of the juvenile justice system was to rehabilitate rather than punish but, at the same time, 73 percent felt that the court was too lenient on youths found guilty of serious crimes. Actually, the juvenile justice system is expected to pursue a variety of goals: to "rehabilitate" without being "too soft," to be tough enough to deter potential offenders while addressing the underlying problems that bring youths into the system.

The juvenile justice system is expected to do a little bit of everything. Imprisonment satisfies some of these expectations as a means for incapacitating offenders, as a form of punishment, as a threat to others, and as a means for keeping youths under control while "rehabilitating" them. Whether imprisonment has such consequences and the degree to which youths should be isolated from the community is still being debated. In this chapter we examine imprisonment and the wide range of correctional experiments designed to facilitate rehabilitation while confined or to provide alternatives to traditional forms of confinement.

It is important to put contemporary debates and discussions in context since many of the arguments that encouraged the invention of such institutions are now made to challenge confinement of juveniles. The progressive ideas of one era can readily become the outdated and backward ideas of another era. Responses to delinquency which were attacked at one time may later regain popularity. The use of imprisonment as a tool for correcting, deterring, or punishing offenders was itself an aspect of various reform efforts.

Development of the Prison

In historical context, imprisonment was often viewed as a benevolent advancement over *corporal* (bodily) and capital punishment. One review of corrections in America describes the use of confinement or incarceration as a phase in "the continued search for alternatives to brutality" (Carter et al., 1975). Until the 1800s the major means of punishment took the form of flogging, mutilation, branding, torture, banishment, removal to penal colonies, or some form of restitution for the damage or harm done to the victim and the state. Imprisonment was a prelude to the actual punishment, not the punishment itself. It was also used as a penalty for political prisoners of high rank and as a means of coercing payments of debts (Johnston, 1973).

Schrag (1971) has noted that in twelfth-century England jails were used to detain the accused while they awaited trial and to punish offenders as well. Beginning in the sixteenth century, "houses of correction" and "workhouses" were established in Europe for minor offenders, beggars, and vagabonds. Such institutions were widespread by the seventeenth century. Such houses were not specifically designed to deal with criminals but were repositories for an assortment of minor offenders, the destitute, and the unemployed (Sykes, 1978). Execution, corporal punishment, and banishment were the preferred methods for handling serious criminals (Fox, 1972).

In the American colonies, jails and houses of correction were erected along European lines. Jails were used primarily to house individuals awaiting trial, and houses of correction were institutions for drunkards and vagrants. The conditions in early American jails (and in their European counterparts) were deemed appalling. The following is an account of the conditions in the Walnut Street Jail in Philadelphia shortly after the Revolutionary War:

> It is represented as a scene of promiscuous and unrestricted intercourse, and universal riot and debauchery. There was no labor, no separation of those accused, but yet untried, not even of those confined for debt only, from the convicts sentenced for the foulest crimes; no separation of color, age or sex, by day or night; the prisoners lying promiscuously on the floor, most of them without anything like bed or bedding. As soon as the sexes were placed in different wings, which was the first reform made in the prison, of thirty or forty women confined there, all but four or five immediately left it; it having been a common practice, it is said, for women to cause themselves to be arrested for fictitious debts, that they might share in the orgies of the place. Intoxicating liquors abounded, and indeed were freely sold at a bar kept by one of the officers of the prison. Intercourse between the prisoners and those without was hardly restricted. Prisoners tried and acquitted were still detained till they should pay jail fees to the keeper; and the custom of garnish was established and unquestioned; that is the custom of stripping every newcomer of his outer clothing, to be sold for liquor, unless redeemed by the payment of a sum of money to be applied to the same object. It need hardly be added, that there was no attempt to give any kind of instruction and no religious service whatsoever. (Gray, 1847:15-16)

The conditions of jails and houses of correction in both Europe and America prompted efforts at reform, which in America led to the development of the *penitentiary* in the late 1700s. The very word "penitentiary" is a clue to the religious origins of the institution. The Walnut Street Jail just described became the first institution based on the Quaker idea that restraint and isolation would lead inmates to contemplate the error of their ways and to do penance for their sins. Rather than flogging, physically branding or inflicting pain, imprisonment itself was to be both punishment and a means to interpersonal reform. In Quaker philosophy, sin and crime were synonymous. Life in an austere and disciplined environment, meditation, and Bible reading would strengthen the moral and spiritual fibers of the inmates. To facilitate penitence, inmates were kept in single cells, were not allowed contact with other inmates, and were made to carry out their assigned work in isolation. This conception of the penitentiary as a means of correction came to be known as the *Pennsylvania system.*

A second school of corrections emerged in New York state in the early 1800s and became known as the *Auburn system.* The hallmark of the Auburn system was not total isolation but, rather, silence. Inmates worked together during the day but were kept in solitary confinement at night. Although there was contact, rules requiring silence were strictly enforced. Prisoners worked in common workshops and ate in a common dining hall but were not allowed to communicate. The Auburn system became the dominant penal system in America, primarily because it was economical and secondarily because of concern over the psychological impact of isolation. The Pennsylvania system called for individual confinement, which entailed the construction of separate living quarters for each inmate. The Auburn system's architectural design was more economical, requiring only common work areas and small solitary cells for sleeping. Prisons such as Sing Sing, built in 1825, followed the Auburn model. The Pennsylvania system was ultimately abandoned in the United States, although European penologists who studied the two systems preferred the Pennsylvania model for prisons in their countries (Fox, 1972).

Although proponents of each of these systems cast aspersions on the other, both systems were based on a similar philosophy. Each emphasized rigid discipline, restraint, isolation, and work as the means to personal reform. At about the same time, a somewhat different correctional philosophy was being implemented in Australia, Austria, Spain, and Ireland (Sykes, 1978:470; Sutherland and Cressey, 1978: 525). In Australia, Alexander Maconochie, superintendent of a penal colony, devised a system called the *mark system.* Under this system, inmates had to earn their release through hard work and good behavior. Prisoners could work for a *ticket of leave,* similar to parole. If the prisoner successfully completed the parole period, he was granted a conditional pardon and, finally, transported back to England as a free man. This progressive method of liberation was imported to Ireland where it became known as the *Irish system*. The Irish system was characterized by the use of an indeterminate sentence (i.e. length of confinement dependent on progress made by the inmate) and the "mark" whereby prisoners could gain their release. Marks were awarded for good behavior and, after earning a set number of such marks, the prisoner was eligible for parole. The system embodied the features of contemporary behavior modification programs which will be discussed later in this chapter.

The Irish system was hailed in this country as the most progressive penal model to date. Its philosophy became the underlying correctional philosophy of prison organization in the United States. In 1870 the National Prison Association was founded under the leadership of Enoch Wines, considered the foremost authority on prisons in the latter part of the nineteenth century (Platt, 1969). Out of the reform efforts of Wines and his organization, a new penal system emerged. Elmira Reformatory, established for offenders between the ages of 16 and 30, opened in New York in 1876. The Elmira Reformatory combined the central features of the Irish system with a strong emphasis on rehabilitation through education and trade training. The goal was not punishment, but treatment and reform. However, according to Sutherland and Cressey (1978), the "treatment" at Elmira was so severe and the use of corporal punishment so frequent that convicted offenders pleaded with judges to be sentenced to the outmoded Auburn Prison rather than the Elmira Reformatory.

The Society for the Prevention of Pauperism was formed in 1817 for the purpose of finding "a practical measure for the cure of pauperism and the diminution of crime" (Dean and Reppucci, 1974). New York City was particularly beset with pauperism and the problems associated with it. Immigrants coming to this country were often stranded in New York City, and the children of destitute families were seen as prime candidates for crime. The Society for the Prevention of Pauperism selected the problem of juvenile delinquency as its major focus.

In 1825 the New York House of Refuge opened as a full-time residence for delinquent, dependent, and neglected children. It was the first attempt to provide separate facilities for young offenders and thereby remove them from the contaminating influence of adult prisons. In 1826 the House of Reformation in Boston was established, followed in 1828 by the opening of the Philadelphia House of Refuge. These early institutions, which were supported by private funds, developed many of the principles of treatment and rehabilitation that would characterize the philosophy of the juvenile court as it emerged at the start of the twentieth century. Despite the rhetoric of the early house of refuge movement, the administrators of these institutions utilized two basic models: one drawn from the public school system, which called for education and discipline, and the other based on the state penitentiary system, which utilized a strict regimen, physical labor, and corporal punishment (Schlossmann, 1977). In institutions for juveniles — variously known as houses of refuge, reformatories, industrial schools, and training schools — coercion, restraint, and discipline became an integral part of "treatment." The enlightened ideology of the reformatory movement gave way to the stark reality of overcrowding, inadequate resources, mismanagement, and disillusioned staff. The distinction between juvenile institutions and adult prisons became extremely tenuous.

The house of refuge actually came to parallel the adult penitentiary, as did the Elmira Reformatory. These products of the reform movement came under attack in the 1850s by "anti-institutionalists" such as Charles Loring Brace and Samuel Gridley Howe, who felt the best means of reform was the family. The family, according to Brace, was "God's reformatory." The anti-institutionalists' critiques and proposals facilitated the development of the "family reform school," an organizational model that was growing in popularity in Germany and France. The family reform school actually represented a compromise between the anti-institutionalists' ideas and the realities of an already existing "institutional establishment" (Schlossmann, 1977:49). Steven Schlossmann has described the system as follows:

> To Americans the essence of the family design was a format whereby anywhere from one to three dozen inmates with similar personality were place in separate small homes or cottages under the supervision, ideally, of a surrogate father and mother. Each family lived, worked, and attended school together, meeting with other inmates only on infrequent ceremonial occasions. This residential arrangement contrasted sharply with the Jacksonian refuge, where children of different ages and dispositions slept in cells or barracks-like dormitories, performed identical tasks according to a uniform schedule, and possessed no close authority figure to appeal to for personal assistance or comfort. (1977:49)

Following the development of the family reform school, the next major phases in the evolution of juvenile justice and corrections were the *Progressive era* and the *juvenile court movement*. As we noted in Chapter 2, there has been considerable debate about whether the accomplishments of that era were in fact progressive. Analyses of the juvenile court movement in Canada (Hagan and Leon, 1977) and the United States (Schlossman, 1977; Finestone, 1976) tend to agree that the most central and significant aspect of the movement was its emphasis on probation. Confinement in reformatories persisted as a response to problem youth, but treatment of youths and their families within the community was a major philosophical emphasis.

It is not clear whether the progressive ideology had any real consequences for the probability that a youth might be imprisoned. For instance, in his historical analysis of the juvenile court movement in Chicago (Cook

County), Anthony Platt argued that "Cook County juvenile court's early records show that institutional confinement was a basic tenet of the child-saving philosophy" (1969: 140). He notes that one-third of all juveniles charged with delinquency were sent to a state reformatory. Platt also contends that institutional confinement was increasingly used to deal with delinquency. In contrast, Schlossman's analysis of the juvenile court system in the neighboring state of Wisconsin led him to the following conclusions:

> Probation accounted for the great majority of dispositions. . . . with the modal period of supervision running about one and a half years. The heavy reliance on probation, especially for male delinquents, is confirmed by records showing a rather small number of commitments to the state reform school at Waukesa during this period. . . . Between 1905 and 1916, the average number of youths committed each year was only thirty. Moreover, although the number of reformatory committals varied from year to year, it clearly did not increase at a rate proportional to rising intake in the court. Indeed, if anything, it decreased. For example, in 1906, 55 boys were committed to the reformatory, out of 536 new delinquency cases; in 1911, 15 boys were committed out of 705. To sum up, the odds of being committed to a reformatory for boys charged with delinquency in the Progressive era were rather small. Despite increases in intake, the court's reliance on long-term committals actually diminished after 1905. (1977:155)

Schlossman warns us that these observations do not necessarily mean that the use of *confinement* declined, since large numbers of children were held in detention centers before, during, and sometimes after their hearings. The proportion of persons detained actually increased during that time. Schlossman argued that detention centers developed into children's jails that allowed institutional control and incapacitation in a system that emphasized probation.

The Progressive era of the early 1900s was also characterized by dramatic increases in resources invested in public reformatories for girls. Schlossman and Wallach (1982) note that twenty-three new facilities for girls opened between 1910 and 1920 compared to only five between 1850 and 1910. Such reform schools were generally small facilities compared to such institutions as the New York House of Refuge which held over 1,000 males. Based on their historical research, Schlossman and Wallach found that female juvenile delinquents were viewed as "fallen women" and a major concern in the juvenile courts and reformatories was to control their sexual precociousness and promiscuity. Girls were to be isolated from males, kept long enough to insure marriageability after release, and taught the skills necessary for a domestic future. The Victorian emphasis on sexual purity and growing concern about biological and mental degeneration of society led to increased confinement of girls at a time when anti-institutionalists were challenging the use of institutions for boys. Girls were actually viewed as less amenable to change through probation and home treatment than boys and incarceration was deemed necessary to control female sexuality. Schlossman and Wallach conclude that the expansion of female reformatories was "part of a larger cultural reaction, an attempt to revitalize Victorian morality and to punish women—prostitutes and sexually promiscuous girls alike— who impeded attainment of that goal" (1982:70).

Thus, by the early 1900s four basic dimensions of juvenile justice and institutional confinement had been established: 1) prison-like reform or training schools, 2) family-cottage reform schools, 3) probation, and 4) detention facilities for the short-term confinement of youthful offenders. Moreover, the use of confinement for females who violated sexual mores and for boys who violated criminal laws developed in this period. The incarceration of female status offenders would not come under serious attack for another half century.

The Contemporary Scene

Since the establishment of a separate juvenile justice system there has been a proliferation in the types of juvenile facilities available. In addition to training schools and detention centers a significant number of youths may spend time at ranches, forestry camps, and farms for delinquent youth or in halfway houses and group homes. Ranches, camps, and farms for children in custody are not as restrictive as training schools and detention centers but do maintain security and isolate youths by virtue of their location. Halfway houses and group homes maintain control over youth but allow structured and monitored contact with the wider community. Youths may live in such homes while attending school or even working at a job but are subject to rules established and enforced by people acting as their custodians.

There are other facilities for children under state custody such as "shelter care homes" which are used primarily for dependent and neglected children but also provide care for young offenders and status offenders who do not constitute security risks. Youth may spend some time in "reception and diagnostic centers" as well. Such centers are facilities for evaluating delinquent youths and their circumstances before an ultimate disposition is made.

While only a small proportion of the juvenile population (92,000 out of about 25 million youths subject to juvenile court jurisdiction) are in custody at a given point in time, many more youths pass through these facilities in a given year. For example, more than twice as many cases are admitted to training schools in a year's time as are resident on a specific day and over thirty-times more pass through detention centers (Galvin and Blake,

1984). In 1987 there were over 590,000 "admissions" to public juvenile facilities and about 126,000 admissions to private facilities— which yields an admissions rate of about 26 per 1,000 juveniles ages 10 through 17. Since many youths pass through the system more than once in a year, that figure does not mean that 26 of every 1,000 youth are dealt with by the juvenile correctional system. However, it does tell us that a sizeable number of youth experience some form of confinement.

Confinement and Juvenile Crime

Data on juvenile delinquency summarized in Chapters 3 and 4 suggest a stable or declining overall crime rate among juveniles beginning in the mid-1970s, with some upturns in violent offenses since the mid-1980s. Whether variation in the confinement of youth has anything to do with variation in juvenile delinquency or youth crime cannot be determined with any accuracy given available data. Systematic, comparative data on juvenile corrections has been compiled sporadically over a short span of time thus making it difficult to answer simple questions about youth confinement over any substantial span of years.

Paul Lerman (1984) has computed the rate of confinement through 1979 and we have updated his results with estimates through 1985 (see Figure 10-2). The rate of confinement per 100,000 juveniles has increased over time from about 71 in 1960 to 105 in 1985. Relative to their contribution to arrests the number of youths confined has varied as well. Lerman's data for 1950 when compared to arrest statistics at that time suggest a very high rate of confinement relative to FBI reports of arrests of persons under eighteen. There were about 35,000 arrests in national statistics and close to that number were confined to long-term facilities. Such figures do not mean that youth who were arrested were certain to be confined. They do suggest that, relative to their contribution to crime, American youth were quite commonly being confined.

In 1960 there were about eight youths in confinement for every 100 arrests of juveniles due to huge increases in juvenile arrests coupled with moderate increases in the number confined. By 1970 the number confined per 100 arrests was down to four and by 1977 it was less than three. The most recent comparable data on both long-term public and private facilities is for 1985 and the ratio of juveniles confined to arrests was back up to about four per 100.

Juvenile court data support similar observations in that there were about nine youth in long-term confinement for every 100 court cases in 1960 as compared to six in 1970 and four in 1979. In the 1982 about five were confined for each 100 court cases and in 1985 about six youth were confined for every 100 delinquency cases handled by the juvenile court.

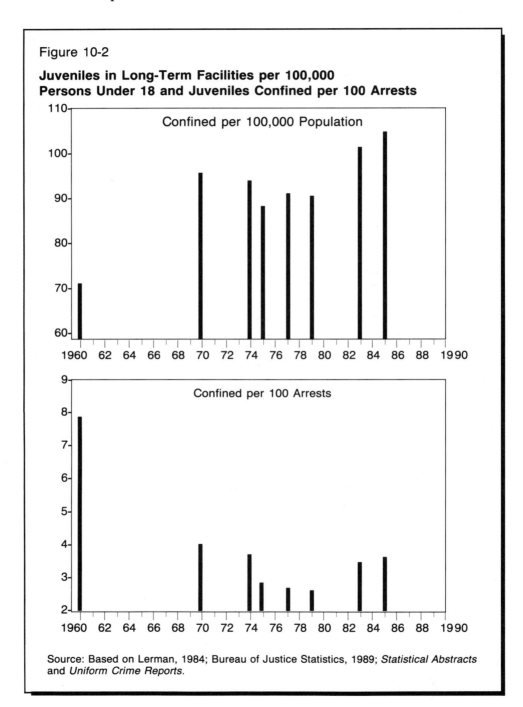

Figure 10-2

**Juveniles in Long-Term Facilities per 100,000
Persons Under 18 and Juveniles Confined per 100 Arrests**

Source: Based on Lerman, 1984; Bureau of Justice Statistics, 1989; *Statistical Abstracts*
and *Uniform Crime Reports*.

In sum, the use of confinement relative to juvenile crime seems to have reached a low by the late 1970s but has been increasing since that time. While juvenile crime rates were low during some historical periods when confinement was relatively common, a wide range of other circumstances were different during those periods as well. Variations in confinement may be one factor affecting delinquency rates but there are other variables, such as the divorce rate (see Chapter 7), which have varied closely with juvenile arrest and referral rates and also have to be considered. At present the available data on juvenile corrections are not adequate for isolating the effects of confinement from the effects of other changes in society.

Variations in rates of confinement or imprisonment may reflect the availability of facilities at different points in time as well as shifts in juvenile justice philosophy. As arrest rates and court cases rose dramatically from the 1960s through the early 1970s the number of youths confined increased but not nearly as rapidly as youth crime was increasing. The justice system, in essence, could not keep up with crime and delinquency. When juvenile crime leveled out and began to decline, the juvenile justice system could begin to "catch up" in terms of facilities and resources available. However, once sufficient facilities were developed confinement became a more likely option than when the system was more seriously overburdened. Moreover, consistent with the growing conservatism of public and political sentiment, juvenile justice officials grew more enamored with "setting things right" with victims, i.e. scaring potential offenders and incapacitating repetitive offenders. Incapacitation, deterrence and restitution developed into key issues among justice scholars and professionals during the 1980s and early 1990s.

The Privatization of Juvenile Justice

One of the most notable trends in juvenile justice in the United States has been the *privatization* of juvenile correctional programs. In 1950 about 22 percent of youths confined in a long-term facility were in private rather than public or government-owned facilities. However, this figure began climbing in the early 1970s and by 1974 about 50 percent of youths under correctional supervision were in a private facility. The figure has hovered around 50 percent since that time. Between 1975 and 1987 the rate of confinement in private facilities of all kinds increased twice as much as the rates of confinement in public facilities (Bureau of Justice Statistics, 1989).

Ironically, the proliferation of private facilities was facilitated by the movement to deinstitutionalize status offenders and to provide community-based alternatives for minor offenders as reflected in government legislation in 1968 (the Omnibus Crime Control and Safe Streets Act) and 1974 (the

Juvenile Justice and Delinquency Prevention Act). The "alternatives" to public training schools and existing forms of long-term confinement were new long-term and short-term programs developed in the private realm. The number of such private short-term facilities increased 35 percent between 1977 and 1985 compared to an increase of only 7 percent in public facilities. Private long-term facilities increased by 30 percent compared to only 3 percent for public long-term facilities. Total growth in the number of private facilities for juveniles increased 72 percent between 1974 and 1987 compared to 27 percent for public facilities (see Figure 10-3). Most of the growth has involved "open" or short-term facilities. There has been little increase nationwide in training school facilities.

Private correctional enterprise was encouraged by the government and moved rapidly to provide new alternatives. Such enterprise was consistent with the commonly-held view that the private sector could provide services

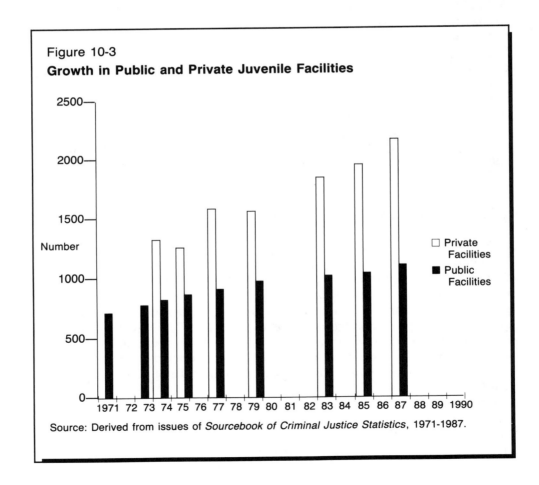

Figure 10-3
Growth in Public and Private Juvenile Facilities

Source: Derived from issues of *Sourcebook of Criminal Justice Statistics*, 1971-1987.

more economically than government bureaucracies. The fact that such programs tended to use existing buildings and housed less serious offenders meant that the high costs associated with reform school security were avoided. Moreover, relative to state-operated facilities and training schools per capita operating costs were lower. For example, in 1975 per capita expenditures in public institutions was $11,471 compared to $9,518 for private institutions. However, this advantage has eroded over the years. The per capita cost in 1982 had increased to $21,300 in private facilities compared to $22,000 for public facilities. By 1987 (the latest summary report when this text was written) the operating costs of private programs exceeded public programs. In sum, the economic advantage of private corrections is now minimal or nonexistent.

There are differences in the characteristics of youths held in public and private settings. About 94 percent of the juveniles in public facilities in 1985 had been adjudicated delinquent as compared to only one-third of juveniles in private facilities (Bureau of Justice Statistics, 1989). Nearly two-thirds of juveniles in private programs are status offenders, youths deemed "in need of supervision" by the court, and other youths whose parents do not want them or who do not want to return home. A greater proportion of juveniles in private facilities are female and a smaller proportion are members of minority groups. The more open nature of such facilities is reflected in the fact that 40 percent of the juveniles in public institutions "never" have access to the community while nearly 80 percent of the residents in private facilities have daily access. This level of access reflects the fact that most private facilities are group homes or halfway houses. In contrast, most public facilities are training schools or detention centers.

Figure 10-4 summarizes the number of males and females in public and private facilities from 1971 through 1987, including 1989 for public facilities. Those data show that there was a decline in the confinement of girls and boys in the early 1970s, most likely reflecting the diversion and deinstitutionalization of status offenders. While the number of boys confined in public facilities started to rise again in the 1980s, girls have never regained the share of juveniles in custody that they accounted for prior to diversion activity in the early 1970s.

Galvin and Blake (1984) have summarized trends in female delinquency as well as the percent of admissions and residents in detention centers and training schools from 1971 through 1982. While the contribution of females to arrest statistics was nearly constant from 1971 to 1982, they have accounted for a declining percentage of admissions and of the daily population in such facilities. Some of the decline is a result of diversion into private short-term and long-term community-based programs (Adler, 1984) as well as the growing number of mental health, welfare, and drug treatment agencies referred to by some as the "hidden" system of juvenile control (see Schwartz et al., 1984).

Figure 10-4

Males and Females in Public and Private Facilities, 1971-1989

Year	Public		Private	
	Male	**Female**	**Male**	**Female**
1971	41,781	12,948		
1973	35,057	10,637		
1974	34,783	10,139	22,104	9,645
1975	37,926	9,054	19,152	8,138
1977	36,921	7,175	20,387	8,683
1979	37,167	6,067	20,512	8,176
1983	42,182	6,519	22,242	9,148
1985	42,549	6,773	23,844	10,236
1987	46,272	7,231	26,339	11,804
1989	49,388	6,734	Not Available	

Source: *Sourcebook of Criminal Justice Statistics, 1985; Children in Custody, 1975-85;* National Institute of Justice Reports, 1991.

The privatization of juvenile justice has been associated with a growing segregation of offenders by race and ethnicity. Blacks and hispanics make up an increasing proportion of youths in secure public long-term facilities (Shover and Eisenstadter, 1989) while white youth have been diverted to alternative programs to a greater degree than minority youth. Scholars may debate which is the more positive or negative experience for youth (see Box 10-1) but it does appear that correctional experiences in the public versus the private realm are differentially distributed by racial or ethnic status. Such segregation is partially a reflection of the types of interpersonal violent offenses that are overrepresented among minority youth but there is also precedent to propose biases in dispositions as part of the explanation (see Figure 10-5). Shover and Einstadter (1989:107) state that "some part of this inequity is due to systematic discrimination."

There is evidence that the recent "war" on drugs in the United States has led to increases in the referral of minority youth to the juvenile court and an even greater increase in detention, though the war has not resulted in increases for white youths (Snyder, 1990). Increases in the imprisonment of drug offenders may generate an ever greater concentration of minority youths in public prisons and training schools.

Box 10-1

"Being Abused at Better Prices?"

It is hard to spend an evening watching television in recent times without encountering advertisements by the health care industry encouraging parents to deal with their children's problems through some sort of medical or psychiatric program. Ira Schwartz (1989:137) reports that in 1980 about 17,000 adolescents were admitted to private psychiatric hospitals but that by 1985 the number had ballooned to 35,000.

Schwartz titled a chapter of his book on *(In)justice for Juveniles* (1989) "Being Abused at Better Prices" because there is little evidence that such intervention is effective and because youths are being committed for problems that do not require hospitalization. He argues that "Hospitals are rapidly becoming the new jails for middle-class and upper-middle-class kids" (1989:143). Indeed, a Rand Corporation review cited by Schwartz found that many such youth are in treatment involuntarily as an alternative to criminal sanctions, that they are often in unsuitable programs and that the methods used assume that the problem is biological or psychological.

Such programs reflect the growing "privatization" and "medicalization" of responses to juvenile problems and have proliferated among hospitals to fill vacant beds and enhance profits through medical treatment of behavioral problems.

Have you or your friends ever been in such a program? Do you think the program made any difference?

The Training School

The proliferation of different types of facilities for juveniles is reflected in recent reports from the Bureau of Justice Statistics where they now categorize facilities as 1) public or private, 2) long-term or short-term, and 3) institutional or open. The traditional "training school" falls in the long-term, institutional category and most of them are public facilities. In 1985 out of 49,322 youths in public facilities, one-half (24,446) were in an institutional, long-term correctional setting.

Because of the security requirements for confining serious offenders, training schools are the most expensive juvenile facilities. In 1987 it cost about $2200 per month to house a juvenile in a public, long-term, institutional facility compared to $2000 in a public long-term open facility. Such differences in cost have been one reason for advocating more open,

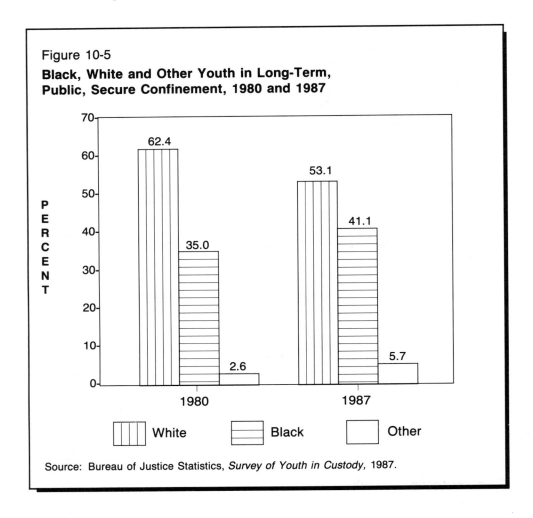

Figure 10-5

Black, White and Other Youth in Long-Term, Public, Secure Confinement, 1980 and 1987

Source: Bureau of Justice Statistics, *Survey of Youth in Custody*, 1987.

community-based programs instead of building more institutional facilities.

While training schools are likely to be viewed by juveniles as the most severe form of incarceration, they take a variety of forms and, ideally, are supposed to provide treatment and education while maintaining security. In 1975 the Children's Bureau described the functions of such schools as follows:

> The prime function of a training school is to re-educate and train the child to become a responsible, well-adjusted citizen. . . . The training schools must be essentially treatment institutions with an integrated professional service wherein the disciplines of education, casework, group work, psychology, psychiatry, medicine, nursing, vocational

rehabilitation and religion all play an important role. Through such an integrated program the child is expected to learn self-discipline, to accept responsibility and act and react in a more socially acceptable manner. (1975:3)

Although the philosophy expressed calls for a dynamic, resocializing environment, several overviews of training schools suggest that they are like miniature prisons that may exacerbate rather than eliminate delinquency problems. In its criticism of traditional juvenile institutions, a Presidential Task Force in the late 1960s stated:

Mass handling, countless ways of humiliating the inmate in order to make him subservient to rules and orders, special rules of behavior designed to maintain social distance between keeper and inmates, frisking of inmates, regimented movement to work, eat, play, drab prison clothing and similar aspects of daily life, all tend to depersonalize the inmate and reinforce his belief that authority is to be opposed, not cooperated with. (President's Commission on Law Enforcement and Administration of Justice, 1967:142)

Such descriptions of juvenile institutions suggest that they may not differ significantly from adult prisons. For instance, in his study of a cottage-type residential treatment center in New York, Howard Polsky (1962) found a stratification system based on toughness and manipulative abilities. The social hierarchy was so pervasive and the code of conduct so strongly enforced that Polsky concluded that the cottage system was culturally and organizationally "delinquency bound." Polsky's research suggested that the cottage lifestyle tends to sabotage the system's treatment programs and that juvenile institutions may suffer from the same type of *prisonization* effects as adult penitentiaries. Prisonization refers to the oppositional "inmate code" adopted by prisoners as a result of socialization by other inmates. Such prisonization is viewed as a barrier to treatment and reintegration into conventional society.

Barry Feld (1981) reached similar conclusions about juvenile institutions in Massachusetts. Youths in ten cottages in two institutions appeared to come into the institutions with negative attitudes and these were compounded with an "inmate culture" that developed within the cottages. However, such prisonization was more evident in the punitive and custodially-oriented cottages than in treatment-oriented cottages.

Many training schools have made a concerted effort to move away from a custodial approach where security and discipline are foremost concerns to a treatment orientation like that advocated by the Children's Bureau. The success of such a move depends on the "mix" of treatment goals and custodial concerns and the degree of cooperation among the staff.

David Street and several colleagues have carried out research relevant to the diversity of juvenile institutions and the relevance of that diversity to the perspectives and social relations of juvenile inmates (Street, 1965; Zald and Street, 1964; Street et al., 1966). They studied four different institutions, nicknamed "Dick," "Mixter," "Milton," and "Inland." Each institution had a somewhat different orientation towards juvenile corrections:

> *Dick* (Discipline)—a large (200-250 inmates) public institution which had no treatment program, whose staff felt no lack because of this, and which concentrated on custody, hard work, and discipline.
>
> *Mixter* (Mixed Goals)—a very large (375-420 inmates) public institution with poorly integrated "mixed goals" of custody and treatment. Some treatment was attempted, but this was segregated from the rest of the activities, and for most boys the environment was characterized by surveillance, frequent use of negative sanctions, and other corollaries of an emphasis on custody.
>
> *Milton* (Milieu Therapy)—a fairly large (160-190 inmates) public institution using not only individual therapy but a range of other treatment techniques. This institution resembled Mixter in its bifurcation between treatment and containment staffs and activities, but by and large the clinicians were in control, used treatment criteria, and influenced the nonprofessional staff to allow inmates considerable freedom.
>
> *Inland* (Individual Therapy)—a small (60-75 inmates) private "residential treatment center" in which clients were virtually in complete control, allowing much freedom to the inmates while stressing the use of psychotherapeutic techniques in the attempt to bring about major personality change. (Street, 1965: 43)

The treatment-oriented institutions were characterized by a higher staff-inmate ratio and contact. Staff at these institutions viewed the organization's goals as rehabilitation and attitudinal change to be accomplished through close, trusting relationships. In contrast, staff in the custodial institutions stressed order, discipline, immediate response to staff, and isolation.

In analyzing data from questionnaires completed by inmates, Street and his colleagues found several variations among inmates in the different settings. First, inmates in treatment settings expressed more positive attitudes toward the institution and its staff. In that sense they appeared less "prisonized" than inmates in custodial settings. Second, inmates in the treatment settings expressed more positive "images of self-change"; that is, they felt they were improving. Third, length of stay in the custodial institutions was associated with an increasing proportion of inmates expressing negative attitudes, while in treatment-oriented institutions length of stay was associated with an increasing proportion of inmates expressing positive attitudes. Fourth, Street and his colleagues found that inmates in treatment settings more often encouraged positive attitudes in other inmates than similar groups in custodial institutions.

Rose Giallombardo (1974) conducted research on incarcerated females based on three models: a custodial, an "intermediate," and a treatment-oriented institution. All three were cottage systems holding between 150 and 350 girls. In all three institutions female inmates created "family" groups with some inmates performing male roles and others female roles. Imprisoned girls were found to create courtship, marriage, and kin relations with other inmates which functioned as "substitutes for normal relationships with family and friends of both sexes" (Giallombardo, 1974: 145). Between 85 and 95 percent of girls belonged to such groups and staff tended to feel that such groups were a bad influence on the girls. Staff at the treatment-oriented institution were least likely to view such groups as a bad influence. No data on prisonization or impact of different orientations were reported.

In sum, the image of juvenile institutions as junior prisons that inevitably generate hostility, opposition, and bitterness ignores the variability in juvenile institutions and the impact of different organizational goals on inmates. At the time of Street's research, at least 50 percent of all public institutions were estimated to be basically custodial (Janowitz, 1966: xi) and about 25 percent treatment-oriented, so it is not surprising that most overviews stressed the opposition-generating aspects of juvenile institutions. We should note, however, that the type of research undertaken by Street and his colleagues does not tell us whether certain types of institutions increase or decrease the chances of youths committing further offenses (i.e. *recidivism*). Of course, whether we believe such an outcome is important depends on our conception of the function that such institutions are supposed to serve.

Reactions to Delinquency: Terms and Objectives

What are the objectives of any organized reaction to delinquency? We use the neutral term "reaction" here because words such as "punishment," "treatment," or "correction" tend to imply that a choice about major objectives has already been made. For instance, if we considered retribution or deterrence the appropriate response to delinquency, then we might call this section "The Objectives of Punishment." On the other hand, if we believed that changing the offender in some positive fashion was the major objective, then we might refer to the objectives of treatment, rehabilitation, or reform. Similarly, the name given to an institution conveys a sense of that facility's purpose. The word "prison" carries a connotation of punishment when compared to "correctional center." The label "reformatory" implies that reform is the institution's main objective, just as "training school" implies an emphasis on learning and "penitentiary" implies an emphasis on penitence. The words we use in discussing "reactions" to delinquency reflect choices about objectives.

Herbert Packer (1968) has outlined two historically developed justifications for reactions to crime: 1) retribution or revenge and 2) the utilitarian view of prevention. When the emphasis is on retribution the dominant concern is with "setting things right" with victims. This philosophy is reflected in the biblical position "an eye for an eye, a tooth for a tooth." The retributive rationale emphasizes punishment commensurate with harm for no other reason than reaffirming a sense of justice. While retribution may have rehabilitative or deterrent consequences such outcomes are not the primary justification for this approach.

The utilitarian position on prevention is often depicted as a more "rational" approach to crime control. The objective in a utilitarian approach is the greatest happiness for the greatest number with a minimal infliction of suffering. Punishments should be no more severe than is necessary to make the costs of offending outweigh the rewards. People may have to be locked up to protect the rest of society and to make the costs outweigh the rewards. If it is possible to change offenders in ways that reduce crime with minimal suffering, then such possibilities should be pursued. A "rational" approach to the control of crime and delinquency can include incapacitation, deterrence, and rehabilitation.

The problem with integrating these objectives is that the programs or facilities which would be conducive to accomplishing one objective may be incompatible for achieving the others. For example, when the emphasis is on incapacitation or protecting society from serious offenders, the primary concern in corrections is security. Secure confinement, virtually by definition, requires that offenders be isolated from potential victims outside of institutions. Yet, most theories of rehabilitation stress the importance of contact with the outside world in preventing "prisonization" and reintegrating the offender into society. Similarly, if the threat of imprisonment is to be a general or specific deterrent, then the experience must appear sufficiently threatening to instill fear in would-be offenders or potential recidivists. The characteristics of institutions which might instill such fear are quite contrary to those believed to be necessary to bring about positive change in offenders.

The response of the juvenile justice system to such dilemmas is to pursue multiple objectives through different programs and facilities. Imprisonment remains the ultimate threat and final recourse for serious and repetitive offenders. However, even in training schools there is an effort to pursue multiple objectives and provide programs to bring about positive change in offenders as well as to incapacitate them. As we will elaborate later in this section, the pursuit of multiple, and often incompatible goals, means that the justice system (for both juvenile and adults) is "inevitably in disfavor'' for ''not doing its job.'' Unfortunately, there is no agreement as to what the job is, how to do it, or how to measure its effects.

The Impact of Correctional Efforts

Have any efforts to save, treat, rehabilitate, or deter youths from further offenses been successful? To answer such a question is far more difficult than most people initially anticipate. Critics often refer to custodial institutions and traditional training schools as ''schools for crime.'' In his book, *Radical Non-intervention*, Edwin Schur has stated such a view as a matter of fact:

> There is now widespread recognition that the legal processing of juveniles, whatever it is called and however it is described, is in fact significantly punitive and potentially stigmatizing. This first became clear in the commitment to institutions, which function as ''schools for crime.'' (1973:127)

However, whether institutions function as ''schools for crime'' is not as clear and unequivocally accepted as critics have implied.

The tendency to denigrate juvenile institutions as schools of crime has been based on assessments of the number of youths who commit offenses after release. In the early 1960s Robert Beverly and Evelyn Guttmann (1962) examined the parole performance of juveniles released from California Training Schools during the first fifteen months after their release. They found considerable variation in recidivism, ranging from a low of 36 percent to a high of 60 percent. A study in New Jersey (Horwitz and Wasserman, 1977) reported 85 percent of boys who were institutionalized were recidivists but none of the girls were arrested again. Studies in England and Scotland yield estimated reconviction rates of between 60 and 70 percent for youth released from institutions (Rutter and Giller, 1983: 288). In Ontario, Canada the recidivism rate for training schools ranges between 54 and 73 percent with a median of 58 percent (Leschied and Thomas, 1985). Such rates fuel criticism of training schools and provide a rationale for pursuing alternatives.

Do such recidivism rates indicate failure of the correctional system? The answer to that question requires *a basis for comparison*. One relevant comparison would be the repetitive delinquency rate of offenders who have *never* been caught and punished. It is conceivable that the repetitive offense rate for those never caught could be greater than the high recidivism rates for youth released from institutions. If that were the case, then *relative to no response*, imprisonment would not be considered a total failure. In most attempts to evaluate the impact of different reactions to delinquency, the comparison is between offenders released from institutions and youths in alternative programs. These sorts of comparisons tell us something about the impact of one reaction compared to another but not the impact of any reaction compared to no reaction.

We will learn more about the impact of training schools relative to alternative programs when we summarize research on correctional experiments later in this chapter. We have already encountered some information relative to the success or failure of training schools in Chapter 9. Thornberry's (1971) study found that youths who had been institutionalized had lower subsequent involvement in delinquency than youths who had received less severe dispositions. A second study is noteworthy here because, as Richard Lundman states, " . . . its findings fly in the face of the near consensus among social scientists and others that institutionalization is an ineffective method of controlling delinquents" (1984: 199).

In a study called *Beyond Probation* (1979) Charles Murray and Louis Cox, Jr. compared 317 serious and repetitive juvenile offenders who had been sent to the St. Charles Training School or Valley View Training School in Illinois with youths sentenced to community-based alternatives. Rather than focusing on the proportion of youths who were caught offending after intervention, Murray and Cox studied the "reduction" in the volume of delinquent offenses. While a youth who was caught for an offense after release from a program would be a recidivist and, traditionally, considered a "failure," Murray and Cox argue that such a stringent definition of failure does not tell us whether the odds of delinquency were reduced more by one program than another. If youths processed through one program were committing five offenses per month before that experience and only one per month after intervention while another program reduced delinquency to three offenses, the former would be the more successful program in terms of the "suppression" of delinquency.

Of course, some changes in delinquency might occur due merely to aging or "maturational" reform and, hence, data on reductions in delinquency are useful for comparing alternative interventions rather than assessing the actual reduction in delinquency compared to no response. Thus, their study is relevant to the comparative suppression of delinquency among alternative interventions. This point is important to remember because summaries of *Beyond Probation* can give the impression that a reduction in delinquency after intervention means that the intervention "worked." For example, with regard to the Illinois research, Lundman states that "Everything worked to suppress involvement in delinquency" (1984: 206). In fact, all that can be said is that delinquency declined regardless of the type of intervention. Whether those declines were a result of the interventions would require data for youths where no intervention occurred at all.

What were the comparative suppression rates for alternative reactions? We have summarized Murray and Cox's results in Figure 10-6. Youths sent

Figure 10-6

Murray-Cox Study: Reductions in Delinquency by Type of Program

	Number of Offenders	Reduction in Arrests (12 mos. Before-12 mos. After)
Department of Corrections Training Schools	317	—68%
Nonresidential Programs	156	—53%
Residential Services	40	—60%
Wilderness Programs	14	—47%
Out-of-town Camp	45	—70%
Intensive Program	11	—82%

Source: Derived from Murray and Cox, *Beyond Probation*, 1979: Table 4.4, p. 118.

to the training schools committed 68 percent fewer offenses in the first twelve months after their release than in the twelve months prior to intervention. This figure represents a greater reduction than nonresidential programs and most alternatives. While some programs did as well or better, the data are contrary to the view that institutions or training schools make youths worse either in an absolute or in a comparative sense.

In short, the view of institutions as schools for crime is no better substantiated than a view of imprisonment as a specific deterrent or as a setting for reform. Advocacy of one or another point of view appears to be more a function of ideology than of evidence. Regardless of its basis in fact or fiction, the view of confinement in institutions as an inappropriate, expensive, and counter-productive force has generated considerable correctional experimentation. As we have already noted, assessing the success or failure of any particular type of intervention is no easy matter, and such is the case for measuring the success of correctional experiments.

Evaluating Correctional Experiments

There are numerous criteria for evaluating correctional programs but the two most common are *effectiveness* and *efficiency*. Program effectiveness refers to the attainment of goals or objectives while efficiency refers to the resources expended in attaining objectives (Adams, 1974). Both are important when making decisions about the investment of resources because they do not necessarily coincide. Expenditures may not appear justified in terms of payoff either in an absolute sense or in comparison to alternatives. For example, James Wilson (1975) has recounted the efforts of the New York City Police Department to curb subway robberies. In 1965 the New York police increased patrols of subways and assigned police to every subway train and station during peak hours for felony offenses. Robberies immediately dropped and in terms of effectiveness the program was a success. Yet, the cost of each felony prevented was about $35,000. Whether this was an efficient use of resources depends on the cost of alternatives.

The same issue is involved when evaluating community-based alternatives to training schools. One type of intervention may do no better or worse than another but, if one expends fewer resources, it may be the preferred response. We use the word "may" because there are other grounds for evaluating the total impact of an intervention other than goal attainment and comparative efficiency. For one, if the focus is on the behavior of offenders after release, a particular intervention may be as effective and efficient as any other but have other consequences that could make it undesirable. For example, some people advocate imprisonment because while the youth is confined citizens are not being victimized. If the number of crimes prevented during imprisonment exceeds the number prevented after participation in a less restrictive alternative, then confinement might come out ahead in terms of total impact. If confinement of some youths deters others from committing offenses for fear of the same consequences, then confinement might be the more effective program in terms of total impact on the delinquency rate in a community. In sum, while evaluation research has concentrated on recidivism of youths processed through a particular program in comparison to alternatives, there are broader considerations of total impact which could affect the relative merits of alternatives.

Of course, the focus on effectiveness and cost reflects the utilitarian approach to program evaluation even if expanded to include consideration of incapacitation and deterrence. If an intervention does not seem appropriate given public evaluations of the offenders or offenses involved, then demonstrations of effectiveness and efficiency may fall on deaf ears. Similarly, a particular intervention might be preferred because it is judged more humane than another. Paul Lerman (1968:63) has suggested that when two alternatives are similar in terms of effectiveness and cost, the most humane response should be chosen. Thus, issues of morality and justice may enter into the assessment of correctional alternatives with contrasting conclusions depending on the values and points of view involved.

Even if the focus is exclusively on recidivism, a researcher should deal with a variety of "methodological" issues before making any claims about demonstrated program effectiveness. One simple, but often ignored, requirement is to establish a basis for comparison. We have already noted that what may seem like a very high recidivism rate in an absolute sense may be low relative to alternative interventions. Such "alternatives" provide a basis for comparison.

Sometimes offenses by the experimental subjects before intervention are compared with offenses after intervention and, in that sense, the "experimental" group is compared with itself. Such comparisons may be meaningful if repeated numerous times and if other possible causes of changes (such as aging or maturational reform) are taken into account. However, ideally, a comparison of before-and-after delinquency among groups subject to alternative interventions and no intervention at all would make the results far more meaningful.

A common problem in correctional experimentation is that the composition of youths in a particular program can make a program look successful when, in fact, it merely had "better" subjects. A true experimental design attempts to solve this problem by assigning subjects to different groups or conditions through a random process. If different groups are created by the "luck of the draw" or some other random process and the number of youth in the groups is large enough, then we can have some confidence that the groups are comparable on all sorts of characteristics which might bias the results. As simple as it sounds, there are serious ethical questions involved in implementing it. Most conceptions of justice are based on the presumption that the response to an offender should be based on characteristics of the offense and the circumstances surrounding its commission. Responses to offenders are not supposed to be random either for the benefit of society and/or the offender. Hence, the only circumstances where random assignment is likely to occur is for trivial offenders or for minor variations in response where issues of justice are not a serious problem.

LaMar Empey and Maynard Erickson (1972) have described the difficulty of implementing an experimental design in the study of a nonresidential treatment approach. Their experiment in Provo, Utah, called for random assignment of boys either to a traditional institutional setting or a probation alternative. In the interest of science, the juvenile court judge initially expressed willingness to participate in the experiment. However, once the program got underway, the judge was reluctant to commit boys to institutions. The judge believed institutions to be harmful and preferred to divert youths. From a scientific perspective, the effects of institutions and alternatives need to be studied and analyzed. However, from a legal and ethical perspective, the random assignment of a youth to an institution or to probation is a violation issue of the delinquent's civil rights.

Correctional research must also confront the question: "How are the outcomes to be measured and evaluated?" Stated another way, what constitutes a success or a failure? Lerman (1968) examined the California Youth Authority's Community Treatment Project and found that youths in the experimental and comparison groups were reacted to differently by probation workers. Boys placed in community treatment who committed a new offense were often given a "second chance," whereas subjects in the comparison groups who broke the law were more likely to have their probation revoked. The criterion for failure was different for the two categories of youth and therefore biased results in favor of the experimental youths.

Several reviews of correctional treatment literature have commented on both the quality and the results of such studies. By far the most controversial review was a report submitted by Lipton, Martinson, and Wilks (1975) to the Governor's Special Committee on Criminal Offenders in New York in the mid-1970s. In a search for available reports on attempts at rehabilitation from 1945 through 1967, they found 231 studies that met a minimum set of standards for a methodologically adequate study. Perhaps the most telling statement about the methodological adequacy of such research is a statement by Martinson in a 1974 article that "it is just possible that some of our treatment programs *are* working to some extent, but that our research is so bad that it is incapable of telling" (1974: 48). This comment was merely a cautionary note to Martinson's more substantive conclusion that the best studies available "give us very little reason to hope that we have in fact found a sure way of reducing recidivism through rehabilitation. This is not to say that we have found no instances of success or partial success; it is only to say that these instances have been isolated, producing no clear pattern to indicate the efficacy of any particular method of treatment" (1974: 49). For purposes of formulating policy, Martinson concentrated on *methods of treatment*. For a treatment program to have policy implications, he believed it should be generally applicable, amenable to implementation in new settings, and should rely on something other than "exceptional" personnel. Martinson did cite some specific programs that appeared to be effective. However, he noted that the determinants of success for those programs did not seem to be the method of treatment per se, but the coincidence of exceptional personnel, subjects amenable to treatment, and enthusiasm for the program. To recommend that exceptional people be hired to do "something" with enthusiasm to subjects ready to change did not strike him as a policy for treatment.

Correctional Experimentation: Some Examples

Even as the review by Lipton, Martinson, and Wilks was published it was outdated, not necessarily in terms of the conclusions reached but in terms of the programs evaluated. Any discussion of correctional experimentation currently in vogue quickly becomes outdated as "innovations" are added and other approaches discarded. For instance, while the dominant theme in the 1970s was the implementation of community-based alternatives, themes which emerged in the 1980s emphasized restitution and deterrence. Restitution and shock therapy programs will be reviewed together with diversion in Chapter 11. In this concluding section we will review some examples of correctional experiments designed to "rehabilitate" or reduce recidivism by bringing about positive change in offenders.

For heuristic purposes, we will identify certain underlying dimensions to correctional experiments and briefly assess some specific programs. One dimension for classifying correctional experiments is the specific *focus* of the treatment effort. Some correctional efforts are directed specifically at the *individual* offender and attempt to deal with specific individual problems through counseling or individual casework techniques. Other programs work through and with *groups*. Sometimes such group-oriented treatment may be nothing more than counseling or discussion in group sessions. However, it may also involve "guiding" the development of groups in a way that can be used to gain control of members' behavior in positive ways and in a wide range of circumstances. Finally, while the ultimate goal is to change the behavior of individuals, modification of the wider social environment is the central focus of some correctional experiments as well. When embodied in an institutional program, such an approach is often called *milieu therapy*. Milieu therapy attempts to use every aspect of the inmate's environment as part of the treatment program (Martinson, 1974:33). It is also the basis for a variety of new programs, such as the "teaching-family" program (which provides a surrogate family, with house parents serving as role models) and related behavior modification or "token economy" programs. When extended beyond the confines of the institutional setting, such environmental approaches are the most global and ambitious of the forms of treatment because they call for a restructuring of relationships between offenders and the wider community.

In addition to the focus of treatment efforts, a second dimension for classifying forms of correctional experimentation is the degree to which they isolate offenders from the community or the degree of confinement involved. Some programs are totally residential with youths living within the confines of an institution while others are community-based with variable degrees of control over the everyday lives of subjects. They may be nonresidential with youths living at home or "semiresidential" with youths attending school, working, and participating in recreational activities in the wider community but, otherwise, living within program facilities.

For the sake of illustration, but at the risk of oversimplification, we will classify certain experimental efforts along two dimensions—the *focus* of the program and the *locus* of the program. Figure 10-7 classifies several

Figure 10-7

Correctional Treatment Approaches

Degree of Confinement	Focus		
	Individual	**Group**	**Environment**
Residential	Training Schools California Youth Authority	Highfields Redwing Cascadia	Project Case Project Ace
Semiresidential	Most halfway houses	Silverlake Experiment	Achievement Place Boy's Town Outward Bound Vision Quest
Nonresidential	California Community Treatment Project	Provo Experiment Buddy System	New Pride Chicago Area Project Oregon Social Learning Experiments

experiments along such lines. The programs identified in this table will be discussed in this section. Correctional philosophy, especially during the 1960s and 1970s, was characterized by arguments that treatment of juvenile offenders should move away from isolation towards community-based treatment and should expand its focus towards the modification of the environment rather than individual therapy.

Working with Individuals in Total Confinement

The study of diversity in juvenile institutions by Street, Vinter, and Perrow (1966) suggested that juvenile inmates' attitudes and attitudinal changes varied by type of institution, with inmates in treatment-oriented institutions exhibiting the most positive orientation and change. However, we do not know whether these attitudinal differences affected recidivism, nor do we know whether characteristics of inmates or characteristics of the institutional programs themselves accounted for these differences. Neither do we know what particular types of treatment programs (if any) might have made a difference.

Rutter and Giller's review of British research leads them to conclude that

"The general picture is one of remarkably similar re-conviction rates in the years immediately following discharge in institutions run on theoretically and practically different lines" (1984:289). They suggest that the features which differentiate successful institutions cannot be delineated in terms of a simple "therapeutic" versus "correctional" emphasis. Rather, the programs that may have a higher probability of success involve "firmness, warmth, harmony, high expectations, good discipline, and a practical approach to training" (291). This opinion is very similar to that advocated in the Martinson report summarized earlier. There are some programs that have higher success rates than others but it does not appear to be the "program" so much as the enthusiasm and energy of the people involved.

Research on the recidivism rates of youths receiving some form of individualized treatment within an institutional context has yielded confusing and unpromising results. The California Youth Authority's Community Treatment Project used personality assessment techniques in setting up treatment plans geared specifically to the needs of individual offenders. A study of a California treatment program that used psychodynamically oriented individual counseling found no improvement in recidivism rates (California Department of Corrections, 1958). Evaluations of psychotherapy for young male offenders (Guttmann, 1963) and female offenders (Adams, 1959;1961b) in California institutions produced the same findings. Two studies have suggested, however, that subjects who are deemed "amenable" to individual psychotherapeutic treatment have lower recidivism rates than nontreated subjects, but that the rates of subjects who are "nonamenable" to treatment are higher than the rates of nontreated (Adams, 1961a). In yet another study, Karl Jesness (1970) classified delinquents into "maturity types" such as asocial, conformist, manipulative, and neurotic. He then randomly assigned one group to an experimental program that formulated a specific treatment according to the needs of the individual and the other group to a traditional institutional program. After both groups of juveniles were released back into the community, Jesness found their recidivism rates virtually identical. Moreover, traditional individual and group counseling methods appear to be no more promising with adults (Kassebaum et al., 1971) than they are with juveniles (Martinson,1974). Martinson has qualified this generally negative conclusion with the observation that such programs may work when they are new, when subjects are deemed amenable to treatment, or when therapists are chosen for special qualities of empathy and warmth. A more recent review of individual counseling studies within institutions reached similar conclusions and actually recommended that individual counseling and psychotherapy be discontinued in the treatment of juvenile delinquency (Romig,1978).

Working Through and with Groups in Total Confinement

One of the earliest alternatives to the traditional institutionalization of juvenile offenders was "therapeutic" treatment through carefully guided group processes. The goal of this type of group therapy is to help deviant groups develop and enforce new social norms. The setting for such a treatment program has usually been a small residential institution, which could also be regarded as a therapeutic milieu. This type of group therapy experience is referred to as *guided group interaction* (GGI). Such programs see the group as the crucial factor in adolescent rehabilitation. According to the Center for Studies of Crime and Delinquency:

> GGI programs involve the delinquent in frequent and intensive group discussions of their own and other members' current problems and experiences. Based on the theory that antisocial youth behavior receives the support and approval of the delinquent peer group, and that substituting acceptable norms for delinquent values and attitudes also requires the support of the peer group, these programs encourage the development of a group culture and the acceptance by members of responsibility for helping and controlling one another. As the group culture develops and the group begins to accept greater responsibility, the staff group leader allows the group a greater degree of decision-making power. Over time, the group's responsibility may extend to decisions involving disciplinary measures imposed on a member or determination of a member's readiness for release. (Public Health Service, n.d.:3)

The best-known residential GGI program is Highfields, which began in 1950 in New Jersey. The Highfields program provides a highly supervised setting. It is limited to serving approximately twenty boys, age 16 and 17, who have not been previously committed to a correctional institution. During the day, the boys work at a nearby mental hospital as orderlies. They are not permitted to attend school. In the evening, two groups of ten boys each meet for guided group interaction sessions. Highfields has a short-term treatment approach that normally does not exceed three months.

The Highfields program was first evaluated by McCorkle, Elias, and Bixby (1959), who reported that the recidivism rate for Highfields "graduates" was only 18 percent, compared to a 33 percent rate for reformatory inmates. Ashley Weeks (1963) compared a sample of reformatory parolees with Highfields parolees and found the recidivism rate for the reformatory group to be 63 percent, compared to 47 percent for the Highfields group.

On the surface, the Highfields program seemed to be a successful treatment approach. However, critical examinations of the data have shown the programs's results to be far less convincing than originally concluded. For example, Paul Lerman (1968) noted that 18 percent of the cases from

Highfields were "in-program" failures who did not complete the program. When this group was added to the group whose recidivism rates were studied, the evidence in favor of the effectiveness of the Highfields program was reduced, although a difference still existed. The results of the Highfields program appear promising, but they are controversial on methodological grounds since youths were not randomly assigned to one or another program.

Guided group interaction techniques have been used successfully to reduce conflicts within large institutions as well. In 1968 Harvey Varruth at the Minnesota Training School (Redwing) for boys adapted the GGI program to a large institutional setting of more than 600 juveniles. At that time the institution had been having severe discipline problems and seemed on the verge of explosion. The new approach was received with great enthusiasm, and the internal conflict subsided. It has also been claimed that recidivism and inmate behavioral problems declined while staff morale improved. Of course, it is important to remember that these claims merely suggest that the introduction of a new set of procedures into an explosive situation can have beneficial consequences.

Sarason and Ganzer (1973) have reported on a project (Cascadia) in Washington State which uses a variety of techniques, including group discussion, modeling, and role-playing, to teach youths the skills necessary for avoiding peer pressure, applying for jobs, and planning their futures. For some groups staff "acted out" certain behaviors which the subjects could use as models for their own performance and role playing. Others participated in group discussions relevant to these same problems and skills. They collected data on recidivism for a period of 33 months after discharge and then again after 5 years. The recidivism rate was lower for both experimental groups for both periods and was especially low for those involved in group discussions. The rate after five years was less than one-half that found for the control group.

In sum, group-oriented approaches seem to show greater promise than individual counseling or psychotherapy. The word "seem" is important because it is possible that the differences observed are a product of pre-intervention characteristics rather than the efficacy of group methods. However, the possibility that the effects are real may be as conclusive as correctional experimentation ever gets and may be a satisfactory basis for advocating such techniques.

Designing an Environment in a Totally Residential Setting

Current environmentally-oriented programs in totally residential settings tend to be based on *behavior modification* techniques derived from Skinnerian operant conditioning theory and, more recently, from social learning theory (see Chapter 5). A major characteristic of behavior modification programs is the systematic manipulation of the environment to create a potential for changing behavior. Cohen and Filipczak (1971) report on a "new learning environment" (CASE) for boys in an institution that included a special environment aimed at expanding the social and academic repertoires of the residents and a token economy that rewarded the boys for academic competence and punished them for academic lethargy. The result of this treatment approach was a significant increase in grade level as measured by the Stanford Achievement Test. There was also a mean increase of 12.5 points in IQ scores after ten months in the program.

A second example of a behavioral program in an institutional setting is Project ACE (Applied Contingency Environment) at the Maryland Training School for Boys. This institution provides cottage housing and a school program for about three hundred delinquent youths. Project ACE was introduced in two cottages that housed the institution's most belligerent inmates. The project involved identifying target behaviors (breaking windows or chairs, assaultive behavior, poor school performance) and establishing a "point economy" system. Subjects could earn points through appropriate behavior and spend them in a "spending room" for such tangible goods as candy, soda, and grooming articles. They could also use them for admission to a game room. The program was effective in controlling the behavior of boys within the institution.

Ross and McKay (1978) reviewed 24 behavior modification-token economy programs within institutions and found only three that provided follow-up data on juveniles, including Cohen and Filipczak's. A follow-up of 27 boys suggested lower recidivism at one and two years but no difference at three years. However, the adequacy of the control group was questionable since there was no random assignment. Another study by Jesness and others (1972) suggested a lower parole violation rate for youths in a token economy experiment than control groups while a third study involving females reported higher recidivism rates for experimental subjects (Ross and McKay, 1976). Such variation in results and doubts about pre-intervention comparability of experimental and control groups led Ross and McKay to state " . . . we can conclude with confidence that behavior modification is not the panacea it was touted as when it was introduced to corrections" (289). However, the implications of such experiments for institutional management are more impressive and more conclusive: "In each of the programs . . . a behavioral approach was found to be successful in either reducing anti-social behavior in the institution" or in enhancing the offender's achievement or industrial productivity (289). Ross and McKay remind us once again that rehabilitation "is only one goal of corrections" and in terms of influence on targeted behavior within institutions token economies appear to work. The problem is "generalizing" the institutional impact to the everyday lives of youth when they return to the community.

Working with Individuals in a Semiresidential Setting

The *halfway house* is a temporary residence for offenders and is usually located within a community. The residents are generally given freedoms that are not possible in a totally residential program. These freedoms include access to community-based employment, education, and recreation. Private charitable organizations began operating halfway houses for offenders in the nineteenth century, and governmental agencies began establishing such programs in the 1950s. One of the purposes of the halfway house is to provide a transitional setting that will reduce recidivism, which tends to be inordinately high during the early stages after release. Thalheimer has described the purpose of a halfway house in the following manner:

> The very name halfway house suggests its position in the corrections world; halfway-in, a more structured environment than probation and paroles; halfway-out, a less structured environment than institutions. As halfway-in houses they represent a last stop before incarceration for probationers and parolees having faced revocation; as halfway-out houses, they provide services to probationers and parolees leaving institutions. Halfway houses also provide a residential alternative to jail or outright release for accused offenders awaiting trial or convicted offenders awaiting sentencing. (1975:1)

Depending on the particular halfway house in question, treatment may consist of an informal family-like atmosphere, formalized group therapy (such as guided group interaction), or individual counseling. Because of the diversity of programs and a lack of good follow-up data, it is difficult to assess the effectiveness of halfway houses per se and the effectiveness of individual therapy within such settings is unknown.

Working Through and with Groups in Semiresidential Settings

The best known experiment with group-oriented techniques in a semi-residential setting is the Silverlake Experiment. The Silverlake Experiment was conducted by LaMar Empey and Steven Lubeck (1971) between 1964 and 1968. Some boys were randomly assigned to a special community-based program, while others were placed in the regular institutional regimen at Boy's Republic, a private residential treatment facility for delinquent boys in Los Angeles. The experimental group, which consisted of no more than 20 boys, lived in a residential home located in a middle-class neighborhood during the week and returned home on weekends. The boys attended high school and had the assistance of a tutor. They also attended daily group meetings that were conducted along the lines of guided group interaction. The experiment lasted three years, with an additional year devoted to the collection of follow-up data.

The overall results indicated no significant difference between the experimental and control group in relative frequency of arrest during the twelve months following release. During that period, there was a 73 percent reduction in the volume of delinquency committed by experimental subjects and a 71 percent reduction in the volume of delinquency committed by the control group. This reduction might mean that both programs were successful but, without other bases of comparison, we cannot reach such a conclusion. Although the Silverlake program failed to show positive results compared to another program, the experiment remains as one of the most careful and sophisticated studies of community-based treatment.

Designing an Environment in a Semiresidential Setting

The image of training schools as prisons for juvenile offenders has given way in many settings to smaller, familylike living quarters without barbed-wire fences, bars, cells, or armed guards. A dramatic example of this change is "Boy's Town" in Omaha, Nebraska. In 1967 Boy's Town adopted a program called the "teaching-family model," which attempts to reproduce a homelike environment for learning new skills and behaviors. The "family" is composed of a husband and wife, who are known as "teaching parents," and five to ten adolescents. The youths and the teaching parents live together for approximately one year. Depending on a youth's needs, the parents attempt to instill new academic, vocational, social, and family-living skills. The system for establishing and maintaining new behaviors is based in part on a token economy. Individuals earn points for behaviors deemed desirable and may exchange accumulated points for goods and privileges. As a youth progresses in the teaching-family program, these motivational aids are gradually reduced.

The setting for the program is much like an ordinary suburban community with attractive individual houses for each family complete with all of the amenities of middle-class life. These houses are part of the Boy's Town community together with older buildings where activities necessary for the maintenance of the community and the development of various skills are provided. The youths in the program contribute to the maintenance of the facilities.

A similar attempt to design a new learning environment and break down barriers between the program and the outside world is Achievement Place. Achievement Place provides residential group care for delinquents and is organized similarly to Boy's Town. Youth in this program continue to attend school, visit parents, and may even earn stays at home. A token economy is used within a familylike environment with teaching parents. Youths are encouraged to work their way out of the token system by demonstrating that they can perform well on their own merits. When they are able to return home parents are given instruction on maintaining appropriate behavior. Thus, the program is based on principles of behavior modification but goes beyond a token economy in the attempt to encourage trustworthy behavior in settings where rewards and punishments are not as explicit or forthcoming as in a token system.

The authors are aware of no evaluative data on the Boy's Town program but there has been some evaluation of Achievement Place. As was the case for behavior modification techniques within more confining institutional settings, such techniques are highly successful in bringing about change in targeted behavior. However, the impact on subsequent delinquent behavior is unclear since nonrandom control groups are used as a comparison. Over a one-year follow-up period, 19 percent of 16 Achievement Place youths had been committed to an institution compared to about 53 percent of youths in the control group (Phillips et al.,1971). Over a two-year follow-up period, 56 percent of 18 Achievement Place youths were found to still be in school as compared to 33 percent of controls matched as "comparable" to these youths by a probation officer. Their recommittal rate was 22 percent as compared to 47 percent for the matched controls as well. While these results are suggestive, the same issues of pre-intervention comparability have to be raised.

Boy's Town and Achievement Place attempt to create a new learning environment by gaining control over reward and punishment and restructuring relationships with the community. A quite different approach with a similar goal is central to a variety of "wilderness" survival and "back-to-nature" programs in the United States and Canada. Such programs attempt to build confidence and skills through activities that are believed to be inherently rewarding and conducive to the development of problem-solving skills.

Two such programs in the United States are Outward Bound and Vision Quest. Outward Bound provides challenges such as backpacking, rock-climbing, sailing, and route-finding which are supposed to both develop a sense of competence and accomplishment as well as cooperation and leadership. The program uses existing environments and activities which are presumed to be challenging, rewarding and rehabilitative in themselves. In a follow-up study in Massachusetts, Outward Bound graduates were found to have a significantly lower recidivism rate after one year than a control group of matched juveniles handled through regular channels. However, the advantage was not significant after five years.

An analysis of a wilderness experience program for probationers in eastern Canada (Winterdyk and Roesch, 1982) yielded less promising results. The Canadian program was based on the Outward Bound philosophy and provided the same sorts of activities to minor or first time offenders. Data on psychological traits and attitudes that were supposed to be affected by the experience were "inconclusive" and both the experimental youths and control youths were found to have a reconviction rate of about 20 percent. There was some indication that the experimental groups' offenses were less severe but the differences were too small to be statistically significant.

Vision Quest is a more diverse program than Outward Bound but embodies much of the same philosophy. It is a private, for-profit treatment program for delinquent and troubled youth and has headquarters in Arizona and Pennsylvania. The program has grown to provide home-based treatment, group homes, and learning centers in addition to wilderness experiences. It is best known for its "wagon train" which makes regular appearances in parades throughout the country. The Vision Quest program has also drawn considerable critical attention (and is the subject of civil lawsuits) for deaths which occurred during one of its sailing ventures. In addition to building self-respect through challenging activities, the program is also known for its use of "confrontational" techniques in which inappropriate behavior is immediately addressed by a staff member and youth are forced to accept responsibility for their behavior. The technique has drawn some criticism since it may involve excessive force and pressure in order to immediately confront the problem. The program publicizes itself as successful and has been applauded by numerous corrections personnel, but it has not been carefully evaluated in comparison to alternative responses.

Working with Individuals in Nonresidential Settings

One of the most highly acclaimed rehabilitation experiments is the Community Treatment Program in California (Warren and Palmer, 1966; Palmer, 1971). In this experiment youths who otherwise would have been sent to California Youth Authority training schools were assigned to an experimental program and returned to their community for intensive treatment. Each member of the experimental group was diagnosed and classified on a scale of "interpersonal maturity." Within each maturity level, or "I-level classification," there were further subclassifications based on measures of the way a delinquent responds to or perceives the world. Categories within the I-levels were based on whether responses were passive or aggressive, conforming or manipulative, neurotic, acting out, or culturally identifying. The comparison or control group were youths assigned to one of the existing institutions of the California Youth Authority.

The initial reports from this project purportedly demonstrated greater success than traditional confinement. After fifteen months in the community, the experimental subjects had a parole violation rate of 28 percent, compared to 52 percent for the control subjects. However, in a critical analysis of this project Paul Lerman (1975) concluded that the most dramatic finding was that the project changed *parole officers' behavior* rather than the youths' behavior. Lerman found that the reported *number of offenses* for the two groups was approximately the same, if not higher for the experimental group, but that the *reactions* of officials to offenses was different. Parole officers for juveniles who were in the experimental group recommended fewer parole revocations than members of the control group. Youths in the community treatment program were more likely to be given additional chances to reform even though the experimental subjects had committed an average of 2.8 offenses in the follow-up period as compared to 1.6 for the control group. This unexpected difference may reflect greater interaction with parole officers for experimental subjects, increasing the chances that a parole officer would be aware of their misbehavior. Such differences make it difficult to draw definite conclusions about either the success or failure of the program.

Working Through and with Groups in a Nonresidential Setting

The basic principles of the Highfields project (GGI) were expanded upon in a nonresidential setting in Provo, Utah, beginning in 1959 (Empey and Erickson, 1972). Each day, following work or school, boys assigned to the experimental program went to a center for guided group interaction sessions. The control groups were to be a random selection of adjudicated youths placed on probation in the community and youths committed to the state training school. However, once the program was underway, the juvenile judge decided against randomly committing boys to the training school, and a new comparison group of youths committed to the training school from other Utah counties had to be used for comparison.

Analysis of the program showed that the experimental group did not have a significantly higher success rate than the probationers. After the first year of the program, the recidivism rates of the two groups was approximately 50 percent and the differences did not change appreciably over the next four years. After four years the recidivism rate for both groups was around 60 percent. However, both the experimental group and probationers did better than youths committed to a training school. After one year, 60 percent of training school youths had recidivated and by the end of four years about 80 percent had done so. Thus, confinement was less effective than two noninstitutional alternatives. Since the training school comparison group was not randomly created from the same population of youth as the probationers and experimental subjects, caution must be exercised in interpreting these findings.

A small-scale experiment in Hawaii called the Buddy System used nonprofessional volunteers to provide new social relationships for youths in their natural environment. Based on the same philosophy as "Big Brother" or "Big Sister" programs, youths with school problems were assigned a "buddy" to serve as a role model, monitor, and confidant. In essence, youths entered into a small group relationship with an older, conventional "buddy." An evaluation of buddy system programs in two cities in Hawaii (Fo and O'Donnell, 1974) found that youth with truancy problems who were referred to the program by schools were truant less often, especially when the volunteer "buddy" controlled a small amount of money which was used as a reward contingent on the performance of the youth.

Modifying the Environment in Nonresidential Programs

The objective in nonresidential, environmentally-oriented programs is to alter the communal or social relationships of the offender. Some alterations have been relatively minor while others have involved major changes in neighborhoods. The Chicago Area Project (Kobrin, 1959), instituted in the 1930s by Clifford Shaw, is the most notable example of an attempt to alter the environment on a rather large scale. The project had the dual objectives of rehabilitating parolees and preventing delinquency in neighborhoods with high crime rates. The core aim of the project was the revitalization of neighborhood identity and pride through local self-help enterprises. Parolees were expected to have a better chance of avoiding future crime if the neighborhoods to which they returned were organized in ways which would increase bonds between offenders and conventional organizations, people, and institutions. Solomon Kobrin has cited evidence that the program did reduce delinquency and a recent assessment by Schlossman and Sedlak (1983) suggests that the arrest rate may have been halved in one of the project neighborhoods as compared to no reduction of the arrest rate in a comparable nonproject neighborhood.

Project New Pride in Denver, Colorado is a difficult program to classify because it involves rather comprehensive attempts to alter the relation between a youth and the community environment, but working primarily through the offender. It does not attempt to reorganize the environment in the sense that the Chicago Area Project did but it does address nearly every aspect of a youth's relation to the community. It is a nonresidential, community-based program for repetitive and fairly serious offenders. Based on the belief that youths who do not want help are not likely to be helped, the program prefers voluntary enrollment and handles about 60 new enrollees per year. The project includes an alternative school and a learning disabilities center and provides intensive counseling, behavioral modification, and contracting and job placement. A follow-up study of New Pride youths found them to have a slightly lower recidivism rate (27 percent) than a control group (32 percent) with some of the success attributable to job placement and re-enrollment in school (Blew et al., 1977). However, it is important to remember that the New Pride youths were volunteers and may have differed motivationally prior to treatment compared to control youths.

Another approach to altering the problem behavior of youth without confinement attempts to alter the behavior of parents in relation to their children. Extensive research on such "family intervention" techniques have been carried out by researchers at the Oregon Social Learning Center (See Patterson et al., 1973; Patterson, 1980; Patterson and Fleischman, 1979). Parents of delinquent youth and aggressive children are taught non-coercive techniques of control and how to interact more positively with their children. The emphasis is on establishing stronger bonds between parents and children, improving parental monitoring, and insuring appropriate reactions to approved and disapproved behavior. One study of youths who had committed theft showed impressive reductions in stealing—from .83 events per week to only .07 per week immediately following treatment (Patterson, 1981; 1982). A subsequent study, however, found that after a year the youths had returned to their original rate (Moore et al., 1979). The family intervention approach has been used with some success to change aggressive behavior and such results appear to be more enduring than the changes produced in the study of theft.

Overview

The correctional experiments summarized in the previous section support several observations. First, few studies are methodologically adequate for reaching definitive conclusions about the impact of a program on recidivism when comparing alternative approaches or doing nothing at all. Second, token economies and behavior modification are effective tools for the management of offenders, the control of contrary behavior *within* a program, and the enhancement of educational, vocational, and other skills. Third, it is extremely rare for a correctional experiment to make offenders worse and most have done no worse than training schools and may have done better. Fourth, programs which attempt to alter the offender's environment, group life, or social relationships while minimizing barriers between the youth and the community show promise of reducing recidivism relative to training schools but may do no better than routine probation.

Richard Lundman (1984) concluded his examination of efforts in the prevention and control of juvenile delinquency, including many of the programs we've summarized, with several recommendations for policy. One recommendation is that *routine probation be retained as the first and most frequent sentencing option of juvenile court judges.* This recommendation was supported by the Provo Experiment since the experiment did no better than probation and cost more. He also recommends that *community treatment programs be expanded to accommodate nearly all chronic offenders.* This recommendation is advocated on the grounds that community treatment does no worse than confinement and is more humane. Finally, Lundman recommends that *institutionalization continue to be used as a last resort reserved primarily for chronic offenders adjudicated delinquent for index crimes against persons.* Cheaper and more humane alternatives are available for the vast majority of offenders and imprisonment is justified when an offender constitutes a continuing threat to the community.

Such recommendations stem from available research but it is important to note that they are based primarily on evidence concerning recidivism. Robert Martinson has noted that the emphasis on rehabilitating offenders has overshadowed other criteria for evaluating programs such as *general deterrence* and *incapacitation.* A particular treatment program might generate lower recidivism rates and yet contribute to a community's crime rate by allowing free movement of offenders and reducing fear of punishment among nonoffenders. Such possibilities are the basis for growing criticism of studies that use recidivism as the sole criterion for evaluating the effects of treatment programs (Martinson, 1976; Wilson, 1975).

A common sociological response to the generally unimpressive impact of treatment experiments has been to question the view that offenders can be changed by programs which tinker with limited aspects of their lives and environments. Sociologists often argue that rather than attempting to reform offenders, we need to institute fundamental changes in social, political and economic arrangements conducive to crime. In fact, it is principles underlying behavior modification that support such a view. If people can be influenced by *new contingencies* of reward and punishment within a correctional program, they will also be responsive to the contingencies operating in the outside world after release. Such observations, together with the question of whether treatment is more effective than doing nothing and with concern over possible labeling effects, have led sociologists to propose policies that combine *radical nonintervention* with efforts at social reform (see Schur, 1973). These two emphases are reflected in the diversion and prevention programs discussed in Chapters 11 and 12.

Box 10-2

Parents' Responsibility for Delinquency

Laws have been passed in several states holding parents responsible for their children's behavior. For example, Charles Gibson, city attorney in Dermott, Arkansas (*USA TODAY*, December, 1989) reports that parents can be charged with misdemeanors for their children's curfew violations. They can also be charged if they allow their children to possess controlled substances. Gibson reports that crime is down as a result.

By David Seavey, USA TODAY

Do you think that parents should be made to pay for the delinquent activities of their children?

Source: Copyright, *USA TODAY*. Reprinted with permission.

Summary

In this chapter we have summarized the history and current status of the imprisonment of juvenile offenders. While the risk of apprehension for a delinquent offense is quite low and the proportion of delinquents who are sent to correctional facilities is small, the use of imprisonment as an appropriate reaction to juvenile delinquency remains a key controversy in juvenile justice. Ironically, imprisonment itself was originally viewed as a humane alternative to physical punishment. Moreover, the imprisonment of offenders came to be viewed as a means of changing, or "reforming" people, rather than as simply a means of punishment. The reformatory emerged as a symbol of a new correctional philosophy but soon generated criticism from "anti-institutionalists." While the emergence of a separate juvenile justice system was characterized by arguments for probation and home treatment rather than reformatories, such institutions were not abolished and, in fact, a new form of short-term confinement, the detention center, was invented. The need for secure, custodial institutions for juveniles is still under attack, although countered in recent years by arguments for imprisonment as a means of incapacitation, retribution, and general deterrence. The rate of confinement has begun to climb relative to juvenile crime after a decade of decline during the 1970s. The actual impact of imprisonment on offenders is not as definite as conveyed by the declaration that reformatories are "schools for crime," but neither has its deterrent or rehabilitative consequences been demonstrated. Similarly, while correctional experiments suggest that community-based alternatives do no worse, and possibly better, than reformatories, it is not clear that they do better than ordinary probation. Numerous programs have produced what appear to be positive results, but these results can often be attributed to the characteristics of the staff or subjects. There is considerable evidence that offenders alter their behavior in response to changes in reinforcement contingencies and social relationships in their immediate environment, but there is less evidence that these changes endure or affect behavior after release.

After forty or fifty years of correctional experimentation we cannot easily counter charges that "Nothing works!" or demonstrate that doing "something" is better than doing nothing. That fact has led some critics to challenge the notion that experimentation with more of the same is the best direction for addressing problems of juvenile delinquency. In the 1970s radical critics advocated policies of minimal intervention, tolerance, and basic social change. Currently, critics with a more conservative bent have advocated a return to an emphasis on the potential deterrent, incapacitative, and retributive functions of imprisonment. Approaches reflecting these different points of view are reviewed in the next chapter where we consider programs that attempt to divert youths, to scare them straight, or to assure that they set matters right with victims.

References

Adams, S. 1959. "Effectiveness of the Youth Authority Special Treatment Program: First Interim Report." Research report no. 5. Sacramento: California Youth Authority.

———. 1961a. "Effectiveness of Interview Therapy with Older Youth Authority Wards: An Interim Evaluation of the PICO Project." Research report no. 20 (January 20). Sacramento: California Youth Authority.

———. 1961b. "Assessment of the Psychiatric Treatment Program: Phase 1, Third Interim Report." Research report no. 21 (January 31). Sacramento: California Youth Authority.

———. 1974. "Measurement of Effectiveness and Efficiency in Corrections." In D. Glaser (ed.), *Handbook of Criminology*. Chicago: Rand McNally.

Adler, C. 1984. "Gender Bias in Juvenile Diversion." *Crime and Delinquency* 30 (July): 371-85.

Allen-Hagen, B. 1991. "Public Juvenile Facilities: Children in Custody, 1989." *National Institute of Justice Reports* No. 223 (January/February): 20-23.

Beverly, R. F., and E. S. Guttmann. 1962. *An Analysis of Parole Performance by Institution of Release 1956-1960*. Sacramento: State of California.

Blew, C. H., D. McGillis, and G. Bryant. 1977. *Project New Pride*. Washington, DC: U.S. Government Printing Office.

Bureau of Justice Statistics. 1989. *Children in Custody, 1975-85*. U.S. Department of Justice.

Bureau of Justice Statistics. 1988. *Report to the Nation on Crime and Justice*. U.S. Department of Justice.

Bureau of Justice Statistics. 1988. *Bureau of Justice Statistics Annual Report, 1988*. U.S. Department of Justice.

Bureau of Justice Statistics. 1985. *Children in Custody*. U.S. Department of Justice.

Bureau of Justice Statistics. 1987. *Children in Custody*. U.S. Department of Justice.

California Department of Corrections. 1958. "Intensive Treatment Program: Second Annual Report." Prepared by H. B. Bradley, and J. D. Williams (December 1). Sacramento. Mimeographed.

Carter, R. M., R. A. McGee, and E. K. Nelson. 1975. *Corrections in America*. Philadelphia: J. B. Lippincott.

Children's Bureau. 1975. *Institutions Serving Delinquent Children*. Washington, DC: U.S. Government Printing Office.

Cohen, H. L., and J. Filipczak. 1971. *A New Learning Environment*. San Francisco: Jossey-Bass.

Dean, D. W., and N. D. Reppucci. 1974. "Juvenile Correctional Institutions." In D. Glaser (ed.), *Handbook of Criminology*. Chicago: Rand McNally.

Emerson, R. M. 1969. *Judging Delinquents*. Chicago: Aldine.

Empey, L. T., and M. L. Erickson. 1972. *The Provo Experiment*. Lexington, MA: Lexington Books.

Empey, L. T., and S. G. Lubeck. 1971. *The Silverlake Experiment*. Chicago: Aldine.

Feld, B. C. 1981. "A Comparative Analysis of Organizational Structure and Inmate Subcultures in Institutions for Juvenile Offenders." *Crime and Delinquency* 27 (July): 336-63.

Finestone, H. 1976. *Victims of Change*. Westport, CT: Greenwood Press.

Flanagan, T. J., and E. F. McGarrell (eds.). 1985. Sourcebook of Criminal Justice Statistics. U.S. Department of Justice.

Fo, W. S. O., and C. R. O'Donnell. 1974. "The Buddy System: Relationship and Contingency Conditions in a Community Intervention Program for Youth with Non-professionals as Behavior Change Agents." *Journal of Consulting Clinical Psychology* 42:163-69.

Fox, V. 1972. *Introduction to Corrections*. Englewood Cliffs, NJ: Prentice-Hall.

Galvin, Jim, and Ken Polk. 1983. "Juvenile Justice: Time for New Direction?" *Crime and Delinquency* 29 (July):325-32.

Galvin, Jim, and Gerald Blake. 1984. "Youth Policy and Juvenile Justice Reform." *Crime and Delinquency* 30 (July): 339-46.

Giallombardo, Rose. 1974. *The Social World of Imprisoned Girls: A Comparative Study of Institutions for Juvenile Delinquents*. New York: Wiley.

Glaser, D. 1964. *The Effectiveness of a Prison and Parole System*. Indianapolis, IN: Bobbs-Merrill.

Gray, F. C. 1847. *Prison Discipline in America*. London: J. Murray.

Guttmann, E. S. 1963. "Effects of Short-Term Psychiatric Treatment on Boys in Two California Youth Authority Institutions." Research report no. 36 (December). Sacramento: California Youth Authority.

Hagan, J., and J. Leon. 1977. "Rediscovering Delinquency: Social History, Political Ideology and the Sociology of Law." *American Sociological Review* 42 (August): 587-98.

Horwitz, A., and M. Wasserman. 1977. "A Cross-Sectional and Longitudinal Study of the Labeling Perspective." Paper presented at American Society of Criminology annual meeting, Atlanta, Ga.

Howard, J. 1780. *The State of Prisons in England and Wales*, 2nd ed. London: Cadell and Conant.

Janowitz, M. 1966. Foreword to Street, Vinter, and Perrow, *Organization for Treatment*.

Jesness, K. F. 1970. "The Preston Typology Study." *Youth Authority Quarterly* 23 (Winter): 26-38.

Jesness, K. F. et al., 1972. *The Youth Center Research Project*. Sacramento, California Youth Authority.

Johnston, N. 1973. *The Human Cage: A Brief History of Prison Architecture*. New York: Walker.

Kassebaum, G., D. Ward, and D. Wilner. 1971. *Prison Treatment and Parole Survival: An Empirical Assessment*. New York: John Wiley.

Kobrin, S. 1959. "The Chicago Area Project: A 25-Year Assessment." *Annals of the American Academy of Political and Social Science* 322 (March): 20-29.

Lerman, P. 1968. "Evaluative Studies of Institutions for Delinquents: Implications for Research and Social Policy." *Social Work* 13 (July): 55-64.

Lerman, P. 1975. *Community Treatment and Social Control*. Chicago: University of Chicago Press.

Lerman, P. 1984. "Child Welfare, the Private Sector, and Community-Based Corrections." *Crime and Delinquency* 30 (January): 5-38.

Leschied, A. W., and K. Thomas. 1985. "Effective Residential Programming for 'Hard-to-Serve' Delinquent Youth: A Description of the Craigwood Program." *Canadian Journal of Criminology* 27 (April): 161-77.

Lipton, D., R. Martinson, and J. Wilks. 1975. *The Effectiveness of Correctional Treatment: A Survey of Treatment Evaluation Studies*. New York: Praeger.

Lundman, Richard. 1984. *Prevention and Control of Juvenile Delinquency*. New York: The Oxford Press.

Martinson, R. 1974. "What Works?—Questions and Answers About Prison Reform." *Public Interest* 35 (Spring): 22-54.

_____. 1976. "California Research at the Crossroads." *Crime and Delinquency* (April): 180-91.

Mauer, M. 1991. "Americans Behind Bars: A Comparison of International Rates of Incarceration." Washington, DC: The Sentencing Project.

McCorkle, L. W., A. Elias, and F. L. Bixby. 1959. *The Highfields Story*. New York: Holt, Rinehart and Winston.

Moore, D. R., P. Chamberlain, and L. H. Mukai. 1979. "Children at Risk for Delinquency: A Follow-Up Comparison of Aggressive Children and Children Who Steal." *Journal of Abnormal Child Psychology* 7: 345-55.

Murray, C. A., and L. A. Cox. 1979. *Beyond Probation: Juvenile Corrections and the Chronic Offender*. Beverly Hills, CA: Sage Publications.

Office of Juvenile Justice and Delinquency Prevention. 1989. "The Juvenile Court's Response to Violent Crime." *Juvenile Justice Bulletin*. U.S. Department of Justice: U. S. Government Printing Office.

Packer, H. 1968. *The Limits of Criminal Sanction*. Palo Alto, CA: Stanford University Press.

Palmer, T. B. 1971. "California's Community Treatment Program for Delinquent Adolescents." *Journal of Research in Crime and Delinquency* 8 (January): 74-92.

_____. 1976. "Martinson Revisited." In M. Matlin (ed.), *Rehabilitation, Recidivism and Research*. Hackensack, NJ: National Council on Crime and Delinquency.

Patterson, G. R., J. A. Cobb, and R. S. Ray. 1973. "A Social Engineering Technology for Retraining the Families of Aggressive Boys." In H. E. Adams and I. P. Unikel (eds.), *Issues and Trends in Behavior Therapy*. Springfield, IL: Chas. C. Thomas.

Patterson, G. R., and M. J. Fleisman. 1979. "Maintenance of Treatment Effects: Some Considerations Concerning Family Systems and Follow-up Data." *Behavior Therapy* 10: 168-85.

Patterson, G. R. 1980. "Treatment for Children with Conduct Problems: A Review of Outcome Studies." In S. Feshbach and A. Fraczek (eds.), *Behavior Change: Biological and Social Processes*. New York: Praeger.

Patterson, G. R. 1981. "Some Speculations and Data Relating to Children Who Steal." In T. Hirschi and M. Gottfredson (eds.), *Theory and Fact in Contemporary Criminology*. Beverly Hills, CA: Sage Publications.

Patterson, G. R. 1982. *Coercive Family Processes.* Eugene, OR: Casalia Publishing Company.

Phillips, E. L., E. A. Phillips, D. L. Fixen, and M. M. Wolf. 1971. "Achievement Place: Modification of the Behaviors of Pre-delinquent Boys within a Token Economy." *Journal of Applied Behavioral Analysis* 4: 45-59.

Platt, A. 1969. *The Child Savers.* Chicago: University of Chicago Press.

Polsky, H. W. 1962. *Cottage Six.* New York: Russell Sage Foundation.

Public Health Service. N.d. *Community Based Correctional Programs: Models and Practices.* Publication no. 2130. Washington, DC: U.S. Government Printing Office.

Regnery, A. S. 1985. "Getting Away with Murder: Why the Juvenile Justice System Needs an Overhaul." *Policy Review* 34 (Fall):65-68.

Romig, D. 1978. *Justice for Our Children.* Lexington, MA: Lexington Books.

Ross, R. R., and H. B. McKay. 1976. "A Study of Institutional Treatment Programs." *International Journal of Offender Therapy and Comparative Criminology* 20: 167-73.

Ross, R. R., and H. B. McKay. 1978. "Behavior Approaches to Treatment and Corrections: Requiem for a Panacea." *Canadian Journal of Criminology* 20: 279-95.

Rutter, M., and H. Giller. 1984. *Juvenile Delinquency: Trends and Prospects.* New York: The Guilford Press.

Sarason, I. G., and V. J. Ganzer. 1973. "Modeling and Group Discussion in the Rehabilitation of Juvenile Delinquents." *Journal of Counseling Psychology* 20: 442-49.

Schlossman, S. L. 1977. *Love and the American Delinquent.* Chicago: University of Chicago Press.

Schlossman, S. L., and S. Wallack. 1982. "The Crime of Precocious Sexuality: Female Juvenile Delinquency and the Progressive Era." In D. Kelley Weisberg (ed.), *Women and the Law: The Social Historical Perspective.* Cambridge, MA: Scherlman.

Schlossman, S. L., and M. Sedlak. 1983. *The Chicago Project Revisited.* Santa Monica, CA: Rand, Schmeiser and Douglas.

Schrag, C. 1971. *Criminal Justice: American Style.* Washington, DC: U.S. Government Printing Office.

Schur, E. 1973. *Radical Non-Intervention: Rethinking the Delinquency Problem.* Englewood Cliffs, NJ: Prentice-Hall.

Schwartz, I. M. 1989. *(In)justice for Juveniles: Rethinking the Best Interests of Children.* Lexington, MA: D. C. Heath and Company.

Schwartz, I. M., M. Jackson-Beeck, and R. Anderson. 1984. "The 'Hidden' System of Juvenile Control." *Crime and Delinquency* 30 (July): 371-85.

Shover, N., and W. J. Eisenstadter. 1989. *Analyzing American Corrections.* Belmont, CA: Wadsworth.

Snyder, H. N., 1990. "Growth in Minority Detentions Attributed to Drug Law Violators." Juvenile Justice Bulletin. Washington, DC: U.S. Department of Justice.

Snyder, H. N., T. A. Finnegan, E. H. Nimick, M. H. Sickmund, D. P. Sullivan and N. J. Tierney. 1989. *Juvenile Court Statistics, 1989*. U. S. Department of Justice: Office of Juvenile Justice and Delinquency Prevention.

Snyder, H. N., J. L. Hutzler, and T. A. Finnegan. 1985. *Delinquency in the United States, 1982*. Pittsburgh, PA: National Center for Juvenile Justice.

Snyder, H. N., and J. L. Hutzler. 1983. "The Serious Juvenile Offender." Summarized in "Juvenile Crime Increase is Moderate, Compared to Adults." *Justice Assistance News* 3 (April): 12-13.

Street, D. 1965. "The Inmate Group in Custodial and Treatment Settings." *American Sociological Review* 30 (February): 40-55.

Street, D., R. D. Vinter, and C. Perrow. 1966. *Organization for Treatment*. New York: Free Press.

Sutherland, E. H., and D. R. Cressey. 1978. *Criminology*, 10th ed. Philadelphia: J. B. Lippincott.

Sykes, G. 1978. *Criminology*. New York: Harcourt Brace Jovanovich.

Thalheimer, D. J. 1975. *Cost Analyses of Correctional Standards: Halfway Houses*, vol. 2. Washington, DC: Law Enforcement Assistance Administration, U.S. Department of Justice.

Thornberry, T. P. 1971. "Punishment and Crime: The Effect of Legal Dispositions on Subsequent Criminal Behavior." Ph.D. Dissertation. University of Pennsylvania.

Tittle, C. R. 1974. "Prisons and Rehabilitation: The Inevitability of Disfavor." *Social Problems* 21 (3): 385-95.

Warren, M. Q. 1969. "The Case for Differential Treatment of Delinquents." *Annals of the American Academy of Political and Social Science* 38: 47-59.

Warren, M. Q., and T. B. Palmer. 1966. *The Community Treatment Project after Five Years*. Sacramento: California Youth Authority.

Weeks, H. A. 1963. *Youthful Offenders at Highfields*. Ann Arbor: University of Michigan Press.

Williams, J. R., and M. Gold. 1972. "From Delinquent Behavior to Official Delinquency." *Social Problems* 20 (Fall): 209-29.

Wilson J. Q. 1975. *Thinking about Crime*. New York: Basic Books.

Winterdyk, J., and R. Roesch. 1982. "A Wilderness Experiential Program as an Alternative for Probationers." *Canadian Journal of Corrections* 24 (January): 39-50.

Zald, M. N., and D. Street. 1964. "Custody and Treatment in Juvenile Institutions." *Crime and Delinquency* 10 (July): 249-56.

chapter 1

Recent Themes
Diversion, Restitution, and Shock Therapy

Does clubbing a man reform him? Does brutal treatment elevate his thoughts? Does handcuffing him fill him with good resolves? Stop right here, and for a moment imagine yourself forced to submit to being handcuffed, and see what kind of feelings will be aroused in you. Submission to that one act of degradation prepares many a young man for a career of crime. It destroys the self-respect of others, and makes them the easy victim of crime.

—John P. Altgeld, *Our Penal Machinery and Its Victims,* 1884

In the last chapter we summarized a large volume of literature on corrections and correctional experiments of various kinds. This chapter will be much more narrow in focus. We will address three themes in juvenile justice that emerged as "new and innovative" approaches in the 1970s and 1980s and which will continue to dominate discussions of delinquency control in the 1990s. In the 1970s the major emphasis was on diverting offenders who had not committed serious offenses to community-based programs. This major programmatic theme became known as *diversion.* However, the concern about protecting some offenders from the presumed trauma of traditional court processing was paralleled by a growing concern for protecting the rights of victims. Matters had to be set right with the victims of crime, and offenders had to play an active role in that process. This "victim-orientation" was reflected in programs requiring that offenders pay the victim and/or society back through their own labor. *Restitution* emerged as a programmatic emphasis in the 1980s. Finally, public, political, and social scientific opinion grew more conservative during the 1970s and 1980s. The emerging victim-orientation was accompanied by an increasing commitment to "getting tough" with juvenile offenders. Youths needed to be dramatically confronted with the potential costs of their transgressions. If adolescents could not be corrected by the system, then maybe they could be *scared straight* by direct exposure to the hazards of prison life. Diversion, restitution, and shock therapy programs were seen as new and innovative approaches for the juvenile justice system. They have intuitive appeal as plausible alternatives to traditional processing of juvenile offenders, but as with all "new and improved" products, we must examine them with a critical eye.

Diversion

While diversion was a key theme in juvenile justice philosophy in the 1970s and 1980s, its underlying philosophy was anything but new. The basic notion that juvenile offenders should be protected from the harshness of the adult criminal justice system was the precise rationale for the creation of a separate juvenile justice system. One of the first attempts at diversion was the very creation of the juvenile court in Cook County, Illinois, in 1899. In the quote heading this chapter, Governor Altgeld was condemning the lack of special consideration for juveniles in the criminal codes of the nineteenth century. In a popular pamphlet published in 1884 entitled "Our Penal Machinery and Its Victims," Governor Altgeld described the criminal justice system as a "crushing process." His forceful indictment of the inhumane treatment of offenders was a catalyzing force in the development of the juvenile court in Illinois. Similarly, in a treatise on prisons, Enoch Wines (1880), a nineteenth century penologist, stated that "human justice is a clumsy machine and often deserves the punishment which it inflicts." Wines advocated a reformatory system for juveniles that would reflect the conditions of home life rather than the harsh and punitive aspects of the penitentiary. The advent of the juvenile justice system may have represented certain regressive and politically motivated social policies, as Anthony Platt's (1969) study of the juvenile court contends (see Chapter 2), but there is also evidence that the emergence of the juvenile court represented a perceived need to divert juveniles from the adult criminal justice system with its institutional modes of treatment (see Hagan and Leon, 1977; Schlossman, 1977).

Therefore, while the juvenile court was created as part of a diversion movement, it also became the focus of diversion efforts. By the late 1960s criticism of the juvenile justice system solidified in a concert of arguments to the effect that many youthful offenders needed to be diverted from the juvenile justice system. In the words of one scholar, the juvenile court had become a "dumping ground" for all of those problems of youth that families, schools, and other agencies could not handle (Emerson, 1969). Some criminologists specifically challenged the scope of the court and of juvenile delinquency statutes. Edwin Lemert (1971) advocated a philosophy of "judicious nonintervention," arguing that the juvenile court should be an agency of last resort for children, to be used only when all other remedies have been exhausted. In devoting time and attention to relatively petty behavioral problems, the juvenile court was less able to deal with far more serious matters.

By the end of the 1960s, disillusionment with the scope of the juvenile court was widespread and the call for diversion and new alternatives developed into a set of policy recommendations. The 1967 report of the President's Commission on Law Enforcement and Administration of Justice was highly critical of the juvenile justice system. It called for the utilization of alternative programs so that contact with the juvenile justice system could be minimized:

> The formal sanctioning system and pronouncement of delinquency should be used only as a last resort. In place of the formal system, dispositional alternatives to adjudication must be developed for dealing with juveniles, including agencies to provide and coordinate services and procedures to achieve necessary control without unnecessary stigma. Alternatives already available, such as those related to court intake, should be narrowed, with greater emphasis upon consensual and informal means of meeting the problems of difficult children. (1967)

This commission advocated limiting the jurisdiction of the juvenile court to criminal cases involving juvenile offenders.

Theoretical Precedents

When the members of the President's Commission on Law Enforcement and Administration of Justice advocated diversion, they made specific reference to the dangers of stigmatization and contamination believed to be inherent in the labeling and legal processing of juvenile offenders. In doing so, they were drawing on two prominent sociological perspectives on delinquency — *labeling* and *differential association*. According to the tenets of labeling theory, juveniles who are processed through the juvenile justice system may become what they are labeled. Diversion policies would presumably avoid or minimize the stigma of being labeled a delinquent by diverting certain categories of juvenile offenders out of the court system.

Similarly, advocates of differential association theory assume that crime, like other behavior, is learned in social interaction. By associating with persons whose attitudes favor law violation, an individual comes to learn those attitudes and gradually becomes a lawbreaker himself. From the perspective of differential association theory, the juvenile justice system creates more delinquency by introducing novice delinquents to the infectious values of "hard-core" delinquents. Differential association theorists would lobby for diversion to prevent any fraternization of "pre-delinquents" with "lawbreakers."

Juvenile Rights and Due Process

Another underlying theme in the development of a diversion philosophy was concern for the clarification of children's rights and the extension of guarantees of due process of law to juveniles. Several critics of juvenile justice had taken the position that the denial of certain rights of due process and the processing of juveniles for trivial and often unspecified transgressions might contribute to a "sense of injustice" (Matza, 1964) and undermine respect for the legal system (Schur, 1973). A concern for juvenile rights and due process was central to the idea of *judicious nonintervention* or what Schur (1973) termed "radical nonintervention" in the lives of the young.

The Attack on Detention

A major concern among the advocates of diversion was to keep as many juveniles as possible out of detention or jail. Juvenile detention is the practice of holding juveniles in secure custody pending court disposition for offenses that range from abandonment by parents, incorrigibility, and running away from home to such serious offenses as homicide, rape, burglary, and aggravated assault. Youths involved in the less serious offenses are often referred to as "PINS," "MINS," or "CINS," which translates into persons, minors, or children in need of supervision. Many who are designated as PINS are dealt with informally but are in need of some temporary care until suitable placement can be found. Those juveniles charged with criminal acts may also be placed in a detention facility as a measure of public protection and to prevent the offender from absconding before the juvenile court can review the case. Thus, adolescents in need of temporary custodial care can range from a first-time status offender to a hard-core, chronic delinquent.

According to the National Center for Juvenile Justice (1990), 230,000 or 20 percent of all delinquency cases in 1987 resulted in detention. Similarly, 10,000 or 12 percent of all status offenders were held in a detention facility at some point between referral to court and case disposition (see Figure 11-1). In some local jurisdictions where no juvenile detention facilities exist, youths may be held in detention by being placed in a separate section of the local jail. Sarri (1983) estimates that 3,000 to 12,000 youths under 18 might be found in adult jails on any given day. She estimates that over a period of a year, 500,000 children are detained in adult jails. A study of incarcerated children revealed that juveniles held in adult jails commit suicide at approximately eight times the rate of youths held in juvenile detention centers (Justice Assistance News, 1981). While the federal government has repeatedly sought to have juveniles removed from adult jails, this has not been completely successful.

In addition to the practice of using adult jails in those locales where no juvenile detention facility exists, a second difficulty with detention is the fact that unlike adults, bail is not used with juveniles. According to the Bureau of Justice Statistics (1989), juveniles placed in detention facilities had an average stay of 12 days. However, this average is misleading because the actual distribution of days in detention clusters either at one day or several weeks. While detention is supposed to be used prior to a juvenile court hearing to hold youths who are a danger to themselves or to others, it is often used as a type of unofficial punishment (Sarri, 1983).

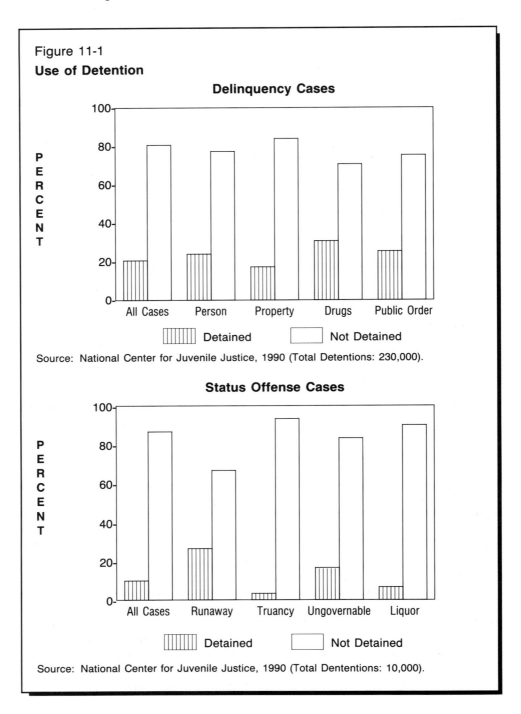

Figure 11-1
Use of Detention

Delinquency Cases

Source: National Center for Juvenile Justice, 1990 (Total Detentions: 230,000).

Status Offense Cases

Source: National Center for Juvenile Justice, 1990 (Total Dententions: 10,000).

Thus, removing juveniles from detention, particularly when the placement is for inappropriate reasons, has been a major objective of diversion advocates.

Economics

Depending on the type of diversion program implemented, removing even a small percentage of noncriminal offenders from the juvenile justice system could save millions of dollars. According to the Bureau of Justice Statistics (1991), the nationwide costs for public juvenile facilities totaled more than $2.1 billion a year, more than doubling in the preceding ten years. The average cost for a one-year stay per resident is now $29,600, ranging from a high $78,800 in Rhode Island to a low of $17,600 in South Dakota. The average per-day cost at short-term facilities like detention centers is $76 ($27,740 annually), but for open environments like shelters or halfway houses, the cost is $81 per day ($29,565 annually). Further, of those juveniles who are held in such facilities, only 17 percent are violent offenders. The rest are property, status, drug-related, and probation violation offenders. By removing even a fraction of these less serious offenders from the formal system, diversion might serve the lofty ideals of human justice, as well as the practical need for economic retrenchment.

The Meaning of Diversion

The exact meaning of diversion is ambiguous in that it has been used to refer to policies as diverse as doing nothing to programs indistinguishable from existing juvenile justice options. It can refer to the simple act of deflecting juveniles away from the juvenile justice system. However, in many other instances, it implies the development of alternative strategies or programs for dealing with juveniles outside of the formal processing mechanisms of the juvenile court. These alternative strategies range from informal, "field adjustment" strategies to sophisticated treatment programs. Finally, to make matters even more confusing, some juvenile justice agencies use the term "diversion" to refer to formal actions taken by the juvenile court that attempt to "minimize penetration into the juvenile justice system" (Cressey and McDermott, 1973). In this instance, the "diverted" juvenile actually remains within the formal system, but attempts are made to reduce the offender's exposure to the juvenile court process. This type of diversion may take the form of an official or semiofficial program in which the standard procedures of the juvenile justice system are somewhat modified. Thus, as simple as the word "diversion" may be, the actual implementation of diversion may entail radically different alternatives.

In the broad sense of the term, diversion may occur within the police department after a juvenile has been taken into custody. Figure 11-2 shows the disposition of juveniles taken into custody and the options that are available to police departments. Of the nearly one million juveniles apprehended each year, only 63 percent were actually referred to the juvenile court. As shown in Figure 11-2, nearly a third of all apprehended juveniles were never brought to the attention of the juvenile court, and were instead referred to a welfare organization (1.9%), to some other police agency (1.1%), or handled within the police department and then released (29.1%). Only 4.7 percent of all apprehended juveniles were referred to adult court. Thus, the police exercise a significant amount of discretion not only in deciding whether or not to take a juvenile into custody, but also how the juvenile is to be dealt with after the apprehension occurs.

On page 106 of Chapter 3 is a flowchart of the juvenile court's processing machinery. Of the 1.1 million adolescents referred to the juvenile court in 1987, 54 percent were nonpetitioned or allowed to bypass the formal court process. The remaining 46 percent were petitioned but 187,000 or 35 percent were nonadjudicated cases and in a sense, also allowed to bypass a formal court appearance. Of the original 1.1 million referrals, 344,000

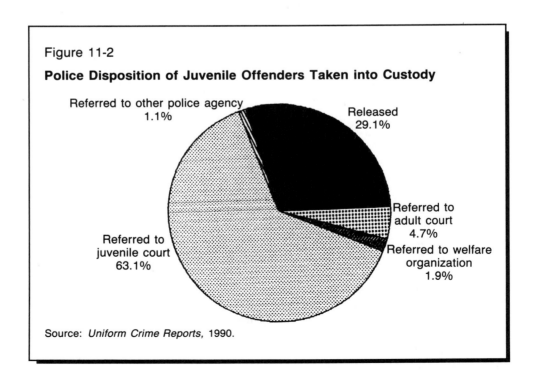

Figure 11-2

Police Disposition of Juvenile Offenders Taken into Custody

Referred to other police agency
1.1%

Released
29.1%

Referred to
adult court
4.7%

Referred to
juvenile court
63.1%

Referred to welfare
organization
1.9%

Source: *Uniform Crime Reports*, 1990.

cases (waived + adjudicated) or 30 percent had a formal court appearance and the remaining 70 percent were processed out of the system. Further, of those who were actually adjudicated, only 99,000 were actually placed in a formal juvenile facility. Assuming that the 11,000 waived cases resulted in some type of formal response from the adult system, and adding to this the 99,000 placements in the juvenile system, we arrive at a total of 110,000 of the original 1.1 million receiving a serious court disposition. In other words, 90 percent of all referrals to the juvenile court result in something other than formal placement, and only 10 percent are either waived to the adult court or sent to a juvenile placement. This would suggest that the juvenile court sends the vast majority of its referrals back to the community and in a sense diverts them from the formal court process.

In an attempt to clarify a muddled concept, Klein (1976) has suggested that the term "diversion" should refer only to the process of turning alleged juvenile offenders away from the formal juvenile justice system. According to this definition, diversion does not require that specific alternatives be prescribed, only that the juvenile not enter the official system. The term "referral" is used to describe the process by which a juvenile who is diverted from the formal system is placed in a program that is not directly related to the juvenile justice system. Much confusion exists regarding the precise meaning of the term "diversion" and while in some instances it may represent a new and innovative approach in dealing with delinquency, in other instances it may be nothing more than bringing the juvenile offender in the side door rather than the front door. Finally, diversion may also refer to the discretionary judgment exercised by the police and juvenile court officials.

Evaluation of Diversion Programs

The ambiguities with the concept of diversion make it difficult to summarize evaluation studies of diversion programs (Rojek and Erickson, 1982b). For some, the success or failure of diversion is simply the removal of juvenile offenders from the formal juvenile justice process. For others, it is what Rutherford and McDermott (1976) refer to as "the minimization of penetration" into the system. That is, offenders are dealt with in a manner that is less formal and less bureaucratic. For yet others, diversion means referring a juvenile to some form of community treatment. Furthermore, can one equate informal and unstructured diversion that occurs outside the official system with "official" diversion that occurs within the juvenile justice system? Some juvenile courts operate diversion programs but these can be more structured and coercive than the informal and less supervised diversion programs that are operated in the community. The diversion philosophy is so popular that a wide variety of different programs can be lumped together under the rubric of diversion. Research is handicapped by an absence of precise operational definitions and clear operational concepts of how these programs supposedly function.

Research Findings

In a previous edition of this text (Jensen and Rojek, 1980) we noted that research findings on the impact of diversion did not support any one conclusion. Some programs may have had their intended impact, minimizing future involvement of diverted youths with the juvenile justice system, while others appeared to make no difference or to do worse than traditional court responses. Since that first edition was published, there has been a national evaluation of diversion programs and several reports issued on specific diversion programs in different regions of the nation. Most reports have shown diversion to do no better or worse than ordinary court responses. Selke (1982) pointed out that diversions programs are highly vulnerable to *selection bias* or what is more commonly called "creaming," where the subjects selected for the program are low-risk offenders. Diversion programs must be carefully examined to be certain that characteristics of the system such as arrest practices or court intake procedures, are not biasing the outcomes.

Published evaluations based on programs in Arizona (Rojek and Erickson, 1982a; 1982b), Connecticut (Rausch and Logan, 1983), Illinois (Spergel et al., 1981) and Florida (Frazier and Cochran, 1986) have been quite consistent. Youths diverted into programs created as alternatives to ordinary court practices do no better or no worse than youths dealt with by traditional means. Moreover, with the implementation of such alternatives, police appear more willing to bring youth in for processing than was the case prior to their creation. Reports from England (see Rutter and Giller, 1985) suggest a similar outcome. Efforts to lessen the severity of juvenile processing tend to result in more cases being processed. Rather than narrowing the range of candidates for intervention, diversion has been charged with "widening the net" (Esbensen, 1984; Klein, 1979).

Given the unexpected outcome of diversion, some critics question whether the results justify the lax attention to issues of due process that may accompany processing. Lundman (1984) argues that diversion can result in large numbers of youth receiving "treatment without trial." Moreover, once created, the existence of diversion agencies depends on cases being assigned to them for service. Rojek and Erickson (1982b) found programs in the county they studied competing for status offenders and accepting any kind of offender into their program to justify their existence. Youths treated were a "mixed bag" of offenders rather than youths who had only committed status offenses for the simple reason that pure status offenders were difficult to find. It was discovered, for example, that diversion programs created for status offenders were also accepting property, drug, violent, and even nonoffenders.

Rojek (1986) examined the issue of inappropriate referrals to diversion agencies. These were cases where community-based programs sought to maximize the number of clients they served by allowing all types of juvenile offenders who were diverted from the traditional court processing into their programs. What invariably occurred was a mismatch between services provided and a juvenile's specific needs. For example, runaway facilities were dealing not only with runaways but also with truants, curfew violators, drug violators, and often nonoffenders. While it might be alleged that some service is better than no service at all, it was found that in those instances where diverted youth were receiving inappropriate "treatment" from a specialized agency, the youth were less well-adjusted after completing the program. Some juveniles who were indiscriminately placed in treatment programs simply to "fill-up the slots" experienced increased frustration and anger.

While these reports challenge some of the rationales for diversion, it is important to note that some diversion programs appear to be more successful than others. For example, a review of diversion projects in California found that in three of eleven programs studied, youths who were diverted into special community-based programs did significantly better than comparison youths dealt with through routine procedures (Palmer and Lewis, 1980). Of course, youths in eight of eleven diversion programs did not do significantly better than comparison youths. Moreover, the lower recidivism rates for the diverted youths did not extend to first-time offenders or youths who had several prior offenses. Palmer and Lewis suggested that diversion may work for youths with slight prior involvement with the justice system and when the programs have the following characteristics: 1) minimal personal distance between workers and youths, 2) high levels of personal concern and acceptance of youth, and 3) high frequency of contact. They also note that the programs that significantly reduced recidivism were more costly on the average than those that had no effect.

The overall assessment of diversion varies. For those who believed that diversion was supposed to reduce the involvement of government agencies in youths' lives, diversion has turned out to be particularly disturbing because it led to greater involvement. However, as noted in Chapter 10, the diversion movement did reduce the number of youths, especially girls, in correctional institutions and, in that sense, diversion was successful.

Binder and Geis (1984) note that while critics of diversion point to increases in the range and number of youth dealt with as an undesirable side effect of diversion, increased attention to problems of youth can be defined as a positive consequence. If organized community attention to youth addresses real needs and problems that would not go away by ignoring them, then the infusion of resources into new programs may be worthwhile. Thus, for those who believe that providing a greater range of programs to a wider range of youth is the rationale for diversion, then diversion may have succeeded. However, it is still the case that the vast majority of programs have not had their intended impact on the future delinquent activities of diverted youths. Although Binder and Geis defend diversion, they do note that, at present, there are more negative findings than positive ones.

Kenneth Polk (1987) sees a much more sinister side to diversion. He argues that:

> The net-widening effects observed with these apparent efforts at "destructuring" are not illustrations of "good ideas gone astray." The widening of the net of social control that results from much of diversion or from such programs as "community treatment" or "community corrections" instead should be seen as a logical consequence of the ideas within which the programs were initially conceived and defined. The persons who controlled the implementation of these efforts, whether they were top-level bureaucrats or line-level staff, were explicitly — and from the beginning — in the business of expanding the treatment or rehabilitative resources of the community. (1987:375-76)

In other words, diversion was supported with the explicit view of bringing more clients into community service organizations. As with any new program, funds were made available to a wide range of community treatment agencies, and this meant a new source of revenue. As stated by Polk "less meant more precisely because that was what was intended" (1987:377). Curran (1988) found that a bifurcated system exists in the United States with public facilities responsible for institutionalized offenders and the private sector concentrating on diverted juvenile offenders. The existing public juvenile institutions were maintained at the same level as before the advent of diversion but the major change was in the private sector. Rausch and Logan (1983) in supporting this contention assert that:

> In essence, the diverted population was drawn from a pool of offenders who, prior to the implementation of diversion programs, would probably have been released or left alone. The effect of such a policy has been to expand control over a larger, less seriously involved sector of the juvenile population. (1983:21)

Binder and Geis (1984) argue that sociologists are rejecting diversion prematurely because of their basic distrust of police, their overidentification with underdogs, and their cynicism about the criminal justice system. Polk, on the other hand, asserts that "It would be easier to take the comments of Binder and Geis more seriously if they had paid closer attention to the empirical record available on diversion" (Polk, 1987:360). Clearly, diversion is a policy that evokes strong sentiment on both sides of the debate. After close to two decades of proliferation of diversion strategies, the evidence is still lacking that diversion is the panacea originally intended. Whether diversion ideology was flawed in its very conception or was simply never properly implemented, the myriad forms of diversion created in the 1970s and 1980s seem to have waned, and formal and more punitive responses by the juvenile justice system have gained popularity.

Juvenile Restitution

A second and more recent theme in dealing with delinquency is restitution. Unlike diversion, where the objective was to protect the juvenile, restitution represents a significant shift to a policy of juvenile accountability. As a sanction imposed by the court, restitution requires the offender to make payment, either in monetary terms or by performing service to the victim or the community. Alfred Regnery of the Office of Juvenile Justice and Delinquency Prevention states:

> No program in juvenile justice has met with greater enthusiasm from courts and communities across the nation than restitution. Perhaps because restitution offers an element of "common sense" to juvenile justice that other approaches seem to lack, it is especially adaptable to a wide variety of program goals and methods. (Juvenile Justice Bulletin, 1985:2)

The growing disillusionment with diversion, along with the repeated "nothing works" doctrine, has spurred interest in restitution. Because this approach is simple, victim oriented, and reasonably inexpensive, restitution programs are currently enjoying immense popularity in the adult and juvenile court systems. Schneider (1986) points out that in 1977 there were only fifteen formal juvenile restitution programs in the United States; currently they exist in nearly every state.

Historical Basis of Restitution

The concept of restitution dates back to ancient civilizations. Some aspect of restitution is found in the code of Hammurabi, the Torah, Greek law, and Roman law. Interestingly, restitution was required in many early societies as a way of protecting the offender from aggressive retaliation by the victim or the community. Anglo-Saxon codes required that a specified amount of "blood money" be paid as a substitute for retaliation (Martin, 1981). Under the Anglo-Saxon code, the offender made one payment to the victim and another to the king for having broken "the king's peace." However, under the Common Law, this early Anglo-Saxon tradition of payment to the victim eroded as the monarchy gained strength. Payment to the crown took a larger and larger share of the final settlement. Eventually, the state replaced the victim and when any crime took place it was considered a violation against all of society. In the process, the concept of compensation or payment of damages to the victim gradually disappeared from criminal code in the Common Law.

Presently, a victim of a criminal act who seeks some type of compensation must turn to the civil code and file charges for tort action. Under the Common Law, such litigation is distinct from the criminal process and usually takes a back seat while the state actively pursues the prosecution of an offender. Even if the state proves that the offender committed the act, there is no provision in criminal law for the victim to receive compensation other than the satisfaction of sending the offender to prison.

Many countries operating under a Civil Law system rather than a Common Law system tend to place the rights of victims above the rights of the state. For example, in the People's Republic of China, the issue of victim compensation is of tantamount importance. In an assault trial in Shanghai attended by one of the authors, an individual was accused of attacking another person with a knife. To the amazement of the Western observers, the victim himself brought in a bag that contained all of the evidence. The victim proceeded to show the judge each article of clothing that was stained with blood, several towels that were blood stained, plus the bicycle tire that had a hole in it. Under the procedures governing criminal law in the United States, such evidence could not be casually brought in by the victim and then presented to the judge. However, in China the trial judge encourages the presentation of such evidence, carefully examines each item, determines its value, and begins to tally up the damages. At the conclusion of the trial, the offender agreed to buy the victim all new clothing, new towels, replace the bicycle tire, pay for medical bills and, finally, pay the victim for the one day of lost wages. The judge gave the offender one year of probation and required him to apologize to the victim.

In the United States, on the other hand, the victims of crimes often find that they are first confronted by their offenders, and then they are "victimized" a second time by having to endure the harshness of a court proceeding and the cross-examination of a defense attorney. The criminal code in the United States does not emphasize compensation to the victim as much as punishment for the offender.

Types of Restitution

Hudson and Galaway (1978) suggest that restitution could include four types of arrangements. One type requires offenders to compensate the victim with monetary payment. A second type of restitution involves monetary payments made by the offender to a community agency such as a hospital or a service agency, a third party such as an elderly citizen who is in need of assistance, or the community at large (for example, purchasing trees for a city park or purchasing playground equipment). The offender could be required to contribute money to a charity when the victim cannot be located or when the "victim" is the public at large. A third type of restitution requires the offender to personally repair whatever damage he or she committed. Finally, the fourth type of restitution, often referred to as *symbolic restitution*, is when the offender is required to provide a service to the community. Typically the offender has to work a certain number of hours in a social service facility like a community mental health agency or a neighborhood recreation program, or address youth groups on the dangers of drug abuse.

Figure 11-3 is an example of a restitution agreement used in the District of Columbia. The juvenile offender agrees to provide direct services to the victim, make money restitution, and perform community service. As long as the juvenile honors this agreement, he or she will remain on probation; any violation of the restitution agreement may result in the revocation of probation.

The Goals of Restitution

According to Schneider (1985), restitution can serve multiple purposes. First and foremost, it allows some sense of victim's rights to play a part in the judgment. In the strictest sense, it does not matter whether the offender, the offender's family, or even the state compensates the victim. The point is that the victim suffered a loss and, for justice to be served, it is imperative that the victim's loss be restored. A second purpose of restitution is rehabilitation. Many restitution programs are organized around the notion that by compensating the victim, the offender is undergoing a type of treatment and learns that crime does not pay. By varying the amount and type of restitution, the juvenile court can offer a treatment program that will serve the needs of the juvenile offender. A third rationale for restitution is accountability. Unlike the *parens patriae* basis of the juvenile court, which tends to excuse juvenile offenders for not being totally responsible for their actions, restitution purportedly "reflects a shift in thinking about youth; one that emphasizes juveniles' individual responsibility and therefore, accountability for their actions" (Schneider, 1985:7). It is argued that by holding the youth accountable, recidivism is reduced and public confidence in the juvenile justice system is increased. Finally, for some, restitution can also be seen as a form of punishment because the juvenile court is imposing a sanction and the offender must

Figure 11-3

Superior Court of the District of Columbia

Social Services Division   Family Branch

Restitution Agreement
Juvenile Community Service Program
Superior Court of the District of Columbia
Social Services Division — Family Branch

I, _____ , agree to participate in the Juvenile Restitution Program. I agree to all the requirements listed below under the checked paragraphs:

DIRECT SERVICE TO VICTIM. _____ was a victim of this offense. I will work directly for   him   her   for a total of _____ hours in the following manner:

MONEY RESTITUTION. As a result of my offense_____ suffered monetary damages. I agree to repay   him   her for the total sum of $_____ to be paid in the following manner:

COMMUNITY SERVICE. I agree to pay the community for my offense by performing _____ hours of community service. I will perform this service in the following manner:

_____
_____
_____
_____
_____
_____

I agree that this agreement will become a condition of my probation and I further recognize that if I break this agreement, the Social Services Division may request that the Court revoke my probation and commit me to the Department of Human Services. I also recognize that I must fulfill other conditions in order to participate on probation in the Restitution Program. These conditions are:

_____
_____
_____
_____

PROBATIONER'S SIGNATURE: DATE:
ATTORNEY FOR DEFENDANT: DIVISION OF SOCIAL SERVICES:
COMMUNITY WORKER: VICTIM:
CORPORATION COUNSEL: MEDIATOR:

pay a price for his or her transgression. Others might argue that restitution is not punishment in the traditional sense because the offender is merely repaying a debt. Strictly speaking, punishment means not merely the repayment of a debt but a sanction that exceeds the proportionality of the debt.

A theoretical basis for restitution can be derived from a perspective called *equity theory*. When someone commits a criminal act, both the victim and the offender find themselves in an inequitable situation. Offenders can overcome that inequity by justifying or excusing the victimization (a "psychological" equity) or they can restore actual equity by compensating the victim. The use of restitution as a sanction may restore the balance that existed prior to the criminal act. According to equity theory, direct restitution from the offender to the victim produces the most psychologically satisfying results while symbolic restitution to a third party provides the least satisfactory results. Schafer (1970:125) states that restitution "is something an offender does, not something done for him or to him and as it requires effort on his part, it may be especially useful in strengthening his feelings of responsibility." Similarly, Martin (1981) suggests that restitution can be devised in such a fashion as to allow the harm-doer the opportunity to neutralize the damage that was done and to become reintegrated into society by doing something positive. The equity rationale avoids the notion of the offender as "sick" or in need of treatment.

Research Findings

It is currently estimated that 52 percent of juvenile courts have formal restitution programs and 97 percent have used restitution at one time or another (Juvenile Justice Bulletin, 1985). Nearly every state currently has legislation that either permits restitution explicitly or implicitly allows restitution under the guise of juvenile court discretion. Moreover, the Office of Juvenile Justice and Delinquency Prevention has spent $30 million in 85 juvenile courts in an effort to promote and evaluate the use of restitution (Staples, 1986). Presently it is sponsoring a new initiative called RESTTA (Restitution, Education, Specialized Training and Technical Assistance Program) to provide practitioners with the information they need to start or expand restitution programs. There is a concerted effort in the U.S. Department of Justice to encourage the wholesale adoption of restitution in the juvenile court.

One of the problems in evaluating restitution programs is that restitution is typically added to other consequences. For example, in addition to being placed on probation, the juvenile offender is also required to repay the victim for the harm that occurred. A youth may succeed in one regard and fail in the other. The terms of probation may be met but the "add-on" stipulation may or may not be met satisfactorily. Schneider, Griffith, and Schneider (1982) found that when restitution is the sole sanction, rather than an "add-on" to probation, youths are more likely to successfully abide by the court order and less likely to commit a new offense. However, in this research, low-risk offenders were found to be given restitution as sole sanction more often than high-risk offenders. The question that arises is whether restitution had an impact or if low-risk offenders by definition are less likely to recidivate. Thus, it has not been conclusively established that restitution as a sole sanction is more effective than restitution as an additional sanction.

More recently, Schneider (1986) examined the outcomes of four studies where juvenile offenders were randomly assigned into restitution or into traditional juvenile court programs, such as detention on weekends or incarceration. In the first study, Schneider found that the restitution group had fewer subsequent offenses than the control group, but the difference was not large. In the second study, Schneider found the restitution group to have lower recidivism scores, but again the difference was slight. The third study produced results that were supportive of restitution rather than probation. Finally, in the fourth study, the restitution group tended to re-offend slightly more than the probation group. Schneider concluded that the "results from the experiments regarding the effect of restitution on recidivism should be viewed as quite encouraging" (1986: 549). While restitution groups had a slightly lower recidivism rate than the control groups in three comparisons, the magnitude of the differences was quite small, varying between 3 and 10 percent. Whether such differences are "quite encouraging" is a matter of interpretation.

Current Assessment of Restitution

As was the case with diversion, restitution makes eminently good common sense and, theoretically, both of these approaches ought to be successful. The arguments in favor of restitution are quite appealing. Unlike incarceration, restitution is relatively inexpensive, the victim is compensated for losses incurred, the negative effects of incarceration are avoided by allowing uninterrupted schooling or employment, reparation might have a rehabilitative effect, and the community becomes an integral part of the overall program. On the other hand, restitution can become just another sanction applied to an increasing range of problems. As with diversion, there is the potential for restitution to be used in a discriminatory manner. For example, upper-class youth may have opportunities to earn money that are not available to lower-class youth. Staples (1986) argues that the unemployment rates for youth are exceedingly high, and since a juvenile offender has the added burden of "being in trouble with the law," they are even more unlikely to find employment and will be unlikely to make monetary restitution. There have been alleged instances of work or service programs that are inadequately supervised and undocumented. In other cases, there have been criticisms of work time assigned that is so excessive as to be self-defeating. After a lengthy review of restitution, Martin concludes: "Like diversion and probation, restitution is a broad concept with theoretical promise, popular appeal, and unsystematic empirical support that indicates that it is a potentially effective sentencing alternative for use with certain types of offenses and offenders" (1981: 492).

Victim-Offender Mediation

A more recent version of restitution brings together the victim and the offender in a face-to-face meeting with a trained mediator, to negotiate the type or amount of restitution. Hughes and Schneider (1989) sought to identify victim-offender mediation programs at the juvenile court level and found 171 such programs in the United States. In attempting to assess the effectiveness of these programs, they found that in most cases both the victim and the offender expressed satisfaction with the outcome, although the offender was less satisfied than the victim. The outcome of the mediation was generally monetary restitution to the victim, but in a few instances community service was required or some type of behavioral change in the offender was proposed, such as improved school attendance or grades. Coates and Gehm (1985) found that in the few restitution/mediation programs that were evaluated up to this point in time, the victims were highly satisfied with the outcome, and indicated that they would participate again. Unfortunately, because victim-offender mediation is relatively new and has not been properly evaluated, little can be said about the overall success of these types of programs. Though reports indicate that the outcome is viewed favorably by the participants and the community, the suggestion that restitution also produces a lower recidivism rate requires much more careful research.

Shock Therapy

The two types of institutional alternatives already discussed in this chapter have not made for exciting reading in the popular press and it is conceivable that most individuals have little awareness of these programs. However, the third "new" approach that we will examine has received enormous publicity and is enthusiastically supported by the public at large. In one sense, shock therapy is both an application of deterrence theory (discussed in Chapter 9) and a prevention approach (discussed in Chapter 12). But, it can also be a form of community-based treatment. Central to the notion of deterrence is the assumption that any rational individual can be deterred from committing a crime if that person is convinced that dire consequences are likely to follow (Lundman, 1984). Shock therapy such as the Scared Straight program, which entails intensive confrontation between adult prisoners and juveniles, sends a simple message: "Mess around with the law and you are going to spend time in jail, and jail life ain't pretty."

Punishment Not Treatment

During the 1980s, a pronounced shift took place from that of the "velvet glove approach" in dealing with juvenile offenders to one that was a "clenched fist." Throughout the 1970s there was a growing concern for the rights of status offenders, but little attention was paid to the problem of rehabilitating serious juvenile offenders. However, in 1984 the National Advisory Committee for Juvenile Justice and Delinquency Prevention recommended that grants which supported programs aimed at the deinstitutionalization of status offenders be discontinued, while a more punitive orientation be taken in the juvenile courts. "Law and order" became a popular slogan and several state legislatures began to revise their juvenile codes to reflect a more punishment-oriented stance. Indeed, juvenile incarceration rates increased 30 percent between 1975 and 1985 (Bureau of Justice Statistics, 1989). Yet this incarceration rate increased in spite of the fact that juvenile arrests for serious offenses remained stable over the same period (Galvin and Polk, 1983).

Clearly, the most discernable change in the attitude toward juvenile offenders has been the Supreme Court's recent decision on capital punishment for juveniles (see the *Stanford v. Kentucky* case discussed in Chapter 2). According to Streib (1987), capital punishment of juveniles is reemerging as an issue of great symbolic importance despite the fact that only 287 out of more than 14,000 people legally executed in American history were below the age of 18. The mere fact that the Supreme Court in the Stanford case ruled on the legality of the death sentence for a 16- and 17-year-old in such a perfunctory fashion supports Streib's contention that there is a pervasive shift toward a more punitive stance for juvenile offenders.

A second area where there is a clear indication of a get tough approach is the juvenile reform legislation calling for mandatory and determinate sentencing of juveniles, as well as the lowering of the upper age of the juvenile court's jurisdiction (Ohlin, 1983). In 1977 the state of Washington was the first state to revise its juvenile code in order to clearly endorse punishment as its primary objective, and step back from the traditional goal of rehabilitation. Incarceration is mandatory for certain offenses, and the length of incarceration varies according to the seriousness of the offense.

New York and Colorado also require mandatory periods of incarceration, and other states may soon follow. Many more states are beginning to restrict the exclusive jurisdiction of the juvenile court and require particular types of offenses to be turned over to the jurisdiction of the adult court. It was out of this national frustration and anger that the Scared Straight program emerged.

The Rahway Prison Project

In September 1976 a group of inmates who were serving long prison sentences organized a Juvenile Awareness Project. These inmates, who became known as the "Lifers' Group" at Rahway State Prison in New Jersey, began to "counsel" juveniles who were becoming more and more involved in delinquent behavior. The basic approach of the Lifers' Group was to expose these juveniles to the harsh realities of prison life and to scare these adolescents into going "straight." Over time, these sessions developed into extremely harsh confrontations and the experience was termed "aversion therapy."

This program was first briefly discussed in a *Readers' Digest* article. A television producer who read the article conceived the idea of producing a documentary film on the Juvenile Awareness Project (Finckenauer, 1982). A documentary film was produced in 1978 entitled "Scared Straight" and was aired in Los Angeles for a local audience. This show received such a phenomenal response that in March of 1979 it was broadcast from coast to coast. "Scared Straight" received virtually every award possible for a documentary film, including an Oscar and an Emmy. Soon after the film was shown, 38 states started or initiated plans for Juvenile Awareness Programs (Cavender, 1981).

Evaluation of Scared Straight

The documentary film entitled "Scared Straight" show a small group of juveniles being escorted into Rahway State Prison where they will have a confrontational encounter with the Lifers. While Peter Falk narrates, the camera shows seventeen street-wise and cocky adolescents casually walking into the prison. Falk points out that these kids represent the dregs of adolescent society. They have been arrested for all kinds of offenses and they are headed for adult prison. One of the girls in the group points out how much fun it will be to watch these "burn-outs" in prison and see what "losers" they are. Upon entering the prison, the juveniles see crowded cells, hear the jarring sound of steel prison doors opening and closing, and walk the prison corridors listening to the verbal taunts of prisoners making sexual advances. In the actual confrontation with the Lifers, the language is crude, crass, and vulgar. The inmates unleash a verbal barrage of the horrors of prison life including sexual assaults, beatings, and even murder. The Lifers take turns haranguing these adolescents and in the process inject an element of fear. After nearly two hours of verbal abuse, the adolescents are then brought back to the waiting bus and taken home. Falk states that three months after this visit, sixteen of the seventeen adolescents have gone straight. The Lifers have allegedly worked with 10,000 juveniles and the documentary claims that 90 percent of these have gone straight. The program is powerful and revealing. By the time "Scared Straight" ends, the average viewer is convinced that the problem of juvenile crime can be solved. Once again, we confront a simple solution to a complex problem.

James Finckenauer (1982) investigated the making of the film along with the policy implications of Scared Straight programs and has written a devastating critique. First of all, Finckenauer points out that the Lifers did not keep very good records. Precisely how they determined that 90 percent of adolescents went straight is somewhat of a mystery. Further, it is not clear how the documentary producer arrived at the conclusion that the seventeen youngsters used in the film were hard-core delinquents. These adolescents were recruited for the filming and were told to be somewhat arrogant going into the prison and somber coming out. No concrete evidence was actually gathered to prove that, in fact, sixteen of the seventeen went straight. Of the 10,000 to perhaps 15,000 adolescents that were subjected to this shock treatment, most of them were recruited from local high schools and the students were under the impression they were going on a field trip. Again, there is no concrete evidence to suggest that these youngsters were delinquent. Most likely they were straight before they went to Rahway State Prison.

The key question is why 90 minutes of abusive language and scare tactics should reform a person for life. This approach assumes juveniles are totally responsible for their behavior and ignores social factors which may play a role in the onset of delinquency. In other words, adolescents get themselves into trouble and they can get themselves out. No follow-up services are provided to the adolescents once they leave the prison setting. In this sense, Vito and Wilson (1985) suggest that Scared Straight was hardly a program. It was more of an effort by a group of inmates with good intentions but who did not have a clear intervention strategy, no theory, no data, and no follow-up procedures.

Finckenauer (1982) showed that about 59 percent of the youngsters who went through the Rahway Scared Straight program had not been charged with an offense in the six months following the "rap" session. However, 89 percent of the control group who did not participate in the program remained free from delinquent activity during the same period. Not only did the program not have the expected impact, it may have "boomeranged" and made things worse. On this basis, Finckenauer questioned the credibility of the film and argued that the Juvenile Awareness Project failed to reduce delinquency.

The State of New Jersey investigated the net worth of the project at Rahway prison and concluded that the warden needed to be transferred, and the program itself drastically changed. A "showtime mentality" had developed at the prison with two sessions being held each day, five days a week. Further, there were hints of excessive abuse and sexual advances. Prison officials decreed that participants had to be "certified" delinquents. The program was modified into a prison tour followed by a discussion with certain inmates.

Other Shock Programs

One of the longest running juvenile awareness programs in the United States is the Squires Program at San Quentin in California. The Squires program is similar to the modified Scared Straight approach. That is, juvenile offenders are brought in for a prison tour and a discussion session with the inmates, but the scare tactics and abusive language are not used. Lewis (1983) evaluated this program using an experimental and control group, and followed these subjects over a twelve-month period. Lewis' results were quite similar to Finckenauer's: the experimental group actually had a higher recidivism rate than the control group, although the differences were not statistically significant.

Buckner and Chesney-Lind (1983) evaluated a Stay Straight program in Hawaii. Once again, it was found that the experimental group had a higher number of subsequent arrests but the authors could not attribute this higher failure rate to the Stay Straight program. They concluded, "It is unrealistic to expect that any single experience, no matter how profound, would have a significant and long-lasting impact on a problem so complicated and intractable as juvenile delinquency" (1983:245).

There are numerous other programs; including JOLT (Juvenile Offenders Learn Truth at the State Prison of Southern Michigan), The Insiders Juvenile Crime Prevention Program (Virginia State Penitentiary), STYNG (Save the Youth Now Group, Milhaven Penitentiary, Ontario, Canada), and JAIL (Juvenile Awareness of Institutional Life, Idaho State Penitentiary). Many of these programs started around the time of Scared Straight, but by the early 1980s they were terminated. Most of these programs failed to gather any data, using instead correspondence or testimonials as follow-up information. In the few instances where they were evaluated, no evidence could be found demonstrating program effectiveness.

The Scared Straight program is a classic example of a "bandwagon" effect that caught the attention of the public but had little substance. As

Cavender (1981) states, it was a "media-generated phenomenon." The proposed solution to crime was superficial, based on distorted facts and exaggerated claims. There was little structure to the program, no attempt to alter the social situation in which these youth lived, and no aftercare service. Lundman (1984) warns that simply scaring adolescents is no solution to delinquency and may even exacerbate the problem. It is important to recognize that the Scared Straight program essentially tries to use the threat of crime and violence within institutions as a deterrent to juvenile crime. Thus, in supporting such a program, the justice system is admitting that it cannot control the problem even within its own secure institutions.

Summary

We have examined three current and popular responses to juvenile delinquency and found all three of them to be less than promising. There is some potential in restitution and diversion but their impact on delinquent behavior has yet to be convincingly demonstrated. Scared Straight programs appear to be ineffective or counterproductive.

Juvenile diversion arose out of the criticism of the juvenile justice system as a stigmatizing and self-depreciating experience. This approach attempted to deflect juveniles from the traditional system and in those instances where youth needed special help, to generate some community-based response.

A review of the literature suggests that:

1. More rather than less juveniles get processed, and many of these are petty rather than hard-core offenders.
2. Community competition for clients can result in inappropriate services and a frenzied recruitment of clients.
3. There are several points of view about the nature of diversion, and evaluation of its success or failure vary depending on conceptions of the form it was to take (e.g., "leave them alone" versus "give them more programs").
4. Diversion may represent an instance of treatment without trial, where the protection of individual rights tends to be ignored.
5. Some programs may reduce recidivism but there are more negative than positive findings.

Restitution programs arose during the onset of disillusionment with juvenile diversion. Restitution has intuitive appeal, combining concern for the rights of victims with notions of responsibility on the part of offenders. Our review of the existing literature suggests the following:

1. The research literature dealing with restitution programs is quite sparse.

2. Many restitution programs are add-ons to traditional probation. There is a need for research on programs that are exclusively restitution-oriented.

3. There is a danger that the stipulations of a restitution program can be excessive.

4. Restitution can be a mere slap on the wrist for upper-class youth and much more demanding for lower-class youth.

5. The research findings to date are inconclusive, suggesting some small differences in recidivism.

6. Participants in restitution/mediation programs expressed satisfaction with the outcome, but evidence suggesting reduced recidivism is slight.

The third approach we examined was shock therapy or, more specifically, the Scared Straight program. Some of these programs were merely prison tours, while others used aversive shock techniques. Our review of the literature revealed that:

1. The "Scared Straight" documentary film made exaggerated, ill-founded claims.

2. A follow-up study found that an experimental Scared Straight group had higher recidivism rates than a control group. It is not clear whether this is simply an artifact of small data sets or whether exposure to prison life encourages delinquent activity.

3. While these shock programs initially appeared in a majority of states, they have been drastically cut back or eliminated. In those instances where the programs are still operational, there appears to be some concerted effort to work only with delinquents and not the general population of adolescents.

4. The Scared Straight philosophy flows from a changing mood in the Supreme Court, state legislatures, and public opinion calling for a more punitive response to juvenile delinquency. This mood will continue to be reflected in programs in the 1990s.

References

Altgeld, J. P. 1884. *Our Penal Machinery and Its Victims*. Chicago: Jansen and McClurg.

Binder, A., and G. Geis. 1984. "Ad Populum Argumentation in Criminology: Juvenile Diversion as Rhetoric." *Crime and Delinquency* 30: 309-33.

Buckner, J. C., and M. Chesney-Lind. 1983. "Dramatic Cures for Juvenile Crime: An Evaluation of a Prisoner-Run Delinquency Prevention Program." *Criminal Justice and Behavior* 10:227-47.

Bureau of Justice Statistics. 1989. *Children In Custody, 1975-1985*. Washington, DC: U.S. Department of Justice.

_____. 1991. *Children In Custody*. Washington, DC: U.S. Department of Justice.

Cavender, G. 1981. "Scared Straight: Ideology and the Media." *Journal of Criminal Justice* 9:431-39.

Coates, R. B., and J. Gehm. 1985. *Victim Meets Offender: An Evaluation of Victim-Offender Reconciliation Programs*. Valpraiso, IN: PACT Institute of Justice, PACT, Inc.

Cressey, D., and R. McDermott. 1973. *Diversion from the Juvenile Justice System*. Ann Arbor, MI: National Assessment of Juvenile Corrections.

Curran, D. J. 1988. "Destructuring, Privatization, and the Promise of Juvenile Diversion: Compromising Community-Based Corrections." *Crime and Delinquency* 34:363-78.

Emerson, R. M. 1969. *Judging Delinquents*. Chicago: Aldine.

Esbensen, F. A. 1984. "Net Widening? Yes and No: Diversion Impact Assessed through a Systems Processing Rates Analysis." In S.H. Decker (ed.), *Juvenile Justice Policy*. Beverly Hills: Sage.

Finckenauer, J. O. 1982. *Scared Straight and the Panacea Phenomenon*. Englewood Cliffs, NJ: Prentice-Hall.

Frazier, C. E., and J. K. Cochran. 1986. "Official Intervention, Diversion from the Juvenile Justice System, and Dynamics of Human Services Work: Effects of a Reform Goal Based on Labeling Theory." *Crime and Delinquency* 32:157-75.

Galvin, J., and K. Polk. 1983. "Juvenile Justice: Time for a New Direction?" *Crime and Delinquency* 29:325-31.

Hagan, J., and J. Leon. 1977. "Rediscovering Delinquency: Social History, Political Ideology and the Sociology of Law." *American Sociological Review* 42 (August):587-98.

Hudson, J., and B. Galaway. 1978. "Introduction." In B. Galaway and J. Hudson (eds.), *Offender Restitution in Theory and Action*. Lexington, MA: Lexington.

Hughes, S. P., and A. L. Schneider. 1989. "Victim-Offender Mediation: A Survey of Program Characteristics and Perceptions of Effectiveness." *Crime and Delinquency* 35: 217-33.

Jensen, G. F., and D. G. Rojek. 1980. *Delinquency: A Sociological View*. Lexington, MA: D. C. Heath.

Justice Assistance News. 1981. "Juvenile Suicide Rates Eight Times Higher in Adult Facilities." Vol. 2: 3.

Juvenile Justice Bulletin. 1985. "Introducing RESTTA." U.S. Department of Justice.

Klein, M. W. 1976. "Issues and Realities in Police Diversion Programs." *Crime and Delinquency* 22 (October):421-27.

_____. 1979. "Deinstitutionalization and Diversion of Juvenile Offenders: A Litany of Impediments." In M. Norris and M. Tonry (eds.), *Crime and Justice*, 1978. Chicago: University of Chicago Press.

Lemert, E. M. 1971. *Instead of Court: Diversion in Juvenile Justice.* Rockville, MD: National Institute of Mental Health.

Lewis, R. V. 1983. "Scared Straight—California Style: Evaluation of the San Quentin Squires Program." *Criminal Justice and Behavior* 10:227-47.

Logan, C. H., and S. P. Rausch. 1985. "Why Deinstitutionalizing Status Offenders is Pointless." *Crime and Delinquency* 31: 501-17.

Lundman, R. J. 1984. *Prevention and Control of Juvenile Delinquency.* New York: Oxford University Press.

Martin, S. E. 1981. *New Directions in the Rehabilitation of Criminal Offenders.* Washington, DC: National Academy Press.

Matza, D. 1964. *Delinquency and Drift.* New York: John Wiley.

National Center for Juvenile Justice. 1990. *Juvenile Court Statistics, 1987.* Pittsburgh, PA.

Ohlin, L. E. 1983. "The Future of Juvenile Justice Policy and Research." *Crime and Delinquency* 29:463-72.

Palmer, T., and R. V. Lewis. 1980. *An Evaluation of Juvenile Diverison.* Cambridge, MA: Oelgeschlager, Gunn, and Hain.

Platt, A. 1969. *The Child Savers.* Chicago: University of Chicago Press.

Polk, K. 1984. "Juvenile Diversion: A Look at the Record." *Crime and Delinquency* 30:648-59.

_____. 1987. "When Less Means More: An Analysis of Destructuring in Criminal Justice." *Crime and Delinquency* 33:358-78.

President's Commission on Law Enforcement and Administration of Justice. 1967. *Task Force Report: Juvenile Delinquency and Youth Crime.* Washington, DC: U.S. Government Printing Office.

Rausch, S. P., and C. H. Logan. 1983. "Diversion from Juvenile Court: Panacea or Pandora's Box?" In J. R. Kluegel (ed.), *Evaluating Juvenile Justice.* Beverly Hills, CA: Sage.

Rojek, D. G. 1986. "Juvenile Diversion and the Potential of Inappropriate Treatment for Offenders." *New England Journal on Criminal and Civil Confinement* 12:329-47.

Rojek, D. G., and M. L. Erickson. 1982A. "Delinquent Careers: A Test of the Career Escalation Model." *Criminology* 20:5-28.

_____. 1982b. "Reforming the Juvenile Justice System: The Diversion of Status Offenders." *Law and Society Review* 16: 241-64.

Rutherford, A., and R. McDermott. 1976. *Juvenile Diversion: Phase I Summary Report.* Washington, DC: National Institute of Law Enforcement and Criminal Justice.

Rutter, M., and H. Giller, 1985. *Juvenile Delinquency: Trends and Perspectives.* New York: Guilford Press.

Sarri, R. C. 1983. "The Use of Detention and Alternatives in the United States Since the Gault Decision." In R. R. Corrado, M. LeBlanc, and J. Trepanier, (eds.), *Current Issues in Juvenile Justice.* Toronto: Butterworth.

Schafer, S. 1970. *Compensation and Restitution to Victims of Crime.* Montclair, NJ: Smith Patterson.

Schlossman, S. L. 1977. *Love and the American Delinquent.* Chicago: University of Chicago Press.

Schneider, A. L. 1985. *Guide to Juvenile Restitution*. Washington, DC: U.S. Department of Justice.

_____. 1986. "Restitution and Recidivism Rates of Juvenile Offenders. Results from Four Experimental Studies." *Criminology* 24:533-52.

Schneider, P. R., W.R. Griffith, and A. L. Schneider. 1982. "Juvenile Restitution as a Sole Sanction or Condition of Probation: An Empirical Analysis." *Journal of Research in Crime and Delinquency* 17:47-65.

Schur, E. M. 1973. *Radical Non-intervention: Rethinking the Delinquency Problem*. Englewood Cliffs, NJ: Prentice-Hall.

Selke, W. L. 1982. "Diverson and Crime Prevention: A Time-Series Analysis." *Criminology* 20:395-406.

Spergel, I. A., F.G. Reamer, and J. P. Lynch. 1981. "Deinstitutionalization of Status Offenders: Individual Outcome and System Effects." *Journal of Research in Crime and Delinquency* 18:34-46.

Staples, W. G. 1986. "Restitution as a Sanction in Juvenile Court." *Crime and Delinquency* 32:177-85.

Streib, V. 1987. *Death Penalty for Juveniles*. Bloomington, IN: Indiana University Press.

Vito, G. F., and D. G. Wilson. 1985. *The American Juvenile Justice System*. Beverly Hills: Sage.

Wines, E. C. 1880. *The State of Prisons and of Child-Saving Institutions in the Civilized World*. Cambridge, MA: Harvard University Press.

chapter **12**

Prevention
Dilemmas of Choice,
Change, and Control

> *We have come of late to the realization that the pace of achievement in domestic programs ranges chiefly from the slow to the crablike— two steps backward for every step forward—and the suspicion is growing that there is something basically wrong with most of these programs. A nagging feeling persists that maybe something even more basic than the lack of funds or will is at stake. Consequently, social scientists like myself have begun to reexamine our core assumption that man can be taught almost anything and quite readily. We are now confronting the uncomfortable possibility that human beings are not very easily changed after all.*
>
> —Amitai Etzioni, "Human Beings Are Not Very Easy to Change After All," *Saturday Review*, 1972

Disillusionment

The last several chapters have concentrated on theory and research relevant to deterrence, labeling, and correctional experimentation, including popular programs to divert nonserious offenders, scare others straight, and set matters right with victims. Some responses to delinquency appear promising while others either make no difference or make offenders worse. It is typically unsettling to people to learn that after years of research, we cannot conclusively state that doing something is better than doing nothing. Yet, the impulse to have a policy, to do something, is quite strong and persistent.

One response to the dismal and uncertain outcomes of correctional experimentation is to stress the *prevention* of delinquency. Whereas efforts to correct and rehabilitate focus on changing the offender "after the fact," the emphasis in prevention is on changing conditions thought to be conducive to delinquency in general or before it becomes a fact. These conditions range from changing in some fashion basic characteristics of individuals to altering the social environment or even modifying the basic features of our social and cultural system.

Given the results of correctional research summarized in Chapters 9, 10, and 11, many readers might predict that a final chapter on prevention is already doomed to failure. It would appear that every possible type of treatment program has been tried and has fallen short, so why should something as ambitious as delinquency prevention have any chance of success? While not specifically addressing delinquency prevention programs, Amitai Etzioni, whose comments serve as the preface to this chapter, reminds us that changing human behavior is not as simple as devising a catchy slogan, using massive advertising, or even developing concerted social campaigns. He cites a massive effort on the campus of Columbia University to save electricity at a time when there was a severe shortage of electricity in New York City. Even though the targeted audience was convinced that this was a vital issue, and the students and professors represented the educational elite who knew the importance of environmental issues, the campaign did not work. What in fact did produce a substantial savings of electrical energy on campus were not slogans, posters, or environmental "teach-ins," but simply having the janitors remove some light bulbs from the classrooms and the corridors. The moral of the story is that basic values, attitudes, and behaviors are not easy to change. Clearly, if campaigns directed at mature professionals fail, then there is good reason to be pessimistic about attempts to reduce delinquency by changing the attitudes, values, and behavior of juveniles and those influencing their lives. We will review efforts at delinquency prevention in this chapter and assess the degree to which such pessimism and disillusionment are justified.

Prevention Revisited

The term "prevention," like the terms "rehabilitation," "deterrence," and "diversion," has no one, unambiguous, agreed-upon definition. At one time or another, virtually all attempts to inhibit the delinquent activity of offenders or potential offenders have been referred to as prevention programs. For example, a review of literature by Wright and Dixon (1977) revealed that of 350 research reports using the words "delinquency prevention" (or their equivalent), a large number were actually programs involving juvenile court probation and parole techniques. In many instances, the court or police were the referral agencies, and participation in the program was a disposition for juveniles processed by the juvenile justice system. However, the arguments for prevention are typically presented in the context of the failure of correctional programs. In our discussion, we use the term prevention in reference to efforts to inhibit delinquency in the populace in general or in special targeted categories of youth who are not currently being processed or dealt with for actual lawbreaking.

An orientation toward prevention is by no means new. It has been proposed periodically for centuries. A prevention philosophy has been central to social reform movements throughout American history, although with considerable variation in views about what needed to be reformed and how change should be accomplished. It has also been central to sociological positions on crime and delinquency. Consider, for example, the following paragraphs from Edwin Sutherland's 1924 edition of *Principles of Criminology*:

> Two methods of reducing the frequency of crimes have been suggested and tried. One is the method of treatment, the other is the method of prevention. The conventional policy has been to punish those who are convicted of crimes, on the hypothesis that this both reforms those who are punished and deters others from crimes in the future. Also, according to this hypothesis, crime rates can be reduced by increasing the severity, certainty, and speed of punishment.
>
> Methods of reformation have been suggested and tried, also. These have been in the form of probation, educational work in prisons, and parole supervision. These methods, like the methods of punishment, have not been notably successful in reducing crime rates.
>
> Prevention is a logical policy to use in dealing with crime. Punishment and other methods of treatment are, at best, methods of defense. It is futile to take individual after individual out of the situations which produce criminals and permit the situations to remain as they were. A case of delinquency is more than a physiological act of an individual. It involves a whole network of social relations. If we deal with this set of social relations we shall be working to prevent crime. It has become a commonplace in medicine that prevention is better than cure. The same superiority exists in the field of crime. (1924:613-14)

Arguments nearly half a century later are much the same. According to C.R. Jeffrey, "Crime cannot be controlled through measures designated for the individual offender, but can be controlled only through the manipulation of the environment where crimes occur" (1971:19). Jeffrey illustrated his argument by comparing the treatment of crime to the futility of trying to eradicate yellow fever without eliminating the swamps where the mosquitoes that carry the disease flourish. The presumed superiority of preventive approaches is that efforts are directed at the fundamental social conditions or personal maladjustments that are seen as the "seedbed" of crime.

Every criminology text written by sociologists advocates an emphasis on prevention in one form or another. This point of view flows quite naturally from the sociological emphasis on the social and cultural circumstances that facilitate crime and delinquency. It is a quite common sociological belief that if the circumstances that encourage delinquency can be identified, then those circumstances can be modified to discourage delinquency. We refer to it as a "belief" because, as we will discuss later, there is a huge gap between the identification of "causes" of delinquency and the development of prevention strategies consistent with those causes.

Prevention Experiments

As we've already noted, the term "delinquency prevention" is often loosely used. As a result, many correctional experiments, such as those discussed in Chapter 10, are included in comprehensive reviews of the prevention literature. Such reviews suggest that the vast majority of reports on programs that aspire to delinquency prevention provide no data on program effectiveness. Steven Lab (1988) surveyed the literature on prevention and found much confusion on the type of subjects, types of crime, intervention strategies, and outcome measures. Similarly, Wright and Dixon (1977) found that of the 350 reports they examined, only 96 contained any type of empirical data. After evaluating those reports that did provide some empirical data, they concluded that "most were of low validity" and of little utility for decision makers. In view of the methodological limitations of these studies and the results reported, Wright and Dixon could find no particular prevention strategy that could be "definitely recommended." Their ultimate conclusions and recommendations for further research were quite similar to the reviews of correctional experimentation that we summarized in Chapter 10:

> We conclude that changing or preventing certain kinds of behavior is a difficult task, that positive results are probably related to quality and quantity of intervention, that any one intervention strategy is probably going to be differentially effective given a heterogeneous population, that theory-based strategies are going to be in a better position to profit from evaluations than are atheoretical strategies, and that sound research design is needed if we wish to be able to attribute changes in delinquency rates to prevention efforts. (1977:60)

Given these sorts of observations (which by now are beginning to sound painfully familiar), one impulse might be to end the chapter here, and simply conclude that prevention is a lost cause. However, if we are to gain any insight into what circumstances might account for the failure of so many prevention programs, we need to consider some of these approaches and assess their philosophical orientation. On the other hand, as we found with many treatment programs, most of the evaluation research that was done was so poor that it is difficult to be certain what works and what does not work. It is possible that some prevention programs are indeed working but poor evaluation research techniques may be distorting the real findings.

Early Identification and Intensive Treatment

Jackson Toby (1965) has observed that one argument concerning delinquency prevention that often strikes people as "breathtakingly plausible" involves early identification and intensive treatment. According to this argument, delinquency can be prevented by developing techniques to identify those who are headed for trouble and providing some form of treatment that would prevent such an unfolding of events from coming true. Such a prevention approach has been the dream of social control agencies.

One of the proposed uses of the personality tests discussed in Chapter 5 has been the early identification of potential offenders. For example, the Minnesota Multiphasic Personality Inventory (MMPI) was developed in the 1940s as an aid in the diagnosis of personality disorders. It was initially created by being administered to hospitalized psychiatric patients and to a group of "normal" individuals. A series of subscales were created that purported to measure specific personality problems such as depression, schizophrenia, hysteria, and paranoia. It was suggested that the MMPI could be an important tool in predicting delinquency. Some degree of success was found by using the schizophrenia subscale, where delinquents scored somewhat high. However, it was found that there was a 76.2 percent error in predicting delinquency four years after testing (Lundman, 1984). Various subscales were combined to increase the accuracy of the MMPI, but even with this improvement there was still a 65.5 percent error rate. Other tests have been used in the attempt to predict who will get into trouble with the law but all of them yield too many false predictions to be used as a basis for early intervention.

The most famous early identification and treatment program was the Cambridge-Somerville Youth Study first begun in 1937. The original goal was for teachers and police officers to identify two groups of boys: "difficult boys," who were viewed as potential delinquents, and "average boys," who were viewed as having no predisposition toward delinquency. By a random process, about half of the predelinquent boys were assigned to an experimental group, while the other half were assigned to a control group. The experimental group received family guidance, individual counseling, tutoring, medical care, and recreational services. The control group received no special treatment. World War II forced an early closure to the study (which was to have lasted ten years) when both counselors and adolescent subjects were drafted into military service. However, the project did last eight years, and provided some test of the effect of intensive counseling and academic tutorial services for youth who were "headed for trouble." An evaluation five years after the completion of the project revealed little positive effect. In a thirty-year follow-up conducted in 1975 using court, mental health, and alcoholism treatment records, Joan McCord (1978) found that "none of the . . . measures confirmed hopes that treatment had improved the lives of those in the treatment group" (1978:289).

Community and Neighborhood Experiments

Sociologists have quite commonly attributed the failure of psychiatrically and individually oriented prevention strategies to their focus on the individual rather than the social environment. John Martin (1961) argued that the basic flaw with "individual-centered techniques" is that "such efforts fail to come to grips with the underlying social and cultural conditions giving rise to delinquency." Similarly, Edwin Schur maintained that "our overall crime picture massively reflects conditions that require collective social solutions" and that "social reform, not individual counseling, must have the highest priority in our program to reduce crime problems" (1969:15).

Somewhere between the two poles of individual treatment and basic social reform are action programs that attempt to strengthen or reorganize certain social relationships in neighborhoods or areas of the city. This type of prevention program tries to overcome factors in the youth's immediate environment that are seen as contributing to delinquent behavior in the neighborhood or community.

Perhaps the best-known prevention program focusing on the social environment is the Chicago Area Project. Developed by Clifford R. Shaw in the 1920s and still operating in some parts of Chicago, the project was based on social disorganization theory (see chapters 6 and 8). It attributed delinquency to a lack of neighborhood cohesiveness and viewed self-help enterprises on the part of residents of areas with high crime rates as the key to prevention. Indigenous community leaders were to serve as conventional role models for youngsters in such areas in the hope of facilitating the growth of an antidelinquent culture.

Measuring the effectiveness of a program like the Chicago Area Project is extremely difficult—if not impossible. Delinquency statistics declined in three out of the four communities where the project was implemented, but since the project had no control groups, its findings were inconclusive. However, the project did pay sufficient attention to the organization, development, and implementation of the area projects to provide some clues as to the conditions under which a total community strategy might be feasible. One analyst (Finestone, 1976) noted that, ironically, it was in communities or neighborhoods with high delinquency rates that the Chicago Area Project had the most difficulty establishing local community committees or organizations concerned with the welfare of the area. On the other hand, the project was quite successful in facilitating the development of active, strong community committees in areas with low rates of delinquency. As Finestone observed:

> Where the disorder characterizing a community was so great as to preclude the existence of established institutions with a stake in the area,

> the area project idea tended to become more form than substance. In
> retrospect it is unrealistic to have expected the area projects to be able
> to develop effective community organizations out of whole cloth.
> (1976:148)

The very problems that sustained a high rate of delinquency limited the
possibility of implementing change.

It is important to note that while design problems precluded a definite
claim for success, the Chicago Area Project may have had significant
impact. As noted in Chapter 10, a reassessment of the evidence by
Schlossman and Sedlak (1983) suggests that the declines in delinquency
were far greater than would be expected, given delinquency statistics for
comparable, non-project neighborhoods.

While the Chicago Area Project could not claim to have demonstrated
a preventive impact on delinquency, it did stimulate many ideas on how
to develop grass-roots organizations in a community. For example, natural
leaders and the human resources of neighborhoods were sought out with
the intent of building from the bottom up rather than the top down.
Programs were not imposed on neighborhoods; but rather, highly
differentiated, flexible, and experimental projects were devised.
Community improvement campaigns were created to instill a sense of pride
in local neighborhoods. Recreation was central to the project because it
served as a springboard for eliciting adult participation, counseling,
employment opportunities, and ultimately the supervision and
involvement of youth in conventional activities. Schlossman and Sedlak
(1983) suggest that the Chicago Area Project remains as the exemplary
model of community organization designed to get at the roots of
delinquency rather than a superficial, bandage approach.

The ideas originally developed in the Chicago Area Project were
implemented in several subsequent projects. One such project was a "total
community" delinquency program carried out in a lower-class district of
Boston from 1954 to 1957 (Miller, 1962). Known as the Midcity Project,
it was concerned with developing and strengthening local citizens' groups
and organizing relationships among agencies and institutions involving
youth. The project also provided an intensive program of psychiatrically
oriented casework for "chronic problem families" and assigned
professionally trained adult workers to work with street gangs in certain
areas of the city. The workers' goal was to help the street gang move in
the direction of conventional, rather than delinquent, activities. Workers
also acted as intermediaries between adult institutions and gang members.
The project used psychiatric clinics, family service agencies, and group
therapy sessions when cases or situations were felt to require such a
response. A variety of techniques was viewed as valuable for testing what
Walter Miller called the *synergism* concept — the idea that the application

of a diverse set of procedures in concert might be more effective than distinct programs operating individually (1962:189). According to Lundman (1984) the major difference between the Midcity Project and the Chicago Area Project was that the latter was unique in its faith that the residents of inner-city neighborhoods could deal with their own problems rather than bringing in "experts."

Given the Midcity Project's intensity and diversity of programs, the ultimate conclusions concerning delinquency prevention generated by this project were surprising. The evaluation of the project, which used a variety of different measures of delinquency, concluded that there was no significant inhibition of either illegal or immoral behavior resulting from this prevention program. In the words of Miller, "All major measures of violative behavior...provide consistent support for a finding of 'negligible impact' " (1962:187). As a qualification to this finding, Miller observed that the project, which had been instituted in response to concern over "rampant gang violence," did appear to mollify those fears and to "calm" the adult community. Moreover, the project did establish new local organizations that survived the project. Miller further noted that there was considerable variability in the responses of different neighborhood groups.

Another community delinquency prevention program, the Mobilization for Youth Project, was created in 1961 in Manhattan's lower east side. This program was built on Cloward and Ohlin's *delinquency and opportunity* theory, and attempted to improve opportunities available primarily to Puerto Rican and black youth in the areas of education, employment, and social services. Employment assistance included job-training programs, subsidized work, and vocational-guidance programs for unemployed, out-of-school youth. Educational programs included a "homework helper" project, tutorial programs, increased parent-school contacts, and curriculum revision geared to help minority students. Recreational programs were developed; a Detached Worker Program sent adults into the streets to mingle with street gangs; a Coffee House Program was established to provide an alternative meeting place for young people. In sum, the Mobilization for Youth Project was a comprehensive, multidimensional prevention program that received substantial funding and widespread support. Unfortunately, while it enjoyed some limited success, it did not have a dramatic impact on delinquency in New York City. Some administrative irregularities were uncovered and the program suddenly lost the support of public officials. Many supporters of this program argued that progress was being made but more time was needed.

In 1962 a smaller-scale project designed to prevent delinquency among "high-risk" black youths was implemented in Seattle's central area. Whereas the Midcity Project worked with existing gangs, the workers in the Seattle Delinquency Control Project were each assigned a set of youths whom they subsequently attempted to organize into groups. The caseworkers, who were trained male social workers, worked with the boys, their families, and the schools. Berleman and Steinburn (1967) evaluated the impact of the program by comparing an experimental group of high-risk boys with a control group of high-risk boys. Cases had been randomly assigned to either group. They also compared the experimental and control groups with boys who refused to participate and with a set of "low-risk" boys. One interesting finding was that at all points in time examined, boys who refused to participate had the highest scores in terms of combined indexes of school and police disciplinary records. There were no significant differences between the experimental or treatment group and the control group. Disciplinary scores for the treatment group appeared to decrease over time as compared to increases in the other groups, but the differences were too small to be reliable. The treatment group's improvement disappeared after termination of service.

Community-oriented projects have been implemented in Canada as well. David Turner (1984) has reported on the Blanshand Community Project in a subsidized housing project that had been a source of a serious delinquency problem. The Blanshand program brought professionals together with people in the community, established "talk groups" of mothers for improving parenting skills, made an apartment into a community center, developed a recreation program and encouraged the development of a community response to juvenile justice issues. A "rent-a-kid" program was also developed to help integrate youths into the community by providing employment opportunities. Turner reported a decline in delinquency complaints from 70 in 1972 to only 17 by 1976. The housing project dropped from first among such projects in delinquency to fifth. Again, while the data do not allow definite claims of preventative success, the decline appears unusual and greater than in comparable projects.

A final type of community prevention program is called *community policing*. Community policing is an example of an informal effort to develop closer ties between the police and local neighborhoods. Police establish storefront centers, hold neighborhood meetings, and distribute information on crime in local neighborhoods. While couched in terms of community prevention, it is not clear whether such programs are designed to reduce crime through processes of general deterrence or by building neighborhood ties. If the emphasis is on strengthening ties between youth and the law or strengthening communal bonds, then the theory behind community policing would be similar to some of the other prevention projects we have discussed. Such deterrence-oriented programs have become quite popular in many cities. Sherman (1986) reviewed many of these programs and found that they tend to be more successful when there is *less* citizen involvement. Sherman found that citizen involvement increases the fear of crime and often creates an exaggerated perception of the crime problem.

Another popular crime prevention strategy is the *neighborhood watch* program. Residents of a particular neighborhood meet to discuss the crime problem in their immediate area, discuss ways to prevent crime, and devise ways to supervise the neighborhood and report suspicious activity to the police. Such neighborhoods proudly display prominent neighborhood watch signs in their homes and on street signs. Rosenbaum (1987) found that neighborhood watch programs in middle class, culturally homogeneous neighborhoods can be reasonably successful. However, in lower class, culturally heterogeneous neighborhoods where residents hold conflicting views, subscribe to different norms, and display varied family styles, these programs do not work well. Even in those neighborhoods where these programs are accepted with great enthusiasm, Lindsay and McGillis (1986) found that with the passage of time, interest in the program declines rapidly. In sum, low-income neighborhoods where crime is more prevalent than in middle- or upper-income neighborhoods, are typically less organized, tend to feel less in control over what happens in their neighborhood, and typically receive little outside support to do much about crime.

Youth Service Bureaus and the Neighborhood Youth Corps

A third type of prevention strategy includes a broad range of services for juveniles. The 1967 report of the President's Commission on Law Enforcement and Administration of Justice recommended the creation of *youth service bureaus* to reduce the role of the juvenile court and to act as central coordinators of various community services for juveniles. The concept of youth service bureaus is not totally clear or precise. Originally they were to be diversion agencies for arrested children, but most youth service bureaus received referrals from nonlegal and nonjudicial agencies. The true potential of youth service bureaus as an alternative to the formalized juvenile court was never realized because of funding cuts. Those youth service bureaus that did not close were incorporated into the juvenile court structure and the program was greatly reduced.

The Neighborhood Youth Corps, operated under the Department of Labor, employs youngsters living in low-income families and provides them with income, work experience, counseling, and remedial education. Gerald Robin summarized the rationale for Neighborhood Youth Corps programs as follows:

> The dialogue supporting such programs has increasingly emphasized their contribution toward reducing delinquency and youth crime by inculcating more positive and socially acceptable attitudes and values in the youths and by constructively occupying leisure time through

employment activities, thereby reducing the inclination and opportunity of its recipients to engage in behavior which would make them objects of law enforcement attention. (1969:323)

Robin reported on evaluations of two such programs. One was a Neighborhood Youth Corps program in Cincinnati that provided jobs to students from poor families. Participants were allowed to work up to fifteen hours per week during the school year and thirty-two hours per week during the summer, earning the minimum wage. The work projects were generally sponsored by school boards and educational institutions. The participants were directed by a work supervisor and assigned to counselors who were to help with any problems. Since there was a large waiting list of equally qualified applicants, the researchers were able to select enrollees randomly, thus creating a control group "of unassailable quality" (Robin, 1969:323). The experimental group was comprised of actively enrolled youths, and the control group consisted of eligible youths who had not been accepted into the program. The other program evaluated was a Neighborhood Youth Corps project in Detroit.

Robin examined offense records for the control group and for enrollees both during and after participation in the program. His findings illustrate the importance of having a control group for comparison. During participation in the Cincinnati Neighborhood Youth Corps program, there was a 33 percent reduction in the proportion of year-round male enrollees with police contacts. This is a type of finding that could easily be reported to the public and funding agencies as evidence of success. However, the presence of a control group allowed a comparison with those youths who did not make it into the program. The startling finding was that for the control group, the reduction was 39 percent. Comparisons of the program enrollees with the control groups indicated that participation in the Neighborhood Youth Corps in Cincinnati and in Detroit neither reduced delinquency during the program relative to nonparticipation nor prevented subsequent delinquency. These findings were true for both males and females. Robin concluded: "Assuming that police contacts are a valid index of variation in illegal behavior, then the putative importance of anti-poverty programs that consist largely of the creation of work opportunities in reducing criminality among juveniles and young people may be more illusive than real" (1969:331).

During the mid-1960s an Opportunities for Youth Project in Seattle used supervised youth employment and teaching machines to try to enhance the self-confidence of boys in four public housing projects in communities with high delinquency rates (Hackler, 1966; Berleman et al., 1972; Hackler and Hagan, 1975). Several experimental conditions were created so that the researchers could isolate the impact of work and teaching machines alone or in combination. Boys worked with an adult in city parks and in the public housing projects on Saturdays. The boys cooperated and attendance at work sessions was around 95 percent. Teaching machines were used two hours on a weekday afternoon under the supervision of a trained teacher. The successful completion of lessons on the teaching machines was supposed to enhance the boys' perception of themselves as adequate, nondelinquent boys.

When the boys were followed over time the work groups actually appeared to do worse than control groups. Hackler and Hagan (1975) reported that the delinquency rate of boys in control groups declined more than those in the work groups. Some decline was expected based on aging alone and evidence of a program impact would have come from a greater decline for boys in the work groups. There was evidence of a greater decline for boys involved with teaching machines than control groups. Further analysis suggested that work made the boys worse regardless of use of teaching machines and that the most disadvantaged youth were the most negatively affected. Teaching machine use appears to be associated with improvement regardless of degree of disadvantage. Finally, the program did have a positive impact on the attitudes of adults in the community (Hagan and Linden, 1970).

School-Based Programs

The programs that we have just described were based in the community and worked with a variety of institutions, including schools. Other delinquency prevention programs have been specifically based in the school. An early example of a school-based experiment was carried out in Columbus, Ohio, and has been documented by Walter Reckless and Simon Dinitz (1972). This particular experiment was based on ideas developed by Reckless and others to the effect that a boy's "self-image" is an important determinant of how he behaves. From such a perspective, a "good self-concept" insulates a youth from pressures and pulls that are conducive to delinquency, while a "poor self-concept" increases susceptibility to such forces. Hence, the experiment sought to develop special teaching programs that would provide attractive conventional role models and, to use Reckless and Dinitz's words, "beef up" the self-concepts of youths who otherwise appeared to be headed for delinquent involvement.

The subjects were incoming seventh-grade boys. They were divided into three subgroups: 1) randomly selected "bad" boys (predicted by sixth-grade teachers or principals to be headed for delinquency) who were assigned to all-male experimental classes; 2) "bad" boys in regular classes; and 3) a sample of "good" boys in regular classes. A select group of teachers was given special training that was intended to facilitate their becoming role models for the experimental youths. The program attempted to improve the boys' reading ability and to implement a disciplinary system based on respect for the rights of others. The program ran for three years with the following results. There were no significant differences between the control group and the experimental subjects in 1) school performances, 2) police contacts, 3) changes in self-concept, and 4) perceptions of law, police, courts, school, teachers, and education. When interviewed, both teachers and students were enthusiastic about the program, but despite this enthusiasm, experimental subjects did not differ from controls on a single outcome variable.

A more recent large-scale program of delinquency prevention focuses specifically on alterations in schools and educational programs that might reduce delinquency. In 1980 the Office of Juvenile Justice and Delinquency Prevention established an "Alternative Education Initiative" based on the theory that delinquency can be reduced by increasing youths' bonds to school and education and their sense of competence and belonging (see Chapters 6 and 7). Seventeen programs were funded under this initiative and evaluations suggest that such an approach does have some merit (see Gottfredson and Gottfredson, 1986).

Denise Gottfredson reported on one of the school-based programs in detail (1986). Project PATHE (Positive Action Through Holistic Education) was carried out between 1980 and 1983 in three high schools and four middle schools in Charleston County Public Schools. Gottfredson describes the rationale for the program as follows:

> The program assumed that delinquency and low attainment have multiple causes. Approaches targeting only selected aspects of the environment would be ineffective, according to this view, because the nontargeted negative forces in the environment would swamp any progress made in the targeted area. Approaches attempting to change the behavior of delinquency-prone individuals without attention to the features of the environment that elevate these students' risk for engaging in delinquent activities would also be ineffective. These ideas are reflected in the program's comprehensive approach. It targeted several aspects of the environment for change, and it simultaneously attempted to ameliorate the academic and social deficits of delinquency-prone students and to alter environmental cues, rewards and punishments, and structural arrangements in the school in ways intended to make undesired behavior less likely to occur. (1986:707)

Thus, in contrast to the prevention experiment evaluated by Reckless and Dinitz, PATHE combined prevention techniques aimed at high risk youth with more basic changes in the school environment as a whole.

The changes to be made were planned and accomplished through a team structure involving staff, students, administrators, parents, and members of the community. Both curriculum and school discipline were addressed and teachers were provided training in innovative teaching and classroom management. Students were involved in the establishment of both classroom and school rules. Mini-courses were developed, student learning teams were created, and a "school pride" campaign was mounted together with an expansion of extra-curricular activities and the development of peer counseling or "rap" sessions. Career-oriented interventions included a Career Exploration Program and a Job-Seeking Skills Program. About 10 percent of the students were eligible for direct services based on academic and behavioral problems. Specialists established behavioral objectives for this high-risk category, provided counseling and academic services, and monitored their progress.

Data on both school-level and individual-level outcomes were collected, including self-reported delinquency, suspensions, and school punishment as well as official school and court records. Researchers also measured academic progress, attachment to school, attendance, educational expectations, self-concepts, and perceptions of general school climate, morale, and discipline. PATHE schools were compared to nonintervention schools and targeted high-risk students compared to other high-risk students who did not receive direct services. The treatment and control high-risk groups were created through random assignment.

Gottfredson reports that, based on both self-reports and official data, the program brought about "a small but measurable reduction in delinquent behavior and misconduct" (1986:705). School climate and students' sense of belonging improved as well. In contrast, the provision of services to high-risk youths did not reduce their delinquency although they did appear to have lower dropout rates, higher chances of graduation, and improved achievement test scores. However, targeted students in the only school where high-risk students received the planned intensity of personal service did engage in significantly less delinquency. Overall, it appeared that organizational-level change relevant to the experiences of all students is more promising than treatment programs aimed specifically at high-risk populations.

The notion that schools play a central role in any delinquency prevention program has become a common theme. However, as reflected in Figure 12-1, schools are not insulated from the problems of American society. The educational system is a microcosm of the society it serves. In 1983 the National Commission on Excellence in Education published a highly critical report entitled *A Nation at Risk: The Imperative for Educational Reform.* The basic conclusion of this report was that students are emerging from the American educational system *less* educated than their parents, scores on standardized tests are declining, students stay longer in school and learn less, and discipline problems are on the increase. Jackson Toby (1984), in a commentary published a year after the *Nation at Risk* report suggested that the age for compulsory school attendance be 15 or lower. Toby argued that alienated students are forced to attend school because of compulsory

Figure 12-1

Excerpts from Juvenile Justice Bulletin, "Weapons in School"

Reading, Writing and Ducking Bullets

Gunfights are replacing fistfights, and bullet drills are replacing fire drills on many campuses. The situation is so serious that superintendents and security officials from the nation's largest urban school districts listed weapons on campus as one of their five top concerns. Several incidents support their fears:

A 13-year-old in Clearwater, Florida threatened to "torture and kill" his social studies teacher after receiving a poor grade. When taken into custody, he had two pistols, a box of bullets, and a switchblade.

An eighth-grader in Portland, Connecticut, who was suspended for refusing to remove his hat, brought an assault rifle to Portland Junior High School, killed the janitor, and wounded the principal and his secretary.

After being bullied and taunted by other students for weeks, a high school senior in Buffalo, New York, placed a pipe bomb in the locker of one of the students, who was severely wounded when the bomb exploded.

A school security officer told a gang conference in Garden Grove, California, about receiving a tip that a student had a weapon on campus. He located the student, wrestled him to the floor, confiscated his duffel bag and found a loaded Uzi 9mm rifle inside.

A first-grader arrived at a Manhattan elementary school with a loaded .25-caliber semiautomatic pistol tucked in his belt. He said he needed something for show and tell.

The 1,600 students at Chester High School, south of Philadelphia, must pass through a metal detector at the school's front entrance.

In Montgomery, Alabama, students may carry only clear plastic or mesh bookbags so that weapons are readily visible.

Sources: Office of Juvenile Justice and Delinquency Prevention.

attendance laws, but by allowing them to drop out, schools might become safer.

Finally, the most current preventative effort centering on schools is an aggressive law enforcement approach called "Drug-Free School Zones" (DFSZ). The objective of this national effort is the passage of legislation in every state that establishes drug-free zones around a 1,000-foot school perimeter, school property, school buses, bus routes, and bus stops. Anyone caught in this zone using, distributing, manufacturing, selling, or trafficking illegal substances will be subject to increased criminal and civil penalties than are normally charged against offenders outside this drug-free zone. Public service advertisements are posted in the community warning people of the significance of a drug-free zone (see Figure 12-2). For example, in Tucson, Arizona, the school system endorsed a "zero tolerance" regarding staff or student use, possession, or distribution of illegal substances. The police established bicycle patrols in order to concentrate their surveillance in drug-free zones. Similarly, in Broward County, Florida, Sorenson (1990) reports that as a result of aggressive police patrols in drug-free zones, "overall crime dropped, drug-related crimes [were] reduced, drug-arrests decreased, and open-air drug markets dispersed" (1990:8). Some states are expanding drug-free zones to include public parks, libraries, and swimming pools. The objective of this legislation is not necessarily the eradication of drugs in the community but the creation of drug-free havens in those areas frequented by school-aged children.

An Overview: Problems in Implementation, Cooperation, and Finance

There is little indication that delinquency can be prevented among high-risk youth, and programs that seem to have promise for youth in general in one setting may fail in another. Some programs do show promise and several have had a positive impact on attitudes and morale of people living in a community. Why have so many such experiments failed to reduce delinquency? If we consider the observations of prevention researchers themselves, we can find some common themes regarding experimental failures.

One recurrent theme is: "The theory is still good, but we need to do what we did with more resources, greater intensity, and for a longer period of time." For example, Reckless and Dinitz concluded that one of the lessons they learned from their prevention program was that they needed to develop more effective methods of presenting role models and of training effective project teachers. Thus, they wrote "There is reason to suspect

Figure 12-2

Sample Drug-Free School Zone Warning

that the exposure to role-model internalization was not intensive enough"
(1972:158). The McCords (1959) felt the same way in their reevaluation
of the Cambridge-Somerville Youth Study. However, it is hard to imagine
creating more intensive prevention programs than those that have already

been attempted. The Boston Midcity Project was no casual, loose, haphazard program; yet it had no significant impact. Reckless and Dinitz's program appears to have been carried out with considerable intensity and to have generated enthusiasm among teachers and students; yet, it made no difference. Gerald Robin found the lack of preventive effect in the Neighborhood Youth Corps programs a "somewhat unexpected finding if for no reason other than -that the program utilized approximately 1,000 hours of what would otherwise have been leisure time and therefore opportunity for misbehavior" (1969:327). Unless the researchers' own descriptions of their programs are misleading, it is hard to believe that more of the same in bigger doses will make the difference.

If the failure of these programs is a problem of intensity, then we have to face the fact (or propose some way to overcome it) that there are political, social, and cultural forces that limit the implementation of prevention programs of any greater intensity than those already described. In fact, the circumstances that limit more intense intervention are quite commonly mentioned as problems in implementing several of the programs that have been tried. In evaluating the Minnesota Youth Advocate Program, Higgins (1978) observed that the funding and ultimate demise of this program was determined by lobbying efforts and conflicts between advocates and school principals, rather than by any evidence of the program's success or failure. Advocates were "going to bat" for youths whom some school principals did not particularly want to see back in school. However, when advocates began encouraging their clients to enroll in private schools, they generated complaints that funds for public schools were being threatened. Very few school principals supported the program.

The PATHE program described by Gottfredson shows promise and appears to have had an impact on the student body but the actual reductions are still described as "small." Moreover, that experiment was carried out in the context of high school consolidations and a 39 percent budget cut to the experimental program. One control high school was closed and the students consolidated with the experimental schools, causing problems for evaluation. One middle school had to be dropped from the program for lack of funds. Thus, even programs that yield some positive results are faced with limitations set by larger economic and political forces.

It often appears that delinquency persists because of the reluctance of many people, groups, and organizations to accommodate changes that might reduce delinquency. Some action programs require a redistribution of power — the "haves" yielding some decision-making power to the "have-nots." It is at this juncture in implementing a new policy that change falls short. For instance, some years ago one of the authors was involved in a Headstart program for Mexican-American children. One of the fundamental goals of the program was to involve parents in the education of their children. Not only was the child to receive a pre-school "head start" in the educational arena, but also, and more importantly, parents were to become involved in a group something akin to a PTA (Parent-Teacher Association). This group included parents, teachers, and school officials, and was to act as an advisory board in running the program. One problem that arose involved the daily diet of "Anglo" food for Mexican-American children who were unaccustomed and unreceptive to this type of food. The advisory council recommended that these children be gradually introduced to new foods lest they refuse to eat altogether. However, the school administration decreed that the Mexican-American preferred food was too high in starches and unwholesome. Even though many of the children were not eating "nutritious" school meals because they were unfamiliar with such foods, the administration refused to yield on this point. The issue was recast into a power struggle between "professional" school administrators and "ill-informed" parents.

A second confrontation between the advisory board and the school administration concerned the employment of Spanish-speaking teachers who lacked a few credit hours for state certification. It was suggested by the advisory board that teachers be employed who could speak Spanish even if they only had provisional teaching certificates. However, the school administration asserted that only fully certified teachers could be hired even though they could not speak Spanish. It was argued that even though these teachers could not communicate with their students, they met the qualifications of the school system.

Eventually the advisory council fell into performing perfunctory chores and never achieved the decision-making role that it was initially intended to have. The school administration was so recalcitrant that even the slightest suggestion was viewed as a threat to its power. Delinquency prevention programs are often confronted with the same dilemma: the solution of a delinquency problem may require some redistribution of power or sharing of resources. Invariably this proves to be too threatening to the power structure, and ultimately nothing is changed.

In addition, internal problems in the implementation of a prevention program may reflect the fact that the program is operating as a small unit in a hostile bureaucratic milieu. For example, Finestone observed that in the Chicago Area Project some community committees began to "distance themselves" from the delinquency issue and that some committee members did not want to associate with persons with delinquent or criminal backgrounds (1976:137). Walter Miller (1958) found that a major impediment to delinquency prevention in the Midcity Project was conflict among the program participants. Miller wrote that the executive board became a battleground for different groups, organizations, and agencies over conflicting causes of crime, disposition of offenders, organizational style, and the hiring of personnel. Miller concluded that such conflict is a major source of difficulty in implementing and carrying out delinquency prevention programs. Similarly, program sponsors, whether they are public or private organizations, have specified orientations and goals that cannot be threatened by funded programs. For example, a delinquency prevention program that encouraged any form of abortion counseling for pregnant teenagers would be in danger of losing its funding. Often times delinquency prevention advocates must be reminded to "work within the system" which means supporting the status quo. Unfortunately, it may be the status quo which exacerbates or creates the problem in the first place. The very nature of a true prevention approach suggests modifying some basic component in the social environment but this can threaten the established order.

On the other hand, we also need to question some of the underlying assumptions of delinquency prevention programs. We have already cited the rationale behind the Neighborhood Youth Corps programs — that the services provided would take up time, as well as inspire new attachments, commitments, or attitudes. However, as we noted in Chapter 6, merely occupying a youth's time does not appear to be an important barrier to delinquency. Delinquent activities are episodic, situational, and require very little time. Moreover, it may be that the types of activities provided by the Neighborhood Youth Corps do not inspire "more positive and socially acceptable attitudes and values" as intended. Too often the work is "busy work" that serves no real purpose. For example, one of the authors was called upon to provide work for Neighborhood Youth Corps enrollees on a research project where extra help was not really needed. However, the Youth Corps staff was desperate for placements. This in turn prompted the youths in the program to view the money they received as a gift that would be awarded regardless of the quantity or quality of their work.

What is ironical about this prevention program is that research has shown that "spending money" is related to many types of delinquency (see Cullen et al., 1985). Jensen (1979) found that students who were in the top half of their high school in terms of spending money were significantly more likely to report alcohol and marijuana use, experimentation with more serious drugs, and a variety of "hell-raising" activities, such as joyriding, dragging, and vandalism. Moreover, this effect persisted regardless of parental social status. No matter what the parents' social standing, the adolescent with more spending money was freer to engage in delinquent activity than the adolescent with less money. As we noted in Chapter 7, having a car also appears to increase the freedom to commit delinquent acts. The point here is not that paying disadvantaged youths is bad or wrong. Given the larger economic system and the larger social world of a program's participants, any delinquency prevention program would probably flounder at the outset without monetary incentives. However, it should be recognized that some aspects of a program may increase the probability of some forms of delinquency.

Overall it appears that the major limitation on both the implementation and potential effectiveness of prevention programs is that the wider system — the real world — "will have its way." It might generate optimism and make us feel better to argue 1) that prevention strategies purporting to be comprehensive must be directed at fairly massive kinds of environmental change, and 2) that rather than focusing on individual delinquents or potential delinquents, delinquency prevention must call for an alteration of those factors in the environment that contribute to delinquent behavior. However, the fact of the matter is that if delinquency programs opting for small-scale change have met strong resistance, it is doubtful that large-scale prevention programs will ever be mounted successfully. The very most that we can anticipate is that small reductions in delinquency might be brought about by well-organized and intensive efforts to partially change communities and/or schools.

Theory, Research, and Policy

A common reaction to researchers looking at the delinquency problem is "So what do you propose we do?" It is assumed that theory and research will have some relevance to public policy. In *Thinking About Crime* (1983), Harvard political scientist James Q. Wilson contends that sociological research on "causes" tends to concentrate on conditions that cannot be readily manipulated or that have little relevance to policy. For example, the focus on age and gender differences is deemed "theoretically important," but of little relevance to policy makers because "men cannot be changed into women or made to skip over the adolescent years" (1983:46). Wilson argued that sociological theory and research has concentrated on conditions "which cannot be easily and deliberately altered." Of course, research on delinquency prevention has shown that conditions that can be easily and deliberately altered have little or no consequence for delinquency.

Charges that scholarly work on delinquency has few policy implications are typically based on a specific conception of what qualifies as "policy." Wilson defines policy analysis as follows and contrasts it with the "causal analysis" dominating the social sciences:

> Policy analysis, as opposed to causal analysis, begins with a very different perspective. It asks not what is the "cause" of a problem, but what is the condition one wants to bring into being, what measure do we have that will tell us when that condition exists, and what policy tools does a government (in our case, a democratic and libertarian government) possess that might, when applied, produce at reasonable cost a desired alteration in the present condition or progress toward the desired condition? In this case, the desired condition is a reduction in

> specified forms of crime. The government has at its disposal certain —
> rather few, in fact — policy instruments: it can redistribute money, create
> (or stimulate the creation of) jobs, hire persons who offer advice, hire
> persons who practice surveillance and detection, build detention
> facilities, illuminate public streets, alter (within a range) the price of
> drugs and alcohol, require citizens to install alarm systems, and so on.
> It can, in short, manage to a degree money, prices and technology, and
> it can hire people who can provide either simple (e.g., custodial) or
> complex (e.g., counseling) services. (1983:49)

Wilson's definition of policy analysis builds in limitations on the amount of change and the means of implementing change that qualify a proposal as a policy proposal. In sum, it is not so much that sociological theory and research have no policy implications, but that their implications are not realistic given current social reality. Yet, it is the same social reality that is under attack as the source of many social problems. What one views as realistic or reasonable may very well depend on how well one has benefitted from that reality. The failure of so many policies that use existing tools at a reasonable cost may lead some people to stress retribution and incapacitation as the only alternatives but lead others to propose more radical changes.

From his studies of low crime rates in Switzerland, Marshall Clinard (1978) arrived at several policy implications that would be deemed "unreasonable." For example, he proposed limiting cities in the United States to under 500,000 population. He also cited Switzerland's mandatory military participation as a factor that kept the youth crime rate down and suggested that a policy of mandatory service might have the same effect in the United States. He noted that political decentralization is another characteristic of Swiss society that may account for the low crime rate. Recommendations to decentralize the United States Government along Swiss lines would be deemed unreasonable in terms of Wilson's definition of policy analysis, as would proposals by radical criminologists that we actively work to change our political economy by revolutionary action if necessary. Moreover, it is not entirely true that findings concerning basic demographic variations have no policy implications. Rather, the implications that they do have would not seem reasonable to Wilson, or to many other people. For instance, we could propose a nationwide program beginning in the primary grades to encourage boys to be more like girls. Research findings do make this a policy implication, but it is one that would be considered unreasonable and certainly would not be easy to implement.

In short, with growing pressure for social scientists to make their work relevant to policy, we have to be careful that we do not so restrict the term that nothing new can be proposed. In fact, it may very well be the case that research that is carried out to test theories or extend our knowledge with little concern for policy implications is potentially more valuable than research directly tied to policy issues. Why? Because research tied to "policy issues" has been limited to policy as it has been defined by governments, bureaucrats, and politicians. In a critique of "child-saving" movements and government programs for preventing delinquency, Anthony Platt (1970) argued that contemporary policies are based on a belief in "the benevolence of government" and differ from earlier child-saving movements mainly in the sense that it is now specialists, professionals, and persons in the child-saving bureaucracy itself who are defining directions, goals, and the limits of policy. We need people who study the social world without being bound to bureaucratic proclamations about what is and is not "reasonable." We need to learn what they discover for good or ill if we are to control our own lives. Moreover, as we will argue in the next section, decisions, choices or "personal policies" of everyday life can make a difference and such choices can be made in view of research findings summarized throughout this text.

Choices: Assessing Our Own Values, Beliefs, and Commitments

Despite the intuitive appeal of listing a series of recommendations for someone "out there" to act on, we need to consider our own stake in this matter. Obviously, there are any number of alternatives that could be selected for a nationwide delinquency prevention program. However, overcoming personal bias, prejudice, or even ignorance while we collectively fashion a plan of action that may ultimately fail is no simple matter. Furthermore, any set of far-reaching proposals that calls for a significant alteration of the social structure very quickly becomes an intensely personal matter. The price of eradicating crime and delinquency may be too painful for us to bear. It is relatively simple to suggest changes in the lives of other people, but far more difficult to alter our own lifestyles. Before we commit society to a plan of action, we need to judiciously assess our own contribution to the problem and consider how much we are willing to sacrifice in order to find a solution. Grappling with choices is what delinquency prevention is all about and why it is so radical, and ultimately, why it is so difficult to implement.

Personal Reform

Adults and most particularly parents serve as critical role models for children and adolescents. We have all acquired a sense of values and attitudes, political orientations, language, behavioral mannerisms, and even tastes that were strongly influenced by key adult role models as we were growing up. Adults and parents can subtly influence not only law abiding behavior but also law violating behavior. It is one thing for adults to bemoan the fact that adolescents are committing all forms of crime, but then again these same adolescents are confronted with endless examples in the daily news of bank fraud, income tax cheating, embezzlement, political corruption, savings and loan scandals, insider trading, property crime, and every conceivable form of violence against persons. If parents and adults can dabble in criminal activity, why can't adolescents?

Erich Goode (1989) has noted that there is a generational continuity to drug use: "Parents who use legal drugs (alcohol, tobacco, and prescription drugs) are more likely to raise children who both drink hard liquor and use illegal drugs than are parents who abstain from drugs completely" (1989:73-74). Similarly, Kandel (1984) states that warnings about the dangers of alcohol will have little impact on teenagers who see their parents consuming alcohol.

Many parents avoid feelings of guilt by viewing their children's problems as the responsibility of governments or schools, even though what goes on in the family and in parent-child relationships appears directly relevant to an understanding of delinquency. There is a growing body of court decisions obligating parents to exercise reasonable control over their children. For example, every state has some type of statute imposing financial liability on parents for acts of vandalism by their children. Geis and Binder (1991) cite two cases where parents were sent to jail for having chronically truant children. In Wisconsin, grandparents are financially responsible for a baby born to their unmarried minor child. Florida makes parents liable for a fine or a prison term if their child uses a gun that was not properly secured in the home. All these instances suggest that the courts and the legislatures are becoming increasingly sensitive to the notion that parents share in the responsibility for their delinquent children.

Personal apathy is very likely a major contributor to the failure of prevention efforts. We have already discussed the fact that victimization reports show that nearly two-thirds of personal and household victimizations are not reported to the police. Similarly, we repeatedly hear stories of bystanders who watched a crime take place and took no action. Even more distressing are accounts of assault, rape, and child abuse that occur because no one intervenes. In terms of prevention efforts, local citizens need to take the initiative in helping to eradicate a festering social problem. For example, volunteer tutorial programs to assist school children tend to operate with a skeleton staff. Success in school and a sense of self-esteem that arises from the mastery of certain subjects are critical barriers to delinquency. Yet, few adults will participate in these programs. Many children from the lower socio-economic spectrum rarely participate in organized sports, general recreation programs, or even visit a zoo or a museum. If every adult could contribute an hour or two a month to some

Box 12-1

The way we react to criminal and delinquent events is often affected more by characteristics of the event than the harm done. The two events in the editorial cartoon below were reacted to very differently. One was national news for several days while the other was not. The cartoon highlights the racial and social status of the offenders.

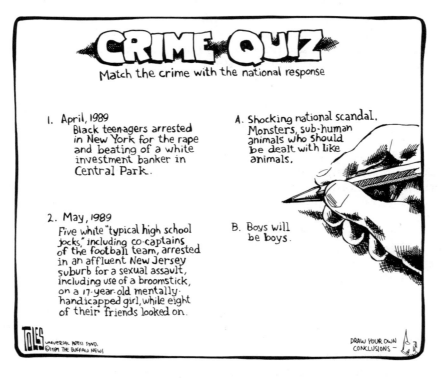

Do you think reactions to and fears about crime are a product of seriousness alone?

type of youth program, some effort could be made at delinquency prevention. Young people experience extraordinary rates of unemployment, even though they will work for less than the minimum wage. Adults could hire adolescents to perform any number of household chores, but this seems to be a rare event. In these examples and innumerable others, adults could take a much more active interest in young people and perhaps in the process make some contribution to the prevention of delinquency. But far too often they stand by the wayside and choose not to get involved.

Since anonymity facilitates crime and delinquency, we need to work to reduce the distance between ourselves, our neighbors, and their children. Locked doors and security devices do reduce the risk of victimization, but excessive social isolation can contribute to juvenile crime as well. Rather than excluding youth from "our territory," adults can work to increase the sense that this territory is shared or, at the minimum, the territory of people who care about them. Depictions of our society as "youth-oriented" are misleading in that it is children who are increasingly excluded from communities. In times of budgetary constraints it is youth programs that are among the first to be cut. When attention is drawn to a "problem" such as drug abuse the problem is likely to be attributed to the young — despite the adult control and dominance of the distribution of legal and illegal drugs and despite the prevalence of drug problems among adults. There may be more evidence of hostility toward youth than any tendency to be oriented toward their well-being.

Schools

As summarized in Chapter 7, certain characteristics of schools are suspect as contributors to alienation from school and, ultimately, involvement in delinquency. If huge schools are more alienating than smaller schools, then we should work toward smaller-scale schools or smaller classroom sizes. If schools where the student body plays a greater role in formulating policy have lower delinquency rates, then greater student responsibility and involvement should be encouraged. We need to experiment and improvise more school-related programs that might serve in a delinquency prevention role, but these programs are often inadequately funded. There is more than adequate evidence to suggest that variations in educational environments may be the most promising direction for delinquency prevention. As the PATHE program analysis suggested, programs designed to benefit all students in a system appear more promising than programs aimed at high-risk students alone.

The PATHE program is based on a set of strategies derived from social control and social learning theories summarized in earlier chapters. Gary

Gottfredson (1981) summarizes strategies within the scope of school action as follows:

1. Increase student attachments to socially appropriate peers by providing multiple opportunities for cooperative interaction both within and outside of class.

2. Increase student attachment to teachers by giving homeroom teachers special roles in advising students, reinforcing success in all areas of school activity, handling student problems, and maintaining contact with parents.

3. Increase student involvement and attachment to the community by giving students roles in helping community members.

4. Give students access to success by rewarding weekly progress, net of past levels of performance, instead of allocating rewards based on relative standing in the school or class.

5. Involve parents in concrete tasks to improve student performance by providing them with reports on student progress in behavior, attendance, and achievement, and teaching them how to reinforce gains in these areas.

6. Make school rules fair, firm, and consistent, and make sure that students understand them and participate in setting them.

Efforts to implement some of these strategies will meet with resistance, but resistance is one price of freedom and diversity.

Schools are also a promising setting for the implementation of "real" diversion programs where problems are handled short of screening and processing by the juvenile court. One such program is the *School Resource Officer* program found in numerous schools throughout the nation. Carefully selected police officers are assigned to junior high schools where they attempt to deal with delinquency problems in and around schools through warnings, interaction with students, and remedies worked out in cooperation with teachers, counselors, administrators, and parents. Processing by the juvenile court is limited to serious and/or repetitive offending and cases where complainants push for legal action. Under such a system diversion becomes more than referral to alternative community agencies and takes on qualities closer to those originally proposed by diversion advocates.

Religion

The relevance of organized religion to the alleviation of social problems is a controversial issue. Some religious groups charge that scientific silence about the role of religion is really advocacy of *secular humanism* wherein the solution to problems rests entirely with the human modification of interpersonal relationships and political, economic, and educational institutions. Such a philosophy, it is charged, does not incorporate ideas of religious salvation and divine control of worldly relationships into the solution or understanding of problems. Indeed, since our focus is on human intervention and change of institutions and social relationships as means of coping with delinquency, it is primarily humanistic and focuses extensively on changes in the secular world. However, religion and religious beliefs are not dismissed as irrelevant to the inhibition and potential prevention of delinquency. As some research findings have shown, religion may play a role in reducing the potential for delinquency. However, as just discussed in the section on personal reform, churches must participate in solving social problems and not stand idly by and point an accusatory finger at youth.

It is unusual for a delinquency text to even address the relevance of religion to delinquency since speculation on the issue can easily be misinterpreted as advocacy of a religious revival or advocacy of a particular set of religious principles. However, the evidence that religious practices and beliefs are correlated with some forms of law abiding behavior suggests that the church could play some role in delinquency prevention. When a faith is characterized by strong prohibitions against certain activities, those most involved in that faith have very low rates of involvement in the prohibited behavior. Drinking and drug use appear to be particularly sensitive to variations in religiosity. Moreover, research on state levels of church membership suggests that religion may function as an integrative force inhibiting crime. If these relationships reflect the relevance of religious doctrine and practice to human choices, then the church does have relevance to contemporary problems.

The implications of such findings for policy, whether personal or political, are not simple and straightforward. For example, some people might advocate forced religious education as a response to adolescent drinking and drug use. However, in addition to the constitutional issues of freedom of religion and separation of church and state, the findings on religiosity and delinquency suggest that it is personal commitments to religion that are most relevant. Forced church attendance or practice is unlikely to inspire such personal commitments. On the other hand, parental encouragement and family participation in religious activities might decrease the odds of some forms of delinquency.

Social Revolution

Radical theorists, drawing heavily on *conflict theory* and *Marxian theory*, argue that delinquency is the product of the perpetual class struggle in capitalist societies. The ruling class creates the conditions out of which delinquency arises, and nothing short of revolution will alter the situation. For instance, the Schwendingers (1985) see the core of the delinquency problem as the marginalization of youth. Capitalism is viewed as a *criminogenic* system that perpetuates inequities based on age, sex, race, and occupation. Thus, merely "tinkering" with the system by investing time and resources into rehabilitation, diversion, or prevention will not rectify the delinquency problem. Only by fundamental alterations in the political economy can the cooperative instincts of the young dominate and a society free of high crime rates emerge. The prescriptions for this revolution are stated in the following manner by Richard Quinney, one of America's most prolific, radical criminologists:

> Our task as students is to consider the alternatives to the capitalist legal order. Further study of crime and justice in America must be devoted to the contradictions of the existing system. At this advanced stage of capitalist development, law is little more than a repressive instrument of manipulation and control. We must make others aware of the current meaning of crime and justice in America. The objective is to move beyond the existing order. And this means ultimately that we engage in socialist revolution. (1974:25)

While the goals of a truly liberated society are clearly articulated by radical theorists, the means of attaining a classless state are not clearly specified. Chambliss and Mankoff have stated that "the ultimate test of a theory's utility is not its logical structure or its 'fit' with empirical data but its ability to create workable recipes for changing the existing set of social conditions" (1976:3). Yet that is the precise bone of contention — what are those "workable recipes"? A search of the literature that expounds the radical doctrine does not clearly articulate any plan of action. One rationale for this lack of articulation is as follows:

> We cannot present a blueprint or an exact specification of how a socialist "utopia" would work; nor should we attempt to do so, since constructing imaginary utopias bears little relation to the actual task of building a decent society. Any real alternative to capitalism will be historically linked to the forces and movements generated by the contradictions of capitalist society itself. New institutions which liberate rather than oppress can only be created by real people confronting concrete problems in their lives and developing new means to overcome oppression. The political movements arising from capitalism's contradictions therefore constitute the only means for society to move from its present condition to a new and more decent form, and only out of these movements will humane as well as practical new institutions be generated. (Edwards, Reich, and Weisskopf, 1974:433)

The authors of this statement go on to say that they can explain the values and goals that would characterize a "decent" society, but a blueprint of how a socialist society would work is not available.

When we consider radical proposals for reform, we can say very little about their probability of success or failure on the basis of research findings. It might be true, as several theorists have argued, that a basic change in our economic arrangements (for example, from modern capitalism to socialism) would reduce some forms of crime. But how are we to test that theory? We might study existing societies and economic arrangements, except for the fact that we do not have reliable comparative data on crime and delinquency and such societies are themselves undergoing considerable change toward a more capitalistic economy. In any case, such theories are rarely couched in terms of existing societies. Proposals for change that go beyond existing variations always sound the most promising, and their arguments ring true for many of us. However, we cannot look to current scientific research for confirmation. The view that the benefits of such change would outweigh the costs is a matter of faith, but faith and utopian vision are no worse than disillusionment, pessimism, and apathy.

Elliot Currie (1985) argues that American society is more punitive and relies more on the formal machinery of punishment than most other advanced societies. Similarly, there is much greater inequality in the United States than in most other societies, a glaring lack of social policies to deal with unemployment, inadequate health care, and substandard housing. Currie states, "we must build a society that is less unequal, less depriving, less insecure, less disruptive of family and community ties, less corrosive of cooperative values . . . we know that many of the conditions that generate criminal violence *are* capable of alteration; other countries have done so" (1985:225-226).

Law Enforcement

While radicals advocate massive change in societal organization, most liberals are likely to emphasize reforms of specific social institutions or limited redistributions of wealth within the existing system as steps in the amelioration of social problems. People of a more conservative political orientation tend to focus on stricter laws and increases in the certainty, severity, and celerity (speed) of enforcement and punishment as the most "realistic" and "reasonable" approaches to the control of crime and delinquency. As was summarized in Chapter 9, there is quite a bit of evidence consistent with the point of view that stiffer law enforcement might reduce delinquency. Such findings are the basis for advocating that the juvenile justice system has to include some consequences certain and severe enough to have general deterrent effects. Moreover, regardless of deterrent effects, some form of imprisonment is necessary for a limited set of offenders who constitute serious risks to the community.

However, the failure of scared straight programs to inhibit delinquency should generate reservations about carrying the deterrence philosophy too far. When the state begins to use the threat of exposure to illegal violence and problems within prison which it cannot control as part of the "threat" of punishment, then it is admitting defeat and its own inefficacy in coping with crime. Indeed, the tendency of youth processed through such programs to do worse than control youth suggests that such an approach is counter-productive. The use of the system's failures as threats may be alienating and disillusioning in the long run. Policies aimed at increasing the threat of sanctions within the limits of the law and with appropriate concern for due process hold more promise for inhibiting delinquency.

We have to recognize that in addition to the limitations of support for deterrence theory summarized in Chapter 9, experiences at school, in the family, and in peer groups are far more strongly related to delinquency than anticipated punishment by the legal system. Such a finding does not mean that law enforcement is unimportant in the control of delinquency but it does require that we put enforcement in perspective. There is some foundation for the belief that youth may make different choices if they perceive legal punishment to be certain and severe. Policies enhancing such beliefs might reduce their delinquent choices. However, there is also evidence that it is anticipated costs to relationships and aspirations in other contexts that gives the legal system its clout. It is doubtful that the threat of legal sanctions can have much of an effect on delinquency if people do not accord the law legitimacy and its agents respect and authority.

Understanding Our Own Fears

The feeling that "We've got to do something!" often occurs in the context of alarm. Whenever a problem escalates into a national panic, the tendency is to create short-term, quick-fix responses that most likely have minimal impact. The fact that something is being done may alleviate some fears whether or not the response is effective. Since alleviation of fear is itself a worthy goal, it is important to assess the relation between our fears and the real dimensions of a problem.

In Chapter 1 we cited several traditional rationales purporting to explain why delinquency is such a pressing problem, including the view that juveniles account for an inordinate amount of crime in America. Several of the presidential task force reports on delinquency and youth crime were written during a period when the crime rate was climbing dramatically. Black Americans were rioting and protesting injustice in America. Students were protesting the war in Vietnam. The post-World War II "baby boom" was passing through adolescence into young adulthood and swelling educational institutions. Girls were no longer "acting like girls" and were beginning to account for an increasing share of the delinquency problem.

However, neither survey data nor official statistics are consistent with such perceptions in recent spans of time. The increase in the older age categories could inflate the incidence of crimes committed by adults, and the crime picture could alter dramatically as we become a more aged population. Midlife crimes, alcoholism, and white-collar crime could be to the 1990s what the delinquency problem was to the 1960s and 1970s.

If the recent respite from perpetually increasing delinquency and crime turns out to be more than temporary, will there be a decline in public concern about juvenile delinquency? Will attention shift elsewhere? The sociological issue to be addressed in responding to these questions is the correlation (or lack of it) between perceptions of social problems and the actual magnitude of the problem. Consider, for example, the findings from the Gallup Poll from 1972 to 1989 shown in Figure 12-3. Most people felt that crime in their area was increasing and very few felt crime was decreasing. Yet, ironically both *Uniform Crime Reports* and victimization data show quite the opposite. The *Uniform Crime Reports* indicate a steady increase in the crime rate in the 1970s but a dramatic drop in the early 1980s. Victimization data show that for violent crimes and property crimes there has been a moderate but consistent decline in the victimization rate for the past 15 years. However, the common perception is that crime is always getting worse. On the average, less than 20 percent saw crime decreasing, which was in fact happening throughout most of the 1980s.

James Hackler (1985) refers to the "we've got to do something" syndrome that is characteristic of juvenile justice policy. It is highly dubious that delinquency is an overpowering threat to society, but action must be taken. Hackler asserts that "harm done to life or limb by juveniles is a tiny fraction of the injuries caused by automobiles or that the economic losses are trivial compared with those resulting from cheating on income tax, and the variety of crimes committed by more affluent members of society. Enduring certain nuisances while concentrating on vital problems has never characterized human society" (1985: 229). Similarly, the studies of Marvin Wolfgang et al., (1972) and Steven Lab (1984) suggest that many juveniles grow out of their delinquency by their mid-teens. In other words, kids grow up and mature on their own accord, and for many what is needed is not massive programs but simple tolerance.

Sutton (1988) in his study of the American juvenile justice system concludes by stating that "juvenile justice reforms are best understood as symbolic efforts to dramatize an ideal vision of social order rather than instrumental attempts to control children's misbehavior" (1988:239). He goes on to call many reformers "socially marginal cranks" or "on-the-make

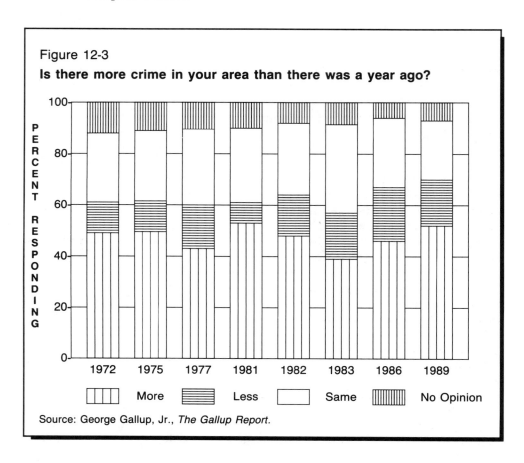

Figure 12-3

Is there more crime in your area than there was a year ago?

Source: George Gallup, Jr., *The Gallup Report*.

professionals" who enjoy revelling in a nostalgic vision of the moral order. The theme that has been repeated throughout this book is that children are by definition immature, and subject to the whims of adult society. One way of dealing with the inadequacy of contemporary society is to blame it all on our recalcitrant youth.

In short, our responses to delinquency and crime are not necessarily based on the actual magnitude and objective nature of the problem. When we stand back and take an objective look at ourselves, our institutions, and our society, we discover that the very problem we abhor and want to do "something" about may be imbedded in our society, institutions, and ultimately ourselves. Commenting on the prospects for reducing delinquency some three decades ago, Jackson Toby concluded:

> Adolescent delinquency may be part of the price industrial societies pay
> for their affluence, their freedom from oppressive social controls, and

their willingness to give young people a relatively long period of preparation for adult responsibilities. This does not mean that high rates of delinquency are inevitable, but it suggests that panaceas are unlikely. The lowering of delinquency rates will come about only if the fuller participation of youth in major institutions becomes a priority value — important enough to justify large expenditures not only for the education and job-training of intellectually marginal youth but also for the development of the civic, marital, and aesthetic potentialities of all adolescents. (1963:25)

Delinquency is shaped and facilitated by aspects of the social world that each of us helps to create and sustain. We may not do so consciously or intentionally since we are each also constrained by the social world. However, an understanding of the forces that shape delinquency and of reactions to delinquency should help us understand ourselves and our own role in the problem. Such understanding does not provide clear and certain answers to the choices we must make, which is why this chapter is subtitled "Dilemmas of Choice, Change, and Control."

If we choose to view delinquency as a serious problem and want to advocate doing something about it, then it is important to learn what has been tried and to consider alternatives in view of past failures. If previous prevention designs did not work because they were not intensive enough or because of vested interests and political limitations, then we will have to overcome such limitations and try these designs again. If they failed because they did not change society sufficiently, then we may choose to alter the system radically and hope for the best. There will be risks and costs involved and no scientific research to tell us with certainty what the rewards and costs of alternative utopias will be. If our actions or inactions contribute to the problem, then we can certainly change ourselves. If we feel we need to know more before deciding what to do, then let's pursue such knowledge and support others in that pursuit. Existing knowledge is a risky and uncertain guide. It can help narrow the options, but it also leaves us in the age-old human position of making choices with no guarantee of success.

References

Berleman, W. C., and T. W. Steinburn. 1967. "The Execution and Evaluation of a Delinquency Prevention Program." *Social Problems* 14 (Spring):413-23.

Berleman, W. C., J. R. Seaberg, and T. W. Steinberg. 1972. "The Delinquency Prevention Experiment of the Seattle Atlantic Street Center: A Final Evaluation." *Social Service Review* 46:323-46.

Chambliss, W. C., and M. Mankoff. 1976. *Whose Law? What Order?* New York: John Wiley.

Clinard, M. B. 1978. *Cities With Little Crime: The Case of Switzerland.* Cambridge: Cambridge University Press.

Cohen, S. 1985. *Visions of Social Control.* Cambridge: Polity Press.

Cullen, F. T., M. T. Larson, and R. A. Mathers. 1985. "Having Money and Delinquency Involvement: The Neglect of Power in Delinquency Theory." *Criminal Justice and Behavior* 12 (June):171-92.

Currie, E. 1985. *Confronting Crime: An American Challenge.* New York: Pantheon.

Edwards, R. C., M. Reich, and T. E. Weisskopf. 1974. "Toward a Socialist Alternative." In R. Quinney (ed.), *Criminal Justice in America.* Boston: Little, Brown.

Etzioni, A. 1972. "Human Beings Are Not Very Easy to Change After All." *Saturday Review* (June):45-47.

Finestone, H. 1976. *Victims of Change.* Westport, CT: Greenwood Press.

Gallup, Jr., George. 1989. *The Gallup Report.* Princeton, NJ: The Gallup Poll.

Geis, G., and A. Binder. 1991. "Sins of Their Children: Parental Responsibility for Juvenile Delinquency." *Notre Dame Journal of Law Ethics and Public Policy* 5:303-22.

Goode, E. 1989. *Drugs in American Society.* New York: Alfred A. Knopf.

Gottfredson, D. C. 1986. "An Empirical Test of School-Based Environmental and Individual Interventions to Reduce the Risk of Delinquent Behavior." *Criminology* 24 (Number 4):705-31.

Gottfredson, D. C., and G. D. Gottfredson. 1986. *The School Action Effectiveness Study: Final Report.* Center for Social Organization of Schools. Baltimore: The Johns Hopkins University.

Gottfredson, G. D. 1981. *Schooling and Delinquency Prevention: Some Practical Ideas for Educators, Parents, Program Developers, and Researchers.* Center for Social Organization of Schools. Baltimore: The Johns Hopkins University.

Hackler, J. C. 1966. "Boys, Blisters and Behavior — The Impact of a Work Program in an Urban Central Area." *The Journal of Research on Crime and Delinquency* 3 (July):155-64.

_____. 1985. "The Need to Do Something" in R. A. Weisheit and R. G. Culbertson (eds.), *Juvenile Delinquency: A Justice Perspective.* Prospect Heights, IL: Waveland Press.

Hackler, J. C., and J. Hagan. 1975. "Work and Teaching Machines as Delinquency Prevention Tools: A Four Year Follow-up." *Social Sciences Review* 49 (1):92-106.

Hagan, J., and E. Linden. 1970. "The Response of Adults to Delinquency Prevention Programs: The Race Factor." *Journal of Research in Crime and Delinquency* 7:31-45.

Higgins, P. S. 1978. "Evaluation and Case Study of a School-Based Delinquency Prevention Program." *Evaluation Quarterly* 2 (May):215-34.

Jeffrey, C. R. 1971. *Crime Prevention Through Environmental Design.* Beverly Hills, CA: Sage Publications.

Jensen, G. F. 1979. "Final Report: Delinquency in a Middle-Class High School." Washington, DC: National Institute of Mental Health.

Kandel, D. 1984. "Marijuana Users in Young Adulthood." *Archives of General Psychiatry.* 41:200-209.

Lab, S. P. 1988. *Crime Prevention: Approaches, Practices and Evaluations.* Cincinnati: Anderson.

_____. 1984. "Patterns in Juvenile Misbehavior." *Crime and Delinquency* 30:293-308.

Lindsay, B., and D. McGillis. 1986. "Citywide Community Prevention: An Assessment of the Seattle Program." In D. P. Rosenbaum (ed.), *Community Crime Prevention: Does It Work?* Beverly Hills, CA: Sage.

Lundman, R. J. 1984. *Prevention and Control of Juvenile Delinquency.* New York: Oxford Press.

Martin, J. M. 1961. "Three Approaches to Delinquency Prevention: A Critique." *Crime and Delinquency* 7 (January):16-24.

Martin, J. M., J. P. Fitzpatrick, and R. E. Gould. 1970. *The Analysis of Delinquent Behavior: A Structural Approach.* New York: Random House.

McCord, J. 1978. "A Thirty-Year Follow-Up of Treatment Effects." *American Psychologist* 33:284-89.

McCord, J., and W. McCord. 1959. "A Follow-Up Report on the Cambridge-Somerville Youth Study." *Annals of the American Academy of Political and Social Science* 322 (March):89-98.

Miller, W. B. 1958. "Inter-Institutional Conflict as a Major Impediment to Delinquency Prevention." *Human Organization* 17 (Fall):20-23.

_____. 1962. "The Impact of a 'Total Community' Delinquency Control Project." *Social Problems* 10 (Fall):168-91.

Platt, A. 1970. "Saving and Controlling Delinquent Youth: A Critique." *Issues in Criminology* 5 (Winter):1-24.

_____. 1974. "The Triumph of Benevolence: Origins of Juvenile Justice in the U.S." In R. Quinney (ed.), *Criminal Justice in America.* Boston: Little, Brown.

President's Commission on Law Enforcement and Administration of Justice. 1967. *The Challenge of Crime in a Free Society.* Washington, DC: U.S. Government Printing Office.

Quinney, R. 1974. *Criminal Justice in America.* Boston: Little, Brown.

Reckless, W. C., and S. Dinitz. 1972. *The Prevention of Juvenile Delinquency: An Experiment.* Columbus: Ohio University Press.

Robin, G. D. 1969. "Anti-Poverty Programs and Delinquency." *Journal of Criminal Law, Criminology and Police Science* 60 (Fall):323-31.

Rosenbaum, D. P. 1987. "The Theory and Research Behind Neighborhood Watch: Is It a Sound Fear and Crime Reduction Strategy?" *Crime and Delinquency* 33:103-34.

Schlossman, S., and M. Sedlak. 1983. *The Chicago Area Project Revisited.* Santa Monica, CA: Rand.

Schur, E. 1969. *Our Criminal Society.* Englewood Cliffs, NJ: Prentice-Hall.

Schwendinger, H., and J. R. Schwendinger. 1985. *Adolescent Subcultures and Delinquency.* New York: Praeger.

Sherman, L. W. 1986. "Policing Communities: What Works?" In A. J. Reiss, Jr. and M. Tonry (eds.), *Communities and Crime.* Chicago: University of Chicago Press.

Sorenson, S. L. 1990. "DFSZs Work! Broward County Study Reveals Effectiveness of Drug-Free School Zones." *Safe Haven* (Spring, 1990):1-2, 8.

Sutherland, E. 1924. *Principles of Criminology.* Philadelphia: J. B. Lippincott.

Sutton, J. R. 1988. *Stubborn Children: Controlling Delinquency in the United States, 1640-1981.* Berkeley: University of California Press.

Toby, J. 1963. "The Prospects for Reducing Delinquency Rates in Industrial Societies." *Federal Probation* 27 (December):23-25.

_____. 1965. "An Evaluation of Early Identification and Intensive Treatment Programs for Predelinquents." *Social Problems* 13 (Fall):160-75.

_____. 1984. "Toby Releases Study on School Violence." *The Criminologist.* 9:304.

Turner, D. 1984. "The Probation Officer and Community Delinquency Prevention: The Shift Out of Reactive Casework." *Canadian Journal of Criminology* 26 (January): 75-96.

Wilson, J. Q. 1983. *Thinking About Crime.* Revised Edition. New York: Basic Books.

Wolfgang, M. E., R. Figlio, and T. Sellin. 1972. *Delinquency in a Birth Cohort.* Chicago: University of Chicago Press.

Wright, W. E. and M. C. Dixon. 1977. "Community Prevention and Treatment of Juvenile Delinquency." *Journal of Research in Crime and Delinquency* 14 (January):35-67.

Author Index

Subject Index

Community treatment, 45, 431, 438-41
Complainants, 79, 80, 109
Compulsory education, 39-40, 41-43
Conditioning, 189-90
  classical, 201-2
  operant, 202-3
Conflict theory, 507-8
Constitutional psychology, 184-85
Containment theory, 218
Contraculture, 213, 222-24, 227, 228
Correctional experiments, 429
  focus, 429
  locus, 429
Cost of crime, 10-15
Criminal families, 190
Criminology
  definition, 20
  science, 19-20
  sociology, 212-15
Cultural conflict theory, 224-26, 235-39

Darwinian theory, 180
Defensible space, 344
Definitions favorable to lawbreaking, 237-38, 244
Delinquency law
  common law, 46, 48
  continuing controversy, 36, 67-70
  current statutes, 61-65
  definition of delinquency, 3, 34, 61
  delinquent act, 34
  dependent child, 34, 62
  detention, 33
  incorrigible child, 31, 34
  jurisdiction, 61-65
  labeling theory, 379, 382
  legal precedent, 40-42, 46
  recency, 4
  status offense, 31, 35, 61
Delinquent
  act, 34
  as myth, 122-23, 134-35, 164
  behavior, 213, 215
  careers, 375, 382
  gangs, 213
  subcultures, 213, 215, 225-26, 229
Denomination, 324-26
Dependent child, 34, 62
Detention, 33, 34, 47, 455
Determinant sentences, 470-71
Deterrence
  absolute, 363
  and criminological theory, 360-62
  capital punishment, 365-67
  certainty, 369-70
  doctrine, 358
  experiments, 370-72
  general, 362-63, 365

general preventive effects, 362
  incapacitation, 362, 364
  marginal efficacy, 363-64
  overload, 369-70
  perception, 372-74
  philosophy, 65-66, 358
  restrictive, 363-64
  severity, 369-70
  socialization, 362
  specific, 363
Diagnostic centers, 410
Differential association, 203, 224-26, 454
Differential reinforcement theory, 203-4
Direct supervision and control, 242
Discretion, 105-6
Discrimination
  gender, 112-14, 116
  race, 107-11, 116
  social class, 111-12, 116
Disposition, 33, 34
Distribution of delinquency, 83
  among groups, 93-96, 98-102
  space, 91-93
  time, 84-91, 115-16, 139-41, 156-59
Diversion, 452
  children's rights, 454
  controversy, 461-63
  detention, 455-56
  discretion, 474
  evaluation, 459-63
  ideology, 453
  meaning, 457-59
  policy, 20-21
  rationales, 454-58
  status offenders, 460-61
  theoretical precedents, 454-57
Double jeopardy, 54-55
Dramatization of evil, 381-82
Drift theory, 219
Dropout, 285-87
Drug use
  and religion, 322-24, 326
  legislation, 375, 376-80
  official statistics, 104, 116
  self-reports, 131-34, 137-41
  subcultures, 377-78
Drug-Free School Zones, 495
Due process of law, 35, 41, 48

Early identification and intensive treatment, 483-84
Ecological research, 345-48
Enculturation, 362
Endocrinology, 188-89
England
  age and crime, 96, 98
  delinquency research, 308
  public reporting, 78